Alexander Hamilton
and the Growth of the New Nation

American Presidents Series

Alexander Hamilton and the Growth of the New Nation
John C. Miller
With a new introduction by A. Owen Aldridge

Conversations with Lincoln
Compiled, edited, and annotated by Charles M. Segal
With a new preface by the editor and
an introduction by David Donald

Eisenhower and the American Crusades
Herbert S. Parmet

George Bush: The Life of a Lone Star Yankee
Herbert S. Parmet

Herbert H. Humphrey: The Politics of Joy
Charles L. Garrettson III

The Illusions of a Conservative Reagan Revolution
Larry M. Schwab

*President Roosevelt and the Coming of the War, 1941:
Appearances and Realities*
Charles A. Beard
With a new introduction by Campbell Craig

Thomas Jefferson: America's Philosopher-King
Max Lerner
With an introduction by Robert Schmuhl

Woodrow Wilson: A Psychological Study
William Bullitt and Sigmund Freud

Alexander Hamilton and the Growth of the New Nation

John C. Miller

With a new introduction by
A. Owen Aldridge

Transaction Publishers
New Brunswick (U.S.A.) and London (U.K.)

New material this edition copyright © 2004 by Transaction Publishers, New Brunswick, New Jersey. Originally published in 1959 by Harper & Brothers.

All rights reserved under International and Pan-American Copyright Conventions. No part of this book may be reproduced or transmitted in any form or by any means, electronic or mechanical, including photocopy, recording, or any information storage and retrieval system, without prior permission in writing from the publisher. All inquiries should be addressed to Transaction Publishers, Rutgers—The State University, 35 Berrue Circle, Piscataway, New Jersey 08854-8042.

This book is printed on acid-free paper that meets the American National Standard for Permanence of Paper for Printed Library Materials.

Library of Congress Catalog Number: 2003047316
ISBN: 0-7658-0551-0
Printed in the United States of America

Library of Congress Cataloging-in-Publication Data

Miller, John Chester, 1907-
    Alexander Hamilton and the growth of the new nation / John C. Miller ; with a new introduction by A. Owen Aldridge.
        p. cm.—(American presidents series)
    Originally published: Alexander Hamilton. New York, Harper, 1959.
    Includes bibliographical references and index.
    ISBN 0-7658-0551-0 (pbk. : alk. paper)
    1. Hamilton, Alexander, 1757-1804. 2. Statesmen—United States—Biography. 3. United States—Politics and government—1775-1783. 4. United States—Politics and government—1783-1809. I. Title. II. Series.

E302.6.H2M57 2003
973.4'092—dc21   2003047316
[B]

To the Memory of My Brother Raymond

No man can by care-taking (as the Scripture saith) "add a cubit to his stature," in this little model of a man's body; but in the great frame of kingdoms and commonwealths, it is in the power of princes, or estates, to add amplitude and greatness to their kingdom: for, by introducing such ordinances, constitutions, and customs, as we have now touched, they may sow greatness to their posterity and succession; but these things are commonly not observed, but left to take their chance.

FRANCIS BACON

Contents

Transaction Introduction ix
Introduction xvii

Part I The Union Against Great Britain

1. The Making of a Revolutionary 3
2. Aide-de-Camp to Washington 17
3. The Struggle Against Inflation 43
4. The Quarrel with Washington 62

Part II The Union Against Chaos

5. Congress and the Army 83
6. Law and the Loyalists 100
7. "A Rage for Liberty" 111
8. Democracy and Banking 120
9. "More Power to Congress" 131
10. The Constitutional Convention (1) 151
11. The Constitutional Convention (2) 171
12. The Federalist 184
13. The Rule of Law 193
14. A More Perfect Union 206

Part III The Union Consummated

15. The First Secretary of the Treasury 219
16. The Report on Public Credit 229
17. "Speculators" vs. "Patriots" 238
18. The Bank of the United States 255
19. The Report on Manufactures 278
20. The Effort to Transform the American Economy 296
21. The Opposition Emerges 311

22.	The Attack upon Hamilton	322
23.	Hamilton's Quarrel with Jefferson and Burr	343

Part IV The Union Against Foreign Aggression

24.	The Proclamation of Neutrality	363
25.	The War Clouds Gather	379
26.	The Whisky Rebellion	396
27.	Jay's Treaty	415
28.	The Election of 1796	435
29.	The Mission to France	451
30.	Second in Command of the United States Army	466
31.	The War That Refused to Come to a Boil	479
32.	The Effort to Avert Peace	493
33.	The Election of 1800	509

Part V The Union Above All

34.	A Prophet of Woe	533
35.	Defender of the Freedom of the Press	544
36.	The Duel with Burr	557
	Notes	577
	Bibliography	623
	Index	641

Transaction Introduction

Until the middle of the twentieth century, a considerable number of biographies portrayed Alexander Hamilton as a romantic hero as well as one of the founders of the American nation. This perspective changed in the 1930s, presumably as one of the results of the Great Depression, and he became associated with the economic policies responsible for that disaster. One of the leading conservatives of the twentieth century, Russell Kirk, attempted to deny him admittance to this company by describing him as "the first American businessman," in contrast to John Adams as "the founder of true conservatism in America." [*The Conservative Mind* (1963)] John C. Miller, in his classic biography, however, restores Hamilton to his proper eminence in the history of the American nation. As one of the authors of *The Federalist*, "he appeared in the guise of a true conservative—the guardian of order, conscious of the history, ideals and traditions of his society, and yet, withal, aware of the necessity of change." [204] Throughout his entire life, Hamilton never engaged in industry or commerce, although he did speculate in land in his later days. In contrast to Adams, who may justly be termed a moral conservative, Hamilton was without a doubt a political conservative. Not only in activities, but also in demeanour and appearance, Miller distinguishes him from the commercial type, represented by one of his distant family members: "a heavy, goutish businessman whose conversation ran largely to stocks and bonds." [464] Miller does not entirely free himself from the cliché about Hamilton, however, at one point affirming that "he always had a soft heart for businessmen." [485] After specifically declaring in the topic sentence of one paragraph, though, that Hamilton "made himself the spokesman" of the business community, Miller, in the final sentence of the same paragraph, modifies this to "he was not the father of American business; rather he found it a lusty infant and taught it to walk." [283] Whether his conservatism in regard to property was a feature of his nationalism or just the reverse is difficult to determine.

Miller's portrayal of Hamilton does not follow the conventions of standard biographies by portraying the protagonist as either hero or villain or by balancing the character, personality, and private life of the protagonist with his relationship toward the exterior world. His highly original study consists primarily of a chronologically arranged analysis of Hamilton's political and economic contributions to the organization and development of the American nation, emphasizing its stability and independence. He cites and exemplifies the general Enlightenment assumption that the function of history is to expose "the constant and universal principles" underlying human behavior and customs. [114] In this sense his work has more in common with a well-written treatise in political science than with most biographies. Miller, for the 1964 edition of this work, changed its title from *Alexander Hamilton: Portrait in Paradox* to *Alexander Hamilton and the Growth of the New Nation*, perhaps because the original title suggests personal and psychological analysis rather than political and economic exposition. Miller, nevertheless, adheres faithfully to the traditional methods of history, the reconstruction and exhibition of past events, not as they actually were, but as close as possible to that end, and garnished with literary devices, new information, and enlightening explanations of ideologies and philosophies. This is in great contrast to the mode of minihistory and reliance on statistics and annals in the postmodern age. Organizing concepts such as "the nation" have been replaced on a large scale today by multicultural topics relevant to races, genders, and ethnicities.

Miller's rich documentation, based upon extensive research, is exceedingly inobtrusive, and much of the enjoyment from reading his work derives from his witty style. Miller reports, for example, that Hamilton at the outset of his career encouraged the rich to "succour the miserable and lay up a treasure in heaven," but he later advised them to "lay up their treasure in United States government bonds." [7] Because of Hamilton's good looks, gentility, and social graces, Miller describes him as "the greatest boon to womankind ever to descend upon the City of Brotherly Love." [281] One of his favorite phrases, used several times throughout the text, describes the Federalists as comprising "the party of the good, the wise, and the rich." [359] It is not clear, however, whether this phrase embodies a degree of irony. At any rate, it is not entirely accurate. Adams, for example, although one of the leading Federalists, was far from wealthy, and Hamilton himself, although enjoying a life of luxury, never acquired a fortune, and he left his wife almost penniless after his death.

One of the paradoxes suggested by Miller's subtitle enshrining Hamilton as one of the major supporters of national union is that he was born in the West Indies beyond the continental boundaries of the United States. [xii] The supreme paradox, however, concerns the formation of political parties, which Hamilton, as the proponent of a tightly-organized union, bitterly opposed. Many of his innovative policies, moreover, led to the formation of sectional divisions, while Jefferson, his arch-rival and proponent of state over national supremacy, seemed at one point about to turn the country into a single party state. [xii] Several other paradoxes may be discerned. In 1771 Hamilton inclined toward Thomas Paine's notion of a government directly influenced by the popular will, in contrast to Adams's concept of a mixed government of executive, judicial, and legislative powers. Ten years later, however, he jumped to the opposite side, becoming an advocate of strong powers of government and rule of "the enlightened few." He was widely regarded as an aristocrat, yet he rejected any claims of superiority based upon inheritance. His conversational French was one of the most elegant among all the nation's founders although he had never stepped foot on the European continent. As a soldier Hamilton shone as brave and resourceful, rising to become second in command under Washington. In reaction to the XYZ affair, however, he showed less belligerence than Adams; he prepared for defense but hoped for a peaceful settlement. [468]

In a famous speech delivered at the Constitutional Convention, Hamilton advocated the allocation of all power without restriction to a central government, favoring unity over liberty. Real liberty, he argued, "is neither found in despotism or the extremes of democracy, but in moderate governments." [164] Only in this sense was he willing to accept some degree of democracy or republicanism. While exposing the potential weaknesses of "a perfect democracy in which virtue, property, and social distinctions would be destroyed," he did not recognize, as Miller points out, that conservatives are "sometimes incapable of ruling wisely." [142] Miller observes, moreover, that Hamilton, throughout his career, emphasized the duties rather than the rights of citizens, a principle not recognized by present historians who adhere to multiculturalism. One of the most controversial elements in Hamilton's Convention speech, the institution of an Electoral College as a device to remove the presidency from popular choice, is still much debated. Hamilton felt that electors as well as congressmen should vote according to their own best judgment without consulting the will of their constituencies, in essence a principle of British government. Obviously the rule of an intellectual aristocracy would be ideal if the men chosen could be trusted always to pursue the path of virtue, justice, and reason, but it is no more possible to find such a guaranteed combination among the rich and well born than among the middle and lower segments of society. Hamilton, however, was never an advocate of monarchy or aristocracy, but merely of the mixing of their best ingredients with the best of republicanism. [168] Here he and his archrival, Adams, also decried by his enemies as a monarchist, were in essential agreement. The major difference between the two was in personality—Hamilton adventurous, compulsive, audacious, and persistent; Adams, cautious, and, to a degree, flexible and ready for compromise. Adams was frequently unjustly accused by his enemies of favoring monarchy while Hamilton, who openly agreed with Montesquieu that only a monarchy was viable for a large country, was never involved in efforts to install a royal regime. [163]

From the perspective of literary expression and philosophical profundity, Hamilton's contributions to *The Federalist* represent his highest attainments. In Miller's summation, "he was not so much a philosopher in politics as a politician with a philosophy." [182] On the surface, Hamilton's political views seem highly undemocratic, faced as they were with the necessity of defeating two widely-accepted theoretical platitudes—that the voice of the people is the voice of God, and that man is capable of perfectibility. Miller makes no effort, though, to reconcile this interpretation of Hamilton's opinions in maturity with a previous statement that in his youth Hamilton fully accepted the notion of immutable laws established by "God and nature," basing his acquiescence on the doctrine of natural rights. Hamilton forcibly denied in *The Federalist* the "possibility of an improvement in man's nature," [198] representing for Miller a manifestation of political Calvinism, not in the sense of a theological doctrine but as a conclusion drawn from extensive study of "the Nature & Character of Man" in history and Scripture as well as personal experience. Without specifically defining class structure by means of the dualities of the few and the many, the rich and the poor, or the rulers and the people, Hamilton rejected the notion that some men are preordained to rule or that one class should automatically have power over any other. Liberty belongs to all, but the guidance of the most virtuous and rational leads to a "balance of power between the classes." [200] Miller applauds Hamilton for proposing the Supreme Court as the arbiter between the executive and legislative powers as well as the protector of the rights of states against the encroachments of Congress. [201] His favorable opinion of judicial review also supports the principle that the Court should consult the will of the people as well as the Constitution in arriving at its decisions. Although Hamilton rejected the doctrine of the perfectibility of man, Miller observes that he held the "great man" view of history, which became the guiding principle of his own career. In promoting his primordial goal—the creation of a united nation—"he was sustained by the convictions that all obstacles to its realization could be overcome by the exercise of wisdom and resolution on the part of a determined man." [228]

Miller suggests that Hamilton considered the principle of unity as basic also to the formation of his economic theory. Although his broad philosophy derives from Locke, his system embraces production, distribution, and investment with the entire continent representing an "economic whole." [15] Miller associates this mercantilist perspective with Hume's principle that the welfare of the state is far more important than the welfare of any individual and that as a consequence the state may properly intervene in any situation. Hamilton also considered the rights of property second only to the rights of man, conceiving of liberty and property as inherently linked. [121, 123] These trends, Hamilton believed, emerged from the study of history, which reveals "the constant and universal principles" underlying human affairs. [114] Although Hamilton is generally associated with federalism, both as a political party and as a device of government, Miller points out that he never considered this kind of loose association as ideal, preferring one much more articulated. [117] For this reason he constantly maintained that the central government should have control of the economy.

In view of Hamilton's disparaging view of a loose governmental structure, it is not surprising that he held more appointive offices during his career than elective ones, the most colorful of all in the military. At the age of twenty he became an artillery captain and served as aide-de-camp to Washington, a rise in eminence probably explained primarily by his aristocratic connections and gentlemanly qualities. [21] Other biographies do not adequately recognize his military acumen and bravery or the prestige he eventually gained as "Second in Command of the United States Army."

Although Hamilton and Thomas Paine are usually considered as exponents of opposing ideas and projects, Miller indicates some of the fundamental areas in which they agreed. Not only did Hamilton in 1777 concur with Paine's concept of a strong central government directly influenced by the popular will, but both men in 1782 made personal efforts to persuade the state of Rhode Island to agree to a federal impost, the only one of the thirteen states to refuse. Although the politicians of the recalcitrant state declared that their reluctance was based on fear of the potential tyranny of the central government and danger of losing their natural rights, Hamilton discovered that Rhode Island was enjoying a lucrative income by taxing residents of Connecticut, who were forced to use Rhode Island's seaports, and that the projected impost would take away this revenue. Unlike other biographers of both Paine and Hamilton, Miller offers a full explanation of this situation. Hamilton, at the urging of a congressional committee, composed a passionate address to the governor of Rhode Island demanding compliance, and Paine made a personal trip to Providence in the same cause, but neither one had the least success. [89-90] Several years later, during Adams's presidency, Hamilton engaged in a vicious quarrel over an alleged declaration of Adams that he would much prefer to be a vice-president under Jefferson "than be indebted to such a being as Hamilton for the Presidency." [519] Hamilton twice demanded in writing an explanation from Adams and, receiving no reply, issued an open *Letter from Alexander Hamilton concernng the Public Conduct and Character of John Adams*. [502] In analyzing its contents, Miller, instead of defending Hamilton, maintains that he does not show that any substantial offenses had been committed against him. [520] This exchange represents a further parallel with Paine, who also published a denunciation of a president of the United States, his better known *Letter to George Washington, President of the United States of America. On affairs public and private*. 1796. Scurrilous and venomous epistles directed toward public officials were by no means rarities in those days, but bitter accusations directed against a sitting president by other eminent personalities equally in the public eye were not at all common.

Miller pays more attention to Hamilton's religion than to any other aspect of his personal life. Apparently emotionally sensitive to appearances of the supernatural, he published while still in his teens a newspaper essay on a tornado that had recently descended upon St. Croix and had thereby aroused personal reflections on man's sinful nature and the wrath and power of the Deity. His Presbyterian schoolmaster was so impressed that he arranged for the budding author to seek admission to the College of New Jersey, later Princeton. The president, Dr. Witherspoon, however, another Presbyterian clergyman, had some misgivings about Hamilton's extreme youth, and as a result he enrolled in the Anglican

King's College, later Columbia, in New York. Several years later, when revolutionary mob violence was directed against the president of King's College, Dr. Myles Cooper, and he was rescued by a group of students including Hamilton, the grateful clergyman mentioned him by name in a poem on the incident, published in the *Gentleman's Magazine*. [17] Religion had relatively little influence in Hamilton's middle years, as his life came to be almost exclusively taken up by political and financial ventures. Miller, however, reports an episode related to group worship during the Constitutional Convention in which he played a minor part. Benjamin Franklin had proposed that a clergyman be called upon to intercede with the Divinity for help in overcoming the acrimony then threatening to destroy the body completely. Miller suggests that Hamilton under other circumstances would have supported the project, but felt that at that time it would be harmful publicity for the impression to be given that the convention was deadlocked. Miller also observes that most of the delegates had more confidence in human understanding than in the intercession of heaven. In a footnote he cites an account, which he labels "suspect," written many years later quoting Hamilton to the effect that, "he did not see the necessity of calling in foreign aid." Franklin's conciliatory proposal was never actually defeated nor was it carried out, as James Madison records, simply because the convention had no funds to pay a clergyman's salary.

Nowhere does Miller suggest that Hamilton, like many of the other heroes of the revolution, ever in any way adopted radical trends of religious thought. Instead of following contemporaries like Franklin, Adams, and Jefferson by entertaining deism, Hamilton in his later days came close to adopting concepts associated today with the religious right, the only episode of his life that Miller seems to condemn. As a measure to overcome the disappointing performance of Federalist candidates, Hamilton proposed the organization of a Christian Constitutional Society to promote religion and the Constitution, its activities to consist of voting Federalist and establishing societies for the relief of immigrants and the training of artisans, localities where, Miller wryly remarks, "the worthy poor would be indoctrinated with Federalist principles as well as with Holy Writ." [552]

Some of Hamilton's sensational biographers make capital out of the only unconventional episode in his life, his liaison with a prostitute that he was forced to admit publicly. Miller places most of the blame on the woman's dissolute husband and suggests that Hamilton was more sinned against than sinning. The circumstances of Hamilton's death, moreover, seem to have convinced Miller that although his Christian faith had dimmed or been seriously neglected at the height of his political activities, he still retained both intellectually and emotionally a strong attachment to the Christian church. Shortly after suffering the wound leading to his demise, he expressed to a clergyman of the Dutch Church his "firm belief in Christianity," and a few hours later he asked to be received into the Episcopal Church, receiving the sacrament from the presiding bishop of New York, thus indirectly manifesting an attachment to his Anglican heritage.

Transaction Introduction

Miller has great admiration for Hamilton, admitting nothing reprehensible in his character, but he also readily admits his faults and weaknesses. His closest approach to condemning him of serious ill behavior comes in regard to his appointment as second in command to Washington in the continental army. Adams, one of his greatest enemies, declaimed bitterly against his candidacy, but Hamilton, intriguing with other notables, succeeded in securing the post for himself. Miller terms this personal victory "a far more damaging blow at the prestige and authority of the presidency than Jefferson ever inflicted upon that office." [478] Miller emphasizes throughout, however, that in addition to his financial and political talents, Hamilton was a gifted essayist, a master of political prose, a scholar, a linguist, a military genius, and, perhaps above all, a man after Washington's own heart. His dress and manners, moreover, turned him into an American Beau Brummell. "Among his friends, Hamilton seemed to be the most generous, eloquent, charitable, patriotic, forceful, and charming of men." [226] Although granting that at times he may have seemed remote from the common man, Miller points out this was not a sign of aristocratic aloofness, but merely an aspect of personality. "Artisans, shopkeekpers and workers of the seaport towns" attributed to his policies the economic prosperity in America during the last decade of the eighteenth century and "acclaimed him as their benefactor." [439] It would be difficult to demonstrate that he was not!

A. Owen Aldridge

Introduction

The period in which Alexander Hamilton lived was an age of great men and great events. In the United States, besides Hamilton himself, George Washington, Thomas Jefferson, James Madison and John Marshall held the center of the stage; while the European scene was dominated by William Pitt, Charles James Fox and Napoleon Bonaparte. And yet, Talleyrand, whose career is a convincing testimonial of his astuteness in judging men and measures and who was intimately acquainted with the leaders on both sides of the Atlantic, pronounced Alexander Hamilton to be the greatest of these "choice and master spirits of the age."

Probably no American statesman has displayed more constructive imagination than did Hamilton. Prodigal of ideas, bursting with plans for diversifying the American economy and obsessed by a determination to make the United States a powerful nation under a centralized government, he left an imprint upon this country that time has not yet effaced. Of some of our institutions it may be justly said that they are the lengthened shadow of one man—Alexander Hamilton.

In Hamilton's comparatively brief span, he lived through three great wars, in two of which he was an active participant. Whenever he looked abroad he found wars or rumors of wars. As a result, the conviction was implanted in him that the survival of the United States depended to a great degree upon its warmaking potential. If this was a harsh and unattractive philosophy, at least it could be said to have been based upon the facts of international life as Hamilton knew them.

Everything depended, he believed, upon strengthening the union: if it perished, Americans would never attain the liberty, material well-being and happiness to which they aspired. Even his financial and economic plans were but means to the great end of solidifying the union; in his hands, capitalism became a barrier against the strong centrifugal forces that threatened to reduce the central government to impotence.

Paradoxically enough, the abounding love of the American union that actuated Hamilton was partly owing to the fact that he was born outside the continental boundaries of what later became the United States. He was thereby preserved against the corroding effects of state loyalty which in most of his contemporaries seriously weakened the springs of nationalism. Even more important, Hamilton's service in the Revolutionary Army impressed upon him the necessity of strong central government capable of acting upon Americans directly rather than through the states. Above all, he realized to a greater degree than any American of his generation that the republic must draw its strength from union. The source of American greatness, he perceived, was continental, not provincial. From first to last, he "thought continentally."

Hamilton's was a strange career—and no one was more conscious of its strangeness than was Hamilton himself. A West Indian by birth and of antecedents that provided his enemies with a never-failing source of scurrility—John Adams called him "the bastard brat of a Scotch pedlar"—he rose to high social, political and military position in the United States. To the cause of American union he gave unstintingly of his energy and devotion, and yet he had little love for the people whose power and material wellbeing he sought to advance. Never, he said, had he expected to find a people born to greatness who more stubbornly resisted their destiny than did Americans. He confessed that he did not understand them and on one occasion he cried out in anguish of spirit that "this American world" was not made for him. Frequently he asked himself to what end he was laboring; but he never ceased to strive to mold the United States in accord with the vision that had been granted him.

The supreme irony of Hamilton's achievement is that the methods by which he sought to lay the economic foundations of the American union actually aggravated political sectionalism in the United States—the very eventuality he most dreaded. There are few instances in history that demonstrate more strikingly how the best-laid plans of statesmen can go awry. Hamilton dedicated himself to the cause of union; yet when he retired from the office of Secretary of the Treasury, the fissures between North and South had begun to assume menacing proportions. True, Hamilton did not bear the sole responsibility for this untoward and, for him, wholly unexpected development; and yet he, more than any other individual, was responsible for the policies which divided the American people and which led to the creation of political parties. It was his archrival, Thomas Jefferson, who united Americans and, until the imposition of the embargo of 1808, seemed on the point of making the United States a one-party state. If the American world were made for Thomas Jefferson, then Alexander Hamilton felt that he stood on foreign ground indeed.

PART I
The Union Against Great Britain

1.
The Making of a Revolutionary

Alexander Hamilton bore neither loyalty nor affection for Nevis, the British island on which he was born, or for St. Croix, the Danish island on which he passed his early youth. An American who spent a few years on St. Croix during the eighteenth century remarked that he felt "much the same anxiety at a distance from it as Adam did after he was banished from the bowers of Eden." For Hamilton, however, the island was a prison from which he could not wait to escape: probably the happiest moment he knew in the West Indies was when, from the deck of a ship, he watched St. Croix drop below the horizon.¹ *

No doubt, much of the aversion Hamilton felt for St. Croix was owing to the unhappiness he experienced there. His father, James Hamilton, the fourth son of the Laird of Cambuskeith, "The Grange," Ayrshire, Scotland, lived in open adultery with Alexander's mother, Rachel Fawcett Lavien, the daughter of a French Huguenot physician and wife of John Lavien, a German businessman who had settled at St. Croix. Although Alexander was born in 1755 (his brother James had preceded him by two years), John Lavien did not get round to divorcing Rachel until 1758. In his bill of divorce, he declared her to be no better than a prostitute. In actuality, she seems to have been an impetuous, ardent and high-spirited young woman, too strong-willed to endure a loveless marriage. But since Rachel was forbidden by Danish law to remarry (she being the offending party), the bar sinister was indelibly fixed upon her two sons.²

To make matters worse, James Hamilton was a ne'er-do-well. His business ventures almost invariably turned out badly; the year Alexander was born, his father went bankrupt. Moreover, most of Alexander's relatives on his mother's side, the most important of whom were the Lyttons, were in financial difficulties. Thus, from his earliest years, it was impressed upon Alexander that while he came of good family—"My blood," he once said, "is as good as that of those who plume themselves upon their ancestry"— and many of his near relatives had been wealthy and respected, times had

* Numbered notes will be found in a group beginning on page 577.

changed for the worse, the money was gone and they were all on the downgrade. As for the family name, it was becoming increasingly apparent that James Hamilton would add no embellishment to it, not even to the extent of handing it down legally to his descendants.

In 1765, shortly after James Hamilton had brought his family to St. Croix, he abandoned Rachel and his sons. He left them almost wholly destitute. Since none of Rachel's relatives were able to help out financially, she was obliged to open a small store while her son James was apprenticed to a carpenter, and Alexander, at the age of eleven, became a clerk in the counting house of Cruger and Beekman. In 1769, Rachel died; she had ceased to call herself "Madame Hamilton" and she was buried as Rachel Lavien. As for James Hamilton, he was last heard of on the island of St. Vincent, where he lived to a ripe and impenitent old age. While thus cutting himself off from his family, he did not make the breach so complete as to exclude charity. Over the course of years he received a considerable sum of money from Alexander, but James Hamilton never indicated any strong desire to see the son whose generosity he had done so little to merit.[3]

Singularly enough, Alexander never blamed his troubles upon his father. He always addressed James Hamilton with filial respect and affection; at no time did he reproach him for his conduct toward his wife and children. Indeed, had James Hamilton been a model of conjugal and parental behavior, he could hardly have evoked a greater semblance of regard from his youngest son. In later life, when Alexander referred to his family—which, understandably, was not often—it was of his father rather than of his mother that he usually spoke.

Hamilton forgave his father this unpaternal neglect because James Hamilton, with all his faults, represented a link with the aristocratic world. Much could be forgiven a lord, or the younger son of a lord; to have broken with his father, to have loaded him with the censures he no doubt deserved, would have invalidated what Alexander came to regard as his passport to good society.

The harrowing experiences of his youth did not embitter Hamilton against the world so much as they instilled in him an inflexible resolution to conquer it. Pride and a fierce determination to succeed—these were the qualities which he derived from his early environment and which he never relinquished. His ambition was whetted by the obstacles it encountered. Many years later he wrote in *The Federalist:* "There are strong minds in every walk of life that will rise superior to the disadvantages of situation, and will command the tribute due to their merit, not only from the classes to which they particularly belong, but from the society in general." Keenly aware of the superiority of his talents as well as of the disadvantages of his situation, Hamilton from an early age put himself in the company of those who by intelligence and industry rise superior to their station in life.

The Making of a Revolutionary

In Hamilton's case, it was an uphill road strewn with obstructions. Nevertheless, his ability, industry and engaging manners soon began to tell: in 1771, owing to Nicholas Cruger's temporary absence from the island, Alexander was elevated from bookkeeper to manager. Here he displayed the acumen, self-confidence and willingness to take risks that later became his distinguishing characteristics in the United States Treasury. But his tenure of authority was short-lived: Nicholas Cruger returned to St. Croix and Hamilton was demoted to bookkeeper, thereby reversing the traditional American success story. Nevertheless, at Cruger and Beckman's, Hamilton gained valuable experience for his later career in business and finance. He learned the importance of method, the ways of the business world and— from the ship captains and supercargoes with whom he was obliged to deal —the seamier side of human nature.[4]

Even though his connection with Cruger and Beckman might have blossomed into a junior partnership, Hamilton chafed at the dull round in which his duties confined him: with the world waiting to be conquered, what was he doing pushing a pen in a stuffy office? Conscious as he was of his ability and ambition, he was no less aware that St. Croix afforded scope for neither. The life of a merchant or planter, however prosperous, did not capture his imagination. His daydreams transported him to a very different world from that which he knew at St. Croix. Almost shamefacedly, he confessed that he built castles in the air; but, although he apologized for wasting his time conjuring up visions of future greatness, he always clung to the hope that such dreams came true "when the projector is consistent."

His friend Edward Stevens did not need to rely upon daydreams to escape from St. Croix: in 1769 he was sent by his father to New York to study at King's College. Being possessed of a "fine Address, & great Merit & Cleverness," Stevens proposed to convert these assets into a bedside manner: after graduating from King's College, he intended to study medicine. With his best friend gone, Hamilton found the island even more deadly than before. In November, 1769, he wrote Stevens that he would willingly risk his life, though not his character, to raise himself out of the rut into which he felt himself slipping. "I wish," he exclaimed, "there was a war."

It was not a war but a hurricane that gave Hamilton his opportunity of severing connections with St. Croix. Fittingly enough, he rode into the North American continent upon a whirlwind. In August, 1772, one of the most devastating hurricanes in the history of the West Indies struck St. Croix. So deeply impressed was Alexander by the force of the winds and the devastation they wrought that he wrote a description of the storm for the benefit of his father. Before sending the letter, however, Alexander showed it to the Reverend Hugh Knox, a Presbyterian clergyman, schoolteacher, apothecary and physician who resided on the island. Knox had already seen in Alexander evidences of a genius that could be brought to fruition only by a college education. Alexander's description of the hurricane so completely vindicated Knox's high opinion of his young parishioner's talents that he published it in the *Royal Danish American Gazette*.

Although Hamilton set down in his "Hurricane Letter" such effective bits of observation as that the rain tasted of salt and that at the height of the storm there was a strong odor of gunpowder in the air, when he warmed to his work he portrayed the horrors of the night with all the flamboyance of a Gothic novelist. "Good God!" he exclaimed, "what horror and destruction—it's impossible for me to describe—or you to form any idea of it. It seemed as if a total dissolution of nature was taking place. The roaring of the sea and wind—fiery meteors flying about in the air—the prodigious glare of almost perpetual lightning—the crash of the falling houses—and the ear-piercing shrieks of the distressed, were sufficient to strike astonishment into Angels." But it was the "reflections and feelings on this frightful and melancholy occasion" to which Hamilton gave expression that caught the attention of the Reverend Dr. Knox and his friends. Hamilton's letter left no doubt that he had faithfully absorbed the religious instruction of his Presbyterian spiritual guide. Contemplating God's power and wrath as manifested in the hurricane, Hamilton was moved to meditate upon the wretchedness and degradation of man: "Where now, oh! vile worm," he exclaimed, "is all thy boasted fortitude and resolution? What is become of thy arrogance and self-sufficiency?" He saw mankind as wholly depraved and damned and God as "an incensed master, executing vengeance on the crimes of his servants."

Upon rereading his letter, Hamilton was troubled lest these thoughts strike his readers as morbid; after all, not every seventeen-year-old boy saw a sermon in a hurricane. The religious bent of his contemplations, he hastened to point out, did not proceed from excessive fear of God's wrath or from "a conscience overburdened with crimes of an uncommon cast"—the possession of which at his age would have been truly extraordinary. These ideas, he explained, were such as would be naturally awakened in "every thinking breast. . . . It were a lamentable insensibility not to have such feelings—and," he added, "I think inconsistent with human nature." It was inconceivable to him that after witnessing the majesty of God, as manifested in a hurricane, thoughts of man's helplessness, baseness and sin should not follow as a matter of course.

This letter likewise revealed Hamilton to be a youth of high emotional intensity, strongly affected by the plight of the poor and downtrodden, particularly women and little children. During the hurricane, he recounted his horror at seeing "whole families running about the streets unknowing where to find a place of shelter—the sick exposed to the keenness of water and air—without a bed to lie upon—or a dry covering to their Bodies." Extracting, as always, a moral from these events, he urged all who "revel in affluence, [to] see the afflictions of humanity, and bestow your superfluity to

The Making of a Revolutionary 7

ease them." At this stage of his career, his advice to the rich was "succour the miserable and lay up a treasure in Heaven." At a later period, his advice to the rich was to lay up their treasure in United States government bonds.

At least partly on the strength of Hamilton's "Hurricane Letter," his friends—notably the Reverend Hugh Knox and Nicholas Cruger—decided to make it possible for the boy to further his education upon the North American continent. Probably other well-wishers contributed small sums of money to the cause. They did not act wholly out of charity: Hamilton contemplated studying medicine and it was hoped that he would return, as Edward Stevens later did, to practice at St. Croix. With fever and other diseases endemic on the island, the citizens could always use another physician. For a brief period, Hamilton actually did study medicine in New York, but the pressure of events soon swept him into the larger world of war and politics.

That world was entering upon one of its most important and decisive periods when in October, 1772, with hope high and ambition unbounded, Hamilton set sail for the American continent.

When Hamilton arrived upon the North American continent he was far from being a revolutionist. Having lived in a remote corner of the world, he had little understanding of the issues that threatened to disrupt the British Empire. His first impulse was to uphold the authority of the mother country: what manner of men were these, he asked himself, that were continually ranting about liberty and trying to break up the Empire into autonomous petty jurisdictions?

The answer to this question was supplied by the men in whose company he moved after his arrival in the continental colonies. Since Hamilton's letters of introduction from the Reverend Hugh Knox were addressed to residents of the Middle Colonies and the commercial connections of Nicholas Cruger were with New York, it was foreordained that the young West Indian would settle in the New York-New Jersey area. His letters of introduction likewise made certain that he would be thrown in with the Presbyterian friends of the Reverend Dr. Knox, most of whom were zealous upholders of the colonial cause. William Livingston, at whose house Hamilton lived for a short time while attending Dr. Barber's preparatory school at Elizabethtown, New Jersey, was a Presbyterian who took his politics almost as seriously as he did his religion—indeed, in some respects, the two were almost indistinguishable. He was the head of the Presbyterian party that had sworn eternal enmity to the Church of England. When it seemed likely that a bishop of the Church of England would be set over the colonies, it was William Livingston and his Presbyterian friends who led the resistance in the name of religious and civil liberty. In this pious, God-fearing company,

Hamilton was not likely to lose the religious zeal that had distinguished him in St. Croix. He was regularly seen at church, and, as a college student, besides attending church regularly, he was said to be on his knees both morning and night offering up fervent prayers for salvation. While an undergraduate, he composed a hymn entitled "The Soul entering into Bliss."

At this point of his career, Hamilton seemed more likely to win renown in piety and good works than in the feats of arms which had preoccupied his adolescent imagination. And yet Hamilton was not a pallid, priggish, censorious youth given to catechizing his friends upon the state of their souls and priding himself upon his own sanctity. On the contrary, he left the impression of being an extraordinarily cheerful, vivacious and friendly young man. Hercules Mulligan, at whose house Hamilton boarded while attending college, recalled that his star boarder "used in the evening to sit with my family and my brother's family and write doggrel rhymes for their amusement; he was allways amiable and cheerful and extremely attentive to his books."[5]

After a year at Elizabethtown, where he probably dropped two years from his age in order to spare himself the humiliation of going to school with boys younger than himself, Hamilton applied for admission to the College of New Jersey, later known as Princeton. But when he asked to be allowed to accelerate his college work, he touched the Reverend Dr. Witherspoon, the president of the college, at a sore spot. A recent arrival from Scotland, Witherspoon felt that Americans were too much inclined to speed up everything, including their educations. He therefore refused to admit Hamilton upon his own terms—with the result that he entered King's College, later Columbia, as an independent student affiliated with no particular class.

All this time, Hamilton was being indoctrinated by his Presbyterian friends with the philosophy of the revolutionary movement. As a result of their ministrations and Hamilton's reading of the works of James Otis, John Adams and John Dickinson, his earlier doubts and misgivings were wholly swept away. But it is significant that Hamilton was never persuaded that each colony should go its own way; if the empire were to be dissolved, he believed from the beginning that it must be replaced by a firm and indissoluble American union.

In 1773, he was given an opportunity to demonstrate the strength of his convictions. A party of Bostonians, disguised as Indians, threw the taxed tea belonging to the East India Company into Boston Harbor. Although little inclined to condone violence, Hamilton defended the conduct of the Bostonians in a speech delivered in the "Fields" of New York City, and in the New York newspapers, arguing that because of the intransigence of Governor Hutchinson, they had no alternative but to destroy the tea or submit to "slavery." Needless to say, the British government took a very different view of the Boston Tea Party. Measures were quickly taken to punish the Bostonians for their contumacy: by the so-called "Intolerable" or "Coercive" Acts passed by Parliament in 1774, the port of Boston was closed to shipping and the government of Massachusetts was brought more directly under the control of the British government. Alarmed by the rigor with which the home government exacted retribution for the Tea Party, the colonies summoned the First Continental Congress to concert organized resistance to British "tyranny." This resistance took the form of the Continental Association—an agreement not to import or consume British goods and to export no colonial products to Great Britain until Parliament rescinded the Intolerable Acts and offered ironclad guarantees that Americans would not again be molested in the enjoyment of their "inviolable liberties"—including the liberty of not paying taxes imposed by Parliament.

Many Americans refused to join in this attempt to coerce Great Britain, endeavoring instead to confine colonial resistance to petitions and remonstrances. In New York, these conservatives found a redoubtable spokesman in the Reverend Samuel Seabury. This Church of England clergyman revealed himself to be one of the ablest propagandists on either side of the controversy. Writing under the signature "A Westchester Farmer," he cut a deep furrow through the already badly divided public opinion of the province and, for a time, seemed on the point of plowing under the radicals.

Instead of tamely surrendering to the Continental Congress the liberty of buying and selling as they pleased, New Yorkers were enjoined by Seabury to treat the enforcement officers of the Continental Association as though they were "a venomous brood of scorpions to sting us to death." When these unprepossessing visitors arrived, he recommended that they be received with "a good hiccory cudgel." This drastic action was justified, he argued, because if the Continental Association were permitted to go into effect, it would injure Americans themselves far more than the English, West Indians and Irish at whom it was aimed. And the principal victims of this ill-advised measure would, he predicted, be the farmers of New York: unable to sell their produce, they would lose their farms by foreclosure to their creditors. If Seabury could be believed, the only people who would profit from the boycott were the moneylenders and merchants: while the bottom fell out of the price of farm products, the businessmen, their shops well stocked for just such an emergency, would be in a position to charge what the traffic would bear. "You had better trust to the mercy of a Turk," he bluntly told the farmers.[6]

Seabury's principal objective was to destroy the nascent union of the colonies: here, he perceived, lay the real menace to the authority of King and Parliament. It particularly pained this excellent clergyman that instead of suffering the privations they so richly deserved, Bostonians were being showered so lavishly with gifts by their sympathizers throughout the colonies that they were growing rich and insolent. Unless Americans pulled the wool from their eyes, he feared that there would be a literal fulfillment of the prophecy that the saints shall inherit the earth. The Bostonians, he declared, seemed to act upon the improbable proposition that "God had made Boston for himself, and all the rest of the world for Boston."

Manifestly, the patriots could not permit this diatribe against the Continental Congress, New Englanders and colonial businessmen to go unanswered. Some of the most redoubtable writers on the patriot side were preparing to lay Seabury low when an unknown published an answer so crushing that the patriots felt that the "high flying priest" had been permanently grounded. Although this pamphlet was first ascribed to John Jay and John Adams, two of the ablest American propagandists, in actuality it was the work of Alexander Hamilton, then an undergraduate at King's College.*

Here, for the first time, Hamilton gave concrete evidence of the precocity that was to make him an object of wonder to his contemporaries. In their eyes, he seemed to have leaped fully armed from the head of Jove. It is undeniable, however, that despite the suddenness of his advent, he had been long preparing for this emergence. He had carefully modeled his literary style upon that of the masters of precise and lucid English prose—Addison and Steele, Jonathan Swift and "Junius"; he had steeped himself in the literature of political controversy; and he had familiarized himself with the doctrines upon which the American patriots grounded their case against British "tyranny." Finally, his firsthand knowledge of the West Indies and his appreciation of the role of economics in the creation of an American union peculiarly qualified him to answer the Westchester Farmer.

Hamilton perceived that it was as the decrier of colonial union that the Westchester Farmer was most to be feared. Lord North, the British Prime Minister, would hardly have given New Yorkers advice different from that proffered by the Reverend Samuel Seabury. The ulterior purpose of the British government was to isolate Massachusetts and to break up the union of the colonies. Although Seabury sold his wares under the trade-mark of liberty, in reality he worked the same side of the street as did the Prime Minister. By identifying freedom with provincial rights and urging New Yorkers to put their trust in the magnanimity of Great Britain rather than in colonial union and economic coercion, he made himself the spokesman of the British government.

As a defender of colonial union, Hamilton undertook to beat the Westchester Farmer at his own game of appealing to the self-interest of the farmers of New York. Whereas Seabury tried to frighten the farmers into

---

* It required two pamphlets, *A Full Vindication of the Measures of Congress from the Calumnies of their Enemies, in Answer to a Letter under a signature of A. W. Farmer* and *The Farmer Refuted; or a more comprehensive and impartial View of the Disputes between Great Britain and the Colonies,* for Hamilton to dispose of the Westchester Farmer. Altogether, he devoted almost 50,000 words to presenting the patriot case and refuting the aspersions of the Reverend Dr. Seabury.

The Making of a Revolutionary

abandoning the Continental Association by picturing the ruin that awaited them if they challenged Great Britain to an economic trial of strength, Hamilton dwelt upon the ruin that would befall them if they submitted to Parliament. Give that body the slightest opportunity, he said, and it would throw the whole tax book at Americans. "Perhaps, before long," he predicted, "your tables, and chairs, and platters, and dishes, and knives, and forks, and every thing else, would be taxed. Nay, I don't know but they would find means to tax you for every child you got, and for every kiss your daughters received from their sweethearts; and, God knows, that would soon ruin you."

If New Yorkers wished to preserve their inalienable right to beget children and to give and receive kisses without interference from the tax collector, Hamilton advised them to support the Continental Congress and the Continental Association to the full. The times were too critical, he declared, for Americans to indulge their sectional jealousies and animosities; if Massachusetts were offered up as a sacrifice to appease the British government, the rest of the colonies, far from purchasing security, would discover that they, too, had been marked for ruin. In that event, he said, the British government would be able to devour them piecemeal—which was precisely how the British Ministry had planned it.

It was not enough for Hamilton to vindicate the policies of the Continental Congress; Seabury had impugned the integrity of the colonial merchants by asserting that they would use the boycott to profiteer at the expense of the public. Since 1770, when the New York merchants had broken the intercolonial boycott that had been begun two years before, they had been under suspicion of using nonimportation agreements to feather their own nests—at the risk, of course, of getting a coat of tar to go with the feathers. Therefore Hamilton, the defender of the American businessman—now cast for the first time in the role he was to play later upon a larger stage—could not hope to carry conviction if he pictured businessmen as honest, high-minded patriots who put the good of the country above profits. He wisely contented himself with observing that "a vast majority of mankind is entirely biased by motives of self-interest" and that businessmen, being influenced by self-interest to a greater degree than any other order of men, would find it to their interest to support the boycott.

And yet, even though the merchants did their duty, many Americans doubted that they could triumph over Great Britain in an economic duel. The colonies were almost wholly dependent upon the mother country for wool and cotton cloth: they produced little wool or cotton and, except for homespun, they manufactured no clothing. Here, therefore, was the crucial question: Would Americans persist in boycotting British merchandise, especially clothing, when they felt the blasts of winter? Would they hate Great Britain in December as much as they did in May?

The Westchester Farmer had made the most of his dismal prospect of winters without end and without breeches, predicting that if Americans refused to buy British goods they would soon be as naked as Indians—and vastly more uncomfortable. Thus would they discover that the state of Nature, far from being the idyllic condition they imagined, was, as Thomas Hobbes had said, nasty, brutish and short.

Even the most optimistic patriots resigned themselves to wearing their old clothes for the duration of the struggle with Great Britain, but Hamilton declared that they would not be obliged to undergo even that small hardship. If Americans were frugal, industrious and wise, he saw no reason why they could not be as well clad as Englishmen—and this without the necessity of importing a yard of cloth from abroad. All the raw materials, he pointed out, were either available or could quickly be brought under cultivation: given the incentive, in a few years the southern colonies might produce enough cotton to clothe the entire continent, and the northern colonies had only to turn a small part of their land to sheepraising in order to make Americans wholly self-sufficient in wool. Nor did Hamilton's optimism fail him when he came to the last and most formidable obstacle—the establishment of factories for manufacture of cloth and clothing. He believed that from the stream of immigrants pouring into the colonies enough skilled workers could be drawn to build and operate factories that could compete successfully with their English prototypes.

While the immediate objective of the Continental Association was to retaliate upon Great Britain, Hamilton viewed it in a much broader perspective. In its blundering, muddling way, the British government seemed to him to be hastening a process that would one day make American colonies rich and powerful beyond the imagination of eighteenth-century men. When he surveyed the magnitude and the diversity of the blessings with which Nature had endowed the North American continent, Hamilton saw evidences of a Divine plan by which the parts were to be indissolubly linked together. It seemed to him that God and Nature had intended that Americans should find their true well-being and happiness in trading with each other, thereby attaining the self-sufficiency that would insulate them from the wars of Europe and guard them against the oppressions of Great Britain.

If Great Britain were so far gone in folly as to provoke war with the colonies, or if—as Hamilton thought more probable—fighting broke out between the New Englanders and the British troops stationed in Massachusetts, he was ready for the event. Having told Americans that they were invincible in an economic struggle with Great Britain, he now endeavored to persuade them that they were equally certain of winning a shooting war with the mother country if for no other reason than that France was certain to come to their aid. French professions of neutrality he pronounced to be "merely a piece of finesse"; "The promises of princes and statesmen," said

The Making of a Revolutionary

this young student of Machiavelli, "are of little weight. They never bind them longer than till a strong temptation offers to break them; and they are frequently made with a sinister design." Reasons of state—and to Hamilton's mind there were none stronger—indicated that France would sooner or later be an active belligerent in a war between Great Britain and its colonies.

But civil war and foreign intervention were not what Hamilton wished for the British Empire: by taking up his pen, his whole purpose, he averred, was to avoid the necessity of taking up his sword. In writing his answer to the Reverend Samuel Seabury he sought to show Americans and Englishmen how the imperial connection could be solidified by "the powerful bands of self-interest"; how Americans could be persuaded to work and multiply for the greater glory of the Empire; and how, in place of broils and contentions, a "perpetual and mutually beneficial union" could be created. Later in his career, Hamilton became the great apostle of American union, but he began as a protagonist of union among the English-speaking peoples. He became an American nationalist only after his vision of imperial federation had faded at Lexington, Concord and Bunker Hill.[7]

The responsibility of preserving the British Empire as a community of free men Hamilton regarded as one of the supreme challenges of British statesmanship. True, up to this time British statesmanship had not given Hamilton much reason to suppose that it would rise to the occasion. But the case was not so desperate as it might appear: he believed that he had the answer to the problems that vexed the Empire, and that if British statesmen could be persuaded to act upon his ideas the colonies would be secured to Great Britain by the most durable ties Hamilton recognized—those of self-interest.

The first and most important step, Hamilton said, was for Great Britain to give Americans as much freedom as they desired. He told Englishmen that they had no reason to fear American freedom: the more liberal they were in this regard, the more prosperous they and the colonists would be. Of course, the application of this principle to the Empire meant that Americans would enjoy complete equality with Englishmen. This was precisely what Hamilton had in mind: had his plans been realized, Americans would have virtually achieved commonwealth status one hundred and fifty years before the Statute of Westminster made the Dominions legally coequal with Great Britain.

In propounding this theory of the Empire, Hamilton did not conceive himself to be a revolutionist. A federal union of sovereign states united by allegiance to the reigning monarch was not something Hamilton proposed for the British Empire as a new venture: he believed that it had existed from the beginning. In his own eyes, he was no innovator attempting to overturn the constitutional relationship between the colonies and the mother country—he was a defender of the established and legal order against the encroachments of Parliament.

The certitude that characterized Hamilton's political opinions sprang from his conviction that his version of the imperial relationship was nothing less than the order established by God and Nature. Here his political philosophy found its ultimate sanction: separated by three thousand miles from its colonies, Great Britain could not tax them without violating those immutable "laws" which decreed that there should be no taxation without representation. It was only by the exercise of local autonomy that Americans could enjoy the rights which God and Nature had intended them to enjoy. All that Hamilton asked of British statesmen was that they conduct the affairs of the Empire in conformity with the will of God.

Like most American patriots of his generation, Hamilton believed that he was fully competent to elucidate the intentions of the Almighty. Conceiving the universe to be essentially mechanistic, governed by laws which the human intelligence could discover and comprehend, it seemed to Hamilton and his fellow patriots that human affairs were likewise controlled by laws which could be reduced to a few simple principles. There were, for example, certain things forbidden to governments by God and Nature; as Hamilton said, "an intelligent, superintending principle . . . the governor of the universe" had erected barriers beyond which governments could not legally go. These barriers were designed to protect the rights of the individual. A beneficent Creator had made the liberties of mankind his special concern; and Infinite Wisdom had defined the limits of governmental authority.[8]

Thus Hamilton embarked upon his controversy with the Westchester Farmer armed with a philosophy of natural rights against which no arguments drawn from the law or the constitution could stand. Indeed, according to his interpretation, the British constitution was simply another version of the laws of Nature; the accumulated wisdom of the centuries which it incorporated seemed to Hamilton to have been evolved from the immutable principles laid down by the Creator for the governance of mankind. With God and the British constitution on his side, Hamilton feared no adversary: he had an irrefutable answer for every argument. "THE SACRED RIGHTS OF MANKIND ARE NOT TO BE RUMMAGED FOR AMONG OLD PARCHMENTS OR MUSTY RECORDS," he declared. "THEY ARE WRITTEN, AS WITH A SUNBEAM IN THE WHOLE VOLUME OF HUMAN NATURE, BY THE HAND OF THE DIVINITY ITSELF, AND CAN NEVER BE ERASED OR OBSCURED BY MORTAL POWER."[9]

Although he assumed that the laws of Nature were cognizable by all reasonable, well-intentioned men, Hamilton recognized that a special revelation might be necessary for the "blind and infatuated" British ruling class. He was right: nothing short of a revelation would have persuaded Englishmen that Americans had correctly interpreted the will of God and Nature.

The Making of a Revolutionary

For it was a peculiarity of the laws of Nature that though they were abundantly clear to all men, all did not read them alike. Nor was the "Mother of Parliaments" ready to recognize her overseas offspring as her equals or, indeed, as her legitimate descendants.

Likewise, Hamilton's vision of a bloodless colonial victory over Great Britain by means of the Continental Association was founded upon a misapprehension of the attitude of Englishmen toward the colonies. Rather than suffer themselves to be coerced by "rebellious peasants" overseas, the majority of Englishmen were prepared to support the claims of King and Parliament to the bitter end. While correctly gauging the colonists' determination to maintain their rights, Hamilton seriously underestimated Englishmen's determination to maintain their sovereignty over the colonies. If, as he assumed, self-interest dictated a policy of conciliation toward the colonies, the government and people of Great Britain were singularly deaf to its promptings. Sovereignty was more precious than even the peace of the Empire. It was not until after seven years of war that Americans attained what Hamilton assured them they would secure after a few months of economic coercion—"the undisturbed possession of our privileges."

In the dispute over the meaning of the British constitution, the rights of Englishmen and the nature of the British Empire, Hamilton played a far more important part than did anyone of his own age on either side of the Atlantic. At a time when expository prose attained new heights of clarity, precision and vigor, and when some of the best minds were engaged in polemics, Hamilton emerged at the age of nineteen as one of the most adept practitioners of the art of persuasion.

Even so, Hamilton contributed no new principles to the controversy. For the most part, he was content to take his stand upon the doctrines then being advanced by the Continental Congress and, like Thomas Jefferson and other patriots, he made John Locke his political Bible. His own writings were largely an exegesis of the sacred text of the "Two Discourses upon Government." Nevertheless, Hamilton did not merely reduce John Locke to everyday terms for the benefit of those who did not take their natural-rights philosophy straight from the source. The arguments by which he sought to prove the economic invincibility of the colonies in their struggle with the mother country; his analysis of the commercial relations between the continental colonies and the West Indies; and his conviction that America formed an economic whole in which the various sections complemented each other in such a way as to indicate that Providence had designed a great and powerful nation upon this continent—these were his real contribution to the American cause. Although Hamilton later changed his political philosophy, his views of the economic basis of the American union were never altered.

Even though Hamilton's pamphlets won the praises of the patriots, among the members of the New York Assembly they made few converts. In that body the conservatives and Loyalists formed a united front against all efforts to enforce the Continental Association; and the Assembly went so far as to refuse to send delegates to the Second Continental Congress summoned to meet in May, 1775. It was not the reasoned arguments of Hamilton and other patriots but the outbreak of fighting at Lexington and Concord that swept New York into the vortex of the Revolution.[10]

2.
Aide-de-Camp to Washington

With the advent of fighting in New England, a wave of mob violence swept the American colonies. In May, 1775, the New York mob, having already emulated the Boston "redskins" by destroying a cargo of East India Company tea, attacked the house of the Reverend Myles Cooper. Admittedly, this was an unceremonious way of treating a clergyman, but the Reverend Doctor Cooper, in the eyes of his adversaries, had forfeited his clerical immunities by becoming a Tory propagandist and a college president. Although Hamilton was fond of sport, he drew the line at Tory-baiting: there were, he declared, wise and good men on both sides of the controversy and he could not "presume to think every man who differs from him either a fool or knave." Suiting his actions to his words, Hamilton and several other undergraduates saved the Reverend Doctor from the mob. No greater love hath an undergraduate for a college professor than Hamilton demonstrated on this occasion. He was properly rewarded by being mentioned in a poem commemorating this incident published by the grateful clergyman in the *Gentleman's Magazine*.

A few months later, in October, 1775, Isaac Sears, a New York patriot, descended upon the city at the head of a body of Connecticut horsemen. His objective was to capture James Rivington, a New York printer guilty of publishing Loyalist tracts. On their way through Westchester County, Sears and his men carried off the Reverend Samuel Seabury. But by the time they reached New York City, Rivington had flown and the patriots had to be content with wrecking his press. Nevertheless, they returned to New England in triumph: it was not every day that Yankees could see a real live clergyman of the Church of England in captivity.*[1]

Instead of warmly welcoming these visiting Sons of Liberty and applauding the forthrightness with which they disposed of his political adversary, Hamilton deplored Sears's raid as a wanton piece of violence and an unlaw-

---
* A sad disappointment was in store for the patriots: no crimes or misdemeanors could be proved against Seabury. And so, upon the demand of the New York Provincial Congress, his captors reluctantly turned him loose. Seabury found sanctuary in England and later returned to the United States, where he became an Episcopalian bishop.

ful invasion of the territorial integrity of New York. It is said that he even harangued the citizens to defend Rivington's press against the "invaders." Not that Hamilton was disposed to accord the Loyalists the privilege of freely expressing their views in print; although his own pamphlets had been printed by Rivington, Hamilton pronounced him to be "detestable . . . in every respect" and his press pernicious beyond all bearing. Nevertheless, he could not condone the practice in which many patriots were beginning to indulge of taking the law into their own hands. Although he had hitherto defended New Englanders as a virtuous, long-suffering and peace-loving people, he now discovered that they were prone "to a spirit of encroachment and arrogance" which led them to treat the local concerns of New York as though they were their own and to attempt—an utterly hopeless undertaking—to remake New York in the image of Boston. Above all, he deprecated invasions of one colony by citizens of another colony, because they tended to inflame long-established animosities and to impede the unification of the country under the Continental Congress.[2]

Radical as Hamilton was in his views regarding the exercise of British authority in America, he was a stanch conservative when it came to mobs and disorders. If the freedom of the press had to be curtailed, it was the duty of the government, not of the mob, he held, to take action. "I am always more or less alarmed," he remarked, "at every thing which is done of mere will and pleasure without proper authority." His idea of the proper authority to deal with Rivington and his kind was the Continental Congress; and when it became necessary to suppress the Loyalists by force, he urged that the Continental Army be called in to do the job. The union of the colonies was less than a year old, yet already Hamilton was advising his countrymen to entrust the central government with the responsibility of maintaining order.

It grieved this young revolutionist that violence and disorder could not be kept out of the revolutionary movement. It was a simple matter to raise a mob, but, he reminded New Yorkers, it was a very different matter to lay one: violence bred violence until it eventuated in a reign of terror. From the "unthinking populace," he perceived, moderation was not to be expected: the very passions that led the multitude to resist tyranny tended to breed contempt of all authority. And once the populace had tasted power, Hamilton was prepared to bid farewell to liberty: lacking "a sufficient stock of reason and knowledge to guide them," the people seemed certain to cast off law and order as so much impedimenta upon the rights of man.

Even intelligent people, Hamilton feared, were prone, under the stress of passion, to run into the same excess as did the multitude. For this reason, in such tempestuous times as the colonies were then experiencing, Hamilton believed that it required the "greatest skill in the political pilots to keep men steady and within proper bounds." Even in the days when hope ran high that a new era was about to open for mankind, Hamilton apprehended that Americans would destroy their happiness by succumbing to their passions and grasping for more liberty than they could wisely use.

A Revolution which, while observing the rules of decorum, upheld the rights of man was the ideal of many Americans besides Hamilton. Nor did his fear of the violence of the "unthinking multitude" necessarily stamp him as a contemner of the common man who revealed even in his youth the qualities that were to make him a champion of aristocracy. Thomas Jefferson had declined in 1774 to approve the Boston Tea Party for the same reasons that made Hamilton deplore Sears's raid: both men wanted to keep the mob out of the American Revolution. When Hamilton said that "Irregularities ought to be checked by every prudent and moderate man," he echoed a sentiment held by most of the leaders of the revolutionary movement. One of the most remarkable features of the Revolution was the extent to which prudent and moderate men like Hamilton were able to prevent the "spirit of licentiousness" from getting out of hand.[3]

Despite the misbehavior of overzealous New Englanders, Hamilton never forgot that the real menace to freedom came from Old rather than from New England. While Americans' ears were "stunned with the dismal sounds of New Englanders' republicanism, bigotry and intolerance," he exclaimed, the British Ministry was preparing to establish in Canada "arbitrary power and its great engine, the Popish religion." In 1774, the British Parliament had enacted the Quebec Act by which the boundaries of that province were extended to include the Ohio Valley; English common law was replaced by French civil law; and the Roman Catholic religion was accorded official toleration. Under different circumstances, these concessions to the customs and religion of the French-speaking Canadians might have been acclaimed as a work of statesmanship; but coming at a time when the British government was attempting to punish Massachusetts, the Quebec Act seemed to Americans to betray a determination on the part of the Ministry to use a host of "Popish" slaves to overrun the Protestant colonies at a signal given by Lord North and the Pope.

Under the firm persuasion that the British government intended to destroy freedom in all the colonies, Hamilton beat the alarm against the insidious advance in the North of "popery" and tyranny. Every liberty-loving Protestant American, he declared, ought to view the Quebec Act as proof positive of the intentions of the British Ministry to reduce all British America to slavery. "They had no more right to do it there than here." As for using Canadian Roman Catholics to destroy American liberty, Hamilton admitted that the Ministry could hardly have chosen a better instrument; "by reason of their implicit devotion to their priests, and the superlative reverence they bear those who countenance and favor their religion," he remarked, "they will be the voluntary instruments of ambition, and will be ready, at all times, to second the oppressive designs of the administration against the other parts of the empire."

This unsparing condemnation of the Roman Catholics of Canada Hamilton soon had occasion to regret. Within a few months of the publication of his tirade against "popery," the Continental Congress was seeking to win the support of the French Canadians to the cause of American freedom. Instead of being denounced as the hirelings of the British Ministry and the servitors of Antichrist, the Canadians were hailed as freemen and adherents to a respectable religion for which Protestant Americans entertained only the friendliest feelings. It is hardly to be wondered that the Canadians were bewildered by this sudden change of front and that they were not quite sure, when the Americans finally invaded Canada, whether they would be massacred as "papists" or embraced as brothers. Their doubts and misgivings had much to do with their failure to give wholehearted support to the American invaders in 1775-76 and with the consequent failure of the Continental Congress to make Canada the fourteenth state.[4]

From the scenes of mob violence which momentarily strained Hamilton's devotion to the Revolution, he turned almost with relief to the more reputable spectacle of war. For, unwanted and unheralded, war had come, and Hamilton lost no time in getting into the thick of it. Although he did not fire the shot heard around the world, he was one of the first Americans of the War of Independence to unlimber a cannon. Thanks to his friends in the New York Provincial Congress, he was appointed a captain of artillery in 1775. But in accord with the practice of the army at this period, Captain Hamilton was obliged to find the men for his company and to provide them with accouterments—no easy matter for a college undergraduate without private means.

In defending Americans' courage against the aspersions of Samuel Seabury, Hamilton had asserted that "there is a certain enthusiasm in liberty, that makes human nature rise above itself in acts of bravery and heroism." He himself had given evidence of this enthusiasm in August, 1775, when he went under the fire of British ships in New York Harbor to help drag to safety the cannon guarding the Battery. But in the subsequent fighting around New York, Hamilton found that something more than bravery and heroism was needed to hold back the British fleet and army. Although Hamilton and his men fired until their cannon were put out of action, they failed to stop the passage of British ships of war up the Hudson. Nor did they have better success in halting the advance of British troops on Long Island and Manhattan. Reeling under successive blows, the American army, with Hamilton's company covering the rear, began the retreat across New Jersey that did not end until it reached Philadelphia.

The war was taking a course not anticipated by Hamilton. He had supposed that the odds—15,000 against 500,000 men—would be far too great for British discipline and military skill to overcome. Moreover, he had assumed that the British army, after twelve years of peace, was full of deadwood, particularly in the higher echelons: "There are many effeminate striplings among the officers . . . and but few veterans, either among the leaders or the common soldiers," he had assured his countrymen. But the "striplings" and the "old women" gave an account of themselves in the fighting in New York and New Jersey that made Americans wonder if they had not grossly underestimated the prowess of their enemy.

Yet after Sir William Howe halted his forces at the Delaware, thereby giving Washington an opportunity to regroup his army and assume the offensive, the war assumed a very different complexion. Hamilton and his company played a conspicuous part in the new phase of the fighting that opened with the crossing of the Delaware by the American army. At the second battle of Trenton he and his gunners prevented the British under Lord Cornwallis from crossing the Raritan while Washington and the main army struck out for Princeton. Hamilton, too, got away from the redcoats at Trenton and his guns harassed the enemy as they retreated northward. Although Hamilton had been denied admission to Princeton, he left his mark upon that institution: he put a cannon ball through Nassau Hall where some British troops were holed up.

It was at this time that Hamilton's star unexpectedly rose ascendant. Probably at the instigation of General Henry Knox, the Boston bookseller who had risen to command of the American artillery, he was invited by General Washington to become his aide-de-camp with the rank of lieutenant colonel. The offer came at a critical moment in Hamilton's fortunes: as a result of battle casualties, desertion and expiration of terms of enlistment, his company was reduced to two officers and thirty men.

Serving as aide-de-camp to the Commander in Chief was an honor reserved for young men of good family and breeding: Washington always set great store by the gentlemanly qualities of his officers and he was particularly insistent that his immediate comrades-in-arms—his "family" as he called them—be gentlemen born and bred. True, Hamilton did not have family in the strict sense of the word, but he did have what sometimes serves as an effective substitute—an easy, ingratiating manner, a lively intelligence and the air of an aristocrat. Moreover, his association with the Livingstons and other prominent families certified him as a gentleman. He already had a foot inside the charmed circle of the aristocracy: with his appointment as Washington's aide, the door began to swing open.[5]

Certainly Hamilton was not regarded as an interloper by the young blue bloods of Washington's staff. Among them, his ardor for military glory and his eagerness to come to grips with the British earned him the sobriquet of "The Little Lion."

Of the "beardless boys" who served Washington as aides, Tench Tilghman and Richard Harison at first enjoyed the greatest intimacy and bore the main burden of secretarial duties. Yet in the course of time Hamilton became closer to Washington than any other man. Some of Hamilton's best friends in later life were likewise his companions in Washington's "family." But there was also Cain: Aaron Burr served as Washington's aide before the disclosure of a surreptitious love affair and his dislike of Washington himself led Burr to seek a wider theater for the display of his talents as a lover and a soldier.

The friendships thus formed in the army were compared by the young men themselves to that of Damon and Pythias, and they expressed their devotion in the high-flown literary language of the day. In their letters it is not uncommon to find them addressing each other in terms certain to provoke a riot in even the best-regulated present-day barracks or mess hall. For example, John Laurens, one of Washington's aides, saw nothing strange in writing to his friend Richard Meade in this strain: "Adieu: I embrace you tenderly. . . . My friendship for you will burn with that pure flame which has kindled you your virtues." Laurens addressed Hamilton as "My Dear" and his letters abound in flowery protestations of undying affection, to which Hamilton responded with the touching declaration: "I love you."

Hamilton and Laurens belonged to a generation of military men that prided itself not upon the hard-boiled avoidance of sentiment but upon the cultivation of the finer feelings. Theirs was the language of the heart, noble, exalted and sentimental. For Hamilton and Laurens were not merely soldiers doing a job; they were classical scholars whose thoughts and actions were colored by the grandeur of antiquity. They lived—and often died—by the code of the heroes of Plutarch.

In consequence of his appointment as aide-de-camp to General Washington, Hamilton stepped from the comparative obscurity of a captain of artillery into the limelight of headquarters. Not only did he now serve under the eye of the Commander in Chief—with all the possibilities of advancement opened up by that proximity—but he also attracted the attention of the political leaders of New York. As a fellow New Yorker, a writer of proved ability and, presumably, a confidant of the Commander in Chief, Hamilton appeared to these civilians as a prime source of military information and a medium through which to impress their views upon headquarters. He was accordingly invited by a committee of the New York legislature to open a regular correspondence relating to the conduct of the war. With a fluency seldom encountered among gentlemen of the sword, Hamilton provided the committee with a running commentary upon the events of the war, an elucidation of the problems confronting the government and an analysis of the international situation. Deeply impressed upon these letters is a strong sense of stewardship: he boldly faced the difficulties confronting the struggling young republic and with characteristic assurance offered a solution for every problem. In this correspondence, he made clear that his opinions were his own, not Washington's. Nor did he hesitate to set his own views against those of the Commander in Chief; he never carried subordination to the point of adopting another man's ideas against his better judgment.

Well aware that time was running out—if the war dragged on, France was almost certain to intervene—Sir William Howe planned in 1777 to crush the rebellion by a two-pronged attack. While General John Burgoyne marched southward from Canada by way of Ticonderoga and Albany, thus cutting off New England from the rest of the union, Howe himself intended to force Washington into a general engagement by moving against Philadelphia, the rebel capital. At the outset, this strategy worked to perfection: Howe sent his army by sea to the Chesapeake and threatened Philadelphia; when Washington attempted to stop the British advance, the Americans were routed at the battle of the Brandywine. Burgoyne easily captured Ticonderoga and the American army in the North was scattered to the winds. But just when the road to Albany seemed clear ahead, the Americans changed commanders—General Philip Schuyler, who had succeeded in alienating the New Englanders under his command, was replaced by General Horatio Gates, a former British officer popular among the Yankees—and a new American army, armed with guns and powder recently received from France, took the field. Burgoyne suffered serious reverses at Bennington and Fort Stanwix and finally, in October, 1777, surrounded and outnumbered by the Americans and harassed by the reckless forays of Benedict Arnold, "Gentleman Johnny" surrendered his army at Saratoga.

In the fighting in the south it fell to Hamilton to carry the news to Philadelphia that the British had broken through the American defenses and that the city was doomed. But while the capital was lost, the army remained intact and in November, 1777, Washington came close to defeating Howe at the battle of Germantown. Despite Washington's good showing, this engagement promised to be his last: although it was public knowledge that Howe was mustering his forces in order to overwhelm the Continental Army before winter put an end to the campaign, Washington's troops, their terms of enlistment having expired, went home in droves. The fate of the Revolution thus seemed to depend upon procuring a large number of fresh troops capable of withstanding the expected onslaught.

In this moment of crisis, Washington looked to General Horatio Gates for reinforcements. The conqueror of Burgoyne, now unopposed by any British force, had at his disposal enough troops to turn the balance in Pennsylvania in favor of the Americans. Theoretically, the Continental troops of the Northern Army were under Washington's command and could be moved wherever he desired. But Washington's authority had been undermined by Gates's assumption—tacitly condoned by Congress—of independent powers: in announcing his victory over Burgoyne, for example, he had communicated directly with Congress, pointedly ignoring the Commander in Chief, and Congress had not seen fit to rebuke him for the slight. Moreover, Washington was in no position to force a showdown of authority upon Gates: as a counterpoise to Gates's victory over Burgoyne, he could offer only defeats and the indecisive battle of Germantown.

Nevertheless, at a council of war it was decided to call the Continental troops under the command of General Gates to the main army in Pennsylvania opposing General Howe. A few troops were to be left at Peekskill and in the Highlands for defense of the Hudson, but otherwise all available regulars were to be brought up to reinforce Washington. To inform Gates of this decision, Hamilton was ordered to post with all speed to Albany, the headquarters of the Northern Army.

Hamilton found Gates in no mood to strip himself of troops in order to oblige Washington. Although prior to Hamilton's arrival Gates had sent several thousand troops, including Morgan's riflemen, southward, he had retained some of the best regiments for the defense of the arsenal at Albany and to forestall any attempt by Sir Henry Clinton in New York to invade New England—and with these men he refused to part. While Hamilton was not convinced that Gates needed all this man power, he decided not to insist peremptorily upon a full compliance with Washington's orders. General Horatio Gates, he perceived, had become a power to be reckoned with: his popularity was unbounded, particularly in New England, and he had many supporters in the Continental Congress. Moreover, as Hamilton admitted, there was always the possibility that Gates would be proved right: Clinton might come up the Hudson or he might turn his army against New England as Gates seemed to fear. If either of these events occurred, the blame would fall upon Washington while Gates would add to his already swollen popularity the prestige of a vindicated prophet.

For these reasons, Hamilton accepted the one brigade of Continental troops offered by Gates. It did not seem a bad bargain: together with the men being dispatched, as he supposed, by General Putnam to the main army in Pennsylvania, Washington would have almost five thousand additional men with which to make head against Howe. Despite the obstructions he had met with, Hamilton still hoped to see Philadelphia in the Americans' hands before the winter put an end to the campaign.

He was preparing to return to headquarters in order to be on hand for the impending battle when an event occurred which put an entirely new complexion upon his relations with General Gates. He learned—from his own inquiries, not from Gates himself—that the brigade of Continental troops to be sent to Washington was the weakest of the three under Gates's com-

Aide-de-Camp to Washington

mand: it consisted of only about six hundred effectives and, although a militia regiment of about two hundred men was attached to it, the period of service of the militiamen was on the point of expiring.

Hamilton immediately concluded that he had been tricked by Gates: he had ventured on his own responsibility to accept less than Washington had asked only to find that the commander of the Northern Army had played him false. Immediately, all Hamilton's compunctions about challenging Gates's authority vanished: he demanded in Washington's name that one of the other Continental brigades be sent south; and he now revealed for the first time that his instructions required him to procure two regiments as reinforcements for the main army. Nevertheless, Hamilton was willing to abide by the terms of his original agreement with Gates provided that a Continental brigade of full strength was detached from the Northern Army.

When the matter was put to him in this light, Gates consented to part with two brigades—the one he had attempted to palm off upon Hamilton, and another with a full complement of men and officers. But Hamilton, put on his guard by Gates's "duplicity," took no chances that these troops would slip through his fingers: he remained at Albany until they had been dispatched to the southward; then, and only then, did he himself set out for headquarters.

It proved to be a journey full of unpleasant surprises. If Hamilton supposed he had encountered obstinacy, pride and wrongheadedness in General Gates, they were as nothing compared with what he suffered at the hands of General Putnam. "Old Putt" was nursing ambitions that could not be reconciled with Washington's orders that reinforcements be marched to Pennsylvania; and in a conflict between ambition and orders from his superior officer, Putnam unhesitatingly chose the course of ambition. Whereas Gates professed to fear an attack by Clinton upon the stores at Albany, Putnam saw in Clinton's weakness an opportunity to capture New York City and destroy the garrison. To this end, he detained at Fishkill all the troops, both Continentals and militia, that came his way. The men Hamilton had supposed were on their way to Washington's camp were still at Fishkill: everything was subordinated to the grand design of taking New York City. That the Commander in Chief disapproved of this strategy was apparently of no consequence whatever: Gates had already set the example, with Congress's approval, of ignoring the Commander in Chief, and Putnam was determined to show that he, too, could wage his private wars.

When Hamilton cited his instructions and ordered Putnam to obey in the name of the Commander in Chief, the cantankerous New Englander declined to believe that a mere boy could represent Washington's views. At last, even he was convinced that this particular stripling really spoke with authority, but other circumstances conspired to delay the marching of reinforcements to Washington's army: the troops were ill, mutinous for want of pay and without supplies—the remedying of which fell upon Hamilton's shoulders.

In the midst of these tribulations, Hamilton fell ill and was confined to his bed for over a week. That the reinforcements finally marched away to Pennsylvania was largely owing to Governor George Clinton, who raised the money to pay the troops and found the necessary supplies to start them on their way. So impressed was Hamilton by Clinton's energy and ability that he suggested to Washington that the governor be put in the place of Putnam, whose "blunders and caprices" seemed certain to cost the Americans dear.[6]

The fact that Washington was not obliged to withstand attack from a reinforced British army under Sir William Howe while the American generals wrangled was owing primarily to the heroic resistance of the defenders of Mud Island, which denied the British fleet access to Philadelphia. When, in the middle of November, Mud Island finally fell, the season was too late to admit of an extended campaign. Although Howe marched out of Philadelphia at the head of his legions and drew up before the American position at Whitemarsh, the two armies were content to exchange angry looks: Howe would not march up the hill and Washington would not come down. And so, upon this indecisive note, the campaign of 1777 ended; Howe had Philadelphia, but he had not succeeded in attaining the objective that had drawn him to Pennsylvania—the destruction of Washington's army—without which Howe knew that victory would continue to elude him.

Thus Hamilton's efforts to rush reinforcements to Washington—an undertaking upon which he believed the fate of the American cause depended—did not materially affect the outcome of the campaign of 1777. Some of the troops he succeeded in bringing to the main army went into winter quarters at Valley Forge—an experience for which they had no reason to be thankful to Hamilton.

The fighting was over for the winter, but there was no rest for the soldiers and the politicians. The contrast between the brilliant victory won by Gates at Saratoga and the stalemate achieved by Washington in the war in Pennsylvania persuaded some citizens, both in and out of Congress, that the time had come to change the high command. These men had long dreaded the overweening popularity of Washington and his insistence upon a large army of regular troops as portents of military dictatorship. Gates, on the other hand, seemed disposed to accept congressional direction of the war with good grace and he was known to set a higher value upon militia than did Washington. As a result, Gates began to be groomed as the "savior" of the American cause from the bad generalship and dictatorial ambitions of George Washington.

The "plot" against Washington—if it ever existed—was thwarted by the indiscretion of two men who wore the buff and blue of the Continental Army

Aide-de-Camp to Washington

—General Thomas Conway and Colonel James Wilkinson. Conway was an Irishman who, having served many years in the French army, had come to the United States to pick up a little easy glory and strengthen his claims to promotion in the French army. An excellent drillmaster, he made his brigade a model for the rest of the army; but he was keenly aware of his superiority and made no effort to conceal his disdain of American officers, including Washington. Many members of Congress were prepared to accept him at his own valuation as a military genius. Moreover, he held a contract signed by Silas Deane, the American representative in Paris, promising him preferential treatment in the American army. When Conway threatened, unless the terms of this contract were fulfilled, to return to France and tell Louis XVI what ingrates the Americans were, Congress meekly agreed to make him a major general with the title of Inspector General of the Continental Army.

Insofar as he was capable of feeling hero worship for anyone besides himself, the Irish officer found General Horatio Gates worthy of homage. In return, Gates ate up Conway's praise, heavily spiced as it was with sneers at Washington. Unluckily for Gates, Conway chose to make him the confidant of some particularly devastating remarks about the Commander in Chief: after the battle of Germantown, which, Conway declared, would have been an American victory had Washington kept his head, he told Gates that "Heaven surely is determined to save the American cause, or a weak General and bad councils had long since lost it."

The letter containing this aspersion was entrusted to James Wilkinson, Gates's aide-de-camp, who, because of the speed with which he brought the news of Burgoyne's surrender from Saratoga to Philadelphia, was raised by Congress from the rank of colonel to brigadier general. As a bearer of glad tidings, Wilkinson was unexcelled; but when it came to carrying confidential letters, he left something to be desired. Having had a few too many in a wayside tavern, he told a fellow officer that Conway was promoting Gates for the post of Commander in Chief and even quoted a few choice passages from the letter he was carrying to his commanding officer.

As might be expected, Washington was immediately informed of this development. Although no one pretended that Gates ought to be condemned for opinions expressed by a correspondent, in an atmosphere as surcharged with jealousy and suspicion as that which existed between Gates and Washington, small things were magnified out of all proportion. To Washington and his entourage, therefore, it appeared that a plot had been laid, with Gates's connivance, to invest the conqueror of Burgoyne with the supreme command.

Having just returned from Gates's headquarters, Hamilton was in a position to speak with authority concerning the attitude of the "Hero of Saratoga" toward Washington. Without hesitation, he gave it as his opinion that Gates was acting out of malice to Washington: puffed up with pride and self-importance, the Northern commander could not bear to see his rival, the Commander in Chief, win a victory over Howe that might diminish the luster of his own triumph over Burgoyne. That Gates had sent two regiments to Pennsylvania when he was informed of Washington's orders seems to have been blotted from Hamilton's memory. "I shall not hesitate to say," he told Washington, "I doubt whether you would have had a man from the Northern army, if the whole could have been kept at Albany with any decency." As for Conway, Hamilton called him "one of the vermin bred on the entrails of his chimera dire, and," he added, "there does not exist a more villainous calumniatory and incendiary"—a description that proves that Hamilton had read *Paradise Lost*.

Throughout this period, when Washington was being assailed by enemies on the home front, Hamilton identified loyalty to the Commander in Chief with loyalty to the Revolution. "All the true and sensible friends to their country," he asserted, "ought to be upon the watch to counterplot the secret machinations of his enemies" to the same degree that they guarded against Tories and other enemies of the state.

In the end, Congress agreed with Hamilton: some members went so far as to say that anyone who displeased the Commander in Chief ought to be removed forthwith from the army. Wilkinson found himself treated so coldly by his fellow soldiers that he resigned his commission as brigadier general; and Conway was badly wounded in a duel before he returned to France. As for Gates, he was sent to an inactive theater of the war and his supporters were given to understand that they could expect no favors from the Commander in Chief. When Gates attempted to patch up the quarrel by protesting that he had had no thought of displacing Washington, he was rebuffed in a manner that indicated that Washington's suspicions were far from being laid at rest.

In 1778, as a result of the Franco-American alliance, the British military position in North America became precarious in the extreme. Hoping to take the British by surprise, the French sent a fleet across the Atlantic before formally declaring war, and had not d'Estaing, the French commander, tarried on the way, the ruse might have resulted in the destruction of the British fleet and army. As it was, the British barely succeeded in evacuating Philadelphia before the French closed the Delaware. The British fleet reached New York before the French could attack, but the British army, attempting to make its way overland to New York, was not so fortunate: the American army was in hot pursuit and, at Monmouth Court House in New Jersey, finally caught up with the retreating enemy.

Obliged to protect a baggage train almost seven miles long, the British army under Sir Henry Clinton seemed vulnerable to an American attack. Washington was eager to take advantage of the opportunity but a council of general officers, summoned to discuss the strategy of the campaign, strongly opposed precipitating a battle with the British. Reluctant to run risks, the generals gave their approval only to harassing attacks upon the enemy.

As Commander in Chief, Washington was not obliged to accept the advice of this council, even though he usually attached considerable weight to its recommendations. In this instance, however, before deciding whether to accept or to reject the counsel of his officers, he sent Hamilton and several other aides to reconnoiter the enemy's dispositions.

Although his opinion had not been asked by the council of war, Hamilton was eager to make a full-scale attack upon the British. He was sure that the American army could overwhelm Clinton; but he found to his dismay that there were more "old women" at headquarters than paladins ready to do and die. The decision of the generals to engage only in harassing attacks upon the British "would have done honor," Hamilton exclaimed, "to the most honorable society of midwives and to them only."

In this frame of mind, Hamilton spent several days and nights in the open country, observing the enemy's strength and movements. He returned to headquarters with a report calculated to send the "old women" into a dither. The British army, he declared, was marching in good order and the rear guard, composed of grenadiers, light infantry and chasseurs of the line, was especially formidable. From this he concluded that the kind of harassing action contemplated by the generals was out of the question: "To attack in this situation," he told Washington, "without being supported by the whole army, would be folly in the extreme.... If the army is wholly out of supporting distance we risk the total loss of the detachment in making our attack."

Hamilton's report, supported by other evidences of the enemy's strength and readiness for battle, convinced Washington that a blow at the British rear guard was likely to turn into a general battle. He made his dispositions accordingly: General Charles Lee with five thousand men was ordered to attack near Monmouth Court House while Washington and the main army remained within supporting distance a few miles away.

Of all the "midwives" in whose hands the campaign seemed to Hamilton likely to miscarry, none had been more active in discouraging a full-scale offensive than had General Charles Lee. This former British officer had joined the rebellion in 1775 only to be captured by the British in the following year. As a prisoner of war in New York he had enjoyed all amenities, including his dogs and his bottle, and was apparently on the point of resuming his allegiance to George III when he was exchanged for several British officers held by the Americans.

At the beginning of the war, Lee had deprecated the courage of British soldiers, but during his captivity in New York he had completely changed his mind on this score. He now went to the opposite extreme of pronouncing the British army to be invincible and the courage of British soldiers superior to any in the world. To meet these men upon anything like equal terms would, he argued, be "folly or madness" certain to end in disaster for the Americans. In fact, if Lee were to be believed, the British had already won the war and the wisest course open to the rebels was to make peace on the most advantageous terms they could extract from their conquerors.

Despite these singular ideas, Lee did not regard himself as disqualified to lead the attack upon the British rear guard. Ignoring Washington's and Hamilton's warning that an attack was almost certain to lead to a general engagement, Lee persisted in his conviction that only a limited action stood any chance of success against the redoubtable redcoats. But even for such an engagement his preparations were defective: he did not trouble to reconnoiter the ground, procure reliable intelligence of Clinton's dispositions, or agree with his subordinates upon a tactical plan.

Dependent largely upon surprise for the success of the kind of operation envisaged by Lee, the Americans quickly discovered that they had not caught the British napping. The forward elements of Lee's army—about fifteen hundred men—found themselves engaged by "the flower of the British army," four thousand strong. Having no stomach for a fight upon such terms, the Americans began to make for the hills, remorselessly pursued by the enemy.

Faulty as were Lee's preparations for the attack, he had apparently made no provision whatever for retreat. He intended to fight only a limited action; the rest he left largely to the inspiration of the moment. Unfortunately for the Americans, Lee was at the moment low on inspiration. Although he knew that the Commander in Chief with the main army was stationed not far away in order to give him support, Lee did not inform Washington of his plight. A veteran of many wars, Lee felt it beneath his dignity to call upon Washington—in his eyes a mere tobacco farmer—for aid.

Anxious to know how the battle was proceeding, Washington sent Hamilton to Lee's corps as an observer. In the thick of the fighting, Hamilton soon found that something more than observation was required of him. He discovered that the British were moving up on the right flank of Lee's troops and that unless this side were strengthened immediately the Americans would be outflanked. When he informed Lee of this danger, the general ordered him to carry a message to Lafayette to reinforce the threatened flank. Hamilton carried out this mission and then hurried back to Washington's headquarters with the news that the Americans were retreating all along the line.

In the meantime, Washington learned from a straggler that Lee had stirred up a nest of hornets and was in full retreat. Picking up Hamilton on the way, and ordering the main army to follow him, Washington rode off in search of General Lee.

Aide-de-Camp to Washington

When Washington caught up with Lee, he descended upon the hapless general like Jove hurling thunderbolts. Lee attempted to defend his conduct but Washington cut him short; and, indeed, since the British were still advancing and the Americans streaming to the rear, little time could be wasted in recriminations or explanations. Washington accordingly ordered the troops to halt their retreat and make a stand against the enemy, whereupon Lee declared that he would set an example to his men by being the last to leave the field. At this point Hamilton charged upon the scene at full gallop. Flourishing his sword, he exclaimed to Lee, "I will stay here with you, my dear General, and die with you; let us all die here rather than retreat."

Such ardor for death took Lee aback; even though the battle was going against him, he was not yet ready to end it all. Looking closely at the agitated young man, Lee decided that Hamilton was "much flustered and in a sort of frenzy of valor." But battles, as Lee knew, were seldom won by heroics and his own taste ran to valor well seasoned with discretion. Resolving to teach this presumptuous aide-de-camp how a true general behaved under fire, he asked Hamilton to observe him carefully and to mark whether he revealed any signs of agitation. When Hamilton replied that Lee seemed tranquil and fully possessed of his faculties, the general declared that he was as ready to die with his boots on as was Hamilton himself, but that his first responsibility lay with his men: when he had looked to their safety, he would be happy to join Hamilton in fighting to the last gasp. Now, if Colonel Hamilton would excuse him for a few moments from dying, he would turn his attention to saving the army.

Actually, the hill on which Hamilton had chosen to expire, while eminently suited for that particular purpose, had little else to recommend it. Washington immediately saw that the army could not make a stand there: ordering Lee to form his troops, the Commander in Chief took a position upon a nearby elevation better adapted for defense.

In the next few hours, Hamilton found no lack of opportunity to meet a hero's death. To the dismay of his friends, he seemed actually to court such an end: even after his horse had been shot from under him, he continued to rally the troops and to charge the enemy. Nevertheless, he came unscathed through every danger. At last, after the Americans had withstood a brief but furious attack by the British cavalry, the battle settled down to a cannonading of the enemy positions by the American artillery. That night the British army decamped and resumed its march to New York, damning equally the mosquitoes, the heat and the rebels.[7]

In recognition of his aide's gallantry on this occasion, Washington included an account of Hamilton's exploits in the account of the battle he drew up for the Continental Congress. But the praise seemed so fulsome to Hamilton that "from motives of delicacy" he asked Washington to omit it from the report. Hamilton regretted this impulse toward self-effacement; later in his career, he would have given much for a commendation from Congress for conduct above and beyond the call of duty.

Although the Americans claimed the battle of Monmouth as a victory, they were hard pressed to explain how it happened that they had retreated and the British had gotten away safely to New York. Obviously, it was not by this kind of triumphs that wars were won. Americans were soon heatedly debating who was to blame for this victory.

Hamilton absolved the common soldiers of any responsibility for the initial reverses suffered at Monmouth. "You know my way of thinking about the army," he wrote a friend at this time, "and that I am not apt to flatter it"; nonetheless, in this instance, he was inclined to give it the highest praise. Never before, he declared, had he seen American soldiers match the order and discipline of the British regulars. And he did not stint his praise of Washington: "a general rout, dismay, and disgrace," he declared, "would have attended the whole army in other hands but his."

It was Lee's generalship—or, rather, the lack of generalship—to which Hamilton attributed the army's difficulties on the day of Monmouth. The more he considered Lee's conduct, the stronger grew his conviction that this singular character was "either a driveler in the business of soldiership or something much worse." He found it hard to believe that a general of Lee's experience and reputation could be as incompetent as he had shown himself to be at Monmouth—an unflattering opinion that led to the even more unflattering conclusion that Lee had deliberately thrown the battle to the enemy. This explanation cleared up so much that was otherwise inexplicable in Lee's behavior that even Washington was inclined to believe that the general was more culpable than unfortunate.

Stung by these charges, Lee wrote an insulting letter to General Washington and demanded a court-martial. At his trial, held in July, 1778, the star witnesses for the prosecution were Alexander Hamilton and John Laurens. Their testimony was calculated to leave Lee not a shred of reputation and hardly a vestige of honor. According to Hamilton's and Laurens' account, Lee was guilty of conducting—if this word could be applied to such a haphazard and desultory operation—a disgraceful retreat. Moreover, Hamilton asserted that during the battle Lee was so badly rattled that he was incapable of commanding troops. This cut Lee to the quick: it was his contention that he had acquitted himself throughout the action with coolness and self-possession and that if anyone had suffered from agitation on that day it was Colonel Hamilton.

Moreover, in detecting these signs of perturbation in Lee, Hamilton and Laurens were alone among all the witnesses who testified during the trial: as Lee caustically remarked, these "boys" saw with "very different optics from those of every other gentleman who had an opportunity of observing me that day." From the weight of evidence, it appeared that lack of composure was not among the weaknesses Lee had revealed at Monmouth.

Nor in other respects was Hamilton's testimony an unqualified success for the prosecution: by dint of close cross-examination, Lee established that his orders had been discretionary, that only a limited attack upon the enemy had been approved by the council and that Lee was not clearly informed of Washington's intentions. Despite these points scored by the defense, Lee was convicted on three counts: disobedience to orders; misbehavior in making "an unnecessary, disorderly, and shameful retreat" and disrespect to the Commander in Chief. He was sentenced to suspension of command for one year—a remarkably mild punishment in view of the heinousness of the offenses of which he had been found guilty.

Lee took his punishment like a man of letters: he rushed into print with a defense of his generalship and an attack upon Washington and the "earwigs," whose aspersions, he declared, "would make Job himself swear like a Virginia Colonel." Hamilton he accused of being a member of that "idolatrous Sett of Toad-Eaters" who perjured their testimony in order to ingratiate themselves with Washington and spat venom at anyone who refused to bend the knee to the Commander in Chief. Lee took comfort in the reflection that sooner or later Hamilton would come to grief: while granting that the young colonel possessed courage, it was not, he remarked, "that sort of valour, unless by practice and philosophy he can correct, which will ever be of any great use to the community."

After the publication of this "Vindication," Lee came to Philadelphia, "damning General Washington . . . and the Congress, and threatening to resign, *aye God damn them, that he would,* and frowning and dancing like a Caledonian stung by a Tarantula." His wrath was specially violent against Hamilton and Laurens, whom he now denounced as Washington's hatchet men. In short, Lee acted like a man spoiling for a duel, and he had no lack of enemies ready and willing to give him satisfaction.

By traducing Washington and those who had testified for the prosecution at the court-martial, Lee incurred no less than three challenges to duels. Baron Steuben, Anthony Wayne and John Laurens demanded a meeting upon the field of honor—from which Lee concluded that Washington's "bravoes" had entered into a compact to kill him and that even if he survived these encounters upon the dueling ground they would assassinate him.

If blood were going to be shed, Lee's adherents were resolved that not all of it should be the unfortunate general's. Major Eustice, Lee's hottempered aide-de-camp, tried to provoke a duel with Hamilton by accusing him of having perjured himself at Lee's trial. One day, the major met Hamilton at the Quartermaster General's office in Morristown, in company with Generals Greene and Stirling. When Eustice entered the room, Hamilton approached him with outstretched hand, but, Eustice later told Lee, "I took no notice of his polite intention, but sat down, without bowing to him or any of the clan.... He then asked me if I was come from Camp. I say'd, *shortly no,* without the usual application of SIR, rose from my chair—left *the room* and *him standing before the chair.* I cou'd not treat him much more rudely," Eustice boasted. "I've repeated my *suspicions* of his *veracity on the tryall* so often that I expect the son of a bitch will challenge me when he comes."

But Hamilton kept his temper under control and Major Eustice was denied the satisfaction of bringing down the "perjured" asperser of his chief. A few months later, Eustice ceased to regret that his brush with Hamilton had ended so tamely: he broke with Lee, to whom he owed money which he did not find it convenient to repay. So outraged was the major by Lee's insistence that the debt be paid in full that he told Lee he would never in the future fight the battles of a man who abused his friendships so callously.

Having no stomach for standing up to Washington's "bravoes," Lee succeeded in placating Steuben and Wayne. But he could not put off Laurens, who, encouraged by Hamilton, was resolved at all costs to vindicate the honor of the Commander in Chief.

After a brief delay occasioned by the injuries Lee had sustained in a fall from a horse and "the quantity of Physick" he had taken "to baffle a fit of the Gout," the two men met on the field of honor just outside Philadelphia, Hamilton acting as Laurens' second. On the first fire, Lee was slightly wounded and, although in evident distress, insisted upon a second exchange. Hamilton and Lee's second, however, were of the opinion that the affair had gone far enough and they finally succeeded in persuading the general to desist. After Lee had explained that his remarks about Washington had referred only to the commander's military ability and had acknowledged that Washington was a gentleman, the participants shook hands all around.

Yet if honor was satisfied, the wounds opened by the controversy remained unhealed. It did not escape observation that despite the strict rule in the army against dueling, Washington delivered no reproof to those who sought to vindicate his good name upon the field of honor, which left Lee to suspect that they would have gotten away with murder without the Commander in Chief's raising a finger to bring them to justice. Declaring that he was "tired of this rascally Planet," Lee finally quitted it in 1782. In his will he directed that he was not to be buried within a mile of any Presbyterian or Baptist meetinghouse. "I have kept so much bad company while living," he explained, "that I do not choose to continue it when dead."

By constituting himself the custodian of Washington's military reputation and honor against Conway, Lee and lesser lights, Hamilton further solidified his position at headquarters. Indignant at the treatment meted out to Gates and Lee, their friends charged that a coterie had gained a fatal ascendancy over the Commander in Chief. Among these evil councilors they listed General Nathanael Greene ("The Favorite"); General Stirling ("The Drunkard"); General Henry Knox, whose three-hundred-pound frame provided him with an obvious nickname; and Colonel Alexander Hamilton ("The Boy"). These men, it was said, were attempting to make Washington into the "Idol of America" preparatory to hailing him as Caesar.

In Hamilton's case, however, there was more policy than hero worship in his praise of Washington. "The Little Lion" stood in no awe of other lions, and his admiration for their prowess was always tempered by his conviction that he was the equal of the best. Nor was he content merely to share in another's reflected glory. To many officers and men of the Revolutionary Army, it was sufficient honor that they had served with Washington; but Hamilton's ardor for fame and glory was not so easily satisfied. Nevertheless, he realized that for the sake of victory, Washington must be built up as a popular hero: the American people needed a symbol and rallying point, and no one was so well qualified to serve that purpose as the Virginian. Accordingly, although it ran much against Hamilton's grain to appear to adulate any man, he was ready to acclaim the Commander in Chief as a military commander of consummate skill and wisdom, and to run down his rivals as incompetents or as "something much worse."[8]

During the War of Independence, American soldiers often suffered privations in the midst of plenty, but they rarely suffered in silence. The men who huddled round the campfires at Valley Forge and Morristown were an extremely vocal lot who let their grievances be known in the forceful language common to all armies. Grousing was one of the favorite occupations of the soldiers; without their outlet for their discontent, they would have found their lot unbearable.

Much of this complaining was directed against the Continental Congress. The "ignorance," "stupidity," "Narrowness of Soul & Shallowness of Head" of congressmen offered an inexhaustible theme to the soldiers. One officer swore that the civilian leaders "and their Puppies were throwing the whole country in a State of Stupidity"; another complained that he was "subject to the censure and reproach of every dirty little politician"; and Anthony Wayne, not having heard from Congress for several months, inquired caustically if the members had "commenced wine bibbers, & forgot that there are troops in the field and Gentlemen who have some right to hear from them?"

These were what Anthony Wayne called the "Blue Devils"; and it took a vast amount of rum and toddy to exorcise them. Hamilton, too, was plagued by these devils, but in his case they did not drive him to the nearest tavern but to writing indignant letters to congressmen and to devising means by which the necessities of the army could be relieved.

Specifically, Hamilton's grievances against the Continental Congress were that it neglected the army and that when it finally got round to acting it "seemed to yield to importunity rather than to sentiments of justice or to a regard to the accommodation of their troops"; that it refused the officers' just demands for half pay for life; and that it permitted "the brat of faction" to distract its attention from the real welfare of the country. "I can never adopt the reasonings of some *American* politicians, deducible from their practice," he exclaimed, "that no regard is to be paid to national character or the rules of good faith." When congressmen ought to be girding themselves for war, Hamilton found them ready to be lulled into inaction by every peace feeler that came their way. He was never one to suffer gladly the dilatoriness of politicians; being always sure himself of what needed to be done, he had a low tolerance point for the timeserving, trimming, and inertia which seemed to mark their conduct of affairs. "Folly, caprice, a want of foresight, comprehension and dignity characterize the general tenor of their action," he declared. ". . . . Their conduct, with respect to the army especially, is feeble, indecisive, and improvident."[9]

What Hamilton could not forgive in the conduct of the Continental Congress was its tendency to regard itself as dependent upon the good will of the states. The diffidence with which it exercised its constitutional powers, the alacrity with which it made concessions to the states and the habit into which it had fallen of requesting instead of demanding its due—by these means, Hamilton averred, it had weakened the springs of national feeling and had imperiled the military position of the United States. He feared that Congress' next step would be to permit the states to assume control of the Continental Army—an event which Hamilton predicted would mark the end of the American union. Deprived of the "solid basis of authority and consequence"—the allegiance of the army—it seemed to Hamilton that the Continental Congress might as well disband and transfer to the states whatever remained of its authority.

Hamilton deplored these shortcomings in Congress not as a monarchist or as an advocate of dictatorship but as a republican and a soldier keenly sensitive to every blemish upon the cause he was defending in the field. In none of his criticism of Congress was there the slightest hint of an intention to disparage its authority; his censures were confined to Congress' failure to use its powers effectively, not that it had too much power for the good of the country. True, he did not always approve of individual congressmen, but the office itself he held to be "the most illustrious and important of any I am able to conceive. He [a congressman] is to be regarded not only as a legislator, but as a founder of an empire." His principal complaint was that these empire builders did not get on with the job.

The Continental Congress took an exceedingly dim view of criticism of its conduct of affairs, particularly when the criticism came from army officers. Fearful of military dictatorship, many congressmen saw the specter of Caesarism in such faultfinding on the part of the military. These same congressmen, on the other hand, deemed themselves the equals of the generals when it came to laying down strategy and, comfortably settled in their armchairs, they freely condemned unfortunate generals as incompetent blunderers.

As the fair-haired boy around headquarters, Hamilton was exposed to all the jealousy, backbiting and denigration that are found in armies as well as in girls' boarding schools. After 1778, the Little Lion was fair game for professional lion-killers in and out of the army; and they had seldom drawn a bead upon a more tempting and—thanks to Hamilton's practice of speaking his mind freely—a more vulnerable target.

In the spring of 1779, it was reported that Hamilton had said in a Philadelphia coffeehouse that "it was high time for the people to rise, join General Washington, and turn Congress out of doors." It required little perception on Hamilton's part to see that if this charge were proved, his career would be at an end. In 1776, an officer accused of having "grossly abused the President and damned him and the Congress"—a less heinous offense than that of which Hamilton stood accused—was stripped of his commission and only escaped more severe punishment by appearing before Congress and humbly begging its pardon. That Hamilton would be treated as leniently seemed unlikely: many members would welcome an opportunity to put the army in its place by making an example of an officer guilty of aspersing the civil government.[10]

No doubt Hamilton had spoken unguardedly about the shortcomings of Congress, but it is exceedingly unlikely that he had ever advocated herding the members out of the Philadelphia State House at the bayonets' point and raising Washington to the purple. Such a highhanded procedure was contrary to everything he had hitherto said or written about Congress and it presupposed an admiration for General Washington that he was far from feeling. With some warrant, therefore, Hamilton suspected that the story was deliberately invented by those who were jealous of his close standing with the Commander in Chief and who were resolved to pay him back for the part he had taken in the humiliation of General Charles Lee and the eclipse of General Horatio Gates.

Nevertheless Hamilton was aware that in the prevailing atmosphere of suspicion and distrust, his reputation could be destroyed by a canard. He therefore immediately set about tracing the story to its source. The trail led him to Francis Dana, a member of Congress from Massachusetts, but Dana declared that his information was secondhand: he had heard the tale from the Reverend William Gordon, a Massachusetts clergyman.

The Reverend Dr. Gordon was one of that "black regiment" of parsons who during the American Revolution converted their pulpits into rostrums and mixed sedition with Holy Writ in about equal proportions. Although he did not go the length of some of his fellow clerics of seizing a musket and rushing to Armageddon in full regimentals, he wrote and preached assiduously against King and Parliament, meanwhile pursuing his avocation of collecting documents for a history of the American Revolution.

Having a sensitive ear for gossip and possessed, thanks to New England congressmen, of a grapevine to Philadelphia, the Reverend Dr. Gordon occupied himself in sending Washington advice on how to win the war, occasionally spicing his words of wisdom with choice bits of scandal concerning officers in the Continental Army. Gordon was among the first, for example, to accuse Joseph Reed, one of Washington's aides-de-camp, of promoting the candidacy of General Charles Lee for Washington's place. Later he elaborated his charges to include treason: "You have some treacherous person about you," he informed Washington in 1778, "that betrays you and our officers to the enemy."

Hot on the trail of malcontents and traitors, Gordon was in too much of a hurry to distinguish rumor from fact and assertion from proof. He sometimes made accusations with no better evidence than hearsay, using the sanctity of his calling and the vehemence of his language to compensate for the absence of any real evidence. As a result, some patriots doubted that the Reverend Dr. Gordon had received a special dispensation to preside as inquisitor over the political beliefs of his fellow countrymen. And before the war was over, Gordon proved that he was more than a mere busybody: beneath his clerical garb and his pedantic manner lurked a menace to the freedom for which Americans were fighting.

Having traced the story to a Massachusetts parsonage, Hamilton believed that he had verified the proverb that "There never was any mischief, but a priest or a woman at the bottom." His concern was now with a priest; later in his career he discovered the infinite capacity of woman for making mischief.

Since it was highly improbable that the Reverend William Gordon had been present in the Philadelphia tavern when Hamilton's alleged outburst against Congress occurred, Hamilton demanded that the clergyman divulge the name of his informant. But to this the cleric raised an unexpected objection: on the ground that such a disclosure would lead to a duel, the Reverend Dr. Gordon refused to mention any names until Hamilton had solemnly sworn that under no circumstances would he demand satisfaction upon the field of honor. With the sententious air that he might have adopted toward one of his youthful and not-too-bright parishioners, Gordon pointed out that it was sometimes improper to reveal the names of "persons of indisputable character" who volunteered information, "and," he added, "I am convinced you will think with me, when you have been more conversant with the world and read mankind more."

Now if there was one thing upon which Hamilton prided himself, it was his knowledge of mankind and his intimate acquaintance of the ways of the world. To be told by an old prig—as he conceived Gordon to be—that he would grow up someday and become as wise as Gordon himself was more than he could endure. Happily for the clergyman, he was not within Hamilton's reach when he read this letter.

As for binding himself not to challenge his calumniator to a duel—the condition upon which the Reverend Dr. Gordon insisted before divulging any names—Hamilton refused to make any promises. Although he decried dueling—"to prove your own innocence, or the malice of an accuser," he said, "the worst method you can take is to run him through the body or shoot him through the head"—he clearly intended to reserve for himself the privilege of doing just that.

The more vehemently Hamilton protested his innocence, the more firmly convinced of his guilt became the Massachusetts clergyman. However, the parson magnanimously offered to intercede with Heaven on Hamilton's behalf: the incident might be ascribed, he observed, to a "sudden transport"— induced, presumably, by alcohol—in which the young officer had been betrayed into expressing opinions which he regretted in his sober moments. Then, too, the good man added, Hamilton was not alone in longing to purge Congress and set up a military dictator: information had reached his parsonage, he portentously declared, which revealed that this feeling was widespread among officers of the Continental Army.

Had not the Reverend William Gordon worn the cloth, it is likely that he would have been obliged to answer to Hamilton over a brace of pistols. But prone as were the young bucks of the day to settle their disputes in the manner approved by gentlemen, they felt a certain compunction about shooting down a man of God. Fortunately for Gordon, Hamilton shared this prejudice.

Finding that his methods yielded no results, Hamilton tried another approach: the whole story, he declared, had been fabricated by Gordon himself, whose "notorious bias . . . to duplicity and slavery" eminently qualified him for the work of a character assassin. These were hard words to apply to a clergyman, but Hamilton believed that in this instance they were fully warranted: beneath his clerical garb, Gordon was as blackhearted a scoundrel as Hamilton had ever encountered among the clergy or laity.

Stung by Hamilton's barbs and more certain than ever of his guilt, the Reverend Dr. Gordon decided to appeal to the Commander in Chief to take his presumptuous subordinate in hand. The parson characteristically assumed the tone of injured innocence: he had been treated in a manner so derogatory to his cloth, he told Washington, that it could not be doubted that the young fire-eater intended to put the army over the religious as well as over the civil power. "In some stations moral character is of little importance," he said, "but in mine it is next to All; and, like female honour must be defended at all adventures." Despite all the provocations to which he had been subjected, the clergyman was still disposed to show charity toward wayward youth: if Hamilton would apologize to him or to General Washington, he offered to reveal the name of his informant to Washington and say no more against Hamilton.[11]

Much to Gordon's chagrin, Washington did not leap at this opportunity to discipline a member of his family. Instead of calling Hamilton upon the carpet, the Commander in Chief wrote a letter to Gordon which would have dampened the zeal of a less self-righteous man for ferreting out subversives in the army. In the icy tone Washington knew so well how to assume, he gave the parson to understand that he set no value upon the kind of tittle-tattle that Gordon retailed. If he saw fit to make any charges against Hamilton or any other officer, Washingon advised him to produce his witnesses before a court-martial; otherwise let him hold his peace and permit the army to get on with the war.

From this brush with disaster, Hamilton learned the importance of circumspection when expressing his views regarding the civilian government. In 1780, General Nathanael Greene, resentful at what he regarded as unwarranted meddling with his department by Congress and reflections cast upon his integrity, decided to accompany his letter of resignation as Quartermaster General with a scorching denunciation of Congress. Before carrying out this plan he asked Hamilton's advice and received in reply a letter which, although Greene was much the elder, made him appear a hotheaded boy who had come to consult a grave and experienced sage. "We are entered deeply in a contest on which our all depends," Hamilton reminded the overwrought general. "We must endeavor to rub through it, sometimes even at the expense of our feelings." And so he advised Greene to tear up his letter and write another in a milder tone.*

A year or so after his quarrel with Gordon, Hamilton had an opportunity to reveal how unfounded the clergyman's aspersions had been. Early in 1780, some members of Congress, despairing of holding the union together and winning the war under the Articles of Confederation, urged that Washington be invested with dictatorial power. This proposal had a precedent in the Roman Republic, where a "constitutional dictatorship"—the temporary concentration of powers for emergency purposes—had proved on several occasions to be the salvation of the republican government. Until Caesar, this method had not led to a usurpation of powers: always the dictator had obediently resigned his authority upon the expiration of the time limit. It was not thought that Washington would reveal himself to be less loyal than an Old Roman.[12]

When Hamilton learned of this "mad project," he attempted to quash it

* Apparently Hamilton did not realize how deeply Greene was involved in speculative commercial dealings that would not bear the light of day.

forthwith. Much as he complained of the shortcomings of the Continental Congress, he never imagined that there was an acceptable alternative to its authority—and least of all was he inclined to save the country by means of a military dictatorship.

Although the front around New York was quiet and, in Hamilton's opinion, seemed likely to remain so, he looked for serious trouble in the southern states, where there were few regulars and the militia a doubtful quantity. In March, 1779, he predicted that the British, having bruised their heads against the stone wall of the Northern Army, would turn their attention to the South and attempt to open another—and more promising—theater of war. Hamilton's surmise proved correct: Sir Henry Clinton was already laying plans for a full-scale invasion of the southern states, where he hoped to find the soft underbelly of the rebellion.

When the war in the South took an unexpected turn against the Americans, the problem of man power became acute in the American army. Few troops could be spared from the Continental Army for the southern theater, yet the militia of the invaded states was weak and divided in its loyalties. How, therefore, Americans asked themselves, could Lord Cornwallis, the "British Hannibal," be prevented from severing the southern states from the union?

Rather than depend upon the white militia of the South, Hamilton advocated that Negro slaves be enlisted into the Continental Army. He did not say that slaves should be forced to fight in order that whites alone might be free. With their swords, he proposed to give the blacks their freedom. "The dictates of true policy" and of humanity enjoined, he said, that the Negro soldiers be emancipated: if the Americans did not offer the slaves something to fight for, the British assuredly would—and the results might be disastrous to the cause of American independence.

Unlike some of the men who later were to denounce him as a reactionary, Hamilton was sensible of the discrepancy between the ideals of the Declaration of Independence and the hard fact of Negro slavery. He held slavery to be morally wrong and he did not agree with Thomas Jefferson, who, at almost this same time, was expressing his conviction that whites were inherently superior to blacks. "The contempt we have been taught to entertain for the blacks," Hamilton remarked, "makes us fancy many things that are founded neither in reason nor in experience"; given equal opportunity, he predicted, it would be shown that "their natural faculties are as good as ours."

If there was no color line in intelligence and ability, the vast difference in the status, education and training of the two races made it essential in Hamilton's opinion that white officers be set over Negro troops. "Let officers be men of sense and sentiment," he said, "and the nearer the soldiers approach to machines, perhaps the better." He believed that even Russians—than whom no people in his estimation were more congenitally stupid—could be made into good soldiers if trained and led by non-Russian officers.

To recommend the use of Negro slaves in the armed forces of the southern states might well be reckoned an act of temerity; and yet this was what Hamilton and John Laurens set out to do in 1779. It was arranged that Laurens, the son of the president of the Continental Congress and, like Hamilton, a lieutenant colonel in the Continental Army, would go to South Carolina and persuade the legislature of that state to raise four battalions of blacks by levying contributions upon the owners in proportion to the number of slaves they owned. At the same time, Hamilton was to induce Henry Laurens, the president of the Continental Congress, to introduce a proposal in Congress recommending that South Carolina raise the troops and promising to take the Negro battalions into Continental pay.

But the South Carolina planters were conspicuously lacking in both the idealism and the ideas of "true policy" held by Hamilton and Laurens. In South Carolina, Laurens found the legislature unalterably opposed to the black levies: "I was outvoted, having only reason on my side," he exclaimed, "and being opposed by a triple-headed monster, that shed the baneful influence of avarice, prejudice, and pusillanimity, in all our assemblies." Nor was the legislature willing to complete the Continental battalions by drafts from the militia: it put its faith in Providence and in the natural obstacles presented by the country. Nevertheless Hamilton continued to insist that the victory would go to the side with the strongest battalions regardless of whether they were black or white.[13]

3.
The Struggle Against Inflation

While rags and a lean, hungry look were becoming the emblems of American soldiers, a few citizens, safe behind the lines, were making fortunes by contracting, privateering, engrossing supplies and speculating in commodities. The principal victim of these practices was the army. By withholding supplies from the market, the profiteers and monopolists increased the price of every necessity to such a degree that the troops were deprived of food, clothing, guns and ammunition even when some of these commodities were in abundant supply. Washington pronounced this "tribe of black hearted gentry" to be more dangerous than the whole military might of Britain. "These murderers of our cause," he exclaimed, "ought to be hunted down as the pests of society, and the greatest Enemies we have to the happiness of America. I would to God that one of the most atrocious of each State was hung in Gibbets upon a gallows five times as high as the one prepared by Haman."

But instead of hanging in gibbets, the profiteers rode in chariots, resided in fine houses and, in general, conducted themselves as though the war were being fought for their exclusive benefit. No laws could curb their cupidity or touch their wealth; the weak governments created by Americans during the Revolution were incapable of preventing the practices against which the patriots protested. Only the army, and, occasionally, the mobs of the cities, gave the speculators cause for alarm.

As befitted a gentleman of the sword, Hamilton at this time despised mere moneygrubbers. Honor, patriotism, generosity, self-sacrifice were the qualities Hamilton looked for in his countrymen; he saw no good in avarice or the other selfish passions which he later made the foundation of his political philosophy. In 1778, he declared that the acquisitive instinct would be the ruin of the country: "When avarice takes the lead in a state," he said, "it is commonly the forerunner of its fall," and he found in the United States, even in its infancy, alarming symptoms of this fatal disease.[1] A few years later he saw in avarice, when rightly directed, the means of salvation for the state.

In 1778, news of the expected arrival in Philadelphia of a French fleet reached Congress. Acting upon this secret information, Samuel Chase, a member of Congress from Maryland, formed a company with some friends for the purpose of cornering the supply of flour, of which the French were known to be in need. Chase's part in the venture was widely rumored, but nothing had been proved against him when Hamilton, armed with evidence that he believed would have convicted Chase in any court of law, undertook to expose the errant congressman in the newspapers.

Hamilton wrote under the name of "Publius," but in actuality his model was "Junius," the unknown master of invective who a few years before had startled England with his poison-pen attacks upon the Ministry of the Duke of Grafton. In the style of the original Junius, Hamilton assailed Chase as a blackhearted, depraved scoundrel, utterly lost to honor and patriotism. "There are some men whose vices are blended with qualities that cast a lustre upon them and force us to admire while we detest," he declared. "Yours are pure and unmixed, without a single solitary excellence even to serve for contrast and variety." With such qualifications, Hamilton believed that Chase was destined to be "immortalized in infamy," but, he admitted, there was a strong competition in the United States for a place upon the roll of dishonor: "Notwithstanding our youth and inexperience as a nation," he said, "we begin to emulate the most veteran and accomplished states in the art of corruption."[2]

This picture might seem to be overdrawn, but in the eyes of thousands of Chase's fellow citizens, Hamilton had produced a recognizable likeness. Moreover, the Marylander later improved upon this picture of total depravity: as a justice of the Supreme Court of the United States, he cut a swathe as a would-be "hanging judge" that led to his impeachment. In 1778, Hamilton might have predicted an inglorious end for Chase; what he could not have foreseen was that he would be on Chase's side when the end came.[3]

Despite Hamilton's righteous indignation against the profiteers, he was not so innocent of economics as to imagine that the problem was to be solved by hanging a few conspicuous offenders. The real enemy, he saw, was inflation—an inflation which swept all the people into its vortex and which defied every effort to bring it under control. He likewise saw that this runaway inflation must be stopped if the United States was to achieve its independence.

It was not difficult to trace the evil to its source. Early in the war, the Continental Congress and the state governments began to print paper money under the assumption that the justice of the cause and the ardor and patriotism of the people would sustain its value. Had the struggle lasted only a year or two, paper money might have carried the country successfully through the war. But the conflict was protracted beyond all calculations; the people lost confidence in the ability of their governments to pay, and

The Struggle Against Inflation

paper money began to depreciate. Whereupon the Continental Congress turned out money faster than before in order to keep pace with the depreciation. But the continued shrinking of the purchasing power of the dollar was melancholy proof that the old magic whereby rags had been converted into gold had ceased to work.

It was not until the summer of 1778, however, that the bottom dropped out of the Continental dollar. Until August of that year, the paper dollar held steady at the rate of four to one specie dollar. But with the news of the signing of the alliance with France and the evacuation of Philadelphia by the British army, the decline began in earnest. Within a few months, the paper dollar had fallen to twenty to one; during the month of May, 1779, prices in Philadelphia doubled in three weeks. Tea sold for four dollars a pound and a pair of stockings cost over a hundred dollars. (They were a bargain at that price: a little later they cost four hundred dollars a pair.) Congress seriously considered moving from Philadelphia into some part of the country less hard hit by inflation, but the spectacle of American statesmen fleeing from the high cost of living promised to have such a disastrous effect upon morale that the plan was abandoned.

Confronted by a problem so appalling and insoluble, Congress could think of no better expedient than to deposit it in the lap of the states, with whom, after all, control of the purse lay. But instead of aiding the Continental Congress, the states tried to save themselves first; indeed, many were in such financial straits that they could not have helped the general government even had they been so inclined. Since the states themselves issued unsecured paper money, the currency of the United States had become a chaos of paper of all kinds and denominations. However varied, it had one thing in common—it depreciated.

Every effort to halt the inflation seemed only to speed its progress. Price-fixing laws produced black markets and taught Americans "the dangerous lesson, that laws may be broken with impunity." Some states went so far as to enact laws which made the refusal to accept paper money or even to speak disrespectfully of it a punishable offense. But the dollar was mortally sick and even this strong medicine could not stop its decline.

Unable to purchase supplies with paper money, the Commissary and Quartermaster departments of the army began to issue certificates in payment of goods and services. Congress had no control over these emissions and they soon created a staggering addition to the already enormous burden of debt. In the hands of these departments, a million dollars proved to be "like a pound of Butter to a Kennel of Hounds." No one knew how many millions had gone to the dogs in this way.[4]

Outside the Continental Congress, there was no place where the inflation occasioned more anxiety than at Washington's headquarters. In November, 1779, Washington declared that he feared nothing but the depreciation of the currency; a reverse in the field was of minor importance compared with the debacle that had occurred upon the financial front. The British army, with plenty of hard money at its disposal, lacked for nothing: many American civilians sold gladly to the enemy the supplies that spelled the difference between life and death to American fighting men.[5]

Probably no officer in the Continental Army devoted more thought to the financial problems confronting the country than did Alexander Hamilton. At headquarters at Valley Forge and Morristown during the long inactive season, he found time to read so excursively that it is doubtful that he would have received a better-rounded education had he remained at King's College. He read Demosthenes, Plutarch, Aristotle, Seneca, Cicero, Rousseau, Bacon, Montaigne and Hobbes—the classics with which every well-educated man in the eighteenth century was acquainted. But in 1778, his studies began to reflect a growing preoccupation with economics and public finance: he made laborious surveys of the mineral resources, land and commerce of the principal countries of the world and read the works of economists like Malachy Postlethwayt, Sir William Petty, Sir William Steuart and David Hume.

Colbert was the statesman whose achievements most completely captured Hamilton's imagination, but in the wider realm of ideas the influence of David Hume was of paramount importance. It is not surprising that Hamilton, a young man in search of a philosophy, should have been drawn to David Hume. His *Political Discourses* (1752) was one of the most influential books of the day, treating of such subjects of engrossing interest to Hamilton as "Commerce," "Luxury," "Money," "Interest," "Balance of Trade," "Taxes" and "Public Credit." The young officer was charmed by the Scottish philosopher's moderate tone, his refusal to concur in the generally accepted dogmas of religion and philosophy (Hamilton himself had lost his religious dogmatism in the army) and the empirical frame of reference he adopted toward all things.

Like a true disciple of the Enlightenment, Hume attempted to do for the "science of human nature" what Newton had done for the science of physics. He assumed that behavior patterns could be traced with mathematical exactitude. His researches led him to the conclusion that while mankind was endowed with the power of reasoning, it played small part in the world: men lived by prejudice, convention and custom; and he accordingly advised statesmen to "govern men by their passions, and to animate them with a spirit of avarice and industry, art and luxury." The greatest of these, Hume said, was avarice: when this passion was harnessed to the service of the state, he thought the nation was on its way to power, opulence and greatness.

Besides serving as a guide to the "science" of human nature, Hume also provided Hamilton with a set of directions through the equally baffling maze of the science of economics. Although critical of some aspects of mercantilism, Hume's philosophy retained an important residue of mercantilism: he accepted the principle of state intervention in the national economy and he upheld protectionism as essential to the national welfare. Like the mercantilists, Hume's objective was to make the nation rich and powerful, capable of surviving in a world of contending, warring states. He placed the greatness of the state above the happiness of its citizens: he would not have held up "the pursuit of happiness" as an ideal to a people who wished to make their mark in the world. Indeed, as he said, there was "a kind of opposition betwixt the greatness of the state and the happiness of the subjects."

These ideas were becoming established in Hamilton's mind at the time he began to see that victory depended not only upon winning battles but also upon winning the fight against inflation. In 1777, he pointed out that one of the worst consequences of the loss of Philadelphia to Sir William Howe would be the depreciation of the American currency, certain to follow upon a serious military reverse. " 'Tis by introducing order into our finances," he remarked a little later, "—by restoring the public credit—not by gaining battles, that we are finally to gain our object. 'Tis by putting ourselves in a condition to continue the war—not by temporary, violent, and unnatural efforts to bring it to a decisive issue, that we will, in reality, bring it to a speedy and successful one."

The more deeply Hamilton probed the causes of the inflation, the stronger grew his conviction that it was large segments of the population rather than a few individuals who were to blame. Paper money came in the guise of "the poor man's friend": debtors found it advantageous to pay their debts with depreciated paper money and businessmen and farmers profited from constantly rising prices. In particular, the farmers seemed to Hamilton to be guilty of undermining the stability of the currency: they refused to sell their produce except at extortionate prices and they bought land on credit with the deliberate intention of paying for it with cheap money. "The farmers have the game in their own hands," he exclaimed; themselves largely self-sufficient, they were in a position to starve the townspeople into subjection. In order to keep these profiteers from utterly destroying the currency, Hamilton recommended that heavy taxes in kind be imposed upon them.[6]

Thus Hamilton grasped the truth that eluded so many of his countrymen: the problem was how to halt an inflation that large numbers of people were actively engaged in whipping on in the belief that the faster it ran, the more they stood to profit. What happened to the country in the meantime seemed to be of slight importance to those who were growing richer on paper every day. A "get-rich-quick" mania had seized upon them; the pursuit of happiness seemed to consist in running after the will-o'-the-wisp of quick, effortless riches.

There was nothing like an uncontrolled inflation, Hamilton discovered, to corrupt the morals of the people. Public spirit could not live where men were forever calculating the value of the dollar (on some days it was worth less in the afternoon than in the morning), trying to overreach their neighbors and seeking to turn public misfortune into private profit. Under the blight of paper money, Hamilton exclaimed, morals were deteriorating as rapidly as the currency itself; instead of producing heroes and patriots, the Revolution seemed to be creating a nation of sharpers. Tom Paine, who fully shared these apprehensions, suggested that the case of paper money ought to be turned over to the society for suppressing vice and immorality.

Some discouraged congressmen began to feel that in combating inflation they were fighting the Devil and all his emissaries, but Hamilton pointed out that the real enemy was human nature—a distinction too finely drawn to afford much consolation to the harassed statesmen. Nevertheless, Hamilton was not disposed to lay the blame wholly upon the frailties of human nature. The dislocations in commerce and agriculture caused by the war; the necessity of taking man power from productive enterprises for service in the armed forces; the effect of the British blockade upon the supply of manufactured goods; the printing of millions upon millions of dollars by the Continental Congress and the states—these in themselves, said Hamilton, would have activated the inflationary forces.

But he was not convinced that the quantity of money in circulation alone explained the rate or the extent of the decline of the purchasing power of the dollar. The basic cause he found in the fact that the people had lost confidence in their money, "A degree of illusion," he observed, "mixes itself in all the affairs of society. The opinion of objects has more influence than their real nature." Opinion being of paramount importance, he reasoned that merely to reduce the amount of paper money in circulation would not restore its purchasing power. Here, too, opinion would prevail, and, rightly or wrongly, the people would not put their confidence in a circulating medium that had forfeited its rights to be considered honest money.[7]

In placing the ultimate responsibility for the inflation upon public opinion, Hamilton gave expression to the growing tendency in the army to blame civilians for the hardships suffered by the men in uniform. For the soldiers were left under no illusion that the war was hell for everyone. The report that civilians were "wallowing in all the luxury of Rome in her declining State" inevitably undermined morale in the army; many officers and men left the service in order to get in line at the fleshpots; and those who remained at camp held the stay-at-homes in open contempt. "Amidst all this boasted Patriotism," said an American general, "the burden has & must fall on a handful of worn out worried Continentals."

As a result, Hamilton began to ask whether Americans had sufficient public spirit to establish a republic. The disquieting thought occurred to him that while Americans might be Romans, they were Romans of the fall, not of the great days of the Republic. In June, 1780, he told one of his friends that "our countrymen have all the folly of the ass and all the passiveness of the sheep in their composition. They are determined to be free and they can neither be frightened, encouraged nor persuaded to change their resolution. If we are saved, France and Spain must save us. I have the most pigmy feelings at the idea and I almost wish to hide my disgrace in universal ruin. Don't think me insane; for the conduct of the states is enough to make a wise man mad." These were "degenerate times" and the evil seemed to stem from human nature itself. "Experience," he remarked in 1783, under the overpowering conviction that Americans had let down their fighting men, "is a continual comment on the worthlessness of the human race. I know few men estimable, fewer amiable."

At one time, Hamilton would have set down as a Tory anyone who expressed such doubts and misgivings about the American people. Even though Hamilton strenuously disapproved of mobs, he had trusted to the wisdom of the people to see the Revolution to a victorious conclusion. As his friend John Laurens said, Hamilton's views were "conceived in the true spirit of a Republican." In fact, they were too republican for the taste of some of his aristocratic friends.

During the American Revolution, one of the hallmarks of a conservative patriot was insistence upon the separation of powers—the division of executive, legislative and judicial functions, each judiciously balanced against the other. Persuaded of the necessity of imposing restraints upon "popular license," John Adams, the spokesman of these conservative patriots, found his ideal in the British constitution as interpreted by Montesquieu and Blackstone; even while rebelling against Great Britain, he clung to the constitution of the mother country. Acclaiming the British government as a "mixed government" in which democratic, aristocratic and monarchical elements were happily fused, he recommended it to Americans as a sheet anchor against rampant democracy.

A radical patriot, on the other hand, was known by his advocacy of unqualified majority rule: he tended to favor a sovereign, popularly elected legislature in which judicial, executive and legislative powers were concentrated. Tom Paine, the leading exponent of this philosophy of government, had no fear of the people; his apprehensions were directed against the "aristocracy" and "monarchism" of the British constitution and he urged Americans, in separating themselves from Great Britain, to make the break complete. Instead of a mixed government of checks and balances, Paine thought that the best government was that which most directly and speedily gave expression to the popular will.

In 1777, Hamilton inclined more toward the radicals than toward the conservatives upon the issue of mixed government versus "simple democracy." He was sure that the evils of democracy had been greatly exaggerated and that majority rule was more to be welcomed than feared. Mixed governments might at first seem to reconcile the contending groups within the state, yet their ultimate effect, he warned, was to "introduce distinct interests, and these interests will clash, throw the State into convulsions, and produce a change or dissolution." Although he did not advocate vesting in the legislature control of the judicial powers, he believed that a representative democracy, in which the people elected the members of the legislative, judicial and executive branches, was likely to be "happy, regular and durable." "I reverence humanity," he exclaimed; in the good sense, republican spirit and virtue of the people he discovered an enduring foundation for stable government.[8]

In this spirit, he criticized the New York State constitution of 1777 for creating a senate which, he declared, "from the very name and from the mere circumstance of its being a separate member of the Legislature, will be liable to degenerate into a body purely aristocratical." The idea of an upper-class senate checking a democratic house of representatives Hamilton rejected as contrary to the principles of republicanism. It was far more important, he thought, to create a government capable of quick and vigorous action than to establish a system of checks and balances which might serve to cripple the government in time of emergency.

At this time, it is clear, Hamilton's paramount concern was not to provide for the security of property but to ensure that government should be capable of giving "long and substantial happiness to the people." He held it to be self-evident that only in a government that adequately represented the people could happiness be pursued.

But even in this, his most democratic phase, Hamilton was not prepared to approve the direct or "pure" democracy that had existed in the cities of ancient Greece. To give all power to citizens assembled in person in the agora was, to Hamilton's mind, to invite "error, confusion and instability" into the public councils. Only a representative system was acceptable to him: the voice of the people was the voice of God only when it was transmitted through enlightened and responsible spokesmen in a well-ordered legislature. In short, in the distinction commonly drawn in 1777, he was a republican rather than a democrat. Republicanism he regarded as the best of all governments; democracy, as the worst. He never changed his opinion about democracy.

Hamilton's aversion to direct democracy extended even to the election of the Chief Executive by the people. "To determine the qualifications proper

The Struggle Against Inflation

for the chief executive magistrate," he declared, "requires the deliberate wisdom of a select assembly, and cannot be safely lodged with the people at large." But in 1777 such reservations regarding the all-embracing wisdom of the people did not necessarily stamp him as a reactionary; most of the leaders of the Revolution believed that the mass of the people were not qualified to elect the governors of their states. Indeed, according to the prevailing theory, they were not qualified to vote at all unless they possessed sufficient property to ensure that they would uphold the rights of property. Thomas Jefferson favored the election of the governor by the legislature rather than by the people; and he held no brief for the popular election of the Senate.

Most of Hamilton's life was spent in combating the ideas he had confidently advanced in 1777. "Unstable democracy," he said in 1777, "is an epithet frequently in the mouths of politicians." In later years, the epithet was in no man's mouth more frequently than in Hamilton's. Between the young officer proclaiming his faith in the wisdom and essential goodness of the people, and their capacity to exercise power with restraint and moderation, and the Federalist spokesman of 1787, portraying in the Constitutional Convention the shortcomings of the people, their proneness to run to extremes and their lust for other people's property, there is a wide gulf. And yet Hamilton made the leap and landed safely on the other side, losing only his principles in the passage. He gained new principles, however, and, in looking back, it seemed to him that he had left the airy and unsubstantial land of wishful thinking for the solid ground of reality.

And yet, had not Hamilton succeeded in living down the comparative radicalism of his youth, he would have played a much less effective part in American history. In 1787, the expression of the views he held in 1777 would have excluded him from the company of the men who drew up the Federal Constitution; and by 1797, had he persisted in his ideas, he would have been set down as a dangerous Jacobin. By virtue of his ability to conform his ideas to the temper of the times, Hamilton escaped the fate of those revolutionaries who cling adamantly to outworn principles while the world moves on.

In 1779, with inflation and war-weariness undermining morale, Hamilton began increasingly to place his hopes of salvation in a strong national government. At the same time that he lost his faith in the people, he acquired a new faith in the powers of government and the "enlightened few." Above all, he now looked to sound financial planning to win the war and preserve the union.

From Hamilton's angle of vision, everything depended upon the speedy restoration of the credit of the government. No pay-as-you-go plan, he pointed out, could possibly meet the necessities of the government: because the Continental Congress had no accumulated wealth upon which to draw, the war must be fought upon credit. Unfortunately, however, the government had almost wholly destroyed its credit: national bankruptcy seemed inevitable and the people had lost confidence in the promises of their own government. It was a situation that seemed to Hamilton to call for daring and imagination; and he met the challenge in 1779-80 with a plan which in many respects foreshadowed the methods by which he later set the government of the United States upon the highroad of financial stability.

Hamilton's ideas were contained in a letter written early in 1780, while he was at Washington's headquarters at Morristown, to an unnamed member of Congress. Hamilton likewise concealed his identity: he wrote under an assumed name and asked his correspondent to address him as James Montague, Esquire, care of general delivery, Morristown, New Jersey. "Though the writer has reasons which make him unwilling to be known," Hamilton wrote, "if a personal conference with him should be thought material, he will endeavor to comply."

The recipient of this letter was probably General Philip Schuyler, late commander of the Northern Army and now a member of the Continental Congress from New York. Although his military reputation was under a cloud—he had been superseded by General Gates at a critical moment of the war—Schuyler was regarded as one of the best-informed members of Congress upon financial matters. To the general himself, this would have seemed faint praise: in his pamphlet *Causes of Depreciation of the Continental Currency*, written in 1779, Schuyler had deplored the ignorance of financial matters displayed by Congress at every turn. "I wish I could say," he remarked, "that there was one member of Congress adequate to the important business of Finance." As a member of Congress, he undertook to repair that deficiency: it was his plan for restoring the value of the Continental currency that was adopted, with slight modifications, in March, 1780.*[9]

In his letter to General Schuyler, Hamilton recommended a measure that Congress had repeatedly denounced as subversive—that the paper dollar be drastically revalued at the then existing rate of depreciation of forty paper dollars to one specie dollar. Thus, by a stroke of the pen, the national and state debts would be reduced from $400 million to $10 million.

Hamilton was too familiar with the vagaries of Continental paper money to imagine that Congress could peg its value at forty to one simply by passing a law to that effect. Only in an absolutism could the government arbi-

* Neither General John Sullivan nor Robert Morris, each of whom is supposed by some historians to have been the recipient, was a member of Congress at the time it was written. Morris left Congress in 1779; Sullivan did not take his seat until late in 1780. General Philip Schuyler, on the other hand, was the ranking financial expert in Congress in the winter of 1779-80. The diffidence with which Hamilton wrote can perhaps be explained on the ground that he was addressing the man he hoped to make his father-in-law.

The Struggle Against Inflation

trarily fix the purchasing power of its currency, and Hamilton was never under the illusion that the government of the United States was an absolutism or that it could conduct itself like one. He did not fail to observe, however, that whatever might be said of George III and his ministers, English money held its head high in the world. The United States, it appeared, was virtuous but its money was almost worthless; Great Britain, on the other hand, was wicked but its currency was sound. Struck by this paradox, Hamilton drew the moral that if American paper money could in some way be associated in the popular mind with the pound sterling, half the battle would be won. To that end, he proposed that new American currency should be issued bearing the denomination of pounds rather than of dollars. "It will," he said, "produce a useful illusion. Mankind are much led by sounds and appearances; and the currency having changed its name will seem to have changed its nature."

While he believed that the people could be fooled up to a point, Hamilton knew that if the currency were to be solidly established, something more than "sounds and appearances" was necessary. Accordingly, besides the fiction that American and British currency were closely related, he projected a combined bank and trading company to be known as "The Bank of the United States." This institution was to be capitalized for $200 million and half the stock was to be owned by the government and half by private investors.

In this plan, the inventiveness and boldness that characterized Hamilton's later financial schemes clearly emerged for the first time. Nothing remotely resembling the Bank of the United States had ever existed in America—in fact, the country did not even boast a bank—nor did any other American propose at this time to combat the inflation and establish the authority of the government by such heroic measures. Obviously, however, Hamilton did not conceive this plan out of thin air. Although he furnished the peculiar blend of audacity and realism that became his hallmark, most of his basic ideas were derived from the Bank of England and John Law. This unlikely juxtaposition of the Old Lady of Threadneedle Street and the Scottish adventurer is typical of the sound financial thinking combined with the willingness to take risks that distinguished all Hamilton's ventures in the field of public finance.

John Law was a Scottish gambler, *bon vivant* and financier who, having killed his rival in a duel, fled to France, where in 1718 he established the Royal Bank of France. He found the kingdom burdened with a crushing debt, the heritage of the wars of Louis XIV, its currency depreciated and its credit at the vanishing point. By means of the Royal Bank of France, Law succeeded in re-establishing the credit of the government and creating a stable circulating medium. But Law was not content with this success: upon the bank he grafted a great trading company—La Compagnie des Indes—a state-managed monopoly which controlled finance and foreign trade and ultimately swallowed up the Royal Bank itself. Before its collapse, La Compagnie des Indes had been converted into what Adam Smith later described as "the most extravagant project both in banking and stock-jobbing that, perhaps, the world ever saw."

Law paid the penalty of failure: the economists were almost unanimous in stigmatizing him as a mountebank who had almost succeeded singlehanded in wrecking the French economy. As a result, his early success was forgotten and the original contributions he had made to governmental finance were generally lost to view.

But they were not lost upon Alexander Hamilton. Having carefully studied Law's writings and career, his imagination had been captured by the spectacle of this Scot arriving in France (much as Hamilton had arrived in the continental colonies) and saving the country from impending ruin (as Hamilton hoped to save the United States). Hamilton, of course, intended to end his resemblance to Law at that point: he had no wish to repeat the last chapter of the unfortunate financier's career.

That Hamilton, against the weight of contemporary authority, saw fit to praise and to emulate John Law is indicative not only of a similarity in certain points of character but of a sound understanding of Law's methods and objectives. No doubt, what most attracted Hamilton to Law was the audacity, resourcefulness and skill in improvisation displayed by the Scotsman in his heyday. What was even more rare, Hamilton also perceived that before disaster overwhelmed Law, he had succeeded in putting public credit upon solid foundation by supporting it with all the resources of the state. It was no inconsiderable matter, Hamilton observed, to have established public faith "in a country that was become a proverb for the breach of it."

Hamilton was not so captivated by John Law as to be blind to the fact that many of the Scotsman's ideas were inapplicable to the United States. Although the combined bank and trading company projected by Hamilton was modeled upon John Law's Compagnie des Indes, Hamilton did not follow Law in utilizing land as part of the capital of the Bank. Nor was the Bank, unlike the Compagnie, to be a monopoly. He advised Congress to take a solemn oath never to grant exclusive trading privileges to the Bank or any other corporation. By means of this prohibition he hoped to secure for the United States all the benefits of large trading corporations, which, by virtue of their capital resources, could undertake enterprises barred to smaller firms, without at the same time destroying "that spirit of enterprise and competition on which the prosperity of commerce depends."

It was above all the example of the Bank of England that saved Hamilton from falling into the pitfalls in which John Law had come to grief. Unlike Law, the Old Lady of Threadneedle Street could not be accused of impropriety: from her, Hamilton learned only the most respectable maxims of

The Struggle Against Inflation 55

finance. This conservative guidance served as a salutary counterpoise to John Law's rashness; and, fortunately for Hamilton, the lessons he learned from the Bank of England were never forgotten.

The Bank of England was a bank of issue whose notes furnished the chief circulating medium of the realm. It is significant that one of the principal functions Hamilton assigned to the Bank of the United States was the issuance of bank notes. He had reluctantly concluded that paper money, no matter how well disguised, could not circulate as honest money so long as it bore the imprint of the government. Credit seemed to wither at the touch of government—paper money, bonds and certificates all shriveled under the blight. Therefore Hamilton proposed to support the new American currency with the combined resources of the government and its more affluent citizens. Thus fortified, the bank notes would replace the debased continental and state paper money: exchanged for paper dollars at the rate of forty to one, the new circulating medium of the United States would hold its own against the efforts of the British, the profiteers and the speculators to undermine it. And, Hamilton predicted, "by a sort of creative power" the bank notes would become "a real and efficacious instrument of trade."

Having bestowed this boon upon the country, the Bank of the United States, like the Bank of England, was expected to loan money to the government. In Hamilton's financial thinking, this function of banks was always given high priority, for he knew that the war could not be won unless the government were able to anticipate its revenues. But he did not ask the Bank to act out of charity to the government: it was to make money available to the government as a requital for the privileges it received in its charter. Moreover, he thought that "very beneficial contracts" might be made between the Bank and the government for supplying the army, in the profits of which the government, as a stockholder, would share.

A bank capitalized for $200 million—a fantastic sum made necessary by the depreciation of the currency—in a country where banks were unknown and capital woefully scarce, raised the all-important question: Where was the money to come from? As Hamilton knew, the available capital of the country was tied up in agriculture, commerce and war, leaving little or no surplus for the establishment of a bank. The government itself had no revenue to devote to such a purpose: the cost of prosecuting the war swallowed up everything and more that the states supplied. Indeed, had the auditors been called in, they would undoubtedly have found that the government was bankrupt; instead of recommending that it launch a bank, they might have advised it to prepare for the deluge.[10]

Hamilton hoped to repair this deficiency of capital by floating a foreign loan, the proceeds of which would constitute a large part of the capital of the Bank. Equally vital to the success of his plan was the enlistment of the rich men of the country in the venture. They alone had the capital and the national point of view upon which a stable circulating medium and a solid union could be built. From 1780 to the end of his life, Hamilton's overriding purpose was to link inextricably the interests of the state with those of "rich individuals," "moneyed men," "men of weight and understanding." Hence his appeal was addressed primarily to the wealthy few; he admitted that his ideas were "not fit for the vulgar ear," for that ear was attuned only to the language of "local views and politics."

It is unlikely that Hamilton's plan was ever presented to Congress and it is even more improbable that it would have been adopted had General Schuyler submitted it to that body. Eager as congressmen were to enlist the aid of the rich, they balked at establishing a bank and trading company along the lines Hamilton recommended. Nevertheless, in March, 1780, Congress was compelled to inform the country what, indeed, it already knew: that the Continental dollar was worth one fortieth of its nominal value. Thus, simply by applying the sponge, Congress wiped out the greater part of the national debt. But the statesmen in Philadelphia did not break away from the dollar, nor did they establish the combined bank and trading company envisaged by Hamilton. Instead, they directed that a new kind of dollar backed by the combined resources of the states and the general government be issued. By September, 1780, however, it was clear that this stopgap had failed to stop the inflation. The new paper money failed to retain its value—apparently the word of fourteen bankrupts was no better than the word of one bankrupt. A wan and shrunken image of its once robust self, the Continental dollar passed at the rate of one thousand to one.

With paper money dead, the country was forced to depend upon barter and upon its slender store of specie to carry on the war and meet its everyday needs. But neither barter nor specie proved an effective substitute for paper money; the necessity of a stable circulating medium grew more acute daily. Having drunk the heady wine of inflation for five years, Americans were now compelled to taste the dregs of deflation. It was a sobering experience, calculated to make the people regret that they had ever taken that first drink.

As went the Continental dollar, so went the authority of the Continental Congress and the morale of the Continental Army. Unable adequately to feed or pay the troops, the Continental Congress seemed on the point of relinquishing control of the army wholly to the states. And well it might: Hamilton declared that the army was "a mob, rather than an army, without clothing, without pay, without provision, without morals, without discipline. We begin to hate the country for its neglect of us. The country begins to hate us for our oppressions of them. Congress have long been jealous of us. We have now lost all confidence in them, and give the worst constructions to all they do. Held together by the slenderest ties, we are ripening for a

The Struggle Against Inflation

dissolution." The only bright spot Hamilton discerned in this otherwise dismal picture was that Nathanael Greene—"a general without an army" —was holding his own in the Carolinas.[11]

Against this ominous background of financial collapse and military reverses, Hamilton took time out from the war—an easy matter in view of the inaction that prevailed in the northern theater—to write a letter to his congressman. This time he selected James Duane, a representative from New York who had long been active in fiscal matters.

A bank and a foreign loan were still in the forefront of Hamilton's mind. As in his earlier plan, he advocated a bank established upon the combined credit of the government and wealthy individuals, authorized to coin money and to issue notes to the amount of its capital. Being under no illusion that the United States could lift itself out of the financial morass by its own bootstraps, Hamilton now recommended that the United States bluntly inform France that unless a loan were immediately forthcoming, the Continental Congress would come to terms with Great Britain. This electrifying announcement, he hastened to add, was intended "not as menace, but as a candid declaration of our circumstances" and would be taken by the French in that spirit. "We need not fear to be deserted by France," he said. "Her interest and honor are too deeply involved in our fate, and she can make no possible compromise."

The main burden of Hamilton's letter to Duane was that a bank and even a foreign loan would be of little avail until radical reforms had been effected in the powers and structure of the general government. Congress, he declared, "should have complete sovereignty in all that relates to war, peace, trade, finance and the management of foreign affairs"—a plenary authority that would establish its supremacy over the states and put it in full command of all phases of the war effort. Armed with this authority, Congress would be in a position to draft men for the duration of the war; abolish the system by which the Army was made dependent upon the states for supplies; and grant half pay for life to the officers. By thus teaching the officers and men of the Continental Army to look to Congress for their pay, supplies and pensions, Hamilton hoped to make the army "an essential cement of the Union."[12]

But before Congress could truly act the part of a sovereign, Hamilton recognized that it must slough off the cumbersome and inefficient methods that were vitiating its authority. Surveying this body with the coldly critical eye of an efficiency expert, Hamilton detected many glaring faults in its administrative procedures. The fundamental trouble, he decided, was that Congress, by attempting to do everything and to keep all powers in its own hands, was doing nothing well. In place of the boards and committees to which Congress assigned executive functions, Hamilton urged that departments of war, diplomacy and finance, each supervised by a single individual, be established. To these heads of departments he wished to give the same sweeping powers enjoyed by their counterparts in the French government, from which Hamilton at this time derived his ideal of administrative excellence. By this means, he predicted, one of the chief weaknesses of republican government would be overcome and "we shall blend the advantages of a monarchy and republic in our constitution."[13]

Had Hamilton's ideas been carried out in 1780-81, a cabinet system of government would have been established in the United States. The heads of the departments, according to his plan, were to be responsible to Congress and under its constant supervision. Congress, in turn, was to deliberate upon the plans submitted by these ministers and, if it wished, originate plans of its own—"only observing this rule," Hamilton cautioned, ". . . that they ought to consult their ministers, and get all the information and advice they could from them, before they entered into any new measures or made changes in the old." Only the party system was lacking to make this plan of government a close approximation to the modern British cabinet.[14]

Despite Hamilton's Cassandra-like predictions of impending disaster, the troops suffered patiently, up to a point. The limit of endurance was reached early in January, 1781, when mutinies broke out in the Pennsylvania and New Jersey Lines of the Continental Army. Although the disorders were finally suppressed, there were several agonizing days when the fate of American independence seemed to hang upon the dubious loyalty of hungry and unpaid soldiers.

It was a narrow escape and, as Hamilton said, it proved that "the republic is sick and wants powerful remedies." He was far from certain that the warning would be heeded by the people. Among civilians, hope seemed to spring eternal that peace was just around the corner: contemplating the felicity that awaited them as a free and independent people, they prepared for peace in time of war. "If the idea [of peace] goes abroad," said Hamilton, "ten to one if we do not fancy the thing done, and fall into a profound sleep till the cannon of the enemy awaken us next campaign. This is our national character."

In the spring of 1781, Hamilton undertook to awaken his countrymen from their lethargy before the cannon opened up. Writing from the vantage point of the headquarters of the Continental Army at New Windsor, Hamilton published, under the signature "The Continentalist," a series of newspaper articles calculated to dispel all the complacency and wishful thinking to which he believed Americans were prone. Great Britain, he reminded his countrymen, was a nation "whose government has always been distinguished for energy, and its people for enthusiasm"—hardly the opinion he had held at the beginning of the war. Nor should Americans flatter themselves that victory was assured because France was on their side: alliances, he pointed

The Struggle Against Inflation

out, were always weakened by conflicts of interests and differences of opinion. The United States would find its only security, he concluded, in preparing for a long and obstinately fought war.

As "The Continentalist," Hamilton made an eloquent and closely reasoned plea for a closer union of the states under the aegis of the Continental Congress. Unless the powers of that body were vastly increased, he warned his readers that their dream of "a great Federal Republic, closely linked in the pursuit of a common interest," would vanish before the reality of "a number of petty States, with the appearances only of union, jarring, jealous, and perverse." With the union dissolved into separate confederacies, each a satellite of a great European power, Americans would learn—unhappily, said Hamilton, too late—that the union was their rock of salvation.

But this calamity, Hamilton hastened to assure his readers, could yet be averted. True, it required a revolution in the American mind: the people would have to renounce their excessive partiality for their states and become what they had boasted they were in 1776—"a race of Americans." The next step, Hamilton said, was to summon a Constitutional Convention and rewrite the fundamental law in such a way that Congress would possess all powers necessary to win the war and preserve the union in time of peace. By Hamilton's definition, these powers must include the right of Congress to tax Americans directly rather than through the agency of the states. As long as the general government was dependent upon the states for revenue, he saw no hope that the United States could enjoy "dignity, vigor, or credit." How could Americans expect foreigners to loan them money, he asked, when the United States government lacked the power to tax its own citizens?

Although nothing came in 1781 of Hamilton's call for a Constitutional Convention, Congress itself made some of the changes he had advocated in "The Continentalist" and in his letter to James Duane. Departments of War, Finance and Foreign Affairs, each headed by a single individual, were established. Of these departments, the most important was finance. Perhaps because he had been impressed by Hamilton's letters to Schuyler and Duane, General John Sullivan, who had recently taken his seat as a delegate from New Hampshire, decided to put Hamilton's name in nomination for the newly created post of Superintendent of Finance. Before doing so, however, he asked Washington his opinion of the young lieutenant colonel's qualifications as a financier. The Commander in Chief was startled to learn that his aide-de-camp was under consideration, for he had no idea that Hamilton was a financial expert. Nevertheless, he gave Hamilton a high recommendation: there were few men of Hamilton's age and position, he told Sullivan, who had "a more general knowledge than he possesses, and none whose soul is more firmly engaged in the cause, or who exceeds him in probity and virtue."

Armed with this character testimonial, Sullivan was on the point of proposing Hamilton's name to Congress when Robert Morris was put in nomination. Concluding that the young officer did not stand a chance against the merchant-financier, Sullivan threw his support to Morris.[15]

Being strongly under the conviction that he possessed the key to the country's salvation, Hamilton's first act when he learned that Morris had been appointed Superintendent of Finance was to write a letter. Hamilton wrote from De Peyster's Point across the Hudson from headquarters at New Windsor, where in April, 1781, he had taken lodgings with his wife. Like his previous communications to Schuyler and Duane, this letter combined self-confidence, resourcefulness and courage with a pervasive tendency to think on a grand scale. The letter to Morris contains the most elaborate and comprehensive plan drawn up by Hamilton prior to his Report on the Public Credit in 1790.

In contrast to his earlier schemes, Hamilton now put forward views that bear close affinity to modern concepts of fiscal policy. He projected a quasi-public bank whose principal functions were to lend, issue notes in pound denominations bearing interest, accept deposits, act as the fiscal agent of the government, contract for military supplies and loan money to the government. The amount of the bank's authorized capital was now reduced to a more practical figure—three million pounds sterling in the form of specie, "European funds" and real-estate mortgages. The bank was to be chartered for thirty years, during which period it would enjoy a monopoly of all banking functions in the United States. One half of the capital stock was to be assigned to the government and it was to have the privilege of appointing four of the twelve directors. Finally, the bank was to be a national institution with offices in Pennsylvania, Massachusetts and Virginia.

Even at this early period, it is clear that Hamilton contemplated making a public bank not only an instrument for creating a stable currency but of attaining a proper balance among agriculture, commerce and manufacturing—all with the overriding purpose of concentrating political power in the central government. The experience of commercial nations demonstrated, he observed, that banks were "the happiest engines that ever were created for increasing trade." They achieved this purpose, he thought, primarily by creating money; money, in turn, stimulated capitalistic enterprise; and capitalistic enterprise, if rightly directed, promoted nationalism. To bring the moneyed men of all parts of the union to look upon the Continental Congress as their benefactor; to promote intercourse among citizens of the various states; and "to link the interests of the public more intimately with the bank"—these were the great ends Hamilton hoped to achieve in 1781 by means of a public bank.

Hamilton's letter did not inspire Robert Morris to rush out and establish a bank: he had long before made up his mind that a national bank was

The Struggle Against Inflation

essential in peace as well as in war. His own plans for the Bank of North America were already formulated; the prospectus was published in May, 1781, less than a month after Hamilton committed his ideas to paper. Nevertheless, the Superintendent of Finance politely thanked Hamilton for his suggestions, assuring him that in many particulars they coincided with his own views and had strengthened his confidence that he was on the right track. At least, Morris now knew that there was a young officer on Washington's staff who was thinking deeply about the financial problems confronting the government.[16]

Within a year, Hamilton had produced three plans for saving the country. In these plans he revealed himself to be resourceful in devising expedients, daring at the same time that he built solidly, and absolutely certain in his own mind as to what had to be done. If his ideas were overambitious, he was basically right in thinking that government and private wealth must be joined in the struggle to establish a strong national government and a stable circulating medium.

It is clear that by 1781 Hamilton had settled upon a program of action and that he was supremely confident of his ability to carry it into execution. His public career was largely an application of this program to the changing conditions and needs of the United States. His principles, objectives and, to a certain degree, his methods were now formulated. The great question that remained unanswered was: Would the times and the man meet?

In 1780-81, there was some reason to fear that Hamilton was out of touch with the times. His convictions regarding the necessity of a strong national government supported primarily by men of wealth was not an idea likely to endear him to his countrymen. Moreover, much as Hamilton emphasized the importance of public opinion, he failed to reckon sufficiently with the opposition that was certain to manifest itself against a bank such as the one he proposed. A great moneyed corporation, monopolizing the banking functions of the country, holding vast areas of choice land and conferring wealth and power upon affluent citizens, was no part of the democratic vision that inspired many Americans to fight for liberty. Hamilton may have had necessity on his side, but arrayed against him were potent ideals and aspirations that not even the harsh experiences of the war could appreciably weaken. He never succeeded wholly in overcoming these ideals and aspirations; he was still struggling against them at the end of his life.

4.

The Quarrel with Washington

War and finance were not the only subjects on Hamilton's mind in 1780-81. At headquarters, particularly during the long inactive winters, he had ample time to plan his future, and, as with most soldiers, his thoughts turned to what he would do when the war was over and he was out of uniform. Never in these daydreams did his thoughts stray far from the necessity of establishing a connection with a rich and influential family.

The kind of connection Hamilton had in mind was, of course, marriage. While his charm, good looks and ability had taken him a long way, Hamilton was under no illusion that he could attain the summit with their aid alone. To reach the heights to which he aspired, he knew that family backing was essential. He was not one to lose the world for love and deem it well lost. There was little likelihood that he would throw himself away on a tavernkeeper's daughter; the insistent voice that reminded him that he bore the bar sinister, that he was poor, and that his abilities were not given full scope constantly kept before him the importance of marrying well.

By thus making marriage serve ambition, Hamilton revealed how well he understood the aristocratic bias of eighteenth-century society. To rise in politics or law, family connection was well-nigh indispensable; and nowhere was this more true than in New York, where a few families held the keys to political power. In that state, certainly, family ties were as important as talent; and so Hamilton, who had no intention of making his rise more difficult than need be, appraisingly surveyed the field of eligible young ladies. To his mind, there was nothing mercenary in this procedure: he did not intend to marry anyone he did not love, but he did not intend to love anyone who was not a good match for a young man on his way to the top. As between a great love and a great career, Hamilton would no doubt have chosen the career. Happily for him, he was never called upon to make the choice.

Hamilton's requirements in a wife were so exacting that he was in serious danger of condemning himself to bachelorhood. "She must be young," he said, "handsome (I lay most stress upon a good shape), sensible (a little learning will do), well bred (but she must have an aversion to the word *ton*), chaste, and tender (I am an enthusiast in my notions of fidelity and fondness), of some good nature, a great deal of generosity (she must neither love money nor scolding, for I dislike equally a termagant and a economist). In politics I am indifferent what side she may be of. I think I have arguments that will easily convert her to mine. As to religion a moderate stock will satisfy me. She must believe in God and hate a saint." He seems not to have been aware that the girl he was describing was a saint herself.

And yet Hamilton never pretended that these virtues alone would suffice to fix his choice. The girl he married, he frankly admitted, must not only be a paragon—she must have money, the more the better. "Though I run no risk of going to Purgatory for my avarice," he said, "yet as money is an essential ingredient to happiness in this world, and as I am very little calculated to get more either by my address or industry, it must needs be that my wife, if I get one, bring at least a sufficiency to administer to her own extravagancies."

He found all these desiderata in Kitty Livingston, the daughter of Governor Livingston of New Jersey, in whose house Hamilton had lived while attending preparatory school. Shortly after his appointment as Washington's aide-de-camp he opened with her a correspondence which, although it remained upon the level of fun and mock amorousness, might well have led, had the lady been willing, to an excursion into what Hamilton called "the flowery walks and roseate bowers of Cupid." With her he discussed the nature of women; and the young philosopher delivered himself of the aphorism that the weaker sex was "not a simple, but a most complex, intricate and enigmatical being." To penetrate the defenses of this unfathomable creature, Hamilton tried flattery; he declared that when he showed one of Miss Livingston's letters to a fellow officer he was ecstatic: "'Hamilton,' cries he, 'when you write to this divine girl again, it must be in a style of admiration—none but a goddess, I am sure, could have penned so fine a letter!'" Playfully, Hamilton suggested that his friend intended to make himself a rival.

The favor of such a "goddess" was not to be won without propitiation. When Miss Livingston expressed her abhorrence of war, Hamilton gracefully accommodated his opinions to hers. "Were it not for the evident necessity and in defence of all that is valuable in society," he wrote, "I could never be reconciled to a military character." He protested that he yearned for peace, not least because it would remove the obstacles "which now lie in the way of that most delectable thing, called matrimony—a state, which, with a kind of magnetic force, attracts every breast to it, in which susceptibility has a place, in spite of the resistance it encounters in the dull admonitions of prudence." Obviously, Hamilton was working up to an avowal of his passion.

But at this point her letters abruptly ceased and Kitty Livingston later married another suitor. Apparently Hamilton had made no progress toward solving the puzzle of that "enigmatical being" known as woman. Even so, this abortive affair did not leave Hamilton with an abiding sense of the fickleness of goddesses, whether of love or of fortune, possibly because another goddess so quickly happened along.[1]

Hamilton probably first met Elizabeth Schuyler at headquarters at Morristown, where she visited her aunt and uncle in 1779. Prior to this meeting he had no doubt heard of her charms from his friend and fellow aide-de-camp Tench Tilghman, who, while staying with General Schuyler in 1775, had been much taken by the general's second daughter. "I was prepossessed in favor of this young Lady the moment I saw her," Tilghman reported. "A Brunette with the most good natured lively dark eyes that I ever saw, which threw a beam of good temper and benevolence over her whole Countenance. Mr. Livingston informed me that I was not mistaken in my Conjecture for that she was the finest tempered Girl in the World." In an age when fashionable young ladies were given to "vapors" and frequent swoonings, Betsy Schuyler was a refreshing outdoor type: in climbing a hill, "she disdained all assistance," reported the amazed young officer, "and made herself merry at the distress of the other Ladies." Even after being exposed to the coquettish charms of Miss Rensselaer, the belle of Albany, Lieutenant Colonel Tilghman continued to sing the praises of Betsy Schuyler.

Finding that his specifications for a wife had been so generously fulfilled, Hamilton embarked upon a whirlwind courtship. Within a few months, he had won a victory of greater importance to his career than any of his exploits upon the field of battle: Elizabeth Schuyler had promised to become his wife.

For the benefit of his good friend John Laurens, who had never met Betsy Schuyler, Hamilton set down a description of the young lady he intended to marry. "She is a good hearted girl who I am sure will never play the termagant," he remarked, "though not a genius she has good sense enough to be agreeable and though not a beauty, she has fine black eyes, is rather handsome and has every other requisite of the exterior to make a lover happy." Hamilton was aware that this inventory of Miss Schuyler's charms might seem more actuarial than passionate; his dry assessment was hardly that of a lover sighing like a furnace and composing sonnets to his mistress' eyebrow. For this reason, he felt obliged to add by way of postscript: "I am a lover in earnest although I do not speak of the perfections of my Mistress in the enthusiasm of Chivalry." In his letters to Betsy Schuyler, however, he wisely did not curb his enthusiasm. "I am too much in love to be either reasonable or witty," he declared; "I feel in the extreme; and when I attempt to speak of my feelings I rave. Love is a sort of insanity and everything I write savors strongly of it."

Had Hamilton married wholly out of calculation and put his affections where they would do him the most good, he could hardly have chosen better. It was a marriage over which Hamilton's friends, especially the French officers, went into raptures. "You will get all that family's [Schuyler's] interest," exclaimed Colonel Fleury. ". . . You will be in a very easy Situation & happiness is not to be found without a Large Estate." To marry for money and position as well as for love seemed to them the height of felicity. And Hamilton himself was inclined to agree that love, money, social prestige and ambition had met in happy conjunction.

There was reason to doubt that General Schuyler would regard the match in this light. Elizabeth's father was a gouty old aristocrat, noted for his proud and imperious bearing, his strong conviction that New Englanders were socially not much better than Yahoos, and his fondness for family trees. True, Hamilton was not a New Englander, but, on the other hand, his family tree would have presented some knotty problems to a genealogist. It is probable that if the subject was brought up by the general, Hamilton dwelt upon his father's aristocratic descent and the respectability of his mother's family. Much as Hamilton praised and practiced candor, he did not feel obliged to advertise the fact that he was a bastard.

Fortunately for Hamilton, there were other topics upon which he could open himself more fully to his prospective father-in-law. They were agreed upon the necessity of a strong central government; they deplored the decline of the authority of the Continental Congress; and they recognized the necessity of drastic financial reforms. (It is possible that Hamilton revealed himself as the author of the letter on finance Schuyler had received in the spring of 1780.) Moreover, the military incompetence of General Gates—a theme sweet to the ears of General Schuyler—furnished them with the subject matter for many a cozy tête-à-tête. For the loss of the command of the Northern Army in 1777 deeply rankled Schuyler and he loved to hear his rival run down. In Hamilton, he found a young man whose opinion of Gates was lower, if possible, than his own and who had played a prominent part in exposing Gates's part in the "plot" against the Commander in Chief.

In August, 1780, Gates confirmed everything Hamilton and Schuyler had been saying for years about his military incompetence when he did not have Benedict Arnold to fight his battles for him. Out of favor at Washington's headquarters, Gates had powerful friends in Congress who were able in 1780 to put him in command of the Southern Army. He met the enemy in the person of General Cornwallis at Camden, South Carolina; and the American army was completely routed. Gates did not stop his flight until he had put over a hundred miles between himself and the battlefield, thereby displaying, Hamilton sarcastically said, "that age and the long labors and fatigues of a military life had not in the least impaired his activity." It was a heavy price to pay for exploding an inflated reputation, but Hamilton consoled himself with the hope that the Hero of Saratoga would henceforth be known as a Man Who Ran Away; and that Americans would learn from disaster the necessity of strengthening the regular army and the authority of the Continental Congress.

And so, strongly prepossessed in Hamilton's favor, General Schuyler accepted his daughter's suitor with scarcely less enthusiasm than did Betsy herself. Before Hamilton's charm, urbanity and intellectual brilliance, the old general's hauteur melted. Far from condescending to the young West Indian, he acted as though Hamilton did him honor by consenting to marry his daughter. "You cannot my dear Sir, be more happy at the connection you have made with my family than I am," he told Hamilton. "Until the child of a parent has made a judicious choice his heart is in continual anxiety; but that anxiety was removed the moment I discovered on whom she had placed her affections." In Schuyler's eyes, Hamilton was the exemplar of all the virtues, including social grace. Instead of recommending that his child read Lord Chesterfield's letters to his son, General Schuyler urged him to model himself upon Alexander Hamilton, "the ornament of his country"—certainly a much better example of decorum than Philip Stanhope. Some, at least, of this advice seems to have sunk in: when young Philip Schuyler fell in love, he said that it would be "the height of presumption" for him to attempt to describe the young lady— only the pen of the inimitable Alexander could do her justice.

Impatient, as always, to get things done, Hamilton would have married Elizabeth then and there had not General Schuyler remonstrated against such precipitancy. He, too, he said, was eager to see the lovers united, but because Mrs. Schuyler had missed her eldest daughter's wedding she insisted upon seeing Betsy led to the altar. Hamilton obligingly bridled his ardor and on December 14, 1780, Mrs. Schuyler had the satisfaction of seeing her daughter married in the family mansion at Albany.[2]

Having solidified his social position by a brilliant marriage, Hamilton nearly threw everything away by engaging in an insensate quarrel with Washington. Had he deliberately set out to blast his prospects of military and political advancement and to make Washington his enemy, he would hardly have acted differently than he did in February, 1781. If the outcome was not that dire, it was owing almost entirely to Washington's forbearance rather than to any exercise of prudence on Hamilton's part.

For Hamilton, Washington went out of his way, as he did for no other man, to show his affection. There was something almost paternal in his

The Quarrel with Washington

attitude toward his aide-de-camp; having no son of his own, the Virginian seemed inclined to bestow upon Hamilton the feelings that, despite Washington's austerity and reserve, he felt with no less force than did more demonstrative men.

By Hamilton's own admission, Washington's efforts to put their relationship upon the footing of intimate friendship were anything but welcome to the younger man; all the while his enemies were accusing him of prostrating himself before the Commander in Chief, Hamilton was actually engaged in keeping him at arm's length. No doubt he was flattered by Washington's practice of asking his advice (but not always deferring to it) and of taking him into his confidence; no aide-de-camp could fail to be gratified by such attentions from his superior officer. But there were two circumstances that tended to diminish the satisfaction he otherwise would have taken from these pleasing attentions: he had no high opinion of Washington's ability as a general and he had begun to feel something akin to dislike for this slow and methodical country gentleman who insisted upon consulting his general officers before undertaking an important action.

In part, Hamilton's resentment was owing to the fact that Washington refused to give him an active command in the field. It was as though the Commander in Chief regarded Hamilton as too valuable a property to be risked in battle; certainly it is true that he would have had to look far for another aide who suited him as well as did Hamilton. Washington once said that an aide-de-camp ought to possess the soul of his superior officer —and in this respect, he felt that Hamilton could not be improved upon. With the young West Indian there was no need to waste precious time in laborious explanations: so quick was Hamilton's comprehension that a word often sufficed to make Washington's wishes clear. Furthermore, his skill in arranging, analyzing and presenting arguments and his knowledge of the technical side of the military art made him invaluable at headquarters. Distrustful of his own literary powers, Washington fell easily to the habit of turning his correspondence over to Colonel Hamilton; and the habit thus acquired during the War of Independence was carried over into the period when the relationship between the two men was that of President of the United States and Secretary of the Treasury.

Undeniably, there were compensations in occupying the position of Washington's most trusted aide. On several occasions, Hamilton was employed to carry out important missions and, after the Franco-American alliance, thanks to his fluent command of French, he acted as liaison officer between American headquarters and French generals and admirals. Washington himself knew no French. When he was urged to study the language, he replied that he was too old to learn a foreign tongue; and he later declined to go to France because, among other reasons, he would be obliged to converse through an interpreter, which, he said, "upon common occasions, especially with Ladies must appear so extremely awkward, insipid, and uncouth, that I can scarce bear it in idea." He might have taken encouragement from the fact that Benjamin Franklin had made a little French go a long way, especially with the ladies. But it was left to Franklin to disport himself with the Parisian beauties: Washington's only rendezvous were with French officers.

Hamilton also served on commissions to arrange with the British for the exchange of prisoners. At these meetings, Hamilton conceived a low opinion of British officers: in his estimation, they abused the Englishman's privilege of taking his pleasures, including his liquor, sadly. And sad spectacles they were when, after a night of heavy drinking (the objective was to outdrink the other side), they were picked off the floor and hoisted on their horses. But this was not the kind of combat of which he had dreamed while a boy at St. Croix. "You know I shall hate to be nominally a soldier," he wrote his friend General Nathanael Greene; unless he were given an opportunity to "act a conspicuous part in some enterprise that might perhaps raise my character as a soldier above mediocrity," he protested that he would know no peace of mind. He envied James Monroe, who in 1779 left Washington's service to go to the southern theater of the war where, Hamilton said, he would be given "some employment, that will enable him to get knocked on the head in an honorable way." Even though it was not likely to lead to such a glorious end, Hamilton was prepared in 1780 to undertake a diplomatic mission to France (Lafayette offered to give him some inside information that would open doors at the Court of France), but the appointment went instead to John Laurens. And, although Hamilton wrote the letter requesting a loan that Laurens carried to France, it was Laurens who secured the loan and returned to receive the commendation.

More and more, "The Little Lion" grew restive in the gilded cage of headquarters. Suffering from a frustrated longing for fame and glory, he often considered resigning from the staff and seeking service in the line. But a command commensurate with Hamilton's opinion of his deserts did not present itself, and Washington declined to make a place for him. Moreover, his friends never ceased to assure him that he was indispensable at headquarters and that by remaining with Washington he was sure to attract some of the reflected rays of the great man's fame. This was poor consolation to offer a man who was already restive under the shadow cast by the heroic figure of the Commander in Chief, and who was crying out against the injustice that permitted one man to enjoy such a disproportionate share of renown.

In the inactive months of winter and early spring, time hung particularly heavy upon the hands of Washington's aides. To relieve the boredom of inactive war, they amused themselves in writing mock-heroic poems ridi-

The Quarrel with Washington

culing their sedentary mode of life. In one of these effusions, Colonel Harison received special mention: "His sedentary exploits are sung in strains of laborious dulness," Hamilton observed. "The many breeches he has worn out during the war are enumerated—nor are the depredations which long sitting have made on his _____ unsung."

But, happily, not all the sitting was done before a desk wielding a quill. Many evenings were spent around a table well laden with wine, drinking toasts and "sentiments"—high-flown tributes to the charm and beauty of the young lady who had won the soldier's heart. Presiding at the table as Hamilton sometimes did during Washington's absence, he seemed to be a master of the social amenities: James Madison, who saw him in a large company, pronounced his manners fit to adorn the most polished circles of society, not excluding the court of Frederick the Great. Beneath this superficial glitter, however, most observers saw the man of action, yearning for higher things than drawing-room gallantries.[3]

Restiveness alone does not account for Hamilton's growing impatience with Washington. Temperamentally, Hamilton was not suited to be a private secretary: his inclinations ran strongly to command and to execute, not to carry out the orders of another. His contempt of subservience, his refusal to curry favor with any man, were symptomatic of a pride and self-confidence that made it impossible for him to pay sincere homage to what the world called greatness.

During this inactive period of the war, when Hamilton feared that he would perish from sheer boredom, an event occurred which revealed that he could be taken in by a beautiful woman and that his relations with Washington had reached a dangerous point of strain.

For Benedict Arnold, Hamilton had always professed high esteem as an officer who understood that the business of a soldier was fighting, not the practice of midwifery. He was willing to award Arnold all the credit for the victory at Saratoga, fully aware, of course, that by magnifying Arnold's achievement he depreciated Gates's merit. But after the capture of Burgoyne, Arnold, temporarily out of action because of battle wounds, retired to the comparative obscurity of the military governorship of Philadelphia. The gallantry he had displayed on the battlefield was now tarnished by moneymaking; and his marriage to Peggy Shippen linked him with the Tory element in Pennsylvania. In 1779, the man whose courage at Quebec and Saratoga had earned him rank among the great military leaders was brought to trial charged with prostituting his official position for the sake of private profit. Shortly after, he made treasonable overtures to General Clinton.

Having contrived to be appointed commander at West Point, Arnold was in a position to sell that key fortress to the British. But at the last moment the plot went awry: Major John André of the British army, serving as Clinton's agent in his negotiations with Arnold, was arrested by some militiamen and documents were found in his possession which revealed Arnold's part in the plot.

At this juncture, Washington and Hamilton were returning to West Point from Hartford, where they had been conferring with General Rochambeau, the commander of the French forces in the United States. Hamilton, who had posted on ahead of Washington and his party, was present at Arnold's headquarters when the news was brought to Arnold that André had been taken prisoner. Excusing himself to Hamilton and his other guests, the traitor paused only long enough to inform his wife of the disaster that had befallen before hurrying down to the river and boarding H.M.S. *Vulture*. A few hours later, Hamilton learned from the captured documents the truth of Arnold's treason. He immediately set out after the fugitive, but Arnold was already on his way to New York City. Fearful that Clinton would launch an attack upon West Point, Hamilton took it upon himself to order General Nathanael Greene to march to the defense of the fortress. This precaution proved unnecessary: although Arnold had deliberately weakened the garrison, the British were not yet ready to execute their part of the plan.

While Arnold had made good his escape, he had left his wife as a hostage to fortune. This clever, beautiful and unscrupulous woman proved herself to be more than equal to the occasion. Assuming the role of an innocent wife and mother, she effected an immediate conquest of Washington and Hamilton. She received them in bed surrounded, the impressionable young colonel was quick to observe, "with every circumstance that would interest our sympathy." These included tears, entreaties, swoonings, well-timed hysterics and an arresting display of negligee.

Hamilton's spirited championship of Mrs. Arnold did more credit to his heart than to his head. He revealed himself to be a man of sensibility, quick to respond to the spectacle of beauty in distress, but with much to learn about the avarice, treachery and duplicity that are sometimes concealed by a fair face and fine manners.

For the other principal in Arnold's plot, Hamilton conceived an admiration almost as strong as his feeling for Mrs. Arnold. The soldierly and gentlemanly virtues exhibited by Major John André—the quiet dignity with which he bore his fate, his vigilance in all that concerned his honor—persuaded Hamilton that knighthood was still in flower and that André was one of its fairest specimens. For fortitude, delicacy of sentiment, accomplished manners and high-mindedness, Hamilton had never seen the equal of this British major.

But by one of the ironies of war, it was John André who was sentenced to die ignobly, while Benedict Arnold—in Hamilton's eyes the embodiment of all that was base and detestable—eluded the Americans' vengeance. Rather

The Quarrel with Washington

than see the wrong man suffer for Arnold's crime, Hamilton toyed with the idea of proposing to General Clinton an exchange of André for Arnold. Although he could not bring himself to suggest this plan to André himself —Hamilton declared that had André accepted he would have forfeited all esteem—Hamilton as a last resort did write to Clinton urging such an exchange. As Hamilton had foreseen, both Clinton and André rejected the scheme.

All hope of an exchange having been abandoned, Hamilton reluctantly acknowledged that André must die: even for such a paragon of the soldierly and gentlemanly virtues, the rules of war could not be suspended. Yet when André asked to die before a firing squad rather than by hanging— the punishment usually meted out to spies—Hamilton strongly favored granting this last request of the condemned man. It could make little difference, he argued, to permit André to meet his fate genteelly as a British officer instead of ignobly as a spy. But Washington insisted that the law be carried out in its full rigor: since André had been captured in civilian clothes within the American lines, he must die by hanging.

Among his friends, Hamilton made no secret of his disapproval of the Commander in Chief's decision. Never before had Washington appeared to Hamilton in so unfavorable a light: a stern, hardhearted, obstinate, bigoted martinet, insensible to the finer feelings of a gentleman and intent upon exacting an eye for an eye. "Some people," he remarked, with cutting scorn that struck uncomfortably close to the Commander in Chief, "are only sensible to motives of policy, and sometimes, from a narrow disposition, mistake it."[4]

Even keeping up appearances was difficult for Hamilton after Washington had ordered the execution of John André. As might have been expected, it required only a trivial incident to ignite this smoldering resentment. In February, 1781, everyone at headquarters was under severe strain: the recent mutinies of the Pennsylvania and New Jersey Lines had shaken the Revolution to its foundations; enlistments were slow and civilians were becoming increasingly apathetic toward the war; and Washington was badly worried over Cornwallis' success in Virginia. One morning, oppressed by these cares, Washington met Hamilton on the stairway of the house at New Windsor which served as headquarters. Washington told his aide that he wished to speak to him, and Hamilton replied that he would return as soon as he had delivered a letter. On his return, he was stopped by Lafayette and they talked for a few moments. Hamilton then continued on his way, but instead of finding Washington in his room he encountered him at the head of the stairs. In an angry tone of voice, the Commander in Chief exclaimed: "Colonel Hamilton you have kept me waiting at the head of the stairs these ten minutes. I must tell you sir, you treat me with disrespect."

It would have been easy for Hamilton to have given an explanation of his absence and he could see that Washington was obviously overwrought, for it was highly unusual for him to forget decorum in addressing his aides. Instead, however, Hamilton blazed back at the Commander: "I am not conscious of it, sir," he said; "but since you have thought it necessary to tell me so, we part." Washington was astonished at this reply, but he answered coolly enough: "Very well, sir, if it be your choice." With this the two men separated.

In the Revolutionary Army, officers were accustomed to resign because of failure to win promotion, fancied slights or plain homesickness, but Hamilton's readiness to break with Washington on so trivial a pretext indicates how deeply the canker of frustrated ambition had undermined his self-control. For years, he had held himself tightly reined, dreaming of military glory while pushing a pen at headquarters. At a few ill-considered words from Washington, the rein had snapped.

When Washington succeeded in mastering his resentment, he saw that he had been at fault in addressing Hamilton in the peremptory tone of a drill sergeant. Deeply distressed by his own breach of good manners and eager to make amends to the offended young man, Washington gave Hamilton to understand that he was willing to forget the unseemly squabble and resume their friendship upon an even more intimate basis. Through one of his aides, he proposed a meeting, but the young West Indian, still simmering with resentment, stiffly declined his commander's offer. His resolution to part company with Washington was, he declared, "unalterable."

While still in a state of extreme agitation, Hamilton wrote a letter to his father-in-law, seeking to vindicate his part in the quarrel with the Commander in Chief.* He accused Washington of bad temper, inordinate vanity and want of respect for the feelings of his subordinates. While he was willing to concede that the root of the trouble was a conflict of personalities, he did not admit to any fault other than pride and quickness to resent ill treatment.

If Hamilton hoped by this means to justify his conduct in the eyes of his father-in-law, he was rudely disappointed. Despite his admiration for the young man, General Schuyler could not believe that Hamilton did justice to Washington's character; he himself knew the Virginian too well to fail to see that Hamilton had let his temper run away with him. But even granting that Hamilton were right, General Schuyler was dismayed to find his son-in-law willfully ruining his career because of a trifling rebuke. Hoping to induce Hamilton to take a sober second look at the consequences of a quarrel with Washington, the general set forth his arguments, not omitting an appeal to Hamilton's vanity. Should he leave headquarters,

* A letter written by Hamilton at Washington's order on February 17, 1781, bears evidence of agitation: there are several mistakes and the handwriting is not as firm as usual.

Schuyler pointed out, the cause of freedom would suffer a grievous blow: Washington would lose the only aide capable of giving him wise counsel; and the general greatly feared that, deprived of an interpreter as skilled in French as was Hamilton, our relations with France would be adversely affected. As a final sop to Hamilton's pride, he pointed out that Washington regarded himself as the aggressor and repented of his rudeness to Hamilton. "It falls to the lot of few men," Schuyler concluded, "to pass through life without one of those unguarded moments which wound the feelings of a friend; let us then impute them to the frailties of human nature."[5]

This was the first but unhappily not the last time that General Schuyler experienced the unpredictability and rashness that so strongly marked the character of his favorite son-in-law. As the general learned, no man could dissuade Hamilton from a course of action he had decided upon: having resolved to break with Washington, he ignored General Schuyler's advice and rejected all overtures toward a reconciliation. It was only the concluding remarks in Schuyler's letter that he seems to have taken to heart: he was very ready to impute his difficulties to the frailties of Washington's character.

Hamilton justified his incivility to Washington on the ground that since he had mortally offended the Commander in Chief, any concessions that the latter might make to heal the breach would be dictated solely by his desire to keep Hamilton on his staff. So little did Hamilton value his commander's magnanimity and sincerity. Yet it flattered Hamilton's ego to suppose that Washington's apparent eagerness to smooth over the quarrel was owing to his realization that Hamilton was indispensable at headquarters. Pride and vanity could hardly have led Hamilton into a more egregious error.

In actuality, Washington's generosity stemmed from his conviction that as the aggressor in the quarrel it was incumbent upon him to propitiate Hamilton. He had, too, a certain sympathy for his talented but headstrong subordinate. As a young man, Washington himself had exhibited the same characteristics that made Hamilton so difficult to deal with: pride, quick temper, ambition and love of military glory. So sensitive was he that within a period of four years during the French and Indian War he resigned his commission seven times. Like Hamilton, he found something soul-satisfying in battle: "I heard the bullets whistle," he said, "and, believe me, there was something charming in the sound." By nature, Washington was fierce and irritable: when Gilbert Stuart studied the first President's face preparatory to painting his portrait, he discovered that all Washington's features were "indicative of the strongest and most ungovernable passions." The artist was sure that if Washington had been a savage, he would have been one of the most redoubtable chiefs of his tribe.

The essential difference between Hamilton and Washington was that the older man had almost wholly succeeded in mastering his passions. Washington discerned his weakness and resolved to conquer it. In his youth he studied *The Rules of Civility and Decent Behavior*—an eighteenth-century gentleman's manual that, among other precepts, laid down the rule: "In all cases of Passion admit Reason to govern." Washington subjected himself to such rigorous self-discipline that he was able "at the dictate of reason," said Gouverneur Morris, "to control his will and command himself to act." Few men of the age better exemplified the eighteenth-century faith in reason and distrust of emotion.[6]

Perhaps for that reason Washington understood Hamilton better than Hamilton himself—that his display of temper was occasioned by his impatience with the routine duties at headquarters which denied him all chance of glory. To a young man passionately determined to display his valor upon a battlefield much, Washington seems to have felt, could be forgiven.

A few weeks after their quarrel, Washington invited Hamilton to attend a private conference with Rochambeau, inscribing himself "yours sincerely affectionately." Most men would have been appeased by Washington's offer of friendship: it was a side of the Commander in Chief which few of his associates ever saw. But still Hamilton did not melt: seemingly unaware of Washington's magnanimity or of his own churlishness, he regarded himself as the injured party, of whom it was quite proper that Washington should beg forgiveness.

At Hamilton's request, Washington made no mention of the incident on the stairs, expecting, of course, that Hamilton would likewise say nothing. He was therefore not a little disconcerted when he learned that Hamilton had told Lafayette the whole story. To a less forbearing man, it might have seemed that Hamilton was trying to put his version of the quarrel before his friends while swearing his adversary to secrecy, but Washington did not choose to view Hamilton's conduct in that light. Instead, he let Hamilton have his say while he buried the incident. His only comment was: "Why this injunction on me, while he was communicating it himself, is a little extraordinary: but I complied, and religiously fulfilled it."[7]

Despite the grave weaknesses Hamilton believed that he discerned in Washington's character, he had no intention of exposing these faults to public view. As he told his father-in-law, although he could never feel the slightest friendship for Washington, he would continue to treat him with correct, albeit formal, courtesy. But, he implied, putting up with the Commander in Chief ought to be accounted an act of patriotic self-sacrifice; only because Washington was indispensable to the cause of independence would Hamilton forbear from declaring publicly that the feet of this idol were composed of Virginia clay. "These considerations," Hamilton said, "have influenced my past conduct respecting him, and will influence my future. I think it is necessary he should be supported." This, he informed General Schuyler, was as far as he would go: he would not be found among those

The Quarrel with Washington

who burned incense at the shrine of this so-called great man. The seat of his trousers might be worn thin, but never his knees.

For several months after this incident, Hamilton remained at headquarters, maintaining all the while what he considered to be the proper stiffness and formality in his relations with the Commander in Chief. It was at this time that he wrote his letter to Robert Morris and the first numbers of "The Continentalist." Washington, on his part, was seemingly content to accept Hamilton on the Colonel's own terms: he made no effort to break the ice that had congealed their relationship. Washington did not have to be told twice by Hamilton that his friendship was not wanted; although he continued to respect the younger man's ability, he knew that Hamilton would never stand in closer relationship to him than that was made necessary by their official status. But thanks largely to Washington's self-mastery, this incident did not become a festering sore which poisoned the future relations of the two men.

Nevertheless, Hamilton continued to plead for a command quite as though he had not just given the Commander in Chief an excellent reason to reject his suit. Moreover, Hamilton could not conceal from himself the dismal fact that even if he secured a command, there was little likelihood of his seeing much fighting. The impending campaign seemed almost certain to be defensive on the part of the Americans: in the spring of 1781, recruiting was slow, the French troops in the United States had failed to win any notable success, and the British navy was still in command of the sea. Time and glory were running out, and Hamilton faced the bleak prospect of ending his military career with hardly a single heroic action to his credit.

That he had not wholly forfeited the good will of Washington was evidenced in April, 1781, when he received a commission in the line as a lieutenant colonel. He was still unattached to any regiment, however, and when he asked Washington for a command befitting his rank, he received, as usual, the Commander in Chief's polite regrets. Admitting Hamilton's merit, ability and deserts, Washington nonetheless was unwilling to provoke the resentment of other officers, equally meritorious and deserving, by appointing Hamilton over their heads. Even if another corps of light infantry were formed—an eventuality which Washington deemed unlikely—it would be composed in all probability of New England troops; and no New Yorker could expect to command Yankees as long as New England officers were available. "While I adhere firmly to the right of making such appointments as you request," Washington told Hamilton, "I am at the same time obliged to reflect that it will not do to push that right too far, more especially in a service like ours, and at a time so critical as the present."

Such nicety did not raise Washington in Hamilton's esteem: he continued to insist that his case was exceptional and that therefore the Commander in Chief ought to have no scruples about giving him a command. As for the times being critical, Hamilton took that to be the clinching argument for calling him into active service. The war in the South was going against the Americans—therefore he ought to be assigned to that theater of action; and, since he already had Lafayette's invitation to take command of the artillery in Virginia, all he needed was Washington's approval to be off to the wars.

But Washington showed no sign of yielding to Hamilton's importunities. Finally, disgusted by the Commander in Chief's temporizing, the young man returned his commission and prepared to resign himself to the life of a civilian, hoping to find in law and politics some compensation for the fame and glory that had eluded him in the army.

By this action, Hamilton forced Washington to decide once and for all what to do with this hotheaded young man whose passion for glory knew no bounds—not even of decorum. Washington could no longer conceal from himself the hard necessity of choosing between giving Hamilton a command, and thereby risking trouble with the officers who had better claims than had Hamilton, or of alienating him and losing his services to the army. His eagerness to conciliate Hamilton and to keep him in the army determined his decision: he returned the commission to Hamilton, accompanying it, the young officer wrote exultingly to his wife, "with an assurance that he would endeavour by all means to give me a command, nearly such as I could have deserved in the present circumstances of the army."

Shortly after Hamilton was promised his command, Washington and Rochambeau agreed upon the strategy of the coming campaign: the attempt to capture New York was abandoned in favor of a march to the Chesapeake, where, aided by de Grasse's fleet, the allies hoped to bag Cornwallis. This decision gave Hamilton the opportunity for which he had been waiting for years: the light companies of the first and second regiments of New York together with two other companies were formed into a battalion and on July 31, 1781, Hamilton was given command of this body of men. Later, on August 19, just before the march to the Chesapeake, two companies of the Connecticut Line were added to Hamilton's command and this augmented force was attached to the light infantry division under General Lafayette.

The siege of Cornwallis' army at Yorktown was conducted in accord with the formal siege tactics of eighteenth-century warfare. Impatient with these dilatory methods and stung by the contempt which British regulars had often shown toward "rebellious peasants," some American soldiers took it into their heads to display their disdain of British marksmanship. One militiaman mounted the parapet in full view of the enemy and "d——d his soul if he would dodge for the buggers—and brandished his spade at every ball that was fired, till, unfortunately, a ball came and put an end to his capers."

Having recently made an excellent marriage, it might have been thought that Hamilton would be the last man to emulate this caper, particularly as it seemed to prove that Americans took altogether too low a view of British marksmanship. And yet, with so much to live for, Hamilton characteristically proceeded to risk his life for glory. With Hamilton, prudence ended at the altar.

Not to be outdone in audacity by a militiaman, Hamilton ordered his troops, engaged in constructing trenches under enemy fire, to mount the parapet, form in line and, to the roll of drums, go through the manual of arms. Although the shot had been becoming thick and fast before Hamilton gave his order, the dumfounded British gunners held their fire while the American troops executed their drill.

The devil-may-care young gentlemen of the army—those who wore their hats at a damn-my-eyes cock—were delighted by Hamilton's bravado: here was a commander of dash and spirit who in exposing the lives of his men did not hesitate to put his own life to the hazard. His exploit set off a series of similar madcap demonstrations: Colonel Philip van Cortlandt of New York paraded his men with flags flying and drums beating only a few hundred yards from the main British positions. When the British opened fire, Baron Steuben saved the day by ordering a diversionary attack upon another sector of the line. But the Baron himself caught the infection: later that same day he mounted the parapet and put his men through their exercises in full view of the British gunners.[8]

Glorious as Hamilton's exploit seemed to many of his fellow soldiers, it could hardly be regarded as war. The British positions were not to be reduced by Americans wantonly offering themselves as targets, particularly since the British did not seem to believe that sportsmanship required them to hold their fire while the rebels strutted their defiance.

Meanwhile the serious business of the siege went forward. A second parallel was constructed close to the outlying British redoubts and preparations were made to capture these positions by storm. It now became apparent that Hamilton was in an excellent position to see the action he craved. Lafayette's light infantry division, composing the right wing of the allied army, was assigned an advanced position near two of the most exposed British redoubts. The assault upon one of these fortifications was entrusted to the French troops holding this sector of the line, and Lafayette's division was assigned the task of reducing the other redoubt.

The honor of commanding the assault party was given by Lafayette to Lieutenant Colonel Gimat, a Frenchman who had served since 1777 as Lafayette's aide-de-camp and who had fought gallantly in the Virginia campaign. His ability and experience gave him strong claim to the command and, since he had been designated by Lafayette and approved by the Commander in Chief, Gimat's place seemed assured.

Hamilton alone was dissatisfied with this arrangement. Although he was designated to take part in the action, his thirst for glory was not appeased by serving in a subordinate capacity to Colonel Gimat: his ambition demanded that he command the assault party.

Fortunately for Hamilton, the attack was set for a day on which it was his turn to serve as officer of the day. Making the most of this turn of fortune, he asked Lafayette to relieve Gimat of the command and give it to him, in whose hands, as officer of the day, it rightfully belonged. Despite his friendship for Hamilton, the Marquis declined to oblige him, saying that it was impossible to interfere with arrangements already approved by the Commander in Chief.

With his chances of military glory again slipping through his fingers, Hamilton appealed directly to Washington, happily forgetful of the hard things he had said about the Commander in Chief. He based his claim to the command upon military punctilio, declaring that his honor as an officer would suffer irreparable injury if he were passed over. Washington again demonstrated that he bore his former aide-de-camp no ill will: when apprised of all the facts, he declared that Hamilton, as the officer of the day, was entitled to the post of honor.

To placate Colonel Gimat, his battalion was designated to lead the attack, to be followed by Hamilton's battalion and Laurens' company, Hamilton being in command of the corps. Thus, although Gimat might be the first man over the parapet, Hamilton would have the honor and glory—if any there were—of commanding the assault. From his caper on the parapet, it could be seen that Hamilton had no intention of directing operations from the rear: his opportunities of acquiring renown had been too few to permit him to neglect this last chance of covering himself with glory.

At eight o'clock on the night of October fourteenth, after a diversionary attack had been made on the right of the enemy's lines, the troops under Hamilton's command left their trenches and crept toward the British redoubts. They were unobserved by the enemy until they reached the abatis, where they were challenged by a sentry. Before he could give the alarm and without waiting for the engineers to remove the abatis, they lifted each other over the pickets and swarmed over the British troops in the redoubt. Not a shot was fired by the attackers; following the example of the British, who in the Paoli Massacre had wiped out Mad Anthony Wayne's command, they relied exclusively upon their bayonets. These proved sufficient to rout the defenders of the redoubt: although Colonel Gimat received a bullet in his foot and seven men and officers were killed and fifteen wounded, virtually the entire British force was captured, Colonel Campbell, the British commander, being taken as he attempted to make his way to the main British lines. The entire action lasted only ten minutes and, although three colonels

The Quarrel with Washington 79

on the American side were wounded, Hamilton came through without a scratch.

While these events were taking place, the French grenadiers, under the command of Baron Vumenal, carried out an assault upon the other British redoubt. In this action, although the French were successful, they suffered twice as many casualties as did the Americans. This disproportionate loss was owing to the early discovery by the British of the approach of the attacking force and to the fact that the French waited until their engineers had cut down the abatis before they attempted to penetrate the main defenses of the redoubt.

With the redoubts in the allies' hands, the engineers moved up and began digging trenches to connect the redoubts with the American lines. Before they could get under cover, the Americans and French were subjected to a heavy fire from the now active British howitzers. The casualties among the allies were heavy, but here again the Americans, working in light and sandy soil, suffered much less than did the French.

The loss of the two redoubts, from which the Americans could enfilade the British lines and command the river between Yorktown and Gloucester, left Cornwallis in a highly vulnerable position. Despairing of a last-minute rescue by Clinton and the British fleet, he decided on October seventeenth to run up the white flag and two days later the formalities of surrender took place.[9]

With Cornwallis and his army prisoners of war, Hamilton did not long remain in Virginia and he never returned to the state. Had he not been married, he perhaps might have been tempted to tarry: as one northern officer observed, the girls were "handsome & witty & what is still better they have fortunes—very great loadstones. I have a mind to pay my addresses to eight hundred acres of good land and twenty or thirty *black* Negro's." But Hamilton could think only of returning to Betsy and the child they were expecting, and to resume his law studies, which, he grimly pointed out, "to avoid inferiority, must be laborious."

PART II
The Union Against Chaos

5.
Congress and the Army

Home from the wars, Hamilton settled down to the study of law in the office of Colonel Robert Troup, a lifelong friend. Having attained a modicum of glory, he seemed to have put all such thoughts from his mind: "You cannot imagine," he confided to a friend, "how entirely domestic I am growing. I lose all my taste for the pursuits of ambition. I sigh for nothing but the company of my wife and baby." Securely enmeshed in these delightful domestic toils, he declared that he asked no more of life than a home, a family and a reasonably profitable law practice.[1]

Yet the circle of Hamilton's felicity was not so easily drawn. Several times in his career, Hamilton tried to persuade himself that he could be happy and contented as a plain New York attorney, but on each occasion the goad of ambition and the necessity of saving the country propelled him into the thick of the political struggles of the day. In 1781, he could hardly fail to observe that neither the domestic hearth nor the law library was quite the place for a man who had just given six years of his life to the winning of American independence. For the country was not yet in a situation to admit of an exclusive devotion to the pursuit of happiness. Indeed, Hamilton was already beginning to ask himself whether independence would prove a blessing or a curse.

While Hamilton was savoring the pleasures of home and busying himself with getting on in the world, his letter to Robert Morris suddenly bore fruit. True, it was not a particularly juicy plum that dropped into Hamilton's lap, but it was one of the best at the disposal of the Superintendent of Finance. Hamilton was offered the post of Receiver of Continental Taxes for the State of New York.

Since Congress had no authority to lay and collect taxes—that was a privilege reserved exclusively to the sovereign states—Robert Morris appointed officials to receive the money collected by the states for the general government and to act as representatives of the Treasury in its dealings with the states. Although these duties seemed simple enough, Hamilton hesitated before accepting Morris' offer: he had given many years to the public service and he was desperately anxious to get on with his civilian career. But when he was assured that acting as Morris' agent in New York would not unduly interfere with his law studies, he promptly accepted.[2]

Hamilton discovered that before he could hope to receive any considerable sums from the State of New York it was necessary to reform the method of assessing and collecting taxes. Although he applied himself energetically to this task—he even drew up a complete fiscal system for the state and pressed its adoption upon the state leaders—his work went largely for naught. "Mountains of prejudice and particular interest," he lamented, had to be leveled before the state could be brought to contribute its quota to national needs. In vain he quoted "the sentiments of the celebrated Mr. Neckar" to the legislators: "I found every man convinced that something was wrong," he reported to Morris, "but few that were willing to recognize the mischief when defined and content to the proper remedy." No one was really suffering except the Continental Congress and the army, and it was devoutly hoped that there was a special providence that would take care of their needs without the necessity of taxation by the states.

Of the $8 million requested by Congress from the states for the year 1782, the Continental Receivers turned in only about $400,000. Despite Hamilton's efforts, New York was one of the most backward of the states in paying taxes to the general government. Nevertheless, judged by the energy and initiative he displayed in his attempts to reorganize the fiscal tax system of New York and to bring order out of the chaos of the state's finances, he was highly exceptional. Many of Morris' appointees became discouraged and threw up their jobs, particularly after Morris began to draw upon them in anticipation of their receipts.[3]

In July, 1782, Hamilton was saved from the vexations, frustrations and unpopularity of a tax receiver's life by the action of the New York legislature in electing him to the Continental Congress—an appointment undoubtedly owing in large part to the fact that he was General Schuyler's son-in-law. Not that going to Congress spared him from either vexation, frustration or unpopularity: yet at least it could be said that he was now moving onto a stage which afforded greater scope to his talents and a wider audience to his ideas. He now knew the nature of the enemy he must overcome—his experience as a tax collector had taught him, he said, that in all his plans of reform he had overlooked one cardinal fact—"the universal reluctance of these States to do what is right."[4]

Even while serving in the army, Hamilton had come to the conclusion that the Continental Congress had become the main theater of action and that the war would be won or lost in the council chambers of the republic. Under that conviction, he had urged his friends in the army to hang up

Congress and the Army

their swords and don the toga. In particular, he wished to see John Laurens in the Continental Congress, where, said Hamilton, he would find the odds no less heavy than those he had encountered in battle. But Laurens died in 1782, his life thrown away in an obscure action.

As a member of Congress, Hamilton was obliged to renounce the domestic joys which he had briefly tasted in New York. While Betsy remained in Albany with their young son, Philip, Hamilton, like most congressmen, lived in a boardinghouse near Independence Hall where Congress held its meetings. While nothing could compensate for the comforts of home, Hamilton found that Philadelphia had undeniable attractions: there were frequent balls, dinners and horse races, the last being particularly well attended by southern congressmen.

Among the members of Congress to whom Hamilton was instantly drawn by an affinity of interests and ideas was James Madison of Virginia. A graduate of the College of New Jersey, where the president had never known him "to do or to say an improper thing"—which set him apart from all other undergraduates before or since—he outgrew his priggish youth as, indeed, all politicians must. Of an even slighter physique than Hamilton and without the West Indian's erect military bearing, this shy, reserved, scholarly young man who dressed habitually in black, and who, except when he rose to speak, was intent upon making himself as inconspicuous as possible, seemed destined for a cloistered life. Yet he married one of the most glamorous women of the day. Truly, this was the Age of Philosophers when even beautiful women delighted to pay them the final act of homage.

Madison made his way in American politics by sheer intellectual brilliance—he was by far the best-informed man in Congress—by his skill in the thrust and counterthrust of debate, and by an engaging, ingratiating manner that disarmed his opponents. It was said of Madison that he united "the profound politician with the scholar": while Jefferson praised "the rich resources of his [Madison's] luminous and discriminating mind," he also depended upon his acumen as a practical politician.

In the course of his long career in politics, many men disagreed with Madison but few hated him. He stirred neither the passion of hero worship nor of hatred as did Hamilton. More profound than Hamilton, he was less daring: when Hamilton acted, the Virginian was sometimes still engaged in assessing the risks. Hamilton found his true being in action; Madison was more inclined to realize himself in study and contemplation. The breadth of Madison's erudition, the clarity and precision with which he expounded his ideas, the zeal with which he devoted the acquisitions of study to the public service, were never equaled by Hamilton.

When Hamilton took his seat in Congress, Madison had been a member for two years and had acquired the skill of a seasoned parliamentarian. Like Hamilton, he was an ardent nationalist: all his energy and learning were devoted to the supreme task of furthering the solidarity of the nation.

Had Robert Morris succeeded in restoring the credit of the government, the lives of Alexander Hamilton and James Madison might have been spent in quieter days and their talents might have been overshadowed by the towering reputation of the Superintendent of Finance. For, in essentials, Morris undertook to introduce into American fiscal policy the methods and objectives that later became known as Hamiltonianism. But he had the misfortune to act before the country was prepared to accept this dispensation and he paid the penalty—in the form of failure and obloquy—of being ahead of his times. In all probability, Hamilton would have met with the same fate had he attempted as Superintendent of Finance to put into execution the plans that a decade later were to bring him acclaim as a worker of financial miracles.

Since Robert Morris was a self-made man, Congress was hopeful that he would be able to do as much for the country as he had done for himself. Moreover, as the richest man in the country, he was expected to use his personal fortune to bolster the credit of the United States government. Had Croesus been an American he no doubt would have been drafted for the job of Superintendent of Finance—and only Croesus could have footed the bill.

A man of highly sanguine temperament, Morris thought that by appealing to the patriotism of the states and to "the sacred bonds of national faith and honor" the requisition system could be made to work. He quickly learned his error: it was, he said, "like preaching to the dead." He began by believing that the states would do what was right when their duty was pointed out to them; he ended with the conviction that they would never cease to do wrong.

Disillusioned by the ill success of his efforts to revive the requisition system, Morris looked increasingly to men of wealth to restore the government to solvency: it was necessary, he now said, for government to support the rich in order to persuade the rich to support the government. With the affluent citizens on the side of the government, Morris believed that the country could be united "more closely together in one general money connexion"—and from this union would come order and stability.

In order to consummate the union between the wealthier citizens and the government, Morris established the Bank of North America in 1781. This institution incorporated most of the basic principles laid down by Hamilton in his three letters on finance written in 1780 and 1781, with the notable exceptions that its notes were not issued upon landed security and that no provision was made for a trading corporation. Otherwise, in broad essentials, Morris' views coincided with those expressed by Hamilton: the Bank of North America was a quasi-public bank; the government provided the bulk of the capital and enjoyed the right of inspection; the management was in the hands of the private stockholders; and the bank loaned the government money in anticipation of revenue.

With little aid forthcoming from the states or private individuals, Morris was obliged to depend upon foreign loans. As long as Morris confined himself to borrowing money abroad, he enjoyed a certain measure of popularity at home. Americans had no objection to striking the rock of European resources—all they asked was that the government keep its hand out of their pockets. But, as Hamilton remarked, for European governments or capitalists to loan money to the United States required "a degree of credulity not often to be met with in the pecuniary transactions of mankind and little reconcilable with the usual sharpsightedness of avarice."

Informed by France that the United States could expect no more loans, Morris urged that taxes be imposed upon the people by the Continental Congress rather than by the states. The burden, he warned, would not be light: there must be poll taxes, land taxes, an excise and tariff duties upon imports. He did not omit even the final horror of a stamp tax.

With keener insight into the state of public opinion and less understanding of the financial requirements of the government than was possessed by Robert Morris, Congress eliminated everything from his recommendations except the tax on imports. This tax—the so-called impost—would permit the general government to levy a 5 per cent duty upon foreign commodities imported into the United States. Since the revenue derived from this duty would not even pay the interest on the foreign debt, Robert Morris dismissed it as hardly more than "a Tub for the whale." To satisfy that Leviathan—the foreign and domestic creditors of the United States—he believed that the American people would be obliged to pay taxes until it hurt.

Nevertheless, to an upholder of the sovereign rights of the states, the impost represented a revolutionary shift of power from the states to the central government. Not only was the Continental Congress to be given the authority to tax directly—it was to enjoy the privilege of appointing the collectors of the impost. Since this proposal entailed a change in the fundamental law, it required the unanimous approval of the states. The Articles of Confederation established the rule of unanimity: better that there should be no action at all than that there should be action which lacked the approval of all parties to the compact.[5]

This was the situation when Hamilton took his seat in the Continental Congress in the autumn of 1782: the impost had been adopted by most of the states, the army was unpaid and the creditors of the United States were clamoring for their money. Considered solely as a source of revenue, the impost was in Hamilton's estimation little more than a palliative. It did nothing for the civilian creditors whom Hamilton hoped to attach to the government by the bonds of self-interest—they, it was said, must wait their turn, trusting in the meantime to "the Sympathy of their Countrymen." Moreover, the impost was intended to discharge only the interest on the debt owing foreigners—how the principal was to be repaid, no man could say. And yet, Hamilton believed that it might prove to be the means of endowing Congress with a substantial revenue. "Important operations," he remarked, "might be engrafted upon it towards the extinguishment of the domestic debt." In short, the impost might serve as a precedent for future taxation by Congress; once that right had been conceded by the states, Hamilton believed that it would only be a question of time before Congress was made financially independent of the states.

Viewed as an entering wedge, the impost seemed to Hamilton to have many merits. In the first place it was a hidden tax—a weighty recommendation in view of Americans' well-known aversion to paying any taxes they could see. It fell upon those best able to pay: "The rich," he observed, "must be made to pay for their luxuries, which is the only proper way of taxing their superior wealth"; and it promoted frugality by taxing extravagance. And lastly, but far from least in his estimation, by encouraging domestic manufactures, it tended to make the United States more self-sufficient.[6]

The impost ran the gamut of twelve states, leaving only Rhode Island unheard from. But this small state presented an obstacle to the impost out of all proportion to its size. In the fable, the mouse saved the life of the lion, but Rhode Island was in a lion-killing mood.

Their experience as British subjects was too fresh in Rhode Islanders' minds to permit them to view the impost merely as a revenue-producing measure. Having rebelled against a central government that sought to tax them, they were inclined to suspect any central government, including their own, of harboring evil designs upon their freedom and pocketbooks. If the Continental Congress ever succeeded in making itself financially independent of the states, these patriots did not doubt that it would lord it over them as imperiously as ever did the British Parliament.[7]

Although the Rhode Islanders based their opposition to the impost upon pure and disinterested devotion to the rights of man, Hamilton made it a practice to look closely into the motives of men who talked about liberty. In the case of Rhode Islanders he discovered that although they had many reasons for opposing the impost, liberty was the least of them. As an importing state, Rhode Island levied tribute by means of its tariff duties upon the citizens of Connecticut, who, lacking an important seaport of their own, were compelled to buy their goods from Rhode Island suppliers. This system enabled the farmers of Rhode Island to place the main burden of taxation upon commerce, leaving their lands relatively untouched. The liberty which these farmers extolled consisted largely, therefore, in the privilege of making other people pay the taxes.

In April, 1782, writing under the signature of "The Continentalist," Hamilton marshaled all the arguments in favor of the impost. He did not deny that its immediate effect would be to benefit some states and to injure other states, particularly those which derived a considerable share of their revenue from tariffs. But he refused to admit that this circumstance justified opposition to the impost: some degree of inequality would be found in every revenue law operating upon the country as a whole. Unless Americans took a "continental" view of their problems, Hamilton predicted that "we shall never be a great or a happy people, if we remain a people at all."

As a member of a congressional committee appointed for the purpose, it fell to Hamilton to answer Rhode Island's objections to the impost and to press its adoption upon the reluctant legislators. Addressing himself to the governor of Rhode Island, he adopted a peremptory and vehement tone which, he hoped, would mark a salutary departure from the deference and humility which Congress sometimes assumed when addressing the sovereign states. He bluntly informed the governor that the cantankerous behavior of his state was endangering the existence of the union: "The increasing discontents of the army, the loud clamours of the public creditors, and the extreme disproportion between the current supplies and the demands of the public revenue," he said, "were so many invincible arguments for the fund recommended by Congress." He boldly stated the doctrine of implied powers; asserted that Congress could not possibly devise a more equitable plan; and insisted upon the compulsory nature of congressional requisitions. Should Rhode Island reject the impost, he predicted "calamities of a most menacing nature"—for which this benighted state would bear the sole responsibility. Unless Rhode Island wished to have the blood of the American republic on its hands, he urged the governor to recommend to the legislature the immediate adoption of the impost.[8]

In some quarters, Hamilton's letter was welcomed as a long-overdue piece of straight talking to a "perverse sister" whose waywardness threatened to break up the family. But upon the opponents of the impost it made a very different impression: their worst fears that Congress was "lusting after power" now seemed confirmed. After reading Hamilton's letter, the Connecticut House of Representatives declared that it was obvious that Congress was seeking to possess itself of both the sword and the purse—presumably in order to cut up American liberty by the roots.

No doubt, had Hamilton's letter been laid before the Rhode Island legislature, it would have aggravated hostility to the impost: Rhode Islanders were not likely to thank Hamilton for suggesting that the necessity of the impost was so "invincible" that their arguments were not worth listening to. But the impost was defeated without the aid of Hamilton's letter: before it was received in Providence, the legislature had killed the plan. As a counterblast to the Continental Congress, the Rhode Island legislators declared that they considered it "the most precious jewel of sovereignty that no State be called upon to open its purse but by the authority of the State and by her own officers."[9]

In Rhode Islanders' eyes, their conduct, far from requiring an apology, entitled them to the gratitude of future generations of Americans. For had they not saved liberty from a tyrannical Congress and preserved the United States as "the glorious Seat of undiminished Freedom"? The United States might be bankrupt but it was free!

Less obliging than Goliath, the Continental Congress refused to fall down dead before Rhode Island. Instead, as was its custom when in doubt, it appointed a committee. As a member of this committee, Hamilton was in a strategic position to influence the policy of Congress. Although the Rhode Islanders had imposed a "unanimous and final veto" upon the impost, Hamilton continued to believe that the arguments in favor of it were so unanswerable that it was impossible that a body of responsible men could fail to feel their force. Accordingly, he proposed that a congressional delegation should be sent to Rhode Island to persuade the legislators to change their minds.

Being in a mood to clutch at straws, Congress adopted Hamilton's plan and a delegation was sent off to Providence. At the same time, Tom Paine, a vigorous champion of the cause of a "more compact union," the advocate of a constitutional convention to revise the Articles of Confederation, and a defender of banks and bankers, undertook a journey into the heart of "the enemy's country" upon the same mission. All he achieved by his pains, however, was to be publicly denounced in Providence as an agent of Congress. Even the great propagandist of the American Revolution could make no impression upon these intractable Yankees.

No doubt, the congressional committee would have met with an even cooler reception, but Congress was spared that indignity at the cost of an even more bitter humiliation. Before the delegation reached Providence, Virginia announced that it had repealed its assent to the impost. Since not even Hamilton was prepared to send delegations far and wide over the country to convert the obdurate and keep the faithful in line, the Rhode Island committee was ordered to return to Philadelphia.

And so victory lay with one of the smallest states of the union, joined at the last moment, it is true, by the largest state. Liberty—assuming that it consisted of local rights and privileges—was safe, but the triumph had been won at the expense of the authority and prestige of the Continental Congress. Nor did the public creditors have any reason to acclaim the Rhode Islanders as the heroes of the struggle for freedom: the national debt seemed to be one of the casualties of that struggle.[10]

Congress and the Army

While the sovereign state of Rhode Island defied Congress to do its worst—which, Hamilton admitted, was likely to cause little inconvenience to anyone—the Continental Army took a hand in the proceedings. At first, Hamilton did not know whether to rejoice or to take alarm at this turn of events: the soldiers had guns in their hands and, what was more disconcerting, seemed disposed to use them to enforce their demands upon the civil government. But Hamilton was inclined to regard the army as an old, albeit somewhat unpredictable, friend: if it were wisely handled, he believed that it could be made to serve the purpose of those who wished to make the Continental Congress a power in the land.

Yet even Hamilton could not pretend that the army was in a manageable frame of mind. In December, 1782, a delegation of officers headed by General Alexander McDougall came to Philadelphia to lay the officers' demands before Congress. Having just seen the hope of the impost go glimmering, congressmen were not in the mood to extend a warm welcome to these visitors. But there was little good in wishing that they would go away: the army had grievances and it insisted upon redress.

One of the most pressing of these grievances had to do with the half pay promised by Congress in 1778 and 1780. By 1782, with the war apparently won and the army no longer essential to the security of the country, some civilians began to repent of Congress' generosity and to argue that it was not necessary to honor promises made under the duress of war. Let the states take care of their own was the cry set up by these citizens, and the slogan was adopted even by some members of Congress.

This effort to break the agreement regarding half pay struck Hamilton as a new low in national dishonor. Would Americans never learn, he asked, that contracts were sacred and that if the government hoped to enjoy any credit or repute it must faithfully execute its promises? He recognized that the control of the army was at stake: if the officers and men of the Continental Army could be brought to look to the states rather than to the Continental Congress for justice, the forces of localism would win a decisive triumph. Hamilton always believed that victory would incline to the side which won the allegiance of the army.

Even though Hamilton was disposed to deal generously with the army, Robert Morris declared that nothing could be done for the officers and men. To prove his point, he had only to open the books of the United States Treasury: there all could see that the government was heavily overdrawn in Europe and that a mere trickle was coming from the states. The utmost that Morris could do was to promise that if Congress would authorize him to make further drafts upon the American ministers in Europe, he would see that the soldiers would receive one month's pay in cash. Since in many cases three years' pay was owing the soldiers, this offer could not be regarded as exactly munificent.

Resolved that the loyalty of the army to the Continental Congress must be preserved at all costs, Hamilton, Robert Morris and Gouverneur Morris undertook to unite the soldiers and civilian creditors in a "phalanx" that would overwhelm the opponents of the impost and make the Continental Congress supreme over the states. To this end, Hamilton, supported by James Madison and James Wilson, urged that Congress ask the states to permit it to levy a poll tax, land tax, a house and window tax, an excise and an impost. Endowed with this "general revenue," Congress would be in a position to do justice to all its creditors, civilian as well as military, state as well as federal, and to attach them by ligaments of self-interest to the general government. For it would be to the immediate personal gain of every soldier and civilian who held claims against the United State government to support measures calculated to increase the revenues and authority of the Continental Congress. Thus would be created "a mass of influence" throughout the union upon which a nation could be built. This was the paramount consideration in all Hamilton's fiscal planning—self-interest was to be made to contribute toward transforming a loose association of states into "one great republic."

While Hamilton, Madison and the Morrises were laboring to unite the army and the civilian bondholders, other members of Congress were working to divide them. Since Congress could not pay both the army and the civilian creditors and since the army was much the most dangerous of the two, it was moved in Congress that a second impost be proposed to the states with the proviso that all revenue derived from it be appropriated exclusively to the benefit of the officers and men of the Continental Army. In support of this motion it was argued that the impost would be acceptable to the states only if the army were made the sole beneficiary: "No civilian creditor," it was said, "would dare to put his claims on a level with those of the army."

This proposal elicited strenuous objections from Hamilton. Even though he acknowledged that the soldiers were "the most meritorious class of creditors" and that he was so outraged by the wrongs inflicted upon the army that he was almost prepared as a last resort to sanction the use of force—"I feel a mortification," he exclaimed, ". . . that sets my passions at variance with my reason. . . . I have an indifferent opinion of the honesty of this country, and all forebodings as to its future system"—he feared that paying the troops without at the same time providing for the civilian creditors would mean the defeat of all his larger objectives. The union of creditors upon which he rested his hopes of creating a strong national government would be broken: finding themselves discriminated against in favor of the soldiers, the civilian creditors could be expected to oppose the impost in the state legislatures, thus depriving the general government of its most faithful (because most interested) friends.

Nor did Hamilton believe that by making the army the beneficiary of the impost the credit of the government would be strengthened. He never lost sight of the end to which the impost was merely a means: "The question," he reminded Congress, "was not merely how to do justice to the creditors, but how to restore public credit." Since the objective was to put the government in a position to borrow from its own citizens and from foreign countries, it was clear to Hamilton's mind that the payment of the army alone would incline neither affluent Americans nor foreign governments to loan money to the United States. If the government were to attract their capital, it was more important to cherish the civilian creditors than the soldiers; for, he argued, the civilians had the capital with which to make loans to the government, whereas the soldiers, even if they were paid, would have little surplus, after they had paid their debts, to lay out in government securities.[11]

In view of the recent rejection of the impost, Hamilton's plan of a general revenue seemed to have little or no chance of success: the recalcitrant states had given no sign of a change of heart and Rhode Island was still celebrating its victory over congressional "tyranny." Here was where the army entered into Hamilton's calculations: although the Rhode Islanders were as brave as lions when dealing with unarmed civilians, would they display equal courage when they found themselves confronted by determined men with guns in their hands?

If the army were called in as an auxiliary in the struggle against the states, it was essential to determine how far the officers and men were to be encouraged to go in asserting their demands. Apparently the Morrises thought that a little violence might not be entirely amiss: after all, force seemed to be the only language the state leaders understood. Hamilton, on the other hand, was too intimately acquainted with the temper of the army to imagine that if force were once resorted to it could be kept within bounds: a show of violence, he declared, "might end in the ruin of the country, and would certainly end in the ruin of the army." A manifesto from the army declaring its intention of standing beside the civilian creditors would perhaps have best answered his purpose.[12]

Properly to play the part Hamilton assigned it, the army needed the guidance of a firm hand. In General Washington, Hamilton found the man best qualified to unite the army with the civilian creditors and at the same time keep the officers and men "within the bounds of moderation." Not for the last time, Hamilton proposed to use Washington as an "aegis" for the execution of plans of far-reaching significance for the future of the republic.

From the sidelines in Philadelphia, Hamilton tried to coach Washington in diverting the suffering and discontent of the army toward the goal of a general revenue. But the stratagems that appeared so full of promise to the young congressman bore a very different aspect when viewed by Washington at Newburgh. While the Commander in Chief agreed that a general revenue was indispensable, he differed with Hamilton as to the methods of attaining it. Washington regarded the army as "a dangerous instrument to play with," even for the most laudable and patriotic ends. In his opinion, the quickest way to produce a mutiny was to give the soldiers grounds for believing that they were being made "mere puppets to establish continental funds." It was not more difficult, he assured Hamilton, "to still the raging Billows in a tempestuous Gale, than to convince the Officers of this Army of the justice or policy of paying men in Civil Offices full wages, when *they* cannot obtain a Sixtieth part of their dues."[13]

Nor was Washington inclined to agree with Hamilton that the "fools" in the states were so insensible that only the threat of an "enraged soldiery" would overcome their objections to give Congress adequate funds and powers. He was confident, he told Hamilton, that the states were not "so devoid of common sense, common honesty and common policy as to refuse their aid on a full, clear, and candid representation of facts from Congress." Just how Congress could make its representations to the states more clear and candid than it had already done, he did not say.

Although Washington declined to play Hamilton's game of using the army as a trump to force the adoption of the general revenue, he did advise the soldiers not to disband until the money due each officer and private had been ascertained and provided for by Congress. Washington had learned from experience not to trust the promises of the government; if the troops laid down their arms and went home, he feared that the adage of out of sight, out of mind would apply to the army. As long as the men kept their arms they were in a strong bargaining position. Even though he had no intention of permitting them to turn their guns against their countrymen, he likewise did not intend to permit their countrymen to defraud them.[14]

In the meantime, the emissaries dispatched to Newburgh by the "friends of the army" in Philadelphia were engaged in directing the soldiers' wrath against the state leaders. But Major John Armstrong, a fire-eater who nursed a grudge against all civilian authority, took upon himself in his Newburgh Addresses to urge the officers to carry their appeal "from the *justice* to the fears of government," even if it necessitated setting up a military dictatorship. This was more than Hamilton had bargained for: an uprising of the Continental Army against the Continental Congress had no place in his strategy. The real culprits, Hamilton had tried to impress upon the soldiers, were in the states, not in the Continental Congress; and while "fools" had to be intimidated, it was unnecessary to go to the extremes advocated by Major Armstrong—they frightened much more easily than that.

The task of undoing the damage wrought by the "friends of the army" fell upon Washington. While the Commander in Chief succeeded in preventing the officers from acting upon Major Armstrong's advice, it was only by promising that Congress would do them justice. At last Hamilton began to see the wisdom of Washington's policy. "Republican jealousy," Hamilton lamented, "has in it a principle of hostility to an army, whatever be their merits, whatever be their claims to the gratitude of the community." So powerful was this jealousy that it began to appear that the army was actually prejudicing the cause of the civilian creditors.

As the spokesman of Robert Morris in Congress, Hamilton was suspected by the soldiers of being in the "plot" to aggravate the sufferings of the army in order to promote his scheme of a general revenue. Hamilton had worried about Washington's popularity with the army; it was now time for Washington to worry about Hamilton's reputation. He warned the young congressman that by persisting in his efforts to unite civilians and soldiers he had come close to driving the troops to mutiny or into the arms of the states. Lest Hamilton be counted among those who were ready to "open the flood Gates of Civil discord, and deluge our rising Empire in blood," the Commander in Chief advised him to concentrate his efforts upon satisfying the demands of the army, leaving the civilian security holders to make their terms with Congress at a more propitious time.[15]

Balked in his efforts to enlist the active support of the army, Hamilton did not cease to work for a general revenue. Indeed, the necessity of such a revenue was daily becoming more apparent: "If the war continues," he pointed out, "it would seem that the army must, in June, subsist itself, *to defend the country*. If peace should take place, it *will* subsist itself to *procure justice to itself.*" Congress, in short, was in its usual position of looking down the horns of a dilemma.[16]

Upon the necessity of a general revenue, James Madison was in complete agreement with Hamilton. Nevertheless, the Virginian felt that his friend, being a newcomer to Congress, had much to learn about the facts of political life. Accordingly, he undertook to instruct Hamilton in that engrossing yet delicate subject, "What Every Congressman Should Know."

The essence of Madison's homily was that laws of Congress were not made in Heaven. Even the wisest and most salutary measures, he thought, required a *deus ex machina* which, reduced to the mundane level where, after all, politics were played, consisted of logrolling, "sweetening" and other such devices designed to make unpalatable bills appear attractive. In the case of Hamilton's plan for a general revenue, it seemed to Madison that his friend had omitted the ingredient upon which everything depended —the sugar. Not a trace could Madison find, and for this reason he feared that the measure stood no chance of adoption by the states. In order to make little bills grow into laws, it was necessary, Madison held, to give them a large dose of "sweetening."[17]

Accordingly, under Madison's direction, a generous measure of sugar was added to the bill. The proposed general revenue was coupled with a demand that the states cede their western lands to Congress; that the requisitions levied upon war-ravaged states be reduced; that the general government assume all war costs incurred by the states with or without the sanction of Congress; and that requisitions upon the various states be based upon population rather than upon the basis of land valuations, as the Articles of Confederation provided. And, lastly, no part of this omnibus bill was to be binding unless the whole was adopted by all the states.

Armed with a bill that fairly dripped sweetening, Hamilton urged that the hall of Congress be thrown open to the public even though the disclosure of the financial plight of the government was certain to give aid and comfort to the enemy. Hamilton invoked the right of a free people to hear their representatives in open debate, but it was suspected that he really had in mind packing the gallery with vociferous supporters—particularly security holders—of his general revenue scheme. Rather than expose itself to such pressure, Congress rejected Hamilton's proposal and the doors remained locked and guarded while the fate of the general revenue was decided.

It was soon apparent that Hamilton sorely needed the support of the security holders. Many members of Congress, apprehensive of suffering a second defeat at the hands of the states, wished to drop the general revenue plan altogether and to modify the impost to conform with the conditions laid down by the states. This meant that the impost would be restricted to twenty-five years' duration and that the states rather than the Continental Congress would be given the power to collect the duties. These concessions struck Hamilton as an abandonment by Congress of essential rights: the duration of the impost could not be limited, he observed, because the debt itself was not limited; and if the collection of the revenue were entrusted to the states, he predicted that the utility of the measure would be wholly defeated. Without a uniform collection, the impost seemed certain to operate as an unequal tax unless, as Hamilton considered probable, the states refused to collect money for the benefit of a government they regarded as a rival. In that event, of course, equality would be achieved between the citizens of the various states, but the national government would perish in order that no one paid more than his due.

In the heat of debate, Hamilton permitted his fervor to get the better of his discretion. When the question whether Congress or the states should appoint the collectors of the impost, Hamilton declared that, because the general government lacked sufficient authority to unite the states, "it was expedient to introduce the influence of officers deriving their emoluments from & consequently interested in supporting the power of Congress."[18]

Nothing was more certain to alarm the upholders of the rights of the states than this frank avowal of an intention to subvert the existing—and constitutional—relationship between the states and the general government. Observing the startled expression upon the faces of some congressmen when Hamilton made his remarks, Madison concluded that his colleague from New York had let the cat out of the bag.

But even if Hamilton had been a model of discretion, his cause was plainly doomed. Even James Madison abandoned his friend and joined the majority. Over Hamilton's objections, Congress decided that the revenue bill "must be accommodated to the sentiments of the States, whether just or unreasonable." In April, 1783, suiting its action to its words, Congress recommended to the states that it be authorized to levy an import duty of 5 per cent, reserving to the states themselves the appointment of the collectors, who were to be amenable to and removable by Congress. As a further concession it was agreed that the proposed impost should be limited to twenty-five years. At the same time, the states were asked to supplement this revenue by contributing one and a half million dollars more than the sum requested by Congress in the form of requisitions.

Knowing full well that he would be in the minority, Hamilton voted against the bill. He thereby placed himself in strange company: the Rhode Island delegates, protesting to the end that liberty was in danger, voted with him. Although Hamilton had salved his conscience, he took care not to put matters of conscience above the survival of the union. On the ground that as between the revenue plan recommended by Congress and no plan whatever "the obligations of national faith, honor and reputation" took precedence, he advised New York to adopt the proposal. More importantly, he called upon Washington to put the weight of his popularity on the side of the impost. If the Commander in Chief would write a circular letter to the states, candidly stating his opinion of the Articles of Confederation "and of the absolute necessity of a change," Hamilton flattered himself that the opposition would be overwhelmed. In September, 1783, Washington reluctantly acted upon this advice, but the reception accorded his letter was not calculated to induce him to make a practice of stepping out of his military role to instruct his countrymen in their civil duties.

Congress had deferred to the wishes of the states, but the army remained to be dealt with. As usual, Congress looked to the Superintendent of Finance to extricate the country from its difficulties by working some financial miracle. But Morris protested that the age of miracles was over and that he was as little able to meet the demands of the army "as to make bread of stones."

His hopes of a general revenue having gone glimmering, Hamilton became as eager to get rid of the army as he had once been to frighten "fools" with it. It was now Hamilton's turn to be frightened as he contemplated the alternatives before the government. To disband the army while the

British were still in force in the United States was, he knew, to invite disaster, yet it was at least as probable that the American army would mutiny as that the British would attack.

Hamilton was now acting as Washington's spokesman in Congress. On May 28, 1783, Congress adopted Hamilton's or, more properly, the Commander in Chief's plan, by which the troops were offered one month's pay in cash, three months' pay in certificates and an immediate furlough. In actuality, furloughing was an euphemism for disbanding the army: it was devoutly hoped in Congress that the troops would go home and no longer trouble the civilian government—unless, of course, the peace negotiations failed and their services were again urgently required.[19]

Although the soldiers at Newburgh went in peace, those stationed in Philadelphia and Lancaster refused to take their pittance and begone. Instead, they mutinied against their officers, seized control of the city and threatened the Continental Congress and the Supreme Executive Council of Pennsylvania. Because the Pennsylvania authorities refused to call out the militia to keep order, Congress felt that it had no alternative but to evacuate Philadelphia. But the representatives of the government of the United States did not dare to march out of Philadelphia in proud defiance of the mutineers. On June 24, 1783, they slipped quietly out of town by back alleys. All made their getaway except the Rhode Islanders, who stayed behind "to show their courage." President Boudinot set the delegates a fine example of prudence by leaving the proclamation announcing Congress' departure on his desk to be opened after he had reached safety in Princeton.

On his part, Hamilton rode out of Philadelphia cursing the folly that had prompted the Pennsylvania Executive Council to refuse to call out the militia and the precipitancy that had led Congress to abandon the city before it had become untenable. What he would not have given for a few pieces of artillery with which to clear the streets of this "licentious soldiery"! "The conduct of the executive of this State was to the last degree weak & disgusting," he wrote Washington. ". . . I regard the whole of this business as a most unfortunate one, in which, probably, none of the actors will acquire great credit." He was right: Congress lost immeasurably in prestige by its flight and for several years it was obliged to wander about the country, a government in search of a capital.

The bulk of the army having been sent on its way, Congress was free to turn its attention to the problem of a peacetime army. After some debate, it had been agreed that the United States could not safely dispense with an army, and in April, 1783, Hamilton had been appointed to a committee charged with the responsibility of drawing up plans for embodying and regulating the armed forces of the United States.

In the report of his committee, Hamilton recommended the retention of six regiments, including one regiment of artillery incorporated in a corps of engineers; the construction of fortifications; and the establishment of government-owned factories for the production of munitions and weapons of war. Even though it were more expensive to produce these articles at home than to import them from abroad, Hamilton believed that the government ought to undertake their manufacture on the ground that "every country ought to have within itself all the essential means of defence; for to depend on foreign supplies is to render its security precarious." By utilizing the labor of soldiers in these state factories, he contended, the United States would ultimately be able to supply itself cheaper than by buying abroad.

In submitting these recommendations, Hamilton imagined that he had cut the peacetime army to the minimum strength compatible with national security. Even so, he had not sufficiently reckoned with Americans' prejudice against a "standing army" or with Congress' passion for economizing. When that body had finished trimming his estimates, only three regiments remained and no provision was made for a national manufactory of arms and ammunition. While the United States Army did not die, it faded away almost to nothingness. As James Madison said, with the danger passed, it became unpopular "to *mention* that there was an American army, during the *late* war."

Hamilton intended that the few troops remaining in the Continental Army should be stationed at West Point and the frontier posts, but here he encountered a storm of protest from his own state. New York insisted upon garrisoning the posts that lay within its territory with its own troops and it stoutly asserted its intention of resisting any effort by the Continental Army to "invade" the state. Despite the instructions sent by the government of New York, Hamilton refused to present his state's demands to Congress: "Federal rather than State provision," he declared, "should be made for the defence of every part of the Confederacy, in peace as well as in war." Even so, a conflict between New York and the United States government was avoided only because the British refused to surrender the posts in question.[20]

As Hamilton had predicted, the authority of the general government declined rapidly with the advent of peace: Americans could not wait until the last shot had been fired before beginning to strip the Continental Congress of its powers. After 1783, the question uppermost in Hamilton's mind was whether the general government could survive the peace and the resurgence of the states to which it gave rise.

6.
Law and the Loyalists

When Hamilton first came to Congress in 1782, he hoped to find in that body wisdom, decision and energy. Only by the exercise of leadership on the part of Congress did he believe that the republic could be saved. A year in Philadelphia, however, confirmed all of Hamilton's fears that congressmen themselves were much too deferential toward the states to play a commanding part in the newly created "American empire." They were, he now admitted, "not governed by reason or foresight, but by circumstances"—and circumstances seldom worked in their favor. As a result, he declared, Congress was no place for a man of vision, boldness and zeal for the public good: among the timeservers and trimmers who made an art of evading responsibility, Hamilton feared that he would experience only frustration. As one of his friends wrote him at this time: "if you could submit to spend a whole life in dissecting a fly you would be in their opinion one of the greatest men in the world."

Rather than purchase fame by such means, Hamilton decided not to stand for re-election to Congress. It was a wise decision; probably he could not have been re-elected had he wished. For a radical change had taken place in the attitude of the prevailing party in New York toward the general government and toward the policies advocated by Hamilton himself. As a result, politically speaking, New York became for Hamilton the enemy's country.

During the early part of the war, Hamilton and Governor George Clinton of New York had been political allies. The governor had been a vigorous and uncompromising nationalist; indeed, he was prepared to go even further than was Hamilton in strengthening the hand of the central government: in 1780, he recommended that Congress be given power to coerce recalcitrant states with military force. Under Clinton's leadership, New York had been one of the first states to approve the impost. And Hamilton had gone to Congress in 1782 authorized by his state—Hamilton himself was the author of the proposal—to move for a Constitutional Convention.

Law and the Loyalists

But all this had changed by the summer of 1783, when Hamilton decided to abandon his political career. The state completely reversed itself on the all-important question of augmenting the powers of the Continental Congress. With the fighting at an end and the British about to evacuate New York, Governor Clinton and his adherents sloughed off their earlier nationalism and adopted an extreme state-rights point of view. In 1782, Hamilton had set out from New York as a young knight-errant eager to break a lance for nationalism; he returned to the state in 1783 to find himself denounced as an enemy by the very people who had sent him forth to battle.

Another shock awaited Hamilton in New York. In 1783, the state was swept by a wave of hatred for the Loyalists. As early as 1782, while Hamilton was in Philadelphia attending the meetings of the Continental Congress, he had begun to hear disturbing reports of a Loyalist exodus from New York. Thousands of "Tories" hastened to remove their persons and property out of the reach of the patriots; even the wilderness of Nova Scotia and Canada seemed preferable to New York. Seven thousand Loyalists sailed in the spring of 1783; and in November, 1783, the British army evacuated New York City, carrying with it more thousands of Loyalists. Nevertheless, a considerable number remained behind, trusting to the guarantees made them in the treaty of peace. Accordingly, when the American army marched into New York City in November, 1783, the patriots came face to face with their fellow Americans who had sided with the King and Parliament.

To banish these "atrocious and incorrigible offenders" from the country was regarded by Governor Clinton and his partisans as treatment much too mild for their crimes: such "Imps of Hell," they declared, ought to be given a foretaste in this world of the wrath that awaited them in the next. As a dispenser of punishment, Governor Clinton was not likely to err on the side of clemency.

Even though Hamilton had no reason to love Loyalists, he could not enter into the spirit of the Tory witch-hunt led by Governor Clinton. During the war, when the suppression of the Loyalists could be justified as a military necessity, Hamilton had refused to condone wholesale persecution. In 1777, while complaining that the government was too lax in its treatment of Loyalists and urging that "exemplary punishment" be meted out, he was careful to add that the punishment ought to be inflicted by the government rather than by mobs and that only heinous offenders ought to be made to suffer. Nothing was worse, he pointed out, than to impose penalties indiscriminately upon all suspected of loyalism: better to exterminate them altogether, he said, than to embitter them against the government and still leave it in their power to do injury. By way of illustrating his meaning, he quoted the advice given by a Roman general when he was asked whether the army ought to be destroyed utterly or dismissed with honor and respect: "By the first method, says he, you disable the Romans from being your enemies, by the last you make them your friends. So with respect to the Tories," said Hamilton; "I would either disable them from doing us any injury, or I would endeavor to gain their friendship by clemency. Inflicting trifling punishments only embitters the minds of those on whom they fall, and increases their disposition to do mischief without taking away the power of doing it."*

If this was the part of wisdom during the war, it seemed to Hamilton to be even more imperative now that peace had been made. He was persuaded that the majority of Loyalists had acted "from accident, from the dread of the British power, and from the influence of others to whom they had been accustomed to look up." Obviously, such men were not beyond redemption: it required only fair treatment to make them good citizens. Once these erring brethren had been made to see that it was to their interest to support the new government, Hamilton was certain that they would cease to be troublemakers. If, on the other hand, the objective was to make them eternal enemies of the United States, Hamilton confessed that Clinton's policy of proscription, confiscation of property and deprivation of civil rights could hardly be improved upon.

And so, instead of crying good riddance upon the Loyalists, Hamilton deplored their departure as a grievous loss to the community. For, he pointed out, the capital the Loyalists carried with them was vital to the well-being of the United States; and the country was suffering from a shortage of wealthy, substantial conservative-minded citizens. To make matters worse, while the United States was weakening itself, Canada and Nova Scotia were increasing in wealth and population at the expense of this country. And finally, with thousands of embittered Loyalists taking refuge in the North, Hamilton saw little prospect of preserving peace with Great Britain.[1]

Finding that the common people, their resentments inflamed by Governor Clinton, "breathed nothing but the bitterness of vengeance, and would hear of no forgiveness," Hamilton undertook to calm the public mind by writing a series of newspaper articles under the signature of "Phocion."†

---

* Compare with Machiavelli: "Men must either be caressed or else annihilated; they will revenge themselves for small injuries, but cannot do so for great ones; the injury therefore that we do a man must be such that we need not fear his vengeance."

† Hamilton's choice of pseudonyms casts a revealing light upon the processes of his mind. For example, according to Plutarch, Phocion was an Athenian leader who espoused "the cause of those who differed most from him, when they needed his patronage'. . . . and distinguished himself by advocating the recall and forgiveness of those who had been banished. So far was he from humoring or courting the people that "he always thwarted and opposed them"; "and when once he gave his opinion to the people, and was met with the general approbation and applause of the assembly, turning to some of his friends, he asked them: 'Have I inadvertently said something foolish?'" Although he attained the name of "the Good," he was finally forced to drink hemlock.

Here he addressed himself to "the good sense of the people," hopeful that this appeal to reason would dispel "all the furious and dark passions of the human mind" that had been stirred up by the governor. He reminded his countrymen that "passion and prejudice" were the inveterate enemies of the ideals for which they had fought; that the eyes of the world were upon the United States; that the future of republicanism not only in the United States but throughout the world might be determined by what occurred in this country; and that the stipulations in the Treaty of Peace respecting Loyalists were sacred and inviolable.

Manifestly, only a man who disdained the kind of popularity that is purchased by truckling to the "popular passions" would have come to the defense of the Loyalists. Except for raising a cry for George III and Old England, there was probably no more certain way of incurring obloquy: as a traveler remarked, it was held to be "a crime unpardonable to think in any way different from the crowd" upon this matter. Inevitably, therefore, by championing the Loyalists, Hamilton exposed himself to the charge of being a Tory-lover. It was said that he swooned with joy whenever a blue-blooded monarchist gave him a civil word. He was accused of being "the bell-wether of the flock" of the Loyalists and of being in British pay. Newspaper writers speculated as to the number of pieces of silver for which he had sold his country. If this "little, pompous, stripling delegate—the Jack Daw of public affairs" were given a free hand, it was predicted that he would "blast the fruits of our exertions, and make the blooming garden of our revolution as forlorn and desolate as the barren and inhospitable wilderness."

According to Plutarch, Phocion, the Athenian statesman, once remarked that "he had been the author of much safe and wholesome counsel, which had not been followed." The same might be said of Hamilton's "Phocion" essays. In May, 1784, an "Act to preserve the freedom and independence of this State" was passed by the New York Assembly. Under the sanction of this lofty purpose, all those who had voluntarily remained within the British lines during the war were disfranchised—the very measure Hamilton had sought to prevent by his newspaper articles. In thus proscribing the Loyalists, no effort was made to distinguish between the innocent and the guilty: the condemned were accused of no wrongful acts or even of wrongful words; their place of abode sufficed to place them under the ban. Thus the governor and his followers established the doctrine of guilt by residence and proceeded to apply it in full rigor against the Loyalists.

Manifestly, Clinton was actuated by more than blind hatred of those who had sided with the enemy: the governor intended to perpetuate his ascendancy by disfranchising a large part of the opposition. In New York as in other states, the Loyalists were the victims of "avarice cloaked in the cover of patriotism, or private passion and prejudice, under the presence of revenging the wrongs of the country." Moreover, Clinton was astute enough to see that by posing as the savior of the people against "Tory aristocrats," he would add immeasurably to his already formidable reputation as a stern and incorruptible patriot.

True, the act disfranchising the Loyalists provided that they might secure exemption from its penalties by swearing to an oath that they had not been guilty of acts calculated to give aid and comfort to the enemy. But so tender of civil liberties was Hamilton, at least in this instance, that he denounced this procedure as inquisitorial. No more heinous oath could be devised, he held, than one which required a citizen to swear that he had not been guilty of past offenses. Even in England, he reminded the Clintonians, oaths had been limited to testing present dispositions toward the government; and he pointed out that it would be more in conformity with the pretentions to liberalism to which the United States laid claim to abolish oaths altogether than to carry them to the lengths New York had done.

Not content with disfranchising Loyalists, the Clintonians insisted upon requiring oaths of Roman Catholics that effectually debarred them from holding public office. Again Hamilton inveighed against such an inquisition into matters of conscience: "Why," he asked, "should we wound the tender conscience of any and why present oaths to those who are known to be good citizens?" The policy of the governor and his adherents in multiplying tests and oaths seemed to Hamilton to constitute a danger to all citizens: against the exercise of arbitrary power, no one could feel secure in his liberty. To drive home this peril to the people of New York he posed a hypothetical case: supposing, he said, that the majority of the New York legislature consisted of rich men and that this majority, possessed of unlimited power, enacted a law that no man without an estate of £10,000 should be eligible to sit in the assembly—in that event, what recourse would the people of New York have against a tyrannical law?

At the same time, Hamilton reminded New Yorkers that Europe, owing to religious bigotry, had lost thousands of its most enterprising citizens. He feared that political bigotry might prove equally costly to the United States. Unless a spirit of moderation and toleration in politics replaced the existing insistence upon conformity to the lowest common denominator, he predicted that the United States would never attain order, peace and prosperity. True Americanism, he said, was "generous, humane, beneficent, and just."

Among the rights of man to which Hamilton laid claim was the right of criticizing to the fullest extent the actions and policies of those in power. As befitted an opposition leader, he exalted freedom of speech and of the press into a bulwark of liberty. "There is no danger," he declared, "that the rights of a man at the head of the government . . . can be injured by the voice of a private individual. There is as little danger that the spirit of the people of this country will ever tolerate attempts to seduce, to awe, or to clamor them out of the privilege of bringing the conduct of those in power to the bar of public condemnation." In republican governments, officials were servants of the people and could claim no immunity from criticism and, where it was warranted, from censure. Fine words—but the real test of Hamilton's devotion to the principle of freedom of speech and of the press was to come after he himself was in power and his conduct was scrutinized by unfriendly and prejudiced individuals.

No doubt, some of the zeal displayed by Hamilton in behalf of the Loyalists was owing to the fact that in many instances they were wealthy and conservative members of society to whom he looked for aid against the radicalism that seemed to threaten the established social order, the rights of property and the integrity of the union. The attack leveled against Loyalist property rights struck him as the prelude to the destruction of all property rights. Consequently, under the rule of George Clinton, Hamilton increasingly felt a sense of kinship with the Loyalists, who, even though they had chosen the wrong side in the struggle, were closer to him in many other respects than were the radical patriots.

In March, 1783, the New York legislature passed the so-called Trespass Act, according to the terms of which Loyalist and British occupants of patriot property within the British lines were made legally responsible for all damages and accrued rent during the entire period of the British occupation of New York City and its environs. No British subject was permitted by this act to plead that he acted under the authority of the British military or civil power: the mere fact that he had been in possession of property belonging to an American patriot was sufficient to make him liable to the penalties of the law.

Shortly after the passage of this law, Mrs. Elizabeth Rutgers, a patriot widow, brought suit against Benjamin Waddington, a British merchant, for the rent of her brewery which Waddington had occupied from 1778 to 1782. As a widow and a patriot, it seemed impossible that she would fail to recover against a British subject in a New York court. Who would deny the widow her mite—in this case the accrued rent for a period of five years—when she came to court to plead her patriotism, her indigence and her rights as defined by the New York legislature?

And yet Alexander Hamilton was hardhearted enough to assert that Mrs. Rutgers was asking more than her due. Unlike those patriots who could not see the legal and constitutional principles at stake for the widow's weeds, Hamilton insisted that the Trespass Act upon which Mrs. Rutgers founded her case was a palpable violation of international law and the treaty of peace. Under this persuasion, Hamilton undertook Waddington's defense. Associated with him as counsel were some of the leading members of the

New York bar: Brockholst Livingston and Morgan Lewis. Mrs. Rutgers' attorneys were no less distinguished: John Lawrence, Robert Troup, and Egbert Benson, the Attorney General of the State of New York. From the array of legal talent assembled by both sides it was apparent that *Rutgers* v. *Waddington* was regarded as a test case of far-reaching significance.

The case came to trial in February, 1784, before the Mayor's Court of New York City, consisting of the mayor, aldermen and recorder of the city. Before these magistrates, Hamilton argued the case upon much the same grounds that he might later have taken before the Supreme Court of the United States. He treated it as a controversy in international law: the rules of war laid down by Pufendorf, Vattel, Burlamaqui, Wolfe and Grotius, by which it appeared that a conqueror was privileged to appropriate personal property and the rents and profits of real property during the period of occupancy, were in his opinion decisive. But the counsel for the plaintiff, while complimenting Hamilton upon his erudition and skill in marshaling authorities, declared that the principles of international law were irrelevant and immaterial to the case at issue since the War of Independence was not an ordinary war to which the laws of nations applied. By pillaging, burning, raping and committing other enormities, the British, it was said, had placed themselves beyond the pale of civilized society. They had broken all the rules and yet the counsel for the defendant was claiming for them the immunities, rights and privileges of the law of nations. The patriots of New York were not buying *that* doctrine from lawyer Hamilton even though he asserted it was based upon "the maxims of eternal truth" and "the immutable law of moral obligation."[2]

Hamilton did not deny that the British had been guilty of atrocities: to suggest in a company of American patriots that the late enemy had waged war decently and humanely was the quickest way of bringing down the roof. Instead, he contented himself with quoting Vattel to the effect that the justice or injustice of a war had no bearing upon the case: the rights of the belligerents remained unimpaired.

But it was as a violation of the treaty of peace between the United States and Great Britain by which claims of citizens of the United States and Great Britain growing out of the war were reciprocally canceled that Hamilton made his most telling points in behalf of his client. Under the conviction that the issue in *Rutgers* v. *Waddington* was essentially whether the states of the Continental Congress were to control foreign policy, Hamilton made in his speeches a rousing plea for nationalism. He contended that the United States began its existence as a united nation: the union came prior to the states and the Declaration of Independence was a fundamental part of the constitution of every state. Although the Articles of Confederation professed to create merely "a league of friendship," Hamilton asserted that as regards foreign affairs they made the general government sovereign. Every state was

Law and the Loyalists

therefore bound to execute without demur all the treaty obligations of the United States government. Upon the strict observance of treaties, he declared, depended the authority of the Continental Congress, the ability of the government to borrow money, the security of the country and its acceptance as a respectable member of the family of nations.

Upon these grounds, Hamilton urged the judges of the Mayor's Court to interpose their authority by voiding the Trespass Act as a violation of the Articles of Confederation and of international law. That the judges possessed the right of declaring invalid acts of the legislature Hamilton had no doubt. Final authority in determining the constitutionality of laws did not reside, he asserted, in the legislature but in the courts: judges rather than legislators were the guardians of the fundamental law. This was a novel doctrine in 1783; Hamilton was one of the first Americans of his day to invoke the "judicial power" as a curb upon the authority of the state legislatures and as a means of subordinating the states to the fundamental law from which the powers of the general government were derived. Up to this time, no state court, much less a Mayor's Court, had ventured to declare a law unconstitutional.[3]

If the judges of the Mayor's Court boldly asserted their prerogative in the case of *Rutgers* v. *Waddington,* Hamilton promised them a rich reward of honor and fame: "It will remain a record," he said, "of the spirit of our courts and will be handed down to posterity." But the judges were inclined to look not to posterity but to Governor Clinton and the New York legislature for their cue. Despite Hamilton's exhortations, the judges were not convinced that they possessed the powers which he urged them to exercise, and they knew that Clinton and his party were emphatically not of Hamilton's way of thinking.

On the other hand, the judges of the Mayor's Court were not prepared to abdicate their function of subjecting laws to the test of reasonableness. Under this right, only limited discretion was permitted the courts: they could do no more than give expression to the legislature's intent. The literal application of the law could be prevented only when it was assumed that the legislature had not intended to require the performance of unreasonable or impossible acts. In such instances, the judges were "in decency" to assume that any untoward consequences of the act were not foreseen by the legislature.

Acting under this authority—a very different thing from judicial review—the Mayor's Court acknowledged that there were certain ambiguities in the Trespass Act which required judicial interpretation. It was not reasonable to suppose, the judges held, that the legislature had intended to set its own authority against the law of nations and the treaty of peace—therefore, whatever discrepancies existed between the statute and the law of nations and the treaty must be assumed to be accidental. Applying this principle to the case at issue, the court ruled that during the period when Waddington had held Mrs. Rutgers' property under the authorization of the British military—that is, from 1780 to 1783—he was not obliged to pay rent to Mrs. Rutgers. But for the two years from 1778 to 1780, he was compelled to reimburse the widow.

In this way, either explicitly or by implication, the Mayor's Court upheld most of the points contained in Hamilton's brief: that treaties are the supreme law of the land; that the Continental Congress had full and exclusive power to make peace and war; that no state could alter or abridge the Articles of Confederation or the Treaty of Peace with Great Britain; and that acts done in relation to war are, by the law of nations, consigned to oblivion by a treaty of peace. On the other hand, the judges went to considerable pains to exculpate themselves from the charge of having exercised the function of judicial review. "The supremacy of the legislature need not be called into question," they asserted; "if they think positively to enact a law, there is no power which can control them. Where the main object of such a law is clearly expressed and the intention manifest, the judges are not at liberty, although it appear to them *unreasonable* to reject it: for this were to set the *judicial* above the *legislative*, which would be subversive of all government."

Nevertheless, the outcry against the Mayor's Court raised by the Clintonians would hardly have been more strident had it claimed and exercised the right of setting aside acts of the legislature. Rather than submit to "Judicial Tyranny," the New York Assembly censured the Mayor's Court and reaffirmed the Trespass Act. It was moved in the New York legislature to remove the mayor and recorder of New York City; although the motion was defeated, the legislature denounced the decision of the court as "subversive of all law and good order," calculated to produce "anarchy and confusion." In 1785, a New York patriot sued General Tryon of the British army under the Trespass Act and recovered five thousand pounds for damages done his farm during the war—considerably more than the farm was worth. Cases continued to be brought under this statute and verdicts for exorbitant rents and damages were found in almost every instance. Not until 1788 was the Trespass Act finally removed from the statute book.

Waddington was relieved to have gotten off so lightly; but when Mrs. Rutgers' attorneys announced her intention of appealing the case to the state supreme court, Hamilton advised his client to make a settlement with the widow out of court. Knowing the attitude of the judges of the supreme court toward judicial review and their reluctance to cross swords with Governor Clinton, Hamilton expected little aid from that quarter. He had won a partial victory in the Mayor's Court and with that he was obliged to be content until the adoption of the Federal Constitution afforded him a second and vastly more important opportunity to plead the case for judicial review.

The significance of *Rutgers v. Waddington* was out of all proportion to the amount of money involved. The arguments of counsel and the opinion of the court were published in a pamphlet, and the case was noted and commented upon by the newspapers. The continuing necessity of preventing the states from transgressing the terms of the treaty of peace gave increasing importance to the doctrine of judicial review. In 1786, John Jay, the Secretary of Foreign Affairs, urged Congress to adopt the position taken by Hamilton in *Rutgers v. Waddington*—that a treaty ratified by Congress became binding on the whole nation without "the intervention, consent or fiat of the state legislatures" and that the state judiciary be given power to decide all cases arising under the treaty.

But judicial review, as Hamilton envisaged it, required the existence of an independent, forceful and nationally minded judiciary. Unfortunately for the success of Hamilton's plan of making judges lions under the Continental Congress, few states had a judiciary capable of challenging the supremacy of the legislature. Worse still, the general government had only one court, the Court of Appeals in Cases of Capture. Sitting as an admiralty court, these federal judges heard appeals from the state courts. With the ending of the war, however, its functions almost wholly ceased. In June, 1783, hoping to give greater scope to this vestigial organ of federal authority, Hamilton proposed in the Continental Congress that its powers be broadened. His efforts went for naught, however; although the court lingered on, it was compelled to depend upon state officials to enforce its decrees—a circumstance which the states turned to their advantage by assigning its powers to their own courts.

Above all, judicial review could not gain a foothold until it was recognized that political authority was inherent in the people, that legislatures were mere agents of the sovereign will and that the fundamental law was superior to legislative acts. In short, judicial review waited upon the victory of the views of Lord Coke over those of Judge Blackstone.[4]

As though defending Loyalists and British subjects in the courts of law was not enough to sink him in the estimation of the Clintonians, Hamilton undertook to represent Loyalists and British subjects in bringing suits against patriots. For example, Stephen De Lancey, one of the most notorious of the Loyalist leaders, solicited Hamilton's aid in distraining his "wicked Tenants" for unpaid rent. By accepting such cases, Hamilton gave some patriots occasion to wonder just who had won the war. One merchant, threatened with imprisonment for debt by his British creditors, complained that he faced the dismal prospect of being "dragged to prison by hungry British Agents (brutal and barbarous as the Savages) who . . . hover like

Cormorants over the devoted Carcasses of their captive Debtors." And when his fellow Americans undertook to shoot down these birds of prey, lawyer Hamilton posted "No Hunting" signs!

Nevertheless, it could not be said that by appearing as counsel for British and Loyalist litigants Hamilton did his practice any harm. As he said in 1784, "Legislative folly has afforded so plentiful a harvest to us lawyers that we have scarcely a moment to spare from the substantial business of reaping." While doubts were cast upon Hamilton's "Americanism," his devotion to property rights was not questioned: in this regard, all conservatives, patriots and Loyalists alike, looked upon him as their champion.

And yet, Hamilton might have had even more briefs had he joined in the hue and cry against the Loyalists. By an act of 1779, all lawyers licensed prior to 1777 had been suspended from practice in the New York courts until they had been certified as loyal by a court of inquiry. As a result, some of the leading practitioners at the bar were disbarred and their business handed over to fledglings like Hamilton himself. Even so, he felt the injustice of this law so keenly that he endeavored to procure its repeal and to open the legal profession to former Loyalists.

In 1786, partly as a result of Hamilton's efforts, the acts disbarring Loyalist lawyers and disfranchising Loyalists who had remained in the state were repealed. Heartened by this success, Hamilton attempted in the New York legislature to secure the repeal of all laws discriminating against Loyalists in contravention to the treaty of peace. In 1788 he finally carried his point. After that date, the statute books of the State of New York were purged of all laws regarding Loyalists; for the first time, the treaty of peace could be said to be honored in New York both in the letter and in the spirit.

Hamilton's labors in behalf of the Loyalists had important political consequences. An alliance was effected between New York City, Long Island and Albany whereby the conservative citizens of the state were united in support of Hamilton's policies. It was not merely coincidental that the former Loyalist areas of the state warmly supported the Federal Constitution in 1788. Common interests born of social, economic and political necessities proved in the end more potent than the disruptive effects of war and revolution.[5]

7.
"A Rage for Liberty"

During the War of Independence, Americans had been sustained by the hope that the United States would create a new and invincible "empire of freedom" against which despotism, even of the enlightened variety, could not stand. The peoples of the earth were invited to throw off their yokes and join Americans in the pursuit of happiness; and it was expected that even Englishmen, benighted as they were held to be, would catch a spark of freedom from their revolted subjects. But these inflated hopes were punctured by the course of events that immediately followed the attainment of independence. The United States, it is true, afforded a spectacle to the world—but what nation, Hamilton asked, would be tempted to follow the wavering, unsteady footsteps of the tottering American republic? To effect a revolution in the minds of men he held that it was first necessary to demonstrate that republicanism worked in one country. From the way things were going in the United States, Hamilton thought that Americans were more likely to verify the theory that men were not competent to govern themselves—"that they must have a master, and were only made for the reins and spur." If that proved to be the outcome of the revolution, "with the greatest advantages for promoting it [Liberty] that ever a people had," he exclaimed, "we shall have betrayed the cause of human nature."

Alexander Hamilton was a gadfly who kept reminding his countrymen that by weakness and disunion they were jeopardizing everything they held dear; the pursuit of happiness, he said, must wait upon the creation of a "solid, coercive union." At the same time, he undertook to point out to them the cause of their tribulations. It was the Articles of Confederation, he declared, that threatened to put a premature end to the republican experiment in the United States. The trouble was organic; it was lodged in the frame of government itself; and it required a sure hand and a sharp knife to excise the evil.

The Articles of Confederation bore little resemblance to the kind of government that Hamilton, had he been given a free hand, would have devised for the United States. This frame of government was shaped in large part of Americans' experience as British colonists—an experience that had taught them to fear centralized government and to exalt their local governments as bulwarks against tyranny. The maxims that power corrupts, that it is the nature of government constantly to encroach upon the liberty of the individual and that strong government invariably degenerates into tyranny—these precepts Americans had learned by going to school under George III. His Britannic Majesty was a good teacher: his subjects overseas mastered their lessons so well that when they came to establish their own government they applied to it all the "self-evident truths" that the British government had driven home.

As a result, the Founding Fathers of the Articles of Confederation created a league of sovereign states rather than a unitary state. The Continental Congress functioned as a council of ambassadors. In general, it was allowed only so much power as the colonists had been willing to grant the British Parliament. The analogy between the new American government and the old empire was complete even to the extent of preserving the requisition system, thereby leaving the general government dependent upon the voluntary contributions of the states. Not only did the Articles of Confederation narrowly define the powers of the general government; they likewise denied Congress the means necessary to carry its enumerated powers into effect. To all intents and purposes, Congress was reduced in several vital areas of government to giving advice to the states. If wise counsel could have prevailed, the Articles would have been a notable success; but as a patriot observed, the injunctions of the best and wisest of mankind, even when clothed in the sanctity of Holy Writ, were honored more often in the breach than in the observance.[1]

That this was a true government, Hamilton always denied: "A mere treaty, dependent on the good faith of the parties," he said, ought not to be confused with a government which was "only another word for POLITICAL POWER AND SUPREMACY." Nevertheless, in the states themselves, the road to popularity was to depict the Continental Congress as a potential tyrant and to keep the people in a perpetual fret for their liberties. Politicians who had attained power in the states were unwilling to surrender any part of it to the general government; from their point of view, the Articles of Confederation had established the best of all possible governments and they were resolved to defend it to the bitter end. Many of these politicians had won office on the strength of their unsparing denunciations of British authority and they seemed intent upon retaining power by denouncing congressional authority in much the same terms. Some state politicians appeared to regard Congress as though it consisted of "men annually chosen by the Emperor of Morocco, and sent over to enslave us" and who nourished "deep laid designs to ruin the people, and create themselves so many aristocratic lords."² This may have been the shortest way to attain political office, but, as Hamilton pointed out, it was fatal to national unity. The state politicians' game, he remarked, was "to inspire jealousies of the power of Congress, though nothing can be more apparent than that they have no power; that for want of it, the resources of the country during the war could not be drawn out, and we at this moment experience all the mischiefs of a bankrupt and ruined credit." Only a people immoderately enamored of liberty and incorrigibly hostile to nationalism, Hamilton decided, could suppose that the Continental Congress menaced their freedom. The members of Congress were chosen annually by the state legislatures; they were debarred from serving more than two years successively or more than three years in seven; and they were subject to recall at any time by their states. Under these circumstances, to talk of "republican jealousy" of government, the corrupting effects of power, the danger that the Continental Congress would encroach upon the rights of man, and the other "imaginary dangers from the spectre of power in Congress" was, in Hamilton's opinion, to tilt at windmills while a host of real enemies overran the state.

As long as the states held the purse strings, Hamilton saw no prospect that the general government would ever be anything more than a mendicant, dependent upon handouts from thirteen jealous, close-fisted sovereignties. And well might the states keep Congress upon short rations: by ignoring the requisitions of the general government they exhibited their independence, humiliated a rival and saved themselves money. Under this system, Hamilton marveled how the general government existed—or were Americans trying to prove that they could enjoy free government in the sense that no one paid for its support?

The defects of the Articles of Confederation Hamilton attributed to the "rage for liberty" that seemed to possess Americans: having almost no other view than to devise safeguards against tyranny, it was not surprising, he remarked, that they made government weak and inefficient. "The circumstances of a revolution quickened the public sensibility on every point connected with the security of popular rights," he observed, "and in some instances raised the warmth of our zeal beyond the degree which consisted with the due temperature of the body politic." Unwilling to risk the abuse of power, Americans incurred the even greater risk—to Hamilton's way of thinking—of doing away with power. Instead of recognizing that governments must be able to act, Americans took refuge in the comforting illusion that "all is safe because nothing improper will be likely to be done." Thus, said Hamilton, "we forget how much good may be prevented, and how much ill may be produced, by the power of hindering the doing what may be necessary." He insisted that there was "a happy mean between too much confidence and excessive jealousy in which the health and prosperity of a State consist. Either extreme is a dangerous vice. The first is a temptation to men in power, to arrogate more than they have a right to; the latter enervates Government . . . breeds confusion in the State, disgusts and discontents among the people, and may eventually prove as fatal to liberty as the opposite temper."

In Hamilton's eyes, the sight of a nation without a government worthy of the name was "an awful spectacle," comparable, perhaps, to Niagara flowing upstream. Some Americans took comfort in the belief that the evil would effect its own cure and that it was merely a matter of waiting for the people to come right. Hamilton admitted that there was some reason to hope that "when prejudice and folly have run themselves out of breath, we may return to reason and correct our errors," but he saw that the course of prejudice and folly was long and that it was doubtful if virtue and wisdom could go the distance.

Manifestly, powerful centrifugal forces were at work in the United States —forces which the Articles of Confederation were wholly unable to counteract. The principle of self-determination applied by the United States against Great Britain might well be applied by the individual states against the United States. In short, the same explosive principle that had disrupted the British empire now threatened the existence of the American republic.

In the eighteenth century, it was generally assumed that the principal purpose of the study of history was to reveal "the constant and universal principles" underlying human affairs. "History," said David Hume, "furnishes examples of all kinds; and every prudential, as well as moral precept, may be authorized by those events which her enlarged mirror is able to present to us."

It was in this spirit that Hamilton approached history: he studied it to determine the nature of the laws which controlled human affairs. He always sought to point a moral, to extract some useful lesson and to chart the course of future events. He was persuaded that if history were rightly read, "the plain principles of human nature" would be brought to light. To read history, in short, was to be forewarned of the pitfalls that lay in store for every organized society.

For Hamilton, the glory that was Greece was forever blighted by the inability of its statesmen to establish a stable, orderly and peaceful union. The consequence of that failure was the wars of the Greek city-states, by which the way was paved for foreign conquest. It was the absence of an effective and enduring union, capable of restraining the ambition and greed of the cities, he asserted, that in the long run had cost Greece its freedom.

In the turmoil, internecine war and "licentiousness" of classical Greece,

"A Rage for Liberty"

Hamilton saw prefigured the history of the United States. Although he did not pretend that Americans took their democracy quite as strenuously as did the Greeks, he believed that his countrymen had it in them to outdo even the Athenians in this regard. For Hamilton assumed that the "laws" governing human behavior were the same at all times and places—hence if Americans persisted in their present course they would inevitably meet with the same kind of disaster that had overwhelmed Athens, Thebes and Sparta. When he surveyed the state of the American union, he had the disquieting feeling that the stage was being set for another tragedy such as the Peloponnesian War: in his mind's eye, he saw Massachusetts and Virginia, each surrounded by its satellites, playing the part of Athens and Sparta in the downfall of the American commonwealth.[3]

Because of the strong attachment of the people to the Articles of Confederation, Hamilton was confronted with the question: Was it possible to hold the union together under the Articles until a more effective government could be brought into being? He was prepared to believe that they could be made to serve this purpose—provided that they were subjected to the same kind of broad interpretation that he later gave the Federal Constitution of the United States.

In all his plans for a national bank, Hamilton had assumed, despite the silence of the Articles of Confederation on this point, that Congress was competent to charter a bank. He argued that since a bank was indispensable to the management of the country's finances and since the constitution did not expressly forbid the incorporation of such an institution, the Continental Congress possessed the implied power—as valid as any express grant of power—to establish a national bank.

Although he disagreed with Hamilton about the power of Congress to charter a bank, in other respects James Madison subscribed to the doctrine of implied powers. Among these powers he included the right of the general government to coerce recalcitrant states. Despite the fact that the Articles made no mention of this right, Madison held it to be plenary and ineluctable, but, to settle all doubts on this score, he urged that the states be asked to authorize Congress "to employ the forces of the United States as well by sea as by land" to force delinquent and obdurate states to comply with its directives. Among other things, Congress was to be expressly authorized to seize the vessels and merchandise of the citizens of the offending states and to prohibit their trade and intercourse with other states and with foreign countries.

Toward this proposal, Hamilton displayed a notable lack of enthusiasm. Not that he questioned the right of Congress to coerce refractory states; he agreed with Madison that it was an essential attribute of sovereignty and that the Continental Congress possessed it as indubitably as though it had been written into the Articles of Confederation. Nevertheless, he saw no advantage to be gained from pressing Congress' claim to a power which seemed more likely to produce civil war than revenue.

Who would tremble, asked Hamilton, if Congress donned the grim visage of war? Certainly not the larger states: they would be able to put into the field an army that would gobble up the handful of men that wore the Continental uniform. Nor could Congress depend upon the aid of other states: "Considering the genius of this country," he remarked, ". . . they [the states] would always be more ready to pursue the milder course of putting themselves upon an equal footing with the delinquent members by an imitation of their example. And the guilt of all would become the security of all." And under what circumstances, he inquired, would Congress feel justified in resorting to force? If the refusal of a state to obey Congress' requisitions were deemed sufficient to warrant armed intervention, then Congress could be sure of being at war with the states, singly or collectively, most of the time. He later pronounced the idea of coercing the states to be "one of the maddest projects that was ever conceived"—for it meant government by the sword, of all forms of government most abhorrent to the people of the United States.[4]

If implied powers and the use of force were denied the general government, the Articles of Confederation offered little hope of keeping the union intact. And, indeed, impotent as the government was, it was steadily growing weaker. "What is become of the Federal Government?" Hamilton was asked by a friend in England; and some discouraged patriots feared that the time might come when it would be necessary to send out a search warrant for this poor derelict government, without a permanent place of residence and so straitened in its finances that it could not even afford a small library for the use of its members. The balance of power was on the side of the states, and the encroachments of these sovereignties upon the authority of the Continental Congress seemed destined to make the American Revolution a triumph of provincialism rather than of nationalism. When Americans of this generation spoke of their "country," they frequently meant their state. They were Virginians, Carolinians and New Englanders first: they seldom permitted their allegiance to stray very far from home.

Even the national debt, which Hamilton considered to be one of the strongest sinews of the union, was proving itself to be a disruptive force within the confederacy. Rather than see the states swallowed up in the "congressional vortex," some Americans urged that the national debt be divided among the states, each free to pay its share in its own way without interference from outside authority. Then, it was predicted, the people would willingly pay taxes and the country would be happily delivered of an insupportable debt, without the necessity of giving revenue to a government that might make itself a menace to liberty.

The threat of state assumption of the national debt struck almost as much alarm in Hamilton as if the United States had suffered a serious reverse in the field. Had the national debt been a precious acquisition, he could hardly have guarded it more jealously from the states; and he protested against every effort to alienate it, as though Congress was being attacked in a vital point of sovereignty. In his plans, the public creditors figured as the chief prop of the general government—if that pillar were kicked away, he feared, every man would cast his lot with his state, the Continental Congress would cease to maintain the fiction that Americans were a united people, all revenue would be cut off from the general government, and the name "American" would refer to a continent, not to a people.

At the same time that the states usurped the national debt—and with it the powers and prestige of the Continental Congress—they denied the general government the revenue that might have enabled it to put the nation's finances in order. The requisition system was a reed upon which the statesmen in Philadelphia leaned at their peril, for, as Robert Morris' experience proved, the states were impervious to appeals to patriotism when it came to paying for the support of the general government. The words "recommendation" and "requisition" in the mouth of the Continental Congress were to the states empty sounds signifying nothing.[5]

The predicament of the Continental Congress, bedeviled as it was by an unworkable system and the obstructionism of the states, strongly prejudiced Hamilton against a federal system of government. In every case, he believed, it produced an irrepressible conflict between the head and the members.[6] The local jurisdictions seemed to be driven by their inveterate jealousy of the central government to usurp its prerogatives until it had become a thing of shreds and patches, naked to its enemies. Or, not content with slowly stripping the central government of its powers, the largest and most populous states united and thereby put it to a violent and speedy end. Always, however, the result was the same: the states triumphant, the national government prostrate. "This," said Hamilton, ". . . is the real rock upon which the happiness of this country is likely to split."[7]

If, as Hamilton supposed, the states were actuated by ambition, pride, and lust of power and dominion, it could easily be foreseen that the United States might become another Europe in which peace hung precariously upon the maintenance of a balance of power. But what, it might be asked, would Americans fight about: could they not live in peace and amity if they chose to set up separate confederacies? Hamilton's answer was that there was enough potential cause of conflict to keep Americans embroiled for generations: the public debt, western lands, economic rivalries, and the influence of leaders who were ready to "sacrifice the national tranquillity to personal gratification." Men were by nature so "ambitious, vindictive and rapacious" and actuated by "the love of power or the desire of preeminence and dominion" that Hamilton believed that if no cause of war existed they would invent one. Human nature itself, in brief, provided "abundant sources of contention and hostility."[8]

As early as 1781, Hamilton had come to the conclusion that "the present futile and senseless Confederation" ought to be scrapped forthwith. In its place he proposed to establish a national government endowed with complete sovereignty "in all but the mere municipal laws of each State." Such a government would have been vastly more powerful than the federal structure created by the Constitution of 1787. The "solid union" envisaged by Hamilton in 1781 would have shifted the center of gravity so radically in favor of the central government that the states would have survived as little more than administrative districts. Toward this ideal Hamilton never ceased to labor, even after the adoption of the Federal Constitution.[9]

It was not merely because Hamilton was born in the West Indies that he lacked the strong feeling of state loyalty that distinguished most Americans of his generation. During the War of Independence, the army was the school of nationalism: the men who went hungry, ragged and unpaid for years on end were not apt to share civilians' fears of strong government or to decry the authority of the Continental Congress. No better corrective to the state-rights philosophy existed than a tour of duty in the United States Army. The freemasonry of common suffering and common devotion to an ideal erased the insularity of American fighting men. Many of the later advocates of a more perfect union were weaned of provincial attachments at Valley Forge and Morristown. Two of the favorite toasts in the army were "A hoop to the barrel" and "Cement to the union." The men who fought for the independence of the United States hoped by their sacrifices to make it a powerful nation, not a "Monster with Thirteen Heads."[10]

Feeling no state attachments himself, Hamilton could not comprehend why his fellow countrymen permitted these sovereignties to have first place in their affections. Among the Americans of his day, outside the army, Hamilton felt himself to be almost an alien—because he was so much more truly American than they.

In his insistence that Americans become wholehearted nationalists, Hamilton was asking too much of his fellow citizens. Their economic interests were too diverse, their experience of living apart upon a vast continent of too long standing, and their ways of life too variegated to permit them to slough off immediately their provincialism and assume a continental outlook. The United States had declared its independence less than a decade before—hardly a sufficient time to engender the kind of nationalism Hamil-

"A Rage for Liberty"

ton wished to see. As Gouverneur Morris said in 1784: "A national spirit is the result of national existence, and although some of the present generation may feel colonial oppositions of opinion, yet this generation will die away and give place to a race of Americans."[11]

To this counsel Hamilton replied that unless the present generation acted with vigor and decision in the work of building a nation, there might be no nation for the next generation to cling to. Far from believing that time was on the side of nationalism in the United States, he thought that it was on the side of the states. While the central government withered away, he saw the states growing more powerful and more impatient of restraint. The danger, as he saw it, was that the "race of Americans" would become extinct. In the struggle between the states and the national government, he believed that the people would support the states—in their eyes, the guardians of their rights and liberties against a central government which, by its very nature, would always seem alien and removed.

The people of the United States, as Hamilton visualized them, were a provincial-minded lot, incapable of seeing beyond the boundaries of their states and incurably devoted to village-pump politics. To wait for national feeling to develop among such as these struck him as the counsel of despair: long before the people saw the light, the confederacy would have fallen apart. And so, little of the love that Hamilton lavished upon his country was expended upon his countrymen. To the end, it remained a mystery to him how a people could be so indifferent to their opportunities of attaining national power and greatness. Americans asked whether it was better to be "good than great—better to be free than powerful." When Hamilton told them that they could be both free and powerful, they were openly incredulous.

That there was greater danger of dismemberment in attempting to bind the Union than in preserving a looser, more flexible form of government which allowed for the existence of separate and divergent sectional interests —this Hamilton never acknowledged. His idea was a nation, one and indivisible, in which the people were not citizens of the various states but were "Americans" who knew no allegiance save to America. He did not wish to see a United *States* of America; his affection encompassed the nation and found room for only one supreme loyalty.

8.
Democracy and Banking

Americans ushered in their independence with a depression. As a result of British restrictions upon the trade and shipping of the United States, a postwar buying spree in which Americans went heavily in debt to British merchants, and the deflation which followed the inflation of the war years, the new republic was obliged at the outset of its existence to contend with economic difficulties that would have taxed the resources of a far stronger government than that which had been created by the Articles of Confederation.

For those who had gone in debt while money was cheap and the country was prosperous, the deflation was a chastening experience. They found themselves obliged to pay their debts and taxes at a time when money was almost unobtainable, paper money being completely discredited and specie having taken wing to Great Britain. As a result, thousands of once-prosperous Americans farmers were faced with ruin at the hands of their creditors or the tax collectors. At the same time it began to appear that the merchants, speculators and profiteers who had taken advantage of the opportunities afforded by the war for money-making were the material heirs of the Revolution: a new ruling class had stepped into the shoes of the expropriated Loyalist aristocracy. Americans no longer located the seat of tyranny three thousand miles away: it had moved its residence, they declared, to the countinghouses, banks and great landed estates of the wealthy. From these new "headquarters of oppression," they believed, emanated the taxes which bore more heavily upon the poor than upon the rich, the laws which put debtors at the mercy of their creditors, and the favoritism of the courts of justice to privileged members of the community.

Instead of accepting this state of affairs as the inexorable consequence of the workings of economic laws, the victims of the depression demanded that something be done to meliorate its effects. Accordingly, when debtors gained control of a state they enacted laws designed to restore prosperity. These measures took the form of stay laws (which imposed a moratorium upon the collection of debts); tender acts (which permitted debtors to pay their debts in commodities rather than in money); and paper money (which enabled them to pay their debts, sometimes at a fraction of the original sum).

The small but—from Hamilton's point of view—troublesome State of Rhode Island again demonstrated its claim to the title of "erring sister" of the confederacy by the abandon with which it prostituted itself to paper money, stay laws, tender acts and the whole paraphernalia of debtors' legislation. Rhode Island was perhaps harder hit by the depression than any other state and, in consequence, a large part of the business community tended to favor easy money. The state became a debtors' paradise in which creditors were compelled to accept depreciated paper money at its face value. Thus was worked the miracle by which delinquent debtors pursued their creditors; but for the final miracle by which prosperity would be restored, Rhode Islanders waited in vain.[1]

These were the times that tried the souls of the good, the wise and the rich. They had not intended to exchange the rule of King and Parliament for a "popular despotism" that undertook to "rob the industrious of the fruits of their labor and . . . enable the idle and rapacious to live in ease and comfort at the expense of the better part of the community." It was now conservatives' turn to cry out that government was becoming too powerful, that it was being perverted to the purposes of faction and class and that liberty was in danger. As a defense against the confiscatory propensities of the state governments, they invoked the bills of rights in the state constitutions which expressly prohibited the governments from encroaching upon civil and property rights. But majorities could not be restrained by paper guarantees of liberty; in effect, their will became the Constitution.[2]

In the light of this development, Hamilton concluded that although the laws of God and Nature had decreed that property should be sacred, the message had not gotten through to American democrats.* These men did not hesitate to deprive their fellow citizens—particularly those who belonged to an unpopular minority—of their "indefeasible" and "inalienable" rights quite as though God and Nature had no say in the matter.[3] Nor was it of any avail to appeal from popular majorities to the laws of nature; apparently, for democrats, nothing was sacred. They acted upon the theory that they could do as they pleased and that what they pleased to do was always right.[4]

It was now clear to Hamilton that the philosophers and statesmen of the Revolution, preoccupied as they were in asserting the rights of man, had given insufficient attention to safeguarding the rights of property. They had assumed that the two were virtually identical; it had not entered their minds that Americans, engaged in a struggle to defend property, would

* In *Oceana*, James Harrington had defined democracy as "being nothing but intire Liberty." Hamilton seems to have accepted this definition.

assail it under the guise of protecting liberty. And so they had failed to endow property with the means of keeping off democratic majorities; the few "No Trespassing" signs they had erected had been quickly trampled underfoot.[5]

As Hamilton himself acknowledged, his station and prospects in life had something to do with his attitude toward debtors' legislation. Had he been a debt-ridden, struggling farmer or a down-at-heels officer of the Continental Army, he might have taken a different view of the dangers to be apprehended from the rule of the majority. Even so, he did not oppose all reform: he approved of the abolition of primogeniture and entail because, as he said, an equal division among the children of their parents' property "will soon melt down those great estates, which, if they continued, might favor the power of the few." Nor did he make property a graven image before which all must blindly worship; he never asserted that Mammon could do no wrong. All property rights which were "contrary to the social order and to the permanent welfare of society," ought, he said, to be abolished. "Whenever, indeed, a right of property is infringed for the general good," he continued, "if the nature of case admits of compensation, it ought to be made; but if compensation be impracticable, that impracticability ought not to be an obstacle to a clearly essential reform." He advocated one of the most daring invasions of property rights that was ever made—the abolition of Negro slavery.*

Contrary to the impression Hamilton sometimes conveyed, this was not a struggle between a few enormously rich individuals and a mass of dispossessed and rebellious peasants. Rather, it was a quarrel within the house of capitalism: there were property owners on both sides and the "democrats" had almost as great a material stake in the country as did the "aristocrats." One party was composed of those who had inherited wealth or profited from the Revolution by speculation, privateering, monopolizing, army contracting or business acumen, while the other party was made up of small farmers, ex-soldiers, tax delinquents, purchasers of Loyalist property who wished to pay off their debts to the state government with cheap paper money, and many perfectly honest citizens (including many merchants and planters) who were being pinched by the acute scarcity of a circulating medium. Excluding the slaves, the population of the United States did not consist of a few rich and many poor: it was a middle-class society in which radicalism drew its strength principally from an economic depression which threatened to impoverish many middle-class citizens.

It was small comfort to Hamilton to be told that he was not dealing with

* Although Hamilton was a member of the New York Manumission Society, he held slaves throughout his life. As chairman of the Society he proposed that the members enfranchise their slaves, but his proposal was rejected. Nathan Schachner, *Alexander Hamilton* (New York, 1946), p. 183.

Democracy and Banking

a propertyless proletariat: these debtor-farmers might be respectable middle-class citizens, but in his eyes they were not much better than a mob bent upon razing the foundations of society. And if radicalism flourished among propertied farmers, what, he asked himself, was in store for the United States when the population would be largely composed of a multitude of laboring poor?

In upholding the rights of property, Hamilton was not merely defending the cozy world of silk stockings, powdered wigs and coats of arms against the assaults of hornyhanded egalitarians. Nor was he in his own eyes playing the part of a counterrevolutionary thwarting the legitimate aspirations of the American people. As he saw it, he had remained true to the principles of the Revolution, whereas the advocates of paper money, stay laws and tender acts had betrayed the cause. John Locke had taught that private property antedated the state and that the primary purpose for which government was instituted was to protect property in the hands of those who possessed it. Hamilton sought to call Americans back to this fundamental principle of the revolutionary creed. For he recognized no real distinction between liberty and property: in his philosophy, it was syllogistic that if property were not secure, men were not free. Under a government that could invade property rights at will, none of the other rights of man had any real worth because they, too, existed at the sufferance of arbitrary power. "If everything floats on the variable and vague opinions of the governing party," he said, "there can be no such thing as rights, property or liberty." Viewed from this perspective, property rights appeared to be the first line of defense of civil rights; the rights of man stood or fell together; if one right were permitted to go down, the others could not long endure.[6]

It was the propensity of democracy to invade property and other rights that led Hamilton to condemn it as hostile to true liberty. Brief as had been its course in the United States, he already saw the marks of the beast: no form of government seemed less friendly to dissent, more insistent upon conformity and more inclined to override minority rights. Hamilton knew of no more oppressive tyranny than that which emanated from "a victorious and overbearing majority." True, he might have changed his mind had he visited Turkey and Russia, but Hamilton was speaking from his own experience and from his reading of history. Nevertheless, it was true, as he pointed out, that while even an absolute monarch might be restrained by fear of public opinion, a popular majority, because it was a majority, felt no curbs upon its power.

If Americans had any doubt what was in store for them, Hamilton advised them to look at the history of Greece. Here they would find, he said, that all the "pure" democracies degenerated into "mobocracies." "Their very character was tyranny," he remarked of these governments. ". . . When they assembled, the field of debate presented an ungovernable mob, not only incapable of deliberation, but prepared for every enormity." Here was democracy in its most turbulent, oppressive and repellent form: "the giddy and fluctuating populace" ostracized leaders to whom a short time before they had raised statues; demagogues whipped the poor into a frenzy against the rich; and the laws were prostituted to the selfish purposes of a single class. Following Aristotle's cyclical theory of history—that governments move from democracy to anarchy to tyranny—Hamilton gave democracy but a brief life expectancy. Tyranny was democracy at the end of its journey; although the passage was rough and full of perils, it could at least be said that it did not last long—the tyrant quickly put democracy out of its misery and the people acclaimed him as their hero and savior.

Thus it was made to appear that tyranny sprang from the excessive love of the people for liberty: they killed the thing they loved because they were not content to possess it in moderation. Confusing licentiousness with liberty, they ran to such extremes that everything fell into chaos until, in order to escape from a situation more intolerable than that of the state of nature, they gladly submitted to a master. The cry of the Athenian populace that "they must not be hindered from doing what they pleased" seemed to Hamilton to sound the knell of freedom; anarchy could not be far away and the shadow of the despot already lay darkly upon the land.

Observing democracy in action and studying it in history, Hamilton came to the conclusion that it was government by the worst passions of the worst men. He discerned in the mass of the people, particularly during periods of crisis, a fatal propensity toward electing unworthy men to public office. In particular, they seemed wholly unable to resist the blandishments of demagogues: when a plausible, backslapping politician came along, the people fawned upon him and rushed to do his bidding. In a democracy, he found, nothing succeeded like demagoguery: a sovereign people, uncontrolled by law and swollen with a sense of power, was always "liable to be duped by flattery, & to be seduced by artful and designing men."

A demagogue, in Hamilton's opinion, was the lowest form of political life: a parasitic animal that lived by "working on the passions and prejudices of the less discerning classes of citizens," inflaming their jealousies and hatreds and beguiling them with hopes of Utopia. These were the men, he exclaimed, who brought the beast from its lair by inveighing against the rich and promising an equal division of property and the abolition of debts. And so the fools and the knaves, the weak and the wicked, the dupes and the charlatans—the whole crazy mob rushed down the road that ended in dishonor and beggary, kicking their creditors and tearing up contracts as they went.

The career of Governor George Clinton provided Hamilton with the case history of a demagogue, the methods by which he attained power and the uses to which he put his authority. The pity of it all, said Hamilton, was that

Clinton had begun well: in his early days he was an honest man and a patriot but, having tasted popularity and power, he degenerated into a vote-getter whose only concern, said Hamilton, was "what will *please*, not what will *benefit* the people"; "instead of taking a lead in measures that counteract a prevailing prejudice, however he may be convinced of their utility, he either flatters it, or temporizes. . . . Here," he exclaimed, "we find the general disease which infects all our constitutions—an excess of popularity."

The spirit against which he protested did not merely take the form of an attack upon the rights of the individual; it was likewise directed against the authority of the national government. A democrat seemed to be known by his loyalty to his state as well as by his hatred of his betters and to be no less intent upon depriving the general government of its rightful powers than upon despoiling the rich of their property. Hamilton could hardly fail to remark that Rhode Island, the state whose legislature was "the picture of a mob," and where "the art of cheating Creditors" was carried to the highest pitch of perfection, was also the state that had singlehandedly upset the impost in 1782 and had consistently distinguished itself by brazenly defying the Continental Congress.

For this reason, Hamilton's ambition of seeing the United States take its place among the great powers would in itself have alienated him from democracy—a form of government which seemed to condemn the country to insignificance, weakness and contempt. Increasingly, he tended to identify conservatism with nationalism. As he saw it, "the men who think continentally" were the business and professional men of the United States. On the other hand, the common people seemed to be imbued with a bitter and narrow provincialism: their political horizon did not extend far beyond the village pump.

Hamilton's conservatism in questions affecting property was largely a means to an end: in order to create a more perfect union, he saw that it was first necessary to make property rights sacrosanct. For it was upon private property that Hamilton proposed to build the edifice of union. Any weakening of the institution of private property promised to destroy Hamilton's plan of creating a strong, prosperous and closely integrated nation. It followed that if the rich were to be made pillars of the national government, their wealth could not be left at the mercy of delinquent debtors in the states.[7]

Nor, without security of property, did he believe that there could be any opportunity for the free play of individual initiative, industry or the accumulation of capital. The foundation of all order and prosperity seemed to him to rest upon the principle that every man ought to be left in the peaceful enjoyment of what he acquired by his fortune and industry. Like Blackstone, Hamilton thought that nothing "so generally strikes the imagination and engages the affections of mankind, as the right of property," and that it tended "more powerfully than any other cause to augment the national wealth." His vision was that of a nation in which property was beyond the reach of envy, contracts were sacred, the financial obligations of the government were strictly honored and the people were immune to the wiles of demagogues.[8]

The result of this conflict between debtors and creditors was to administer a serious setback to Hamilton's hopes of uniting the country by means of a stable monetary and economic system. But even in these "atrocious breaches of moral obligation and social justice," Hamilton found a grain of comfort. In comparison with the state governments, the Continental Congress appeared virtuous and chaste: it had not been debauched by demagogues and led into the ways of financial sin. Accordingly, conservatives tended more and more to cling to this pillar of rectitude against the "anarchy, ignorance and knavery" rampant in the states. This was as Hamilton wished: against the radicalism of the states he always sought to set the conservatism of the national government.

Hamilton never advocated letting the depression run its course unimpeded by the countervailing measures of the government. A firm believer in "energetic government," he favored a program of action more vigorous and far-reaching than any adopted by the states. But his plan differed markedly from theirs: instead of leaving the separate states to attack the depression singlehanded, Hamilton wished to meet it with the full force of a rejuvenated national government. With a strong central government empowered to act for the national welfare, Hamilton believed that the foundations of an enduring prosperity could be laid in the United States. A more perfect union, he held, was a prerequisite to a more perfect economy. Throughout this period, he acted upon the theory that the depression could be successfully combated only with a funding system, a stable circulating medium of bank notes and a national government capable of controlling the national economy. What the country needed, he thought, was not more lenient bankruptcy laws or longer debtors' holidays (although he did vote in 1787 in the New York legislature in favor of bills postponing execution on debts owed British merchants and virtually abolishing imprisonment for debt), but the assurance that property rights would be respected, that the national debt would be paid and that the states would not be permitted to make themselves masters of the household. Then foreign capital would be attracted to the country and the energies of the people would be stimulated and guided by the government into the most productive and beneficial channels.

As a means of strengthening the position of the class that embodied the forces of nationalism in the United States, Hamilton knew that there was nothing quite as effective as a bank. Through its agency, the wealth of many individuals was made available to entrepreneurs and a stable circulating

Democracy and Banking

medium was provided the business community. It had long been Hamilton's ambition to found a bank, but the honor of establishing the first American bank had fallen to Robert Morris. The high dividend rate paid by the Bank of North America whetted the appetite of American capitalists for the seemingly easy profits of banking. For the duration of the War of Independence, the Bank of North America enjoyed a monopoly of banking in the United States, but with the advent of peace the way was cleared for the incorporation of other banks.

As a result, it was toward a state bank rather than a national bank that Hamilton's thoughts now turned. Although the idea of founding a state bank had certainly occurred to him before 1784, a succession of events early in that year impelled him to act sooner, perhaps, than he had intended.

By virtue of his marriage, Hamilton was trebly blessed: not only did he possess an amiable wife and a rich father-in-law but he had a brother-in-law who was on the way to becoming one of the wealthiest men in the United States and who was not averse to cutting in Hamilton on some highly profitable deals. John Barker Church was an Englishman who, having come to the United States during the war, married a daughter of General Schuyler and made a large amount of money supplying the American and French armies. Having increased his fortune handsomely by canny speculations in Great Britain, Church decided to invest part of his wealth in the United States. His idea was to buy British goods, sell them for cash in the United States and use the proceeds to establish a bank in New York City. Associated with him in this enterprise was Jeremiah Wadsworth, a Connecticut capitalist who had been Church's partner in purveying to the American and French armies. The son of a Hartford minister, Wadsworth represented the new type of businessman who owed his wealth chiefly to speculation and finance rather than to shipping and trade. Like Church, he was on intimate terms with some of the leading capitalists of Great Britain and the continent. With these kindred spirits he speculated in the national debt, engaged in banking and helped establish new industries in the United States.[9]

Church intended to establish a bank in New York and he instructed Hamilton accordingly; but soon thereafter he learned that a bank was being organized in Philadelphia to rival the Bank of North America. This institution—bearing the name of the Bank of Pennsylvania—seemed to Church to offer better investment possibilities than the bank he contemplated in New York. He and Wadsworth therefore instructed Hamilton to buy a controlling interest in the projected bank, enjoining him to observe the strictest secrecy lest the price of stock be run up beyond its real value. For the times, this was high finance indeed, and Hamilton congratulated himself upon being associated with financiers as venturesome as himself.

When Hamilton learned that a new bank was being established in Philadelphia, his first impulse was to give it his blessing. As he knew, the Bank of North America was insufficiently capitalized for the needs of Philadelphia businessmen: those who were not so fortunate as to own stock in that institution met with considerable difficulty in procuring loans. He accepted Adam Smith's dictum that if banking capital were divided between several institutions, there would be less danger of catastrophic loss in case one bank went under. Moreover, he believed that competition among banks was salutary: it tended to reduce the interest rate and thereby stimulate trade and investment.*

He had no opportunity, however, to carry out Church's orders that he buy a large block of stock in the Bank of Pennsylvania. Finding that it could not destroy the proposed bank, the Bank of North America absorbed its rival and thereby preserved its monopoly. The capital of the Bank of North America was augmented and the projectors of the Bank of Pennsylvania were permitted to become stockholders in the enlarged institution.

While the Bank of North America was engaged in preserving its monopoly in Philadelphia, Hamilton was drawing up plans for the Bank of New York. Before they were out of the blueprint stage, however, a rival institution entered upon the scene. Chancellor Robert R. Livingston, one of the largest landowners and most important political leaders of the state, threw the weight of his influence behind a plan to create a land bank; and, before Hamilton could effectively organize his forces, the Chancellor had all but persuaded the New York Assembly to give an exclusive charter to his bank.

This bank was conceived primarily in the interests of the large landowners, the purchasers of confiscated Loyalist property and the more conservative businessmen of New York City. One third of the bank's capital was to be composed of specie and two thirds of land, and one of the chief functions of the bank was to loan money to landowners on mortgage. New York being largely an agrarian society, the Chancellor pointed out, it was proper that land should serve as the capital of a bank; in such an institution, farmers as well as merchants could be accommodated to their mutual advantage, whereas from a purely specie bank farmers could derive little or no advantage.

In 1781 Hamilton himself had proposed to utilize land as part of the capital of a national bank, but he now pronounced Livingston's plan to be "wild and impracticable" and destructive of all sound principles of banking. No doubt, this change in Hamilton's views was owing to the unexampled success of the Bank of North America, a specie bank, and to his association with the merchants and professional men of New York City. Their experience during the Revolutionary War with depreciating paper money had

* Hamilton soon changed his mind about the desirability of another bank in Philadelphia. He decided that there was not enough capital available to warrant more than one bank.

Democracy and Banking

made them distrustful of currency unsupported by gold and silver. Land banks had functioned successfully during the colonial period but they, too, had suffered in the estimation of many businessmen as a result of the irresponsible issuance of paper money by the states.

It was typical of the state of enlightenment among the advocates of the land bank, Hamilton sarcastically observed, that they should acclaim this institution as "the true philosopher's stone that was to turn all their rocks and trees into gold." Nevertheless, he was prepared to permit the landowners to share in some measure in the benefits of banking. According to his plan, one fifth of the capital of the specie bank would be set aside for loans on landed security to the counties of the state, the quota of each county to be determined by the state legislature. But he was careful to specify that no part of the capital of the proposed bank should be in land and that all payments should be made in gold, silver or bank notes.

The unexpected popularity of the land bank compelled Hamilton to drop his own project and join forces with a group of New York businessmen whose plans were further advanced than his own. Strengthened by this alliance, Hamilton conducted an effective campaign against the land bank among the "most intelligent merchants, who," he said, "presently saw the matter in a proper light and began to take measures to defeat the plan." His new allies insisted upon a specie bank pure and simple with no frills added for the benefit of farmers. Hamilton yielded with such good grace to their demands that the merchants commissioned him to write the charter of the Bank of New York and to become a member of the board.

In one important respect, however, Hamilton had his way. The original plan of the bank imposed a limit upon the number of votes allowed a shareholder regardless of the number of shares he held. Knowing that this would not meet with Church's and Wadsworth's wishes—they aspired to control the bank—Hamilton inserted a clause allotting one vote for every five shares above ten. Hamilton did not benefit personally from this ruling—he held only one share of stock.

The Bank of New York, like all the banks in which Hamilton was concerned, was a public bank. Though the management of the bank was private, its functions were intended to benefit the public quite as much as the individuals with whom it dealt. Its facilities were placed at the disposal of the state: it received deposits of state funds and it loaned, or was expected to loan, money to the state. Finally, the state was invited to become a stockholder and to exercise the supervision to which it was thereby entitled.

The Bank of New York issued bank notes which served the business community as a circulating medium. In Hamilton's financial thinking, this was one of the primary purposes of a bank: "for the simple and most precise idea of a bank is a deposit of coin or other property as a funding for circulating a credit upon it which is to answer the purpose of money." But

Hamilton insisted upon restraining the expansion of bank liabilities; in the charter of the Bank of New York he established a multiple ratio between liabilities and capital, thereby injecting into American banking the principle of fractional reserves.

The men responsible for the establishment of the Bank of New York were almost wholly merchants. The first American bankers were businessmen who sought to advance their own interests by pooling their capital to provide the credit they required. Consequently, the loans made by the Bank of New York were to merchants, usually for short terms. Commerce prospered under this system, but farmers, who generally required long-term loans, were able to make little use of the facilities of the Bank of New York. In consequence, they were obliged to pay usurious interest rates to private lenders. It was not until 1792, when an act of the New York legislature created a State Land Office where the state's surplus funds were loaned on landed security, that a small beginning was made toward solving one of the most pressing of the farmers' problems—the need for credit facilities comparable to those enjoyed by businessmen.

Although Hamilton and his friends were able to prevent the establishment of a land bank in 1784, they were not strong enough to secure immediately a charter for the Bank of New York. Not until 1792 did the state legislature finally yield to the pressure of the bank for incorporation. During this interval, the bank carried on its business—including the payment of dividends —without benefit of a charter, tolerated but not officially sanctioned by the government.[10]

In this institution, Hamilton again found himself hobnobbing with Loyalists. While the patriotism of the president of the bank was impeccable— Alexander McDougall had attained the rank of general in the United States Army—and the board of directors included patriots of the caliber of Isaac Roosevelt, Nicholas Low, John Vanderbilt and Hamilton himself, there were at least four members of the board who had remained in New York City during the British occupation and who were therefore under suspicion of Loyalism. This suspicion was particularly strong in the case of William Seton, the newly appointed cashier of the bank, who in 1784 was sent to Philadelphia—the School for Bankers in the United States—to acquaint himself with the methods and procedures of the Bank of North America. A Scotsman, Seton had remained in New York City during the British occupation but, more fortunate than many of his fellow Loyalists, he had preserved his property from confiscation.

It was the patriots' boast that most of the Loyalists had been driven to Hell, Hull and Halifax. But Hamilton's only regret was that more of them had not remained in the United States. They made such excellent allies against democrats!

9.
"More Power to Congress"

Among the causes of dissension and potential civil war in the United States, Hamilton had always given primacy to the rivalries among the states for land. If the West offered hope of a stronger union and financial relief for the general government through the sale of land, he perceived that it also contained the seeds of embroilments between the states—seeds that in 1786 produced in the Wyoming region of Pennsylvania a localized war between the rival claimants from Pennsylvania and Connecticut. New York was likewise engaged at this time in a dispute with Vermont that posed a serious threat to the peace of the confederacy. The Vermonters demanded independence from New York and, like other Americans of their generation, they were prepared to fight for their freedom when it was denied them. Since New York, no more than Great Britain, would not permit its lawful "subjects" to go in peace, a border war broke out in the North.

From a defense of their homes and lands, the Green Mountain Boys, under the command of Ethan Allen, went over to the offensive and began to encroach upon the territory of New York. This alarming development led New York to appeal to the Continental Congress to take the obstreperous Vermonters in hand. But this, Hamilton learned when he took his seat in Congress in 1782, was "a business in which nobody cares to act with decision" and which everyone was eager to foist upon someone else. It was soon made plain that the Yorkers and Yankees could not depend upon the Continental Congress to settle their quarrel.

From the beginning, Hamilton deprecated any attempt to coerce the Vermonters. As Burgoyne had learned to his sorrow, Vermont was not a healthy region for an invading army; and Hamilton was inclined to profit by the example of the British general. Nor did he overlook the fact that the independence of Vermont was warmly supported by the New England states and that an army sent against the mountaineers would have to reckon with the "whole tribe of Yankees." Even though New York's victory were certain, Hamilton would have opposed war, for, in that event, he pointed out, his state would be obliged to hold down some of the most cantankerous citizens in the union—a task which only New York's enemies would wish upon it. His final and decisive argument against war was the attitude of public opinion: "the scheme of coercion would ill suit even the disposition of our own citizens," he remarked. "The habits of thinking to which the Revolution has given birth, are not adapted to the idea of a contest for dominion over a people disinclined to live under our government."

Some of Hamilton's closest friends had bought heavily in Vermont lands and stood to lose their investment if the Vermonters triumphed. James Duane and Richard Harison, for example, owned considerable real estate in the Grants and, in consequence, they were ardent supporters of the policy of rooting out the "nest of Vipers" that was playing havoc with land values in the area. Gouverneur Morris likewise wished to see Vermont reduced by conquest—"success will sanctify every operation," he declared. "Forty victims to public *justice* or *wrath,* and submission from the rest of the people, will convince everybody."

Among these advocates of a forcible solution to the dispute was Governor Clinton of New York, who, despite his professions of good will to the common man, was prepared to take the side of speculators where his own interests were concerned. And in this particular matter, his interests were vitally affected: he was one of the largest land claimants. Rather than yield New York's rights to the region, Clinton was prepared to recall the state's delegation from the Continental Congress and to use New York troops serving in the Continental Army against the Vermonters.

Against these warlike counsels, Hamilton urged the New York legislature to make a compromise with the Vermonters. But the legislators were resolved to have all or nothing, and the Green Mountain Boys, for their part, swore that rather than see their state divided like Poland between neighboring states, they would fight to the last man.

In March, 1787, convinced that Vermont was lost to New York beyond the possibility of recovery and that by obstructing the admission of that state into the confederacy New Yorkers were encouraging civil war and British intrigue, Hamilton introduced a bill into the New York legislature calling for the recognition of the independence of Vermont. The New York land claimants strenuously resisted this proposal and were given permission to present their case at the bar of the New York Assemby through their chief counsel, Richard Harison. In his speech, Harison took the position that New York was obliged to employ all the means in its power to recover and protect the rights and property of its citizens and that the New York legislature was constitutionally debarred from dismembering the state. The sacred rights of property and the no less sacred duty of government to act in self-preservation thus became the principle issues in the controversy.

This was delicate ground for Hamilton to tread: everything he had said concerning the rights of property in general and Loyalist property in particular seemed to place him on Harison's side. And yet, generally speaking, Hamilton was not a doctrinaire; he appreciated the necessity of allowing for changes in circumstances; and in this instance he believed that principle must yield to expediency. As for the obligation of the state to preserve its territory from violation, Hamilton observed that in this instance the state had already been dismembered by force. "It was in fact a revolution," he declared, "it was not the Duty of the State, nor was she bound by the fundamental principles of the social compact to engage in a cause which must prove disastrous & fruitless." In short, the state was under no compulsion to destroy itself in order to uphold a hopeless cause.

Convinced perhaps less by Hamilton's arguments than by the course of events in Vermont, the speculators themselves were by this time beginning to realize that they were unlikely to make good their claims against the opposition of trigger-happy Green Mountain Boys. Accordingly, they offered to surrender their titles provided that they were compensated for their losses by the State of New York. But those members of the legislature who had no claims to lands in the disputed area refused to reward speculators at the expense of the state. Here, again, Hamilton declined to uphold the narrow interpretation of the rights of property: the state, he held, was under no obligation to reimburse the claimants for losses suffered as a result of a revolution.

Throughout this controversy, Hamilton assumed that the revolution was an accomplished fact. The bill he introduced into the New York legislature in 1787 therefore purported merely to recognize an existing situation—that Vermont had won its independence. While this bill passed the House of Representatives, the governor and his fellow speculators managed to kill it in the Senate. Even though many of his friends joined the governor on this occasion, Hamilton set down the incident as another example of how "the pride of certain individuals has too long triumphed over the public interest."

In 1789, Hamilton worked out a settlement with the Vermont leaders whereby the New York claimants were to be compensated by a cash appropriation by Vermont of thirty thousand dollars. Despite the fact that the arrangement was opposed by Clinton, it was adopted by the New York legislature. Ultimately the claimants who had suffered property loss in consequence of this dispute were compensated by a grant by New York of an eighty-mile-square tract in western New York. Thereupon New York dropped its opposition and Vermont came into the union in 1790 as a state. Thus Hamilton's policy of conducting negotiations in an atmosphere of peace and compromise prevailed. It was a triumph of statesmanship that effectually refutes the accusation frequently leveled against him that he thought only of the rights of property and that he always advocated the use of force when those rights were invaded.[1]

Next to its inability to impose taxes, the most palpable deficiency in the powers of the Continental Congress was its lack of control over commerce. The general government undertook to make treaties of commerce with foreign nations on terms of "the most perfect equality and reciprocity," but it was notorious that it had no power to compel the states to observe such treaties. Congress could not establish a customhouse; it could not prevent the states from imposing tariff duties of their own; it could not lay an embargo; and it could not prohibit the importation of any article of foreign produce or manufacture.

In 1784, acutely aware of this defect in its powers, the Continental Congress formally asked the states to invest it with control over commerce. Because this measure entailed a change in the fundamental law, the rule of unanimity applied. Therefore, having made its request, Congress sat back anxiously to await the verdict of the thirteen.

While the states weighed the dangers to "liberty" inherent in this proposal, it became increasingly doubtful that if and when they agreed to grant Congress control over commerce there would be any American shipping left for Congress to regulate. The heavy losses sustained during the War of Independence had not been repaired; American ships were excluded from trade with the British West Indies, one of their principal prewar markets; and shipbuilding had received a severe setback by the refusal of the British government to permit American-built ships to be sold in Great Britain or the empire.

The argument in favor of making this grant of power to Congress that appealed to the largest number of Americans was that it would injure Great Britain. Resentful against the late mother country for its refusal to surrender the northwest posts, to make a treaty of commerce with the United States and to offer compensation for the slaves emancipated by the British army, many Americans were willing to give Congress control of commerce—provided that it was used to retaliate upon British shipping and manufactures.

No doubt, the easiest way of stimulating national feeling among Americans was to preach hatred of Great Britain. The people were strongly predisposed to believe that George III and his ministers were at the bottom of all the republic's troubles. King George had not outlived his usefulness as a scapegoat for American republicans: the memory of his "crimes" against liberty was still fresh and it could be safely assumed that the baffled despot meditated new enormities. Apparently Americans needed some pressing common danger to lift them out of the rut of provincialism—and what better bogey was there than His Britannic Majesty?

Hamilton was never prepared to purchase American nationalism at the price of exacerbating Anglo-American relations. For him, Great Britain did not assume the guise that it did to many of his countrymen—the eternal enemy that had been as yet only partly punished for its "crimes." Rather, the late mother country impressed him as a valiant nation which, despite its recent misfortunes, was making a notable comeback. He was already of the opinion that Americans could learn much by following Great Britain's example: its constitution, commercial wealth and empire entitled it to the respect and emulation of mankind.

As early as 1781, Hamilton had advocated giving Congress the power of regulating trade by imposing duties, granting bounties and laying embargoes. The effect of his plan would have been to authorize Congress to enact a navigation system comparable to those of European powers and to have put Congress in a position to direct the national economy. But the Continental Congress was much more modest in its requests: in 1784, it asked only for power to lay prohibitions upon the entry of ships and goods of countries that did not have commercial treaties with the United States.

Hamilton was under no illusion that this power—even assuming that the thirteen states agreed to grant it—would solve the problems confronting the United States. He had probed too deeply into the weaknesses of the Articles of Confederation to suppose that a single change would restore the body politic to health and vigor. Nevertheless, he supported the proposal as he did every other effort to strengthen the Articles of Confederation. Inadequate as the Articles seemed to Hamilton, he never forgot that they were the bond of union that held the states together. Until a more satisfactory form of government was in prospect, he was not willing to see them collapse.

In the meantime, impatient with the helplessness of Congress and obduracy of Great Britain, some states began to retaliate upon the former mother country by levying duties upon its shipping and manufactures. As a result, the people residing in states that had few ports and ships complained that as consumers they were being taxed—without benefit of representation—by the commercial states. In self-defense, they opened their ports to British ships and goods. Thus each state seemed bent upon creating a navigation system, complete with tariffs, bounties and other governmental regulations, of its own. The interests of the nation as a whole were almost wholly forgotten.[2]

Despite all that Hamilton could do, New York was one of the worst offenders in this exploitation of the citizens of the uncommercial states. Through New York City passed a large part of the British merchandise consumed in Connecticut and New Jersey. In their efforts to squeeze profits from their neighbors, New Yorkers went too far: the farmers of New Jersey and Connecticut attempted to throw off their "bondage" to the Yorkers by boycotting merchandise imported from that state; and New Jersey declared that it would not comply with the requisitions laid by Congress until New York had reduced its tariff.[3]

And so it went: each state pursuing its own local interest while the authority of the Continental Congress dwindled and the United States became a mosaic of different kinds and degrees of tariff, taxes and prohibitions. Americans seemed destined to apply the phrase "free and independent states" against each other as well as against Great Britain. Surveying this scene of domestic discord, Hamilton wondered if Americans would learn from anarchy the necessity of a superintending national government. But he feared that they would learn only from bloodshed: "If these States are not united under a Federal Government," he predicted, "they will infallibly have wars with each other."

Although eleven states eventually agreed to give Congress the right to lay prohibitions upon imports from countries not having commercial treaties with the United States, two states stood pat upon the Articles of Confederation. As a result, Congress could do no more than wring its hands at the spectacle presented by the United States of a nation whose shipping had not yet recovered from the ravages of war, whose commerce was obstructed in both the French and British West Indies, whose flag was insulted and whose "few Mariners, who venture on the Ocean" were "exposed to linger out their days in all the bitterness of Captivity, from a barbarous and hostile Power," the Barbary corsairs.

In 1786, certain in his own mind that chaos lay directly ahead, James Madison proposed and the legislature of Virginia adopted a plan calling upon the states to send delegates to a convention at Annapolis, Maryland, for the purpose of considering the commercial plight of the union and making recommendations for its amelioration. A meeting of this kind, strictly limited in its agenda, had some attraction for the dominant party in New York. Averse as this party was to strengthening the Continental Congress, it was even more eager at this particular moment to inflict economic reprisals upon Great Britain for its refusal to surrender the northwest posts. As a result, Hamilton and Egbert Benson, a lawyer of nationalistic outlook, were appointed by the New York legislature to go to Annapolis. Two men less representative of the state-rights philosophy prevailing in New York could hardly have been found in the state.

Even though Hamilton considered the Annapolis Convention to be no more than a stopgap, he did not for that reason publicly minimize its importance. It was only by improvisations and makeshift contrivances, he perceived, that the union could be kept afloat until rescue, in the form of a constitutional convention, arrived. Rigid and inflexible as regards his larger objectives, Hamilton was capable of accommodating his policy to the main chance—and in this instance the main chance dictated that he clutch at every straw. Without losing sight of his cardinal objective—the creation of a truly national government—he was willing to let expediency be his guide in attaining it.[4]

When Hamilton arrived in Annapolis in September, 1786, he found that few delegates had preceded him. The town was strangely empty of the businessmen with whom he had expected to discuss the commercial affairs of the country. Somewhat disconcerted, Hamilton settled down to wait the coming of the representatives from the other states. But the prospect was discouraging: four states, including Maryland, did not even trouble to appoint delegates. Altogether, only five states were represented at the meeting; and of the so-called "commercial states," New York and Pennsylvania alone sent delegates.

Eager as were northern merchants to obtain the carrying trade of the southern states, many distrusted a meeting called by Virginia to discuss the commercial affairs of the union. Since when, they asked, had the Old Dominion devoted itself to promoting the welfare of American businessmen; and what credence could be placed in the professions of planters that they wished to encourage the growth of an American merchant marine? Nor did the fact that the convention had been summoned to meet in Annapolis, far removed from the "marts of trade," help to allay the suspicion of northern merchants that the Virginians were playing a deep and devious game. In some quarters it was believed that the purpose of the convention was to thwart the attempt to effect sweeping changes in the Articles of Confederation. Hamilton himself was not universally trusted by the merchants: some thought that he cared far more for the public creditors than for businessmen and that he would bend his efforts toward raising a revenue rather than toward advancing the cause of commerce.

As a place for a meeting that had nothing to do, Annapolis was unexcelled: the town afforded a round of gay parties, horse races and beautiful women—enough to keep the delegates occupied as long as they chose to remain. But Hamilton and his colleagues were not men to play the horses while Rome burned: they chafed under the pleasures of Annapolis and yearned to get down to business.

Small as was the gathering, Hamilton found himself in the company of kindred spirits: most of the delegates agreed that the union was *in extremis* and that palliatives were no longer of any avail. George Read of Delaware, for example, advocated a national government that would swallow up the states; and Tench Coxe, the delegate from Pennsylvania, expounded his favorite theme that a national union, to be enduring, must have a solid economic basis. Thus, the delegates fortified each other's resolution to stop the drift toward "national insignificance" through disunion.

Yet it could not be pretended that the delegates were sufficiently numerous to draw up any proposals regarding commerce that would carry weight with the states. This rump convention might recommend—but who would listen? Certainly not the commercial states that had boycotted the meeting: insofar as they were concerned, the meeting could be written off as a failure.

At this juncture, Hamilton revealed the audacity that was his most distinctive characteristic as a soldier and statesman. He proposed that the convention should recommend to the states that another convention be summoned to meet in Philadelphia and that this meeting be authorized to take into consideration all the problems—financial, commercial and political—confronting the country.

Since the agenda of the Annapolis Convention was limited to devising recommendations for a uniform system of commercial regulations among the states "to their common interests and permanent harmony" and Hamilton and Benson were bound by the instructions of the New York legislature to confine their attention wholly to this purpose, they were not in a position to propose officially that the states be called upon to appoint delegates to a constitutional convention. Fortunately for the success of Hamilton's plan, the New Jersey delegates had not been bound by such precise instructions. Accordingly, by prearrangement, Abraham Clark of New Jersey rose to introduce a resolution that a convention be summoned to meet in Philadelphia in May, 1787.

There were not a few delegates who questioned the wisdom of such a course of action. Desiring, yet despairing of achieving immediate changes in the Articles of Confederation, they believed that the timing of a call for a constitutional convention was all-important and that it was better to move gradually than to risk everything upon such a dubious step at the present juncture of affairs. They could not forget that the Annapolis Convention itself was "utterly unknown to the Constitution." How, therefore, they asked, could an extralegal assemblage composed of a "very few delegates from a very few States" undertake to recommend "a great and critical object, wholly foreign to their commission?"[5]

Fearful that Hamilton's boldness might recoil upon the cause of nationalism, Madison at first wanted no part of the plan of making the failure of the Annapolis Convention a steppingstone to a constitutional convention. His colleague, Edmund Randolph, shared his apprehensions: in the opinion of both these Virginians, Hamilton was too inclined to gamble upon a turn of fortune. Having suffered a reverse, they appreciated the need of caution in future efforts to revise the Articles of Confederation. Seeking to restrain Hamilton's impetuosity, Madison now argued that the enemy was too strongly entrenched to be dislodged by the tactics that had served his friend so well at Yorktown: ignorance and iniquity, he said, were leagued against the forces of nationalism and therefore it behooved good men to walk softly.

On the other hand, there were equally patent hazards in winding up the convention and accepting defeat at the hands of the states. In that event, the chances of effecting any reforms in the Articles of Confederation would be dim indeed; the next step might well be the dissolution of the confederacy by the northern states bent upon attaining commercial salvation in their own way. Rather than expose the country to such dangers, the Convention decided to adopt Hamilton's plan of making the abortive meeting at Annapolis a sounding board for calling a constitutional convention. As the leading advocate of this course of action, Hamilton was designated to write an address to the states.

Had the inditing of this address been left wholly to Hamilton, his acute sense of the inadequacy of the Articles of Confederation might have led him to emit such a stentorian call for their overthrow that the confederationists would have taken alarm. His first draft revealed only too clearly that he had not succeeded in resisting this temptation. Fortunately for the success of the cause he had at heart, the more cautious members of the Convention insisted upon toning down his exhortation. As a result, in its final form, the address to the states proved to be a masterpiece of temerity concealed by reserved and oblique language. The Convention pointed out that there were "important defects" in the Articles of Confederation that required "adjustment," but what these defects were and how much adjustment was required, it wisely did not say. The address recommended that the states empowered their delegates to make such changes as were in their opinion "necessary to render the constitution of the Federal Government adequate to the exigencies of the Union." But whether this could be done within the framework of the Articles of Confederation was left to the imagination.

One thing the report of the Annapolis Convention made clear—that the purview of the proposed convention must embrace all matters pertaining to the union. No one power, Hamilton asserted, could be granted to the general government without requiring "a correspondent adjustment of other parts of the Federal System." The Annapolis Convention, it was implied, had been condemned to failure because it was authorized to discuss only one of the manifold problems facing the country.

Despite the circumspection with which Hamilton clothed his appeal for a constitutional convention, nationalists had no difficulty in penetrating his meaning: this was the long-awaited signal to converge upon Philadelphia all the forces of conservatism and nationalism. After having dissipated their energies upon schemes of partial reform, the supporters of a strong central government were apparently to be given an opportunity to accomplish at one stroke what had been proved to be unattainable by means of a series of requests for grants of specific powers.[6]

In his early plans of government Hamilton was apparently content that the Continental Congress should remain a unicameral legislature in which all the powers of government—legislative, executive and judicial—were concentrated. Not until 1783 did he advocate what in 1787 became one of his cardinal objectives—the division of the federal government into distinct executive, legislative and judicial branches each independent of and yet dependent upon the others. As a result, it fell to others first to propose the system of government that Hamilton later expounded so brilliantly in *The Federalist*.

Perhaps this omission was owing to his preoccupation with the financial difficulties of the country and to the importance he attached to calling a Constitutional Convention. Certainly he was familiar with the concept of a division of powers: no student of Harrington, Blackstone, and Montesquieu could have overlooked that point. But Hamilton's reading was seldom a decisive force in establishing the convictions upon which he acted: here, as elsewhere, it was his experience that taught him the necessity of a division of powers in the federal government. As his friend James Kent later said, Hamilton's views "grew more & more enlarged & comprehensive as we approached the crisis of our destiny."[7]

It was also true that Hamilton's emphasis upon the separation of powers grew as his confidence in the wisdom and good intentions of the people diminished. As a unicameral legislature possessing all executive and judicial powers, the Continental Congress was vulnerable to the same debtor farmers who had gained control of the state legislatures. In establishing an energetic central authority, Hamilton had no intention of creating a supergovernment that would strip the wealthy of their property with more dispatch and efficiency than even the state legislatures had displayed. His ideal was a central government capable of stemming the force of popular majorities both in the states and within itself.

Viewed in this light, the Continental Congress appeared to Hamilton to be an unsafe repository of political power. It was a saving grace, he later admitted, that this unicameral legislature had so little actual power—otherwise it might have made itself dangerous to liberty and property.

If this were true, Hamilton had been laboring for a cause from which he had nothing to fear so much as success. He had made the slogan of the nationalists "More Power to Congress"—yet Congress, as he now admitted, was unworthy to exercise even the powers it enjoyed under the Articles. His efforts had been ostensibly directed toward propping up a moldering anomaly; had he achieved his purpose, the radical defects of the Articles might have remained untouched.

Furthermore, the strategy of piecemeal reform promised to postpone the day when the frame of government could be subjected to a thoroughgoing revision. Success in the policy of gradual change would have merely blunted the wedge which Hamilton hoped to drive into the heart of the Articles. "Is it not to be feared," asked James Madison, ". . . that these little meliorations of the Government may turn the edge of some of the arguments which ought to be laid to its root? Every days delay settles the Govt. deeper into the habits of the people, and strengthens the prop which their acquiescence gives it."

The nationalists themselves were far from unanimous in believing that the hour had struck for summoning a Constitutional Convention. Because of their failure to achieve even a modest measure of reform, some nationalists had become firmly wedded to caution; others thought that the country must be allowed to drift into greater confusion, even to the point of anarchy, before the people could be brought to see the necessity of a strong central government. Therefore, ran their argument, let the friends of strong government hold their hand until the people, in terror and despair, turned to them for succor. Then a truly national government might be erected: even a king and nobility were thought by some to be within the realm of possibility.

This plan of plucking the flower of strong government from the nettle of anarchy did not find favor with Hamilton. His inclination was always to control events rather than to permit them to control him; and he knew that by waiting for time and catastrophe to force a settlement, there was no certainty that the final arrangements would be to his taste. Always there was the danger, he pointed out, that European powers would take advantage of the quarrels and weaknesses of Americans and divide the United States between them—with the result that when the nationalists were ready to intervene there would be no nation for them to save.

Among the nationalists, Hamilton's prestige was steadily mounting; unquestionably he was the boldest and most active of the advocates of a strong national government. It remained to be seen whether boldness would succeed any better than had caution; certainly, it seemed to Hamilton, it could not do less.[8]

Hamilton's credo that fortune smiled upon audacity was never more strikingly vindicated than when he urged the Annapolis Convention to issue a call for a Constitutional Convention. In September, 1786, an attempt to make the general government dominant over the states stood little chance of success; but in May, 1787, the Constitutional Convention assembled in Philadelphia and proceeded to rewrite the fundamental law of the land. Obviously, events must have conspired to favor Hamilton's designs. Events usually did!

While it is true that Hamilton was not responsible for the occurrences to which the success of his policy was so deeply indebted, that does not detract from the measure of his achievement. This important and decisive fact is that he had a policy with which to meet these contingencies; they helped produce the results desired because he knew what he wanted. Having determined upon the objectives, he was prepared to make events contribute toward their realization.

At almost the same time that Hamilton called upon the states to summon a Constitutional Convention, Daniel Shays summoned the New England farmers to rebellion. Although Shays knew nothing about the plans that had been laid at Annapolis, had he wished to further those objectives, he would not have acted differently.

Hamilton returned to New York to find the work of the Annapolis Convention overshadowed by the news from Massachusetts: county conventions assembling and demanding the abolition of the Massachusetts Senate and the relocation of the state capital in the western part of the state; mobs closing courts of justice and terrorizing creditors in very much the same way that the patriots had dealt with Loyalists a few years before; and "desperate debtors," "bankrupts and sots, who have gambled or slept away their estates," and "a multitude of tavern-haunting politicians," demanding paper money, stay laws and tender acts.

In Hamilton's hierarchy of abominations, Massachusetts temporarily replaced Rhode Island as a portent of the wrath to come. In the latter state, the paper-money faction had gained control; but in the Bay State, Americans could see to what lengths "villains & fools"—a well-nigh unbeatable combination—would go to seize power from constituted authority.

When confronted by rebellious farmers, Hamilton's impulse was usually to damn them as pestilential democrats and to ascribe their discontents to the "spirit of licentiousness" that seemed to possess these misguided tillers of the soil. Without pausing to inquire into the nature of the farmers' grievances or the justice of the reforms they advocated, Hamilton uncompromisingly condemned the uprising and called for its suppression by force of arms. In so doing, he found himself in the company of Sam Adams, a seasoned revolutionist who now upheld the established order as vigorously as he had once undermined it. Even George Washington, when he learned of the uprising in Massachusetts, exclaimed: "What, gracious God, is man! that there should be such inconsistency and perfidiousness in his conduct?"

Although as General Steuben said, "when a whole people complains . . . something must be wrong," Hamilton did not draw the moral that conservatives were sometimes incapable of ruling wisely. He thought, rather, that the uprising in Massachusetts proved that the masses were the natural prey of demagogues and that strong government was the only security against popular "licentiousness." "If Shays had not been a desperate debtor," he observed, "it is much to be doubted whether Massachusetts would have been plunged into a civil war." Under the circumstances, it first seemed necessary to set the people right by a little wholesome chastisement—then their grievances, if any, might be looked into. He believed that these grievances would prove upon examination to be largely unfounded: the real objective of these disturbers of the peace, he said, was the abolition of all debts, the abrogation of contracts and a new division of property—in short, "a perfect democracy" in which virtue, property and social distinctions would be destroyed.[9]

Alarmed by the growing disaffection of the western farmers, Massachusetts instructed its delegates to ask Congress for military aid. Since the federal armory in Springfield was one of the objectives of the insurgents, Congress was obliged to take measures for its protection. Moreover, the disturbances in Massachusetts gave Congress an opportunity to demonstrate that despite the low esteem into which it had fallen, it was still capable of preserving order in the states. Accordingly, in October, 1786, Congress resolved to increase the size of the regular army, giving as the ostensible reason for its action the menacing attitude of the Indians along the northwest frontier.[10]

True enough, all was not quiet on the frontier and additional troops were needed to keep the Indians out of the frontiersmen's hair. But Congress' subterfuge—intended to prevent the Massachusetts farmers from proceeding to extremes before strong forces could be brought up—deceived neither the Indians nor the Shaysites. Thousands of armed men prepared to attack the federal armory at Springfield, where enough arms were stored to give Shays and his men undisputed control of the western counties.

All the secrecy with which Congress sought to clothe its efforts to aid Massachusetts proved unnecessary: no Continental troops ever reached the scene of trouble. The truth was that Congress had no money with which to raise and equip an army. Indeed, at this time, it was scraping the bottom of the Treasury in order to pay the annual allotment it had promised some of the French officers who had served in the War of Independence; and the troops along the frontiers were half-mutinous for want of pay. Daniel Shays and his men had nothing to fear from the Continental Congress. For all it could do, they might have captured Boston and set up their standard over the State House.

No thanks to the Continental Congress, the rebellion was suppressed and insurgents were either disarmed or sent in headlong flight to New York, Vermont and Rhode Island. This was entirely the work of Massachusetts state troops: four thousand men were drafted from the militia and placed under the command of General Lincoln. This force routed the Shaysites and saved the armory at Springfield.

Gratified as Hamilton was to see the rebellion suppressed, his satisfaction was considerably diminished by the fact that it had been put down by Massachusetts rather than by the central government. More than any other single event that occurred during the so-called "Critical Period," Shays' Rebellion drove home to Americans the truth Hamilton had been trying to impress upon them for years: that the general government was a mere shadow incapable of giving security to property and the other rights of man. He might have taken consolation, on the other hand, in the fact that Daniel Shays had incidentally demonstrated that even the state governments were dependent upon men of wealth. The army that took the field against the insurgents was largely raised and equipped with money contributed by the wealthy merchants and landowners of the state.[11]

But, above all, Hamilton was indebted to Daniel Shays for a rare fund of propaganda with which to assail the Articles of Confederation and to support the case for calling a Constitutional Convention. Massachusetts, he pointed out, had escaped disaster by the narrowest margin: it was clearly another instance of how Providence came to the aid of Americans. But how long, he asked, would Americans tempt Providence; did they suppose that they would always be saved at the eleventh hour from the consequences of their own folly? There was no good in writing off Shays as an incompetent leader: "Who can determine," he asked, "what might have been the issue of her [Massachusetts] late convulsions, if the malcontents had been headed by a Caesar or by a Cromwell? Who can predict what effect a despotism, established in Massachusetts would have upon the liberties of New Hampshire or Rhode Island, of Connecticut or New York?" Who could tell how many village Cromwells and Caesars were at the moment nursing dark ambitions that would lead them to the destruction of their country's liberties?[12]

Just as there seemed to be no lack of demagogues and would-be despots in the United States, neither did the country seem to want for the conditions that made possible their rise to power. What had happened in Massachusetts, Hamilton declared, could happen anywhere in the republic. In North Carolina and Pennsylvania, he reminded Americans, the people had the same grievances and suffered from the same distresses that had produced rebellion in Massachusetts: all that was needed was "the trumpet of some bold leader" to set the people in motion. Massachusetts' difficulties were in part owing to its efforts to pay off its internal debt at too rapid a rate—a condition which, Hamilton observed, might be reproduced in every state that attempted by its own efforts to relieve itself of its financial burdens. The problem of state and national debt, he concluded, must be solved upon the national level.[13]

Even the restoration of order in Massachusetts did not lay the specter of demagoguery and the subversion of the laws. In the spring of 1787, Governor Bowdoin, under whose administration the rebellion had been crushed, was defeated for re-election by John Hancock. At the same time, a large number of Shaysite sympathizers were returned to the Massachusetts legislature. Having been worsted in the field, the rebels won such a decisive victory at the polls that Hamilton began to fear that they would yet carry their program through the legislature. The full measure of popular caprice was now revealed to Hamilton: apparently the people ceased to follow a demagogue like Daniel Shays only when a more insidious demagogue like John Hancock came along.* [14]

───────────

* Madison said that John Hancock's policies were "not a little tainted by a dishonorable obsequiousness to popular follies."

The uprising in Massachusetts did not incline Hamilton, as it did some frightened conservatives, to put his faith wholly in coercion. Although he continued to believe that every government must have sufficient force at its disposal to compel obedience in emergencies, he did not contend that force provided the whole answer to the problem of governing men. Self-interest and the "passions" of men, if put to the service of the state, still seemed to him to offer the best security of preserving order and union. The means of compulsion ought, he said, to be held in reserve, for the likes of Daniel Shays; knaves and fools had to be shown that the long arm of government packed a punch.

Nor did Hamilton deduce from Shays' Rebellion that republican government was "impracticable and absurd." On the contrary, he argued that a strong national government could effectively bridle "the lusts and passions of mankind" and divert them into productive channels. The evils of the day he traced to "want of energy" in the government quite as much as he did to "popular licentiousness"; under the conditions prevailing in the United States, he could not believe that republicanism had ever been given a fair trial. But it had been abundantly demonstrated, he said, "how little the rights of a feeble government are likely to be respected, even by its own constituents . . . how unequal parchment provisions are to a struggle with public necessity."[15]

After Shays' Rebellion, there was little disposition on the part of conservatives to question that the time had come to strike for a strong central government. Even those who advocated waiting for anarchy before taking action were ready to admit that the "horrors of anarchy and licentiousness" were at hand. "The flames of internal insurrection were ready to burst out in every quarter," it was said; ". . . from one end to the other of the continent, we walked on ashes, concealing fire beneath our feet." Fisher Ames of Massachusetts looked forward with gloomy certainty to the day when Americans would revert to the state of nature and take rank among the savages "somewhere below the Oneida Indians."[16]

Important as was Shays' contribution toward crystallizing the opinion of conservatives, it was largely owing to the work of Hamilton, Madison, Washington and others who shared their views that these hopes were fixed upon a Constitutional Convention. For seven years or more, Hamilton and his fellow nationalists had been telling the American people that their salvation lay in a strong national government. Had it not been for these exhortations, it is possible that Americans would have sought some other escape from their predicament—the most likely being a breakup of the union into two or more confederacies.

If force became necessary to put down the democrats, protect property and hold the union together, there was an organized body of men in the country prepared to take action. This was the Society of the Cincinnati, established immediately after the Revolutionary War by the officers of the Continental Army. The purposes of this society were to create a charitable fund for the support of needy officers, their families and dependents, and to preserve a bond of brotherhood between the officers of the American army and their French comrades-in-arms. Most important of all, from Hamilton's point of view, the Order of the Cincinnati was intended "to promote and cherish between the respective States that Union and National Honor, so essentially necessary to their happiness and the future dignity of the American empire." In order to perpetuate the Society beyond the lives of the officers themselves, it was provided that membership should descend to the eldest son or, in failure thereof, to collateral branches which might be deemed worthy of the honor.

Upon this "self-created" society of officers, Americans vented all the "hatred for soldiers" which Hamilton had repeatedly found occasion to deplore. In the Cincinnati these confirmed antimilitarists beheld "A Race of Hereditary Patricians" who, it was feared, would make themselves supreme over the civil government. Thomas Jefferson and John Adams stigmatized the Society as a baleful offshoot of European aristocracy and predicted that the liberties of Americans would not be safe as long as the organization existed.

Alarmed by these demonstrations of hostility to the Society, Washington, as president of the Cincinnati, persuaded the general meeting held in Philadelphia in 1784 to recommend to the state societies the renunciation of all political activity, including even the general meetings; the abandonment of the principle of hereditary descent; and the surrender of the funds of the state branches to the control of the legislatures of the several states. Little more than the charitable and fraternal aspects of the Society remained. By thus deferring to public opinion, Washington hoped to convince his countrymen of the rectitude and patriotism of the officers; had not the French officers been already invited to join, he declared, he would have favored the abolition of the Society.

It remained only for the state branches to carry out the decisions of the general meeting, but here Washington's policies encountered vigorous opposition. The state societies, with New York leading the van, refused to adopt the recommendations of the president. Whereupon Washington wrote to Hamilton and other prominent members of the Cincinnati urging them to aid in effecting the reforms that would permit the officers to live at peace with their fellow citizens.

To some of the changes adopted by the general meeting, Hamilton agreed. Hereditary succession by the eldest son was open to the objection, he admitted, that *"it refers to birth what ought to belong to merit only*: a principle inconsistent with the genius of the Society founded on friendship and patriotism." The distinction between honorary and regular members was likewise contrary to the spirit of an organization "where the character of patriot ought to be an equal title to all its members." But beyond these reforms Hamilton was unwilling to go. If primogeniture were abolished, he insisted that some provision be made for continuing the society beyond the lives of its original members. To make the existence of the society depend upon charters granted by the states was, he warned, to put it at the mercy of a legislative majority; the most that the Cincinnati ought to ask of the states was permission to appoint trustees to hold its property for charitable purposes. Above all, he would not consent to expunge the clause in the constitution which pledged the members to promote the cause of union and national honor. "America can never have cause to condemn an Institution," he asserted, "calculated to give energy and extent to a Sentiment, favorable to the preservation of that Union by which she established her liberties, and to which she must owe her future peace, respectability and property." Therefore, he contended, the general meetings of the Society ought to be continued and the members welded into an even more effective phalanx for political action.

Although the general meetings of the Society continued to be held and the principle of hereditary succession was upheld by the state branches, the Cincinnati failed to become the kind of political organization Hamilton envisaged. It was by means of a party rather than a semimilitary body that Hamilton was to achieve his objectives.[17]

By 1786, twelve states had ratified the impost proposed by the Continental Congress in 1783. Since amendment to the Articles of Confederation required the consent of all thirteen states, the financial position of the general government remained no better than before. Neither the foreign nor the domestic creditors of the United States were visibly impressed by Congress's near misses in its efforts to win the unanimous approval of the states for its revenue schemes.

Even Rhode Island, for once, was numbered among the "chaste sisters." It was New York that now frustrated the will of twelve states—or, as Governor Clinton's partisans said, thwarted the tyranny of "King Cong," their favorite name for the Continental Congress.

Having been elected to the New York Assembly in 1786, Hamilton was in a position to make his voice heard in opposition to Clinton. While he still regarded the impost as a mere stopgap and his hopes were centered upon a Constitutional Convention, he recognized that the immediate task was to use all available means to keep the confederacy intact. Accordingly, in a speech delivered in January, 1787, he attempted to convince New Yorkers that they were jeopardizing the union and injuring themselves by opposing the impost. If this measure did not take effect, he warned, New

York might become the sole support of the tottering Continental Congress. "Are we willing to be the Atlas of the Union, or are we willing to see it perish?" he rhetorically asked the Assembly. The union had indeed reached a low point if its survival depended upon the governor of New York and his followers.

Hamilton's eloquence did not make the slightest impression upon the Clintonians. After he had concluded his speech they sat stolidly in the seats and, without deigning to answer him, proceeded to kill the impost. Nevertheless, Hamilton's speech on the impost, more than any other act prior to his appointment as Secretary of the Treasury, brought him into the public eye. Widely reprinted in the newspapers, it marked the beginning of his emergence as a national leader: his reputation, like his ideas, now embraced the United States.[18]

The Connecticut Wits, a group of young Yale graduates some of whom had acquired in the army a strong nationalistic bias, celebrated Hamilton's speech on the impost in their epic poem, the *Anarchiad*. Here Anarch, having been vanquished by Hesper, is pictured plotting to regain his power with the aid of his friends in New York; Hamilton appears as the young hero

> Ardent and bold, the sinking land to save
> In council sapient as in action brave,

who gives battle to Anarch but who is finally overcome by his antagonist aided by the "band of mutes" in the New York Assembly. In celebration of this victory, Anarch prepares to restore the happy days "when those plagues to society, law and justice shall be done away with; when everyone shall be independent of his neighbor, and when every rogue shall literally do what is right in his own eyes."*

But "Old Anarch" rejoiced too soon: the defeat of the impost proved to be his last gasp, not the beginning of a new reign of power. In failure, Hamilton won a greater triumph than would have been possible had he secured the adoption of this measure. For Hamilton, defeat often proved to be the steppingstone to a decisive victory.

* The soliloquy of Anarch:
> Ardent and bold, the sinking land to save
> In council sapient as in action brave,
> I fear'd young HAMILTON's unshaken soul,
> And saw his arm our wayward host control.
> Yet, while the Senate with his accents rung,
> Fire in his eye, and thunder on his tongue,
> My band of mutes in dumb confusion throng,
> Convinc'd of right, yet obstinate in wrong,
> With stupid reverence lift the guided hand,
> And yield an empire to thy wild command.

In rejecting the impost, Governor Clinton might have justified his action on the ground that the country was recovering from the depression. The bottom was reached in 1786; after that dismal year, commerce and building began to revive as new trade routes were opened up to China and the East Indies. Americans no longer plunged recklessly into debt in order to buy imported merchandise; "industry and frugality," it was observed, were becoming the order of the day. The Ordinances of 1785 and 1787 inaugurated a new policy toward the West which promised to open up vast areas to settlement. Altogether, the economic prospects of the country had not looked brighter since the United States won its independence.[19]

If the economic crisis was easing in 1787, the same could not be said of the political crisis which, in the form of a struggle for power between the states and the general government, had existed since the beginning of the Revolution. Here, Hamilton said, "things are continually growing worse: having long kept Congress on short rations, the states seemed about to deny it sustenance altogether. Only two or three states honored even part of the requisitions of Congress and several states no longer even took the trouble to discuss the requests of that body; they were certain to be rejected anyway. It was said that no one could be elected constable in Connecticut "if he was to declare that he meant to pay a copper towards the domestic debt." By 1787 the requisition of 1781 had not been paid by some of the states; and from 1784 to 1786, the total sum received by Congress from the states did not exceed half a million dollars. Small as this sum was, it was steadily growing smaller: from June, 1787, to June, 1788, the states contributed less than two hundred thousand dollars to the Treasury of the United States. A few states kept the general government alive by their contributions, but it was a precarious existence that might be terminated at any moment.[20]

Thus, while the country was coming out of the trough of the depression, the ship of state was wallowing helplessly and, as Washington said, "without the aid of one friendly star to guide us into port." There was no indication that when prosperity returned, the general government would share in it; whether the times were good or bad, the union threatened to break up into "insignificant and wretched fragments of Empire."

If Hamilton took too dark a view when he said that the United States had reached "the last stage of national nothingness," the end was clearly in sight. When the Secretary of War applied for one thousand dollars for ammunition badly needed by the military posts on the Ohio River, the Board of Treasury declared that it was unable to make even this "pitiful advance." At the end of 1787, the Continental Congress was over ten million dollars in arrears of interest on the national debt, and a good share of this was owing foreign creditors. Moreover, what Hamilton called "the tremendous process of compound interest" was adding millions to the debt every year. Congress was caught in the ever-contracting vise of a shrinking income and increasing debt. When a new minister arrived from France, he cast a chill upon the welcome that had been prepared for him by reminding Americans that they owed his country a large sum of money and that His Christian Majesty expected payment in full.[21]

As though this were not a heavy enough cross to bear, Congress was committed to begin payments in 1787 on the principal of the foreign debt. Since it was not able to pay even the interest except by borrowing abroad, Congress had no alternative but to throw itself upon the mercy of its creditors. But the quality of mercy was already being strained by Americans' debt-dodging. To France and Holland, the spectacle of the Continental Congress paralyzed by the negative vote of one state inspired about as much confidence as did the Polish Diet or the latter-day Holy Roman Empire. But even had the American government looked like a good financial risk, France was not in a position to make another loan. The hardheaded private bankers of Holland were therefore the government's last hope.[22]

At this critical moment, John Adams and Thomas Jefferson succeeded in floating a loan in Holland, thereby preserving, at least for the time being, the credit of the government. Yet had it not been for the efforts of Hamilton and other nationalists to create a government capable of paying its debts, it is unlikely that the Duch bankers would have made this timely advance.

Borrowing from Holland to pay France was not a permanent solution of the financial problems of the United States: at best, it was a palliative that kept a sinking government afloat a little longer. Nevertheless, any good news tended to weaken Hamilton's arguments in favor of a stronger national government. It was probably fortunate for him, therefore, that the political crisis of the union occurred before the economic recovery had fully manifested itself. Had Hamilton waited—as some nationalists wished to do—until conditions became worse, they might have found themselves outflanked by a resurgent prosperity.

No doubt, Hamilton was guilty of exaggerating the economic plight in which the United States found itself as a result of a weak central government and the postwar depression. But he did not overstate the nature and scope of the political malaise that threatened to prostrate the government. By Hamilton's diagnosis, the trouble was fundamentally political and therefore a political remedy had to be found. The immediate objective was not so much to restore economic prosperity as to preserve the United States and to bind the states together with both political and economic ligaments. "The union, the peace and the happiness of America" seemed to Hamilton to be one and indivisible.

10.

The Constitutional Convention (1)

New York's veto of the impost marked Hamilton's last effort to achieve the reform of the Articles of Confederation. Henceforth he devoted himself to the only course which he had long believed held any prospect of success—a Constitutional Convention authorized to devise a wholly new frame of government.

Since it was apparent that the approval of the Continental Congress was essential to the success of this plan—a number of states, New York among them, declined to participate on the ground that the Convention lacked constitutional sanction—Hamilton proposed in the New York legislature that the state instruct its delegates to move that the Continental Congress give formal approval to the Philadelphia meeting. On February 17, 1787, the New York legislature adopted this resolution, but before it could be presented to the Continental Congress that body had already decided to give the project its blessing. It was the rejection of the impost by the New York legislature that led Congress to approve the Constitutional Convention: after that dismal news only the revision of the Articles of Confederation afforded hope of averting disaster.

Having taken a leading part in persuading New York to send delegates to Philadelphia, Hamilton's next objective was to secure for himself a place on the delegation. But in view of the fact that the New York legislature was under the control of his political enemies and that his record in the Continental Congress and the Annapolis Convention was in Clinton's opinion a complete misrepresentation of the attitude of the state toward national concerns, Hamilton's chances of going to Philadelphia seemed remote. The expedition to the City of Brotherly Love promised to be a wholly Clintonian excursion with no room aboard for a nationalist like Hamilton.

So Clinton intended and, had not General Schuyler intervened, the governor probably would have had his way. Rather than permit Clinton to pack the delegation with his followers, General Schuyler resolved to send his favorite son-in-law to Philadelphia to represent the views of the New York nationalists. Therefore when the Clintonians proposed that the delegates be elected by joint ballot of the two houses—a procedure certain to result in a solid slate of Clintonians—Schuyler organized the Senate for resistance. He was sufficiently successful to compel the Clintonians to agree to a compromise: the election was to be by joint ballot, but it was settled beforehand that one member of the delegation should be chosen by the Schuyler-Livingston coalition.

As a result, Hamilton was elected on the first ballot, standing second in the poll. It was far from certain, however, that General Schuyler had done his son-in-law a service. With Hamilton were yoked two reliable party wheelhorses, Robert Lansing and John Yates, who were expected, if Hamilton showed any inclination to take the bit in his teeth, to pull vigorously in the opposite direction. Since they outvoted Hamilton two to one, the vote of the State of New York in the convention was certain to reflect the views of George Clinton. And, to tie Hamilton's hands even more effectively, the delegates were instructed to confine themselves "to the sole and express purpose of revising the Articles of Confederation." A motion by Robert Yates that the delegates should be instructed to agree to no alterations in the Articles of Confederation "repugnant to, or inconsistent with, the constitution of this state" failed of passage by only one vote.[1]

Feeling alone and friendless in such company, Hamilton attempted to secure the appointment of two additional delegates. Since his purpose was to give the nationalists a majority vote in the delegation, his first choice was John Jay, the onetime Secretary of Foreign Affairs. But the Clintonians insisted upon strictly adhering to the terms of the agreement they had made with General Schuyler. As a result, Jay's nomination was defeated in the Senate and Hamilton was condemned to the unhappy position of a minority of one.[2]

Rather than submit to such a humiliation, a lesser man might have thrown up the appointment in despair. And, indeed, the more closely Hamilton studied the colleagues with whom he had been saddled, the less tenable his position appeared. There was no possibility of converting Yates and Lansing to his views: both men had voted against the impost and had otherwise distinguished themselves by their inflexible opposition to everything that savored of nationalism. Yates even questioned the legality of his and his colleagues' appointment: the joint vote of the New York legislature he held to be unconstitutional since, as he said, "acts of the least consequence, even for the yoking of hogs require to be passed under the formalities of a law."[3]

The composition of the New York delegation augured so ill for the nationalists that some of Washington's friends advised him not to hazard his reputation by attending the Convention. Even James Madison doubted if Washington should come to Philadelphia until it had been determined whether other states were going to follow New York's example. But if Hamilton had any doubts or reservations regarding the Convention, he kept them

The Constitutional Convention (1)

to himself. Even though he occupied the most unenviable spot of any delegate, his hopes of success ran high: *he* did not advise Washington to remain at Mount Vernon and wait to see how the land lay.[4]

At this particular juncture Washington badly needed an infusion of the courage, optimism and determination displayed by Hamilton. The former Commander in Chief was nagged by uncertainty and misgivings: the damage his hard-won reputation might suffer from a fiasco at Philadelphia was constantly in his mind. And yet, had not Washington yielded to the importunities of Hamilton and other nationalists, the Constitutional Convention might have failed as dismally as the faint of heart feared it would in the early spring of 1787. Washington was slow to see that his presence was indispensable to the success of the venture upon which the nationalists had staked their hopes; Hamilton knew it from the beginning.

Hamilton came to the Constitutional Convention armed with a philosophy which eminently qualified him to be the spokesman of a new order. He was a complete and uncompromising nationalist: no vestige of state loyalty impaired his devotion to the union. He was convinced that the American people, in pursuit of a happiness that emphasized the rights rather than the duties of citizens, had stumbled to the brink of disaster. He viewed human nature with the skepticism of a disillusioned revolutionary and he was prepared to redress the balance which had been weighted heavily on the side of faith in the essential goodness of man. Everything considered, he was as much in the mood to effect a revolution as he had been in 1776.

It seemed to Hamilton that the meeting at Philadelphia was the last clear chance for reason to exert its sway before chaos took over; if the Convention failed, he expected that the next act in the drama would reveal the awful spectacle of republicanism in its death throes. "If we did not give to that form [republicanism] due stability and wisdom," he said, "it would be disgraced & lost among ourselves, disgraced & lost to mankind forever."[5]

Obviously, Hamilton did not subscribe to the doctrine that men were the helpless victims of blind forces which shaped their destinies to preordained ends. The drift to anarchy, he was persuaded, could be stopped; a stable government could be erected in the United States and the union could be freed of the incubus of state rights. But if these things were to be done, he knew that reason would have to exert its sway quickly: the country could no longer be permitted to be swept along wherever "passion and prejudice" led it.

For Hamilton, the pursuit of happiness led straight to a strong national government. But he no longer pretended that it could be attained within the Articles of Confederation; a sound and enduring government, he observed, could not be built upon rubble. He considered the Articles to be designed for a league of nations, not for a nation; nationalism could not live within that narrow and oppressive framework.

He was resolved to change the league into an effective centralized government, clothed with high sovereign powers for national objects and operating directly upon the people as individuals—in short, a government capable of dealing with national problems in a national way. But standing squarely in Hamilton's path were the Articles of Confederation, still the fundamental law of the land.

The delegates had no more than taken their seats before Hamilton made clear that despite his respect for constituted authority, he was not averse to doing it violence when his objectives could not otherwise be attained. He solemnly declared that the Articles of Confederation had died of "a mortal disease": he had taken their pulse without detecting the slightest flutter. It remained therefore only decent to inter the unlamented dead and get down to the business of creating a new frame of government.[6]

Having thus summarily disposed of the Articles and the instructions of the New York legislature, Hamilton saw the way clear to the creation of a government adequate to the national needs. He asserted that the delegates were at liberty "to form such a national government as we think best adapted to the good of the whole. . . . The great question is what provision shall we make of the happiness of our Country? . . . We ought not to sacrifice the public Good to narrow Scruples. All America, all Europe, the World would condemn us. The only enquiry ought to be what can we do to save our Country."

It is fair to say that this would have been news to the American people. It was generally expected that the Constitutional Convention would do no more than recommend changes in the Articles of Confederation. Virtually all the discussion that had taken place prior to May, 1787, had revolved round the question of revitalizing the Articles; little had been said of establishing a wholly new form of government. The utmost that was anticipated from the Philadelphia meeting, therefore, was a recommendation to the effect that the states grant Congress the impost and limited control over commerce. The members of the Convention were not expected to play the part of "Founding Fathers": they were called in not as the architects of a new order but as journeymen to renovate an essentially sound and "perpetual" structure.[7]

Hamilton could advocate the exercise of discretionary powers by the Convention because he admitted that this body did not have the power to bind the country in any way. The Convention, he conceded, could only recommend; although the people had called in the experts, they were not obliged to take the experts' advice. For this reason, he argued, the delegates ought to regard themselves at liberty to recommend whatever they deemed necessary to the welfare of the union, "convinced that the Pressure of unavoidable Circumstances will direct the public mind."[8]

The Constitutional Convention (1)

In effect, Hamilton was suggesting that the Convention assume constituent powers, ordain a government and demand a plebiscite. He did not claim the right of revolution for the Constitutional Convention, but he did assert it as a prerogative of the people—a prerogative which he wished to see them exercise to the full. "The fabric of American empire ought to rest on the solid basis of THE CONSENT of the people," he declared; it was therefore the duty of the convention to decide what was necessary for the people's welfare and to submit its decision to their sovereign will.[9]

The men who assembled in the Philadelphia State House in May, 1787, were not philosophers on a holiday from their ivory towers, with a glint of Utopia in their eyes and a sheaf of visionary plans in their pockets. Rather, they were practical men of affairs, versed in business, law, politics and the management of plantations. When they approached the problem of how "the energy and dignity of government may be combined with the just and equal Rights of Man," they were more inclined to rely upon experience and the lessons of history than upon pure reason. They viewed human nature through a glass darkly; and in that somber light they undertook to give the American people another, and perhaps a final, opportunity to disprove the age-old saying that men were "unequal to the task of governing themselves, and therefore made for a Master."

It remained to be seen whether the delegates were prepared to interpret as broadly as did Hamilton the powers with which they had been invested. Hamilton lost no time in settling this crucial question. Early in the Convention, he asked whether the delegates were agreed that the United States "were susceptible of one government, or required a separate existence connected only by leagues offensive and defensive and treaties of commerce"— the equivalent, in his mind, to asking whether the Convention was prepared to draw up a wholly new frame of government or stick with the Articles until death did them part. The response was gratifying: not a single member was prepared to embrace the latter alternative, although it is probably true that some did not understand what Hamilton meant by "one government."* Clearly, most of the delegates had arrived at the conclusion that no amount of shoring and propping could sustain the tottering government of the confederacy: something was rotten in the very structure of the state and it was therefore necessary to raze it to the ground. As James Wilson of Pennsylvania said: "To give additional weight to an old building is to hasten its ruin."[10]

Any apprehensions that Hamilton may have felt that the Convention would confine itself to doing a face-lifting job on the Articles of Confederation ought to have been removed by the Virginia Plan, which, introduced

---

* It is doubtful that Hamilton ever made a formal motion to the Convention to this effect.

in the opening days of the Convention, provided the basis of discussion during the succeeding months. For the Virginia Plan—largely the work of James Madison—proposed to create a highly centralized federal government which operated directly upon the people and in which the states were accorded a distinctly subordinate status. According to its terms, a National Legislature was authorized to legislate in "all cases to which the separate states are incompetent, or in which the harmony of the United States may be interrupted by the exercise of individual legislation"—a sweeping and undefined grant of power which in practice would have approximated the authority claimed by the British Parliament over the colonies. As if to carry this analogy a step further, the National Legislature was given the right to "negative all laws passed by the several states contravening in the opinion of the national legislature the articles of union." With good reason, therefore, one delegate inquired, after Edmund Randolph had finished expounding the Virginia Plan, "whether it was intended to annihilate the State governments?"[11]

In its final form, the Virginia Plan provided that members of the House of Representatives were to be elected by the people for a term of three years, whereas members of the Senate were to be chosen by the National House of Representatives for a term of seven years from lists of candidates submitted by the state legislatures. The President was to be chosen by the National Legislature for a term of seven years and to be ineligible for a second term; he was removable on impeachment and he was to possess a qualified veto which might be overridden by two thirds of each branch of the National Legislature. Finally, the judges of the Supreme Court were to be appointed by the Senate and were to hold office during good behavior.

With some of the provisions of the Virginia Plan Hamilton was heartily in accord. He welcomed the abandonment of the principle of the equality of the states in Congress: "it shocks too much the ideas of Justice, and every human feeling," he remarked, that Virginia and other large states should be obliged to submit to equality with the smallest states in the union; he rejoiced in the prospect of a strong central government capable of curbing the states; and he had long advocated a plan of government that incorporated the principle of the separation of powers.[12]

Nevertheless, Hamilton made little effort to conceal his opinion that the bad outweighed the good in the Virginia Plan. Only a "high toned government," he thought, was adequate to the exigencies of the union. In this respect, the Virginians seemed to him to have fallen woefully short: fearful of alienating public opinion, they had produced a plan that even the people would despise. Despite the fact that the dish had been prepared by his friend James Madison, Hamilton considered it to be the mixture as before—"the same pork with a change of the sauce."

The pork which Hamilton found so distasteful was federalism and democracy. Under the Virginia Plan the federal structure of the government was preserved: the state boundaries were left untouched and the states were made the foundation upon which the superstructure of the general government was erected. From this system Hamilton foresaw nothing but endless contention between the states and the general government. How, for example, he asked, could Virginia be expected to accept a subordinate place when its territory was already almost "imperial" in extent and the end of its expansion was not yet in sight; within twenty-five years it might contain a million inhabitants? "The national government cannot long exist when opposed by such a weighty rival," he predicted; large or small, the states were the eternal enemies of the national government and they could never rest until they had brought it under their dominion. Plainly, Hamilton was neither a large-state nor a small-state man: he was essentially a no-state man.

By admitting federalism into the national government, the Virginia Plan seemed to Hamilton to have opened the door to its deformed and malignant twin, democracy. The last thing Hamilton wished to do was to establish a powerful national government that might become the instrument of unchecked majority rule. Emphatically, he had not come to the Constitutional Convention to help erect a government for the benefit of debtors bent upon despoiling the well-to-do. Nevertheless, the Virginia Plan, viewed from his angle of vision, seemed to provide a vehicle for majorities to ride roughshod over law and order. What else could be expected, he asked, from a government that ordained that "a democratic Assembly is to be checked by a democratic Senate, and both these by a democratic chief magistrate?" He never supposed that the cure for democracy was more democracy.

It was enough, Hamilton thought, that one branch of the government be surrendered to the direct control of the people—that was all any people who wished to be truly free had any right to ask. If the people dominated every branch, as the Virginia Plan envisaged, he was prepared to see the government become a theater for the exhibition of "the amazing violence & turbulence of the democratic spirit." It would all end, he felt sure, with liberty done to death, despotism triumphant and the people in chains.

Obviously, the Convention had to be made to see the pitfalls toward which it was moving!

Nevertheless, for the first three weeks, Hamilton said little upon the floor of the convention. This unwonted silence, out of character in a young man never hitherto known to hide his light behind a bushel, Hamilton later ascribed to his reluctance to differ publicly with statesmen of "superior abilities age & experience" and to the anomalous position in which he found himself in the New York delegation. Anything he might say was certain to be contradicted by his colleagues, who croaked dismally about "tyranny" and "oppression" every time the subject of strong government was mentioned.

The votes cast by the State of New York therefore seldom reflected the opinions of Alexander Hamilton. New York voted against a single Executive; against giving the Executive an absolute veto upon acts of the legislature; against a negative in the national government upon all state laws; against referring the proposed constitution to conventions rather than to the state legislatures for ratification. On the other hand, New York voted in favor of state equality in the Senate and of the appointment of the Senate by the state legislatures. All these things were anathema to Hamilton, yet, outnumbered two to one, he was compelled to see the vote of New York go the other way.

Although Hamilton made no set speeches, he sufficiently indicated the channel in which his mind was moving. On June 4, when James Wilson moved that the Executive be given an absolute veto upon the proceedings of the legislature, Hamilton seconded the motion, asserting, among other things, that there was little danger that this power would be abused by the President. Witness the monarch of Great Britain, he exclaimed, who had not used his absolute negative since the Revolution. By broaching the subject of an absolute veto, Hamilton and Wilson stirred up a hornets' nest. Colonel George Mason of Virginia, apostrophizing the "genius of the people in favor of democracy," asked Hamilton if he really imagined that the people would ever willingly consent that the President should ape the ways of George III. Benjamin Franklin entered the debate by pointing out that while it was true that the royal veto had fallen into disuse, it was not because kings had become more just but because they had found other means of bending Parliament to their will. Bribery and corruption, he declared, were now doing the King's business more effectively than had the more open and forthright methods employed by the Stuarts: Parliament was in a state of "complete subjection to the will of the Executive" and the behests of the King's ministers had virtually the effect of law. The inference Franklin drew from this state of affairs was that an American President, if given an absolute veto, would use it freely unless he, like his counterpart across the waters, found it more convenient to stoop to corruption.

Hamilton made no effort to parry these thrusts: he sat silent while his critics cut his arguments to pieces. When the vote was taken, only Gouverneur Morris, Hamilton and Wilson were found to be in favor of an absolute veto for the President.

On the rare occasions when Hamilton took the floor, it was usually in order to amend the Virginia Plan in the direction of greater centralization of authority and more power in the presidency. But, obviously, his heart was not in the Virginia Plan: he was inclined to believe that a scheme of government so fundamentally wrong did not merit serious consideration. Inevita-

The Constitutional Convention (1)

bly, in Hamilton's attitude toward the proceedings of the Convention there was a certain superciliousness that gave offense to some delegates: he held himself aloof from the debate as though it were beneath his attention. "His manners are tinctured with stiffness, and sometimes with a degree of vanity that is highly disagreeable," observed an otherwise well-disposed delegate.[13]

During the first two weeks of the Convention, Hamilton was completely outshone by James Madison. The Virginian had taken the lead in drawing up the Virginia Plan and in elucidating and defending it before the Convention. As a result, Madison was well on the way to winning the reputation of being the most redoubtable debater and the best-informed man in the assemblage: "Every person," it was said, "seems to acknowledge his greatness"—a tribute that was the more easily paid because of his modesty and singular sweetness of temper.

Nevertheless, Madison's nationalism, bound up as it was with the primacy of the large states, encountered vehement resistance. Hamilton was not alone in finding fault with the Virginia Plan: to the delegates from the small states assembled in Philadelphia, the Virginians' proposals were as abhorrent as they were to Hamilton. But for a very different reason: the small states feared that Virginia and the other large states wished to put teeth into the national government the better to devour the small states. The small states were not disposed to submit to the slaughter without a struggle. On June 16, William Paterson of New Jersey introduced into the Convention a plan of government designed to protect these lesser sovereignties from their larger neighbors.

With two plans before the Convention, Hamilton was presented with the opportunity of essaying the role of a Great Compromiser. But Hamilton's talent did not consist in conciliating opposite points of view and in assuaging the heats of party dissension. The plan of government he favored did not stand midway between the Virginia and New Jersey plans: on the contrary, it was so far removed from either that he was in danger of becoming a minority of one, not only in the New York delegation, but in the Convention as a whole.

From the beginning of the Convention, Hamilton had been keeping such a plan under wraps. Before leaving for Philadelphia he had worked out with General Schuyler the framework of a scheme of government for the United States which transcended anything that had been laid before the Convention. As a nationalist, General Schuyler was not far behind his son-in-law; as an enemy of democracy, he yielded to no man. Sharing these convictions, Hamilton found his father-in-law more of a kindred spirit than any member of the Convention. The plan that they devised between them probably represents the closest approximation Hamilton ever came to his ideal of a national government.

According to the Schuyler-Hamilton plan, a new central government was to be created with unlimited power of legislating for all the states. Although the states were to be preserved, their legislatures were to be restricted to improving roads and preserving the order. All taxes and laws were to be imposed by and to run in the name of the central government. In short, the relationship of the states to the central government was to reproduce the relationship between the English counties and the British Parliament—that is, they were to be no more than "magistratical bodies to execute the laws of a common sovereign."

Having brought these ideas with him to Philadelphia, it is not surprising that the Virginia Plan impressed Hamilton as being little more than milk and water. He was strongly inclined to cry a plague upon both the Virginia and New Jersey plans. Of course, the New Jersey Plan struck him as much more objectionable than the Virginia Plan, inasmuch as it borrowed more heavily from the Articles of Confederation; and he was nettled by Paterson's assertion that the people would refuse to accept any radical changes in the government. Finally, the fact that Yates and Lansing had spoken in support of the New Jersey Plan compelled Hamilton to speak in rebuttal lest the impression be created that he approved the measures under discussion or, equally intolerable, that he did not dare to take issue with his colleagues and that New York had no spokesman for nationalism in the Convention.

Hamilton believed that the Constitutional Convention was one place where he might speak his mind without fear of public disfavor. There was no intention of making the proposed Constitution a covenant openly arrived at. The work of the Convention was carried on in the strictest secrecy: the members were sworn not to divulge its proceedings and soldiers were posted at the doors of the Pennsylvania State House in which the delegates met. As a result of these precautions, the American people knew next to nothing of what was transpiring behind the locked doors of the State House.

When Hamilton rose to speak on June 18, it was soon apparent that he intended to take full advantage of the opportunity afforded by the rule of secrecy to make a candid and explicit avowal of his opinions. Without ceremony, Hamilton threw out the Virginia and New Jersey plans: with such trifling variations on the old theme of state sovereignty he wished to have no part. He candidly admitted that he did not "think favorably of Republican government" and that he doubted the country could be united under it. While acknowledging that the Convention ought to confine itself to the possible, he did not altogether reject the visionary: "Our situation," he said, "is peculiar—*it leaves us Room to dream* as we think proper."

His dream took the form of a President and Senate, elected by an electoral system, whose tenure of office was during good behavior; a President with an absolute veto upon the acts of the legislature; a central government with the power of appointing state governors; and state governors authorized to

The Constitutional Convention (1)

negative state laws. Most significant of all, illimitable sovereign power was concentrated in the central government: like the British Parliament before 1776, it could bind the people of America in all cases whatsoever.[14]

Although the plan of government Hamilton laid before the Convention on June 18 was hardly more than a sketch, it revealed that a fundamental change had occurred in his political philosophy. Up to this time, Hamilton had devoted himself not only to aggrandizing the powers of the general government but to protecting the individual against the exercise of arbitrary power. He had feared "absolute government," whether of a monarchical or democratical cast, as an evil thing that, however benevolently it began, always degenerated into oppression. One of his fundamental postulates had been that the sovereign could not overleap the bounds established by the Constitution without destroying the foundation on which its authority rested. During the American Revolution, he had regarded the claim of the British Parliament to bind the colonies in all cases whatsoever as proof of its intention to reduce them to slavery.

But in the frame of government he now devised for the United States there was a notable absence of a fundamental law which said to government: "Thus far and no further." There was no enumeration of the powers of government, no Bill of Rights, no safeguards for the "natural rights" of man against the state. Instead, the national government was empowered to pass all laws whatsoever: sovereignty, absolute and uncontrollable, was vested in the government of the United States. The Constitution was not made superior to the government.[15]

This radical departure from the concepts to which Hamilton had hitherto adhered was owing to his experience under the Articles of Confederation with a government limited to powers expressly delegated, to his fear of the power of the states, to the revelation of human depravity afforded by Shays' Rebellion, and to his perception of the necessity of "energetic government." A government of enumerated powers he now held to be incapable of fulfilling the ends for which it had been instituted; bound to the letter of the fundamental law, it could not cope with the unforeseen emergencies which occurred despite the best efforts of prevision to guard against them. Because the objects confided to the care of the national government were illimitable, Hamilton reasoned that the powers of the national government must likewise be illimitable. Nor would a national government such as Hamilton projected in his speech of June 18 need to live in dread of encroachments upon its authority by the states—those sovereignties would be deprived of all power of doing harm.

Had Hamilton seen his way clear, he no doubt would have recommended the abolition of the states. Certainly he left no doubt of his own inclinations: he bluntly informed the Convention that there was no security for the national government short of obliterating "State distinctions and State operations." If the states were permitted to remain in their existing form and in possession of their existing powers, he predicted that within twenty-five years "national attachment to the general government" would be extinct. Nevertheless, he admitted that the time was not ripe for wiping the states off the map: necessary as was such action, the American people were sure to take it amiss. And so, instead of raising against the states the cry of *delenda est,* he did not even advise the Convention to reduce them to uniform size. At least for the time being, he observed, the nationalists must resign themselves to suffering these troublesome jurisdictions; as yet, they could only dream of the day when the states did not exist and the people knew allegiance only to the national government.

He left no doubt, however, that the states were to be rendered harmless to the national government. When one is compelled to share the society of serpents, he believed, it was always advisable to extract their fangs. This necessitated, in the case of the states, depriving them of all sovereign powers that might enable them to challenge the authority of the national government. Preserve the states in form if we must, Hamilton told the Convention, but reduce them to mere administrative districts of the general government —the same kind of relationship that existed between the counties and the state governments. He enjoined the Convention to divest the states of military and naval forces and bring the militia under the sole direction of the national government. And, according to one source, he urged that the national government establish its own courts throughout the union "so as to make the State governments unnecessary to it."[16]

Hamilton's strategy, it is clear, was to weaken the states as much as possible in the Constitution; then, as the central government gained strength, the finishing blow might be administered. Americans might awake one morning and find themselves living under a consolidated government in which the states were mere geographical expressions.

When this event occurred, Hamilton anticipated no injury to the liberty of the individual. Although the state leaders made it appear that the rights of man depended upon the survival of the states, Hamilton denied that civil rights would be adversely affected. A strong central government, constructed according to his specifications, he regarded as in no way inimical to liberty; indeed, insofar as it promoted stability and advanced the general welfare, he believed that it would subserve the cause of freedom.

Nor was he willing to concede that the disappearance of the states would prove injurious to the economy of the country. The states were not essential, he asserted, "for any of the great purposes of commerce, revenue, or agriculture": on the contrary, their "vast and expensive apparatus" stifled enterprise and increased taxes. By getting rid of these anachronistic encumbrances, he told the Convention, the country would enjoy peace, prosperity and

The Constitutional Convention (1)

security, and no one but the state politicians would have cause to complain.

To guard further against "caprice and contumacy, and to secure obedience to the national will," Hamilton stipulated that all laws of the states contrary to the Constitution or laws of the United States were to be "utterly void" and, the better to keep the states under surveillance, the governors of the states were to be appointed by the central government and were to possess an absolute negative upon the laws passed by the state legislatures. In exercising this veto, the state governors were authorized to act upon any law which seemed to them, as representatives of the central government, inimical to the national interest. A central government could hardly ask for a wider latitude of power.

Whereas most Americans thought in terms of liberty, Hamilton was preoccupied with the necessity of drawing tighter the bonds of union. He was in favor of the kind of government that promised to unite the United States most effectively; the union was the touchstone of his political philosophy and empiricism was his guide when he undertook to judge which variety of government was best suited to the needs of the United States. The first question he asked of republicanism was: Could it preserve the union against the disruptive forces that threatened to destroy it? If it could be shown that republicanism was incapable of achieving this end, Hamilton was for calling off the noble experiment and giving some other form of government a try.

He did not often acknowledge that he was at a loss how to act, but when he contemplated the immense area covered by the United States he confessed to the Convention that he was "much discouraged by the amazing extent of Country in expecting the desired blessings from any general sovereignty." Montesquieu had observed that only a monarchy was suited for a large country, and all Hamilton's experience under the Articles of Confederation seemed to confirm the dictum of the French philosopher. And, large as the United States was, it promised to become larger with the passage of time: he told the Constitutional Convention that it must extend its range of vision not only to "thirteen independent sovereign States, some of which in territorial jurisdiction, population and resources, equal the most respectable nations of Europe, but likewise to innumerable States yet unformed, and to myriads of citizens who in future ages shall inhabit the vast uncultivated regions of the Continent." It was primarily because he doubted that this "great empire" could be effectively governed under a republican system that he pronounced republicanism to be "radically defective."[17]

Despite this weighty objection to republicanism, Hamilton did not pronounce it beyond redemption. Even though he was not a republican by conviction, he acknowledged that he was one by necessity. In view of the ineradicable prejudice of the people of the United States for republicanism, Hamilton was driven to the conclusion that it would be "unwise to change that form of government." He contented himself with advocating that it be rendered adequate to the exigencies of the union by "a skilful & judicious Structure of the republican machinery of Government." When he addressed the Convention on June 18, he believed that he knew how republicanism could be rendered adequate to those exigencies. In essence, his speech was a plea to give that form of government a chance to show what it could do after it had been taken in hand by an expert.

He always insisted that the sketch of government he proposed to the Convention was essentially republican. He had not departed, he said, from the fundamental principle that governments derive their just powers from the consent of the governed; he had provided that all branches of the national government, with the exception of the judiciary, were to be elected directly or indirectly by the people. He made no provision for hereditary distinctions or property qualifications for voting and officeholding. "Let the People be represented according to numbers," he remarked; "the People will be free: every Office will be equally open to all and the majority of the People are to make the Laws."*[18]

Nor is it true that Hamilton wholly condemned democracy. In every wellordered government, he said, there was an admixture of democracy. His purpose was not to eliminate it altogether but to regulate and control it—above all, to prevent it from becoming the whole of the government. The problem as he saw it was: How could democracy be made safe for the United States? His solution was to dilute it liberally with monarchism and aristocracy: "The occasional Violence of Democracy and the uniform Tyranny of a Despot," he said, "are productive of the same Consequences. . . . Real liberty is neither found in despotism or the extremes of democracy, but in moderate governments." Here, at least, he had the majority of the Convention on his side; as he said, "the members most tenacious of republicanism . . . were as loud as any in declaiming against the vices of democracy." By his own reckoning, there was no better friend of freedom than he in the Convention; and the proof of his devotion was that he advocated a government sufficiently strong to withstand the onslaught of ephemeral majorities.

At the head of this government of unlimited powers, occupying a position not very far below the British monarch in dignity but much above him in point of real power, Hamilton placed the President of the United States.

* Hamilton's definition of republicanism accorded with that held by other members of the Constitutional Convention. Washington said that a republican government was one "in which all power is derived from, and at stated periods, reverts to" the people; Madison declared that it was "a government which derives all its powers directly or indirectly from the great body of the people, and is administered by persons holding their offices during pleasure, for a limited period, or during good behavior."

The Constitutional Convention (1)

As a bulwark against demagoguery and popular licentiousness—the besetting weaknesses of republics—the President, in Hamilton's scheme of things, was expected to save the people from their worst enemy—themselves; and, as the apex of the national government, he was called upon to unify the "American empire" much as George III furnished a bond of union to the British Empire. Hamilton always acted upon the assumption that the way to make republicanism an effective form of government was to graft a monarchical Executive upon the main republican stem. There is no doubt that if in Hamilton's plan the presidency was tailor-made for George Washington, the cut of the garments was deliberately borrowed from George III.

Hamilton endowed the President with monarchical powers because his function, as Hamilton conceived it, was essentially monarchical. In the British government, the monarch served as a check upon the democracy of the House of Commons and the aristocracy of the House of Lords: by this means, it was said, the balance was maintained between the two great conflicting groups in society, the many and the few. "Amidst the agitations which are the unavoidable attendants of Liberty," remarked a Swiss observer of the British constitution, "the royal power, like an anchor that resists both by its weight and the depth of its hold, ensures a salutary steadiness to the vessel of the state." In the same manner, the President was expected to preserve a balance between the democratic House of Representatives and the aristocratic Senate: he stood above the struggle of parties and classes and arbitrated their differences.[19]

But Hamilton did not intend that this potent Chief Executive should spend all his time merely sitting on the lid of a rampant democracy. "Strongman government" was essential in Hamilton's way of thinking, not only to preserve stability, but to carry the authority of the central government to the furthest reaches of the union. It had not escaped his observation that the British Crown served to "consolidate the whole into one compact indissoluble body." So with the President of the United States—he, too, would fuse the United States into an indivisible whole.

Since the national government was given unlimited powers in Hamilton's plan, he deemed it essential to invest the President with an absolute veto. The best security against the tyranny of the majority seemed to him to consist in a Chief Executive capable of imposing a final and irrevocable check upon the legislature. By this means, he hoped to have an omnipotent government and at the same time give security to the rights of person and property.

If the presidency was to be a stabilizing and nationalizing force in the Constitution, Hamilton saw no alternative but to give him tenure during good behavior, which, in most instances, meant for life. Secure in his eminence and under no necessity of engaging in electioneering, the Chief Executive would presumably survey the American political scene with impartiality and unalloyed devotion to the general welfare. Such a President, he argued, would consult "the true interest and glory of the people" and would therefore be less dangerous to popular liberty than a President elected for seven years; and, by no means least, the "incalculable mischief" of frequent elections would be avoided if the President served during good behavior. In possession of all the power to which he could legitimately aspire, the President would be under no temptation to ask for more; nor would he be inclined to intrigue to maintain his authority. A weak executive, on the other hand, Hamilton feared, would constantly seek to enlarge his powers by corruption, intrigue and, finally, force.

Distrusting as he did the voice of the people, Hamilton had no desire to hear its strident tones in elections for the President. The further the final vote could be removed from the people, the more probable, he thought, that a man of wisdom and integrity would be elected to office. Accordingly, for the President he devised an especially complicated method by which the people elected electors; the electors in turn elected other electors, who, now two removes from the people, chose the President. At each stage in this process, Hamilton expected that some of the dross of passion and prejudice that vitiated the popular choice would be removed and that a reasonable approximation to pure reason would remain.[20]

A Senate holding office during good behavior promised to eliminate one of Hamilton's fundamental objections to republicanism in the United States —the necessity these representatives were under to consult with their constituents in the remote parts of the country.[21] A senator who held a life expectancy in his office would not feel obliged to travel across the country to take the public pulse or to mend his political fences—he voted as he wished and the folks back home liked it. And if Hamilton's conception of the proper function of members of the House of Representatives had prevailed, they too would be under little compulsion to spend their time on the road, working their horses into a lather for the dubious pleasure of shaking hands with the voters. For Hamilton believed that it was the duty of a representative to vote according to his own convictions, not as his constituents wanted him to vote. When the people elected a man to office they were in effect asking him to use his powers of judgment for their best advantage, not to run to them whenever he felt the need of advice.[22]

In effect, Hamilton was advising the delegates not to fritter away their time with the Virginia or New Jersey plans but to take the British constitution as their model. In place of the same old pork, he wished to offer the American people a slice of English mutton.[23] He pronounced the British constitution to be "the best model the world has ever produced"; he called the House of Lords "a most noble institution"; and he declared that he

The Constitutional Convention (1) 167

doubted whether anything short of the British constitution "would do in America." In Great Britain, he exclaimed, was to be found the only government in the world where an "energetic" government was combined with a high degree of individual liberty. As such, it was worthy of imitation by Americans, and Hamilton confessed that he for one was willing to pay the British that supreme compliment.[24]

It was natural that a storm-tossed American conservative should look upon the British constitution as a safe haven. The British constitution was then at the height of its prestige: upon the European continent, the victims of despotism acclaimed it as a charter of human freedom and held it up as a model for mankind. Unlike other monarchies, the British government did not require a standing army to keep the people in awe; instead, stability, security of property, justice and the rule of law prevailed in the midst of liberty. Hamilton and his fellow delegates regarded themselves as the victims of oppression; the fact that this oppression came from popular majorities did not make the British constitution seem less like a refuge against arbitrary government.*[25]

Hamilton's praise of monarchy was therefore not so much of monarchy in general as of the constitutional variety that had evolved in Great Britain. A limited monarchy blended of democratic, aristocratic and monarchic parts, guaranteeing liberty under law, was in Hamilton's estimation as near to perfection as mortals were likely to come.

For absolute monarchy, on the other hand, Hamilton had no kind words. He made abundantly clear that he preferred a free government—despite its occasional lapses—to any kind of absolutism. "The tendency of a free government to interest the passions of the community in its favour," he observed, "beget public spirit and public confidence"—without which, no enduring tranquillity could exist. The principal fault he found in the United States was that public spirit and public confidence, such as they were, were almost wholly directed toward the states rather than the national government.

In Hamilton's opinion, the English were a twice-blessed people—not only did they possess a monarch who embodied the authority of the state but their central government was obliged to deal with nothing more formidable than counties. No refractory, unmalleable sovereign states existed in England; the counties existed for administrative purposes only. The counties of England might disappear—as Hamilton hoped the states of the United States would disappear—and yet the government of England would go on.

Moreover, he was profoundly impressed by the fact that the British people

---

* In the Virginia ratifying convention, Patrick Henry, the great zealot for liberty, declared that the British constitution was in many respects "superior to any government that ever was in any country," and he singled out for special praise the House of Lords, which, he said, prevented encroachments by the King or Commons.

enjoyed a government of action. Upon the King and Parliament were imposed no cumbersome restrictions such as those that had vitiated the Continental Congress under the Articles of Confederation; instead, the British government could act at discretion whenever the national security or welfare was concerned. This, in essence, is the system Hamilton wished to introduce into the United States.

At no time did Hamilton say that the United States ought to establish a government of king, lords and commons. He was content to observe that the British constitution furnished "the best model the world has ever produced"—a very different thing from proposing that George Washington be made king and that the mercantile and landed gentry of the country be raised to an American peerage. The theme of Hamilton's speech was not that the Convention should plump for a monarchy but that it should screw up its courage and recommend a "high-toned" republican government to the country. To all intents and purposes, he proposed to take the best of both worlds—monarchism and republicanism—and to combine them into a single system of government.

It was not without regret that Hamilton acknowledged that the whole order and conjunction of circumstances in the United States was hostile to a king, lords and commons. It would have been so much easier for his purposes had Americans been willing to imitate the government of their late mother country. By so doing, he believed that they would escape the buffetings that awaited them on the uncharted seas of democracy. But he resigned himself to the fact that a people's destiny lies in their national character—and the character of Americans seemed to lead inevitably to democracy. And this point, Hamilton was inclined to say: "Let us pray."

When Hamilton submitted his outline of a plan of government to the Convention, he did not expect to stampede the delegates into adopting his views. While he hoped to induce the Convention to adopt a "high-toned system," he hardly hoped that they would go as high as he had just soared. He declared that his sketch was intended "not as a thing attainable by us, but as a model which we ought to approach as near as possible." Desirable as were a unitary government and a President and Senate holding office during good behavior, he confessed that they were more to be wished for than expected in a country such as the United States.

Nevertheless, he was persuaded that the people of the United States were ready to embrace something much more elevated than the Virginia and New Jersey plans. "I am convinced," he said, "that the public mind will support a solid plan"; even if it were not quite ready to go quite as far as he wished, he detected "certain circumstances now progressing which will give a different complexion to it." Among these circumstances he attached particular importance to the fact—as he saw it—that "the people are

The Constitutional Convention (1) 169

gradually ripening in their opinions of government. They begin to be tired to an excess of democracy." So swiftly was public opinion veering toward strong government that Hamilton expected that the time would soon come "when others as well as himself would join in the praise bestowed by Mr. Necker on the British Constitution, namely, that it is the only Government in the world which unites public strength with individual security."

In the light of later events, perhaps the most remarkable thing about Hamilton's speech to the Constitutional Convention was his conviction that his plan or anything remotely resembling it stood a chance of success. For he did not contemplate a *coup d'état*: the people, he acknowledged, must pass upon any plan of government drawn up by the Convention.

And yet, sanguine as it was, there was much to be said for Hamilton's assessment of the trend of public opinion. Who would have predicted in the summer of 1786 that a Constitutional Convention would meet in Philadelphia and that its first act would be figuratively to tear up the Articles of Confederation? In Hamilton's career, audacity had paid off handsomely; his life seemed to prove that the valorous were the favorites of fortune. He was simply inviting the Convention to do what he had done repeatedly —to aim as high as possible and to strain every nerve to attain the goal.

Even though public opinion was not prepared to support his plan, this was no reason, Hamilton argued, for the Convention to condemn it as impracticable or visionary. For the important question was not what kind of government the people would accept at that moment but what they would accept in six months' time when they would be called to act upon the plan recommended to them by the Convention. In short, said Hamilton, if the meeting saw fit to consider public opinion at all, it ought to take the public opinion of six months hence as its guide. With the scales dropping from the people's eyes, he believed they were beginning to see that the promises of democracy were a snare and a delusion. This, therefore, he exclaimed, was the moment for which the nationalists had long waited of "rescuing the American empire from disunion, anarchy and misery."

In thus baring his innermost political convictions to the Convention, Hamilton had no intention of taking the American people into his confidence. He had addressed himself to an assemblage of wise men bound to secrecy, and he had no idea that his words would go beyond them. Had the debates been divulged to the people, he pointed out, "much food would have been offered to inflammatory declamation. . . . Every infallible declaimer, taking his own ideas as the perfect standard, would have railed without measure or mercy at every member of the Convention who had gone a single line beyond his standard." Indeed, with the possible exception of James Madison, no member of the Convention had more to lose than did Hamilton from a publication of its proceedings; certainly no other delegate had done more to prejudice by his outspokenness the chances of the successful adoption of any plan the Convention might agree upon. Had Hamilton's speech been published in 1788, the declaimers against the proposed Constitution would have been given a whole arsenal of weapons with which to combat it.

And yet, as Hamilton soon learned, the Constitutional Convention was not the place to make a confession of political faith. Seldom has a statesman paid a higher price for having dared to express unpopular views honestly held. As Gouverneur Morris said, Hamilton's "generous indiscretion" in speaking his mind "subjected him to censure from misrepresentation. His speculative opinions were treated as deliberate designs." His speech in the Constitutional Convention continued to plague him for the rest of his life: what he had said in favor of republicanism was forgotten while his "speculative opinions" regarding monarchism were never permitted to be interred.

In later years, he described as "propositions made without due reflection" some of the ideas he had propounded in his speech of June 18. He repented his errors but, unfortunately for his political career, he did not learn from this experience the importance of keeping his unpopular political opinions to himself. Among these ill-advised "propositions," Hamilton gave prominent place to the idea of a President during good behavior. Very early in the history of the republic, Hamilton was forced to face the problem of how undesirable characters could be kept out of the presidency and vice-presidency. George Clinton, Thomas Jefferson and Aaron Burr—than whom in Hamilton's eyes no more dangerous malcontents existed—were soon pressing their claims for these high offices. A lifetime of either of these "enemies of order" was more than Hamilton cared to contemplate. Much of the despair he experienced after the election of 1800 was owing to his fear that Jefferson would occupy the presidency for life.

11.
The Constitutional Convention (2)

Although Hamilton spoke on June 18 with such magisterial and provocative assurance that some delegates felt that no young man had a right to imagine himself to be as right as Hamilton obviously did, his oratorical effort was generally well received. The longest speech delivered in the Constitutional Convention, it established his reputation as the Orator of Nationalism. "This American Cicero," later remarked an admirer, "is indeed one of the most remarkable geniuses of the Age. His Political knowledge exceeds, I believe, any Man in our Country, and his Oratorical abilities has pleased his friends and surprized his Enemies." For advanced ideas trenchantly and lucidly expressed, it was admitted, Hamilton was the man to listen to.

Of Hamilton's speech, one of the delegates observed that although the delegate from New York was praised by everyone, he was supported by none. In truth, however, Hamilton was not praised by everyone and he was supported by some.

By no means all the delegates approved of Hamilton's ideas even as pure theory. Such stanch supporters of the sovereign rights of the states as Luther Martin, Elbridge Gerry, George Mason, John Lansing and William Yates were horrified by Hamilton's suggestion that the states he reduced to administrative districts of the general government. Some of these same delegates felt that the gentleman from New York also deferred too much to the people. For, in general, the champions of the states wished to debar the people from directly electing any branch of the legislature: Roger Sherman of Connecticut, for example, wished that "the people should have as little to do as may be about the government. They want information and are constantly liable to be misled." After all, it was the people who had brought pressure upon the state legislatures to emit paper money and enact laws in favor of debtors. With these "crimes" against property fresh in their minds, few members of the Convention were inclined to give the people an unqualified vote of confidence; Hamilton's proposal that one branch be turned over to the people therefore seemed to be equivalent to admitting the enemy within the gates.[1]

The first reaction to Hamilton's speech came from the nationalists, the men upon whose support, it might be supposed, he could most confidently rely. In actuality, however, Hamilton had succeeded in putting Madison, Wilson and the other advocates of centralized government in an awkward position. For if the impression were established in the minds of the delegates that the nationalists intended to abolish the states, the partisans of the states could muster sufficient strength in the Convention to defeat any plan of centralized government. With good reason, therefore, Madison exclaimed that Hamilton was up to his old trick of letting the cat out of the bag; and this time the cat was a particularly ugly specimen that seemed quite capable of breaking up the Convention. To aggravate Madison's exasperation, he felt that Hamilton was gratuitously stirring up opposition to the Virginia Plan: until Hamilton undertook to take the Convention into his confidence, the supporters of that plan had been careful to avoid any imputations of seeking to establish a monarchy or a consolidated government. The bag Hamilton incautiously opened to the Convention contained nothing to which Madison was willing to admit ownership: the cat was a stray that the New Yorker had picked up somewhere—certainly not in Virginia—and smuggled into the Convention.

To undo the damage wrought by Hamilton's speech became to the nationalists an urgent necessity. Both Wilson and Madison took the floor to register their disapproval of the policies recommended by their colleague from New York. Madison declared that he prized the rights of the states as highly as he did civil liberties and James Wilson offered assurances that the states would not be swallowed up by the general government. The coexistence of the states and the federal government Wilson declared to be essential to good government in the United States: the country was too extensive to be ruled by a single authority; and if the states did not exist, the Convention would have to invent them. "Rome in her most powerful imperial state," he declared, "could not effectually pervade and protect every part of its dominions nor could the United States."

From the expostulations of his friends, Hamilton realized that he had spoken too candidly of his plans for centralizing power in the United States. He had laid violent hands upon the holy of holies, the sovereignty of the states, and the temple rocked upon its foundations.

Although the general tenor of his remarks tended to create the impression that he had recommended the annihilation of the states, in actuality, he had stopped short of that drastic measure. With the air of a man who seeks to put the record straight, Hamilton therefore took the floor to deny that he had ever advised "a total extinguishment of the State governments"; on the contrary, he said, he wished to preserve the states as administrative districts for the convenience of the general government. This was something less than reassuring to the partisans of the states; and Hamilton undid what-

The Constitutional Convention (2)   173

ever favorable effect his explanation might have achieved by adding that "even with corporate rights the States will be dangerous to the national government, and ought to be extinguished, new modified, or reduced to a smaller scale."[2]

Despite Madison's and Wilson's efforts to portray themselves as friends of the states, between them and Hamilton the proponents of state rights found little to choose. No members of the Convention were more eager than Madison and Wilson to give the federal government a negative upon state laws in all cases whatsoever; and Madison agreed with Hamilton that it was better to prevent the passage of a state law than to declare it void after it had been passed. True, Madison, Wilson and Morris did not propose to abolish the states, but they would have made them subordinate jurisdictions which, in the course of time, would probably have become little more than adjuncts of an all-embracing centralized government. With some justice, therefore, a member of the Constitutional Convention compared the nationalists' strategy to "the conduct of a number of jockeys who had thirteen young colts to break; they begin with the appearance of kindness, giving them a lock of hay, or a handful of oats, and stroaking them while they eat, until being rendered sufficiently gentle they suffer a halter to be put round their necks." Hamilton's approach, on the other hand, was to break the spirit of these mettlesome colts with a whip and then lock them up in the stable.[3]

Hamilton sinned less against the convictions of the nationalists than against their sense of the possible. Much as he deplored the Virginia Plan as the same old pork from which the Articles of Confederation had been cut, most of the delegates recognized that the American people were accustomed to this diet and would gag at the dish Hamilton proffered them. Despite his conviction that public opinion was moving rapidly in his direction, it was the impression of the Convention that he would remain well ahead of the procession for a long time to come. The delegates were aware that this was not a conclave of philosophers bent upon devising the best of all possible constitutions but that, like Solon, they were restricted to drawing the best frame of government the people would accept. "America," said Washington, "is like a distempered Patient, whose recovery depends upon the skill of the Physician," but the delegates perceived that the patient, far gone as he was, was still capable of resisting the medicine and throwing the physicians out of the door.

Hamilton's plan of making the states administrative districts of the central government had at least the merit of resolving the struggle between the large and small states. As he said, "the more close the Union of the States, and the more compleat the authority of the whole, the less opportunity will be allowed to the Stronger States to injure the weaker." The small states would have nothing to fear from their larger neighbors: they would all be in the same boat struggling for survival against Leviathan.[4]

Not surprisingly, therefore, Hamilton's ideas found advocates among some of the more nationally minded delegates from the small states. In particular, George Read of Delaware distinguished himself by the zeal with which he supported the gentleman from New York. Read had come to the Convention resolved to uphold the equality of the states; if it proved necessary to abandon this ground, he was prepared to make a strategic retreat to an all-powerful central government in which the sovereignty of the states was utterly dissolved.[5]

Fearful that the adoption of the Virginia Plan would lead to the annihilation of the small states, Read saw in Hamilton's plan a straw at which to clutch.* Rather than see the large states placed in a position to crush their smaller neighbors, Read told the Convention that he would support Hamilton's efforts to reduce the states to mere administrative districts, all of which would be equally impotent before the overtopping majesty of the central government. He even went beyond Hamilton in advocating the obliteration of the states.[6]

As an ally, Read was anything but a tower of strength to Hamilton. His speeches, remarked a member of the Convention, were "fatiguing and tiresome to the last degree; his voice is feeble, and his articulation so bad that few can have the patience to attend to him." After he had spoken it was seldom that anyone took the trouble to answer him; apparently he was written off as a harmless eccentric or as the Convention bore.

Except for these brief flare-ups, Hamilton's forensic effort created little stir. Having cleared themselves as well as they could of the charge of being Hamilton's accomplices in a plot to do away with the states, the nationalists were happy to drop his plan. In the main, his ideas had merely served to distract the Convention from its business of framing a Constitution that stood some chance of ratification by the people.[7]

After Hamilton's speech, the Convention turned its attention wholly to the knotty problem of state equality. Even though the New Jersey Plan was rejected, the delegates from the small states refused to yield in their demands for equality in both houses of Congress. It was plain that Hamilton's ultranationalistic ideas had not made the Virginia Plan appear by comparison more palatable to the champions of the states: Lansing declared that Hamilton's speech had confirmed his suspicions that the Virginia Plan

---

* A week before Hamilton spoke, George Read had declared that the only cure for the evils that plagued the country was to do away with the states altogether, "uniting them all into one great Society." Pierce Butler of South Carolina declared that if certain conditions were met, he was willing to "unite with Delaware (Mr. Read) in abolishing the State Legislatures and becoming one nation instead of a Confederacy of Republics."

The Constitutional Convention (2)

would establish a centralized despotism in which the states would be as effectually destroyed as even Hamilton could desire.[8]

Instead of pushing his own plan in the Convention, Hamilton found himself defending the Virginia Plan against the worrisome little terriers that nipped at its heels. He attempted to calm the small states by pointing out that Virginia, Massachusetts and Pennsylvania were so widely separated by geography, economic interests and social conditions that no combination among them was possible. Equally important, he reminded the delegates, was the fact that the struggle between the large and small states was "a contest for power, not for liberty." By accepting inequality, he conceded, some states would lose power—but this was inevitable because states as well as individuals, upon entering into society, "must give up a share of liberty to preserve the rest." Yet he would not agree that the citizens of the small states would be less free than the citizens of the large states under a consolidated national government.

It was of little avail to point out to the spokesmen of the small states that it was a contest for power—they already knew it and they were determined not to permit the large states to make off with the lion's share. The large states, on their part, insisted upon proportional representation in both houses of Congress; they, too, were in quest of power and they knew that power went to those strong enough to take it.

When the quarrel between the large and small states had reached a pitch of acrimony that threatened to break up the Convention, Benjamin Franklin, citing these differences of opinion as "a melancholy proof of the imperfection of the Human Understanding," suggested that the members call in a clergyman and pray for Divine assistance. Under different circumstances, Hamilton might have welcomed a resort to prayer, but at this stage of the proceedings he deemed it inadvisable for the Convention to allow the public to get the impression that the Convention was deadlocked. This, together with the fact that most of the delegates were more inclined to trust to human understanding, imperfect as it was, than to the intercession of Heaven, led to the defeat of Franklin's motion.*[9]

Nevertheless, it seemed that nothing short of Divine revelation could persuade the delegates of the small states that the large states would not join forces against them. Equality in both houses of Congress they held to

---

* An account written almost forty years later has Hamilton saying that "he did not see the necessity of calling in foreign aid!" Whereupon Washington is said to have "fixed his eye upon Hamilton with a mixture of surprise and indignation." But there are so many errors in this account as to render suspect the story, which is not mentioned in any contemporary version. During the Convention, Hamilton treated Franklin with marked respect, seconding a motion made by the old statesman to the effect that government officeholders be unpaid—"with the view," Hamilton said, "merely of bringing so respectable a proposition before the Committee, and which was besides enforced by arguments that had a certain degree of weight."

be essential to their survival: it was pointed out Nature had given the power of self-defense to "the smallest insect of the creation"—so why should it be denied Delaware? "Every argument which shows one man ought not to have more votes than another because he is wiser, stronger or wealthier," it was said, "proves that one state ought not to have more votes than another, because it is stronger, richer or more populous."

With the Convention stalemated over the issue of state equality, Hamilton perceived that there was no hope of winning the delegates to his views. Moreover, he was still obliged to carry those two old men of the sea, Yates and Lansing. They watched his every move with a vigilance that warmed the heart of Governor Clinton. Nothing he said upon the floor of the Convention that could be construed into evidence of his enmity to republicanism and the sovereign rights of the states was permitted to go unrecorded in their little black books.

Frustrated at every turn, Hamilton began to think of the wife and children and law cases he had left behind him. No longer willing to serve as a delegate without a vote—for this in effect was the consequence of the unit rule of state voting—Hamilton decided late in June to leave the City of Brotherly Love—now, unhappily, strife-torn—for the quieter atmosphere of New York City.

Shortly after Hamilton returned to New York, Yates and Lansing walked out of the Convention, swearing that there was a plot afoot to establish a "consolidated government" and that Hamilton was one of the chief conspirators. Their departure left New York unrepresented; nor did the state ever again cast a vote in the Convention. This was a far more serious loss to the state-rights faction than to the nationalists, for New York had long since been abandoned to the enemy by Madison, Wilson and Morris. Perhaps Madison even felt a certain relief in seeing Hamilton take the stage for New York—there were still some cats in the nationalists' bag that he was not eager to put on public display.

When Hamilton left Philadelphia on the morning of June 30, although the newspapers were saying that all was going well in the Convention and that the delegates were unanimous, in actuality, Madison admitted, they were "on the verge of dissolution, scarce held together by the strength of an hair." Having escaped from this unpromising scene, all too likely to become the graveyard of reputations, Hamilton was an object of envy to those who remained in Philadelphia: his friend Rufus King said that if he had gone with Hamilton he would have "escaped much vexation, enjoyed much pleasure and have gratified the earnest wishes & desires of Mrs. King." Washington, too, repented that he had ever agreed to attend the Convention; Mount Vernon had seldom seemed more attractive to him.

The situation, Washington wrote Hamilton on July 10, was rapidly growing worse and hardly a hope remained that a satisfactory frame of government would materialize unless every supporter of a strong government,

The Constitutional Convention (2)   177

including Hamilton, put his shoulder to the wheel. Washington's determination to establish a "high-toned" government had not diminished: "If to please the people," the Virginian asked, "we offer what we ourselves disapprove, how can we afterwards defend our work? Let us raise a standard to which the wise and honest can repair. The event is in the hands of God. . . . I am sorry you went away. I wish you were back." It was observed that Washington was even more solemn than usual: "his eye was fixed, and seemed to look into futurity." He did not like what he saw.

From the beginning of this dispute, the basis of compromise was apparent to both sides: if proportional representation were adopted as the rule for the House of Representatives, the equality of the states might be admitted in the Senate. But rather than accept this compromise, Hamilton, Madison, Wilson and the other nationalists were prepared to risk the breakup of the Convention. They intended the Senate to be the representative and custodian of property rights, not of state rights; and they were bent upon erecting a truly national government no part of which was derived from the states. In their eyes, state equality was the rotten part of the Articles of Confederation; to it they traced most of the evils of the day; and they assumed that any union of equal states was doomed to suffer the fate that overtook all confederations.

Hamilton's opposition to all measures that seemed likely to impair the powers of the central government became even more strenuous after his return to New York. His conviction that the people were ripe for a really "energetic" plan of government was reinforced by what he found in New York: "The prevailing apprehension among thinking men," he wrote Washington a few days after leaving the Convention, "is that the Convention, from a fear of shocking the popular opinion, will not go far enough. . . . No motley, or feeble measure can answer the end or will finally receive the public support. Decision is true wisdom and will be not less reputable to the Convention than salutary to the Convention than salutary to the Community." At the rate the Convention was jogging along, he feared that public opinion would leave it far in the rear. And this state of affairs, he exclaimed, was owing to a failure of nerve, a mistaken fear of offending the people. If only the members could feel, as did Hamilton, "the impulse from one extremity of the United States to the other" toward strong government, the Convention might yet take fortune at its flood.[10]

It was fortunate that the Convention did not permit itself to be persuaded by Hamilton's optimistic samplings of public opinion. At this time, the form of government under discussion was radically different from that which was finally adopted: it still incorporated a negative on state laws and gave virtually unlimited powers to the national government. Undoubtedly the small states were right: the plan as it then stood would have been rejected incontinently by the people and the Convention's work would have gone for naught.

Had Hamilton remained in the Constitutional Convention, there is little doubt that he would have resisted the adoption of the Great Compromise of July 16 by which proportional representation was made the rule in the House of Representatives and state equality was institutionalized in the Senate. Neither Washington, Franklin, Madison, Wilson or Gouverneur Morris favored this settlement; indeed, Madison continued to try to upset the compromise long after it had been adopted. It was not improbable that he would succeed, for the compromise was carried by the narrow margin of five states to four.

With the Convention still engaged in hammering out a Constitution—for the Great Compromise did not put an end to all differences of opinion among the delegates—Hamilton was eager to get back into the struggle. But returning to the Convention was not as simple as leaving it: if he went back with Yates and Lansing, he would be outnumbered; if he went without them, New York would not have a vote. When Lansing and Yates declined to accept Hamilton's invitation to return to Philadelphia, he decided to attend the Convention alone: New York would not be officially represented, but at least Hamilton could hope to affect the outcome by the weight of his personal influence.*

Certainly the delegates appeared to Hamilton to stand in need of an injection of boldness, courage and resolution. He returned to the Convention to find that his idea of a Senate to serve during good behavior had fallen stillborn. Gouverneur Morris, who, Madison remarked, shared Hamilton's fondness for "avowing his opinions when most at variance with those prevailing in the Convention," enthusiastically endorsed Hamilton's plan of life tenure for senators. Indeed, he made it his hobby and rode it so indefatigably that he left even Hamilton, who was by this time prepared to compromise on a nine-year term for senators, far behind. However, the Convention rejected Morris' plan for a Senate for life; six years was the term finally fixed upon.

But the sharpest conflict in the Convention occurred over the powers and the method of electing the President. For these problems, it is true, Hamilton had provided a solution, but it found little favor among the delegates. The prevailing opinion was that the President should be elected by the National Legislature for a term of seven years and should thereafter be ineligible for a second term. This, of course, was the method specified by the Virginia Plan, which even after the adoption of the Great Compromise continued to provide the delegates with a framework.

On September 6, the Convention adopted the report of a committee which, as regards the Executive Branch, almost wholly rewrote the Virginia

---

* Hamilton was in and out of the Convention during the month of August. About the middle of the month, he went to New York but returned to Philadelphia on September 5 or 6. His appeal to Yates and Lansing was made on August 20.

The Constitutional Convention (2)   179

Plan. The President was to be elected for a term of four years; he was to be eligible for re-election; and the choice of President and Vice-President was given to an electoral college elected by the people. At the same time, the powers of the President were enlarged at the expense of the Senate. That body was now associated with the President in functions over which it had hitherto been given exclusive jurisdiction: the President was now accorded a part in the treaty-making power and he was endowed with authority to appoint the members of the Supreme Court with the consent of the Senate.

The presidency, as it took form during the last days of the Constitutional Convention, represented a triumph for the ideas of Madison, Hamilton, Morris and Wilson. And yet, like all Hamilton's political victories, it was won in the shadow of George Washington. As a delegate remarked, the Convention would not have invested the President with such incalculable powers "had not the members cast their eyes towards General Washington as President; and shaped their ideas of the powers to be given to a president, by their opinion of his virtue." Hamilton's vision of philosopher-President was not altogether fanciful: the reality seemed in fact to be at that moment presiding over the deliberations of the Constitutional Convention.

In creating the Electoral College, the members of the Convention did not believe that, except in the case of General Washington, the electors themselves would make the final choice of a President. Because of sectional and state loyalties—every state was expected to put forward a favorite son—it seemed improbable that a majority of the Electoral College would be able to agree upon a candidate. In that event, it would devolve upon the Senate —the body to which the Convention at first assigned this function—to select the President and Vice-President from among the five highest candidates. The real President-maker, therefore, would not be the Electoral College but the Senate.[11]

This prospect alarmed Hamilton: if the Senate elected the President, he would be dependent for his existence upon a single house of the legislature and brought within the orbit of the states. Between the Senate and the President, Hamilton pointed out, there already existed a close connection: the President was empowered to make appointments with the advice and consent of the Senate. "Here then," he exclaimed, "is a mutual connection and influence, that will perpetuate the President, and aggrandize both him and the Senate."*[12]

* This was the more certain because of the requirement inserted in the Constitution that the electors should vote for two persons for President, one of whom should not be of the state voting. Although the Convention adopted Hamilton's suggestion of indirect election of the President by the people, the Electoral College was not of his contriving. Hamilton wished to divide the country into electoral districts without regard to state boundaries, but the plan devised by the Convention provided that the number of electors allotted to each state should be determined by the number of senators and representatives sent by the state to Congress.

Rather than turn over the election of the President to either house of Congress, Hamilton wished to give the office to the man who received the highest number of votes in the Electoral College, even though he fell short of a majority. A President elected by a minority of the Electoral College was to him infinitely preferable to a President elected by a majority of the Senate alone. But here, as in other instances, the Convention was obliged to effect a compromise between the demands of the large and small states, with the result that it ordained that the election should ultimately devolve upon the House of Representatives, each state voting as a unit.

During these final days of the Convention, Hamilton's efforts were not directed solely toward strengthening the monarchic and aristocratic elements in the plan of government. Fearing, as he said, that "the connections between the President and Senate would tend to perpetuate him, by corrupt influence," he tried to make the House of Representatives a more effective check upon the President and Senate by increasing the number of representatives. "He held it essential," he declared, "that the popular branch of it should be on a broad foundation. He was strenuously of the opinion that the House of Representatives was on so narrow a scale as to be really dangerous, and to warrant a jealousy in the people for their liberties"—a sentiment hardly to be expected from a man who has been accused of planning a system of government in which the poor and the rich had mutual checks, "with the rich doing about four fifths of the checking."[13]

In actuality, Hamilton sought to make the House of Representatives as democratic as possible—to concentrate, as it were, all the passions, prejudices and "volatile humors" of the body politic in one branch where it could be controlled by the aristocratic and monarchic branches of the government. The House of Representatives would thus become a sort of hospital for incurable democrats: here demagogues could rant and "middling politicians" play party politics without doing essential damage to the state. As long as there were adequate safeguards against "democratic licentiousness," Hamilton did not fear even manhood suffrage. In fact, he welcomed it, for as he later said, "The fabric of American empire ought to rest on the solid basis of THE CONSENT OF THE PEOPLE. The streams of national power ought to flow immediately from that pure original fountain of all legislative authority." His ideal was a system in which all the advantages of democracy could be enjoyed without the pains and penalties usually associated with that state— a system in which the people had confidence in the government and yet were unable to bend it to their will. Then—and only then—would democracy be made safe for the United States.*

---

* In the closing days of the Convention, Hamilton indicated what changes he would like to see made in the Constitution. One of the most significant alterations he proposed was to elect the House of Representatives by manhood suffrage. This innovation reflected his conviction that the franchise was "one of the most important rights of the subject, and,

The Constitutional Convention (2)

The Articles of Confederation required the unanimous approval of the states for any change in the fundamental law. Yet nothing was clearer to the members of the Constitutional Convention than that the approval of all thirteen states would not be given the new plan of government: Rhode Island, New York or some other state was certain to raise the cry of "Liberty" and strangle the Constitution at birth. Therefore, rather than condemn its work to certain oblivion, the Convention decreed that the new government should go into effect after nine states had ratified.

Hereupon Hamilton, the daring young man who had dazzled the delegates with the audacity of his ideas, unexpectedly displayed a sudden regard for legality. Although he did not demand that the unanimous consent of the thirteen states be required for the adoption of the Constitution, he refused to go along with those who held that the assent of nine states was sufficient. The latter course he pronounced to be too flagrant a violation of the Articles of Confederation to be acceptable to the states: instead of facilitating the ratification of the Constitution, it seemed to him to condemn it to defeat. There was no getting round that phrase which declared the Articles of Confederation to be "perpetual," he said; and no plea of necessity could alter the fact that it was "wrong to allow nine states to institute a new Government on the ruins of the existing one." He therefore proposed a compromise: each state legislature ought to be asked to propose to the state convention that the Constitution, if adopted, should take effect as soon as nine states had ratified. By this gesture, he believed that the onus of illegality would be removed and that the Constitution would be carried to triumph, for, he predicted, "no convention convinced of the necessity of the plan will refuse to give it effect on the adoption by nine states."

Never had Hamilton's friends expected to see him display such squeamishness. The young hotspur who had pronounced the Articles of Confederation dead beyond recall now seemed unaware of the fact that the Convention was in reality invoking the right of revolution. Hamilton's efforts to preserve some shreds of legality, while they could not disguise the nature of the deed,

---

in a republic, ought to stand foremost in the estimation of the law. It is that right by which we exist as a free people." He defined liberty in another place as the right to share in the government: "being naturally equal," he said, men ought to enjoy equality in rights: "every man having evidence of attachment to and permanent common interest with the society ought to share in all its rights and privileges."

As a counterpoise to the democracy of the House of Representatives, Hamilton stipulated in his second thoughts on the Constitution that only landowners were to be permitted to vote for senatorial electors and that land ownership or personal property to the value of $1,000 was to be required of those who voted for presidential electors. To his specially qualified electorate winnowed from the masses was assigned the duty of ensuring that the Senate should "come from and represent, the wealth of the Nation" and that the President would be a man of wealth who possessed a deep sympathy for and understanding of the problems of the rich. The Senate and the President were expected to bridle the turbulent democrats in the House of Representatives, thereby achieving a synthesis of those irreconcilable elements—democracy and stability.

might very well succeed in defeating it. Thus, exclaimed James Wilson, "after spending four or five months in the laborious and arduous task of forming a government for our country, we are ourselves at the close throwing insuperable obstacles in the way of its success." The Convention's decision was to stand upon the ground that its work was merely recommendatory; everything was to be submitted to the people for their approval and "the disapprobation of this supreme authority would destroy it forever; its approbation blot out antecedent errors and irregularities."[14]

When the completed Constitution was laid before the delegates, many were obliged to make an agonizing reappraisal of their political convictions. If a declaration expressive of total satisfaction with the Constitution and confidence in its workability had been exacted of every delegate before signing, there would have been very few signatures affixed to the document. It was wholly satisfactory to none, and the views of no section or interest had prevailed completely. Many delegates took the Constitution as did Gouverneur Morris: for better or for worse, as a man takes a wife; but, what few men do with their wives, taking it knowing all its bad qualities.

Few members present found the plan of government further removed from their own ideas regarding the kind of government the country needed than did Hamilton. He believed that the Convention had given the people the government not most conducive to their happiness but most acceptable to their prejudices. Nevertheless, he had never taken the position that he would refuse to approve a frame of government that fell short of his ideas: from the beginning, he was resigned to accepting something short of perfection. He was not so much a philosopher in politics as a politician with a philosophy: above all, he was a realist who recognized that when the ideal was unobtainable, it was necessary to make do with the second best.

Even though he disdained to claim any paternity for the poor starveling that the Convention was about to send forth into the world—"no man's ideas," he said, "were more remote from the plan than his were known to be"—he did not refuse to sign the birth certificate. On the contrary, he told the Convention that he would support it before the country as zealously as though it were his own work. Whatever private doubts and misgivings the delegates might feel toward the frame of government they had created, Hamilton advised them to look upon it as a choice "between anarchy and convulsion on one side, and the chance of good to be expected from the plan on the other." On the ground that a vote against the Constitution was a vote in favor of anarchy and convulsion, he urged the delegates to sign unanimously.[15]

Three members of the Convention felt such an unconquerable aversion to the projected frame of government that they refused to affix their signatures. As for Hamilton, although he had no power to sign for New York—

The Constitutional Convention (2)

that state was not officially present at the Convention—he signed as an individual. This action took courage: as Hamilton said later, he was well aware at the time that he was going "against the prevailing weight of the official influence of the state, and against what probably would be the opinion of a large majority of his fellow-citizens, till better information should correct their first impressions." As a result, the Constitution was ratified by the unanimous assent of eleven states and Colonel Hamilton of New York.

The fact that Hamilton suppressed his misgivings about the Constitution and became one of its most ardent advocates does not prove that he was an adventurer. He did not prostitute himself to serve a cause in which he did not believe, for he had dedicated himself to the cause of union. To him, the Philadelphia plan was a means to an end: if it was not the perfect union of which he dreamed, it represented a step in the right direction. No doubt, as a practicing attorney, Hamilton was capable of serving as counsel for a client about the justice of whose cause he entertained private doubts. But this was not his attitude toward the Constitution: if he lost this case he feared that the union would be condemned to suffer the extreme penalty. Never before had he taken a brief upon the outcome of which so much depended.

By volunteering to defend the Constitution despite his strong preference for a form of government more closely approximating that of Great Britain, Hamilton revealed that "spirit of accommodation" to which Washington attributed the success of the Convention. It is perhaps the most convincing evidence of statesmanship that he ever gave. "If mankind were to resolve to agree in no institution of government, until every part of it had been adjusted to the most exact standard of perfection," he observed, "society would soon become a general scene of anarchy, and the world a desert." A more immediate consequence would be the destruction of the American union. For these reasons, he concluded that it would be "the extreme of imprudence to prolong the precarious state of our national affairs and to expose the Union to the jeopardy of successive experiments, in the chimerical pursuit of a perfect plan."

Expediency alone would have counseled Hamilton to champion the cause of the Constitution. Had he sulked in his tent because he did not agree with the Convention's work, he would have forfeited all hope of playing a part in the new government and his influence upon the shaping of the American future would have been inconsequential. When that future came to be molded, Hamilton had no intention of being a mere bystander.

12.

The Federalist

When Hamilton engaged himself in the last days of the Constitutional Convention to support the Constitution, he was making no idle promise. Indeed, even while the Constitution was in an embryonic stage, Hamilton had come to its defense. He was often accused of impetuosity and precipitancy, and the charge never seemed to be better founded than when he undertook to plead the cause of the Constitution before he or anyone else knew what form it would take. In fact, at the time Hamilton first spoke out, it seemed probable that the Convention would have nothing whatever to show for its labors.

In July, 1787, when Hamilton reported from New York that the tide of nationalism was running strong and that a "high toned" government was within the reach of the Convention, he was obliged to admit that Governor Clinton was still stubbornly breasting the current. After Yates and Lansing returned to New York with the news that a plot was afoot in Philadelphia to establish a consolidated government, Clinton was certain that his worst fears were about to be realized. Privately he told his friends that he expected that if the Convention produced a plan it would "only serve to throw the country into confusion." In that event, Clinton advised his followers to rally round the Articles of Confederation, which, with a few minor changes, offered the best hope of peace and freedom to the country.

When Clinton's remarks were reported to Hamilton—he never claimed that his information was anything more than hearsay—he was outraged that a mere "demagogue" like Clinton should presume to set his own judgment against that of the "collected wisdom" of America and attempt to prejudice the people against a Constitution that was still on the drafting table. In order to disqualify the governor as a critic of the finished product, Hamilton charged in the New York *Daily Advertiser* of June 21, 1787, that Clinton was guilty of prejudging the work of the Constitutional Convention. From such an inveterate enemy of nationalism, Hamilton asserted, the people of New York would never receive the dispassionate, unprejudiced, reasoned judgment that the occasion required.

The Federalist

As Hamilton expected—and had in a sense ensured by his newspaper article—Clinton, writing in the New York newspapers as "Cato," attacked the Constitution soon after it made its appearance. Hamilton, in turn, answered "Cato" under the pseudonym of "Caesar." In choosing this name it is possible that Hamilton had in mind the fact that Cato committed suicide at the approach of the victorious Caesar. However historically appropriate, Hamilton's decision to appear in the guise of Caesar was unfortunate. Even more unfortunate were the words he put into the mouth of "Caesar."

As "Caesar," Hamilton made sure that he, for one, would never be mistaken for a demagogue. He candidly avowed that he was "not much attached to the majesty of the multitude" and that he would never seek to gain "influence by cajoling the unthinking mass . . . and ringing in their ears the gracious sound of their absolute Sovereignty. I despise the trick of such dirty policy." Instead of flattering the people, Hamilton announced his intention of instructing them in salutary "truths" regardless of how unpalatable they might be. Obviously, by adopting this course he was certain to make himself unpopular, but Hamilton always acted upon the assumption that in an argument with Governor Clinton to be unpopular was to be right.

In actuality, Hamilton relished this opportunity of speaking his mind—frankness was always his strong point and he was happiest when he was laying bare his inmost political convictions. "I know this is blunt and ungracious reasoning," he declared, "but since my own heart does not reproach me, I shall not be very solicitous about its reception."

How little solicitude he felt on this score was shown by the enthusiasm with which he gratuitously impugned the wisdom of the sovereign people. The construction of a Constitution, involving as it did the erection of safeguards against arbitrary power on the one hand and "popular licentiousness" on the other, was not, he remarked, a task to which the people could do justice: only a group of experts such as that which had been assembled in Philadelphia had the knowledge and skill necessary for such an exacting undertaking. With this proposition there could be little disagreement; but Hamilton, not content with stating a mere truism, advanced to more questionable ground. Not only were the people incompetent to draw up an effective Constitution: they could not even pass intelligently upon its merits. To those of his countrymen who fancied that Americans were a cut above the common run of mankind, Hamilton administered a nasty shock: "The mass of the people of America," he asserted, "(any more than the mass of other countries) cannot judge with any degree of precision concerning the fitness of this New Constitution to the peculiar situation of America." Such judgment, he said, required "men of good education and deep reflection"—by definition, a small part of the population. The sooner the people recognized their shortcomings, Hamilton implied, the better it would be for all concerned: instead of presuming to judge that which they did not understand, they would be well advised to accept the Constitution from the hands of their wise men and offer thanks for the gift of this "bark that may, by the blessings of Heaven, carry them to that port of rest and happiness" to which they aspired. "Gratitude and approbation" were all that he asked of them; they could mar but never improve the proposed instrument of government.

If the people refused to "just take it as it is and be thankful," Hamilton intimated that they might find something worse forced upon them at the bayonet's point. It was better, "Caesar" ominously remarked, that Washington should be induced to accept of the presidency of the new government, than that he "should be solicited again to accept of the command of *an army*." He hardly needed to remind Americans that armies seldom paid regard to civil liberties and that a constitution drawn up by the victors in a civil war was not likely to give satisfaction to the losers.

In uttering this warning, Hamilton was not animated by fondness for military coercion but by a conviction that Clinton's tactics would lead to anarchy and bloodshed, thus assuring that the army would be called upon to restore order. "The misguided people never reflect during this frenzy," he declared, "that the moment they become riotous, they renounce, from that moment, their independence, and commence vassals to their ambitious leaders." Under such circumstances, he thought that they might account it a blessing if they were relieved from the tyranny of Clinton and other demagogues by an army. But his purpose was to ensure that the change of government should be effected peacefully, not by an army, even though it were led by a Cincinnatus like Washington.[1]

By raising the subject of military despotism as an alternative to the adoption of the Constitution, Hamilton gave Clinton an opportunity to portray him as something far more sinister than a brash and intolerant young man. "Caesar," Clinton exclaimed, was living up to his reputation as an advocate of forceful methods of persuasion. "If perchance you should happen to differ from Caesar," asked the governor, "are you to have Caesar's principles crammed down your throats with an army?"

In the exhilaration of flaying Governor Clinton and exposing the delinquencies of the people, Hamilton seemed to have lost sight of the main objective—securing the adoption of the Federal Constitution. Certainly this end was not furthered by branding the governor a demagogue and his followers dupes; the people of New York were not likely to take kindly to being called fools or to think more highly of the Federal Constitution because one of its warmest advocates insisted upon reviling the governor who, incidentally, was the most popular man in the state. Inadvertently, Hamilton had hit upon a method almost certain to bring about the defeat of the Constitution. At the Constitutional Convention, he had missed his oppor-

The Federalist

tunity of becoming one of the leading architects of the new government; now he seemed about to throw away his chance of being an effective advocate of the Constitution.

As "Caesar," Hamilton appeared in the guise of a dogmatic, swaggering, intolerant young man, fond to a fault of parading his opinions as irrefutable truths. Had this been the sum total of his personality, he would have been deservedly set down as an insufferable egotist. And yet, even though he generally succeeded in keeping it under control, this *was* an aspect of Hamilton's character; and it was always just below the surface, ready to propel him into a false position.

Having penetrated Hamilton's disguise, the Clintonians started a backfire against him by spreading the report that this self-styled "Caesar" was a mere adventurer who had palmed himself off upon Washington but who, when his true character was made apparent to the Commander in Chief, had been kicked out of headquarters. This was shrewd strategy: nothing could have been more damaging to Hamilton at this juncture than proof that he had lost Washington's esteem. Moreover, there was enough truth in the charge that he had insulted Washington to make him regret bitterly that he had ever permitted his temper to run away with him at Morristown. When Hamilton pleaded with Washington to refute the canards that were being disseminated by the Clintonians, the former Commander in Chief left no doubt that in his eyes the whole affair was a deplorable lapse from the high standards that ought to prevail among public men, however great their differences. The situation of the country urgently required unanimity, he told Hamilton, and "Gentlemen of talents and character" should seek to compose their quarrels in the interests of national harmony. However, he did give Hamilton a statement denying that the younger man had attempted to worm his way into confidence at headquarters and that he had forfeited Washington's confidence. Armed with this testimonial from Mount Vernon, Hamilton defied the Clintonians to produce "a single instance of his conduct, public or private, inconsistent with the strictest rules of integrity and honor."[2]

While Hamilton, imperfectly concealed under the sobriquet of "Caesar," was exchanging blows with George Clinton, the opponents of the proposed Constitution began to rush into print. In the autumn of 1787, Elbridge Gerry, George Mason and Richard Henry Lee undertook to prove to the American people that they were being asked to surrender their liberties to a "consolidated government." With critics of such caliber subjecting the work of the Constitutional Convention to hostile scrutiny, it was obvious that the friends of the Constitution could not afford to waste their shot upon George Clinton.

Although some of Hamilton's friends applauded "Caesar's" efforts to "stem the torrent of folly and iniquity"—at this time, his name appeared prominently in a list of names published in a New York newspaper of distinguished Americans worthy of consideration as the first President of the United States—others deplored the turn the dispute had taken. "Caesar's" tactics were not the way John Jay and James Madison planned to win friends for the Constitution. At the same time that Hamilton was disparaging the wisdom of the people, Jay was saying that there was "a degree of intelligence and information in the mass of our people which affords much room for hope" and that the best hope of securing the ratification of the Constitution lay in rational argument rather than in the vilification of its opponents; the merits of the new frame of government were of greater moment than the demerits of George Clinton and his party.

To permit Governor Clinton—or, indeed, anyone else—to have the last word ran against Hamilton's grain. But he could hardly fail to see that he had embarked upon a fruitless controversy with the governor and that it was time to strike out upon a wholly new line of argument. Accordingly, in his second "Caesar" article, he announced that this would be the last time that he would enter the lists against "Cato"—an admission which the Clintonians seized upon to prove that "as soon as ever 'Cato' came freely to discuss the merit of the Constitution, 'Caesar' retreated and disappeared."[3]

Hamilton retreated but he certainly did not disappear. Before the Clintonians had finished celebrating their triumph he was back in the fight under a new name and with a much more formidable weapon than "Caesar" had ever put into action. Ten days after Hamilton buried "Caesar," the first number of *The Federalist* appeared in the New York *Independent Journal* of October 27, 1787.

With a happier choice of classical nomenclature than he had revealed in the case of "Caesar," Hamilton chose to address the public under the name "Publius." The original Publius Valerius was the hero who established a just and stable republican government after the fall of Tarquin, the last king of Rome. Of this champion of free government, Plutarch said: "He resolved to render the government, as well as himself, instead of terrible, familiar and pleasant to the people" by assuaging their fears of oppression.

Nothing more strikingly revealed the protean character of Alexander Hamilton than the speed with which he cast off the toga of "Caesar" and donned that of "Publius." As a quick-change artist, he had few peers among public men. With this change, the controversy was abruptly transferred to another plane: from a name-calling tavern brawl—"a torrent of angry and malignant passions"—it became a penetrating analysis of the proposed Constitution, conducted in the atmosphere of a calm and dispassionate enquiry into truth. While Hamilton was at home in both worlds, he was well advised to quit the rough-and-tumble of popular debate in which Clinton excelled for the empyrean heights of constitutional discussion

The Federalist

where the governor and his hatchet men could not follow him.

"Caesar" and "Publius" are the two personalities which struggled for mastery in Hamilton: the highly emotional, arrogant, and intolerant spirit that inspired his outburst against Clinton and the fair-minded apostle of reason that was "Publius." While "Caesar" had seemed more inclined to crush forcibly all opposition to the Constitution than to argue the case, "Publius" wrote in the great tradition of political literature.[4]

While Hamilton had never before called upon his friends for literary aid, he saw that the work of moving the "mountains of prejudice" that stood in the way of the adoption of the Constitution in New York was more than he could accomplish singlehanded. His first choice of a collaborator was John Jay; and, as the plan expanded, he called upon Gouverneur Morris and William Duer. Although Morris had been an active member of the Convention—he had spoken at greater length than any other delegate—Duer had not been in Philadelphia and knew no more of the proceedings of the Convention than Hamilton and others chose to tell him. But Morris declined the honor and Duer, after contributing a few articles signed "Philo-Publius," was dropped from the team.

Jay, Morris and Duer—obviously Hamilton's purpose was to enlist the services in this enterprise of men acquainted with the peculiar problems of New York. Since at this time Hamilton intended to address New Yorkers upon the subject of the proposed Constitution, it was natural that he should try to assemble a group of writers composed largely of citizens of that state. Morris's refusal, and Hamilton's recognition that Duer's talents as an expounder of the Constitution left much to be desired, obliged him to look further afield for a collaborator. His eye fell upon James Madison of Virginia, who was in New York City attending the session of the Continental Congress.

The selection of Madison vastly enlarged the scope of the undertaking. Not only was Madison a Southerner and therefore unable to approach the Constitution from the point of view of a New Yorker, but he also contributed a broad philosophical insight that helped to elevate these essays far above the polemical writings of the day.

No state secret could have been more closely guarded than was the authorship of *The Federalist* papers. Even Hamilton's best friends did not know what he was doing; if he seemed busier than usual, it was ascribed to the flourishing state of his law practice. Only to Washington did Hamilton reveal that he was "Publius" or a part thereof, but even here he displayed a reticence almost unprecedented among men of letters when discussing their work.

Although he could hardly be said to have acted in the capacity of a general editor, Hamilton did establish a rough division of labor. Each writer worked in the field with which he was most familiar and competent. Particularly this was true of John Jay, to whom, as the former Secretary for Foreign Affairs, was allotted the discussion of the relations of the proposed federal government with foreign powers. To himself Hamilton assigned the task of exposing the deficiencies of the Articles of Confederation—a task as congenial as it was familiar. While Hamilton prided himself upon his knowledge of Greek and Roman history and had often put it to good advantage in drawing analogies between ancient and modern confederacies, he now professed himself eager to quit "the dim light of historical research" in order to follow "the dictates of reason and good sense." Perhaps this decision was prompted by the fact that Madison was even better equipped as an historian than was Hamilton; the Virginian had long acted upon the advice of Aristotle that a statesman who seeks to remedy an existing constitution must be familiar with all forms of government. In consequence, to Madison was allocated the discussion of ancient, medieval and modern confederacies—a theme which afforded him an unexampled opportunity of displaying his erudition, somewhat at the expense, it is to be feared, of making proselytes to the Constitution.[5]

In keeping with the authors' aristocratic predilections, *The Federalist* was addressed to a select audience: only men of good will and open minds who joined "to a sincere zeal for the happiness of their country, a temper favorable to a just estimation of the means of promoting it" were worthy of "Publius's" attention. Hamilton declared that he spoke "to all men of reflection, who can divest themselves of the prepossessions of preconceived opinions" and "to dispassionate and discerning men"—by his standards, a small minority of the population.[6]

The nature of the audience determined the tone in which *The Federalist* was written. Since "Publius" did not aspire to reach the mass mind, Hamilton dropped the knockdown arguments which as "Caesar" he had deemed suited for popular consumption and adopted instead the rounded periods, the opulence, the stateliness and the magisterial air that distinguished the prose of the Augustan age. In *The Federalist,* the stylistic overtones were supplied by Gibbon, Bolingbroke and Dr. Samuel Johnson; and so steeped were Hamilton, Jay and Madison in these literary conventions that their respective essays were practically indistinguishable in style.*[7]

By addressing themselves to "the men of intelligence, patriotism, property, and independent circumstances," Hamilton and Madison supposed that they

* In 1804, among Hamilton's unsettled affairs was the question of the authorship of the essays that had appeared under the signature of "Publius." With death not far away, Hamilton's thoughts turned to *The Federalist* papers, his only hope of enduring literary fame. Two days before he was to meet Burr, Hamilton called upon his friend Egbert Benson and concealed, in such a way that it was certain to be found sooner or later, a slip of paper indicating the author of each of the eighty-five essays. Presumably owing to his hurry and agitation of mind, Hamilton claimed credit for writing sixty-three of the essays, thereby relegating Madison and Jay to the status of assistants.

The Federalist

were contributing far more toward the adoption of the Constitution than if they had tried to write down to the level of the popular mind. There still existed in the United States a tradition of aristocratic leadership handed down from colonial times; deference was paid the educated, well born and the rich, and the common people were expected to take their political opinions from their betters, especially in such complicated matters as those contained in the Constitution. As Madison said, "There are subjects to which the capacities of the bulk of mankind are unequal, and on which they must and will be governed by those with whom they happen to have acquaintance and confidence. The proposed Constitution is of this description." Instead of consulting the collective wisdom of the people, therefore, the authors of *The Federalist* sought to inform the more intelligent part of the population, persuaded that by this means wisdom would filter down to the masses. And since it was assumed that all "sober & steady people, even of the lower order," were so weary of the injustice, folly and mutability of democracy that they would welcome any change that promised stability and repose, they would be the more willing to listen to their superiors in rank, wealth and education when the proposed Constitution was brought up for discussion.

It may have been true, that in Virginia, as Madison said, the mass of the people were "accustomed to be guided by their rulers on all new and intricate questions." But in New York, the popular leaders were Governor Clinton and his partisans; if they were permitted to make the decision, the proposed Constitution would be given short shrift indeed. Of necessity, therefore, Hamilton had to appeal from the rulers to the people, but "the people" were an intellectual elite which spoke the same language as "Publius."[8]

It was Hamilton's intention that the three writers should meet at his house at the corner of Wall Street and Broadway for consultation before dispatching their work to the printer. But the necessity of meeting the printer's deadline soon put an end to this happy arrangement: the papers were frequently dispatched without benefit of prior discussion. As a result, sometimes the left hand of "Publius" did not know what the right hand was doing. Hamilton apologized for "the violations of method and repetitions of ideas which cannot but displease a critical reader" inevitable in the haphazard and unsystematical way in which *The Federalist* came into the world, but the most remarkable thing about this work is not that it is marred by repetitions, abrupt transitions and lapses in continuity but that these faults are not more apparent.[9]

Despite the appearance of leisured, philosophical calm, *The Federalist* papers were actually written in hot haste in moments snatched from the exacting duties of a law practice or attendance upon the Continental Congress. It is said that Hamilton wrote the first number on the deck of a sailing vessel on which he was traveling up the Hudson. If that is true, some of the later essays were written under far less felicitous circumstances.

"Publius" at first appeared twice a week, but Hamilton soon saw that the pace must be stepped up if the ground he had set for himself and his colleagues was to be covered. After a brave start, Jay fell ill and made no further contribution except No. 64. Nevertheless, Hamilton announced that "Publius" would be published four times a week—let any Antifederalist try to match that output. None did, but on the other hand, the effort nearly killed him. The weekly stint taxed Hamilton so heavily that on several occasions the printer waited in the anteroom while the harassed author dashed off the concluding paragraph or gave his work a last-minute polishing. The press devoured his work as fast as he could turn it out; at times, "Publius" might well have seemed to Hamilton to be an inexorable taskmaster from whom he yearned to be free.

Hastily written as *The Federalist* papers were, they were not the product of hasty thought. On the contrary, they stemmed from the experience, the hard thinking and the intensive study of comparative government that Hamilton, Madison and Jay had engaged in during the preceding years. Their ideas were clearly formulated and organized when they sat down to write, and Hamilton and Madison had the added advantage of being able to draw upon their firsthand knowledge of the debates that had taken place in the Constitutional Convention.[10]

"Publius" grew far beyond the dimensions Hamilton had originally contemplated. When he first contracted with Archibald McLean, the printer, for printing and binding *The Federalist,* he projected twenty, at the most twenty-five, essays. In actuality, eighty-five essays were written, and the cost of publication, at first estimated at £30, reached £220.

With the beginning of the winter term of the New York Supreme Court on January 8, 1788, Hamilton took a long vacation from "Publius" in order to attend to his law practice and to his duties as a member of the Continental Congress, to which he had been elected early in 1788. In his absence, Madison wrote Nos. 37 to 58 without a break. Thus, while Hamilton was pleading cases at law and sitting in the Continental Congress, the work of rendering the work of the Philadelphia Convention "familiar and pleasant to the people" devolved wholly upon Madison. But in March, 1788, Madison left New York, leaving Hamilton, the sole survivor of the four collaborators, with the responsibility for keeping the presses supplied with material.

Madison's departure meant that some of the most important sections of *The Federalist*—among them, the detailed exposition of the Constitution—fell to Hamilton. As a result, it was Hamilton who undertook to elucidate the powers of the Chief Executive, the Senate and the Judiciary, and who expounded the theory of judicial review. In dealing with these vital matters, Hamilton was to all intents and purposes "Publius." To this accident was owing some of the most distinctive features of American federalism.

13.

The Rule of Law

Despite the strong aversion Hamilton felt for federalism, he now gladly took the name of "Federalist." By so doing he was not as inconsistent as might appear: the Constitution created a new kind of federalism—a mixture of nationalism and federalism which stands as the most distinctively American contribution to the science of government. Sovereignty was divided between the general and state governments and each was made independent in its sphere; some functions were placed exclusively in the hands of the central government, others were assigned wholly to the states and a third group of powers was shared concurrently by both jurisdictions.

If it was the part of wisdom for Hamilton and his party to take the name "Federalists," it was nothing less than a master stroke to call the opponents of the proposed Constitution "Antifederalists." With considerable justice, the "Antifederalists" asserted that they were the real Federalists and that the proponents of the Constitution had appropriated a name to which they had no title. In the struggle over the Constitution, both sides claimed to be federalists: apparently there were neither Antifederalists nor Nationalists in the country.[1]

At the beginning of *The Federalist,* Hamilton sounded the note of high solemnity that pervaded the entire work. The questions to be decided by the American people, he said, were as important as any that had ever confronted a people: whether the union was to survive and whether "societies of men are really capable or not of establishing good government from reflection and choice, or whether they are forever destined to depend for their political constitutions on accident and force." A wrong decision, therefore, could be accounted a "general misfortune of mankind"; what Americans did and said at this critical moment of their history might well decide the fate of free government throughout the world.[2]

Despite the urgency of the occasion, "Publius'" proselyting was pitched in a calm, restrained and moderate key: he consistently appealed to the reason rather than to the emotions of his readers. It was the very antithesis of the technique of the supersalesman. In keeping with this spirit of temperate advocacy, "Publius" did not pretend that the Constitution was perfect: while it was "more perfect" than the Articles of Confederation, it admittedly fell considerably short of perfection. If this were damning with faint praise, "Publius" was prepared to incur that fault rather than claim more for the Constitution than he himself believed. He did insist, however, that on the whole it was a good Constitution and certainly "the best that the present views and circumstances of the country will permit."

Lest Americans reject the Constitution in the belief that they could go on comfortably under the Articles of Confederation, "Publius" pictured the state of the nation in the most dismal light. The government, he asserted, was "in a state of decay, approaching nearly to annihilation," its credit rating was hardly better than that of "bankrupts and fraudulent debtors," commerce was sinking under the weight of restrictions imposed by the states which the general government was powerless to remove, farmers were complaining of the low price of land, British troops were on American soil, American citizens were debarred from the free use of the Mississippi, and the states were busily engaged in undermining the general government "till the frail and tottering edifice seems ready to fall upon our heads, and to crush us beneath the ruins."[3]

When this crazy edifice collapsed, "Publius" was certain that Europe would rebuild the country in its own image—a "pernicious labyrinth" of spheres of influence, wars and power politics. Europe, he exclaimed, was the enemy: it could not endure to see the United States prove to the world that men could govern themselves. Nor could Europe tolerate the spectacle of a rising merchant marine and naval power in the Western Hemisphere. No wonder, therefore, he said, Europe "sought to clip the wings by which we might soar to a dangerous greatness."

Dire as was "Publius'" view of the plight of the country, there was another side to the picture: merely by reversing it from "Disunion" to "Union," the prospect brightened immeasurably. Peace, prosperity and freedom emerged triumphant; Europe retreated baffled into the background while the United States took advantage of its "insulated situation" to make itself "the admiration and envy of the world." And this felicity would not be disturbed, "Publius" predicted, by a large standing army; once Europe had been convinced of the hopelessness of its efforts to extend its influence over the United States, it would presumably content itself with plundering Asia and Africa.[4]

Having no romantic illusions about republicanism, Hamilton did not imagine that the adoption of the Constitution would ensure perpetual peace. Simply for the reason that they were administered by men, republics would continue to wage war; for, said Hamilton, "the fiery and destructive

The Rule of Law

passions of war reign in the human breast with much more powerful sway than the mild and beneficient sentiments of peace." "To model our political systems upon speculations of lasting tranquility," he concluded, "is to calculate on the weaker springs of the human character."[5] But to remain under the Articles of Confederation was in his opinion to invite war of the worst kind—civil war. If the Constitution were rejected, he predicted, the union would quickly dissolve into "an infinity of little, jealous, clashing, tumultuous commonwealths, the wretched nursuries of unceasing discord, and miserable objects of universal pity or contempt."

With this grim prospect confronting the country, "Publius" addressed himself to the task of persuading Americans to cut loose from the Articles of Confederation. To that end, he undertook to prove that the kind of government envisaged by the Constitution was essential to the security and happiness of the people, that it would not abuse its powers, that it was not hostile to freedom, that the states would not fall victim to a Leviathan central government and that—most difficult of all—in the interests of true liberty, the people must accept restraints upon their freedom to do as they pleased.

The principal theme of *The Federalist* is that the purpose of the Constitution is the establishment of an energetic and efficient national government notwithstanding the powers reserved to the states. Even though Hamilton deferred to the new kind of federalism created by the Constitution, it is clear from his essays that his sympathies lay wholly with nationalism. Reference to "the streams of national power" and "the Fabric of American Empire" reveal that even while he was justifying the federalist system he was dreaming of the centralized system that he hoped would emerge from the chrysalis of federalism.[6]

Sensible that human affairs are always subject to the vicissitudes of fortune, "Publius" contended that the general government must be made capable of coping with all emergencies. "As I know of nothing to except this portion of the globe from the common calamities that have befallen other parts of it," he said, "I acknowledge my aversion to every project that is calculated to disarm the government of a single weapon, which in any possible contingency might be usefully employed for the general defense and security." Since the nature and extent of future crises were incalculable, the national security seemed to require that the federal government be given power commensurate with its object—"there ought to be no limitation of power," he said, "destined to effect a purpose which is itself incapable of limitation." In particular, he held it essential that the taxing powers of the federal government be unconstrained: in the emergencies he foresaw, nothing would suffice but a blank check upon the national resources.[7]

In writing *The Federalist*, one of Hamilton's most essential tasks was to persuade the American people that they could have a strong central government without suffering tyranny at its hands. Here, after all, was the rock upon which the proposed Constitution threatened to founder: the widespread and almost ineradicable fear that the plan of government conceived in Philadelphia spelled tyranny. As "Publius," Hamilton therefore directed his efforts toward removing this apprehension by showing that the enumeration of powers, the system of checks and balances, and the extensive jurisdiction reserved to the states constituted guarantees that no man would be disturbed in the enjoyment of his liberties.

Certainly Hamilton was here speaking with full sincerity. He never believed that the federal government would ever menace popular freedom: in his experience, it was the states that had lent themselves to the tyranny of the majority. But "Publius" took much more satisfaction in treating of the positive advantages of union. He rejoiced in the opulence, security and national power that awaited the American people once they gave their unreserved confidence to the general government. In his hands, "union" became a talismanic word that opened all doors—and the vista, wherever one turned, was breathtaking in its sweep and grandeur.

In *The Federalist*, it was not the "silent, powerful and ever-active conspiracy of those who govern" that was emphasized; as might be expected from "Publius'" background, he was chiefly concerned with the reluctance of the governed to submit to the restraints of government and with the demagogues who attained power by seducing unquiet souls. With Aristotle, "Publius" believed that men attained their highest happiness in subordinating themselves to a law of their own choosing. But he knew from experience that men were not easily persuaded to accept such a law and that restraints upon the popular will were often swept away by a sovereign people.

He did not deny that power, like every other good thing, might be abused, but the possibility of abuse, he said, ought never to be made an argument against lodging it with some responsible department of government. It was far better, he observed, to entrust power to a government than to leave it to be usurped by some power-hungry individual or group. "Jealousy of power"—to which Americans were singularly prone—could be easily overdone; in an atmosphere of suspicion and distrust, efficient government could not exist. By indulging their fear of power, the people might be reduced to "an unfathomable abyss" of "absolute scepticism and irresolution" in which, he warned, they would lose all their powers of action.[8]

While he acknowledged that wisdom and integrity were not always found in high places, "Publius" was of the opinion that there were always enough able men in office to prevent the saturnalia of corruption and the misuse of power which the Antifederalists feared. He felt that public men were a much maligned and misunderstood breed of men: the good they did was too often obscured by the mistakes of which they were sometimes guilty. Taking them as a whole, he was persuaded that they embodied some of the

The Rule of Law

most engaging aspects of human nature; the flesh was weak but public office often had a tonic effect upon its fortunate incumbents. If the Antifederalists were right in believing that every man in office would sooner or later prove himself to be a scoundrel, then, said "Publius," "human nature must be a much more weak and despicable thing than I apprehend it to be." There were people in the United States who took a lower view of human nature than did Hamilton and it is significant that they were opposed to the Federal Constitution.[9]

Against the corrupting effects of power, "Publius" set the equally corrupting effect of being out of power. All virtue and moderation did not belong to those who raised the cry of "liberty"; sometimes "Publius" informed his countrymen, opposition to the government sprang from envy, hatred of authority and the all-too-human weakness of coveting one's neighbor's goods.

Despite Americans' partiality for their states, "Publius" did not wholly despair that they were lost to nationalism. The forces of custom, habit and the tendencies of human nature might be counteracted, he believed, by demonstrating to the people the benefits of a strong national government. "It may be laid down as a general rule," he observed, "that their [the people's] confidence in and obedience to a government will commonly be proportioned to the goodness or badness of its administration." By this course of reasoning, the better—and the more—the national government governed, the more it would win the respect and loyalty of the people and the less necessity it would be under to resort to the "violent and perilous expedient of compulsion." From which it can be seen that if Hamilton's ideals were realized, the federal government would dedicate itself to proving to the American people that the best government was that which most energetically promoted the general welfare.

"Publius'" most difficult task was to persuade Americans to accept a frame of government that placed restraints upon majority rule—which meant upon the people themselves. Americans were being asked to consent to limitations upon their sovereign right to do as they pleased. It therefore was incumbent upon Hamilton, Madison and Jay to show why such restraints were necessary and what compensations the American people would derive from this signal act of abnegation.

This they did with a frankness rare in the annals of politics. Making, as usual, a virtue of candor, Hamilton held nothing back: the people were told that they were "ambitious, vindictive, and rapacious"; that they did not always know what was best for themselves; that they were often, particularly in moments of passion, egregiously wrong; and that they were apt to fall under the sway of irrational impulses which had "a more active and imperious control over human conduct than general or remote considerations of policy, utility or justice." Even the apparently altruistic acts of men seemed to him to be a disguised form of selfishness.[10]

If men as individuals were prone to be overmastered by their passions, how much worse, exclaimed "Publius," were men in the mass. Worst of all, when this mass became a majority, it usually succumbed to "the effort in human nature towards tyranny"; and when that occurred, no considerations of either justice or equity were permitted to stand in the way of the gratification of its passions. And when this occurred, nothing was to be gained from ethical exhortations: to beseech a majority, ravening after the property or civil rights of a minority, that it should observe moderation in all things was too much like counseling a tiger to be a considerate and humane animal. "We may preach, till we are tired of the theme," Hamilton once remarked, "the necessity of disinterestedness in republics, without making a single proselyte."

The idea that the voice of the people was the voice of God was a popular fallacy, said "Publius," that had led many free governments down the primrose path to destruction. Puffed up with the pride of omniscience and infallibility, the people fell into the error of believing that they could do no wrong. In the grip of this illusion, they perpetrated one injustice after another until they had created a thoroughgoing tyranny masquerading as liberty and equality.

The doctrine of the perfectibility of man "Publius" set down as a preposterous fiction. His view of human nature presupposed that men in all ages and all places have been actuated by essentially the same desires and passions and that they would always continue to act in the same way. There was no possibility of an improvement in man's nature: the mold had been fixed for all time and the laws governing human behavior were as immutable as the laws of nature.

Viewing Americans in this cold and caustic light, "Publius" concluded that they were not paragons of virtue, a race set above the common run of mankind, but men subject to all the frailties of human nature. True, they could withstand adversity: "There is perhaps not another nation in the world," Hamilton remarked, "that would have shown equal patience and perseverance in similar circumstances" to those that had prevailed during the War of Independence. But the mere capacity to take punishment was not sufficient to make a people great; the history of the United States under the Articles of Confederation demonstrated to "Publius'" satisfaction that no more than any other people could Americans be left without the restraint and guidance of a strong government.

Hamilton derived his view of human nature from "the Study of the Nature & Character of Man," as revealed by history, experience and Scripture. The zeal with which he flayed reprobates and held up to men the mirror of their iniquities would have charmed a Puritan; and, indeed, the old Calvinistic strain again seemed to have become dominant. But with this significant difference, no longer did a wrathful God threaten the people

The Rule of Law

with perdition—they brought destruction upon themselves by giving way to their worst passions. The people created their own purgatory but the flames did not for that reason singe and sear them less cruelly.[11]

"Publius" was here portraying Democratic Man—man in the state which permitted the free play of all his evil propensities. But having laid bare the seamier side of human nature, "Publius" did not draw the conclusion that a free government is beyond the reach of mankind. He derived neither his premises nor his solution from Thomas Hobbes. The message of *The Federalist* is not that men are so hopelessly sunk in bestiality that they are doomed to drag out their short span in anarchy and war unless they submit themselves to the mercies of a Leviathan state. "Publius" said that men can be the architects of their future; that they are capable, through the exercise of reason and the teachings of experience, to establish a government in which the rights of the individual are secure.

Manifestly, "Publius" did not contend that men were wholly vicious: although evil always lurked below the surface of society, there was a modicum of good in mankind upon which a stable social and political order could be erected. "The supposition of universal venality in human nature is little less an error in political reasoning, than the supposition of universal rectitude," "Publius" observed. ". . . There is a portion of virtue and honor among mankind." Upon this side of human nature, "Publius" placed a cautious confidence. The people were possessed, he admitted, of a "cool and deliberate sense" which enabled them on occasion to elect good men to office and to act like rational beings. "In the general course of things," he observed, "the popular views, and even prejudices, will direct the actions of the rulers."[12]

But when the people went wrong, they went terribly wrong—and there was no hope of combining order with liberty until the people were prevented from giving free rein to their passions. The people sober might be trusted, but when they became drunk—and history proved that they went on such binges with distressing frequency—they behaved like tyrants. It was the peculiar merit of the Federal Constitution, according to *The Federalist*, that under its benign auspices the people, even when they lost possession of their faculties, were constrained from running amuck.[13]

In effect, "Publius" was saying that the proper study of a statesman was the depravity of man. The injunction had been heard before: Spinoza had remarked that "experience has taught them [statesmen] that there will be vices as long as there are men. They study to be beforehand with human depravity." Machiavelli had enjoined those "who lay the foundation of a State and furnish it with laws" to "assume that all men are bad, and will always, when they have free field, give loose to their evil inclinations." But "Publius" did not have to go to Spinoza and Machiavelli for proof that men would do wrong when they had the opportunity: in his eyes, it was exemplified at every turn in the history of the United States during the period of the Articles of Confederation.[14]

Perhaps the readers of *The Federalist* papers, being the upper crust of society, exempted themselves from these strictures upon human nature: they nodded approvingly when "Publius" delivered a particularly shrewd thrust against Old Adam, but they would have indignantly rejected the idea that they shared in these weaknesses. If so, they found no sanction in *The Federalist* papers for such complacency: "Publius" rejected the concept of an elite entitled by birth, wealth or education to be the rulers of mankind. Far from being supermen to whom mankind owed obedience, the "opulent minority" remained in the rut of human nature. Having read widely in political theory and history, Hamilton could not easily believe that the rule of the rich produced the kind of stability he wished to see established in the United States. The history of Greece, for example, demonstrated that if political power were lodged exclusively in the hands of either the few or the many, the result was "a constant scene of the alternate tyranny of one part of the people over the other, or a few usurping demagogues over the whole"—certainly not a state of affairs he wished to reproduce in the United States. The substance of "Publius'" philosophy is that no one class was sufficiently disinterested to be trusted with power over other classes.

Rejecting class rule, "Publius" argued that liberty and order could be reconciled by establishing in the government itself a balance of power between classes. Hamilton summed up this theory in the maxim "Give all power to the many, they will oppress the few. Give all power to the few, they will oppress the many. Both therefore ought to have power, that each may defend itself against the other."

If each class were thus given "a distinct, permanent share in the government," "Publius" contended that those blessed with large possessions would be protected against the poor and that the poor would have no reason to complain of the oppressions of the rich. When the poor discovered that the rich were firmly entrenched in the government, they would presumably cease their efforts to expropriate them; while the rich, discovering in turn that they were beyond the reach of the masses, would recognize that it was to their interest to maintain the *status quo*. Having nothing to fear from the established order and everything to fear from change, Americans would settle down as a peace-loving, orderly people.[15]

Despite the care taken by the framers of the Constitution to prevent popular majorities and the states from overriding the fundamental law, Hamilton was far from uncertain that they had been effectively bridled. With classes and interests and the state and national governments jostling for primacy in the United States, Hamilton felt the necessity of some power capable of arbitrating between them. Simply by setting constitutional

The Rule of Law

bounds to the power of the people was not, he realized, a wholly satisfactory means of keeping them under control; nor did he imagine that the states would be dissuaded from encroaching upon the authority of the national government merely because the Constitution forbade them from so doing. He was clear in his mind that something more was needed to secure "the permanent interests of the country" against the assaults of democrats and to place the powers of the federal government beyond the reach of the states.

From this conviction sprang one of the most daring and significant acts of Hamilton's career—an attempt to make the United States Supreme Court the expounder of a higher law which restrained popular majorities and the states alike from transcending their constitutional powers.

One of the most crucial questions raised by the Constitution in Hamilton's mind was: By whom was this instrument of government to be interpreted? If it were left to the legislature to determine the nature and extent of its own powers, Hamilton would have attached little value to the checks and balances established by the Constitution—for in that event, he knew that the legislature would quickly make itself dominant over the other branches of the government. And, conversely, if the states were permitted to judge of their powers, the federal government would soon be rendered as impotent as the Continental Congress. Thus it was made plain to Hamilton some branch of the federal government other than the legislature must be entrusted with this prerogative, in order to maintain the balance between the departments and to preserve the authority of the federal government against the encroachments of the states.

Hamilton was at no loss where to place this power. He had long advocated that the interpretation of the fundamental law be committed to the judiciary. By permitting the courts to adjudicate statutes of the state and federal governments, Hamilton hoped to put democracy in tutelage to judges and to establish the supremacy of the national government over the states. Thus would be created a check upon democracy and localism by means of an organ of government not subject to popular control.

In *The Federalist,* the American people learned for the first time that the Constitution established the principle of judicial review. The Constitution itself does not make such an explicit grant of power to the Supreme Court and no formal vote was ever taken in the Constitutional Convention upon the subject. Nevertheless, the concept of judicial review was not something that Hamilton smuggled into that document in a last desperate effort to forestall the triumph of popular sovereignty. The idea had been discussed in the Constitutional Convention, but had been omitted from the frame of government partly because it was a controversial subject certain to make difficulties for the Constitution in the state conventions. In the last days of the Convention, Hamilton and Gouverneur Morris had been appointed to the Committee on Style and Arrangement, to which was entrusted the work of giving literary polish to the document. Although Gouverneur Morris did most of the labor, it is probable that Hamilton was not chary in giving advice. If that were the case, the section dealing with the judiciary was one of their happiest efforts. So adroitly was this worded that Gouverneur Morris later boasted that it was the only part of the Constitution that passed the Convention without objection.[16]

Even though the Constitution does not expressly so state, the power of interpreting the document fell logically to the judges. Since the Constitution was proclaimed to be the supreme law of the land, it devolved upon men trained in jurisprudence to interpret and construe it. In the Philadelphia Convention the way had been cleared for judicial review by separating the branches of the government and enumerating the powers of the federal government. Without a fundamental law and a separation of powers, judicial review is impossible; with these, judicial review becomes an inevitable corollary of the rule of law.*

Judicial review presupposes that there is a higher law than the legislative will and that this higher law is embodied in the Constitution. Where statutes come into conflict with the Constitution, the supreme law must prevail. Government does not possess ultimate sovereignty; there is a pre-existing and superior law to which governments must conform if their acts are to be accounted legitimate. This fundamental law—the laws of God and Nature that Hamilton had used so effectively during the American Revolution— is above the will of the government.[17]

Having some acquaintance with Americans' love of liberty, Hamilton was aware that they would not willingly submit to the rule of judges over whom they had no control if this rule was presented to them as an exercise of naked power. During the American Revolution, the people had claimed for themselves the right of determining what acts were unconstitutional and therefore not binding upon them. He could not, therefore, baldly state that "We are under a Constitution, but the Constitution is what the judges say it is"; democrats would not take kindly to be held in tutelage by judges. Manifestly, it was necessary to persuade Americans that judicial control was not only in their own interest but that they participated, at least vicariously, in the judicial function. In short, judicial review had to appear to be the expression of the sovereign will of the people.

Accordingly, Hamilton was careful in *Federalist* No. 78 to make clear that he was not exalting the judicial above the legislative power. Judicial review, he said, "only supposes that the power of the people is superior to both, and that where the will of the legislature, declared in the statutes,

---

* Judge Learned Hand has observed that while the power of judicial review is not a logical deduction from the structure of the Constitution, it is "a practical condition upon its successful operation." Learned Hand, *The Bill of Rights* (Cambridge, 1958), pp. 14-15.

stands in opposition to that of the people, declared in the Constitution, the judges ought to be governed by the latter rather than by the former." In other words, Hamilton wished it to be believed that when the judges declared an act of the legislature void, it was not because they were superior to the legislature but because the act was repugnant to the will of the people embodied in the Constitution.[18]

To carry conviction, it was necessary for Hamilton to distinguish between the transitory and fluctuating will of the people expressed in statutes passed by the legislature and the permanent will of the people embodied in the Constitution. As the interpreters of the permanent will of the people, judges speak for the better side of human nature and for the permanent, fixed opinions of mankind, arrived at after long and careful deliberation. It is as though they are designated to save the people from the rashness, irresponsibility and passion which, Hamilton lamented, had made human history largely a record of folly, rapine and bloodshed.

Hamilton never claimed that the judges were more than the penultimate expositors of the Constitution. The final authority—the sovereign power that could amend or dissolve the Constitution—resided in the people. Judges, he made clear, could not change the Constitution—they could merely bring it into harmony with the sovereign will incorporated in the fundamental law. If judicial rule were to prevail, it was essential that the Constitution be regarded not as an agreement between thirteen states but a fundamental ordinance or law established by a sovereign people.

Thanks to judicial review, Hamilton succeeded in limiting the exercise of sovereignty by the people at the very time he paid obeisance to the principle of popular sovereignty. The people were not wholly free to do as they pleased at all times and under all circumstances—and yet their ultimate sovereignty was not impaired. One of the cardinal purposes of the new Constitution was to ensure that in a government of the people, popular caprice, impulse and transitory passions would not be translated into statute law—thereby preventing the people from becoming a law unto themselves. Invested with the power of invalidating statute law, the judges were expected to keep a tight rein upon "popular passions" while acting in the name of the people themselves.

Judicial review held for Hamilton the peculiar virtue of placing both the national legislature and the state governments under the restraints of a fundamental law. Against the impending onslaught of the states upon the powers of the federal government, he hoped to make the Supreme Court an invincible bastion of nationalism. From it the judges would sally forth to do battle with the enemies of national supremacy and, if Hamilton were to be believed, the judges fought under the banner of the people.[19]

Hamilton had no fear that judicial review would lead to judicial tyranny. The judiciary was the one department which in his opinion posed no threat to the other departments: it was the weakest, the most vulnerable and the least aggressive of all the branches of the government. Judges, he supposed, would have less reason and less opportunity to aggrandize their powers than did the officers of the other departments: they had no force with which to support their pretensions and they harbored no aggressive designs against either the executive or the legislature. The judges might be lions under the throne, but from Hamilton's description there was some danger that they would be mistaken for lambs.

And yet it was undeniable that if the judges were to withstand the force of contagious mass emotions, they would need the courage of lions. For there was little in either Hamilton's experience or his view of human nature to warrant the hope that the American people would consent to be bound by a supreme law even when it was solemnly promulgated by an entire bench of judges. Judicial review presupposed a long history of legalism, an established regard for law and a willingness to subordinate the popular will of the moment to ordinances of the Constitution as interpreted by the courts. As Hamilton said, it required of the people recognition of the principle that "no man can be sure that he may not be to-morrow the victim of a spirit of injustice, by which he may be a gainer today." In the ultimate analysis, the success of judicial review depended upon the willingness of the people to submit to law—in other words, to the unenforceable.

Much as he deplored Americans' hankering for democracy, Hamilton paid them the compliment of crediting them with sufficient self-restraint to accept the rule of law. In 1788, this seemed to be a long chance, but Hamilton, always ready to gamble upon unlikely looking horses, took it.

Although Hamilton never fully realized it, in *Federalist* No. 78 he touched a profoundly conservative chord in the American mind. The distrust of omnipotent government, the growing respect for law, the tendency to rely upon the adjudicatory process, the veneration for the Constitution— all these circumstances operated powerfully in favor of judicial review. As a result, constitutionalism became what Hamilton never expected it would be—"one of the most persistent and persuasive characteristics of American democracy." And of this conservatism the Supreme Court became the great archetype. Visiting the United States two generations later, de Tocqueville found that the American aristocracy occupied the judicial bench and the bar: if there was a *noblesse* in the United States, he observed, it was the *noblesse* of the robe.[20]

As the exponent of judicial review, Hamilton appeared in the guise of a true conservative—the guardian of order, conscious of the history, ideals and traditions of his society, and yet, withal, aware of the necessity of change. In serving as the spokesman of this kind of conservatism, Hamilton was giving expression to one of the fundamental concepts of the American Revolution. Never was he more faithful to the ideals of that Revolution

The Rule of Law

than when he wrote *Federalist* No. 78; nowhere is the continuity between the Revolution and the Constitution more apparent. "A government of laws, not of men" was one of the most deeply cherished objectives of American revolutionaries; the Revolution itself was conceived in opposition to acts of the King and Parliament which Americans refused to admit possessed the force of legality. Americans took the position that the authority of Parliament could not constitutionally be carried beyond its assigned powers and they alleged that acts of Parliament which exceeded its powers were contrary to Magna Charta, the laws of nature "and therefore, according to Lord Coke, null and void." This attitude toward law is not often found among subverters of the established order; because it was held by Americans even in their most revolutionary phase, it was made the easier for Hamilton and other conservatives to proclaim themselves heirs of the revolutionary tradition at the very time that they fought on the side of conservatism.

The position taken by Hamilton as "Publius" was more consistent with his previous thinking than were the ideas he had advanced in his speech of June 18. In many respects, he seemed in *The Federalist* to resume the ground he had taken before he spoke his mind in the Constitutional Convention. And, of even greater moment, the course charted by "Publius" was consistently followed by Hamilton thereafter. What he said in June, 1787, is far less important than what he did from 1788 to 1804.

14.

A More Perfect Union

Upon the early state conventions, *The Federalist* made little impression. The leisurely beginning and the elaboration with which "Publius" developed his themes ensured that the more important essays—those dealing with the most controversial parts of the Constitution—did not appear until five or six conventions had met and passed upon the plan of the Philadelphia Convention. Certainly *The Federalist* was not essential to the success of the Constitution in these state conventions: here the Federalists carried the day without the aid of "Publius." Far more potent than anything written by Hamilton, Jay and Madison in securing the adoption of the Constitution was the fact that Washington and Franklin had approved it. Of these worthies it was said by an Antifederalist that "the honest and uninformed *freemen* of America entertain the same opinion . . . as do European *slaves* of their Princes—that they can do no wrong."

While it was often said that *The Federalist* profoundly affected the "reflecting few," no one claimed that it had such effect upon the "unreflecting multitude." When Washington received the first of "Publius'" essays he was so struck by their lofty tone that he sent them to Richmond to be reprinted in the local newspaper. He recognized immediately that here was something more than an ephemeral tract thrown up by political controversy. "When the transient circumstances and fugitive performances which attended this Crisis shall have disappeared," he observed, "that Work will merit the Notice of Posterity, because in it are candidly and ably discussed the principles of freedom and the topics of government—which will be always interesting to mankind so long as they shall be connected in Civil Society." But Washington did not pretend that *The Federalist* would do more than "produce conviction on an unbiased mind."[1]

The Antifederalists were content to leave the unbiased minds to "Publius"; as long as they had the bias of the country on their side, they did not ask for more. No Antifederalist writer attempted to answer the essays of "Publius" in detail. Their own propaganda efforts were pitched in a very different key from his. When Elbridge Gerry's pamphlet, *Observations on the New Constitution and on the Federal and State Conventions*, was republished by the New York Antifederalists for distribution in that state, the Albany committee complained that Gerry's style was "too sublime and florid for the common people in this part of the country." Had "Publius" been an Antifederalist, it is doubtful if he would have gotten into print at all.[2]

Even some Federalists complained that "Publius" was too recondite for the masses: a writer with more of the common touch, they said, would do more good than all "the elaborate works of 'Publius.'" A champion of the Constitution who was not afraid to rough it up with the Antifederalists was more to their taste; in the present contest, they pointed out, victory was not likely to go to the side that boasted the most gentlemanly manners. Worst of all, "Publius" seemed to be going over the heads of the common people: whereas the Antifederalists served up red-hot propaganda, "Publius" gave the people a cold collation consisting largely of disquisitions upon the science of government. For these reasons, when Rufus King wished to bolster the New Hampshire Federalists, he sent them a copy of John Jay's "Address to the People of New York"—more suited to the popular taste, he supposed, than the highfalutin "Publius."[3]

The fact that *The Federalist* was not written exclusively for local consumption tended to weaken its impact in New York. As Hamilton acknowledged in the first number, so many local and particular interests had obtruded themselves into the debate over the Constitution that "views, passions and prejudices little favorable to the discovery of truth" threatened to decide the issue. Certainly it was true that local considerations often prevailed over national concerns; how the proposed frame of government would affect a particular locality or state was usually the first question Americans asked themselves in 1787-88. To this all-important question, "Publius" did not provide a convincing answer: too often for the taste of his readers, he preferred to dwell upon the question how the proposed frame of government would affect the country as a whole.[4]

Even though *The Federalist* did not have as wide a sale or as galvanizing an effect as its authors hoped, it was probably more widely read and more influential than any other Federalist tract. In the two state conventions where the Constitution was most bitterly contested and where its fate hung most precariously in the balance, "Publius" was a potent force on the Federalist side. In May, 1788, when the complete text appeared in book form, Hamilton sent fifty-two copies to Virginia for the use of the Federalist members of the Virginia convention. In both New York and Virginia *The Federalist* served as a handbook for the proponents of the Constitution. When the Antifederalists insisted upon a clause-by-clause examination of the proposed Constitution, they played into the hands of the Federalists, who in "Publius" had a ready-made answer to every objection raised against the frame of government.

But, above all, what gave the Federalist its enduring value was that its interpretation of the Constitution was adopted by the federal judiciary. Generations of commentators upon the Constitution—John Marshall, Daniel Webster, Joseph Story among them—ranked *The Federalist* second only to the Constitution itself; and in determining the jurisdiction of the national government and the powers of the various departments of that government, they followed Hamilton, Madison and Jay with implicit confidence. In the hands of Chief Justice John Marshall, "Publius' " interpretation of the Constitution was invested with all the sanctity pertaining to an exposition of the views of the Founding Fathers themselves. Thanks to Marshall and other jurists of his political persuasion, the philosophy of the Federalist party persisted long after the party itself had ceased to exist.*

As "Publius," Hamilton wrought better than he knew: when he sat on the deck of the Albany sloop in October, 1787, he had little idea that he was writing the first chapter of one of the classics of political literature. Nor did he foresee the profound effect *The Federalist* was to have in shaping the political institutions of the United States. Nothing would have astonished Hamilton more than had he been told at this time that a cult of Constitution worship would one day exalt the Constitution to the status of a sacred ark. In 1787, assuming that the Constitution were adopted, Hamilton would not have given it a life expectancy of more than twenty years. In making possible the surprising longevity of that instrument of government, Hamilton's work was of high importance: "Publius" buttressed the Constitution with all the force of great and enduring literature.[5]

In the autumn of 1787, Hamilton made a remarkably acute assessment of the strength of the various sources of opposition to the Constitution. While he predicted that it would be ratified by the necessary number of states, he foresaw an arduous struggle. The reception accorded the Constitution in the first state conventions made Hamilton seem unduly pessimistic: three states adopted it unanimously and opposition in several other states was easily brushed aside. Bostonians were reported to be "in raptures with it as it is, but would have liked it still better had it been higher toned." So would Hamilton!

---

* *The Federalist* was first cited in a Supreme Court case by Attorney General Bradford in 1795, and in 1798 Justice Chase in Colder *v.* Bull referred to "Publius" as an authority upon the Constitution. Among the rules of interpretation laid down by "Publius" perhaps the best known is the dictum that "the power is exclusive in the national government where an authority is granted to the Union, to which a similar authority in the states would be absolutely and totally contradictory and repugnant." *The Federalist*, together with the commentaries that derived from it, exerted a powerful influence upon the jurisprudence of the states, tending to create uniformity in laws and legislation.

A More Perfect Union

But the auguries were far less propitious in New York than in Boston. In Hamilton's state, a large party led by Governor Clinton was hostile to the Philadelphia plan. "Publius" was a voice crying in an Antifederalist wilderness. During the Constitutional Convention, Hamilton had remarked upon the difficulty of opening the eyes of people "who have been in certain habits of thinking," but it remained for the New York Antifederalists to reveal to him how unalterably fixed in opinion some people could be.

It was not until more than three months after "Publius" had made his appearance that Governor Clinton and his partisans decided to permit the calling of a ratifying convention in New York. And, to make sure that the Constitution would be completely snowed under, the Clintonians ordained that manhood suffrage should be the rule in the voting for delegates to the convention. With the common people on his side, the governor felt himself invincible: "Publius" could have the rich, the wise and the well born, but the ark of liberty and state sovereignty was safe as long as the people were permitted freely to register their opinion at the polls.[6]

Hamilton uttered no protest against the decision to throw down all the barriers to the exercise of the suffrage. He had often expressed his conviction that the new government ought to be as broadly based as possible; and, although he was startled by the thoroughness with which the Clintonians took him at his word, he continued to stand by his principles.[7] And, indeed, he was likely to lose little by so doing: George Clinton had most of the agricultural areas of the state so thoroughly sewed up that the Federalists could not hope to take them away from him. On the other hand, manhood suffrage would open the polls to the mechanics and artisans of New York City, Albany and the smaller towns of the state, whose enthusiasm for the proposed Constitution was the most cheerful sign in this Antifederalist "desert."[8]

Despite Clinton's maneuvers, Hamilton continued to consider the adoption of the Constitution probable, although he admitted that there would be "nothing astonishing in the contrary." Indeed, in the United States, he later remarked, he had ceased to be astonished by anything. He took comfort at this time in the hope that *The Federalist* and John Jay's "Address to the People of New York" had won the "good Sense and Shining Abilities" of the state to the side of federalism. The ticket drawn up by the Federalists for the election seemed to vindicate Hamilton's confidence: some of the most distinguished men in the state, including Chancellor Livingston, John Jay, James Duane, Nicholas Low, Isaac Roosevelt, Richard Harison and Hamilton himself, were named as Federalist candidates.[9]

The election results revealed that Hamilton had overestimated the effect of *The Federalist* and underestimated the strength of the rural vote. Thanks to the farmers, the Antifederalists won a sweeping victory in all save the four lower counties of New York. Probably less than one fourth of the qualified voters of the state favored the Constitution, and only nineteen Federalist delegates were elected out of a total of sixty-five.[10]

On June 16, two sloops sailed from New York City, one carrying the Federalist delegates, the other bearing the Antifederalists to the convention at Poughkeepsie. As the Federalist ship passed the Battery, it was saluted by a discharge of thirteen cannon. Despite an exuberant send-off from their friends and well-wishers in New York City, the Federalist deputies were thoughtful and subdued as they sailed up the Hudson to Poughkeepsie. This small band of gentlemen felt the weight of an almost unbearable responsibility: upon them depended bringing one of the most important states into the union. Hamilton, in particular, gave evidence of the strain under which they all labored: "The more I can penetrate the views of the Anti-federal party in this State," he remarked, "the more I dread the consequences of the nonadoption of the Constitution by any of the other States—the more I fear an eventual disunion and civil war."[11]

At Poughkeepsie, on June 17, when they took their seats in the convention and beheld the Antifederalist host in full panoply, their spirits took another drop. At no time since the Revolution, it was observed, had the rich and well born "felt and appeared so uninfluential, as they feel and appear at this Time and Place. *How are the mighty fallen!* is an Apostrophe applicable to their desponding Circumstances, and ought at least to teach their High flown Imaginations a Lesson of Humility in future." Hamilton did not easily learn humility, but he did perceive that he was in serious danger of suffering a chastening reverse at Poughkeepsie.[12]

Although outnumbered, the Federalists were not outgunned. Had the issue been decided by persuasive oratory and lucidity and acuteness of reasoning, the Federalists might have scored an easy victory. But these things were not decisive: to defeat the Constitution, all the Antifederalists had to do was to sit tight and vote as Clinton directed.

Being the only member at Poughkeepsie who had signed the Constitution, Hamilton felt obliged to assume the burden of debate. He spoke as a republican and ardent lover of liberty; the confessional mood was no longer upon him and he felt no compulsion to express the doubts and misgivings that had assailed him in Philadelphia. The establishment of a republican government in the United States was, he said, "an object, of all others, the nearest and most dear to my own heart." For the states, he had only sweet charity: he declared them to be integral parts of the general government and "essential, component parts of the Union." In the spirit of "Publius" rather than in that of the uncompromising young nationalist of the Constitutional Convention, Hamilton solemnly assured the delegates that the states and central governments could peacefully coexist under the Federal Constitution. "That two supreme powers cannot act together," he declared, "is false. They are inconsistent only when they are aimed at each other, or at one indivisible object." The states were essential to the working of the national government and therefore it could never be the interest of the national government to destroy them: such an act, said Hamilton, would prove "political suicide." Although it probably cost him a pang to say it, he predicted that "the states can never lose their powers till the whole people of America were robbed of their liberties. These must go together; they must support each other, or meet one common fate."[13]

Nor did any hint appear in Hamilton's remarks to the Convention that he had ever uttered kind words for monarchism. He declared that "the principles of republicanism are founded on too firm a basis to be shaken by a few speculative and skeptical reasoners." Montesquieu's doctrine that only a monarchical government could exist in a large country no longer posed difficulties for him: the Federal Constitution, he predicted, would prove the Frenchman wrong by combining vigor and order with freedom. If republics had hitherto failed, it was mainly owing, he now said, to the fact that they had been established on false principles. And, finally, the censures he had cast upon "popular licentiousness" were now tempered by his acknowledgement that the people, hitherto led astray by the search for a "fantastical Utopia," were now seeking liberty under law. On the strength of this promising development, Hamilton was prepared to admit that they were in the process of becoming "exceedingly enlightened and refined."[14]

In this debate, Hamilton repeatedly pleaded for a calm, dispassionate and candid examination of the Constitution. Nevertheless, he himself "frequently made pathetic & powerful appeals to the moral Sense & Patriotism, & the fears and Hopes of the Assembly, in order to give them a deep sense of the Difficulties of the Crisis." On one occasion, he cried out: "O save my country, Heaven"—a piece of "pathos" that his admirers found extremely moving. He became particularly emotional when the Antifederalists charged that the adoption of the Constitution would lead to the rule of an aristocracy. "I declare," exclaimed Hamilton, "I know not any set of men who are to derive peculiar advantages from this Constitution. . . . I have my friends, my family, my children, to whom ties of nature and of habit have attached me. If to-day, I am among the favored few, my children, to-morrow, may be among the oppressed." "These dear pledges of my patriotism," he told the assembly, ought to prove his disinterestedness and "it could be relied upon that no reasonable man would seek to establish a government unfriendly to the liberties of the people."[15]

But upon the Antifederalist majority, Hamilton's flights of oratory made little impression: "Our arguments confound," he ruefully remarked, "but do not convince." No matter how soundly Hamilton beat them upon the field of argument, the Antifederalists came back stronger than before: this "set of ignorant Dutchmen," a Federalist exclaimed, seemed to know the meaning of only one word—no.

In these debates, Hamilton gave the Convention so many arguments straight out of "Publius" that Governor Clinton sarcastically enquired if the young knight-errant of federalism was planning to bring out a second edition.* But, in truth, the Constitution had been so thoroughly canvassed that little new could be said by either side. The Antifederalists themselves played only minor variations upon the familiar theme of "consolidated government," aristocracy and tyranny. In the dearth of new material Hamilton himself furnished the liveliest subject of dispute.[16]

Hamilton's efforts to assume the garb of a friend of the states and an apostle of popular liberties were not permitted to pass unchallenged. As might have been expected, it was Lansing and Yates who appealed to the record: both men had kept journals of the debates in the Constitutional Convention and in these documents Hamilton figured as a hardened antirepublican. Armed with this evidence, Lansing dropped his bombshell: Hamilton, he told the convention, had declared that the states ought to be reduced to mere corporations and that "even in that situation, they would endanger the existence of the general government."

By dint of skillfully cross-examining Lansing and Yates, Hamilton freed himself from this tight corner. Later in the meeting, Hamilton "described in a delicate but affecting manner the various injurious attempts to prejudice the minds of the Convention against him" and "called on the world to point out an instance in which he had ever deviated from the line of public or private duty." Not an Antifederalist accepted the challenge.[17]

Despite the strong feeling excited by the debate, the delegates displayed remarkable moderation and good temper. Although a riot occurred in Albany on July fourth between the rival parades of Federalists and Antifederalists, and eighteen participants were carried off the field, the convention members celebrated the glorious day by dining at separate taverns and drinking toasts to the accompaniment of volleys of artillery. Both on and off the floor of the convention, Hamilton conducted himself with rare courtesy and consideration for the opinions of those with whom he disagreed. On one occasion, he apologized to the convention for having let his feelings run away with him. "If such has been my language," he said, "it was from the habit of using strong language to express my ideas, and, above all, from the interesting nature of the subject. . . . On no subject has my breast been filled wtih stronger emotion, or more anxious concern."[18]

The Clintonians could afford to be magnanimous: everything seemed to be going their way. The wealth and talents of the convention seemingly made no converts; after weeks of debate, the Federalists were hardly more numerous than when the convention opened.

* Melancthon Smith remarked that Hamilton "speaks frequently, very long and very vehemently—has, like Publius, very much to say not very applicable to the subject."

To procure the ratification of the Constitution by New York, Hamilton banked heavily upon favorable action by the New Hampshire convention, which was meeting concurrently with New York's. So confident was he that New Hampshire would ratify and that this action would break the ranks of the New York Antifederalists that he arranged for a post rider to bring the good news from New Hampshire to Poughkeepsie. He was not disappointed in one respect: New Hampshire acceded and thereby became the ninth state to adopt the Constitution. The new frame of government was now the law of the land but the New York Antifederalists showed no signs of weakening. To Hamilton's arguments that the great debate was over, John Lansing replied: "Since nine states have acceded to it, let them make the experiment." Even when Virginia ratified shortly after New Hampshire, the New York Antifederalists were still prepared to go it alone.

In several states the Constitution had been ratified with the recommendation that amendments be made to the frame of government. But Governor Clinton refused to accede to the Constitution on these terms; he would consent to ratify only on *condition* that amendments were adopted. If the Constitution were not amended to his satisfaction, the governor insisted upon New York's right to withdraw from the union.

Not all the governor's supporters were prepared to carry their opposition this far; and it was upon these moderates that Hamilton labored with arguments, dinners, free drinks at the tavern bar, and threats that New York City would secede from the state. In the Convention, he moved the adoption of recommendatory amendments, even going beyond the Antifederalists themselves in offering guarantees to individual liberty. Insofar as amendments were designed to safeguard "the great, essential and inalienable rights of freemen," Hamilton was prepared to give the Clintonians everything they desired. But even this concession failed to break the ranks of the opponents of the Constitution, for George Clinton still held out for conditional ratification.

Despite the deadlock in the convention, on July 23 the Federalists celebrated in New York City the ratification of the Constitution. Applauded by thousands of enthusiastic citizens, the good ship *Alexander Hamilton,* built by the shipyard workers and carpenters of New York, was pulled through the streets on a carriage. This miniature ship, the replica in every detail of a regular seagoing vessel, was reported to have made "a fine appearance, sailing with flowing sheets and full sails, down Broadway, the canvass waves dashing against her sides," the Antifederalists looking all the while "as sour as the Devil." A slight accident, it is true, marred the event: in launching the ship the arm of the figure of Hamilton on the prow had been broken off. It was accounted portentous that the broken arm was the one holding the Constitution.

There was reason to fear that the New York Federalists had celebrated prematurely and that the good ship *Alexander Hamilton* might have to be put into moth balls.[19] In July, 1787, touching the depths of discouragement, Hamilton asked Madison's opinion of a compromise whereby New York would ratify the Constitution while reserving the right of withdrawing if amendments were not adopted within a certain number of years. Although usually it was Madison who favored conciliation and Hamilton who displayed intransigence, the Virginian gave Hamilton no hope that such a settlement would be acceptable: "The Constitution," he declared, "requires an adoption *in toto* and *for ever*. . . . Any condition whatever must vitiate the ratification." Ratification subject to prior amendments would mean that every state which had adopted the Constitution would feel obliged to reexamine its position. Forty amendments had been proposed by the Virginia Convention alone, and it was probable that every state would consider itself entitled to propose at least an equal number.[20]

The only alternative to conditional ratification that the Antifederalists would consider was the calling of a second Constitutional Convention to revise the Constitution in accord with the amendments suggested by the states. From the time a second Constitutional Convention had been first proposed by Edmund Randolph at the Philadelphia meeting, Hamilton had regarded this project with dread and foreboding. "Let a convention be called tomorrow," he told the delegates at Poughkeepsie; "let them meet twenty times—nay, twenty thousand times: they will have same difficulties to encounter, the same clashing interests to reconcile." Such a convention, he predicted, would make the Constitution a thing of shreds and tatters, wholly unfit for the needs of the nation.

Even so, he was compelled to admit that a second Constitutional Convention was preferable to the rejection or conditional ratification of the Constitution. Largely as a result of his assiduous work behind the scenes, the Clintonians agreed to ratify the Constitution with the understanding that a circular letter should be sent to the other states urging the calling of a second Constitutional Convention to consider the question of amendments. Thirty-two amendments were recommended for the consideration of the proposed convention, and with this agreement the Constitution was ratified. But even so there was no rush to get aboard the good ship *Alexander Hamilton:* when the final vote was taken, thirty members voted for ratification and twenty-seven were opposed. Two votes cast the other way would have meant, at best, conditional ratification.

Upon John Jay was thrust the unwelcome duty of writing the address to the states urging them to join in calling a second Constitutional Convention. But it was Hamilton who was blamed by the Federalists for having yielded to the Clintonians. Madison, who had been consulted upon this matter by his friend, declared that outright rejection would have been preferable to the agreement entered into by the New York Federalists: in

A More Perfect Union

that event, Federalists everywhere would have awakened to their danger, the other states would have brought pressure upon New York, and the Antifederalists would have been compelled by public opinion to summon another state convention. Washington feared that Hamilton's imprudence had "set everything afloat again"; it was, he said, like "dashing the cup of national felicity just as it had been lifted to our lips."

But Hamilton was confident that the slip could be averted by the exercise of a little finesse. "The rage for amendments," he observed, "is in my opinion rather to be parried by address than encountered with open force . . . the mode in which amendments may best be made, and twenty other matters" might be converted into pretexts for postponing the promised Constitutional Convention. On the other hand, he did not reject the idea of amending the Constitution by the methods prescribed by that document itself. As long as the amendments did not emasculate the powers of the federal government, he was willing to give satisfaction to the Antifederalists. "That there will be a reconsideration of parts of the system, and that certain amendments will be made, I devoutly wish and confidently expect," he said. "I have no doubt that the system is susceptible of improvement, and I sincerely desire that every prudent means may be used to conciliate the honest opponents of it."[21]

Thus, after encountering seemingly insuperable obstacles, the Constitution cleared the last hazard. The "miracle" that had produced the Constitutional Convention in 1787 had turned out to be a miracle indeed: the United States was launched upon the full tide of a new experiment in republican government. Upon that tide floated the *Alexander Hamilton*. The pilot was aboard, the sails were beginning to fill and the course was charted. Not all Americans knew where they were going, but Hamilton was never in doubt: the destination was the creation of a great, united and powerful nation.[22]

PART III

The Union Consummated

15.
The First Secretary of the Treasury

Hamilton was under no illusion that the new government was to be a government of laws rather than of men in the sense that it would function automatically, in the way *The Federalist* had described, regardless of the men who administered it. He had frequently observed that the success of the government depended upon the quality of the men who occupied the key offices—whether they were the "first characters" in the country or "middling politicians" might spell the difference between the success or failure of the republican experiment.

In view of the importance attached by Hamilton to the presidency, it was to be expected that he would attempt to fill it with the first character in the United States—George Washington. But an office which to most men would have been an eagerly sought honor was to Washington merely another nail in the crucifixion of public service. Enjoying a surfeit of fame, he was unwilling to hazard his dearly bought reputation by embarking upon the sea of trouble he saw ahead. "It is my great and sole desire to live and die, in peace and retirement on my own farm," he said to those who urged him to assume the presidency. His course would be decided, he told Hamilton, by the answer to the question: "Whether there does not exist a probability that the government would be just as happily and effectually carried into execution without my aid, as with it." He was inclined to believe that no man was indispensable and that a government that depended upon a single individual was not likely to endure.

But there was no rest for the Father of His Country as long as Hamilton had need of him—which was as long as breath remained in his body. At the end of Washington's life, Hamilton was trying to draft him for a third term in the presidency. In 1788 Hamilton believed that the late Commander in Chief was as essential to the success of the new government as he had been to the victory of the United States in the War of Independence. "I am not sure that your refusal would not throw everything into confusion," he said. ". . . . Circumstances leave no option." Having contributed to the winning of independence, Washington could not retire with the battle only half won: "It is of little purpose to have *introduced* a system,"

Hamilton remarked, "if the weightiest influence is not given to its firm *establishment* in the outset."

This argument, addressed to a man governed by a consuming love of country and a stern sense of duty, proved decisive. Even so, when Washington made up his mind to renounce the peace and tranquillity of Mount Vernon for the busy haunts of politicians he said that he felt like a culprit on the way to his execution.[1]

In *The Federalist,* Hamilton had made clear that he regarded the Electoral College—the part of the Constitution which he could most justly regard as his own handiwork—as an almost foolproof method of selecting men "preeminent for ability and virtue" for the presidency and vice-presidency. "A small number of persons [electors] selected by their fellow-citizens from the general mass will be most likely," he observed, "to possess the information and discernment requisite to such complicated investigations." Thanks to this indirect method of choosing the two executive officers of the government, he thought that the people would gladly acquiesce in the verdict of their intellectual superiors and that presidential elections would pass off without tumult or "cabal, intrigue and corruption."[2]

Despite Hamilton's fondness for this institution of his own begetting, he could never resist the temptation to manipulate the Electoral College; much as he valued the wisdom of the electors, he valued his own wisdom more. In no less than three elections—those of 1788, 1796, and 1800—he personally intervened to bring about the election of candidates of his own choice. In two of these instances, he deliberately sought to counterwork the will of the people insofar as that will was expressed in the Electoral College.

Having disposed of the presidency to his satisfaction, Hamilton turned his attention in 1788 to the more knotty problem of the vice-presidency. It was generally agreed that the second office of the government ought to go to a Northerner inasmuch as the presidency was to be given to a Virginian. The leading contender for the post was John Adams of Massachusetts. A signer of the Declaration of Independence, American minister to Holland and Great Britain, a member of the commission that negotiated the treaty of peace with Great Britain and the author of an influential book on political science, Adams was one of the most distinguished statesmen in the United States.

Nevertheless, in Hamilton's scale of values, these qualifications were outweighed by Adams' quirks of personality, the "wrongheadedness" of which he was sometimes guilty, and the low esteem in which he was reputed to hold George Washington. In his long political career, Adams had distinguished himself as the very archetype of the civilian: during the Revolutionary War, he freely criticized the American generals, insisted upon the subordination of the military to the civilian government and advocated the annual election of commanding officers by the Continental Congress. Understandably, therefore, John Adams was not a popular figure at headquarters.

Hamilton suspected that this crusty, intractable and opinionated New Englander had helped to make life miserable for the army during the war and that he had conspired to remove Washington as Commander in Chief. Certainly it was true that Adams was jealous of Washington: like Hamilton, he felt that the Commander in Chief, together with Benjamin Franklin, had monopolized the glory of the Revolution. For these reasons, Hamilton feared that if Adams were placed in the vice-presidency, he would intrigue against Washington and that the administration would be rent by the broils and contentions of its two highest officers.[3]

It was therefore "deemed an essential point of caution," Hamilton later said, "to take care, that accident, or an intrigue of the opposers of the government, should not raise Mr. Adams instead of General Washington, to the first place." Hamilton's method of avoiding a miscarriage in the Electoral College was to make sure that the electors voted unanimously for Washington and that votes were withheld from John Adams. To accomplish his second objective he induced a few prominent politicians in Connecticut, Pennsylvania and New Jersey to throw away the electoral votes of those states. From Hamilton's point of view, the plan worked to perfection: Washington received a unanimous vote in the Electoral College; John Adams fell far short of unanimity.[4]

John Adams did not take kindly to this jockeying of the vote in the Electoral College: he swore that there was a "dark and dirty intrigue . . . to spread a panic lest John Adams should be President." Fortunately for Hamilton, the irascible New Englander did not know who was responsible for his discomfiture. On his part, Hamilton could not forgive the man he had injured for displaying such peevishness, jealousy and vanity as to complain because a few votes were withheld from him to make certain that George Washington would be elected President.

The leadership of the House of Representatives passed almost without question to James Madison, the dominant figure in the Constitutional Convention. Since many members of the House of Representatives had served as delegates to that assemblage, there existed, as regards both leadership and membership, a strong continuity between the Constitutional Convention and the first Congress. To a marked degree, the men who had drawn up the Constitution were now faced with the responsibility of coping on a practical level with the necessities that in 1787 had produced the Federal Constitution.

Chief among these necessities was revenue, the lack of which had been primarily responsible for the downfall of the Articles of Confederation. It was here that Madison first exerted his powers of leadership over Congress.

In a plan submitted to Congress in April, 1789, he indicated how revenue could be raised expeditiously without at the same time alienating the taxpayers from the new government. Madison proposed that import duties on foreign goods and tonnage duties on foreign ships be made the financial mainstay of the federal government. To that end, he recommended that a 5 per cent ad valorem duty be imposed upon all imports and that protective duties, ranging as high as 50 per cent, be assessed upon certain enumerated articles manufactured in the United States.

Second only to revenue, Madison placed the necessity of reinvigorating the American merchant marine. Depleted by the War of Independence and hampered in its recovery by the restrictive laws adopted by Great Britain, American shipping in 1789 seemed to Madison to stand in urgent need of the "fostering care" of government. He urged that this care be provided by means of a sliding scale of tonnage duties which favored American over foreign ships with a view of creating an American merchant marine sufficient to the needs of the United States.

In essence, Madison attempted to erect one all-embracing mercantilist system in the place of the thirteen different systems that had hitherto existed in the United States. But he did not rest here: he sought to use the powers granted the federal government to effect a fundamental shift in American trade from Great Britain to France by imposing discriminatory duties upon British ships, merchandise and raw materials. His purpose, he made clear, was to install France in the position occupied by Great Britain as the principal market and source of supply of the United States. That this would involve commercial warfare with Great Britain Madison freely admitted, but he was certain that the United States would be able to impose its will upon the former mother country. In the meantime, he held out to French and American merchants and manufacturers the delectable prospect of succeeding to the markets and profits wrested from the British.

Madison did not attempt to conceal the fact that the financial burden of this economic struggle with Great Britain would fall largely upon southern planters. Since most of their agricultural produce was carried to market by British ships, the higher freight rates that would inevitably result from a switch to American ships would have to be borne by southern producers. In Madison's opinion, it was a price well worth paying: the growth of northern shipping and manufactures would break the "shackles" that bound the economy of the United States to Great Britain. Among these shackles he included British credit, which, his friend Jefferson said, had rendered southern planters "a specie of property annexed to certain mercantile houses in London."[5]

As "Publius," Hamilton had made the necessity of taking reprisals against Great Britain one of the arguments for the adoption of the Constitution. If the United States government were in a position to exclude British ships from American ports—which, under the Articles of Confederation, it was not—Hamilton predicted that the republic could negotiate "with the fairest prospect of success, for commercial privileges of the most valuable and extensive kind, in the dominions of that kingdom." Hamilton had been even more specific in his predictions of the blessings to come: rather than see their trade ruined by the United States, the British would open the West Indies to American ships and grant concessions to Americans in the British Isles themselves.[6]

But when in 1789 he saw the drift of Madison's proposals, he was thunderstruck. What malign spirit, he asked, had moved Madison to introduce such proposals into the House of Representatives? Nothing could be more ill-timed, in Hamilton's estimation, than a trade war with Great Britain while the republic was struggling to get on its feet. Without a continuation of peaceful commercial relations with Great Britain, Hamilton saw no hope of attaining financial solvency: only from import and tonnage duties—largely paid by British merchandise and ships—could the United States draw sufficient revenue to pay the national debt.

Equally inimical to the welfare of the republic, Madison's plan seemed certain to destroy what small foundation already existed in the United States for the expansion of its agriculture, manufacturing and shipping. As Hamilton knew, that foundation was provided by British credit: deprived of this mainstay, the entire economy of the republic seemed likely to collapse. In Hamilton's eyes, this was equivalent to killing the goose that laid the golden eggs. While he was not surprised to find southern congressmen in full cry after that wonder-working fowl, it shocked him to see James Madison trying to strangle it.

On the other hand, Hamilton applauded Madison's eagerness to draw tighter the bonds of economic union between the North and South. He was likewise charmed by Madison's willingness to see the South bear the brunt of the economic burden incidental to building up northern shipping. His only regret in this respect was that there were not more Virginians who shared this inclination to make financial sacrifices in such a good cause.

To undo what he supposed to be the harmful effects of Madison's anti-British policy, Hamilton emphatically dissociated himself from the sentiments expressed by his friend. To the unofficial British agent then in New York, he apologized for Madison's apparent backsliding into the spirit of '76. "The truth is," he told Major Beckwith, the British agent, "that although this gentleman [Madison] is a clever man, he is very little acquainted with the world. That he is uncorrupted and uncorruptible I have not a doubt; he has the same end in view that I have, and so have these gentlemen who act with him, but their mode of attaining it is very different." For his part, he continued, he had never supposed that a trade war was the way to obtain concessions from Great Britain. Moreover, he acknowledged that

England had accorded American shipping certain indulgences which would be forfeited if the United States attempted to gain its ends by coercion. For these reasons, he told the British agent, he was "decidedly opposed" to joining Madison in challenging Great Britain to a commercial war.

In this stand, Hamilton received support from an unexpected quarter—the northern merchants and shipowners, whom Madison proposed to enrich, rejected the proffered boon. Made cautious by returning prosperity, the northern merchants were now more disposed to count their blessings than to enumerate their grievances. Such complaints as they had against British commercial practices—and the exclusion of American ships from the British West Indies especially rankled—they were inclined to settle by negotiation rather than by a resort to economic warfare. To ward off that evil, they even deplored the injustice that would be done southern planters who would be compelled to foot the bills for aggrandizing the mercantile interests of the North.

As for excluding British ships from American ports, they protested that they could not fill the demand for cargo space; and they could not promise that they could build ships fast enough to meet the emergency, particularly if they were deprived of British credit. That resource had never seemed more essential to them: the trade recently opened up between the United States and China and the East Indies required large amounts of capital which only the British could supply.

Although the House of Representatives voted in 1789 to discriminate against British shipping and manufactures, the Senate rejected Madison's bill. As a result, the Tariff and Tonnage Acts of 1789 imposed no discriminatory duties upon British shipping: while American ships were given a favored position, French and British merchant vessels were placed upon an equal footing in American ports in accord with the most-favored-nation principle, despite the fact that France had made treaties of alliance and commerce with the United States.*

The part played by Madison in this business led Hamilton to conclude that his friend was really a Virginian under the skin and, what was even worse, a Virginia politician. The idea of retaliating upon Great Britain seemed to Hamilton to bear all the marks of having been conceived upon a Virginia plantation by men who hated their creditors for having loaned them money. Equally alarming, Hamilton detected in Madison signs of a "speculative philosopher" who put theoretical considerations before the real needs of the country.

Madison attributed the defeat of the discriminatory part of his bill to "New York influence." But in reality this plan created misgivings in the

* By this act, American shippers gained a considerable advantage over their foreign competitors. A duty of six cents a ton was levied on American ships as against fifty cents a ton on foreign ships. At the same time, American shipping was given a monopoly of the coasting trade, and goods imported in American ships were given a discount of 10 per cent of the duties.

minds of both southern planters and northern businessmen. The planters did not share Madison's willingness to aggrandize the North in the interests of the national security and welfare; and northern businessmen had no desire to hurl themselves upon the British trident just when they were beginning to get their heads out of water. They were satisfied, at least for the time being, with the substantial benefits conferred upon them by the tariff and tonnage acts. But the same could not be said of the southern planters: from them emanated a steadily mounting chorus of complaint that they were saddled with a disproportionate share of the tax burden of the new government.[7]

In the summer of 1789, while Congress was engaged in establishing the various departments of the Executive Branch of the government, Hamilton deliberately made himself available for the post of Secretary of the Treasury. When his friends urged him to stand for election to the United States Senate or to indicate his willingness to serve as Chief Justice of the United States Supreme Court, he declined the honor, alleging pressing private business. When they exhorted him to run against George Clinton for the governorship of New York, he "steadily rejected the idea in the most explicit manner." He had a score to settle with George Clinton, but he preferred to smite that Antifederalist leader with the powers of the federal government rather than to engage in dubious battle with the governor in his own bailiwick.[8]

Few men would have willingly chosen the Treasury as their reward for services rendered to the Constitution. It was the graveyard of reputations, a bourn from which no man returned with his name unsmirched. As in 1781, the state of the national finances appeared to be "a deep, dark, and dreary chaos," the ordering of which might well have been added to the labors of Hercules. Moreover, there were few men in the United States with sufficient training and experience to undertake the duties of the Secretary of the Treasury. In the arts of war, government, science and painting, Americans had produced men of genius, but it was wryly admitted that they "were not well acquainted with the most abstruse science in the world [public finance], which they never had any necessity to study." In the United States, it was said, "a good financier is as rare as a phoenix"; financial crises were perennial, but financiers appeared only once or twice in a century.[9]

By 1789, Washington was persuaded that if his former aide-de-camp was not exactly a phoenix, he was certainly a rare bird. Therefore when James Madison and Robert Morris urged him to appoint Hamilton to the Treasury —Morris said that the young man was "damned sharp"—Washington gladly sent Hamilton's name to the Senate. The appointment was quickly confirmed and in September, 1789, Alexander Hamilton became the first Secretary of the United States Treasury.[10]

In accepting this office, Hamilton was aware that he was putting to the hazard his own financial security as well as his reputation. It was the first consideration that seems to have given him momentary pause: could he afford to take a post that paid only $3,000 a year? Hamilton was not a rich man; he had a growing family to support; and he was just beginning to reap the full reward of his law practice. For these reasons, some of his friends advised him to decline the appointment. To them Hamilton replied that "his going into public life would materially affect his pecuniary prospects, but he thought it would be in his power, in the financial department, to do the country great good; and this consideration outweighed, with him, every consideration of a private nature." "In undertaking the task," he said in October, 1789, "I hazarded much, but I thought it an occasion that called upon me to hazard." Danger was his element and he plunged in with an ardor and self-confidence hardly matched by William Pitt when he became Prime Minister of Great Britain at the age of twenty-four.

With Hamilton on the threshold of his career as Secretary of the Treasury, the American people would have been well advised to take a close look at this young man who was so relentlessly bent upon doing them good. They would have seen a smallish man—he was about five feet seven inches—whose deficiency in height was compensated by his slenderness and his erect military bearing. He had a fine presence: always elegantly dressed in the height of fashion—and this was an age in which the male came closest to resembling the peacock—he stood out in all companies by the bold colors he affected in waistcoats and the dashing air with which he wore his lace and ruffles. In the eighteenth century, women affected to admire "a well-turned leg" in men; and Hamilton's legs, decked out in the finest stockings, were the envy of the beaux. Certainly there has never been a more sartorially resplendent Secretary of the Treasury—or one more calculated to set female hearts fluttering. Here was no dry-as-dust statistician, spouting facts and figures like a walking encyclopedia, but a figure of romance whose impeccable manners would have won approval from Lord Chesterfield himself.[11]

Hamilton's features, if not exactly handsome, were strong and well-defined; the angle of his jaw denoted a purposeful nature and his eyes were deep-set and piercing. Certainly he was not a man to suffer fools gladly or to defer to men less well endowed intellectually than himself. He impressed not a few people as vain and arrogant—there was a certain stiffness and formality in his manner, it was observed, which reduced his effectiveness as a political leader. Certainly there was nothing of the hail-fellow-well-met about him. On the other hand, among his friends, Hamilton seemed to be the most generous, eloquent, charitable, patriotic, forceful and charming of men. They could not say enough in praise of his "lively imagination—a quick and almost intuitive perception—profound and comprehensive views, a ready invention of expedients in cases of difficulty, with a solid & correct judgment." He ruled by virtue of his intellectual pre-eminence and the

The First Secretary of the Treasury

ardor and conviction with which he propounded his ideas. In the select circles of his intimates, it was remarked that Hamilton was "so much trusted, admired, beloved, and adored, that his power over their affections was entire."[12]

While Hamilton disdained the arts of popularity and the more commonly accepted methods of influencing the mass mind, his best qualities were displayed in a small group of his peers. Here the very characteristics that alienated popular support—his candor, his contempt for the low shifts of politics, his partiality for the company of the rich, the well-born and the educated—were seen to best advantage. As a political leader, Hamilton conducted himself like a general of an army: instead of dealing directly with the rank and file, he operated through hand-picked subordinates; he was primarily a policy maker and leader of leaders. Holding demagoguery in abhorrence, Hamilton leaned so far in the opposite direction that he almost succeeded in disqualifying himself from becoming an effective popular leader.[13]

Some of Hamilton's friends found him too inflexible in his ideas: Gouverneur Morris, for example, traced most of Hamilton's difficulties to "the pertinacious adherence to opinions he had once formed." It is true that Hamilton's convictions were strongly held and that he seldom changed his mind; but, at the same time, he was capable of moving slowly and patiently toward his objective, and he possessed a sense of timing that, at least in the early and most constructive period of his career, did not play him false. And yet it remained true that while Hamilton was capable of compromise, he could not conciliate: it was not for him to hold a party together by bridging differences between divergent groups or sections. By temperament as well as by the intensity with which he sought to realize his objectives, Hamilton was best fitted to be the leader of a small group of devoted followers.[14]

If the American people did not already know it, they were soon to be made acutely aware of the fact that Hamilton's credo was audacity and yet more audacity. Where others temporized, calculated the risks and paused in indecision, Hamilton acted; he was above all a man of action, not a philosopher seeking some elusive abstract truth. Whether consciously or not, he based his life upon a maxim of Machiavelli: "I certainly think that it is better to be impetuous than cautious," said the Florentine statesman, "for fortune is a woman, and it is necessary, if you wish to master her, to conquer her by force; and it can be seen that she lets herself be overcome by the bold rather than by those who proceed coldly. And, therefore, like a woman, she is always a friend to the young, because they are less cautious, fiercer, and master her with greater audacity." But as Hamilton perhaps insufficiently recognized, this goddess, after lavishing favors upon her worshipers, was also capable of destroying them utterly.

An even less sanguine man than Hamilton might have been forgiven for imagining that he was a favorite of fortune. He had repeatedly made audacity pay off richly: when he assumed the post of Secretary of the Treasury, if experience could be trusted, there was nothing to which he might not aspire. Hamilton had come a long way by pushing his luck, and he thought that the United States ought to act upon the principle that had guided him in the conduct of his own life. Certainly he believed that the United States was the last place in the world where caution ought to be accounted a virtue; and, almost to the last, the events of his career vindicated his philosophy of risking, venturing and striving.

Despite his keen appreciation of the part played by economic forces in the shaping of men's destiny, Hamilton held the "great man" view of history. He tended to glorify the hero, the great state builders, the daring and farsighted who had brought order out of chaos and raised nations to the pinnacle of power. He did not think that the people had leadership, political wisdom and initiative in themselves—leadership came from the exceptional individuals, the "natural aristocrats" and the rich and educated. Leadership, he held, could not wait for the pressures of public opinion: the impulse must be communicated from the government to the masses. In short, it was incumbent upon a stateman to act for the national welfare, and he could not evade this responsibility by thrusting it upon the people or their representatives.

During the Revolutionary War, Hamilton recorded in his Artillery Company Account Book a quotation from Demosthenes' orations that might be regarded as the guiding principle of his career: "As a general marches at the head of his troops, so ought wise politicians, if I dare use the expression, to march at the head of affairs. . . . They ought not to wait the event, to know what measures to take; but the measures which they have taken, ought to produce the *event*." In the writings of Plutarch and Machiavelli he found a wealth of examples of leaders who, dedicating themselves to a great cause, had triumphed over adversity. Hamilton, too, had found his cause—the creation of a nation—and he was sustained by the conviction that all the obstacles to its realization could be overcome by the exercise of wisdom and resolution on the part of a determined men.[15]

16.
The Report on Public Credit

With a new and untried Constitution, a crushing burden of debt, and two states still out of the union, it might well have seemed advisable for the government to feel its way cautiously toward the "more perfect union" envisaged by the framers of the Constitution. James Madison, for one, believed that in order to establish the government firmly in the affections of the people, it was essential that the administration adopt a mild and conciliatory policy. The Bill of Rights represented his contribution to the spirit of amity.

In *The Federalist,* Hamilton had given the impression that he, too, was resigned to moving slowly toward his objectives. Acknowledging that the union was fundamentally federal in nature, he declared that "'tis time only that can mature and perfect so compound a system, can liquidate the meaning of all the parts, and can adjust them to each other in a harmonious and consistent WHOLE." He had frequently made light of the fear that the federal government would aggress upon the states: content with its powers of commerce, finance, peace and war, he contended, it would be under no temptation to invade the powers reserved to the states, because such powers "would contribute nothing to the dignity, to the importance, or the splendor of the national government."

And yet Hamilton was not a man to wait for time to effect the consummation he devoutly wished—the triumph of the national government over the states. He had observed that the Constitution was "a fabric which can hardly be stationary, and which will retrograde if it cannot be made to advance." Neither the national government nor the states could afford to stand still, for a constitutional equilibrium was unthinkable between sovereign powers engaged in a life-and-death struggle for power.[1]

Some nationalists took comfort in the thought that the Constitution had created "a great Oak which is to reduce them [the states] to paltry shrubs," but Hamilton feared that for this very reason the states would not rest until they had hewn down the monarch of the forest. He was certain in his own mind that the only way to prevent them from doing so was to lay the ax to the root of state sovereignty. Nothing that had occurred in the United

States since the adoption of the Constitution had altered his opinion that "the centrifugal is much stronger than the centripetal force in these States—the seeds of disunion much more numerous than those of union." All the passions which governed men—ambition, avarice and self-interest—appeared to him to attach the people to the states, thereby ensuring that they would always be an overmatch for the general government. Not until there had been established "such a compleat sovereignty in the general Government as will turn all the strong principles & passions" to its side was Hamilton disposed to pronounce the union out of danger.

Of all the problems confronting the Washington administration, none was more complex, more urgent and less understood than was the national debt. And yet the success of the Constitution and the very existence of the republic depended upon the skill with which the financial obligations of the government were handled. Hamilton had always contended that the government could not endure without credit "commensurate with the utmost extent of the lending faculties of the community"; but credit could not be established until provision had been made for the existing debt. Little could be done toward disposing of the existing debt, however, until the government had regained its ability to borrow. Truly, the finances of the United States were a dilemma wrapped in a paradox.

If Hamilton was impelled by some inner compulsion to reduce chaos to order, the finances of the United States offered ample scope for that propensity. The domestic debt consisted of a chaos of virtually worthless paper money; loan-office certificates; IOU's signed by the Quartermaster and commissary generals; lottery prizes (the government had conducted lotteries but had been unable to pay the winners in cash); certificates given to soldiers and officers in lieu of pay; indents (paper certificates representing interest paid on the debt); Treasury certificates; and various other evidences of debt. Hardly a means of going into debt known to the governments of the eighteenth century had been omitted by the Continental Congress: and it enjoyed the unenviable distinction of having more creditors than any other government in the world.

When Hamilton came to the Treasury, the foreign debt of the United States was about $10 million, plus $1,600,000 in arrears of interest. The domestic debt Hamilton estimated to be slightly over $27 million, not including $13 million in accrued interest. The total debt therefore stood at slightly over $50 million. But there was no certainty in these figures: how much debt in the form of certificates had been contracted by the various agencies of the government—the commissary and quartermaster accounts were especially confused—was known, as one congressman observed, only to the Supreme Being. Although commissioners had been appointed by the Continental Congress to settle the accounts of individuals holding claims

The Report on Public Credit

against the government, their work had not been completed. Nor had the claims of the states against the general government been ascertained: here was a terra incognita, an impenetrable wasteland of unliquidated debt.

To a less sanguine and resolute man than Hamilton, the national debt might well have appeared more like an albatross hung about the neck of the federal government than a sword with which to vanquish the states. For this mass of paper seemed to lie like a dead weight upon the national economy, stifling governmental credit and diverting into speculation capital which might have been more profitably employed in business enterprise. And, despite all that the government could do, the debt was constantly increasing: revenue was inadequate to meet even the interest which the government had pledged itself to pay.[2]

Under these circumstances, some Americans were of the opinion that the government ought to repudiate the national debt and start out with a clean financial slate. Why, they asked, should the federal government bankrupt itself in order to repay money that had served its purpose and from which everyone had profited in the form of independence of Great Britain? It seemed to them perfectly proper for the government to inform its creditors that, through no fault of its own, the debt was cancelled.[3]

As an exponent of strong government, Hamilton did not deny that under some conditions the government was privileged to repudiate its debts. The highest law of the state, he admitted, was self-preservation; when its existence was at stake, a government could alter the terms of contracts, discriminate between various groups of creditors and declare its obligations null and void. But he emphatically did not agree that this right ought to be applied to the existing debt. In his opinion, the federal government was capable of fulfilling in all essentials the terms of the contract it had made with its creditors and was therefore debarred from entering a plea of abatement.

Besides the purely legal aspect, every consideration—morality, justice and expediency—seemed to Hamilton to require that the government dealt honestly with its creditors. "Establish that a government may decline a provision for its debts, though able to make it," he said, "and you overthrow all public morality.... You have anarchy, despotism, or what you please, but you have no *just* or *regular* government." For governments, the first commandment was: honor thy financial obligations. According to the gospel preached by Hamilton, if "the dead corpse of the public credit" was to be resurrected, it would not be by a miracle but by the observance of probity and sound bookkeeping.[4]

In October, 1789, Hamilton was given an opportunity to put these ideas to the test. Having received petitions from the public creditors asking that funds be set aside for the payment of the national debt, Congress requested the Secretary of the Treasury to submit a plan for "the adequate support of the public credit." Hamilton gave full latitude to this directive: in his Report on Public Credit he undertook to show how the debt could be paid, to whom it should be paid and what was to be done with the state debts dating from the Revolutionary War.

Displaying an optimism to which nothing in the previous financial experience of the United States gave warrant, Hamilton took the position that the tariff could be made to furnish the government with sufficient revenue to liquidate the national debt and at the same time pay the operating expenses of the government. He admitted of no doubt that the foreign debt must be paid in full, accrued interest and all, but at the same time he declared his determination to stretch every resource of the government in order to do justice to the domestic creditors. Everything he had said and done up to the time of his appointment as Secretary of the Treasury indicated that he held the satisfaction of these claims to be a prerequisite to the success of the Federal Constitution.[5]

If the domestic creditors were to be paid, the question inevitably arose: which creditors? For in 1789, the securities of the United States government were for the most part not in the possession of the original holders: they had been transferred—often at a fraction of their nominal value—to purchasers who bought them for speculative or investment purposes. As a result, the evidences of governmental debt had gravitated into the hands of a few, most of whom were residents of the northern states. A class and a section therefore stood to profit from the payment of the debt. In view of this change of ownership, Hamilton was confronted with the question whether the original holders or their assignees ought to receive the windfall that would descend when the government redeemed its securities at face value.[6]

Hamilton had long since made up his mind that the possessors of these securities, whether original holders or purchasers, were entitled to the full usufruct. The certificates themselves stated that the amount thereon specified should be paid to the bearer, thereby creating, said Hamilton, a contractual relationship that made them as much the property of bona fide purchasers "as their houses or their lands, their hats or their coats." Moreover, the Continental Congress had assured foreign capitalists that there would be no discrimination between original holders and assignees—and upon the strength of this promise, Dutch bankers had purchased securities worth many thousands of dollars. If the federal government now attempted to discriminate in the name of equity between different types of creditors, Hamilton was prepared to renounce all hope that foreigners would ever again trust their money to the perfidious republicans across the Atlantic.[7]

All Hamilton's plans for the financial and economic development of the United States were founded upon the assumption that government bonds would be freely transferrable—otherwise they could not serve as a supplementary circulating medium, nor could they be used to stimulate capitalistic

The Report on Public Credit

enterprise. If discrimination were adopted, Hamilton saw an end to this prospect: the pledges of the government would carry no weight with men who had learned from experience that it broke its promises to suit its convenience; and no man could buy a certificate in the confidence that he was acquiring a good title.[8]

Although he did not say so in his Report on Public Credit, Hamilton's attitude toward the men who were engaged in engrossing the national debt had undergone a sea change since the days of the Revolutionary War. The righteous warmth of that earlier period had been succeeded by a coldly realistic view of the advantages of speculation and concentration of wealth in a capitalistic economy. In many respects, the speculators were men after his own heart: these were the kind of capitalists he wished to see take over the direction of the national economy. At a time when the government's credit had almost reached the vanishing point, they had staked their money upon a hazard the success of which "turned on little less than a revolution in government." Men willing to risk their wealth on long chances he deemed indispensable to a flourishing capitalism; he liked his capitalism spiced with audacity and he found this particular ingredient abundantly among the purchasers of government securities. Moreover, with a perspicacity not always evidenced by twentieth-century statesmen, Hamilton saw that if capitalism were to prosper, capitalists were indispensable. Since he knew of no effective substitute for capitalism, he believed that one of the principal duties of a government dedicated to the general welfare was to foster capitalism by affording every facility to the accumulation of wealth. And, since the United States had few large aggregations of capital, Hamilton thought that the government ought to take an active part in creating wealth and in making sure that it got into the hands of those able to make the best use of it.[9]

Thus, from Hamilton's point of view, an equal distribution of the government's largesse would not have advanced his purpose. As David Hume had observed, capital was of comparatively little value to the economy and to the state "if it is dispersed into numberless hands, which either squander it in idle show and magnificence, or employ it in the purchase of the common necessaries of life." Hamilton was primarily concerned with those individuals who possessed a disposable surplus of capital which could be devoted to the support of the government and to the furthering of economic enterprise. To an eighteenth-century statesman bent upon creating the conditions in which capitalism could flourish, the "improvident majority" was of little importance.[10]

Even conceding that equity required that something be done for the original holders, Hamilton took the position in his Report on Public Credit that it was wholly impracticable inasmuch as many of the original records had disappeared or, in some instances, had never existed. He therefore felt justified in saying that any attempt to ascertain and reimburse the original holders would produce endless fraud and perjury and, "beyond all powers of calculation, multiply the evils of speculation."[11]

The impracticability of discriminating between original holders and purchasers, while decisive in most cases, did not apply to the army. Here a semblance of bookkeeping had been preserved: the names of the soldiers and the amounts paid them in certificates had been set down and were open for inspection. Moreover, it was notorious that the soldiers had been compelled to sell their certificates for a pittance. Under the circumstances, it would be an injury indeed to force them to pay taxes for the enrichment of speculators.

Many Federalists, including President Washington, had supposed that one of the first acts of the new government would be to do justice to the soldiers. As a former officer and member of the Cincinnati, Hamilton could be expected to share this feeling. Moreover, for the conditions that had compelled the soldiers to sell their certificates for what they would bring, Hamilton was in no way responsible. Had his plans been adopted in 1783, much of the evils of speculation would have been avoided. At that time, Hamilton was the champion of the soldiers and civilians to whom the government was then indebted. He deplored speculation in government securities as "a pernicious drain of our cash from the channels of productive industry" and he disdained to buy soldiers' certificates at the prevailing price—it was too much like blood money.[12]

And yet, where reasons of state were concerned, Hamilton was capable of closing his mind to the promptings of the softer side of his nature. When he was compelled to choose between strengthening the authority of the government and inflicting inequities upon individuals, Hamilton never hesitated to act as the interests of the state dictated. He later said that Talleyrand was "the greatest of modern statesmen, because he had well known it was necessary both to suffer wrong to be done and to do it."[13]

As a soldier, Hamilton had suffered wrong; as Secretary of the Treasury, he found it necessary to inflict wrong upon his former comrades-in-arms. He refused to make any exception in his opposition to discrimination in favor of the officers and men of the Revolutionary Army. Herein he demonstrated an indifference—unprecedented among politicians—to the soldiers' vote; but this was only one instance among many in which he proved that he would rather be right, according to his lights, than to win votes.

Besides the mass of depreciated securities and paper money issued by the Continental Congress, the people of the United States labored under a heavy load of state debts. Like the national debt, the evidences of state indebtedness had followed the well-worn course from original holders to

The Report on Public Credit

speculators and investors. Hamilton's constant objective was to bind these men to the national government by the durable ties of "*Ambition* and *Avarice*"; but as matters stood in 1789, ambition and avarice tended to attach the state creditors to the state governments. As long as the states possessed their debts, they were certain to compete with the federal government for the allegiance of the creditor class and for the citizens' tax dollar. The result, Hamilton feared, would be that the states would attempt to pre-empt (as the Constitution, by recognizing concurrent taxation, permitted them to do) the remaining objects of taxation and that the affluent citizens of the United States would be divided against themselves, the state creditors seeking to strengthen the states while the holders of federal securities endeavored to aggrandize the powers and the revenues of the national government.*

It can be said of Hamilton that whenever he saw a Gordian knot, he attempted to cut it forthwith. In this instance, he called in his Report on Public Credit for the assumption by the federal government of $25 million of state debts incurred in the prosecution of the War of Independence. Here he acted upon the principle that "if all the public creditors receive their dues from one source, distributed by an equal hand, their interest will be the same. And, having the same interests, they will unite in the support of the fiscal arrangements of the Government." Thus the most valuable members of the community—valuable because they were the most liberally endowed with the goods of this world—would bestow their affections and, Hamilton hoped, their money upon the federal government. With all the creditors, state and national, gathered into the fold of the federal government, Hamilton's vision of a powerful national government, supreme over the states, would begin to assume concrete reality.[14]

But was not the federal government inviting financial ruin by taking upon itself $25 million of the debts of the states? If Hamilton's plan were adopted, the debt of the United States government would soar to $80 million or more. At one time, Americans had been in the habit of talking in terms of hundreds of millions of dollars, but that was in the piping days of paper money when, as a member of Congress remarked, a million dollars was like a sprat in a whale's belly. Hamilton was clearly not thinking of the kind of money that was fed whales, or, as was more often the case, used as wallpaper. Furthermore, only a confirmed optimist could have struck the rock of national resources in the expectation that streams of revenue would gush forth: when tapped previously, it had given forth only a hollow sound,

---

* Hamilton regarded concurrent taxation as "the Gordion-knot of our political situation." In *The Federalist* he observed that the only way concurrent taxation could be made workable was for each government to exercise "reciprocal forbearance" by respecting the rights of the first occupant. As Secretary of the Treasury, Hamilton left no doubt that he intended the federal government to do the occupying, while forbearance was to be practiced by the states.

as of a great void. Even Hamilton went through a long and painful period of doubt before he could bring himself to cast the die. His state of mind was that of a soldier resolved at all costs to storm the enemy's entrenchments. "In a personal view," he remarked, "it would have been pusillanimity and weakness to have stopped short of a provision for the aggregate debt of the country." It remained to be seen whether he had not overreached himself in his anxiety to consolidate the debt and the political power it connoted in the federal government.[15]

Hamilton's confidence that he had not overtaxed the resources of the federal government was based largely upon the system of funding the debt he proposed in his Report on Public Credit. And, indeed, the funding system was the very heart of Hamilton's financial planning. Instead of annual appropriations by the legislature toward debt retirement, the creditors of the United States government were offered by Hamilton permanent appropriations inviolably dedicated to the payment of interest and principal. Every guarantee possible under the Federal Constitution against popular "instability" and "caprice" was given the public creditors: barring "one of those extraordinary crises of nations which confound all ordinary calculations," when all branches of the federal government might be "infected at one time with a common passion, or disposition, so manifestly inimical to justice and the public good," Hamilton assured the security holders that they might safely count upon the prompt payment of their obligations.[16]

In exchange for the security afforded by the funding system, Hamilton proposed to take what he called "a stout Slice" from the accrued interest owing the public creditors. This cut was contrary to his principles and wishes alike, but he felt that the payment of the full interest owing the security holders would require "the extension of taxation to a degree and to objects which the true interest of the public creditors forbids." Roughly, this deduction amounted to an interest rate of $4\frac{1}{2}$ instead of 6 per cent upon the national debt. While Hamilton did not attempt to disguise the fact that the creditors were offered less than their due, he took consolation in the thought that in the course of years the prevailing rate of commercial and governmental interest in the United States would fall to 4 per cent or less, thereby lessening the loss to the public creditors.*[17]

So punctilious was Hamilton in everything that pertained to the financial integrity of the government that he couched this proposal not as an ultimatum but as an appeal to the self-interest of the public creditors. Good faith, he declared, required that the creditors be left free to accept or reject

* Hamilton proposed that the public creditors should exchange their old securities for new certificates issued by the federal government. Upon some of these new bonds (the word was not used in the eighteenth century) the interest was cut to 3 per cent and in some other instances it was deferred until 1800.

the proffered terms. He refused to make their necessities a lever with which to extract better conditions; when he asked them to surrender a part of their claims, he offered them a fair equivalent in return. Hamilton was resolved to avoid any appearance of unilateral modification of the terms of the debt on the part of the government; he ruled out as an infringement of contractual rights anything that resembled coercion.*

Therefore he gave the security holders a wide choice of alternatives, including the privilege of standing upon the original conditions of the loan. He suggested no less than six different methods of payment, any one of which the creditors were privileged to accept. Their rights were in no way altered, abridged or impaired; they were entitled to a full 6 per cent interest and they could have the full measure if they insisted upon it. His whole objective seemed to be to conciliate the creditors; it was their pleasure that he consulted; and when he could not see his way clear to giving them their due, he offered them apologies and generous compensation. Seemingly his only regret was that he could not do more for these estimable men.

That the public creditors would accept these alterations in the terms of their contracts Hamilton felt certain. He believed that he was dealing with men capable beyond the ordinary run of mankind of discerning their true interest. "Those who are most commonly creditors of a nation," he observed, "are, generally speaking, enlightened men. . . . When a candid and fair appeal is made to them, they will understand their true interest too well to refuse their concurrence in such modifications of their claims as any real necessity may demand." Moreover, being men of affairs, they would not fail to see that the resources of the government were limited and that the terms offered them were the best that could be made.[18]

To anyone acquainted with the working of British government and economy, Hamilton's report had a familiar ring. Great Britain bore witness how a funded national debt could be converted into a national blessing by binding men of wealth to the government, stimulating capitalistic development and promoting financial stability. The ability of the British government to pay its debts had become "in the British mind," Hamilton marveled, "an article of faith, and is no longer an article of reason." He was now prepared to believe that the credit of that government was immortal. His task was to confer a similar immortality upon the credit of the United States government without, he lamented, the benefit of the British constitution and British capital.[19]

* In 1789, William Bingham of Philadelphia, one of the wealthiest men in the United States and the holder of many thousands of dollars of government securities, returned from England where he had observed at first hand the fiscal reforms introduced by William Pitt the Younger. On the strength of this indoctrination in British finance, he urged Hamilton in November, 1789, to emulate Pitt by consolidating and funding the debt, creating a sinking fund and establishing a national bank. All the ingredients of what came to be known as Hamiltonian finance were contained in this letter. *Journal of Business and Economic History*, III, 672-673.

17.

"Speculators" vs. "Patriots"

Just before Hamilton submitted his report to Congress, President Washington was congratulating himself upon "the growing unanimity and encreasing goodwill of the Citizens to the Government." The President had never felt more optimistic about the prospects of a quiet and prosperous administration: crops were good, commerce was thriving and manufactures were increasing, and opposition to the new government was melting away. As John Marshall later said, "the apprehensions of danger to liberty from the new system . . . were visibly wearing off; the popularity of the administration was communicating itself to the government; and the materials with which the discontented few were furnished, could not yet be efficaciously employed."

Upon this happy scene, Hamilton's report fell like a bolt from the blue, utterly destroying the President's hope that his administration would inaugurate an era of good feelings. In John Marshall's words, Hamilton's financial program "seemed to unchain all those fierce passions which a high respect for the government and for those who administered it, had in a great measure maintained." Before the storm blew itself out, some Americans were seriously considering disunion. And this two years after the creation of "a more perfect union"!

On January 9, 1790, Hamilton informed the House of Representatives that his report was ready for its consideration. But the House was not ready to receive Hamilton's work, for immediately the question was raised whether the Secretary's report should be made in writing or in person. Elias Boudinot of New Jersey, beginning his career as one of Hamilton's spokesmen in the House, argued that the report should be made in person "in order to answer such inquiries as the members might be disposed to make, for," he added, "it is a justifiable surmise that gentlemen would not be able clearly to comprehend so intricate a subject without oral illustration." No doubt, Hamilton would have welcomed an opportunity to elucidate his plan to the House. But Fisher Ames and Elbridge Gerry, both well disposed toward Hamilton, contended that the report should be made in writing in order to give it permanency and to prevent misunderstandings. Congress decided in favor of reading the Secretary's report rather than hearing him in person—and thereby set a precedent which became one of the established forms of the national government.[1]

Almost a month elapsed between the presentation of Hamilton's report and the formal opening of debate. On February 8, 1790, the subject of the public debt was taken up in the Committee of the Whole and the Secretary's report was declared to be before the House.

Hamilton had expected opposition—his report contained elaborate arguments designed to refute all possible criticism of his plans—but he had not expected opposition from the quarter in which it came. For in February, 1790, James Madison declared his intention of speaking against Hamilton's report.

Nothing except the defection of President Washington could have given Hamilton a more unpleasant jolt. When he learned of Madison's decision, he exclaimed that it could not be true—he had already cleared his report with Madison and the Virginian had promised his support. So acute was his dismay that Hamilton declared that if he had known Madison was to oppose him, he would not have accepted the post of Secretary of the Treasury.

In actuality, Hamilton had at no time received positive assurance of Madison's aid; rather, he inferred such support from what he knew of the Virginian's views and from his silence while Hamilton was drawing up the Report on Public Credit. In November, 1789, Hamilton had solicited Madison's views regarding the financial problems confronting the country. In reply, Madison had suggested, among other things, the imposition of a direct federal land tax. Knowing that Madison had previously favored the assumption of state debts and the funding of the national debt, Hamilton had assumed that since his friend did not touch upon these matters in his letter of November, 1789, his attitude remained unchanged.

But Madison did not consider himself to be inviolably committed to these policies and he always reserved the right—of which he took full advantage—of changing his mind. In the case of the funding of the national debt, he was troubled by the fact that most of the benefit of that measure would go to Northerners and to a kind of Northerner he specially disliked—the speculators. Since Hamilton's report had been submitted to Congress, the speculators had been busy buying all the securities in sight, even going to the length of chartering ships to carry their agents to the southern states before the news of Hamilton's report reached that region. As a result, said Madison, the funding of the debt bore a totally different complexion from the days when he had favored that measure. As for the assumption of state debts, Madison found that Hamilton's plan worked such injustice upon Virginia that he could not consent to be a party to it.

In view of their long and intimate relationship, Hamilton ought to have known that Madison was not a Hamiltonian in the sense that word was defined in 1790. Although he had labored for a more perfect union, Madison had no confidence in a government that depended upon avarice for its principal support. He had never warmed to Hamilton's plan of converting the rich into pillars of the federal government by making them the recipients of the largesse of that government. On the contary, Madison feared that if advantage were given "the sagacious, the enterprising, and the moneyed few over the industrious and uninformed mass of the people," the few would oppress the many. He recoiled from the "impatient avidity for immediate and immoderate gain" in which Hamilton saw a potent force that might be made to work in the interests of union. Although he spoke quite as much as did Hamilton of "the fostering hand of government," he conceived the primary function of government to be that of holding a balance between the various conflicting interests and factions; and he insisted that government ought to be controlled from within in order to render it incapable of "setting up an interest adverse to that of the whole Society." "Justice" was a word frequently used by Madison to describe the operations of the federal government; Hamilton, on the other hand, dwelt largely upon national power and greatness. Finally, Madison was a Southerner and an agrarian and, like so many of his fellows, he held a public debt to be a public curse. For him, the "opulent minority" which the Constitution was designed to protect was composed of southern planters and farmers as well as of northern businessmen and capitalists; he held no brief for a government that singled out a certain kind of capitalist for special treatment. When he saw northern merchants and speculators gaining an advantage over the planters and farmers, his hackles rose: if the agrarians went down to defeat before the urbanized North, "what then," he asked, "will become of your government?"[2]

By 1790, Madison was pondering a more immediate problem—the deterioration of his political position in Virginia. He could not but be aware that he had carried his nationalism far beyond that of his constituents. In 1788, the voters had rebelled against his leadership and had rejected his candidacy for the United States Senate. It is clear that had he supported Hamilton's Report on Public Credit he would have forfeited all standing in Virginia; Patrick Henry would have denounced him in every corner of the state, and Madison almost certainly would have failed of re-election to the House of Representatives. No wonder, therefore, that Madison trimmed his sails to the breeze blowing out of Virginia, even though it meant taking a reef in nationalism.

In February, 1790, Madison launched his first attack upon Hamilton's report. He began by criticizing the nondiscriminatory feature of the funding system, dwelling at length upon the plight of the widows, orphans and ex-

"Speculators" vs. "Patriots"

soldiers who had been defrauded by unconscionable speculators. What would it profit the federal government, he asked, if in gaining the rich, it lost the affections of the people—the certain consequence of permitting this "shower of gold" to fall upon the rich alone? To avert such a miscarriage, Madison advocated a compromise whereby both the original holders and the purchasers of government securities would share in the profit that under Hamilton's plan would go to the speculators alone.

Undeniably it was a moving speech: strong congressmen were seen to weep as Madison pulled out the stops of pathos. But his plan lacked the one ingredient that would have recommended it to Congress—economy. As John Marshall said, Madison appealed to such considerations as generosity, justice and philanthropy, "the operation of which can never be very extensive." Congressmen eager to pare down the national debt found nothing to cheer about in Madison's proposals to make an equitable distribution between the original holders and the purchasers of the national debt. Indeed, between the bookkeeping, the searching of old records and the opening up of opportunities for fraud, Madison's plan promised to be more costly than Hamilton's solution of giving everything to the actual holders of the debt. And so, while applauding Madison's humanitarianism and eloquence, Congress voted down his proposals by a large majority.

Yet the significance of this event could not be wholly measured in terms of votes. As a result of his stand in favor of the rights of the original holders, Madison won the reputation throughout the country of a champion of the common man against the "moneyed interest." One of Madison's admirers urged the painter John Trumbull to depict the Virginian "pleading the cause of Justice and Humanity in Congress, an angel whispering in his ear, and a group of widows, orphans & decrepid soldiers, contemplating him with ineffable delight."

A very different allegorical portrait was designed for Hamilton. Surrounded by jackals, speculators and other predatory beasts of prey, he was pictured loading wealth upon his favorites while in the background lurked the sinister figures of a king and lords. "You enabled the proud speculator to roll along in his gilded chariot," it was said, "while the hardy veteran, who had fought and bled for your liberties, was left to toil for his support, or to beg his bread from door to door." Hamilton, it seemed, was acting upon the principle that to the speculators belong the spoils.

Although Madison carefully avoided casting any reflections upon the integrity and patriotism of the Secretary of the Treasury, this difference of opinion over discrimination "laid the foundation," Hamilton later observed, "of the great schism which has since prevailed." In Madison's concern for the welfare of the common people was the germ of the Republican party which he was later to lead; in Hamilton's insistence upon creating a powerful centralized government and a wealthy class which supported and was in turn supported by that government was prefigured the Federalist philosophy.[3]

Hamilton was given only a brief moment in which to rejoice that his report had weathered its first test. For Madison had merely begun to fight. He hit out next against the assumption of state debts; and here he could hardly miss, for Hamilton had laid himself open to criticism by insisting that the state debts accruing from the War of Independence be assumed in the sums at which they stood at the time he submitted his report. He took no account of the fact that, by disposing of their debts by taxation or, as was more often the case, by inflation and repudiation, some states had comparatively small debts in 1790, and that other states, supposing themselves to be creditors of the federal government for expenditures incurred during the war, expected their debts to be extinguished when a settlement was made. As a result, if Hamilton's plan were carried out, a few states, notably South Carolina and Massachusetts, which had debts of over $4 million each, would be immensely benefited; on the other hand, a state like Virginia, with a comparatively small debt (provided its claims against the federal government were validated), would receive only a small amount.

In his report, Hamilton had sought to anticipate the objections to which this feature of his plan was certain to give rise by pointing out that the state debts were in reality an obligation of the federal government and that the states which would profit most from assumption were those which had exerted themselves most zealously during the war. It could not be denied, however, that the citizens of some states would be obliged to pay taxes in order to pay the debts of certain favored states.

Unwilling that Virginians should help liquidate the debts of Massachusetts and South Carolina, Madison advocated that the federal government assume all the war debts—paid and unpaid—of the states, a measure which, while conferring undoubted benefits upon Virginia, would have almost doubled the amount of debt Hamilton was prepared to assume. Even though Madison's plan was not adopted—again the House boggled at the expense—he succeeded in throwing the legislature into a state of deadlock that lasted for five months. To add to the confusion, at one point Madison revived his attempt to impose discriminatory duties upon British ships and merchandise despite Hamilton's agonized cries that it would destroy the entire financial structure of the federal government. On another occasion, the debate was interrupted by a Quaker petition against slavery. This ill-timed measure further exacerbated Southerners' suspicion and distrust of their northern colleagues: a powerful central government, which would almost certainly be created by the adoption of Hamilton's financial plans, might constitute itself a menace to slavery.[4]

If Madison's objective were to put an end to speculation, his actions in Congress had exactly the opposite effect. Delay and indecision in Congress worked in favor of the speculators who snapped up securities at bargain prices while the congressmen debated. Moreover, as a result of Madison's opposition to Hamilton's plan, the conviction was established, particularly in the South, that the funding-assumption bill would be defeated. Richard Henry Lee advised his friends to sell their state and federal obligations on the assumption that the bottom would shortly fall out of the market, and even John Marshall, who had hitherto shown exemplary confidence in the government, disposed of his securities at this time. Consequently the price of state securities declined markedly in April and May, 1790, as holders unloaded.[5]

When Hamilton introduced his report, he did not anticipate an eight months' delay in its adoption. At that time, he urged prompt action in order to forestall speculation, particularly by foreigners: "Delay, by disseminating doubt," he warned, "would sink the price of stock; and, as the temptations to foreign speculation, from the lowness of the price, would be too great to be neglected, millions would probably be lost to the United States." But this advice was ignored, and in consequence the state securities, together with the outstanding Continental paper money, which Hamilton proposed to redeem at the rate of seventy-five to one (at one time it had sold for almost waste-paper prices), rapidly winged their way to Europe and to Philadelphia, Boston and New York. It was a peculiarity of these birds of passage that they flew only in one direction: never were they known to migrate South once they had made their home in the more congenial northern environment.[6]

Much of the frenzied buying and selling the spring of 1790 was the work of a relatively small number of speculators.* Because of the strong opposition encountered in Congress by Hamilton's report, wary security holders began to hedge against a possible failure of the funding-assumption bill. As a consequence of this hedging, the impression was created that a large amount of new securities, fresh from the hands of the original holders, was being thrown upon the market. But it was closer to the truth to say, as was remarked at the time, that the speculators "vulture-like, are looking out to see where they shall *perch* to the greatest advantage." As they fluttered about from state to federal securities and back again, following the trend of the voting in Congress, the air seemed filled with speculators—with the result, said Hamilton, that "a few hundred thousand dollars appeared like as many millions."[7]

Unquestionably, the smell of money was in the air. As one of Hamilton's enemies said, it was a rank odor calculated to attract the get-rich-quick

---

* Not all the speculators were in favor of Hamilton's plan. The land speculators, for example, were threatened with serious loss if the government securities with which they were buying land rose appreciably in value.

gentry to the national debt like "crows round a carcass." It was a question in many Americans' minds whether the Secretary himself had not pointed out this carrion to his friends and was himself engaged in carrying off some particularly savory morsels.

When he accepted the Secretaryship of the Treasury, Hamilton was aware that his every act would be subjected to unfriendly scrutiny—the experience of Robert Morris as Superintendent of Finance would have dispelled any doubts on that score. Profiting from Morris' example, Hamilton resolved to keep his own hands clean of all dubious connections: "I am not interested more than the felicity and prosperity of this vast continent are concerned," he declared; and, to silence all caviling, he sold the few government securities he had accumulated. He proposed to model his conduct upon that of Caesar's wife: he would disarm his critics by living his official life above suspicion.[8]

It was not enough that Hamilton took Caesar's wife as his model: before he could hope to live beyond the pale of slander, it was necessary that he surround himself at the Treasury with men of unquestioned integrity. After all, Pompeia had been known by the company she kept—a circumstance of which Hamilton seems to have been insufficiently aware. In any event, he appointed as Assistant Secretary of the Treasury a man whose antecedents and conduct in office might have invited comparison with Claudius' wife.

William Duer was an Englishman who had thrown in his lot with the American rebels and had made a fortune in the process. Educated at Eton—his father was a West Indian "nabob"—he entered the British army, served in India and the West Indies and finally settled in upper New York, where he became a neighbor and friend of General Schuyler. During the War of Independence, he was elected to the Continental Congress and in 1779 he married Catherine Alexander, otherwise known as "Lady Kitty," the daughter of William Sterling, the self-styled "Earl of Sterling."

Lady Kitty did not come down in the world by marrying a commoner: having made a very large amount of money by contracting supplies for the American and French armies, Duer lived in a style befitting his wife's social position. He was known to serve fifteen different kinds of wine at dinner; with his fifteen liveried servants, a coat of arms emblazoned upon his carriage and his luxurious mansion in New York City, he lived in almost ducal magnificence. Probably at none of the houses where Hamilton was entertained did he see a more ostentatious display of wealth: as one of the grandees of the new republic Duer set the fashion for the nouveaux riches who had stepped into the shoes of the departed Loyalists.

Among his admirers, Duer acquired the reputation of possessing the golden touch; and, indeed, down to 1792, his career was an almost unbroken record of financial coups. It did not wholly escape observation, however, that when Duer appeared to be tempting Fortune, he was actually often acting on a sure thing. For Duer made a practice of using confidential information acquired from government sources to further his speculations. As a member of the Treasury Board, he was in a strategic position to procure such information and to use his influence for the benefit of himself and his friends.[9]

Duer traveled with an international set of bankers and speculators who tried to manipulate the American debt to their private advantage. In 1788, with Andrew Craigie, Brissot de Warville and others, he formed a syndicate of European and American capitalists for the purpose of buying the American debt from France. Since Duer occupied at this time the strategic position of Secretary of the Board of Treasury, he was assigned the task of procuring the ratification of this transaction by the United States government. That the deal fell through was not owing to any scruples on Duer's part: he always acted upon the precept that public office was private gain. He was also the moving spirit in the "Scioto speculation" by which the government granted to a land company of which Duer was a large stockholder a tract of public land totaling more than five million acres.[10]

Hamilton had known Duer since 1778, and the acquaintance which began while Duer was a member of Congress had been solidified by marriage. Duer's wife, Lady Kitty, was cousin to Elizabeth Schuyler Hamilton. That Hamilton knew of Duer's shady dealings is certain: in 1788, Hamilton had been invited to become a partner in the syndicate that was angling to buy the American debt to France. Nor was he such an innocent as to be unaware of the part that Duer, as a member of the Treasury Board, was expected to play in this transaction. It is to Hamilton's credit that he declined to participate in the plan.

Ostensibly, Hamilton appointed Duer to the Treasury because of his experience in public finance, his ability as a businessman and his wide acquaintance among the men whose financial support Hamilton hoped to enlist on the side of the government. But, knowing Duer as Hamilton did, he could hardly doubt which course the Assistant Secretary would take when the chips were down—that of rectitude or of personal profit. In Duer's case there was no agonizing struggle with his conscience: he had his conscience well in hand and it did what he told it to do.

Apparently it told him to plunge boldly into the security market and to let his friends in on a sure thing. As a result, many of those who seemingly risked their capital upon a long chance in the autumn of 1789 were actually acting upon tips hot from the sanctum sanctorum of the United States Treasury. William Bingham of Philadelphia, one of Duer's confidants, was reported to have borrowed £60,000 sterling in Holland, which he invested in American government securities.* [11]

For his part, Hamilton kept strictly to the path of rectitude: when his friend Henry Lee of Virginia pressed him for information, he refused to give Lee any inkling as to the plans being drawn up in the Treasury. And yet, while the Secretary of the Treasury observed the highest standards of probity, the Assistant Secretary had no standards whatever. In consequence, the tone of the administration tended to sink to the level upon which Duer operated.[12]

There was one small matter which Duer apparently overlooked when he used his office for purposes of private gain—he had violated the law which prohibited any officer of the Treasury Department from buying and selling the securities of the federal government. Rather than remain and face the music, Duer handed in his resignation in April, 1790. He could justify this somewhat precipitate withdrawal on the ground that the office of Assistant Secretary was no longer necessary to the conduct of his private affairs, which now included contracting for the United States Army.

In May, 1790, President Washington fell ill and for a time his life was despaired of. Hamilton knew only too well that the President's death would tie up the funding-assumption bill indefinitely in Congress: even though the President did not actively intervene in Hamilton's behalf, the mere fact that he was known to hold him in high esteem was worth many votes to the Secretary of the Treasury. While it is not true that the Secretary rode upon the President's coattails, he always tried to keep Washington in the forefront when the going became rough: "He was an aegis," said Hamilton, "very essential to me."

By early June, however, the President was sufficiently recovered to go on a three days' fishing trip with Hamilton, Jefferson and a few others. Off Sandy Hook, the party ran into a school of sea bass and blackfish, and the fish seemed to vie with each other to get on the hooks of the statesmen-fishermen.

Despite this run of luck, Hamilton probably found it difficult to keep his mind on the fish in the sea, for mentally he was engaged in frying some specimens more toothsome than any that were pulled in off Sandy Hook. Perhaps as he watched Jefferson land one whopper after another, he began

* Although it was never proved that he gave information to speculators, Secretary of War Knox was engaged at this time in buying government securities. In 1791, General Schuyler owned over $60,000 in government securities. During the debate on the funding system it was said that the opposition speakers caused Schuyler's hair to stand "on end as if the Indians had fired at him." Hamilton's enemies charged that the Secretary of the Treasury had no secrets from General Schuyler: apparently there was a different standard for Caesar's wife when Caesar's father-in-law was involved. But the truth is that Schuyler was a security holder of long standing: as early as 1782 he had attempted to win support for Hamilton's plan of funding the debt.

to consider the possibility of baiting his hook for the Secretary of State himself.

At this time, it seemed probable that Hamilton would be obliged to admit in his next report to Congress that the biggest one of all had gotten away. On five different occasions, the funding-assumption bill was rejected by the House, but each time the margin was so narrow that the Hamiltonians were encouraged to hope that they might yet carry the day. Because of the evenness of the strength of the two groups in Congress, it was proposed by the opponents of the funding-assumption bill that the question be postponed until the next session in order to give the members an opportunity to consult their constituents. This proposal, Hamilton gave his supporters in Congress to understand, must be resisted at all costs: if action upon the debt was deferred, the public creditors would be thrown into despair, the price of securities would toboggan and those who had bought at the prices that had prevailed for the past few years would be ruined.

Holding their breath, Hamilton's friends watched the daring young Secretary on the financial trapeze as he swung from funding to assumption and back again. They were far from certain that he would land on his feet: "such bold politics," exclaimed a Federalist leader, "are rather unfitted to its infant resources . . . I hope to God he [Hamilton] may not be too sanguine. We cannot be too cautious of any future breach of faith." Even the speculators feared that the Secretary had overreached himself in joining the assumption of state debts to the funding system: by grasping for too much he seemed destined to lose everything. The assumption of state debts, it was now said, was "a millstone about the neck of the whole system which must finally sink it."

By the middle of June, 1790, the great gamble seemed to have been lost; the ranks of the Hamiltonians in the House of Representatives were broken; the representatives agreed to separate funding from assumption; and the funding bill, shorn of assumption, was sent to the Senate. Although the Treasury forces held firm in the upper house, the adoption of the bill was so narrowly averted that it began to be said that any further discussion of assumption was like whipping a dead horse.

Despite these reverses, the old guard of the Treasury forces showed no signs of surrendering. The little knot of New England and South Carolina gentlemen which constituted the hard core of the Hamiltonian "phalanx" declared that rather than relinquish assumption they would prevent the passage of the funding bill—a step certain to cripple and perhaps to destroy the federal government. Although Hamilton had not expressly advised his followers to adopt this strategy, he had connected assumption with funding in a manner that left little doubt that the two must stand or fall together. It was enough for his supporters that he had insisted upon the assumption of state debts: "If this is not done," they declared, "New England and Carolina will fly off, and the Secretary's scheme is ruined. We must, we must adopt it." Some disgusted New England delegates wished to fly off immediately, leaving the foreign and domestic debts to Southerners, thus proving, a senator observed, that if the Hamiltonians were not permitted to "milk the cow their own way, they will not suffer her to be milked at all."

While the lines in Congress held firm, Hamilton began some frantic behind-the-scenes maneuvers to break the impasse. Having led his followers down what was beginning to appear more and more like a blind alley, it was incumbent upon the Secretary to get them out. He saw only one road to take, but whether it would lead to Philadelphia, the Susquehanna or to Conococheague on the Potomac, he could not tell. For, although it did not actually belong to him, Hamilton had at his disposal something more precious to congressmen than silver or gold. The Secretary was in a position to barter the future residence of Congress and, by July, 1790, he was prepared to put it upon the block.[13]

The location of the national capital had been a subject of controversy almost from the beginning of the American union. Feeble and despised as the Continental Congress was, the states had vied with each other in offering it shelter: at various times, the hard-pressed statesmen had taken up residence in Philadelphia, York, Annapolis, Trenton, Princeton and New York. When the federal government was organized in 1789, New York City was its seat. Hamilton had always tried to impress upon New Yorkers the advantages they derived from having Congress in their midst; when Governor Clinton deprecated that body as a source of luxury and dissipation that was lowering the moral tone of New York City, Hamilton answered that New Yorkers had never been more moral and frugal than since Congress had been established among them. In actuality, however, morality had nothing to do with it: for Hamilton, the decisive consideration was the benefit derived by the commercial and financial community from having the national government conveniently at hand. Consequently, he was at first so averse to entering into negotiations that looked toward the removal of the capital from New York that a disgruntled Pennsylvanian exclaimed that the Secretary apparently intended to keep Congress "suspended like Mahomet's coffin, by the equal attraction of the different states."[14]

It was apparent that this trick of levitation could be performed only against the opposition of southern congressmen. If the "agricultural interest," and with it republicanism, were to survive in the United States, they thought it essential that the seat of government be moved from the commercial, money-making atmosphere of New York City—"Hamiltonople"— and fixed in the agricultural South where, easily accessible to southern senators and representatives and exposed to the purifying influence of farmers, the federal government would drop its city ways and its city friends and renew its republicanism in the simple joys of country living. James

"Speculators" vs. "Patriots"

Madison declared that "those who are most adjacent to the seat of Legislation will always possess advantages over others," and Southerners' brief acquaintance with Hamilton's fiscal policies seemed amply to confirm that dictum. If the moneychangers could not be driven from the temple, the temple must be moved bodily from the moneychangers.

By July, 1790, it was plain that if Hamilton hoped to pull the funding-assumption bill out of the fire kindled by James Madison, he could delay no longer. He must come to terms with the Virginians—but where could he find a Virginian willing to bargain? Certainly not James Madison: although he did not oppose either funding or assumption, he would not touch them in the form proposed by the Secretary of the Treasury. But there was another Virginian upon whom Hamilton had begun to look with quizzical interest—Thomas Jefferson, the Secretary of State.

Between Hamilton and Jefferson there was as much difference in outward appearance as there was in the cast of their minds. Jefferson—tall, angular, loose-jointed, awkward, ill at ease in company and reserved in his manners—was confronted by a small, well-shaped, meticulously dressed young man who exuded energy, youthfulness and high spirits. Despite the fact that Jefferson had spent several years in the most polite circles in Europe, his ill-fitting clothes—they always seemed too small for him—his lounging, careless manner—he sprawled rather than sat in a chair—made him appear rather like a frontiersman playing the Virginia gentleman and who still had a long way to go before he mastered the part. Even some of Jefferson's friends felt that he abused a philosopher's privilege of negligence in dress. But Jefferson, the born aristocrat, was sure of himself and of his position in society, whereas Hamilton was a parvenu who could never afford to let down his guard; his family closet contained several skeletons over which he was compelled to mount guard.

Although Hamilton never made the mistake of taking Jefferson to be a kindred spirit, he did not at this time regard him as an enemy. The Virginian's objections to the Constitution had been largely removed by the Bill of Rights; he held *The Federalist* in high esteem; he liked to think of commerce as the handmaiden of agriculture; he was a nationalist who favored making the federal judiciary supreme over the state judges; and he was no friend of an "elected despotism" such as had prevailed in some states during the period of the Articles of Confederation. Most important of all, he had not committed himself formally on the issues raised by Hamilton's report.[15]

And so, when Hamilton encountered Jefferson one day near the President's house, he seized the opportunity of sounding out the Secretary of State. Even though Jefferson was on his way to keep an appointment with the President, Hamilton buttonholed him and began to talk at length about the crisis produced by the impasse in Congress. Later, Jefferson recalled that his colleague's appearance was markedly different from his usual spruceness: "sombre, haggard & dejected beyond description, even his dress uncouth & neglected"—evidence of the strain he was undergoing. But he had lost none of his eloquence and persuasiveness: as he walked with Jefferson before the President's door, he urged him to save the union by inducing a few of his friends in Congress to switch their votes in favor of assumption. Three or four votes, he pointed out, were sufficient to carry the measure—and then "the machine of government, now suspended, might be again set in motion." He did not say who, in that event, would be in the driver's seat.[16]

The way Jefferson later described this event, he was at this time a virtual stranger in town, knowing little or nothing about the funding-assumption bill and an easy mark for a subtle and unscrupulous politician. True, he had been abroad and he had arrived in New York to assume the duties of Secretary of State after Hamilton presented his report to Congress. But no one could hold high office in the federal government and be as ignorant of the issues involved in the funding-assumption bill as Jefferson professed to be. Even if the State Department had been an ivory tower, Jefferson had too many contacts with the outside political world, particularly through his friend James Madison, to be oblivious to the import of the struggle going on in Congress.

In actuality, Jefferson had made up his mind regarding the merits of the dispute—and his decision was not in Hamilton's favor. He had come to New York believing that Madison was "the greatest man in the world," and nothing that occurred during the spring and summer of 1790 changed his opinion. Jefferson had closely followed the debates in Congress and in June, 1790, he had privately urged the adoption of Madison's plan of assuming the entire war debts of the states, paid as well as unpaid.

There was good reason, however, why Jefferson could not openly espouse Madison's plan of discriminating between original holders and purchasers. While serving as United States Minister to France, Jefferson had endorsed the principle of nondiscrimination. In 1785, he assured the Dutch bankers that they might buy certificates in the certain knowledge that they would receive the full price when the certificates were redeemed. "Were I the holder of any of them," he said at that time, "I should not have least fear of their full paiment."

Nor is it true that Jefferson was an innocent, guileless farmer who had fallen into the hands of a city slicker in the person of Alexander Hamilton. Jefferson was fresh from five years in Paris, where he had acquired a good working knowledge of the ways of the world. He was fond of playing the role of the country gentleman in town, but actually he was a shrewd politician—far shrewder, as the event was to prove, than the man with whom he now was called upon to match wits.[17]

In this memorable conversation in front of the President's house, Hamilton apparently offered Jefferson only the consolation of saving the union: although Hamilton undoubtedly had in mind some arrangements having to do

"Speculators" vs. "Patriots" 251

with the site of the national capital, he did not broach the subject at this time. It was at dinner the next day, attended by Jefferson, Hamilton and Madison, that the matter was brought up; and it was Madison and Jefferson who set the price for the passage of the funding-assumption bill—the permanent location of the national capital on the banks of the Potomac. And, since assumption could not be carried without the support of the Pennsylvanians, it was agreed that Philadelphia should be made the temporary residence of the government for ten years.[18]

That Hamilton should stoop to bargaining to achieve his objectives struck some of his friends as beneath the dignity of a statesman. Rufus King, who as an United States senator ought to have known better, told Hamilton that "great & good schemes ought to succeed on their own merits and not by intrigue or the establishment of bad measures." But Hamilton was not such a babe in the political woods as to imagine that the purity of his intentions and the rectitude of his measures were a guarantee of success. Putting first things first, he told King, was a policy he had found to yield excellent results: "The funding System, including the assumption is the primary national object; all subordinate points which oppose it must be sacrificed; the project of Philadelphia & Potomack is bad, but it will ensure the funding System and the assumption." To carry that point, Hamilton probably would have been willing to put the national capital in an even hotter spot than the Potomac in mid-August.[19]

In making the national capital a matter of sectional bargaining, Hamilton was playing fast and loose with what many New Yorkers regarded as the dearest interests of their state. To retain the capital in New York was in their estimation essential to the dignity, wealth and commercial importance of the city and state; for where Congress went, did not good society and money-making opportunities follow? New York had gone to considerable expense to make Congress comfortable, £18,000 (New York currency) having been expended upon buildings in Wall Street, of which a New Yorker with more local pride than information declared, "there is nothing equal to it in any part of the world." When the question came up for debate in Congress, the gallery of the House was crowded with ladies whose smiles were reserved for those who spoke in favor of New York. "A severe trial for susceptible minds," exclaimed a congressman, "and a very unfair . . . whilst the abundant beauty of Philadelphia had not an equal opportunity of shewing its wishes."

Despite this handicap, the deal consummated over a bottle of wine with Jefferson and Madison was made good by Congress. Herein Jefferson and Madison gave a signal demonstration of their ability to produce the necessary votes: two Virginians (one of whom gagged violently) and two Marylanders —more than enough to carry the measure—agreed to vote in favor of assumption. Their sacrifice spared Madison the necessity of changing his vote —to the end, his ballot was cast against the bill.

For his part in this famous deal, Jefferson later suffered agonies of contrition. That he should have been a party to a transaction by which over $20 million was thrown to "the stock-jobbing herd" while the farmers went empty-handed and by which the South was sacrificed to the North seemed to him to be the worst error of his political career. His love of the union, he exclaimed, had been adroitly played upon by his adversary: believing that he was saving the country, he had—he now saw—been "most ignorantly & innocently made to hold the candle," the better to enable Hamilton and his plutocratic friends to rob the public.[20]

Had Jefferson been certain that the capital would actually be removed to the Potomac, his pangs of remorse would have been much allayed. But here, precisely, was the rub; he could not be certain that the terms of the bargain would be kept. Hamilton had achieved his purpose—the passage of the funding-assumption bill—but would he ever consent to banish the capital into a wilderness where capitalists, speculators and businessmen were rarely seen? Jefferson suspected that the government would never be permitted to leave Philadelphia: hence his cry of fraud and duplicity.[21]

Though Hamilton, no doubt, hoped that the plan of erecting the national capital on a muddy flat near the Potomac would fall through—in 1788, he predicted that "place the government once down in Pennsylvania, and Pennsylvania will, of course, hold fast"—he never attempted to go back on his bargain with Jefferson. The government stood committed to the Potomac, mud or no mud; little as Hamilton relished the prospect, he was compelled to honor the terms of his agreement. He could not have escaped had he wished, for President Washington had set his heart upon making that unlikely spot the commercial and political center of the union.

The funding of the national debt and the assumption of state debts left Americans, according to Hamilton's definition, the happy possessors of eighty million blessings. The per capita indebtedness of the people of the United States stood at about $20—a staggering sum for the times. Moreover, most of the revenue of the government was "mortgaged," in Hamilton's word, for the liquidation of the debt. If this was "national felicity," some Americans were at a loss to define a "national curse."

And yet Hamilton insisted that the country had never been in better shape. Affluent citizens looked to the federal government for the payment of the interest and principal owing them; the allegiance of the state creditors had been transferred to the general government; the securities of the United States now constituted a circulating medium which might be used to activate the national economy; these securities were concentrated in the hands of those best able to make effective use of them; and the government itself was in a position to turn its attention to attaining "the perfection of the social organization." In short, the United States seemed to Hamilton to be standing on the threshold of a period of unparalleled expansion. And he did not doubt that the men who thought "continentally"—the businessmen, bankers and speculators whose foresight had been so signally rewarded by the funding-assumption act—would take full advantage of the boundless opportunities opening up before them.[22]

As for the national debt, Hamilton saw no reason for alarm. How any man, sensible of the natural resources of the country and the enterprising nature of its citizens, could take a despairing view of the national finances passed Hamilton's understanding. He described it as "a mockery of truth to represent the United States as a community burthened and exhausted by taxes": the entire national debt was no larger than the annual expenditure of the British government; the federal government had not yet tapped the source of direct taxes; and the interest rate was certain to drop. If this were not enough, the increasing productivity and wealth of the country would make the debt seem trivial to future generations. He perceived, as his critics did not, the connection between national income and the national debt and he recognized that there was no more certain way of disposing of the debt than by stimulating the productive forces of the country.

Not least among the effects of the funding system was that it became the means of drawing from Europe large sums of money which were added to the active capital of the United States. No longer an object of speculation, government bonds became increasingly attractive to European investment capital. True, the United States paid interest on money invested in this way; but as Hamilton pointed out, Americans could well afford to pay 6 per cent for money which, invested in productive enterprise in this country, could be made to yield as high as 20 per cent. After the outbreak of the War of the French Revolution, large amounts of European capital took flight—and ultimately came to rest in the United States. By the end of 1794, the United States had the highest credit rating in Europe; some government securities were selling at 10 per cent above par. As Talleyrand told his friends, only in the United States were found bonds that were "safe and free from reverses. They have funded in such a sound manner and the prosperity of this country is growing so rapidly that there can be no doubt of their solvency." By May, 1795, foreigners held over $20 million in the domestic debt of the United States; and by 1801, their holdings had increased to $33 million.

Finally, the funding system provided the means of creating wealth. Every three months, almost a million dollars was pumped into the national economy; and this money, drawn from the taxpayers of the United States, made possible capitalistic enterprise on a scale hitherto unknown in the republic. And the fact that the money thus extracted from the taxpayers was concentrated in a comparatively few hands accelerated the growth of capitalism: it made available for purposes of investment and exchange a sum estimated at ten times the amount of all the specie circulating in the country. Thus

Hamilton activated the springs of national credit and a torrent began to roar down the dry creek bed.

Although Hamilton's plan provided for the extinguishment of the debt in twenty-five or thirty years, he saw positive advantages in extending it over a longer period: even a perpetual debt such as Great Britain's had no terror for him. For he knew that the necessity of collecting revenue in order to pay the public creditors ensured that the federal government would not wither away from desuetude and that as long as the security holders received their payments from the government they were not likely to listen to the sirens in the states. True enough, he wished to reduce the debt to more manageable proportions, but he had no desire to see it wholly liquidated. He would have agreed with—indeed, he may have inspired—Gouverneur Morris' observation that "we have more reason to fear the payment, than the increase of our debt."[23]

18.

The Bank of the United States

The funding of the national debt and the assumption of state debts had become law, but the price in the form of sectional and personal ill will came high. The national debt, instead of cementing the union politically, acted as a divisive force, and alarming fissures began to appear in the united front that the Federalists had presented to the Antifederalists in 1788.[1]

From a purely financial point of view, Hamilton was entitled to be regarded as one of the greatest benefactors of the states: he had arranged for the federal government to assume their debts and he had paid them handsomely. Seemingly, he acted upon the maxim that nothing was too good for the states; yet he gained no honor in Virginia, where the funding-assumption law was regarded as a victory of northern speculators over the honest part of the community. One of the most forceful of Patrick Henry's objections to the Constitution was that it would make the southern states "the milch cow out of whom the substance would be extracted." The legislation adopted by Congress in the summer of 1790 appeared to many Virginians to be a milking machine invented by a Creole for the enrichment of the northern "moneyed interest."*[2]

These discontents found expression in two resolutions adopted by the Virginia House of Representatives late in 1790 in which certain aspects of the funding system were condemned as "dangerous to the rights and subversive of the interests of the people" and the assumption of the Virginia state debt pronounced to be "repugnant to the Constitution of the United States." For these reasons, the Virginia House of Representatives petitioned Congress to amend the funding act and to repeal the assumption law.[3]

This call for action by the Virginia Assembly affected Hamilton like an alarm bell in the night. When urging the adoption of the Constitution, Hamilton had pictured the state legislatures as sentinels who would "sound the alarm if any thing improper should occur in the conduct of the national

* There was more truth in this charge than Hamilton liked to acknowledge. In 1795, citizens of Massachusetts received over $300,000 in interest on United States securities, whereas citizens of Virginia received only $62,000.

255

rulers," but he was now disposed to regard the stand taken by the Virginia legislature as a harbinger of the dissolution of the union. "This," he declared, "is the first symptom of a spirit which must either be killed, or it will kill the Constitution of the United States." Kill or be killed—it was in this dichotomous light that Hamilton viewed the struggle between the states and the national government.[4]

He had always expected that if the national government were done to death, the crime could be laid to Virginia. This great state—an empire in itself, he frequently lamented—loomed in his eyes as the inveterate enemy of the federal government. Sooner or later, he was firmly convinced, there would have to be a showdown between Virginia and the central government; and he was inclined to believe that when the showdown came, it would be upon a battlefield.

There was some advantage, Hamilton believed, in having it out with Virginia before that state became so powerful that it could overpower the federal government. Under that conviction, he sent copies of the resolution of the Virginia legislature to Chief Justice John Jay. But Jay did not rise to the bait; unwilling to risk a quarrel with the largest state of the union in the infancy of the federal government, he advised Hamilton to take a calmer view of this admittedly unpropitious event. Jay was of the opinion that the Assembly's resolution was merely a way of letting off steam and that to treat it otherwise would give it a wholly unmerited and undesirable dignity and importance. "Every indecent interference of the State assemblies will diminish their influence," Jay told Hamilton; "the national government has only to do what is right, and, if possible, be silent. If compelled to speak, it should be in a few words strongly evinced by temper, dignity and self-respect."[5]

Even though Hamilton was far from persuaded that forbearance and charity ought to be shown Virginia, he agreed to let the incident drop. He continued, however, to keep a watchful eye on the Old Dominion; henceforth there was no doubt in his mind that the planters were sharpening a sword which one day would be plunged into the vitals of the federal government.

How little inclined was Hamilton to appease Virginia was revealed in 1791, when he recommended to Congress a second assumption of state debts. The first assumption had not been effected in exactly the way Hamilton had recommended in his Report on Public Credit. Instead of assuming prescribed amounts from each state, as Hamilton had wished—to each according to its debt might well have been his slogan at this time—Congress indulged in a bit of logrolling by means of which the states themselves apportioned the federal largesse, the division being based not solely upon the amount of the existing state debt but upon such considerations as the size of its debt in 1783, the amount of debt redeemed and its voting strength in Congress.

The Bank of the United States

Without this compromise, the funding-assumption bill would not have passed Congress, but it was the work of Roger Sherman of Connecticut rather than of Alexander Hamilton.

This settlement was not wholly satisfactory to Hamilton and after the adoption of his report he again raised the question of assumption by calling the attention of Congress to the fact that South Carolina and Massachusetts still had large debts. Congress obliged in 1792 with a second assumption act. By these two measures the states were overpaid by the federal government: when the commissioners appointed for the purpose of ascertaining the balances owing by the states to the general government finally brought in their report, it was disclosed that several states had received hundreds of thousands of dollars more than they were entitled to. But this was a small matter to Hamilton: for him the decisive consideration was that the state creditors had been attached to the federal government.[6]

At the time Hamilton was revolutionizing American governmental finance, the British national debt had reached a total of £272 million—"a sum," exclaimed a journalist, "which the human mind can hardly form an idea. Were it to be laid down in guineas in a line, it would extend upwards of four thousand three hundred miles in length." By 1791, Americans were already beginning to speculate how far *their* debt would extend. It was highly fortunate, therefore, that a seemingly foolproof method of reducing governmental debt had been invented during the eighteenth century. Money was appropriated by the government for the purchase of its own securities; and the interest on these redeemed certificates, accumulating at compound interest, was used for the purchase of more securities. This was called the sinking fund. It was the essence of a sinking fund that the revenue appropriated for the purchase of government bonds be made permanent and that the fund thus created be rendered inviolable. Annual appropriations by the legislature were not sufficient; and if the government were permitted to dip into the accumulated reserves whenever its necessities prompted, the fund was certain to fail of its purpose.[7]

A sinking fund had been built into the British fiscal system and Hamilton did not rest until the United States had a similar fund. Not that he expected the wonders that were sometimes claimed for this device: it was mainly for its salutary psychological effects that he valued it. "The effects of imagination and prejudice cannot safely be disregarded in anything that relates to money," he said; and he recognized that a sinking fund would help to inspire confidence in the eventual payment of the funded debt and thereby buttress the credit of the government.

In 1790, at Hamilton's instigation, Congress created a fund for the purchase of government securities, but it was too small to reduce the debt materially. In 1791-92, Hamilton therefore recommended that a larger fund be established, that the Commissioners appointed to administer this fund be given greater authority, and that the principles of a true sinking fund be rigorously enforced. Congress obliged with the act of May, 1792, whereby a system modeled upon Pitt's sinking fund of 1786, with permanent revenues and inviolable funds, was ordained.[8]

Since some government securities were still selling below their nominal value, many of the congressmen who voted to establish the sinking fund expected that the government would materially reduce the national debt by buying its securities at the prevailing market price. Certainly, they reasoned, there was no cheaper or more expeditious method of disposing of the government's obligations than for the government itself to buy them at a depreciated price.

These congressmen did not sufficiently reckon with the deep-laid plans of the Secretary of the Treasury. Occupying a dominant position among the commissioners, Hamilton was in a position to determine the fiscal policies of the government—and it was not his purpose to liquidate the national debt by buying it at low prices in the open market. The Secretary's objective, it was soon made clear, was less to pick up bargains for the government than to ensure that the price of these securities was raised for the benefit of investors and to oblige foreigners to pay the full price for government securities. Although the commissioners spent about $2,300,000 from 1792 to 1796 in the purchase of certificates, the chief beneficiaries were the security holders.[9]

The adoption of Hamilton's fiscal system gave the adage about death and taxes more cogency than it had ever before possessed for Americans. The debts of the United States, it could no longer be doubted, were to be paid and the American people would do the paying. But one indispensable element was still lacking: the country had no circulating medium sufficient to the needs of taxpayers, much less to that of the capitalism Hamilton had made to blossom in the wasteland of the national debt.

In *The Federalist,* Hamilton had defined money as "the vital principle of the body politic . . . that which sustains its life and motion, and enables it to perform its most essential functions." As the official responsible for the collection of taxes in the United States, Hamilton was constantly reminded of the implications of that definition. Everyone complained of the scarcity of money: there was little gold or silver and no paper currency, and the notes of the state banks seldom circulated far beyond the confines of the cities in which they were issued. Until something was done to relieve this shortage, it was certain that interest rates would remain high, business would be retarded and the government would be unable to collect the taxes upon which its credit and, indeed, its existence depended.[10]

As a result of his experience with paper money issued upon the mere

The Bank of the United States

pledge of the government to redeem it in gold or silver at some unspecified day, Hamilton had conceived a deep distrust of money bearing the imprimatur of the government. For it seemed inherent in the nature of all governments that whenever they were hard pressed financially they resorted to devaluation, repudiation and inflation until they utterly destroyed all confidences in their promises. Nor were governments capable, in Hamilton's opinion, of learning from their mistakes: "What nation," he asked, "was ever blessed with a constant succession of upright and wise administrators?"

Hamilton was no believer in an all-powerful, all-embracing, all-doing state in which the individual existed only for the purpose of executing orders handed down by a supreme authority. In some areas of human activity, not even Thomas Jefferson was more insistent upon keeping the government at arm's length. True, Hamilton recognized that a little government was a dangerous thing, but he also saw that too much government might be an even greater evil. "Government," he said, "being administered by men, is naturally, like individuals, subject to particular impulses, passions, prejudices, vices . . . to inconstancy of views and mutability of conduct." As long as human nature remained what it was there was no salvation in the Leviathan state.[11]

Of all forms of government, Hamilton thought that wisdom and uprightness in financial matters were found least in those of a popular cast. Always prone to pursue the course of least resistance, these governments preferred to print paper money and to "anticipate and mortgage the resources of posterity, rather than encounter the inconveniences of an increment of taxes." So apprehensive was he that this propensity would gain the upper hand that he wished to keep in abeyance the power of the federal government to issue paper money. The states were prohibited from making paper money legal tender "and," Hamilton remarked, "the spirit of that prohibition ought not to be disregarded by the government of the United States. . . . The wisdom of the government will be shown in never trusting itself with the use of so seducing and dangerous an expedient."[12]

Despite Hamilton's disillusioning experience with paper money "issued by the mere authority of government," he did not draw the inference that all paper currency, together with tender acts and stay laws, ought to be consigned to perdition. From his study of the writings and career of John Law he had learned that a rapid circulation of money was the secret of a prosperous and expanding economy. Of course, Americans and John Law himself had permitted paper money to get out of control—and had incurred disaster for their negligence. Nevertheless, Hamilton believed that Law had hit upon a truth from which the United States could still profit. The way to stimulate a sluggish economy, he reasoned, was to increase the quantity of money in circulation: a controlled inflation could be of infinite benefit to a country that had just experienced a ruinous deflation.[13]

As so frequently happened, Hamilton found what he was seeking by looking across the Atlantic to Great Britain. The Bank of England afforded him an example of a quasi-public bank that controlled credit and currency in the interests of a stable yet expanding economy. The financial integrity, wealth, prosperity and national power for which eighteenth-century Britain was renowned Hamilton attributed to the excellence of its institutions—and of these institutions none was more important in his eyes than was the Bank of England.

The Bank of England provided the country with a circulating medium, furnished the merchants loans and other facilities, and advanced money to the government on both a long- and short-term basis. It was not an ordinary bank of deposit and discount: Adam Smith described it as "a great engine of state," and Lord North—in appreciation of the services it had rendered the government during the War of American Revolution—called it a part of the British constitution. In truth, it was so closely interwoven in the fabric of the state that the interests of the bank and the British government were almost indistinguishable. Through its agency, the government serviced the national debt; its notes were accepted as the equivalent of specie; and it imposed its policies upon all the lesser banks in the realm.[14]

Despite its close association with the government, the Bank of England was in form a private bank: the directors were chosen by the stockholders and upon these officials rested the responsibility of maintaining the private and public credit of the country. Imbued with a high sense of their responsibility to the community, they generally kept a restraining hand upon the issuance of bank notes and set a reasonable limit upon the Bank's dividends. In consequence, the notes of the Bank of England did not depreciate even though the quantity in circulation exceeded the specie reserve. In England, therefore, bank notes were exempt from the worst faults of paper money— the successive glut and famine of the circulating medium—that in the United States had contributed alternately to produce inflation and deflation.[15]

The Bank of England having shown the way, Hamilton concluded that banks might rush in where no government had ever safely trod. Accordingly, late in 1790, he drew up a report calling for a public bank, to be known as the Bank of the United States. In this institution, Hamilton hoped to embody his ideal of a partnership between government and the business community by which government would stimulate and direct the activities of businessmen and receive in return part of their capital in the form of loans. The capitalization of the Bank of the United States was set at $10 million— an impressive sum considering that the combined capital of the three state banks then in existence was hardly more than $2 million. In a country as deficient in investment capital as was the United States, it might have been supposed that the point of saturation had already been reached and that

The Bank of the United States

the proposed national bank would either fail to attain its scheduled capitalization or would ruin the existing state banks in its voracious appetite for capital.[16]

This difficulty Hamilton sought to overcome by stipulating that the securities of the United States government should constitute three fifths of the Bank's capital, the remainder being in gold or silver.* Upon this security, the Bank was to issue notes that would provide the country with a circulating medium. It was also intended to serve as a bank of deposit, to act as the fiscal agent of the government, and to loan the government money. In return, the government was to purchase $2 million worth of stock. Whatever might be said against him by his enemies, Hamilton was not a slavish imitator of all things British: the British government did not have a proprietary interest in the Bank of England.[17]

Despite the extensive powers to be conferred upon this Bank, Hamilton stipulated that it should be managed by private citizens. "To attach full confidence to an institution of this nature," he declared, "it appears to be an essential ingredient in its structure, that it shall be under a *private* not a public direction—under the guidance of *individual interest*, not of *public policy*." Generally speaking, Hamilton believed that it was sufficient for government to keep businessmen on the right track by a system of rewards and penalties, always bearing in mind that their initiative must not be paralyzed by too many directives and too much officiousness. It is typical of the tenor of his thinking that he was more concerned over the harm the government might do the Bank than the harm the Bank might do the government: lest the government try to milk the Bank dry by means of excessive loans, he set a limit to the amount it could borrow from the institution.

And yet, despite his good opinion of the workings of self-interest, Hamilton was careful not to give private bankers a wholly free hand in regulating the country's economy. For they, too, were men and therefore subject, in more or less degree, to all the passions that actuated mankind. Every denomination of men, no matter how respectable or affluent, he believed to be under the constant temptation to sacrifice the public good to private interest. Even in a bland and imperturbable banker, Hamilton knew, the Old Adam might sometimes peep through. The only way of keeping this enemy out of the national economy, he argued, was to give the government a check upon the private bankers. To that end, Hamilton insisted that the bank notes issued by the Bank be made redeemable in coin, thus preventing the overissue of its notes. Moreover, he gave the government the right to take an active part in the management of the Bank. The government was

---

* It is also true that by this means Hamilton hoped to raise the price of government securities. Convertibility into bank stock would naturally make them more attractive to the moneyed men of the country.

permitted to appoint five of the twenty-five directors and to purchase 5,000 of the 25,000 shares of the Bank's stock. Finally, the Secretary of the Treasury was authorized to inspect the books of the Bank of the United States. If these powers proved insufficient to secure compliance with the government's wishes, Hamilton advocated that as a last resort it should exert pressure through its power of conferring future benefits, including rechartering, upon the Bank.[18]

Notwithstanding Hamilton's insistence upon private control of the Bank of the United States, he was resolved that the Bank should be run mainly for the benefit of the public. While conceding that unless the interest of the stockholders were consulted the bank could not exist, he contended that "it does not follow that this alone is to be consulted, or that it even ought to be paramount. Public utility is more truly the object of public banks than private benefit." In other words, the directors of the Bank of the United States were not permitted to assume that what was good for the stockholders was necessarily good for the country.*

Sensible of the strength of the opposition to banks and bankers in the United States, Hamilton made the report he submitted to Congress on December 13, 1790, a treatise on banking. Thanks to his wide reading—he had thoroughly covered the ground from the mercantilists to Adam Smith—the Secretary of the Treasury was well qualified to instruct his countrymen in the intricacies of public finance. In this report, as in his earlier Report on Public Credit, he endeavored to anticipate and to answer the objections likely to be raised against his plan and to supply his supporters in Congress with an impressive array of facts, figures and arguments in its favor.

In contrast to the funding system and assumption of state debts, Hamilton's plan of a national Bank made little stir outside of Congress. The country was prosperous; the Bank affected few individuals directly; and there was a strong prepossession in its favor among businessmen. As one of the opponents of the bank said, "it was one of those sly and subtle movements which marched silently to its object: the vices of it were at first not palpable or obvious." As a result, one morning the American people awoke to find that they were part owners of a Bank—or as some republicans put it, that the bank owned the people.

In February, 1791, the bill chartering the Bank of the United States passed the House of Representatives. The vote was thirty-nine to twenty, a sizable majority compared with the narrow margin by which the funding and assumption measures had scraped through the legislature. But the voting was now much more sectional in character: only one member from the states

---

* As an added guarantee that the directors would not abuse their trust, Hamilton provided in the charter of the Bank of the United States the condition that the bank's debts should never exceed the amount of its capital stock—another evidence that Hamilton had clearly in mind the principle of fractional reserve requirements which has proved to be of fundamental importance in American banking.

The Bank of the United States

north of Maryland voted against the bill and only three members from the states south of Maryland voted in its favor. Fifteen of the nays came from Virginia, the Carolinas and Georgia. The vote in the Senate followed this sectional pattern. In every respect, therefore, it appeared to be a triumph, engineered by Hamilton, of the North over the South; and, unlike the bargain by which the assumption of state debts had been consummated, the South received nothing to sweeten the pill administered by the Secretary of the Treasury.

If Hamilton fancied that with this victory the way was clear for the Bank of the United States, he quickly learned his error. In actuality, the passage of the Bank bill by Congress proved to be the least of the gamut of obstacles the Bank of the United States was obliged to run. Most formidable of all was the roadblock thrown up by James Madison and Thomas Jefferson—a roadblock quarried from the Constitution itself.

When Hamilton wrote his Report on the Bank of the United States, he little imagined that the question of its constitutionality would prove decisive. After all, the Bank of North America had been chartered by the Continental Congress, and it would not have been easy to convince Hamilton that the federal government enjoyed less power than did the government of the Articles of Confederation. Therefore, he had not related the Bank to any specific, enumerated power of Congress; apparently he was content to rest his case upon the general powers of the national government.[19]

Here he underestimated the resourcefulness of Jefferson, Madison and Attorney General Edmund Randolph. Firmly convinced that the adoption of the funding-assumption plan had dangerously weakened the position of the "agrarian interest," the three Virginians were resolved to let nothing get by that would further damage the cause of the farmers. Overborne in the House of Representatives and the Senate, they had no choice but to challenge Hamilton's report on the score of constitutionality. This Jefferson and Randolph did in opinions submitted to the President after the Bank bill had passed both houses of Congress.

Like the Declaration of Independence, the Constitution is replete with generalities which, in content and significance, have varied greatly from generation to generation. Although comparatively free of ambiguities, it speaks in very general terms—a characteristic which has caused it to be described as "hardly more than paragraphs of precepts which are to be defined and executed according to a strict or liberal interpretation." In such a succinct and compressed instrument of government, construction becomes all-important—a truism which was clearly perceived by some of the framers. When Gouverneur Morris was told by a friend that the Convention had made a good Constitution, Morris replied: "That depends on how it is construed."*[20]

* So susceptible of varied interpretations is the Constitution that it has given sanction equally to Hamilton's nationalism and to the opposite theory that the general government is merely the agent of the state governments.

The impossibility of defining the powers of the Federal government with such precision that all contingencies would be provided for had been recognized by the members of the Constitutional Convention. Nevertheless, the three Virginians, Randolph, Jefferson and Madison, now took the position that Congress could act only upon its enumerated powers and that it was limited in its choice of means to measures *indispensably necessary* to give effect to its powers. Relating this dictum to the proposed Bank, they concluded that this institution was patently unconstitutional: the Constitution said nothing about a bank and it could not be regarded as indispensably necessary to give effect to any general power given to the federal government. As for relating the Bank of the United States to Congress' power to regulate trade, Madison dismissed the question with a rhetorical flourish: "What," he asked, "has this bill to do with trade? Would any plain man suppose [a bank] had *anything* to do with trade?"

This kind of constructionism recognized the existence of nothing that was not clearly expressed in the Constitution, took the language used in its exact and technical meaning, and admitted of no equitable considerations. It would have certainly led to the triumph of the states over the federal government, for the states would have rushed in to fill the vacuum created by the self-denying ordinances imposed by Jefferson, Randolph and Madison upon the government.[21]

It had not always been thus with James Madison. In 1787, he had been the first to acknowledge that it was impossible to confine a government to the exercise of express powers: "There must necessarily be admitted powers by implication," he said, "unless the Constitution descended to recount every minutiae." This was a far cry indeed from the narrow constitutionalism he saw fit to promulgate in 1791. But Madison's purpose was no longer to create a dominant national government: he had become the exponent of a brand of federalism which in 1787 he would have scorned as unworthy of consideration by the Constitutional Convention.

To Hamilton's dismay, the arguments invoked by Randolph, Madison and Jefferson visibly affected President Washington. The President was not a man of quick, intuitive judgment: when called upon for an immediate opinion, he was often at a loss and, as Jefferson said, appeared "unready, short and embarrassed." Washington needed time to think, but that did not mean that he was dominated by the confident, strong-willed men by whom he was surrounded. Very early in his relations with Washington, Hamilton learned that the older man could not be bent to any man's will. As Hamilton said, Washington "consulted much, pondered much, resolved slowly, resolved surely." But he did not always resolve as Hamilton wished.

While the President was persuaded of the utility of a national Bank, he could not deny the force of the constitutional objections raised against the measure. Perhaps, too, he shared the fears of many Southerners that if the

The Bank of the United States

Bank were established in Philadelphia, the national government, instead of going to the Potomac, would remain fast-anchored in the City of Brotherly Love. Tormented with these doubts and weighed down by the responsibility thrust upon him, Washington told Hamilton that, as matters stood, the bill would not receive his approval. Hamilton was dumfounded: he exclaimed that he had "never dreamed of Washington's doubting; that had he known *that* he would not have written his report and recommended the course adopted." Had Hamilton been able to read the future, neither his Report on Public Credit nor his Report on the Bank would, by his own account, have seen the light of day.

But Hamilton's expostulations were not enough to change Washington's mind: he bluntly informed the Secretary that unless he could answer Jefferson's, Madison's and Randolph's arguments, the bill would not become law. Plainly, it was incumbent upon the Secretary of the Treasury to produce a closely reasoned argument that would match that of the Bank's critics point for point.

Well aware that much more than the fate of the Bank of the United States was involved in this dispute, Hamilton determined to make his answer a major effort. If Randolph's, Jefferson's and Madison's method of strictly construing the powers of the federal government prevailed, Hamilton was prepared to write off the Federal Constitution as another failure in mankind's efforts to achieve free government. He knew that a constitution, however detailed, could not possibly enumerate the powers essential to meet all emergencies: "unexpected invasions, long and ruinous wars," he remarked, "may demand all the possible abilities of the country. . . . The contingencies of society are not reducible to calculations. They cannot be fixed or bounded, even in imagination." And yet Jefferson and Madison seemed bent upon fixing and bounding them within such a narrow compass that no government, thus constricted, could function effectively.

If the federal government were to cope with the needs of a rapidly growing nation, Hamilton believed that it must be supreme as to the objects delegated to it and that it must possess all the powers necessary to attain the objects legitimately within its control. While he conceded that the federal government was a government of limited, enumerated powers, he contended that every power given carried with it the means of attaining the object intended. His method of interpreting the Constitution presupposed that incidental as well as express powers must of necessity belong to every government and that when power is given to accomplish certain objectives, all the known and usual means not expressly prohibited may be considered as having been given incidentally. If an institution was useful in carrying out an enumerated power of the federal government, Hamilton concluded that there was a strong presumption in favor of its constitutionality: "Little less than a prohibitory clause," he observed, "can destroy the strong presumptions which result from the general aspect of the government. Nothing but demonstration should exclude the idea that the power exists." And, finally, he held that the right of determining whether or not the means were essential lay with Congress: "The national government like every other," he said, "must judge in the first instance of the proper exercise of its powers."

Underlying Hamilton's exegesis of the Constitution were three presuppositions: that the Constitution was ordained by the people and was intended for their benefit; that it was designed to endure for a long period of time and therefore must be "adapted to the various crises of human affairs"; and that while the national government was one of enumerated powers, it was sovereign as to those powers. Given these premises, it could hardly be doubted that the Bank of the United States was a necessary and proper means of carrying into effect the regulation of commerce between the states and of providing for the public credit and defense. It was, he held, a right of sovereign powers to erect corporations; by its silence upon this subject, the Federal Constitution did not debar Congress from exercising this power —it merely indicated that the corporations erected by Congress should be devised to carry out effectually a specified power. Viewed in this light, the case for the Bank of the United States could be reduced to a syllogism: a power is the ability or faculty of doing a thing; the ability to do things is the power of employing the means necessary to its execution; the proper means of executing such a power are necessary and proper laws.*

It was not Hamilton's contention that the federal government had the power to do whatever it considered "necessary and proper." This clause, he took pains to point out, dealt only with the means, not with the substantive powers themselves; and its sole purpose was to render those powers effective. He never claimed that the federal government had more power than was sufficient to attain those ends, but, on the other hand, he was never willing to settle for less power.[22]

From February 6, 1791, when Washington called upon him to answer the constitutional objections raised by Randolph, Madison and Jefferson, the Secretary of the Treasury gave every moment he could spare from his duties to formulating his answer. After a week of rehearsing in his own mind all the arguments in favor of the constitutionality of the Bank, he called upon William Lewis, one of the leading lawyers of Philadelphia. While Lewis listened, Hamilton went over his argument point by point. The entire afternoon was spent in this fashion, the two men pacing Lewis' garden as they talked. When they parted company, Hamilton was satisfied that the case for the Bank of the United States was as strong as it could be made.

* Chief Justice John Marshall, paraphrasing Hamilton, later observed: "If the end be legitimate and within the scope of the Constitution, all the means which are approximate, which are plainly adapted to that end, and which are not prohibited, may be constitutionally employed to carry it into effect."

The Bank of the United States

His mind thus primed with arguments, Hamilton went home to write his opinion on the constitutionality of the Bank of the United States. It is said that he spent the greater part of the night of February 22-23 working on his draft; and, although the copy he preserved does not bear the marks of haste, the story may well be true. For it is clear that the draft was already in Hamilton's mind when he sat down to write: it was simply a matter of transcribing on paper the ideas he had long been pondering. Even so, it was a monumental labor, eloquently attesting to the fact that as John Marshall said, "to talents of the highest grade, he united a patient industry, not always the companion of genius, which fitted him in a peculiar manner for the difficulties to be encountered by the man who should be placed at the head of the American finances."

Hamilton's opinion reached the President shortly before noon on February 23. This left Washington only about forty-eight hours in which to digest Hamilton's arguments and to come to a decision regarding the Bank bill. Although his doubts were not wholly set at rest by Hamilton's state paper, he decided to sign; accordingly, on February 25 the Bank bill became law.[23]

To the construction and interpretation of the Constitution, Hamilton brought a high order of statesmanship, penetrating awareness of the present and future needs of the government, and a creative imagination. His ruling passion was to give to the American people a structure of government in which the national spirit could expand and flourish; and by the application of his rules of interpretation, the Constitution has fulfilled this purpose. Whatever might have been said in the eighteenth century in defense of Jefferson's dictum that no law was authorized by the Constitution which was not indispensably necessary to give effect to a specified power, it is clear in the twentieth century that Jefferson was imposing a crippling restraint upon the federal government. Had it not been for the doctrine of implied powers, that government could not have preserved the people of the United States against the storms and stresses that they were called upon to endure.[24]

Having already incurred the suspicion of abetting speculators, it might have been supposed that in the case of the Bank of the United States, Hamilton would have taken every precaution against provoking a repetition of the speculative frenzy of 1789-90. Nevertheless, he did little to minimize this evil and some of his policies played directly into the hands of the speculators.

Eager that the Bank stock should move briskly when it was put upon the market, Hamilton required only a $25 cash down payment for the purchase of Bank scrip. (Scrip was a receipt for the initial payment which entitled the owner to buy Bank stock at par.) By thus making it possible to buy stock at a small cash outlay, Hamilton was perhaps thinking of the advantage to be derived from broadening the base of the ownership of the Bank of the United States. Certainly he did not intend to bestow upon a few wealthy individuals complete control of the Bank's affairs—witness his efforts to provide against "a combination between a few principal stockholders, to monopolize the power and benefits of the bank," by giving no single individual or corporation more than thirty votes in the Bank's direction regardless of the amount of stock owned.*

In his report, Hamilton set April 1, 1791, as the day on which the stock would go on public sale. But Madison objected to this date on the ground that it would not permit those living at a distance from Philadelphia to take advantage of the opportunity to buy scrip. In consequence, the day of the public sale was postponed until July 4, 1791.²⁵

For a week or more prior to the Fourth of July, Philadelphia was crowded with strangers who had obviously descended upon the City of Brotherly Love with something in mind other than the celebration of the great and glorious day. Rumors were rife that the stock of the Bank of the United States would pay dividends of 12 per cent or more and that the price of the stock would quickly go above par. In this expectation, the *Gazette of the United States* assured its readers in May, 1791, that "no equal object of speculation is perhaps presented in any quarter of the globe." What wonders had this enterprising Secretary of the Treasury provided for his countrymen!

As soon as the Bank doors in Philadelphia were opened, on July fourth, the crowd "rushed in like a torrent," swarmed over the clerks and within two hours had oversubscribed by four thousand shares the amount of stock available to the public. "If a golden mountain had been kindled, emitting from its crater a lava of the purest gold," it was said, ". . . the crowd would not have been greater, or exhibited more intense eagerness to share in the plunder."

Austere patriots watched this scene with consternation: that on the Fourth of July, 1791, fifteen years after the Declaration of Independence, the streets of Philadelphia should be crowded with men engaged "in a mere scramble for so much public plunder" indicated that the American spirit had suffered a drastic change since the equality of all men had been proclaimed to the world. "The men who had resigned their lives in the war, or who had parted with their patrimonies or hard earned estates, to save the public liberty," it was said, "stood at a distance, and with astonishment beheld the singular and unexpected phenomenon."†²⁶

But this was merely the beginning of an orgy of speculation the like of

* One share was entitled to one vote, three shares to two votes, ten shares to five votes, and one hundred shares to twenty votes.
† Limited amounts of stock were also sold in New York and Massachusetts. So quickly was this stock subscribed that it was said that four times the amount could easily have been sold.

The Bank of the United States

which had not been seen before in the United States. Philadelphia was reported to resemble "a great gaming house": "At every corner," it was said, "you hear citizens talking of nothing but Script, 6 per cent, 3 per cent, deferred debt, etc." The President of the Philadelphia Stock Exchange was said to have made $40,000 in one month by buying and selling scrip, and several brokers claimed a turnover of several thousand dollars in a morning's transactions. Inspired by such stories of sudden wealth, merchants, shopkeepers, clerks, apprentices, farmers and members of Congress begged or borrowed money in order to partake of the Great Barbecue.

As might be expected, the price of scrip shot skyward; by August 10, 1791, the same certificates that had cost $25 in July were selling for $325. Government securities enjoyed an only slightly less spectacular rise, the 6 per cent bonds attaining par and the 3 per cent bonds reaching 75 per cent of their face value. Many purchasers hoped to resell these bonds to European investors, now popularly supposed to be eager to pay virtually any price for the prime government securities of a country as stable and prosperous as was the United States.[27]

Amid all this tumult of buying and selling, it was evident that most of the stock of the Bank of the United States was being snapped up by citizens who resided north of the Potomac. For this ominous turn of events—ominous because it rendered more acute the division in the house of American capitalism—Hamilton disclaimed all responsibility: it had been his wish, he declared, that the Bank stock "should be generally diffused throughout the States" in order to give every section a stake in the prosperity and well-being of the Bank. His plans had gone awry, he later told some Virginia Federalists, because he had not anticipated the embarrassment of riches that was showered upon the Bank, "it not having been foreseen, any where, that so rapid a subscription would take place." By underestimating the speculative zeal of his countrymen, he acknowledged, he had unwittingly permitted the concentration of control of the Bank by one section of the union.[28]

Regardless of anything that Hamilton might have done, it is probable that ownership of the stock of the Bank of the United States would have centered in the North. Southern planters did not have sufficient disposable capital to permit them to buy considerable quantities of this stock; nor, after listening to Madison and Jefferson, were they inclined to trust their money to an institution that bore the stigma of unconstitutionality. Most important of all, they rightly believed that the Bank of the United States was intended to strengthen the position of the businessmen of the North. The planters were therefore understandably reluctant to underwrite an institution that seemed designed to encompass their own downfall.

Up to a point, Hamilton took satisfaction in the scrambling of speculators and investors for stock in the Bank of the United States. The fact that the price of that stock had been raised above par in a short period of time appeared to him as gratifying evidence of the progress made by American capitalism under his tutelage and of the confidence now reposed by "the moneyed & trading people" in the government. In this development he saw an augury of the day when the credit of the United States government would be as solidly established as that of Great Britain and the Bank of the United States would take rank alongside the Bank of England.[29]

But as the "delirium of speculation" mounted, the man who had uncorked the genii became more and more alarmed. A little speculation was in Hamilton's opinion an excellent thing for the Bank, the government and the country: it tended to raise the price of government securities and thereby made more capital available for investment. But he was only moderately bullish on Bank of the United States stock: if the scrip sold for around $190 and government bonds reached par or a little above, he declared, he would be satisfied.* Certainly, as he now said, he had not intended to set afloat another South Sea Bubble.

In the hope of deflating the bubble before it burst, Hamilton published in the *Gazette of the United States,* under the signature of "A Real Friend to Public Credit," a warning that the craze for Bank scrip might prove "ruinous to the fortunes of many individuals, and, for a time, hurtful to the public credit." Bright as were the prospects of the Bank of the United States, Hamilton predicted that its dividends were unlikely to run more than 8 per cent. Even government bonds, he remarked, were experiencing a too rapid rise: European investors, discouraged by the high prices prevailing in the bond market, were switching their investments to land. The clear implication of Hamilton's remarks was that Americans would be wise to settle for a moderate profit in their stock-market operations.[30]

If Hamilton's exhortations were to have any effect, it was essential that they be taken to heart by his old friend and former Treasury aide, William Duer. With money borrowed in part from Secretary of War Henry Knox, Duer was buying Bank scrip and government bonds with the obvious intention of cornering the market. Everything was going up and Duer acted as though he expected it would go on forever. An old hand at blowing bubbles, Duer expected to ride this one to the heights of fortune.

Sensible of the importance of winning Duer's support, Hamilton sent him a personal appeal to keep the stock-market boom within bounds. He reminded Duer of the dangers of excessive speculation: financial ruin for himself, the destruction of the government's credit and the ruin of Hamilton's own reputation. "A bubble connected with any operation is, of all the

* Previously, government securities were selling for 82 cents on the dollar for the 6 per cent stock and 42 cents on the dollar for the 3 per cent stock. The comparatively low price of these securities worked to the advantage of purchasers of Bank of the United States stock since government securities were accepted at par value in exchange for stock in the Bank.

enemies I have to fear, in my judgement is the most formidable," he told Duer. Having opened the floodgates of public credit, Hamilton was now concerned lest he be swept away in the torrent.[31]

But as the Secretary ought to have known, the public welfare or the reputations of his friends were of little concern to William Duer when they stood in the way of his ambition of making himself the richest man in the country. He brushed aside Hamilton's pleas and plunged more deeply than before into speculation.

He plunged, but he struck bottom with a crash heard in every security market in the country. Hamilton had delayed too long in issuing his caveat against speculation; the price of scrip had risen to such a height that a collapse was overdue when Hamilton sounded his warning. In its fall, Bank scrip dragged down the price of government securities and the panic was on.

With hundreds of speculators facing ruin, Hamilton took the opportunity to demonstrate that the government of the United States did not let down its friends and supporters in their hour of need. Acting through the agency of the Bank of New York, the Treasury Department entered the bond market in August, 1791; before the emergency was over, it had spent over $200,000 from the sinking fund to support the price of government bonds.

As a result of the prompt action on the part of the Treasury, the panic was short-lived. Except for wiping out a few speculators, the incident seemed to have no untoward results. The government and bank securities soon settled down to a price level well above that which had prevailed before the boom began; by October, 1791, stock in the Bank of the United States was selling for $500 a share and government 6 per cent securities were above par. Unfortunately for Hamilton, the pricking of the bubble did not shake his confidence in or his friendship for William Duer. The financier's only fault, the Secretary decided, was that he was a bit too sanguine. Coming from a man who prided himself upon his deep understanding of human nature, this was truly a charitable judgment.[32]

The speculative fever that accompanied the launching of the Bank of the United States proved—if further proof were necessary—that this was to be a bank dedicated to furthering the interests of the possessors of liquid capital. In Hamilton's plans for the Bank, the farmers were left almost wholly out of account. The Bank was intended primarily for the convenience and profit of businessmen; any immediate advantage the farmers might derive from it was incidental.* There was of course no question of making land part of the capitalization of the Bank of the United States; the institution was founded upon specie and government securities. And,

* Hamilton directed that notes of the Bank of the United States were to be received in payment of duties collected upon imports.

as though to divorce the Bank altogether from real estate, Hamilton inserted a prohibition in its charter forbidding it to hold lands or buildings except insofar as they might be necessary for the operation of its business or devolved upon it through the foreclosure of mortgages. He even refused to approve a suggestion that the Bank should loan money on tobacco warehouse receipts and, in its later operations, the Bank consistently disapproved of any commodity loans. Finally, by confining the operations of the Bank to places where there was "considerable Mercantile circulating Capital," Hamilton ensured that it would be almost exclusively a businessman's bank.*

Yet it is probable that under any circumstances the agrarians would have boycotted the Bank of the United States. Holding banking to be no more than the prostitution of money for illicit gain, one Virginia planter swore that he would no more be caught going into a bank than into a house of ill fame. In general, the farmers wanted nothing to do with bank notes: for this newfangled money they exhibited only distrust. As a result, the bank notes of neither the state banks nor the Bank of the United States circulated far from the commercial cities; farmers continued to barter in the old way, quite as though banks did not exist in the eastern seaports. In effect, the United States was divided into two economic systems: one progressive and commercial, the other backward and rural. In 1794, sixty miles from Boston, Talleyrand saw 6,000 feet of timber exchanged for a bullock; while in Boston, he found people buying expensive European luxuries with bank notes and merchants drawing drafts upon London, New York and Philadelphia.[33]

While Hamilton did not create this divergence between the sections, his policies tended to aggravate it. But, for the moment, the Secretary paid little heed to the voices—many of them speaking with a Virginia accent—raised against the Bank of the United States. For he had just succeeded in riveting another jointure between "the moneyed and trading people" and the government, and there was high rejoicing in the United States Treasury. If this was not a perfect basis of union—and Hamilton never pretended that it was—it nevertheless represented to his mind the best that could be achieved under the conditions then prevailing in the United States. A "race of Americans" seemed far in the future: in the meantime, let the rich sustain the union!

As Hamilton envisaged it, not all the benefits of this newly solidified relationship were to go to the "opulent minority." He emphasized that the rich had duties as well as privileges, and high among their duties he placed the unwritten obligation to loan money to the government. One of

---

* In this, Hamilton was not following current British practice. In Great Britain, some three hundred country banks provided credit facilities to farmers and issued bank notes which circulated in rural areas. The notes of the Bank of England did not at this time circulate far from London.

The Bank of the United States

his first acts after the establishment of the Bank of the United States was to float a loan on behalf of the government. Mindful of the heavy financial commitments of the government, Hamilton arranged that it should acquire its stock in the Bank of the United States without the outlay of any cash on the government's part. Simultaneously with the acquisition of this stock, the Bank of the United States loaned the government a sum equal to the purchase price. In this transaction, no money actually changed hands: the government paid for the stock in bills drawn on foreign bankers and the loan was made by the return of the same bills.

The benefits derived by the government from this arrangement did not end here. The loan was made at 6 per cent interest, whereas the Bank was expected to pay at least 8 per cent dividends on its stock. If this expectation was realized, everything above 6 per cent paid in the form of dividends would be clear gain to the government. Moreover, the $2 million owing by the government to the Bank was to be repaid in ten annual installments out of current revenues, a method of payment designed to relieve pressure upon the government.[34]

As a source of loans to the government, the Bank of the United States fulfilled Hamilton's fondest expectations: indeed, so liberal was the Bank in making loans to the government that, contrary to the wishes of the Secretary of the Treasury, a considerable share of its capital was ultimately tied up in advances to the government. Altogether, fourteen loans were made by the Bank of the United States, representing a sum in excess of $13 million.* [35]

Knowing Hamilton as they did, his enemies expected that he would use the Bank of the United States to destroy the state banks if not the states themselves. Such a maneuver would accord with his strong centralizing bent and his well-known antagonism to all evidences of state sovereignty. Moreover, in his report to Congress, he had stipulated that the Bank of the United States be empowered to establish branch banks throughout the country—and it was by means of branch banks that the destruction of the state banks could be most easily effected.

Many of Hamilton's supporters were eager to take advantage of this opportunity to put an end to state banks and to concentrate the financial power of the country in the Bank of the United States. "All the influence of the moneyed men ought to be wrapped up in the Union, and in one bank," they declared; if the state banks were suffered to exist, they would compete with the Bank of the United States and become "dangerous instruments in the hands of State partisans."[36]

These advocates of war to the death against the state banks proved to

---

* The Bank of the United States paid a dividend of 8 per cent, compared with the 12 per cent paid by most of the state banks. This discrepancy was largely occasioned by the fact that the Bank of the United States loaned such large sums of money to the government. The government paid the Bank 6 per cent interest on the money it borrowed, whereas from other borrowers the Bank charged as high as 9 per cent interest.

be more Hamiltonian than Hamilton himself. Although the destruction of the state banks was fairly within his grasp, the Secretary of the Treasury could not bring himself to sign the death warrant. Instead, he proclaimed the extraordinary doctrine—for him—of live and let live. Even though he had insisted upon giving the Bank of the United States the right to establish branches, he wished to hold that power in abeyance, particularly in states where banks already existed. While advocating centralized government, Hamilton seemingly drew the line at centralized banking.

Hamilton's ostensible objections to branch banking were that control over the Bank of the United States would be dispersed, its resources overextended, and the affairs of the branches mismanaged by local directors.* In actuality, however, Hamilton's concern for the welfare of the Bank of New York cannot be left out of account. He might have said of this institution that although it was a small bank, there were those who loved it. Little as he was disposed to permit sentiment to influence his judgment upon economic questions, it is probable that in this instance his fondness for the institution he had helped bring into the world played a part in determining his attitude toward branch banking. The Treasury's relations with the Bank of New York were eminently satisfactory: it served as the agent of the United States government in that city and Hamilton had been able to turn some profitable government business its way. He saw no necessity, therefore, of establishing another bank in New York—least of all a branch bank of the Bank of the United States.

Intimate as were his dealings with the Bank of New York, Hamilton had by this time severed all connection with it. When he became Secretary of the Treasury, he owned $750 of the capital stock of the Bank of New York. Obviously Caesar's wife could not be a stockholder in a banking institution that profited as did the Bank of New York from its transactions with the United States government. Accordingly, William Seton, the cashier of the Bank of New York, was instructed by Hamilton to sell his stock before he was accused of favoring the Bank for reasons of private gain.

Deploring the "extreme delicacy" that led Hamilton to sacrifice valuable stock on a rising market, Seton succeeded in delaying the sale for four months. It was not until August, 1792, that he sold Hamilton's shares—and then at a profit of about $300. But no sooner had he consummated the sale than the price went up sharply. Hamilton, however, was more relieved to be out of the reach of his political enemies than chagrined over the loss of a few dollars' profit; he was now within the law, where, indeed, Caesar's wife belonged.

* The Bank of England had no branch banks. The country banks added to the productive capital of the country through the issuance of bank notes. Thornton, *An Enquiry*, p. 176; Clapham, *The Bank of England*, I, 162-163; McKee, *Papers*, I, 81; Adam Smith, *Wealth of Nations*, pp. 281-282.

The Bank of the United States

Rather than see the Bank of the United States venture into the untried and hazardous field of branch banking, Hamilton recommended that a mutually advantageous amalgamation be effected between the central and the state banks. If the Bank of New York, for example, offered a portion of its stock to the Bank of the United States and purchased in return an interest in the central bank, Hamilton thought that the country would enjoy all the advantages of centralized banking with none of its pains and penalties. By means of interlocking directorates and a consolidation of capital resources, the state banks and the Bank of the United States would function as one: like satellites, the state banks would revolve round the Bank of the United States. Had Hamilton's plans been fully realized, the Bank of the United States might ultimately have become a bankers' bank like the Bank of England; and, like the Bank of England, it would have stood as a tower of strength to banks in financial difficulties and a guarantor of their financial stability.[37]

In his Report on the Bank of the United States, Hamilton had dwelt upon the advantages to be derived from private control of banking. He now began to experience some of the disadvantages of such control: his own wishes as regards branch banking were openly flouted by the directors.

Although Hamilton's enemies pictured him as the master of the Bank of the United States and the directors as his willing tools, actually the Bank was under the direction of men who followed their own bent even though it ran directly contrary to the Secretary's most cherished convictions. Brushing aside Hamilton's objections, they established branches in the important commercial centers of the country, even where a state bank was already doing business. This course of action, said Hamilton, was "begun, continued, and ended, not only without my participation, but *against my judgment*. . . . I was never consulted." He had asked for a bank under the direction of independent businessmen and this he found, somewhat to his consternation, was what he had gotten.*

Particularly disconcerting to Hamilton was the directors' decision to establish in New York City a branch capitalized for almost twice the amount commanded by the Bank of New York. Clearly, Hamilton's first love among banks was in mortal danger: the colossus he had helped to raise in Philadelphia was now reaching out to destroy the state banks. To the astonishment of his friends and enemies alike, Hamilton entered the lists as the champion of the state banks.

The Secretary's avowed purpose was to prevent the branches of the Bank of the United States from swallowing up the state banks, and to that end he placed the influence of the United States Treasury upon the side of the

* In conformity with Hamilton's ideas, however, a large measure of control was retained by the parent bank over its branches. The directors of each branch were annually elected by the Board of Directors in Philadelphia and the cashier of each branch was appointed by them.

state-chartered institutions. In the drawing of foreign bills of exchange and in depositing the government's revenues, he tended to favor them over the Bank of the United States. His favoritism toward the Bank of New York was especially palpable: it is probable that had it not been for Treasury support, the Bank of New York would have gone down before the Bank of the United States and its New York branch.[38]

Partly as a result of Hamilton's intervention, the state banks were preserved. Reprieved from the doom apparently decreed against them by the decision of the Bank of the United States to engage in branch banking, they multiplied rapidly in the last decade of the eighteenth and early decades of the nineteenth centuries. But Hamilton did not find this a cause for rejoicing: instead of allies working in close union with the central bank, the state banks became its rivals and enemies. Jefferson and Madison were soon fostering the state banks and encouraging them to extend their facilities to farmers. Eventually, it was the influence of the state banks that contributed to the downfall of the Bank of the United States in 1811 and again in 1836.

Thus, for once, Hamilton underestimated the strength of the enemy; instead of striking down the state banks when he had the chance, he permitted them to coexist with the Bank of the United States—with fatal results to that institution. Long before these results were fully apparent, he was called to account by some of his own partisans. Had the Federalist Samson, it was asked, permitted his Delilah—in the form of the Bank of New York— to shear his locks? In Hamilton's justification it could be said that he hoped to make the state banks the nucleus of a centralized banking system; but as Hamilton himself frequently remarked, good intentions were never enough in this world.

But this was looking into futurity; for the moment, Hamilton seemed to have won a complete triumph. His objectives were seldom as fully realized as they were in the case of the Bank of the United States. By increasing and stabilizing the circulating medium, making credit available where credit had not existed before, and discounting bills of exchange, the Bank made itself to a great degree "the mainspring and regulator of the whole American business world." It was of inestimable value to the government in paying the foreign and domestic debt, transmitting funds from one part of the country to another and to Europe, collecting revenue, loaning money and serving as a depository for government funds. It facilitated the payment of taxes by increasing the amount of money in circulation, and the directors co-operated with the Treasury in controlling the money market and maintaining the value of its notes.* As a means of raising up a moneyed

* The necessity of the banknotes issued by the Bank of the United States was made even more apparent by the failure of the United States Mint to produce an adequate coinage. Although Hamilton drew up a Report on the Mint in 1791, the United States was unable to accumulate enough gold and silver to make coinage feasible on a large scale.

The Bank of the United States

class, the Bank was second only to the funding system: the high dividends it yielded to stockholders and the opportunities it afforded businessmen to embark upon new ventures made it a potent instrument of capitalism. In August, 1792, after the Bank had been in operation for a little over a year, Hamilton declared that "the most incorrigible theorist among its opponents would, in one month's experience, as head of the department of Treasury, be compelled to acknowledge that it is an absolutely indispensable engine in the management of the finances, and would quickly become a convert to its perfect constitutionality."[39]

19.

The Report on Manufactures

With the establishment of the Bank of the United States, Hamilton reached the pinnacle of his influence and—such as it was—his popularity. He had carried everything before him; the opposition was as yet unorganized; and the businessmen of the country hailed him as their benefactor. In Boston, among the "better sort," those who could claim an acquaintance with Colonel Hamilton were besieged with questions concerning this remarkable young man; and his portrait, painted by John Trumbull for the citizens of New York, was hung in the City Hall. All the wise, the rich and the good delighted to do him homage; in this select circle, it was not deemed improper to rank him with Washington, and there were some who even whispered that the "Little Lion" was the more redoubtable of the two. Hamilton was the golden boy of the Federalist party—the darling of fortune who dazzled the opulent and the well-born by the brilliance and versatility of his talents. So closely were his policies identified with the integrity of the United States government that his supporters considered an attack upon the Secretary as equivalent to an attack upon the laws and the Constitution—a view with which Hamilton was wholeheartedly in agreement.

In American colleges and universities, rapidly becoming strongholds of conservatism, professors marched in solemn procession to pay tribute to Hamilton. In 1790, the honorary degree of Doctor of Laws was conferred upon him by Dartmouth College; and two years later, Harvard University bestowed a similar degree upon the man "to whose Wisdom and unremitted exertions these United States owe so much of their present tranquillity and prosperity, and the national respectability." He was made a trustee of Columbia College and, as a reward for his services in securing the passage of the bill by which Columbia became a university, he was given an honorary M.A. by his alma mater. At about the same time he attained the dignity of having his effigy exhibited at Bowen's Wax Work Museum near the New York Exchange.

Even the ultimate honor of the academic world was awarded Hamilton—a college was named after him. In 1792, Hamilton agreed to act as trustee of a college in upper New York dedicated to providing education for Indians and whites alike. Although Hamilton seems to have contributed only his name to the undertaking, the school was named the Hamilton Oneida Academy. By consenting to have his name used in connection with this institution Hamilton, by implication, at least, put his approval upon the principles—drawn up by Samuel Kirkland, the real founder of the college—this academy was expected to advance: that there ought to be no segregation of the two races; that Indians were the equals of whites; and that "the difference between one nation [race] and another is not so much owing to nature as to education."

The businessmen, if not the college professors, had good reason to acclaim Hamilton, for the country was riding an unprecedented wave of prosperity. In fact, it seemed to be rushing into wealth faster than even Hamilton—"the most sanguine of the sanguine"—had thought possible. In less than five years, the exports of the United States more than doubled in value; in 1794, twice as many ships flew the American flag as in 1790; wheat rose to the unprecedented price of a dollar a bushel; workmen received as much as two dollars a day; and land values increased, as Washington said, "beyond all calculation. . . . No City, Town, Village, or even farm, but what exhibits evidences of increasing wealth and prosperity." Without much exaggeration, Hamilton could describe the national scene as "a spectacle of national happiness never surpassed, if ever before equalled, in the annals of human affairs."

To a large degree, this prosperity was owing to the adoption of the Constitution and the enactment of Hamilton's fiscal program. While it is true that economic recovery antedated the inauguration of the new government, the stability, order and protection given property by the federal government contributed materially to restore the confidence and optimism without which any enduring prosperity would have been impossible; and the creation of a stable circulating medium and the impetus it gave to capitalistic enterprise provided a solid foundation upon which the well-being of the country could be built.

Thanks to this economic upsurge, the government was able to meet promptly the heavy payments of interest and principal to which Hamilton had committed it. Boom conditions at home meant larger importations of European manufactures and this in turn meant larger revenues to the government. A single vessel, for example, arriving in New York in 1790 from the East Indies, paid $30,000 in duties.

In this abounding prosperity, it might be supposed that the people would be so busy making money and enjoying the good things of life that they would have little time to contemplate their political grievances. To some degree, this was the case: in Boston, for example, it was said that few complained, the people's mouths being "stopped with white bread and roast beef." Elsewhere, and particularly in Virginia, Hamilton had succeeded in arraying against himself a roster of enemies of which, said Gouverneur Morris, any self-respecting Federalist ought to be proud. For sheer unpopularity, no other member of the administration could compete with the Secretary of the Treasury: his political theories, his financial policies and his objectives all made him anathema to those who did not share his vision of the American future. "Seldom," said John Marshall, "has any minister excited in a higher or more extensive degree than Colonel Hamilton, the opposite passions of love and hate," and of the two, hate sometimes seemed to be the stronger. Even those who made a merit of Hamilton's ability to make enemies sometimes lamented that he did not have more friends, particularly in the South.

While all parts of the country participated to some extent in the economic upsurge that began in 1786-87, its effects were particularly noticeable in the eastern seaboard cities. Here merchants, professional men, bankers and successful speculators affected a princely style of living. Even though Robert Morris possessed a house in Philadelphia regarded as the most magnificent in the country, he was not content until he had constructed a mansion on Chestnut Street befitting an English nobleman.

Besides being the largest city in the United States, Philadelphia was the intellectual capital of the country, boasting better prisons, more scientific and literary clubs, hospitals, libraries and men of wealth and refinement than any other city in the union. Impressed by the fame of this metropolis, Voltaire expressed the wish in his old age to end his days in the City of Brotherly Love. And end them he would, exclaimed a Frenchman who had visited Philadelphia—he would soon die of ennui. In Voltaire's eyes, it was predicted, the Quakers would have appeared insufferable bores—"he would have yawned in their assemblies, and been mortified to see his epigrams pass without applause." Discomfited by such treatment, he would have been as thoroughly disillusioned about "republican simplicity" as would Rousseau had he journeyed to the New World to live among the "noble savages."

But after 1790, when the seat of government was transferred to Philadelphia, the austerity of the Quakers was overshadowed by the gay, lively and resplendent society that centered around the President. Never before, it was remarked, had so much Madeira been consumed in Philadelphia. Many congressmen, their constituents learned with dismay, "plunge into vortex of dissipation; they do not always escape unhurt, but like the mariners who have been shipwrecked in nine voyages, will venture on the tenth." Mrs. John Adams reported that in Philadelphia the gyrations of the social whirl were even giddier than in New York—"one continued round of Parties upon Parties, Balls and entertainments." It was not uncommon for a lady or gentleman to lose four or five hundred dollars in an evening at loo.

Even French aristocrats who visited Philadelphia were amazed at the profusion and luxury evident on every side, and at least one pronounced the wives and daughters of these solid bourgeoisie to be prettier than Parisian women. At Mrs. Washington's New Year's Day levee, it was "as much crowded as a Birth Night at St. James and with company as brilliantly drest, diamonds & great hoops excepted"; and for pride, haughtiness and ostentation, these aristocrats did not yield to their British counterparts.

The chiefs of the "sacred clan of rich and polished Americans" mixed high society with politics: Thomas Bingham and his wife, arbiters in Philadelphia of all things pertaining to taste, fashion and gentility, made their "Mansion House"—one room of which was decorated "after the style of the Vatican at Rome"—a political headquarters for Hamilton and other leaders of the Federalist party. Bingham himself was a United States senator from Pennsylvania. He found in both the House and Senate a goodly company of businessmen engaged in giving concrete application to the theory that those who owned the country ought to run it.

With a salary of $3,000 a year, it was not easy for Hamilton to move in the company of the socially elect. Nevertheless, by dint of spending every penny of his salary and dipping deep into the savings he had accumulated as a lawyer in New York, Hamilton contrived to become one of the most glittering ornaments of the social life of the capital. While he could not vie with Secretary of War Knox—the richest man, next to Washington, in the administration—in the kind of magnificence that impressed the nouveaux riches, Hamilton lived in a style that led some to doubt if he were really a Scotsman. When he moved to Philadelphia, for example, he was content with nothing less than the house formerly occupied by the President of the Continental Congress. (Later he moved to a more modest house on Market Street.) He was frequently seen at the theater, assembly hall and the card table relaxing from the cares of state. No American statesman ever combined more gracefully the hard-working administrator with the social butterfly. In some ways, he was the greatest boon to womanhood ever to descend upon the City of Brotherly Love: when the gallant Secretary of the Treasury was among the company, it was observed that husbands were never more attentive to their wives.

Anxious to discover what impression the dashing young Secretary of the Treasury had made upon his wife, Christopher Champlain, a member of Congress from Rhode Island, remarked that Hamilton seemed "very trifling in his conversation with Ladies." His wife agreed: "she did not like him at all," she declared. If, in consequence, the congressman slept sounder, he was happily ignorant of the nature of woman.

By means of the assumption of state debts and the funding of the national debt, Hamilton had succeeded in attaining his first objective—the re-establishment of the credit of the national government. In the Bank of the United States, Hamilton had created an institution designed to concentrate the capital resources of the country in a central bank. Thus the United States was prepared for the capitalistic dispensation, but the answer to the question—to what ends were the new-found wealth of the country to be put?—had not yet been handed down from the Treasury. The answer was forthcoming in the Report on Manufactures Hamilton submitted to Congress in December, 1791.

In January, 1791, the House of Representatives requested the Secretary of the Treasury to prepare a plan "for the encouragement and promotion of such manufactures as will tend to render the United States independent of other nations for essentials, particularly for military supplies." As was his settled habit, Hamilton gave the broadest possible interpretation to this directive. In consequence, what Congress received on December 5, 1791, when he submitted his report, was a comprehensive survey of the state of manufacturing in the United States—its extent, variety, the degree of success attained, the obstacles that needed to be overcome, its future prospects, and a disquisition upon the ways and means of promoting manufactures in the Republic.

For much of his information concerning the state of manufactures in the United States, Hamilton was indebted to Tench Coxe, the Assistant Secretary of the Treasury. This equivocal character—like many of Hamilton's friends, he had been a Tory during the War of Independence—had made a survey of manufacturing even before he came to the Treasury in 1790. His findings had been published in a book entitled *A View of the Manufactures of the United States,* in which he pronounced manufactures to be "the means of our POLITICAL SALVATION" and national independence and urged that they be encouraged by government aid in the form of tariffs and bounties, the subsidizing of the fisheries and the introduction of labor-saving machinery. It was in this last field that Coxe particularly distinguished himself as a pioneer: as one of the leading advocates of cotton manufacturing in the United States, he tried to smuggle models of the Arkwright spinning machines out of England. Singularly enough, it was Thomas Jefferson, not Hamilton, who made it possible for Coxe to get his machinery.[1]

To supplement Coxe's survey of the manufacturing potential of the United States, Hamilton instructed the Treasury agents—collectors of the customs, supervisors, and the rest—to examine and report upon the progress of manufactures in their locality. Since, in many cases, they compiled their accounts from information gained from interviews with businessmen and from personal inspections of factories, Hamilton's report offered an authoritative survey of the state of American manufacturing in 1791.*

* Hamilton also consulted books and articles on American manufacturing, notably William Barton's *Remarks on the State of American Manufactures and Commerce.* But, for the most part, he relied upon the information furnished by Treasury agents or by businessmen themselves.

The Report on Manufactures

Even though the economy of the United States in 1791 was overwhelmingly agricultural and commercial, Hamilton found that manufacturing was well advanced in certain areas. In fact, the British consul in the United States was already alarmed at the quantities of nails, iron utensils, farming implements, shoes and hats being turned out by American factories. In these articles, he reported to his government, the United States was rapidly making itself independent of foreign supplies. In the vicinity of Boston alone, some 2,500 people were said to be employed in manufacturing; and of the 8,600 adult males in Philadelphia, one fourth were engaged in factories large or small. In January, 1789, before Hamilton came to the Treasury, Washington estimated that more cotton, wool and iron factories had been erected in the United States in the previous eighteen months than in the entire history of the country. This was not wholly good news: to the consternation of the children of the country, a castor-oil factory had recently been established in New York.[2]

In the petitions presented to Congress by "the manufacturing interest" it was frequently remarked that the United States contained "resources amply sufficient to enable them to become a great manufacturing country, and only want the patronage and support of a wise, energetic government." Much was made of the argument that manufactures, if properly encouraged, would become a cement of union. As early as 1775, Hamilton had projected the idea that the knot of union could be tied with southern cotton manufactured in northern mills. Although by 1791 cotton had failed to achieve this purpose, manufacturing had to some extent become a bond of union: the shipbuilders of the North bought from southern producers tar, pitch, turpentine, rosin and ship timber. Moreover, the country was being unified economically by roads, turnpikes and canals. Between Philadelphia and New York plied four daily stages, and it was possible to travel from Portsmouth to Virginia and beyond by regularly scheduled vehicles. Most of these roads and canals were built by private companies authorized by the state to collect tolls.[3]

It can thus be seen that the business community of which Hamilton made himself the spokesman was already in existence when he sat down in 1791 to write his Report on Manufactures. As Hamilton said, his purpose was to "cherish and bring to maturity this precious embryo" that private enterprise brought into being. He was not the father of American business: rather, he found it a lusty infant and taught it to walk.

And yet, on the basis of the facts and figures received by the Treasury, Hamilton concluded that the United States had hardly done more than scratch the surface of its boundless potential as a manufacturing country. Since he had long been of the opinion that the survival of the republic depended upon drawing together the economic bonds of union and making the country independent of foreign supplies for its war materials, Hamilton was not satisfied with what had been achieved in this sphere. As his report revealed, he would not rest content until the United States had become one of the great industrialized nations of the world.

Despite the progress made in manufacturing, Hamilton considered the economy of the United States to be in a dangerous state of imbalance. The preponderance of agriculture impressed him as a source of weakness: by pursuing agriculture as single-mindedly as did Americans, Hamilton feared that they were perpetuating the very conditions from which they had sought to escape by declaring their independence—a colonial inferiority and dependence upon the more industrialized countries of Europe. National wealth and power, he perceived, were passing rapidly into the hands of those countries that devoted their energies to commerce and manufacturing: here, he believed, was the wave of the future upon which nations would rise to greatness. Those that chose to ride agriculture would end, he suspected, by sinking into the status of second-rate powers.

If, as Thomas Jefferson supposed, a nation of farmers was the closest approximation upon earth to paradise, Hamilton was of the opinion that the time of exodus was at hand. Sooner or later, self-preservation compelled every agricultural community to turn to manufacturing: when men devoted all their energies and capital to the production of foodstuffs, supply tended to outrun demand and unsalable surplus accumulated which produced unemployment, which in turn could be relieved only by industrialization.

Mainly, it was the course of events in Europe that persuaded Hamilton that time was running out for the American agricultural economy. Every important country in the Old World sought to ensure a monopoly of its domestic markets for its own manufactures and to buy as little and to sell as much as possible abroad. The great powers still clung to the mercantilist ideal of an economy closed as tightly as possible against the intrusions of foreigners. In such an economy, the United States could expect to experience increasing difficulty in selling its agricultural products abroad. Great Britain, for example, imported wheat only when the price rose to seven shillings or more a bushel; but because the prevailing price was well below this figure, the importation of American wheat was in effect prohibited. And, to aggravate their predicament, Americans were steadily bringing new lands under cultivation, thereby increasing the agricultural surplus.[4]

Basing his calculations upon conditions as they existed in 1791, Hamilton assumed that, in the not distant future, the European market for American agricultural products would be almost wholly lost. His report on Manufactures was intended to prepare the economy of the United States for the foreseeable day when Americans would be compelled to live unto themselves. As he later told Talleyrand: "We only need two markets but they are indispensable to us: one for the Northern and one for the Southern

States. . . . Mutual wants constitute one of the strongest links of political connection," he went on. ". . . . Everything tending to establish substantial and permanent order in the affairs of a country, to increase the total mass of industry and opulence, is ultimately beneficial to every part of it." Manufacturing would make the United States one nation indivisible, bound together by common wants, common interests and a common prosperity.

If "mutual dependence formed the essence of union," Hamilton believed that an all-wise Providence could hardly have done better by the United States. Because one section was so admirably suited to manufactures and the other sections were equally well adapted to the pursuit of agriculture, it seemed to Hamilton that the economic foundations of union had been solidly laid by God and Nature: it only remained for a statesman to erect a durable superstructure upon them. The Report on Manufactures was intended to provide the blueprints for such an edifice of union.

Hitherto, much of Hamilton's effort had been expended upon consummating a marriage between businessmen and the government. Now, for the first time, he unveiled in his Report on Manufactures the dowry that government proposed to bestow upon its fortunate partner: tariffs, bounties, subsidies and premiums—everything, in short, to make businessmen happy and to unite them inviolably to a government from which such blessings flowed.[5]

By reconstructing the American economy according to the specifications he laid down in his Report on Manufactures, Hamilton intended to prepare the United States for all the eventualities which experience had taught nations to expect. Not least among those eventualities was war—against which, Hamilton had often pointed out, even a peace-loving country was not immune. As the War of Independence had revealed, the United States was largely dependent upon foreign supplies in time of war and these supplies could easily be cut off by an enemy possessed of superior sea power. Thus it had been deeply impressed upon Hamilton that in the eighteenth-century world of warring states, the United States could not afford to remain a backward nation.

Rather than see the United States risk disaster again, Hamilton urged that the government itself undertake the manufacture of arms and munitions. In general he acted upon the principle that government ought not to do things which individuals were doing already but to do those things which were not being done at all. He was not willing to leave these "implements of national defence to the casual speculations of individual adventure." American businessmen had so far shown little interest or organizational ability in this field—although within a few years the names of du Pont and Whitney were to open a new chapter in the history of the manufacture of the implements of war.

Essential as manufactures were in time of war, Hamilton conceived them to be no less important in peace. Only by means of manufactures, Hamilton observed, could the United States prevent the drainage of its specie overseas that up to this time had defeated every attempt to put the finances of the country upon a sound footing. As long as the northern states bought more than they sold to Great Britain, they were compelled to make up the difference by exporting specie. In consequence, the United States suffered chronically from a pound shortage from which Hamilton saw no relief until Americans manufactured more for themselves and bought less from British suppliers.

Sanguine as Hamilton was, he never believed that it was within the power of government to work miracles simply by passing a law. He knew that even the adoption of his report by Congress would leave unanswered the most important question of all—from whence was to come the capital necessary to implement his grand design? For, although the government could give aid and direction, Hamilton always assumed that the principal impetus must come from private capital.

For the first time, the United States seemed to have sufficient surplus capital to make the establishment of manufactures feasible. As a result of speculation in the national and state debts, the country had received a considerable influx of foreign capital. This windfall Hamilton proposed to devote to the underwriting of capitalistic enterprise, particularly manufacturing, before it was dissipated in the purchase of foreign luxuries or consumed in reckless speculation. Among his countrymen, Hamilton detected "a certain fermentation of mind, a certain activity of speculation and enterprise which, if properly directed, may be made subservient to useful purposes but which, if left entirely to itself, may be attended with pernicious effects." Here was where the government stepped in: it made sure that capitalists invested their money in the ways most advantageous to the national welfare.

Of course, Hamilton saw nothing to be gained by appealing to patriotism, altruism or magnanimity. Such sentiments were too rare and insubstantial, in Hamilton's way of thinking, to serve as the springs of action for any group of men, let alone capitalists. As he saw it, self-interest alone could impel men to action and self-interest had to be spelled out for them by those who understood it better than they themselves. On the other hand, when assured of a profit, even "cautious, sagacious capitalists" became as bold as lions; all they asked was a sure thing—and Hamilton was inclined to do everything in the government's power to give it to them. Manifestly, Hamilton divined the essential spirit of capitalism—"the dependence upon an appeal to the money-making and money-loving instincts of individuals as the main motive force of the economic machine." His efforts were largely directed toward giving constructive direction to these instincts.[6]

To that end, Hamilton recommended that Congress appropriate money

The Report on Manufactures

for bounties, premiums and other aids to industry and that a commission be created to allocate these funds. This commission, Hamilton suggested, ought to be guided by five considerations: the extent to which the raw materials used in manufacture were found in the United States, the degree to which machinery could be substituted for labor, the ease of manufacture, the nature of the uses to which the article could be applied, and its value for purposes of defense. Considering the scope of Hamilton's ambition, his immediate objectives were modest: iron, nails, firearms, ardent spirits and malt liquor he rated as the articles in which the United States most readily could make itself self-sufficient. Cotton and woolen cloth could come later.

Other than serving as a guide, benefactor and partner of business, the government, in Hamilton's philosophy, left individual enterprise to itself. He would tolerate no price-fixing, for example, on the ground that competition was a better regulator of prices than governmental edict. Nor did he envisage governmental interference with business to secure social objectives. Hamilton's ideal was a free economy—free, that is, insofar as curbs upon individual initiative were concerned, but not free in that sense that government abstained from interference of any kind. He insisted only that the interference of government be benevolent and in the interests of the national welfare.

In his inventory of the resources of the United States, Hamilton did not omit the distinctive talents and skills of the American people. He was especially impressed by the inventive genius and the "peculiar aptitude for mechanic improvements" displayed by his countrymen. To turn this aptitude to the account of the state was for Hamilton an essential part of his plan for the encouragement of manufactures; accordingly, he urged Congress "to induce the prosecution and introduction of useful discoveries" by a system of rewards and premiums. To those who introduced machinery into the United States from abroad, even in defiance of the laws of foreign countries prohibiting its exportation, he was prepared to give cash rewards and the temporary grant of exclusive manufacturing privileges.

Nevertheless, no matter how elaborate the system of rewards, Hamilton recognized that few businessmen would be inclined to risk their capital in the establishment of factories in the United States without the assurance of an adequate supply of labor. With western lands acting as a magnet that drew potential factory workers from the eastern states, the problem was not to keep Americans down on the farm but to persuade them to live in cities and work in factories. Nevertheless, Hamilton did not despair of providing American factories with a labor force: there was a plentitude of women, children and immigrants which might be used to work the machines. The men of the United States would learn their error when they saw the pay checks brought home by their wives and children; plow-jogging was not to be compared with a good steady job in a mill!

In England, little children were leading the factory owners to the promised land of bigger factories and bigger profits. Blessed were these children, for they worked fourteen hours a day, six days a week, and were never known to engage in union activities. Hamilton carried his admiration of British industrialism even to the point of noting with approval that almost half the workers in British cotton factories were women and children, "of whom the greater proportion were children, and many of them of a tender age." That the United States should copy this example seemed to Hamilton highly beneficial not only for the national economy but even for the women and children involved: "In general," he asserted "women and children are rendered more useful, and the latter more early useful, by manufacturing establishments, than they would other wise be."[7]

The idea of using women and children in American factories did not originate with Hamilton. When he wrote his Report on Manufactures, women and children were already being employed in the United States. In the manufacturing of nails, in which this country was almost self-sufficient, child labor was extensively used; and it was the pride of Philadelphia that the local carpet factory which made the carpets for the President's and Senate's chambers gave employment "to a number of poor women and children." President Washington had remarked in 1789 that the labor of women and children might be utilized in factories "without taking one really necessary hand from tilling the earth"; and he noted with approval that a factory in Boston employed fourteen children, "the daughters of decayed families." Possibly his enthusiasm was partly owing to the fact that, as he told the factory manager, these were the prettiest girls he had seen in Boston. In short, Americans had long since begun to act upon the theory that "a numerous family of children, instead of being a burthen is a source of opulence and prosperity to the parents." Most of the labor of women and children was expended upon field chores and household manufactures. Hamilton—to whom productivity was the measure of all economic things—emphasized how much more beneficial to the state and to the individuals concerned was this labor when it was employed in factories and workshops.[8]

But women and children were not Hamilton's chief reliance for solving the labor problem in the United States. Following the lead of Adam Smith and Tench Coxe, he set great store by machinery as a means of introducing manufactures into a sparsely settled country. Machinery, said Hamilton, had "prodigiously lessened the necessity for manual labor" and had thereby reduced labor costs and the price of manufactured goods. Given the water power available in the United States and the mechanical bent of the American people, Hamilton believed that the republic stood an excellent chance of becoming one of the most advanced industrial countries.[9]

Notwithstanding his zeal to promote manufacturing, Hamilton was

The Report on Manufactures

aware that protectionism could be carried to the point of working serious injury to the national economy. In *The Federalist*, he had warned against giving domestic manufactures a "premature monopoly" of the market; and in his Report on Manufactures he laid down the rule that prohibitive duties ought to be imposed only when "a manufacture has made such progress and is in so many hands, as to insure a due competition, and an adequate supply on reasonable terms."[10] Hence, in many instances, he advocated only moderate tariff duties, and in the case of pig and bar iron he recommended no protection whatever on the ground that the price had advanced to such a point that foreign competition would still leave domestic producers a reasonable profit.[11]

Nor was it Hamilton's intention to turn the protected market over to a few overgrown corporations. Rather, he envisaged a highly competitive economy in which a large number of businessmen, by virtue of their rivalry, would bring down prices "to the minimum of a reasonable profit on the capital employed" and thereby protect the community against monopolistic practices. While he admitted that the initial effect of bounties and tariffs would be to raise prices, he supposed that in the long run they would result in a permanent reduction of the price level. "In a national view," he observed, "a temporary enhancement of price must always be well compensated by a permanent reduction of it." Since competition tended to reduce prices and bounties whetted competition, Hamilton supposed that he had hit upon an infallible method of fostering industrialization without at the same time imposing an intolerable burden upon the consumer and tax payer.[12]

In Hamilton's economic philosophy, the role of government was not confined to conferring favors upon businessmen: it likewise served the public interest as a regulatory and supervising agency. The Report on Manufactures accordingly recommended that a system of governmental inspection of manufactured goods be established to protect the consumer, improve the quality and enhance the reputation of American manufactures in foreign markets.[13]

Thus Hamilton offered Americans wealth and greatness, not by war and conquest, but by the utilization of the human and material resources at their command. Singularly enough, this road to national felicity was marked out by a man enamored of military glory who yearned to be known in history as a military leader. But Hamilton's major accomplishments were not destined to be made upon the field of battle. His Report on Manufactures contained the embryo of modern America: here, if a date can be assigned to a development so amorphous and far-reaching in its consequences, was conceived the grand design by which the United States became the greatest industrial power in the world.

While he spoke the language of conservatism, Hamilton in fact undertook to revolutionize the economic and political life of the United States. His dream was the transformation of the republic into a highly centralized nation in which manufacturing, commerce and agriculture were made to serve the purposes of an overriding nationalism. Far from envisaging the federal government as a guarantor of the existing order, he intended it to play a decisive part in shaping a progressive national economy. No man in the United States had less love for the *status quo* or less reverence for many of the accepted values of the Americans of his generation than did Hamilton; and no man did more to alter fundamentally their existing institutions and way of life.

If Hamilton's plans looked forward to the day when the United States would become a great commercial and industrial nation, the method by which he proposed to attain this goal looked backward to mercantilism. In this sense, he owed more to Colbert, the exponent of mercantilism, than to Adam Smith, the apostle of laissez faire.

It was natural that Hamilton, seeking union, wealth and power for his country, should turn to mercantilism, "the economic first-thought of self-conscious nationalism." Hamilton and the other leaders of his generation had grown up under mercantilism: they were familiar with bounties, drawbacks, and the laws of trade and navigation by which Great Britain had sought to direct the agriculture and commerce of its colonies into the channels mast beneficial to the mother country; and one of the principal benefits expected from the Federal Constitution was the regulation of trade. Even before Hamilton's appointment as Secretary of the Treasury, Congress had begun to apply mercantilistic principles to the shipping and commerce of the United States.

A centralized, controlling government, a favorable balance of trade, the economic unification of the country—these goals Hamilton shared with the mercantilists. Like them, his ruling passion was to augment the power of the state; he conceived of the state in materialistic terms; and he sought to divert the selfish passions of men to its aggrandizement. And yet Hamilton's was not a pure, unadulterated mercantilism. He differed from the eighteenth-century exponents of that philosophy in believing that one nation could be prosperous without beggaring its neighbors. He did not seek to make the United States self-sufficient in such semitropical products as tea, cocoa, sugar, coffee and spices—to mercantilists, the equivalent of the steel, rubber and oil of a later imperialism. Instead of measuring the wealth of a nation by the quantity of precious metals it contained, Hamilton took the yardstick of productive capacity. He did not subordinate every other consideration—including the welfare of the working class—to production for export; nor did he subscribe to the theory that the standard of living of the workers must be reduced to the subsistence level in order that the state might grow rich. His objective was to unify the country economically, make the nation rich and powerful and raise the standard of living—which from the point of view of a seventeenth-century mercantilist was equivalent to eating your cake and having it too.* [14]

As a foil to these ideas, Hamilton's opponents put forward the doctrine of laissez faire. In Adam Smith's *Wealth of Nations*, they found a repository of arguments with which to combat Hamilton's reports. Smith depicted mercantilism as an unholy alliance between business and government for the better exploitation of the public. His ideal was that of a society of individuals free to shape their own ends, to invest their capital where they pleased and to employ their energies without let or hindrance by the state. In the name of equality, liberty and justice, Smith asked for the abolition of bounties, tariffs, rebates and other forms of state aid. Then, and only then, he declared, would individual enterprise be able to reveal the wonders of which it was capable.

Smith supposed that once the productive forces of the community had been released from the dead hand of government, they would be subjected to the far more prescient oversight of Providence. Having implanted self-love and the acquisitive instinct in human beings, Providence had presumably decreed that self-seeking, if given complete freedom of action, would promote the prosperity and well-being of society. In the actions of economic man, Smith detected the intervention of an "invisible hand" which, under the proper conditions, made even the most selfish individual contribute toward the betterment of the whole. "By pursuing his own interest," said Smith, "he frequently promotes that of the society more effectually than when he really intends to promote it." The corollary of this doctrine of a beneficent, self-regulating, divinely inspired economic system was the theory of international free trade. When men were free to follow their own economic bent, it was reasonable to suppose that they would inevitably produce the commodities for which society as a whole had the greatest need.

Thus laissez faire came into the world under the guise of liberalism: it was the philosophy of progress, freedom and prosperity for all. It promised to emancipate man from the repressive control of the state, to release individual initiative from hampering restraints, and to give security to individual liberty. As Locke had been the prophet of political individualism, so Adam Smith was the prophet of economic individualism. And, like Locke, he found devoted adherents in the rising middle class, to whose eagerness to destroy privilege and monopoly in commerce and trade he powerfully appealed.[15]

* A true mercantilist would have opposed the purchase of United States government securities by foreigners on the ground that the country would lose specie as a result of the payment of dividends. Likewise, the bounty system, upon which Hamilton relied to initiate manufactures, was not intended to promote exports and to keep domestic prices high; he recommended bounties upon production, not upon exportation.

Obviously, Hamilton was not likely to fall under the sway of the philosophy of laissez faire. For one thing, he was not persuaded, as were so many of his countrymen, that the freedom of the individual was best provided for by rigorously curtailing the powers of the state. Nor did he accept the doctrine that when each man was intent upon his private gain the public interest would be advanced as a matter of course: the "invisible hand" remained invisible to him even after its benign effects had been pointed out by Adam Smith. Unlike Smith, Hamilton had not lost his faith in the capacity of government to guide the national economy. In certain respects he considered the wisdom of government to be superior to that of individuals in the economic sphere. The all-embracing vision based upon an exact knowledge of the resources and needs of the country—this, he said, was not often granted to individual businessmen. And it seemed to him to be begging the question to refer to a preordained harmony of economic forces.

Nor did Hamilton share Smith's fears of the consequences of a close association between businessmen and government. While the American statesman never denied that businessmen were actuated by self-seeking, he did not agree with the Scottish philosopher that they were cheats and sharpers, always scheming to gouge the public with the aid of the government. As Hamilton saw it, the closer the bond between government and businessmen, the better for the state: in such a connection the government would benefit from the wealth they produced and it would be in a position to direct their acquisitive instincts into channels beneficial to the country as a whole.

Hamilton's invariable rule was to subject all ideas, new as well as old, to this test: were they applicable to the conditions and needs of the United States? In the case of laissez faire, he came to the conclusion that it failed on every count to pass the test. Although attractive as an ideal, free trade, by Smith's own admission, ran counter to some of the strongest forces of the day—nationalism among them. In 1792, Adam Smith seemed to be a prophet without honor in his own country: whatever the views held in academic circles, the British government continued to act upon the very principles that Smith condemned. Naturally, therefore, Hamilton concluded that free trade was a philosopher's version of the best of all possible worlds, not a picture of reality. "Your economists," he told Talleyrand, "made a grand dream, but it is the chimerical exaggeration of people whose intentions were good. Theoretically, their system might perhaps be contested and its unsoundness exposed; but we must leave them their pleasant illusions; the present state of the affairs of this world suffices to prove that, at least for the nonce, their plan cannot be carried out; let us be satisfied with this fact." It was time enough, he added, to think of free trade when the United States had firmly established its industries and attained with Great Britain a commanding position in world trade.

Against the "reveries" of Adam Smith, Hamilton placed the "fostering care" of the British government by which manufactures had been raised to unexampled heights; the "judicious and unremitted vigilance" of the Dutch government that had converted a small country into one of the greatest commercial nations in the world; and the example of "the great Colbert" who had brought France to a high level of commercial and industrial prosperity.

And yet, being of an eclectic and empirical cast of mind, Hamilton did not dismiss all of the *Wealth of Nations* simply because laissez faire appeared unsuited to the needs of the United States. On the contrary, he found much to commend in Smith's book and on many points he was in agreement with the Scottish economist. Both men, for example, held the same objective in view—national prosperity and power. They agreed that hampering impediments ought to be removed in order that individual initiative and the competitive spirit could enjoy free play. They regarded production as the key to national wealth; they recognized self-interest to be the mainspring of human conduct; and they took a skeptical view of all philosophies that credited mankind with a highly developed sense of social responsibility. They were agreed that avarice, far from being a deadly sin. was an integral part of the order of nature. In this respect it might be said of Hamilton, as was said of Adam Smith, that he supposed "there was a Scotsman inside every man."[16]

In essence, Hamilton's plans for the national economy were an application to this country of Adam Smith's concept of an international economy in which each country produced the commodities for which it was best adapted, thereby fulfilling the designs of Nature. Instead of nations, Hamilton dealt with sections; but just as Adam Smith's principles tended to make Great Britain the workshop of the world, so Hamilton's ideas would have made the North the workshop of the union. In such an arrangement, he argued, neither section would be favored because "the aggregate prosperity of manufactures and the aggregate prosperity of agriculture are intimately connected"—a phrase he lifted bodily from the *Wealth of Nations*.[17]

By 1792, Hamilton had received ample warning that this particular "design of Nature" was not going to be realized in the United States without a bitter and protracted sectional struggle. Nevertheless, Hamilton ignored the storm signals flying to the southward; under the firm conviction that the basis of an enduring union must be built upon an economic bedrock, he refused to be deflected from his course. "Ideas of contrariety of interests between the Northern and Southern regions of the union are, in the main, as unfounded as they are mischievous," he said. ". . . . From New Hampshire to Georgia, the people of America are as uniform in their interests and manners as those of any [country] established in Europe. . . . Under the regular and gentle influence of general laws, these varying interests will be constantly assimilating, till they embrace each other and assume the same complexion." He denied that any injury to the South would result from his policies; any arguments that purported to prove the contrary were, he insisted, "unsupported by documents, facts, or it may be added, probabilities." To silence Southerners' complaint that they were paying the bulk of the taxes, he advanced the then novel doctrine that "communities consume and contribute in proportion to their active or circulating wealth, and . . . the Northern regions have more active or accumulating wealth than the Southern."

It is obvious, however, that his plans took too little account of such intangibles as sectional pride, jealousy and long-standing rivalries. Sensible as he was of the disadvantages experienced by an agricultural country in its dealings with foreign suppliers of manufactured goods, he failed to see that the same disadvantages might be incurred by an agricultural section of a country in its economic relationship with a manufacturing and commercial section. That the South should devote itself to the production of raw materials which the North turned into manufactured goods to be sold to southern planters and farmers struck him as a mutually advantageous arrangement. And yet nothing is clearer than that Hamilton required more in the way of patriotism and self-sacrifice from Southerners than, considering his philosophy of human nature, he might reasonably have asked of human beings. He told the farmers and planters to bear in mind the purity and loftiness of his objectives and the ultimate felicity that awaited them, but he was too honest to deny that the immediate profit was to go to northern capitalists, merchants and manufacturers. Despite these assurances of future blessings, the agrarians suspected that when the time came for them to be served, the larder would be bare.

Moreover, Southerners never forgot one of the basic facts of American life—that "the majority of Congress is in the North, and the slaves are to the South." True, Hamilton was no enemy of slavery in the South; he upheld the three-fifths rule and deplored the injection of the slavery issue into the debates in Congress. Nevertheless, in the opinion of southern slaveowners, the forces he represented were profoundly hostile to the peculiar institution. There was no telling when these northern businessmen and speculators would take it into their heads that slavery was bad for business.

Even admitting that Hamilton was averse to interfering with the slaves in the South, it was difficult to believe that he was well disposed toward their masters. And, in truth, he did not feel for them the close sympathy that might be expected from one gentleman to another. From Hamilton's point of view, the United States had a surfeit of agrarians. Whether small farmers or planter aristocrats, their capital was tied up in real estate and their sole objective seemed to be to acquire more land and slaves, thereby sinking the country deeper into the rut from which Hamilton was attempting to extricate it. So strong was his distrust of their managerial ability and their attitude toward national problems that he felt it would be hardly less disastrous to turn the country over to these aristocrats than to the democrats. Improvident, fond of living like grands seigneurs on borrowed money, haters of Great Britain and of the national government, the southern planters impressed Hamilton as being more adept at wrecking than at building a government. From his point of view there was nothing wrong with the South except Southerners—but this was enough to cast a fatal blight upon the region.*

Had Hamilton been a shrewder politician, he would have distributed the benefits of nationalism more equally among the sections. By 1792, he would have been well advised to turn his attention to conciliating the South and attaching Southerners, especially Virginians, to the union by the ties of self-interest. But here Hamilton's prejudice against Virginia and all that the Old Dominion stood for blinded him to political realities. Instead of showering benefits upon that state, he yearned to carve it up into small jurisdictions. He did not play the game of American politics as it subsequently came to be conducted—that is, by creating a coalition of sections based upon a program of broad economic benefits. In his political and economic thinking there was no room for a New York-Virginia axis such as was created by Jefferson, Madison and Burr.

* In 1785, Jefferson remarked that the planters were "careless of their interests . . thoughtless in their expenses and in all their transactions of business"—"vices" which he ascribed to a climate "which unnerves and unmans both body and mind." Yet Jefferson wished to see these men running the government.

20.
The Effort to Transform the American Economy

In view of the constitutional objections that had been raised against the Bank of the United States, Hamilton could hardly suppose that his Report on Manufactures would enjoy clear sailing through Congress. "Unconstitutionality" vied with "liberty" as the popular rallying cry of the Madisonians. To them, exclaimed a disgusted Federalist, "everything is unconstitutional. I scarce know a point which has not produced this cry, not excepting a motion for adjourning." Thus forewarned, Hamilton included in his Report on Manufactures a full constitutional justification of the course of action he recommended; it could not again be said that he had failed to anticipate the counterattack of his adversaries.[1]

To uphold the constitutionality of government aid to manufactures, Hamilton was obliged to take greater liberties with the letter of the Constitution than he had in the case of the Bank of the United States. In that instance, it had then been sufficient for his purposes to demonstrate that the creation of a corporation was necessary to carry out an enumerated power. But in the Report on Manufactures, he was obliged to base his argument upon something far less tangible—the general-welfare clause of the Constitution.*

The phrase "the common Defence and general Welfare" occurs in the Constitution in a context which has given rise to irreconcilable interpretations of the powers it conveys to the federal government. Because it is inserted at the beginning of a clause which enumerates specific powers possessed by Congress, there were at least three different ways in which this clause could be construed: as a separate grant of substantive power to the federal government to provide for the general welfare; as a clause which

---

* By virtue of the close connection between production and commerce, Hamilton also contended that the inspection of manufactures by agencies of the government was sanctioned by the commerce clause.

The Effort to Transform the American Economy

merely served to introduce the enumeration of powers which followed it; or as a grant of power to tax and appropriate for ends conducive to the common defense and general welfare. It was the third method that Hamilton adopted: the general-welfare clause, according to his view of the Constitution, endowed Congress with powers separate and distinct from those later enumerated and was in no way restricted by such enumeration. In effect, he read the general-welfare clause as though it stated that Congress "shall have power to lay and collect taxes, duties, imposts, and excises in order to pay the debts, and to provide the common defence and general welfare of the United States." By this construction, it became possible for Congress to appropriate money for purposes not enumerated, provided that those purposes furthered the national welfare.[2]

At no time did Hamilton say that this clause gave Congress an independent, substantive power to do any act which might tend to the general welfare. "No government," he declared, "has a right to do *merely what it pleases.*" Broadly as its powers might be construed, the federal government was still bound by the instrument of government; and no method of interpreting the Constitution could alter the fact that the government it established was based upon the principle of enumerated powers. Instead of putting forward the untenable claim that the Constitution had created an omnipotent government capable of acting in all cases whatsoever, Hamilton was content to assert that Congress is vested with the prerogative of determining what is necessary for the common defense and general welfare, and that it may appropriate money for purposes that fall within this definition. It followed, according to this reasoning, that Congress could tax and appropriate to attain objectives which were beyond its legislative powers.*[3]

In Hamilton's hands, the general-welfare clause opened up vast vistas of power to the federal government. It was privileged to act, insofar as the appropriation of money was concerned, for the advancement of "whatever concerns the general interests of learning, of agriculture, of manufactures, and of commerce." The only restriction he laid upon the exercise of this power was that the object to which the application of money was made was for general, rather than local, purposes.[4]

Under this sweeping investiture, the federal government could embark, among other things, upon a comprehensive plan of direct aid in the construction of roads and canals and aid private manufacturing corporations by the purchase of stock. As might be expected, he laid particular emphasis upon this last method of advancing the general welfare: "There is no purpose to which public money can be more beneficially applied than to the

---

* In 1936, the United States Supreme Court decided in favor of Hamilton's construction: "The power of Congress to authorize expenditures of public moneys for public purposes," the Court declared, "is not limited by the direct grants of legislative power found in the Constitution."

acquisition of a new and useful branch of industry," he observed, "no consideration more valuable than a permanent addition to the general stock of productive labor."[5]

To Madison and Jefferson, one of the most alarming features of the Report on Manufactures was the evidence it afforded of Hamilton's intention to make himself the oracle that spoke in the name of the Constitution. They declined to subscribe to the proposition that "Mr. Hamilton and the Constitution are synonymous terms"; when Madison had asked in the Constitutional Convention who was to determine in doubtful cases the line between the powers of the states and the federal government, he had not supposed that the answer would be: "Alexander Hamilton."

In effect, Hamilton seemed to be saying that there was no need to worry about the Constitution—he had it safely filed away among his most cherished possessions. As the custodian of that document, Hamilton was in an excellent position to achieve the objectives he had adumbrated in his speech to the Constitutional Convention—and Madison, who had carefully listened to that speech, feared that Hamilton would be content with nothing less.

In actuality, Hamilton did not claim to possess the final voice in elucidating the Constitution—that power, he admitted, was reserved to the Supreme Court. Nevertheless, he recognized that the government could not always wait for the Supreme Court—particularly since it refused to decide questions involving the construction and interpretation of the Constitution unless they were brought before it through regular legal channels. Inevitably, therefore, it fell to the other departments—Hamilton particularly favored the Executive Branch—to determine their own constitutional powers.[6]

In the Report on Manufactures, Hamilton recommended twenty-one increases in the existing tariff rates, five reductions in the rates on raw materials and four government subsidies to industry. Most of the increases in the tariff were designed for the protection of manufactures rather than for revenue; the time had apparently arrived when the government could forgo its quest for revenue in favor of protection.

These recommendations bore fruit in February, 1792, in a congressional subsidy to the whale and cod fisheries and in March, 1792, in a new tariff law which incorporated eighteen of Hamilton's recommended increases and three of the reductions he had suggested in the rates on raw materials. The import duties were increased by slightly over 2 per cent; prohibitive duties were laid upon the importation of foreign hemp and cotton; and the steel and iron of the Middle States was given similar protection.

Of the industries adversely affected by the war and the postwar depression, none were harder hit than the whale and cod fisheries. The ships had been lost to British cruisers and the markets had been taken over by British and French suppliers. For the first time in generations, the great Leviathan plowed the deep unmolested by the stout lads out of Nantucket; indeed, those lads were now on the beach with scarcely a ship fit to put to sea. In 1785, at the height of their distress, some citizens of Nantucket proposed to declare the island independent and to come to terms with the British; but by that time, a large part of the seafaring population had pulled up moorings and gone to France or Nova Scotia.*

Hamilton's prescription for these sick industries was a liberal dose of bounties—the method that had been successfully used by Great Britain and France to promote their own fisheries. Over the opposition of the Madisonians—who stigmatized bounties as unconstitutional transference of "the product of one man's labor . . . to the use and enjoyment of another" and therefore nothing more than "Governmental thefts committed upon the rights of one part of the community, and an *unmerited* Governmental *munificence* to the other"—Congress enacted an emasculated version of Hamilton's proposals. But this partial aid failed to restore the fisheries to their prewar prosperity; after 1798, both the cod and the whale fisheries experienced a protracted decline.

By no means all businessmen in the United States rallied to the support of Hamilton's Report on Manufactures. The industrialists of the Middle States and New England, who had long clamored for a protective tariff, were of course elated that they found a champion in the Secretary of the Treasury; but the merchants and shipowners, whose prosperity depended upon foreign trade, were markedly less enthusiastic. And, contrary to Hamilton's intentions, the tariff rather than bounties and premiums became the principal aid to "infant industries"; bounties and premiums, unlike the tariff, did not yield revenue to the government or permit retaliation upon British shipping and manufactures, and were therefore not popular in Congressional circles.[7]

One of Hamilton's most frequent criticisms of American businessmen was that once they had hit upon a way of making money they tended to become timid, unadventurous and impervious to new ideas. They seemed to be mere creatures of habit, fond of following the course of least resistance in their quest of profits and dominated by "the fear of want of success in untried enterprises." In short, there was no one as fond of things as they were as a satisfied businessman—unless it was a satisfied politician.

Despite the prospect of profit Hamilton held out in the Report on Manufactures, it was hardly to be expected that such timid souls as he conceived American businessmen to be would risk their capital upon his bare

---

* Both France and Great Britain barred American whale oil in order to promote their own whale fisheries.

assurance. Obviously, therefore, something more was required to persuade them to abandon "the certainties they enjoy" for "probabilities depending on untried experiments." Exhibiting another instance of the daring that his countrymen had come to expect of him, the Secretary of the Treasury undertook to show the way to the doubting capitalists of the United States by establishing not a single factory but a whole city of factories.

It was Hamilton's conviction that manufactures would not flourish until they were undertaken on a vastly larger scale than had hitherto been the case and by corporations more heavily capitalized than had yet appeared in this country. To remedy this situation, he proposed to establish the Society for Useful Manufactures, a corporation capitalized for one million dollars—a sum larger than the total assets of all the existing joint-stock manufacturing concerns in the United States.

As the site for this experiment, Hamilton chose Paterson, New Jersey. Here, in a state comparatively thickly populated, with cheap and abundant supplies of food and water power, rich in minerals (the Schuyler family owned copper and silver mines), and without commerce or western lands to serve as distractions to factory workers, he thought that manufacturing could be carried on under the closest approximation to ideal conditions that were to be found in the United States. Besides, the proximity of Paterson to New York and Philadelphia was expected to attract the investment capital of these cities to the new city. In this village, Hamilton declared, there was "a moral certainty of success" in the manufacture of such articles as paper, sailcloth, linen, cotton cloth, shoes, thread, stockings, pottery, ribbons, carpets, brass and iron ware. In short, another Manchester or Birmingham was to arise on the banks of the Passaic.[8]

The prospectus of this colossus among American business corporations was written by Hamilton in the late summer of 1791, and Governor William Paterson undertook to steer it through the New Jersey legislature. It was not thought improper for the Secretary of the Treasury himself to come to Trenton to enlighten the legislators.

Thanks to the intercession of the governor, the Secretary of the Treasury and the stockholders—among whom were numbered some of the members of the New Jersey legislature—all difficulties melted away. The corporation was given a charter which granted substantially everything that Hamilton had asked for. The S.U.M. (as it was generally called) enjoyed, among other things, a perpetual monopoly, tax exemption for a stated number of years and control of water power at the Great Falls of the Passaic. In honor of the governor, whose services were indispensable in securing this charter, the town was named Paterson.*

---

* As an apostle of free competition, Hamilton took considerable pains to answer the allegation that he was creating a stronghold of special privilege. The so-called monopolistic features of the S.U.M., he declared, were intended to serve as a model for other corporations, not to ensure that S.U.M. itself should enjoy a monopoly of the nation's business

Ever since the adoption of the funding system, it had been Hamilton's hope that the securities of the United States government would invigorate the national economy by functioning as capital. In the Bank of the United States he had demonstrated how these securities might be made the foundation of a national bank, and in the S.U.M. he undertook to show how they might serve to promote industrial enterprise. Accordingly, he stipulated that the capital stock of the S.U.M. should consist largely of government bonds and shares of the Bank of the United States. By this means, he intended to raise the value of these securities, prevent the slender specie reserves of the country from being drained away, and attach the stockholders of the S.U.M. closely to the federal government.

Even though Hamilton omitted to mention it in his report, the short history of manufactures in the United States had been studded with failures. Particularly was this true of textiles: a Hartford, Connecticut, woolen factory, for example, which had been established in 1788, was compelled to close because of the high price of raw material, the insufficiency of capital and the inferiority of American machinery to that used in England.[9]

Since textiles were the least advanced, the most precarious and yet, withal, to Hamilton's mind, the most important branch of American manufactures, he resolved to concentrate his initial efforts upon this particular industry. Success in this field promised to inject confidence into the cautious souls who owned the disposable capital of the United States. And, equally vital to the consummation of Hamilton's plans, the union would be solidified when northern cotton mills drew their raw materials from the southern states.

Likewise, in his Report on Manufactures, Hamilton had advised prospective industrialists to pin their faith and their capital to labor-saving machinery. At Paterson, he set out to exhibit the wonders that could be wrought with the newest machinery from Europe. Part of the capital of the S.U.M. was set aside for the importation of machinery and skilled workmen from abroad; and, even though it was contrary to British law, the Secretary of the Treasury actively tried to aid the emigration of British workmen, engineers and managers to the United States.

Thanks in part to the assiduous salesmanship of William Duer, the governor of the S.U.M., stock to the value of $600,000 was quickly sold. And, as Hamilton had hoped, foreign capitalists showed a lively interest in the new industrial empire rising on the banks of the Passaic. Cazenove, agent for a group of Dutch bankers, bought $25,000 worth of S.U.M. stock, the largest single subscription.

---

for itself. Hamilton credited the American businessman with being an imitative animal: if given an example such as the S.U.M., it could be assumed that he would act in "the spirit of imitation."

Besides this large capitalization, Hamilton saw to it that the Society enjoyed every facility afforded by the Bank of New York. He now had two favorites—the Bank and the Society—to play against the field and he saw no reason why they should not benefit and sustain each other. The Secretary was particularly useful to the Society in procuring loans from the Bank of New York on easy terms. In May, 1792, for example, he asked William Seton to authorize a loan to the Society at 5 per cent interest, remarking that it was to the interest of New York City that Paterson become a thriving manufacturing town and that banks "ought to consider it as a principal object to promote beneficial public purposes."

But in soliciting bank loans for the S.U.M. Hamilton could advance arguments more convincing to bankers than the stale theme of promoting the public welfare. Since the Bank of New York was eager to remain a depository for government funds, Hamilton promised that if the directors gave favorable consideration to the Society's requests for loans, they could be sure of equally generous treatment from the Treasury. "I shall not scruple to say *in confidence*," he told Seton, "that the Bank of New York shall suffer no diminution of its *pecuniary facilities* from any accommodation it may afford to the society in question. I feel my reputation much concerned in its welfare."

Fortunately for Hamilton, this letter did not fall into the hands of his enemies. For it was just this kind of evidence of the Secretary's illicit relations with banks and corporations that Jefferson and Madison were trying to lay their hands on. Had they possessed the incriminating documents that passed between Hamilton and William Seton, they perhaps could have driven him from the administration.[10]

Even without the benefit of these letters, the Madisonians made enough political capital out of the S.U.M. to give Hamilton some very uneasy hours. After all, Caesar's wife had never been involved, even remotely, with bankers and industrialists. The S.U.M. was alleged to be a scheme conceived by Hamilton and Duer to enlist "the whole power of the United States to promote their own private views of ambition and wealth"—even to the extent of reducing the workers to slavery and bringing ruin upon the farmers. What freedom-loving American, it was asked, wanted to see Birminghams and Manchesters springing up in this country, disseminating far and wide the immorality and inequality that apparently were the inevitable concomitants of industrialism? If the Secretary were given free hand, Americans were told to resign themselves to the rule of a merciless plutocracy: from their stronghold on the Passaic, the robber barons would extend their depredations over the entire country.[11]

While Hamilton was attempting to persuade American businessmen that the future lay in manufacturing, the country was undergoing another seizure of the speculative mania that seemed to attend all of his ventures. In this

The Effort to Transform the American Economy

instance, although the Secretary had nothing directly to do with the event, his friends played a conspicuous part; and the credit facilities afforded by the Bank of the United States and the state banks contributed to aggravate the distemper. Hamilton could say in his own defense that he attempted to keep down the number of banks and to restrain their inclination to loan money for speculative purposes.

Late in 1791, with a view to providing capital for their speculations and getting their hands upon the surplus funds of the state government, a group of New Yorkers organized a bank called the "Million Bank." Upon this project, Hamilton laid a heavy interdiction: "Its effects," he declared, "cannot but be in every way pernicious. These extravagant sallies of speculation do injury to the government and to the whole system of public credit, by disgusting all sober citizens and giving a wild air to every thing." But Hamilton's condemnation failed to prevent a "Bank Mania" in which thousands of shares—worth on paper millions of dollars—changed hands. Thus from Hamilton's point of view, the new bank was doubly damned: it diverted into speculation capital that he had hoped would be placed at the disposal of commerce and industry and it threatened the primacy of the Bank of New York. When a coalition between the Bank of New York and the Million Bank was suggested, Hamilton declared that such a consolidation would be like grafting a "dangerous tumor" upon a healthy body.[12]

Partly because of Hamilton's opposition, the Million Bank collapsed, but the get-rich-quick mania of which it was a manifestation showed no signs of subsiding. Early in 1792, when a company organized to construct a canal between the Susquehanna and Schuylkill rivers put one thousand shares of stock upon the market, over five thousand people bid for the shares. Later in the year, the Lancaster Turnpike Company offered six hundred shares of its stock, requiring a down payment of $30—with the result that thousands of would-be purchasers besieged the Pennsylvania State House, each clutching $30 or more in cash. About the same time, General Schuyler organized two companies—the Western Inland Dock Navigation Company and the Northern Inland Lock Navigation Company—for the purpose of constructing an all-water route from Schenectady to Lake Ontario. This sudden burgeoning of corporate enterprise and the wealth that seemed to be springing up on every hand prompted one American to exclaim that "this must be the richest country under the sun." It was not quite that, but there were thousands of Americans who were willing to gamble on its becoming such.[13]

From his experience in the panic of 1791, William Duer had learned the lesson not that speculation was risky but that to be successful it must be on a grand scale. His only error, he decided, was that he had not plunged deeply enough—in other words, that he had not altogether thrown caution to the winds.

It could never be said that the plan Duer conceived early in 1792 suffered from this fault. He set out to corner the supply of government bonds.* In this venture he enlisted the aid of Alexander Macomb, a wealthy New York merchant and land speculator. Together they organized the "Six Percent Club," with the objective of securing a monopoly of the government securities currently yielding 6 per cent interest and of unloading them at much higher prices upon foreign capitalists.[14]

Popularly reputed to be a financial wizard who could turn paper into gold, Duer found money for his operations thrust upon him from every quarter: shopkeepers, butchers, market women, widows—"every description & gradation of persons," Madison observed, "from the Church to the Stews" —begged him to accept their savings. "Even the noted bawd Mrs. Macarty" entrusted her savings to Duer, and the financier promised to double the wages of sin within six months.[15]

As a specimen of the kind of businessman that Hamilton hoped to convert into a pillar of the state, William Duer suffered from feet of clay. Obviously, he was far more likely to pull down a government than to provide a solid underpinning to its financial structure. But at least it could be said that there was one man in the country more daring than the Secretary of the Treasury.

With Duer and Macomb engaged in buying up all the government securities and bank stock on the market, Hamilton was given another occasion to ponder the singular aberrations to which the profit motive gave rise. But he could take little satisfaction in these ruminations: he was much too appalled by the immoderation of Duer's ambition and his utter lack of scruple as to the means by which he attained it. Foreseeing that Duer would come to no good end, Hamilton began to worry lest the Treasury Department be held responsible for "the follies and absurdities" of the speculators and that foreigners would snap up government securities and bank stock when the price collapsed. "How vexatious," he exclaimed, "that imprudent speculations of individuals should lead to an alienation of the national property at such under-rates." All the misgivings Hamilton had felt in 1791 now returned upon him doublefold. With a fervor worthy of Madison, he inveighed against the evils of speculation: " 'Tis time," he wrote on March 2, 1792, "there should be a line of separation between honest Men & knaves, between respectable Stockholders and dealers in the funds, and mere unprincipled Gamblers." He called for a revival of morality and a return to the old-fashioned virtues: "The relaxations in a just System of thinking," he said, "which have been produced by an excess of the Spirit of Speculation must be corrected. And Contempt and Neglect must attend those who manifest that they have no principles but to get money."[16]

The acquisitive instinct was not confined to Duer and his friends. A rival

* In 1792, the Stock Exchange was established in Wall Street and New York City became the leading security market in the United States.

group of speculators headed by Brockholst and Edward Livingston and Andrew Craigie sold to Duer and his associates bank stock and government securities for future delivery. Since the objective of the Livingston-Craigie group was to keep the price of these securities low, they cornered all the gold and silver in New York; then, drawing the specie from the banks, they forced down the price of securities, prevented the banks from discounting and obliged them to call in their loans. Duer and his associates, having gone heavily in debt to the banks, were caught in the middle of a ruinous credit squeeze.

The result, as Hamilton said, was "a scene of private distress for money . . . which probably has not been equalled in this country." With government securities and bank stock pouring in upon them, Duer and Macomb were forced to pay usurious rates of interest (as high as 1 per cent per day) to scrape together enough cash to cover their commitments. Too late they found that they had agreed to buy more shares in the Bank of New York than it was capitalized for.[17]

Drawing upon the experience he had gained in the summer of 1791, when he had been confronted by a similar though less menacing crisis, Hamilton instructed William Seton to support the market by purchasing several hundred thousand dollars worth of government securities. At the same time, he urged the banks not to call in their loans and to extend each other as much credit as possible, thereby mitigating the effect of runs that might break them if they tried to stand alone. To ease the money shortage, Hamilton directed customhouse officers to receive from importers notes payable in forty-five days. And he sought to bolster confidence by announcing that the government had just received a large loan from Holland; that the revenues were being collected as usual; that the Treasury was in excellent shape; and that the banks were still open for business. "No calamity truly *public* can happen," he declared, "while these institutions remain sound."[18]

The entry of the Treasury into the security market, together with Hamilton's efforts to raise public morale, were credited with having given "a new face to things and revived the desponding spirits of every one." Unfortunately for William Duer and his associates, these measures came too late to save them from the consequences of their folly. For, with his back pressed to the wall, Duer was assailed from a new and unexpected quarter. Under the Continental Congress, Duer had served as Secretary of the Treasury Board; and when he left office in 1789, a shortage of $238,000 was found in his books. As Secretary of the Treasury, Hamilton had taken an indulgent view of this discrepancy in Duer's accounts and had given the financier time to put his affairs in order. Now, however, in 1792, finding Duer on the verge of ruin, Hamilton and Wolcott took belated action: a suit was instituted against the financier in the federal court of New York for recovery of the missing money. This action, of course, was prompted by the imminent danger that if Duer failed, the Treasury would be accused of laxity or worse.

That Hamilton should have joined his persecutors was for Duer the cruelest blow of all. With his enemies closing in for the kill, he had expected, he wrote Hamilton, that the memory of past services to his country and the ties of friendship would have preserved him from a suit which made his ruin inevitable. Appealing to Heaven to witness his innocence and the purity of his intentions, he begged the Secretary to postpone legal action: "My Public Transactions are not blended with my private affairs," he declared. "Every Farthing will be immediately accounted for."[19]

Hamilton was not unmoved by Duer's appeal: an old friend in distress usually found him ready with sympathy and, where he could afford it, with cash. But in this instance he was convinced that nothing could save his friend: Duer and the other members of the "Six Percent Club" seemed to be irrevocably doomed. Under the circumstances, to call off the government's suit would make little difference in the final outcome. Moreover, instructions had been already sent to the United States district attorney to commence proceedings against Duer, and Hamilton could not have intervened without raising grave suspicions of collusion between himself and the hard-pressed financier. To a Secretary of the Treasury who classed himself with Caesar's wife, Duer had obviously become untouchable.[20]

Although he might justly have pointed out that he had predicted this outcome, Hamilton resisted that very human impulse, giving as his reason consideration for Duer's feelings. "I will not now pain you with any wise remarks," he told Duer, "though if you recover the present stroke, I shall take great liberties with you." However, he did offer some advice to Duer: if worst came to worst, Duer ought to act with fortitude and honor and, when paying his creditors, give precedence to all "institutions of public utility and in the next of all fair creditors."[21]

But Duer needed cash, not advice; and when he failed to get it, his creditors could be put off no longer. The fall of Duer, the "Prince of Speculators," brought down the entire house of cards that speculation had built. Macomb and Walter Livingston went bankrupt and so many speculators fell with them that it was said that one could scarcely enter a house in New York without finding "the woman in tears and the husband wringing his hands." In Philadelphia, Chestnut Street, the headquarters of the brokers and speculators, became known as "Lame Duck Alley."

Chiefly to escape the duped and defrauded citizens of New York, some of whom obviously had a lynching party in mind, Duer took refuge in the city jail. Even here, "snug in Gaol," a special guard had to be posted to prevent the mob from breaking in and dragging him off to a lamppost. Macomb likewise found protection in jail; but other speculators, unwilling to trust themselves to stone walls and iron bars, "fled into remote and desolate parts of New Jersey."[22]

The Effort to Transform the American Economy 307

The pricking of the bubble led to a short-lived depression in which the price of real estate in New York plummeted, credit was curtailed and almost every branch of business suffered to some degree. But speculation, crushed to earth momentarily, rose again in the form of the turnpike, canal and banking "manias." However capriciously it might treat them, Americans seemed resolved "to pursue CHANCE as the only goddess worthy of human adoration." Within a month after the stock-market collapse, a group of American speculators was trying to purchase the United States debt to France (currently worth some $6 million) with depreciated assignats; and in June, 1792, a Philadelphia merchant complained that all his apprentices had left his employ, "having been infected with ye Turnpike Rage. Everything," he lamented, "is now turned into Speculation."

Perhaps because he felt that in the downfall of William Duer he had not played a wholly praiseworthy part, Hamilton refused to join in the chorus of recrimination raised against the ruined financier. To his friends, he described Duer as "a man who, with a great deal of good zeal, in critical times, rendered valuable services to the country," but who had fallen victim to an unfortunate penchant for overextending himself in speculation. Moreover, against the indiscretions of Duer's public career Hamilton set the purity of the financier's domestic life—"a husband who has a most worthy and amiable wife, perishing with chagrin at his situation," and innocent children upon whom the sins of their father had already been amply visited.[23]

In these panics of 1791 and 1792, Americans were introduced to a phenomenon with which they later became painfully familiar: the boom and the bust. Hope of striking it rich had always been a powerful incentive in America, but it remained for the funding-assumption act and easy bank credit to show the way to sudden, effortless wealth. It was, unfortunately, also the way to sudden poverty.

For both the inflation and the bursting of the bubble the banks bore considerable responsibility. The New York branch of the Bank of the United States opened its doors just in time to contribute to the disaster. At first it generously extended credit to the speculators; then, alarmed by the signs that things were getting out of hand, suddenly recalled its loans, thereby helping to produce the money and credit shortage that brought ruin to Duer and his friends. These tactics likewise almost proved fatal to the Bank of New York: as was its right, the branch bank presented the notes of the Bank of New York for payment in specie, with the result that its specie reserve was soon dangerously depleted. Had a run occurred at this time, the Bank of New York would have been unable to meet its obligations.

In this emergency, William Seton appealed to Hamilton to extend the protection of his "all powerful hand" over the Bank of New York. Specifically, Seton asked his friend to refrain from drawing upon the bank for government balances and to use his influence with the Bank of the United States to prevent it from depriving the smaller bank of its specie.[24]

In response to these pleas, Hamilton directed that government purchases for the sinking fund be made through the Bank of New York; and he went out of his way to make it the fiduciary agent of the government and the repository of its funds. As a return for these favors, the Bank of New York later loaned substantial sums of money to the government. And, fortunately for the Bank of New York, a *modus vivendi* was arrived at with the branch of the Bank of the United States. Thanks to the rapid growth of New York, there was soon more than enough business for both banks.

Well aware that many members of Congress were watching him narrowly and would take advantage of his slightest slip, Hamilton decided in the autumn of 1792 to suspend his efforts in behalf of the Bank of New York. Instead of assurances of aid and good will, Seton now received from Hamilton a request for copies of all letters that had passed between them relating to the purchase of public securities. Not that Hamilton thought that he had done anything wrong—as he later said, no bank had received favors from him "which were not in perfect coincidence with the public interest, and in the due and proper course of events"—but he was resolved to give no opening to his enemies.[25]

The collapse of the stock market in 1792 threatened to drag down with it the Society for Useful Manufactures. Some of the men whom Hamilton described as "a confederated host of fanatic and . . . in too many instances, unprincipled gamblers" were stockholders in the S.U.M. Since they had actually paid only a small part of the total amount due on their stock, the Society suffered a crippling loss when they went bankrupt.[26]

Chief among the stockholders in the S.U.M. was William Duer, the governor of the Society. He had been entrusted with $10,000 of the Society's capital with which to procure workmen and machinery from Europe, and he had "borrowed" heavily from the funds of the Society deposited in the Bank of New York in order to finance his speculations. Although Hamilton urged Duer to give high priority to the S.U.M. when making an assignment to his creditors, Duer gave no accounting of his dealings with the S.U.M. Nor did the government recover by bringing suit against the ruined financier: the first great American speculator in stocks and bonds spent most of the rest of his life in prison.[27]

Not all the difficulties of the S.U.M. could be ascribed to the crooked ways of William Duer. From the beginning, the Society was beset by troubles for which Hamilton's Report on Manufactures had hardly prepared American entrepreneurs. For one thing, although the State of New Jersey bought stock in the S.U.M., the Society was obliged to operate without the benefit

The Effort to Transform the American Economy

of government bounties and premiums—the aids which Hamilton in his report had pronounced to be indispensable. Naturally, the directors were dismayed to find that they were obliged to nurse this "infant industry" without pabulum supplied by the government. Hamilton tried to keep up the courage of his associates by pointing out that the financial aid of the government, "though not to be counted upon ought not wholly to be despaired of." Nevertheless, the federal government remained aloof from the undertaking at Paterson—and thereby administered a blow to the Society from which it never wholly recovered.

When he drew up the prospectus of the S.U.M., Hamilton had no intention of playing an active part in its affairs: after the company was fairly established, he would confine himself to giving advice to the directors, a group of New Jersey and New York capitalists, including his friends Elias Boudinot, Nicholas Low, and Philip Livingston. The stock-market crash of 1792 compelled him to change his plans: with disaster facing the society, the directors looked for succor to him as "the founder of the institution" and its moving spirit.

Hamilton responded by taking active direction of the Society's affairs. His energy and organizational ability were manifested on every side: for the first time, things began to hum along the Passaic. L'Enfant, who had been commissioned to draw the plans for the new federal capital on the Potomac, was hired to lay out "the capital scene of manufactures" on the Passaic; buildings were erected and machinery installed; and skilled workers were brought in to operate these newfangled devices. Hamilton personally inspected the sites selected for the various factories, paying special heed to the effective utilization of water power; and on at least one occasion he advanced money out of his own pocket for machinery. More fortunate than some who entrusted their money to the Society, Hamilton got his back.[28]

For it was soon apparent that all Hamilton's skill and energy were required to pull this ailing industry through its infancy. Lack of capital, frequent changes of plan, the indifference shown by wealthy men to manufactures in comparison with less risky forms of capital investment, and the Society's inability to bring enough foreign artisans to Paterson cast a pall upon the undertaking. Hamilton and the directors were imposed upon by self-styled "experts" whose incompetence cost the company dear. Few Americans knew how to operate power-driven machinery or how to manage efficiently the kind of industrial complex that had been created at Paterson. None of the Europeans upon whom Hamilton and his associates relied proved equal to the task. In all probability, however, the plan was faulty from the beginning and even the best management would have been unable to extricate the Society from its difficulties. The decision to concentrate its energy and capital upon cotton manufacture proved to be a mistake which Hamilton and the directors perceived only after it was too late. Even more serious, the Society sunk so much of its capital in machinery, land and buildings that little remained to cover the cost of operations. As an English traveler observed, "their laying out their capital in large buildings and on unnecessary stock of machinery &c. . . . brings a heavy mortgage on the concern, before they actually begin."[29]

By 1795, the heavy losses incurred by the Society led the directors to abandon the attempt to create an industrial empire in New Jersey. All operations ceased at Paterson and the city became almost a "ghost town," reverting to the status of an agricultural village. The stark, untenanted buildings of the S.U.M. remained for many years an object of curiosity to travelers. Although it was never known as "Hamilton's Folly," the town was regarded as a monument to his ill-founded optimism that large-scale industry could be made to thrive in the United States. Many years later, however, Paterson became the industrial center Hamilton had hoped to make it, and it was not until 1945 that the lands and water rights owned by the S.U.M. passed into the hands of the city of Paterson.[30]

As the misadventure at Paterson demonstrated, Hamilton was far too sanguine in his expectations that large-scale manufacturing would solve the problems that had hitherto beset American entrepreneurs. The realization of his dream of an industrial center to which workers and raw materials would gravitate depended upon the existence of a highly developed system of transportation and a plentiful labor supply. During Hamilton's lifetime, the United States possessed neither of these prerequisites; it was not until the development of the railroads that the country's transportation system made possible industry on the scale envisaged by Hamilton; and the United States did not possess a labor supply sufficient to man the country's mines and factories until long after his death.

Moreover, by the time the S.U.M. wound up its affairs, it was apparent that Hamilton had misread the signs of the times. The very prosperity that enabled the United States government to meet its expenses, including the heavy interest charges on the national debt, militated against the success of the experiment at Paterson. Instead of declining, as Hamilton had predicted, the European market for American raw products underwent an unprecedented expansion as a result of the war between England and France which broke out early in 1793. But, on the other hand, war in Europe did not immediately promote the development of American manufactures: instead, by interrupting the flow of European immigrants and European capital to the United States and by encouraging Americans to invest their capital in agriculture and shipping, it tended, at least in its initial effects, to counteract Hamilton's plans for building up manufactures in the United States.

21.
The Opposition Emerges

Had Alexander Hamilton been content to be the spokesman of the majority of the people of the United States and to reflect faithfully their ideals and aspirations, he would never have written his reports or, had they been written, they would have been dedicated to furthering the immediate interests of agriculture. The prevailing ideas of the day were hostile to the kind of financial and economic planning that emanated from the office of the Secretary of the Treasury: Hamilton's plans were conceived by a minority, designed to benefit a minority and carried into execution by a minority. With characteristic audacity, he undertook to run a farmers' republic for the immediate profit of businessmen.

No wonder, therefore, as the planters and farmers beheld the landmarks of agricultural America slipping away, to be replaced by monuments to the "greed and cunning" of businessmen, speculators and bankers, they became increasingly distrustful of the federal government. The "energy" displayed by that government under the direction of the Secretary of the Treasury seemed directed wholly to the furtherance of commerce, manufacturing and the "fiscal faction."[1]

For southern planters, the enemy was essentially the same antagonist that they had always faced. In place of British merchants and manufacturers, they were now obliged to do battle with northern merchants and manufacturers—which could hardly be accounted a victory, they lamented, for men who had fought a seven years' war for freedom. And, as they quickly learned, the "fiscal interest" led by Hamilton was an overmatch for the "agrarian interest." "The Bank has a flush of trumps," exclaimed John Taylor of Carolina. Since Taylor did not credit the farmers with holding more than a pair of deuces, he predicted that the Bank would take over the country—at which time it would presumably be known as the "United States of the Bank."[2]

In some degree, this was a struggle between different kinds of aristocrats. The planters of the South represented the old, established, landed wealth of the country, whereas Hamilton's capitalists and speculators were to a large extent nouveaux riches. Moreover, their wealth was acquired in commerce, trade, banking and speculation in paper—methods of money-getting that a true gentleman of the South held in utter disdain. Many of the so-called "gentlemen" of the North who rode in coaches and whose servants wore livery "would appear more in character," it was said in Virginia, "if they were to parade the streets in buttermilk-carts, or at the arms of bakers' wheelbarrows." In the eyes of southern patricians, Hamiltonianism threatened to saddle the republic with a governing class of parvenus—"the most repulsive of all, as it would have embraced the pride of distinction without its refinements."[3] It therefore struck Hamilton as highly ironical that southern planters should fulminate against the "privileged orders" quite as though they themselves were not conspicuous members of that order. William Giles of Virginia, Hamilton's most vituperative critic in the House of Representatives, declared that "he should view the banishment of the privileged orders from the world as the surest harbinger of the approach of the millennium"—but it is plain that Giles was thinking only of the French, British and Federalist aristocrats, not of the goodly company of southern slaveowners to which he belonged.

If his enemies could be believed, Hamilton's objective was totally to overthrow the "landed interest" and reduce the farmers to the status of slaves to the overlords of business and finance. Since the planters knew from firsthand experience the degradation of slavery, they spoke with peculiar authority about their future lot at the hands of northern masters. Hamilton, on the other hand, although he never professed to any love for Negro slavery, did not admit to any intention of inflicting servitude upon the white slaveowners or, indeed, upon anyone else. Nor did he acknowledge that his plan for the advancement of commerce and manufactures would depress agriculture. On the contrary, he conceded that agriculture was "the best basis of the prosperity" of every other form of industry and that it merited the fostering care of government. Because of the wasteful methods used by American farmers and planters, he thought that the most effective aid the government could give agriculture was to create a Board of Agriculture to instruct farmers in scientific knowledge. He contended that the interests of agriculture, commerce and manufacturing were indissolubly united and that measures which directly benefited one indirectly benefited the others. But he never departed from the position he had taken in 1790—that since commerce and manufacturing had been far outstripped by agriculture, the attention of the government ought to be chiefly directed toward stimulating the lagging branches of the economy.[4]

At the very time that Hamilton was winning his greatest victories over the "agricultural interest" in Congress, agriculture was on the point of strengthening its position in the American economy beyond all expectations.

The Opposition Emerges

A new king had been born before whom manufacturing and commerce were compelled to pay obeisance—a king whose progenitor was a Yankee inventor named Eli Whitney. The invention of the cotton gin in 1793 changed the course of American history more radically than did any of the measures projected by Alexander Hamilton as Secretary of the Treasury. For the cotton gin gave Negro slavery a new lease on life—with all that implied for the future of the American republic. Moreover, the effect of the spread of cotton cultivation in the South was to bind that section economically more closely to Great Britain than to the northern states. The bulk of American cotton was exported to England, where it was manufactured into cloth. In 1861, when the South seceded from the union, Southerners expected that England would aid their bid for freedom, so imperative was its need of American cotton.

During the struggle precipitated by Hamilton's reports, the agricultural order had acquired in Thomas Jefferson a potent spokesman and adroit political leader. As a member of the Cabinet, Jefferson was in a strategic position to make his influence felt both upon Congress and the President, and he took full advantage of his opportunity to counterwork the plans of the Secretary of the Treasury. Not least among Jefferson's contributions to this work was the formulation of a political philosophy that could be set up against Hamiltonianism.

Even though Jefferson declared that he would welcome a revolution every twenty years, he was actually a far stancher champion of things as they were in America than was Hamilton, to whom revolution was a thing of dread. Whenever the primacy of agriculture in the American economy was endangered, Jefferson revealed himself to be a true conservative. Whereas Hamilton embraced the nascent Industrial Revolution, Jefferson recoiled from it. To preserve the old American dedicated to agriculture and the way of life it entailed was Jefferson's fondest hope. And yet he recognized that the people must be left free to find their own salvation: if they chose the way of manufactures and commerce, Jefferson would have acquiesced, albeit reluctantly and with many misgivings, in their decision.

The Federalists prided themselves upon being the good, the wise and the rich; but Jefferson insisted that wisdom and goodness were a virtual monopoly of the plain farmers and the not-so-plain planters of the United States. The tillage and ownership of the soil he credited with imparting a special sanctity; he believed that agriculture was the first employment of man, chosen for him by God Himself.[5]

While Jefferson acknowledged that commerce was the handmaid of agriculture, he feared that manufacturing would prove to be an oppressive and jealous master. As long as he was in opposition to Hamilton, he declared that he wished to see his countrymen engage in commerce only to the extent necessary to convey their surplus agricultural products to market; and he thought that manufactures were most properly carried on within the household. In place of factories and slums, the Virginian offered Americans an Elysium in which each farmer manufactured for his own needs and the labor force was composed not of "degenerate" and "monarchical" immigrants from Europe but of his own wife, children and slaves. Hamilton's ideal of a balanced economy struck no chord in Jefferson; from his viewpoint, Americans already enjoyed the kind of economy best calculated to create a Heaven upon earth. But he feared that the serpent was already at their ear, whispering to them of national wealth, greatness and power.[6]

Dedicated as Jefferson was to preservation of the agricultural order, his conservatism stopped there. He wished to see the various states, particularly Virginia, reform their educational systems, correct inequities in representation in the state legislatures and revise their inheritance laws. Nor was he friendly toward slavery, the foundation of the planting economy of the South. Had Virginia aristocrats not been so preoccupied with erecting defenses against Hamiltonianism they might well have pondered the question whether Jefferson's ideals were not more inimical to their class interests than was Hamilton's program. For whatever else might have been said of Hamilton, he was no enemy of the economic, social and political *status quo* of the South.

With government on the side of businessmen, Jefferson trembled for the fate of the American farmers. Engaged as they were in a struggle with Nature, Jefferson thought that they already had enough on their hands without taking on the bankers and speculators—a "moneyed interest" which, being united, rapacious and utterly unscrupulous, loaded taxes upon the hapless tillers of the soil. The farmers might be the chosen people of God, but it seemed to Jefferson that if Hamilton's policies prevailed the "moneyed men" would inherit the earth. He suspected that every dollar that went into the pockets of a northern speculator came from the pockets of a farmer or planter. If this process continued, it seemed to Jefferson, the rewards of the chosen people would be mortgages, foreclosures and debt, while speculators made off with the wealth of the country.

In the emergence of the Hamiltonian nouveaux riches, Jefferson saw a monstrous inversion of the balance between "natural aristocrats" and "artificial aristocrats." Jefferson believed that there was a natural aristocracy among mankind, the basis of which was virtue and talents and which constituted "the most precious Gift of nature, for the instruction, the trusts, and the government of society." Unfortunately, there was also, he discovered, an artificial aristocracy "founded on wealth and birth, without either virtue or talents," which conferred no benefits whatever upon society. To ensure the free flow of natural aristocrats to the top and to keep the artificial aristocrats from getting there was one of Jefferson's cardinal objectives.[7] To his mind, Hamilton was striving to do the very opposite.

The Opposition Emerges

Nor did the Virginian accept the doctrine that an enduring union could be erected upon the acquisitive instincts. He regarded covetousness as the "sole antagonist of virtue, leading us constantly by our propensities to self-gratification in violation of our moral duties to others." In his philosophy, there was no good government and no union without patriotism and common ideals: to him, nationalism belonged in the realm of the spirit rather than in that of economics. He had no fear of democracy: in his eyes, the people were by nature good and, if educated, wise. His trust in the masses was as pronounced as was Hamilton's distrust; and, as a corollary to his faith in the essential goodness of the people, he believed that men ought to be left as much as possible in the enjoyment of their liberties. Freedom, he thought, brought out the best in man; and he saw good even in such outbreaks of violence as Shays' Rebellion.[8]

Where Hamilton wrote "the people" as an object of distrust, Jefferson inscribed "the government."[9] To his way of thinking—at least while he was in opposition—popular liberty depended upon jealousy of rather than confidence in the government. He assumed that an educated and informed people would generally do right and elect the right men to office, whereas it was the nature of government—and here Jefferson was thinking of the effects of power upon individuals—to extend its authority at the expense of liberty. "The natural progress of things is for liberty to yield and government to gain ground," he asserted; and he believed that in this eternal struggle, Hamilton was on the side of government.[10]

Upon the Executive Branch, Jefferson concentrated all his fear and distrust of political power. Man was naturally good, but when exposed to the manifold temptations of political office, it seemed to Jefferson, all man's imperfections were laid bare. Since power corrupted in proportion to the amount to which the individual was exposed, it followed that the President must be assailed by all the temptations in the book; and the danger was the greater because, Jefferson said, the people of the United States might be "so fascinated by the arts of one man, as to submit voluntarily to his usurpation." He therefore insisted that Congress rather than the President be made the repository of the people's confidence. Not until Jefferson himself became President was Hamilton's concept of the President as the representative of the people accepted at Monticello.[11]

Conscious that his principles were shared by the majority of the American people, Jefferson possessed even in periods of adversity a confidence and serenity of mind that were denied Hamilton in the full tide of his success. Jefferson never doubted that if the people were wrong, they would come right; whereas Hamilton always feared that if the people were right, they would go wrong. Hamilton was aware that he was breasting the current of public opinion; Jefferson thought that he was moving in the center of the stream—or that, regardless how public opinion shifted its course, it would sooner or later come round to him.[12]

Vulnerable as was Hamilton to the charge that he was fostering a plutocracy in the United States, Jefferson did not make this the gravamen of his indictment of the Secretary of the Treasury. Instead, Jefferson chose to picture his colleague as an implacable enemy of republicanism who was eating his heart out because he had failed in the Constitutional Convention to make George Washington king.

It is doubtful if Jefferson could have found an issue more calculated than was "monarchism" to undermine Hamilton's position before the country and, incidentally, to obscure the real issues between himself and the Secretary of the Treasury. For to accuse a politician of hankering after a king and lords was the most serious indictment that could be leveled against a public man in the United States. "Monarchist" or "monocrat" was at this time a term of abuse—as Fisher Ames said, "a substitute for argument, and its overmatch." As a propaganda weapon, therefore, "monarchism" was unexcelled, and Jefferson wielded it with consummate skill.[13]

Viewed from the vantage point of Monticello, Hamilton's financial and economic planning appeared to be merely preliminary to the crowning of an American king and the investiture of an American order of nobility. The "moneyed interest," said Jefferson, was the advance guard of monarchism; at any moment the Hamiltonian "phalanx" in Congress might reveal itself to be the king's men. It sufficed for the Secretary of State that Hamilton was attempting to create a centralized government and a moneyed mercantile class—this was all the proof the Virginian required to convict Hamilton of an inveterate hatred of republicanism. Jefferson assumed that there was a close connection between "stock jobbers & King makers" and that the consolidation of authority in the federal government was the prolegomenon to the creation of a monarchy.

Every rumor that reflected upon Hamilton's republicanism and integrity was assiduously recorded by Jefferson in his notebooks. In these repositories of political tittle-tattle, Jefferson revealed how credulous he could be when talebearers and gossipmongers told him what he wanted to believe. The Secretary of State did not ask for proof: the rules of evidence were apparently suspended when it came to convicting Hamilton of being a monarchist. In fact, Hamilton was adjudged guilty without trial, and everything he said or did was used against him.[14]

On one occasion, Jefferson was shocked to hear Hamilton defend the corruption practiced by the British Crown. It was at a dinner attended by John Adams, Jefferson and Hamilton that the conversation turned to the British constitution, a topic likely to generate among Americans more heat than light. John Adams expressed the opinion that if some of the glaring defects of the British constitution were corrected, "it would be the most perfect constitution of government ever devised by man." Such heresy from the lips of a patriot of '76 Jefferson had never expected to hear; he had hardly

The Opposition Emerges

recovered from his astonishment than he received an even greater shock. Hamilton asserted that there was no need to reform the British constitution: "with its existing vices, it was the most perfect model of government that could be formed; and that the correction of its vices would render it an impracticable government." On the strength of this assertion, which Hamilton had obviously derived from David Hume, Jefferson concluded that Hamilton was "not only a monarchist, but for a monarchy bottomed on corruption" not only in England but in the United States![15]

By dint of ringing these changes, the Republicans made Hamilton appear to be the head of the "Royal Faction" in the United States, an infatuated lover of kings who praised monarchy even in his sleep and sang "God Save the King" every morning at his devotions. It was rumored that he was plotting to make the Duke of Kent, the fourth son of George III, king of the United States; and one newspaper writer ironically proposed that Hamilton be commissioned to serve as the progenitor of a royal dynasty in the United States. With Alexander on the job, the line seemed certain never to suffer for want of issue.[16]

Hamilton was too levelheaded to fail to see that the British constitution was the product of a historical process that could not be duplicated in the United States and that the characteristics which so strongly attracted him to Great Britain were in many cases the peculiar contribution of the British people. He did not imagine that Americans were simply transplanted Englishmen who would revert to type as soon as a king and lords were set over them. Had it been that simple, he would have been better pleased; but he frankly admitted that "the spirit of the country was so fundamentally republican, that it would be visionary to think of introducing monarchy here, and that, therefore it was the duty of its administrators to conduct it on the principles their constituents had elected." To accuse him of attempting to establish a monarchy struck him as proof of the inconsistency—or worse —of which his enemies were capable, inasmuch as they acknowledged him to be intelligent and yet charged him with entertaining a project "which every person in the least acquainted with the genius and temper of the people of the United States, must know was absurd."[17]

Considered solely from the viewpoint of theory, republicanism seemed to Hamilton to be an excellent system of government. "I am affectionately attached to the republican theory," he declared. "I desire above all things to see the equality of political rights, exclusive of all hereditary distinction, firmly established by a practical demonstration of its being consistent with the order and happiness of society." Had he been given to building castles in the air, he would have given them at least a republican façade. He was not a believer in monarchy because of any theoretical preference for that form; a king, lords and commons appeared to him to be the most practical way of coping with the notorious shortcomings of human nature. As an empiricist and pragmatist, he gave his allegiance to monarchy; republicanism always seemed to him to be more suited to a community of angels than of human beings. Still, he recognized that the American people would have no other form of government.

Monarchism, then, was a red herring, but Jefferson and Madison succeeded in hanging it round Hamilton's neck. And there, despite everything Hamilton might say or do, it remained. Nevertheless, it was clear that if Hamilton actually intended to subvert the republican order in the United States, he chose an exceedingly devious method of reaching his objective. By attaching the capitalists to the federal government, he virtually ensured that they would support the established system. As a newspaper writer observed: "It would be a queer blunder for a man of six per cent to join in a plot against a free government, which pays his income. Liberty, therefore, has gained new friends rather than foes in the funding system." Even Jefferson, when he appraised Hamilton's work in a more judicious frame of mind, admitted that "creditors will never, of their own accord, fly off entirely from their debtors."[18]

According to his own lights, Hamilton was engaged in doing the things that had to be done if republicanism were to endure. Since he never supposed that a republican form of government had received special approval from God and that there were preordained forces working toward its triumph, he was the more determined to take measures to ensure its survival in a hostile world. By declaring its independence and establishing a republican form of government, the United States in effect had flung down a challenge to the monarchies of Europe. And, equally important in Hamilton's mind, it had challenged human nature by raising the question whether or not men were capable of maintaining law and order at the same time that they were given almost unprecedented freedom. Hamilton acted upon the premise that a nation which so recklessly defied the laws of probability could not afford to overlook any means of strengthening its defenses.[19]

If republicanism miscarried in the United States, Hamilton felt sure that it would be through no fault of his; but he could not say as much for Thomas Jefferson. He thought that Jefferson would end by killing republicanism, whereas he himself, having diagnosed the causes of its periodic breakdowns, was trying to keep the patient alive. If he wished to destroy republicanism, Hamilton said, he would play the demagogue: "I would mount the hobby horse of popularity; I would cry out 'usurpation,' 'danger to liberty,' etc; I would endeavor to prostrate the national government, raise a ferment, and then ride the whirlwind and direct the storm." He suspected that Jefferson and Madison were planning to do that very thing.[20]

One of the consequences of the struggle over the funding of the debt, the assumption of state debts, the organization of the Bank of the United States

The Opposition Emerges

and the implementation of the Report on Manufactures was the emergence of a political party dedicated to the support of the policies of the Secretary of the Treasury. It had not been generally expected that parties would disturb the felicity of Americans under the new Constitution; thanks presumably to the wisdom of the Founding Fathers, these particular serpents had been excluded from the republican paradise. But, as the Founding Fathers soon learned, they had not sufficiently reckoned with Alexander Hamilton.

Hamilton himself had been one of the foremost in deploring political parties. Although in *The Federalist* he had acknowledged the utility and, indeed, the indispensability of parties in a free government, most of his pronouncements on this subject deal with the evil wrought by parties. He recoiled from "the tempestuous waves of sedition and party rage" and he prayed that the Constitution would deliver the United States from their malign influence. His ideal was government not by parties but by superior persons—an ideal which perhaps came closest to attainment in the rule of the merchant-bankers of Venice and Florence. By means of indirect election and tenure during good behavior, he clearly hoped to put the President and Senate above party; these exalted personages were expected to concern themselves only with the national welfare. In the New York ratifying convention he declared that "we are attempting, by this Constitution, to abolish factions, and to unite all parties for the general welfare."

Pernicious as Hamilton considered parties to be, he admitted that there was an even more iniquitous by-product of political freedom—faction. According to the definition generally accepted in the eighteenth century, a faction was a group of ambitious and unscrupulous men whose sole objective was self-aggrandizement. Hamilton did not always distinguish between faction and party—in his opinion, both stemmed from the same infirmity in human nature—but he never said of faction what he said of party, that under some circumstances it might serve a useful purpose. In his papers he preserved a quotation with which he no doubt was fully in agreement: "The demon [faction] can no more be banished the earth than human depravity, of which it is at once the parent & the offspring."

What compelled Hamilton, contrary to his intentions, to make himself the head and front of a political party was the fact that his program could not be carried through Congress without strong leadership from the Executive Branch. He recognized that Congress had to be given direction lest it dissipate its energy in the kind of hauling and pulling that had rendered nugatory so much of the work of the old Continental Congress. This executive impulse was not forthcoming from Washington during the early period of his presidency. As a man above party, it neither comported with his dignity nor with his views of the strict separation of powers established by the Constitution for the President to descend into the political arena. As a result of Washington's self-imposed abstention from the kind of leadership practiced by present-day Presidents, a vacuum of power was created. Before Congress itself could fill this vacuum, Hamilton rushed in and the air was soon filled with the tumult of party war cries.

In all likelihood, the breakup of the Federalist party would have occurred without the instrumentality of Alexander Hamilton. A party based upon an alliance of northern businessmen and southern planters contained the seeds of dissolution; only by the constant exercise of moderation and compromise could a coalition of such antagonistic elements have been preserved. Nevertheless, it was the Secretary of the Treasury whose policies provided the catalyst that split the Federalist party. As a result of his reports, the political heats and animosities that had been thought dead and buried were suddenly resurrected. It was Hamilton's peculiar contribution to the history of American politics that he made two parties grow where only one had grown before. As was observed at the time, "Whoever forms *one* party, necessarily forms *two*, for he forms an antagonistic party."

These parties were not organized along the lines of modern political parties, with such appurtenances as nominating conventions, campaign chests and party platforms. But even though their organization was embryonic, they did have a set of political doctrines; their objective was to secure or to retain for their leaders the control of the government, and from such control individuals in both parties hoped to win material benefits and advantages.

The party that challenged the ascendancy of the Hamiltonian "phalanx" called itself the Republican party. It was largely the creation of two Virginians, James Madison and Thomas Jefferson, two of the shrewdest political strategists that ever graced the American scene. As the Federalists ruefully admitted, the choice of the name "Republican" was a stroke of genius worthy of the old master himself, Alexander Hamilton. The name became "a powerful instrument in the process of making proselytes to the party," lamented Noah Webster. "The influence of *names* on the mass of mankind, was never more distinctly exhibited, than in the increase of the democratic party in the United States. The popularity of the denomination of the *republican party*, was more than a match for the popularity of Washington's character and services, and contributed to overthrow his administration."[21]

Initially called the "Madison party," the opponents of Hamiltonianism owed more at first to the leadership of James Madison than to that of Thomas Jefferson. Indeed, the Secretary of State seemingly possessed few of the qualifications usually considered necessary for political success: he could not make a moving speech to a crowd; he always tried to avoid quarrels; and he professed himself to be disinterested in politics and eager to get back to his library at Monticello. This mild, disarming and scholarly man bore none of the marks of the demagogue, but Hamilton was not deceived: he

The Opposition Emerges

had found demagogues in strange places—including the Grove of Academe. When Hamilton observed a party arising in opposition to his policies, his first thought was that the old leaven of Antifederalism was at work. Since he believed that his policies were sanctioned in every respect by the Constitution, it followed that opposition to these policies was opposition to the Constitution. This implied—as Hamilton intended it should—that Republicanism was Antifederalism masquerading under a new name and that its objective was to destroy the frame of government established in 1788. Casting himself in the role of guardian of the flame that had been lighted at Philadelphia, he solicitously watched its flaring and flickerings, fearful that every breeze would snuff out this brief candle of union.[22]

Contrary to his wishes, Hamilton seemed to have succeeded in making Americans a race of politicians to whom party slogans and polemics were the breath of life. An English traveler observed that Americans of all classes "are for ever cavilling at some of the public measures; something or other is always wrong, and they never appear perfectly satisfied. . . . Party spirit is for ever creating dissentions amongst them, and one man is continually endeavoring to obtrude his political creed upon another." Banks, taverns and shops were patronized by those who shared the political sympathies of the proprietors and were shunned by political opponents; doctors, clergymen and teachers were rated according to their political orthodoxy. Indeed, it was to be feared that these contentious republicans would raise up parties in Heaven, provided they attained that high place; and Hamilton felt certain that they would find fault with the Administration.

22.

The Attack upon Hamilton

As organized under the Act of September, 1789, the Treasury was the largest of the departments, consisting of an assistant, controller, treasurer, auditor, register and over thirty clerks. In addition, almost one thousand customhouse officers and excisemen were under Hamilton's direction. The Department of State, in comparison, was staffed by only four clerks, a messenger and office keeper; and the War Department boasted only three clerks. Surrounded by this retinue of clerks and customhouse officers, it was natural for Hamilton to regard his department as superior to all others and himself as the highest officer in the government next to the President.

Still, judged by European standards, the Treasury Department made a meager appearance. In 1794, a French visitor, Moreau de Saint-Méry, called upon Hamilton at his office in Market Street. He found "a man in a long gray linen jacket" seated in a room the furnishings of which he estimated to be worth not more than $10. Hamilton's own desk was a common pine table covered with a green cloth; for filing cabinets the Secretary used planks laid on trestles. Saint-Méry came away with the impression that Hamilton was rather overdoing republican simplicity.

If any Federalist merchants or shipowners supposed that Hamilton was their "man" and that he would overlook their infractions of the laws, they were quickly disillusioned. Shortly after taking office, the Secretary of the Treasury instructed the collectors to institute suits against delinquent importers' bonds the very day they became overdue, and collectors who failed to do their duty were summarily removed. A weekly report of collections was demanded of every collector; and although Hamilton stipulated that all complaints should be given a fair hearing, he left no loopholes through which the laws could be evaded. At the same time he devised new and "energetic" methods of collecting the duties. With the practice that had prevailed in some states during the Confederation—relying upon the integrity of individuals to pay their taxes—Hamilton had no patience: when it came to paying taxes, he remarked, honor and patriotism ought to be

The Attack upon Hamilton

treated as nonexistent. Hamilton put his faith in the vigilance of an efficient corps of customhouse officers; under any other system, he believed, "the most conscientious will pay most; the least conscientious least."

While Hamilton insisted upon a large measure of discretion in administrative matters for the higher officers of the government, he was not disposed to extend the privilege to subordinates. Mindful of the deficiencies of human nature, he sought to devise procedures which would protect citizens against "the passions and prejudices of the revenue officers." All laws which admitted of lax or defective execution he held to be "instruments of oppression to the most meritorious"; one of the features he most admired in the British system was that it left little or nothing to the discretion of officers of the revenue. Nevertheless, he admitted that the success of his administration depended in large measure upon the quality of the men he appointed to office: he required a high level of integrity and efficiency in the officials in his department and, in general, he succeeded in attaining it.

When Congress established the Treasury Department, it had not intended to yield control of the nation's finances to the Secretary of the Treasury. Under Hamilton's administration, however, Congress found that while it had asked for a financial expert who knew his place, it had received a bold and imperious leader who took the entire field of government as his province. As Secretary of the Treasury, Hamilton was as deeply involved in politics as he was in finance: he supervised the whole process of legislation from the inception of bills to their passage, securing the appointment of committees friendly to his plans, determining questions of strategy with prominent members of Congress, and marshaling his followers in Congress when heads were being counted. The man who gave "life & vigor to everything" in the government, Hamilton undertook to show Congress the way in such different concerns as finance, foreign and domestic policy, and Indian affairs.[1]

Of all the evidences of the ascendancy Hamilton had won over Congress, none was more galling to the Republicans than was the practice first adopted by Congress in September, 1789, of turning to him for advice upon financial matters. Hamilton invariably responded with a report, and these reports became the principal means by which he exerted his influence upon Congress. The funding system, the assumption of state debts, the Bank of the United States, and the aids given to manufactures all originated in reports submitted by Hamilton to the legislature. Often Congress received more from Hamilton than it had bargained for: plans, projects and far-reaching schemes involving fundamental changes in the nation's economy might owe their existence to a simple request by Congress as to the most eligible way of raising revenue or paying debts.[2]

Even though Hamilton generally confined himself to making reports to

Congress only when he was requested to do so, the Republicans contended that he exerted a dangerous and unconstitutional influence over the legislature. As they saw it, these reports contained so much special pleading and were written with such a pontifical air that honest members of Congress were fatigued, confounded and bewildered; stunned with arguments and statistics, they were "transformed into resistless dupes, incapable of manly investigation and quietly falling down the stream of ministerial influence." In short, they were subjected to a brainwashing that in some cases, it was said, had changed republicans into monarchists; beginning as skeptics, they ended by receiving the words of the Secretary "with as much confidence, as if they had been delivered from Mount Sinai, in the midst of supernatural thunders."[3]

However appropriate this may have been in Biblical times, Republicans insisted that it was not authorized by the United States Constitution. That document unequivocally declared that it was the right of the House of Representatives to originate money bills and to devise ways and means of raising revenue. In defiance of this constitutional ordination, Hamilton seemed to have made the Treasury Department "the efficient Legislature of the country"; from the office of the Secretary emanated the plans upon which Congress dutifully set the seal of its approval. "Congress may go home," exclaimed an agitated senator. "Mr. Hamilton is all-powerful, and fails in nothing he attempts.... Nothing is done without him." It was sarcastically pointed out that if Congress packed up, the taxpayers would be relieved of an unnecessary expense of about $300,000 a year.[4]

Apparently the only way Hamilton could have persuaded the Republican congressmen that they were earning their salaries would have been to efface himself discreetly from the scene, confine the function of his office to supplying the legislators with statistics and leave policy making wholly to Congress. In that event, his reports would have contained no recommendations, no arguments and no interpretations of the Constitution. Instead of a guide and philosopher, the Secretary of the Treasury would have been demoted to a statistician.[5]

Hamilton was not a man to surrender voluntarily the high prerogatives with which he had endowed the Secretaryship of the Treasury. Nor were his followers in Congress willing to see him abnegate his authority: Federalist congressmen, unlike all others of that species, were eager to strengthen the Executive Branch even at the expense of the House and Senate. While the Federalists agreed that Hamilton's reports were models of lucidity and close reasoning, they did not for that reason concede that his influence over Congress was improper. The legislature, they repeatedly pointed out, was free to take or to leave the Secretary's recommendations; the fact that it took them more often than not indicated to their minds that the force of reasoning was on the Secretary's side. With memories stretching back to the

The Attack upon Hamilton

calamitous days of the Confederation, when the Continental Congress had controlled the nation's finances, they rejoiced that a strong hand was at last at the helm.

Madison and Jefferson attributed the overweening influence attained by the Secretary of the Treasury over Congress, to corruption. Hamilton, they asserted, had put himself at the head of a "corrupt squadron" so powerful that nothing—not even the majority—could stand against it. Thus was created, said Jefferson, "a legislature legislating for their own interests in opposition to those of the people." While honest men watched helplessly, speculators and other beneficiaries of Hamilton's measures rallied round the Treasury "as a nobility around a throne," snapping up the loaves and fishes he tossed them. James Madison detected a close affinity between "the speeches and the pockets" of those members of Congress who held government securities; Hamilton seemed to have demonstrated, not for the first or last time, that money could be made to talk with the voice of a legislator.

No doubt, Madison and Jefferson sincerely believed that Hamilton owed his influence to the pervasive influence of money. A man who talked as much about the profit motive as did Hamilton invited the suspicion that he did not exclude its operations from politics. Moreover, he had been frequently heard to justify corruption as practiced upon Parliament by the British Crown. What was more natural, therefore, than to infer that he favored the use of similar methods by the American Executive?

In order to prove Hamilton guilty as charged, it was sometimes necessary to distort the evidence. He had observed, for example, that a public debt, if properly funded, was a public blessing; his enemies found it convenient to omit the qualification he had appended, thereby making it appear that he had said that a public debt was a public blessing. And why should a public debt be a public blessing, asked Jefferson, except that it afforded the Secretary of the Treasury a fund with which to corrupt members of Congress? No wonder, therefore, he exclaimed, that Hamilton sought to enlarge the debt at every turn—every dollar added to the debt enhanced the power of his "phalanx" over the legislature.

It cannot be said that the Republicans were against speculation per se. Their quarrel was not with the acquisitive spirit but with the way it manifested itself in businessmen; although they deplored "the peculiar vices of commerce," they carefully avoided casting any strictures upon speculation in land. And with good reason—for speculation was the very breath of life to the gentry of the South. Travelers were struck by the Virginians' passion for gaming: "Perhaps in no place of the same size in the world is there more gambling going forward than in Richmond," remarked an English visitor. "I scarcely alighted from my horse at the tavern, when the landlord came to ask what game I was most partial to." He was given a wide choice: faro, hazard, billiards and cockfighting were a few of the games by which the citizens of the Old Dominion proposed to relieve him of his guineas.[6]

While the planters deplored the ownership of public securities by congressmen, they did not deny the right of congressmen, or anyone else, to own slaves. Here was a field for interesting speculations regarding original ownership and the rights of purchasers, but southern spokesmen wisely avoided embarking upon it. Since it was never adequately explained to him, Hamilton failed to see that slaves were a respectable and honorific form of property, the ownership of which constituted a qualification for the duties of statesmanship, whereas the possession of stocks and bonds automatically incapacitated a man for public life. "It is a strange perversion of ideas," he said, ". . . that men should be deemed corrupt and criminal for becoming proprietors in the funds of their country." No purer and more virtuous legislative body than Congress existed, he exclaimed; if his enemies saw malfeasance and bribery on every hand, it was because, he said, they arrogated all probity and patriotism to themselves and condemned every man who did not share their views as "an ambitious despot or a corrupt knave."

In actuality, Hamilton's following consisted for the most part of representatives and senators from the states which expected to benefit most from the measures projected by the Secretary of the Treasury. Admittedly, many of these members of Congress owned government bonds and bank stock, but personal profit was not generally the decisive factor in determining their votes: Hamilton's program of centralized government and state-aided capitalism offered them far more in the form of wealth and power than did the profits realized from stock speculation. As for the "corrupt squadron" that Jefferson pictured riding ruthlessly over the honest men in Congress, the voting was so close that a majority of three or four votes sometimes decided questions involving the expenditure of millions of dollars.

In their efforts to uncover the corruption over which, they had no doubt, Hamilton was presiding, the Republicans were led into many strange and devious courses. In 1791, for example, when the Indians took the warpath, an army under General St. Clair was sent against them and met with a crushing defeat. Republican congressmen began looking for a scapegoat and, as might be expected, they found several. Gratifyingly enough, it was not only the unfortunate general but the Secretary of the Treasury who seemed to be responsible. As Secretary of the Treasury, Hamilton had made contracts for army rations, clothing and military stores. Since William Duer had been one of the largest suppliers of the army, Republicans sniffed the reek of corruption in these transactions; and they confidently expected that the trail would lead to the innermost recesses of the Treasury. Accordingly, the representatives instituted a formal investigation into the conduct of the Secretaries of War and of the Treasury.

The Attack upon Hamilton

In actuality, far from being responsible for St. Clair's defeat, Hamilton had given advice which, had it been followed, might have led to a very different outcome. He urged that the army sent against the Indians be composed largely of regulars; having no trust in militia, he wished to relegate them to a mere supporting role. But the Republicans considered militia to be the mainstay of the army and of popular liberty; they would no more part with these civilian soldiers than with their civil rights. One congressman declared that the Indians despised regulars and would shoot them down like wild turkeys. The humanitarian thing, therefore, was to spare the lives of these turkeys in uniform by using the far more redoubtable militia against the redskins. These counsels prevailed: when St. Clair marched, he had with him only two companies of regulars. As Hamilton had predicted, the militia deserted in droves and left the general and the regulars in the lurch on the field of battle.

The result of these disclosures was that Hamilton emerged from the investigation with enhanced prestige. The blame was placed upon Secretary of War Knox, the army contractors and General St. Clair himself. As a mark of confidence in the Secretary of the Treasury, he was given even larger powers over the supply of the armed forces.[7]

Obviously, the Republicans could ill afford to conduct official investigations of the Treasury Department that redounded to the credit of the Secretary. And, however certain in their own minds they might be of Hamilton's guilt, they could no longer flatter themselves that rumor, guesswork and unsupported accusations were enough to convict him before the tribunal of public opinion.

In the autumn of 1792, having long nourished their hopes of removing Hamilton upon the most meager kind of provender, the Republicans finally got something they could really put their teeth into. Two years before, in the summer of 1790, Congress had authorized the President to contract two loans in Europe: one of $12 million, the proceeds of which were to be appropriated solely to the payment of the interest and principal of the foreign debt and to the purchase of outstanding certificates of indebtedness of the United States government; and a second loan of $2 million which was earmarked for the discharge of the interest due on the public debt contracted after 1790 and the current expenditures of the government. On August 28, in pursuance of the authority vested in him by this act of Congress, Washington instructed Hamilton to float two loans totaling $14 million.* With little or no difficulty, the money was raised in the Netherlands, most of it coming from the private banks of Amsterdam.[8]

No doubt, Congress intended that these two loans should be kept separate

---

* Originally it had been intended to place the negotiation and management of these loans in the hands of the Secretary of the Treasury, but at Madison's suggestion this power was assigned to the President.

and distinct: the money designated for the service of the foreign loans was to be kept in Europe, while the funds to be used for the reduction of the domestic debt were to be brought to the United States. But Hamilton made little effort to separate these two loans in his departmental bookkeeping, nor did he strictly apply them to the purposes indicated by Congress. Instead, accustomed as he was to construe his powers broadly, he treated the money raised in Europe as an aggregate fund to be applied where it could be used most advantageously. This, he discovered during the panics of 1791 and 1792, consisted in purchasing government securities in the open market. As a result, some of the $12 million reserved for the payment of the foreign debt was used for a very different purpose. On the other hand, part of the so-called "domestic loan" was diverted to paying interest on the foreign debt. All told, almost a million dollars was juggled in this way between the two loans.[9]

It was Hamilton himself who gave the Republicans the first clue that the Treasury had not observed the injunctions of Congress. In November, 1792, he recommended to Congress that the government pay in full its debt to the Bank of the United States—$2 million in all. He held out the prospect of a considerable saving to the government: by borrowing money at 5 per cent in Europe, the bank loan, carrying 6 per cent interest, could be liquidated, thereby giving the government a clear gain of 1 per cent annually on $2 million.

The Secretary's solicitude for the Bank of the United States immediately put the Republicans on their guard. Since the Bank was supposed to be the center of Hamilton's web of "speculating and monarchical influence," it was suspected that he was seeking to enrich the Bank of the United States in order to increase the fund with which he purchased the votes of members of Congress. If they needed any further evidence of the sinister nature of Hamilton's intentions, it was provided by the eagerness of the Federalists to rush the bill through Congress.[10]

Their suspicions now thoroughly aroused, the Republicans demanded that the Secretary of the Treasury give Congress a detailed accounting of the money raised by loan in Europe. Although thirty-four members of the House were willing to incur a debt of $2 million "upon the mere 'ipse dicit' of the Treasury officer and without any competent understanding of the subject," enough Federalists joined the Republicans to ensure the passage of the motion. Accordingly, on January 4, 1793, Hamilton submitted to the House a report which he supposed would put an end to the matter. But the Republicans were far from satisfied: they pronounced the Secretary's statement "inaccurate, defective and imperfect," and accused him of deliberately trying to keep the lawmakers in the dark regarding the proceedings of the Treasury.[11]

There could be no doubt that Hamilton was guilty of neglecting to keep

The Attack upon Hamilton

Congress informed of what went on within his department. Except for the information he chose to give or that which Congress itself called for, the lawmakers were left to draw their own conclusions regarding the work of the Treasury. Hamilton did not send Congress regular systematic reports on the state of his department; indeed, it was not until 1800 that the Secretary of the Treasury was required by law annually to make such reports. The Constitution merely required that "a regular statement and account of the receipts and expenditures of all public money shall be published from time to time," and Hamilton construed this to mean that the accounting should be in general terms and at lengthy intervals.[12]

To bring the Secretary of the Treasury to "justice," the Republicans selected William B. Giles of Virginia to act as prosecutor in the House of Representatives. Giles was a planter-politician notable for his loathing of Hamilton, his fondness for descanting upon "canvas-back ducks, ham and chickens, old Madeira, the glories of the Ancient Dominion," and for his drinking habits—"wine or cherry bounce from twelve o'clock to night every day." It would have been better for the Republicans, however, if Giles had devoted more time to the study of finance and less to conviviality.

Like most planters of the Old Dominion, Giles seems to have feared that Hamilton was planning to snatch the canvasback ducks, the chickens and the Madeira from the very mouths of Virginians. And, to compound the felony, the Secretary lavished these delicacies upon northern speculators!

A committee of fifteen, of which Giles was a member, was appointed by Congress to enquire into the affairs of the Treasury. Officials of the Treasury were cross-examined, transactions between the Treasury and the banks were scrutinized, and even Hamilton's private accounts with the banks were inspected. But, to the Republicans' disappointment, the committee unearthed no evidence that Hamilton had used public money to finance his own speculations or that there was anything improper in the relations between the government and the Bank of the United States.[13]

The Republicans perforce fell back upon the lesser charge that Hamilton had not kept the two loans separate as Congress had directed. In this financial maneuver, Hamilton's enemies saw a plot to strike down freedom in France. The million dollars he had "drawn" from Europe for domestic purposes had been earmarked for the payment of the foreign debt, of which France held a large share. When it was disclosed that the United States was almost $700,000 in arrears in its payments to France, Republicans could no longer doubt that Hamilton was deliberately starving freedom-loving Frenchmen in order to pamper the stockholders of the Bank of the United States. No doubt, said Madison, Hamilton withheld the money due France in the hope that the Duke of Brunswick would capture Paris and restore absolutism—then, presumably, Hamilton would be delighted to pay the debts of the United States to Louis XVI.[14]

Hamilton's answer to these charges was delivered, complained the Republicans, in a "magisterial stile" of condescension which "spoke the language of a Frederick of Prussia, or some other despotic prince, who had all the political powers vested in himself." He rebuked Congress for having put him to this inconvenience merely for the gratification of party feeling and he caustically pointed out that all the trouble could have been avoided had congressmen come directly to his office instead of publicly accusing him of malfeasance. However, he did not deny that Congress was justified in asking for information.[15]

Hamilton's acerbity sprang from the consciousness of his own rectitude and the feeling that the Republicans were acting in a spirit very far removed from that of fair inquiry. Simply because a party in Congress differed from him about the legal effect of the appropriation laws, he was accused, he exclaimed, of being a malefactor "who did not scruple to sacrifice the public to his private interest, his duty and honor to the sinister accumulation of wealth." And yet the truth of the matter was, he averred, that "no man ever carried into public life a more unblemished pecuniary reputation, than that with which I undertook the office of Secretary of the Treasury; a character marked by the indifference to the acquisition of property rather than avidity for it."[16]

The air of injured innocence with which Hamilton addressed Congress contrasted sharply with the alacrity with which he complied with its directives. The Republicans supposed that they had laid an impossible task upon him: he would not be able to supply the required information until the next session of Congress—and in the meantime, they rejoiced, he would suffer all the imputations of guilt. However, by dint of working night and day—a labor which his friends compared with the labors of Hercules—he succeeded in drawing up a series of reports, submitted to Congress between the fourth and twentieth of February, which effectively answered the charges that he had concealed shortages in the accounts of the United States; that he had favored the Bank of the United States; and that he had drawn money from Europe to this country for the benefit of speculators.*[17]

To the Republicans, Hamilton's herculean labors represented little more than a whitewashing of the Augean stables of the Treasury. Moreover, he seemed to protest too much: instead of disarming suspicion, his self-righteousness convinced his enemies all the more firmly of his guilt. And by what right, they asked, did he "fly into petulance at the becoming effort of our legislature to remove the veil of mystery and obscurity" with which he clothed his operations?[18]

In the happy expectation that the Virginia squires were at last about to

* To answer fully Giles's charges necessitated forwarding to the Treasury an account of the collection of all revenue officers in the United States—a task which could not have been completed in less than nine months.

close in upon their quarry, Jefferson halloed them on with encouragement and advice. The Secretary of State was not inclined to delay the dispatching of a cornered fox, and he earnestly advised his friends to administer the *coup de grâce* forthwith. Characteristically, Jefferson preferred to remain behind the scenes while this unpleasantness was taking place.

Demurely retiring to his study, Jefferson drew up a series of resolutions for Giles to present to Congress, demanding among other things that the office of Treasurer be made a separate department independent of the Secretary of the Treasury and recommending that Hamilton be declared guilty of maladministration and unworthy of holding office under the United States government.[19]

On February 27, 1792—three days before the end of the session—Giles made his arraignment of the Secretary of the Treasury, "sanguine enough to believe," said Jefferson, "that the palpableness of these resolves rendered it impossible the house could reject them."[20] But the bill of complaints submitted by Giles was much watered down from the stiff draught Jefferson had mixed for the Secretary of the Treasury; apparently even Giles, hostile as he was to Hamilton, felt that the Secretary of State had gone too far. Gone was the imputation that shortages in the Treasury accounts existed, and gone also was the implication that Hamilton had rigged the market for the benefit of speculators. The burden of the charges now directed against Hamilton was that he had given neither Congress nor the President notice of his intention to alter the disposition of the funds raised in Europe; that he had negotiated a loan at the Bank of the United States contrary to the public interest; and that he had shown disrespect for Congress by presuming to judge of its motives in calling for information. Conspicuously absent was the allegation that Hamilton had made corrupt use of public funds—the one thing certain to turn the people against the Secretary. Thus an accusation of "portentous speculation and corruption had dwindled down into a mere complaint of assumption of power, exercise of unwarrantable discretion, arrogance and want of politeness toward the House."[21]

Even though the resolutions were bereft of much of their sting, the Republicans still hoped to force Hamilton's resignation. The eighth and last resolution introduced by Giles was to the effect that copy of the resolutions be transmitted to the President—a clear directive to remove the offending Secretary from office. Obviously, the Republicans' strategy was to arraign Hamilton for various crimes and misdemeanors and then to ring the changes until doubts of probity had been thoroughly inculcated in the public mind. For this reason, they had postponed Giles's formal indictment of the Secretary until the closing days of the session.[22]

But when the resolutions were put to the vote, the Republicans were defeated on every count. After the rejection of the third resolution, Giles offered to drop the rest of the charges, but the Federalists, elated with their easy victory, insisted upon carrying through to the end. The result was that Hamilton was vindicated on every point by a comfortable majority; the Republican lines failed to hold, and even some Virginians voted against the resolutions. Giles was able to muster most support (fifteen to thirty-three) on the charge that Hamilton had failed to give Congress official information, in due time, that he had drawn funds from Europe. Only five members of the House voted for all nine resolutions; among them was James Madison.[23]

Congress adjourned shortly after the defeat of the Giles resolutions, the Republicans bitterly lamenting that justice had miscarried again. "It was not to be doubted," said John Marshall, "that their utmost efforts would be exerted, to communicate to their constituents the ill humor." But when Giles reached Virginia, he had not a word to say about Hamilton: he was, it was remarked, "as mute as a fish" and about as happy as one out of water.[24]

Nevertheless Hamilton knew that he had won but a short reprieve and that at the next session of Congress he would again be fighting for his political life. And with his political life was bound up the fate of the funding system, the Bank of the United States, the excise—in short, "all the most material props of the Government." If the keystone—the Secretary of the Treasury—were removed, the whole edifice promised to cave in upon the heads of the "friends of government." But the Samson of federalism had his Delilah, and at this very time Hamilton was happily submitting to the shearing.[25]

All the while that the Republicans were probing hopefully into the affairs of the Treasury, they were right in believing that Hamilton had a guilty secret. But it was not proof of financial irregularities that Hamilton feared his enemies would unearth—his transgressions were of the marital variety. And it was here that the Republicans finally struck pay dirt.

Had he been a wealthier man, Hamilton might easily have gained the reputation of being an "easy touch." Compared with him Jefferson appeared cold, austere and penurious: there was nothing about him to encourage hopes of financial handouts. Hamilton, on the other hand, had frequently to be reminded by his colleagues that charity cases never yet provided a lawyer with a living. When he came to Philadelphia in 1790, his reputation for "Benevolence and Humanity to the distress'd" had preceded him and many demands were made upon his generosity. Among others, Mrs. Mumford, a Philadelphia landlady who ran a boardinghouse for congressmen, asked him for $20 to stave off her landlord: "Should you condescend to comply with my request," she wrote, "or should you wish to satisfy yourself further by seeing the Petitioner you will find her at No. 96 North Sixth Street, but as it is a Step I have taken wholly unknown to my Husband

The Attack upon Hamilton

whose feelings are far too delicate for his own peace in his present Situation, I confide in your Honor that it may not be mentioned."[26]

Had Hamilton contented himself with chivalrously relieving distressed landladies, even without the privity of their husbands, he would have been spared much vexation of spirit and irreparable loss of reputation. Yet it was not in the end his chivalrous or humanitarian instincts that led him to disaster.

In the summer of 1791 there lived in Philadelphia a precious pair, Mr. and Mrs. James Reynolds. Attracted to the metropolis by the prospect of sharing in the spoil upon which the speculators were battening, Reynolds picked up a meager living by preying upon the former soldiers and officers of the Continental Army. That his success was not greater in this usually lucrative business was owing to no scruples over defrauding veterans: he simply lacked the capital necessary to attain the higher reaches of chicanery. While possessed of first-rate talents for swindling, larceny and blackmail, Reynolds sorely felt the need of wherewithal with which to begin his operations. His search for this elusive commodity led him to Alexander Hamilton.

But Reynolds did not contemplate anything as innocent—or as hopeless —as asking Hamilton for a loan. The Secretary may have appeared to be a soft touch, but hardly that soft. Instead, Reynolds proposed to extort money from Hamilton by the gentle art of blackmail.

In the person of his wife, Maria, James Reynolds had some delectable bait for the trap he was laying for Hamilton. Maria Reynolds was a woman of considerable physical attraction and, equally important to the success of Reynolds' plans, a skillful actress and a born adventuress. Possessed of these redoubtable qualifications for the job in hand, Maria Reynolds did not doubt that she could twist Hamilton round her finger.

The plot necessitated the sacrifice of Mrs. Reynolds' virtue, but James Reynolds had already set a cash surrender value upon his wife's honor. His only regret seems to have been that he had only one wife to sacrifice in such a good cause. On her part, Mrs. Reynolds raised no objections to consummating the bargain; after all, Hamilton was a handsome and dashing young man who had fluttered the hearts of many women. If rumor could be credited, Mrs. Reynolds might make herself the object of envy to a large number of New York and Philadelphia beauties. The gratifications to be expected from such an encounter so strongly appealed, in different ways, to Reynolds and his wife that they both entered enthusiastically into the conspiracy against the Secretary of the Treasury.

When everything was in readiness, Mrs. Reynolds called upon Hamilton at his office in Chestnut Street one day in 1791. She appealed to Hamilton as a man of sensibility eager to succor beauty (even though a bit shopworn) in distress: she had come to Philadelphia, she said, "to endeavour to reclaim a prodigal Husband who had deserted her and his Creditors at New York."

Hamilton was visibly touched, but less, it would seem, by her story of misfortune and unmerited neglect than by the promise she conveyed of more intimate revelations to come. In any event, instead of giving her money then and there, he arranged a meeting that evening at her house on Market Street.

Hamilton's instinct did not play him false: that evening the lady yielded with almost disconcerting precipitancy. She led him into a bedroom— Hamilton never pretended that he offered resistance—and there he paid her the money he had promised to bring. These preliminaries being out of the way, "some conversation ensued," Hamilton later recorded, "from which it was quickly apparent that other than pecuniary consolation would be acceptable."

Perhaps the ease with which Hamilton had attained his success ought to have put him upon his guard, but Mrs. Reynolds' amorousness convinced him that he had made a conquest: the lady herself assured him that it was so and Hamilton was not loath to accept an explanation so flattering to his self-esteem.

The farce was played out to its denouement complete with the outraged husband demanding balm for a broken heart. For Hamilton, this was an ugly surprise: up to this point, he had supposed that Mrs. Reynolds' favors were freely given for love alone; now he found that he was expected to pay —and to pay heavily—for his illicit pleasures. Reynolds stormed in, beating his breast and accusing Hamilton of having wrecked his home: "You took advantage of a poor Broken harted woman," he cried. ". . . . You have acted the part of the most Cruelest man in existance. . . . She ses there is no other man that she Care for in this world. now Sir you have bin the Cause of Cooling her affections for me."

Even though his heart was breaking with grief, Reynolds indicated that he was not disposed to be unreasonable: after all, his wife was a pretty woman and it was quite natural that the Secretary of the Treasury should have succumbed to her charms. Putting it on a man-to-man basis, Reynolds declared that he, too, might be solaced. In his case, however, Hamilton was expected to open his pocketbook to provide consolation.

Hamilton's relief at finding that Reynolds was not going to be difficult was somewhat chilled by the price that he set upon his wife's favors. Ominously, he told Hamilton that nothing would ever restore the conjugal happiness he had once known: "If you should give me all you possess would not do it." Nothing less than a sizable chunk of the United States Treasury would content him, but in the meantime he promised that for $1,000 cash he would clear out of town and never again trouble Hamilton and Mrs. Reynolds in their Chestnut Street love nest. Hamilton paid off, although it was so difficult for him to raise the money that he was compelled to make the payment in two installments. With the husband taken care of, Hamilton

The Attack upon Hamilton

continued his surreptitious visits, furtively slinking through the back streets of Philadelphia and exchanging impassioned billets-doux with his Maria.

But Reynolds seems to have felt that Hamilton was getting more than his money's worth; in any event, he was soon back in Philadelphia demanding more balm in the form of "loans." Hamilton complied, although the notes Reynolds gave him in return could hardly have been considered worth more than the paper they were written upon. Still, Mrs. Reynolds obligingly provided the collateral and Reynolds himself offered no objections to payments in kind. Indeed, from the beginning to the end of the affair he proved himself an honest broker; it is difficult to see how a man could do more for his wife's paramour. When Hamilton called at the house in Market Street, Reynolds, who in such matters was the very soul of delicacy, took himself off, leaving Hamilton and Maria alone. The most obliging of husbands professed himself gratified by the happy change he found in Mrs. Reynolds after Hamilton's visits: "I find when ever you have been with her," he told Hamilton, "She is Cheerful and kind, but when you have not in some time she is Quite the Reverse and wishes to be alone by her self."

The change in Reynolds' own disposition after receiving a "loan" from Hamilton was equally remarkable. His only complaints were that Hamilton did not come frequently enough for his wife's and his own peace of mind and that Hamilton insisted upon using the back door. Why was it, he enquired plaintively, that the Secretary did not enter by the front door: was it because he thought that Reynolds was maintaining a house of ill fame or because he was too proud to be seen entering the house of a poor man? "All any Person can say of me," Reynolds declared, "is that I am poore and I dont know if that is any Crime." He might have added that he was taking steps to correct that condition—at Hamilton's expense.

During this period (his dalliance with Maria lasted almost a year), Hamilton was no Antony chained by love to Cleopatra and the Nile while great events marched forward unheeded. On the contrary, he was actively engaged in administering the Treasury Department, overseeing the customs, launching the Bank of the United States, writing his Report on Manufactures, establishing the S.U.M. and trying to remove Jefferson from the Cabinet. Obviously, Mrs. Reynolds was a plaything for the idle hours of a statesman, not an absorbing passion that consumed energies that belonged to affairs of state. The work of strengthening the government and fostering the national welfare went on; and in these majestic endeavors Mrs. Reynolds provided no more than a refreshing change of scene not only from official duties but, it is to be feared, from Mrs. Hamilton.

All this time, Hamilton imagined that things were what they seemed— that Mrs. Reynolds was a neglected wife who had become infatuated with him and that James Reynolds was an injured husband. But as his passion cooled, his suspicions increased apace and his visits to the Market Street hideaway became less and less frequent. Fearing that he had overplayed the part of the complaisant husband, Reynolds abruptly changed his tune: he forbade Hamilton to see Mrs. Reynolds in the future, but at the same time he flattered Hamilton's ego by telling him that a separation was certain to break Maria's heart. "I was in hopes that it would in time ware off," he wrote Hamilton, "but I find there is no hope." Maria herself entreated him to return. "Oh Col. Hamilton," she wrote early in June, 1792, "what have I done that you should thus Neglect me. . . . Let me beg of you to Come and If you never see me again or if you think It best I will submit to It and take a long and last adieu . . . for heaven sake keep me not In Suspence Let me know your Intention Either by a Line or Catline." On one occasion, she threatened to commit suicide unless Hamilton visited her. "All the appearances of violent attachment, and of agonizing distress at the idea of relinquishment," Hamilton ruefully admitted later, "were played with a most imposing art. This, though it did not make me entirely the dupe of the plot, yet kept me in a state of irresolution." He was sick of the affair and the purchased favors of Mrs. Reynolds had begun to pall; yet because her affection for him seemed so sincere, he decided to break off the relationship gradually, hoping thereby to avoid the weeping and wailing he knew that Mrs. Reynolds would give vent to. Reynolds, however, accused him of being so lost to all sense of honor as to abandon another man's wife. He informed the Secretary that after experiencing the pleasures of his company, Maria had said that she would never be content to be the wife of James Reynolds. Whereupon the heartbroken husband asked his wife's paramour for a loan of $30.[27]

Always Reynolds kept suspended over Hamilton's head the threat of laying the whole sordid tale before Mrs. Hamilton. "Mrs. Reynolds more than once communicated to me," Hamilton later said, "that Reynolds would occasionally relapse into discontent at his situation, would treat her very ill, hint at the assassination of me, and more openly threaten, by way of revenge, to inform Mrs. Hamilton." And Hamilton could not be sure that Reynolds was merely making an empty threat: "In the workings of human inconsistency," he remarked, "it was very possible that the same man might be corrupt enough to compound for his wife's chastity, and yet have sensibility enough to be restless in the situation and to hate the cause of it." Truly, the Secretary of the Treasury was upon a Procrustean bed and the torture was being applied by a master of the art.[28]

Seldom has an American statesman risked so much for so little. From his wife and from public opinion he could expect little forgiveness: "Gallant adventures," remarked a traveler in the United States, "are little known and still less practiced. . . . Conjugal disloyalties, on either side, are punished

The Attack upon Hamilton

by ineffaceable infamy." Nevertheless, Hamilton even brought Mrs. Reynolds to his own house when Mrs. Hamilton and the children were out of town. The man who had carefully planned his marriage into the highest social circles of the republic and who deprecated the principle that the world was well lost for love was now risking everything for something not usually dignified by that word.[29]

As long as he continued to serve as a source of income to Reynolds, Hamilton was safe, but the blackmailer's demands seemed never to end. At one time, Reynolds offered to accept a post in the United States Treasury as solace for his bleeding heart, but Hamilton trembled to contemplate what havoc might thereby be wrought in the financial affairs of the government. And so, although there was a vacant clerkship at his disposal, Hamilton declined to gratify Reynolds' ambition of serving his country. For this affront, reflecting as it did upon Reynolds' probity, the blackmailer turned the screws upon the hapless Secretary a little tighter.

The money extracted from Hamilton enabled Reynolds to graduate from swindling soldiers to the more respectable forms of speculation, particularly turnpike scrip. But in the midst of these promising undertakings, his past suddenly caught up with him: he and his partner Jacob Clingman were arrested on a charge dating back to their earlier confidence-men days. A supposedly dead soldier whose claims against the government they had been seeking to recover unexpectedly came to life and denounced them as forgers and perjurers. A warrant was sworn out by Oliver Wolcott, and Clingman and Reynolds were hustled off to the Philadelphia jail.*

Reynolds did not intend to rot in jail: he was certain that if he threatened to talk, Hamilton, to save his own skin, would see that he was released. But, much to Reynolds' surprise, the Secretary refused to intervene: even when Oliver Wolcott (who knew nothing of his chief's relations with the prisoner) came to Hamilton with reports that Reynolds had threatened "to make disclosures injurious to the character of some head of a Department," the Secretary replied that nothing should be done to free Reynolds "while such a report existed and remained unexplored."

This decision, Hamilton knew, made it virtually certain that Reynolds would talk. To make matters worse, it seemed likely that the story would

---

* In 1790, by corrupt means, Reynolds had obtained from the Treasury a confidential list of individuals, most of them former soldiers, to whom money was owing. With the aid of this list, he bought claims for a few cents on the dollar, or showed the ex-soldiers a fraudulent list in which they were set down as creditors for much smaller sums than were actually owing them. Reynolds secured from them a power of attorney to collect these debts and then pocketed the difference.

Ultimately Reynolds and Clingman were released without standing trial. Held for subornation of perjury, they offered, in exchange for a nolle prosequi, to disclose the name of the Treasury official from whom they had procured a list of the names and sums due the public creditors. These terms were accepted by the government and they implicated not William Duer, as Hamilton had half feared, but a clerk in the register's office.

reach the ears of the Secretary's political enemies: Reynolds boasted that he possessed information regarding Hamilton's speculations and swore that "the prosecution was set on foot only to keep him low and oppress him, and ultimately to drive him away, in order to prevent his using the power he had over him [Hamilton]." Nevertheless, Hamilton did not seriously consider any other course: although he sought to purchase Reynolds' silence with his own money, he would not use official influence or money to save himself from exposure. "I was not disposed," he later remarked, "to make any improper concession to the apprehension of his resentment." Justice must take its course with Reynolds even though the heavens fell—as they seemed likely to do—upon Hamilton himself.[30]

Neither Reynolds nor his partner Jacob Clingman, who had also landed in jail, were strangers to the Republican leaders. As early as April, 1790, Madison had been informed that Reynolds might be persuaded to tell what he knew about the misdeeds going on in the United States Treasury. To Madison, this meant that Reynolds had information linking Hamilton with William Duer. That Duer was in jail and Hamilton still at liberty struck the Republican leaders as a rank miscarriage of justice: the accessory had been compelled to take the rap for the principal in crime.

But in December, 1792, their probings into the Treasury seemed about to be rewarded. Jacob Clingman, despairing of Hamilton's intercession in Reynolds behalf, let it be known to his former employer, Congressman Frederick Muhlenburg of Pennsylvania, that he was ready to talk. Muhlenberg lost no time in getting to the Philadelphia prison, where he was told by Clingman and Reynolds that they had it in their power "to hang the Secretary of the Treasury, that he [Hamilton] was deeply concerned in speculation, that he had frequently given money to him [Reynolds]."[31]

Although hanging Hamilton was a more drastic penalty than the Republicans had contemplated—they would have been satisfied to send him to prison for a long term—they were not inclined to split hairs when it came to meting out punishment to the Great Embezzler.

Muhlenberg immediately told the news to his good friends and fellow congressmen James Monroe and Abraham Venable. The three Republicans immediately constituted themselves a committee of inquiry and called upon Reynolds in prison and Mrs. Reynolds in her house on Market Street for further information. From these interviews the congressmen emerged with even graver suspicions of the probity of the Secretary of the Treasury: the Reynoldses not only talked—they produced letters written by Hamilton which seemingly proved him guilty of speculating in government securities while occupying the office of Secretary of the Treasury.

So damning did the case against the Secretary appear that the three Republican congressmen contemplated going directly to the President and demanding Hamilton's dismissal forthwith. However, since fair play seemed

The Attack upon Hamilton 339

to require that Hamilton be given an opportunity to speak in his own defense, it was decided to confront the accused with the allegations and documents furnished by Reynolds. Not that they gave the Secretary much chance of wriggling out of this tight corner: much as they respected his ability to take advantage of loopholes, they now believed that he was securely entangled.

Accordingly, on the morning of December 15, 1792, without preliminary warning, Monroe, Muhlenberg and Venable called at Hamilton's office. After the barest formalities had been observed, Muhlenberg declared that he and his friends had learned that *"a very improper connection"* existed between Hamilton and Reynolds. "Extremely hurt by this mode of introduction," Hamilton "arrested the progress of the discourse by giving way to very strong expressions of indignation." Whereupon the congressmen explained that "they did not take the fact for established" but that, unsolicited by them, information, supported by documents, of dealings between Hamilton and Reynolds had come to light. Their purpose in paying this visit, they explained, was to give the Secretary an opportunity to clear himself.

Somewhat mollified by these professions of good will—so different from Muhlenberg's opening remarks—Hamilton asked to see the evidence that had come into the committee's possession. When Muhlenberg produced a letter to Reynolds written in a disguised hand, Hamilton promptly acknowledged it to be his. Realizing the precariousness of his position, he assumed a more conciliatory attitude toward the congressmen. He declared that he was ready "to meet fair enquiry with frank communication" and that he possessed written evidence that would establish beyond doubt the nature of his relations with Reynolds. For the presentation of this evidence, a meeting was arranged for that evening at Hamilton's house.

Hamilton had imagined that the worst he had to fear was exposure as an adulterer; he had not foreseen that Reynolds would attempt to incriminate him as an accessory in speculation. Fortunately he had the forethought to preserve the letters sent him by James and Maria Reynolds. These letters proved conclusively to any unprejudiced person that there was nothing to Reynolds' story that Hamilton had used government funds for speculative purposes.

That evening, with Oliver Wolcott present as a witness, Hamilton bared to the three congressmen the whole story of his affair with Mrs. Reynolds and the blackmail plot of which he had been made the victim. He proved every point by reference to the letters sent him by Reynolds; and so convincing was his documentation that, before he was half through, Venable and Muhlenberg declared themselves satisfied and begged him not to go any further. But Hamilton insisted upon completing his unedifying tale, and the congressmen heard him to the end.

Seemingly Hamilton succeeded in acquitting himself to the satisfaction of all concerned. It was agreed that no facts had been brought to light which ought to reflect upon Hamilton's character as a public official or impair confidence in his integrity, and the three congressmen pledged themselves never to breathe a word of the affair.

Thus the Republicans found themselves possessed of the means of wrecking Hamilton's political career but bound by a promise not to use them. At a time when politicians were also gentlemen, there was little reason to fear that Muhlenberg, Monroe and Venable would sacrifice honor to political expediency. Therefore, although Monroe's attitude was not so friendly and sympathetic as that of the other congressmen, Hamilton was confident that they would never divulge his secret.

Hamilton was at last free of the Reynoldses—at some damage to his reputation, it is true, but with his home and his career still intact. Presumably he never saw either of them again: James Reynolds dropped from sight and Maria won a divorce in 1793, Aaron Burr serving as her attorney. She immediately married Jacob Clingman, Reynolds' former business partner and cellmate. Hamilton had imagined that he was playing a part in the eternal triangle, but it is probable that he was really playing in a quartet.[32]

Although the trail opened up by Reynolds had led to a boudoir in Market Street rather than to a stockjobber's office, the Republicans soon again picked up the scent of Treasury corruption. William Duer was reported to have declared that if "certain Persons" did not secure his release from prison, he would "enfold such a scene of villainy as would astonish the world." The Republicans naturally assumed that Duer was referring to Hamilton—who else, they asked, practiced villainy upon such a grand scale? But Duer failed to turn state's evidence against the Secretary of the Treasury and thereby lost his opportunity of becoming a hero to the Republican party.[33]

Even though Duer failed them, the Republicans were seldom without an informer or two who was ready to swear that he could put Hamilton behind bars. In 1793, for example, Andrew G. Fraunces, a former clerk in the Treasury Department, declared that he had so much on his former chief that "he could, if he pleased, hang Hamilton." These were welcome, if somewhat familiar words to the Republicans; if Hamilton were obliged to pay the penalty of the law, it seemed that there would be no lack of executioners. Fraunces spoke with the kind of assurance that might have been expected from Hamilton's accomplice in crime: he declared that the Secretary had agents in Philadelphia whose duty it was to purchase government securities on his account; that Hamilton sold these securities at a higher price to the Commissioners of the Sinking Fund; and that Hamilton employed him (Fraunces) as a go-between in these shady dealings. All this—and more—Fraunces declared that he could prove by means of documents and witnesses.[34]

The Attack upon Hamilton

When Hamilton learned that Fraunces was in communication with the Republican leaders, the Secretary began to betray signs of what the Republicans hopefully took to be a guilty conscience. He called in Jacob Clingman, who boasted of an acquaintance with Fraunces, and tried to pump him for information regarding Fraunces' intentions. Clingman told John Beckley, a Virginia Republican who enjoyed the confidence of Madison and Jefferson, of this interview, adding the piquant detail that Hamilton was attempting to buy from Fraunces for $2,000 all letters and papers relating to his (Hamilton's) speculations with Duer. On the strength of this information, the Republican leaders began to lay plans for Hamilton's impeachment. John Beckley, certain that Hamilton was at last caught redhanded, went to New York "to unravel this scene of iniquity," warning Monroe to lay low lest the Secretary of the Treasury take alarm.

His ego inflated by the court paid him by the Republicans, Fraunces threatened to publish a full account of the corruption he alleged to be rampant in the Treasury. Hamilton was not intimidated: "The attempt to induce me to depart from a rule of public conduct, adopted on mature reflection by the menace of an appeal to the people," he told Fraunces, "is perfectly contemptible. I can imagine no letters nor documents which are not forgeries, about the publication of which I ought to have the least solicitude." Obviously, there was no Mrs. Fraunces involved in this case, and Hamilton was therefore free to dismiss his accuser as a man who "spoke much at random and drank." The reasons for Hamilton's confidence were fully manifest when Fraunces, prompted by the Republicans, published his *Appeal against the Conduct of the Secretary of the Treasury*. This pamphlet proved to be a tissue of improbable mendacities: drunk or sober, Fraunces was apparently incapable of concocting a plausible lie. The former Treasury clerk destroyed his own credibility as a witness by his admission that he himself was a speculator who, having bought securities at a depreciated price, had turned against Hamilton when the Secretary refused to accept them at the Treasury, thus depriving Fraunces of his anticipated profit. As a result, Hamilton emerged with his reputation for probity enhanced: he had refused to connive with a speculator and he had rigidly observed the letter of the law. Even the Republicans were compelled to admit that there was nothing in Fraunces' unsupported charges. Early in 1794, the Secretary of the Treasury was absolved by a congressional committee of any blame in this matter.[35]

Thus, time after time, assuming that Hamilton's political goose was surely cooked, the Republicans had prepared to carve it up—only to find that the elusive bird had taken wing, leaving the hungry crowd below. Chagrined as they were by these repeated disappointments, the Republicans' conviction that Hamilton was guilty as charged was not affected in the slightest. "His [Hamilton's] speculations will only come to light," gloomily predicted John Taylor of Caroline, "when his light is extinguished, and it may be a consolation perhaps to reflect that his children will enjoy them, and he will enjoy them, and he will have escaped an impeachment before our chief justice."[36]

Incensed by what he called "the malicious intrigues to stab me in the dark," Hamilton asked on several occasions for a congressional investigation of his official conduct, certain in his own mind that he would be vindicated. But it was the strategy of the Republicans to spread suspicion and distrust rather than to conduct a formal investigation of his department. They, too, thought that the Secretary would be acquitted—but only because of his consummate skill in covering his tracks in the labyrinthine ways of the Treasury. Thus Hamilton received another confirmation of the hard fate visited upon those who tried to serve the people in a republic. "The triumphs of vice are no thing under the sun and, I fear, till the millennium comes, in spite of all our boasted purification and light, hypocrisy and treachery will continue to be the most successful commodities in the political market," he said. "It seems to be the destined lot of nations to mistake their foes for their friends, their flatterers for their faithful servants."[37]

23.

Hamilton's Quarrel with Jefferson and Burr

As Secretary of the Treasury, Hamilton had not lost sight of the importance of influencing public opinion by "sensible and popular writings." He was a frequent contributor to the newspapers, and it was observed that the policies of the Secretary of the Treasury found no more vigorous vindicator than the Secretary himself. Of all the newspapers in the United States—there were twelve in Philadelphia alone— Hamilton's favorite, and the one which most frequently contained his work, was the *Gazette of the United States*. This newspaper, stentorianly Federalist in tone, came closer to enjoying a national circulation than did any other newspaper of the day. Established in 1789 before Hamilton came to the Treasury, the *Gazette of the United States* received printing patronage from Hamilton's department, and on several occasions Hamilton loaned money to the editor, John Fenno. He got full value for this outlay: no printer more fulsomely praised the talents and virtues of Alexander Hamilton. Dedicated to the task of endearing "the GENERAL GOVERNMENT to the PEOPLE," the *Gazette of the United States* helped materially to advance the policies of the Secretary of the Treasury. For that reason, Jefferson fulminated against it as "a paper of pure Toryism, disseminating the doctrines of monarchy, aristocracy, and the exclusion of the influence of the people"; and he winced whenever he encountered in its pages the "hymns & lauds chanted by Fenno" in honor of Hamilton.

This deification of Hamilton presaged to Jefferson the next step in the Secretary of the Treasury's plans for the United States—his own elevation to the presidency. With some justice, Jefferson felt that Hamilton had already made himself Prime Minister and that the State Department had been converted into a little more than an adjunct to the Treasury. As a counterweight to Hamilton and the *Gazette of the United States*, a Republican newspaper with a national circulation was in Jefferson's opinion a prime necessity. It so happened that at this moment Philip Freneau, the so-called

"Poet of the Revolution" was on the point of deserting journalism in New York City for the greener pastures of New Jersey. Freneau, who mixed his printer's ink liberally with vitriol, saw eye to eye with Madison and Jefferson when it came to "Hamiltonianism"; but he had set his heart upon a little home and newspaper in the country, and even when Jefferson offered him a post as translator in the State Department, Freneau declined to come to Philadelphia. (With characteristic caution, Jefferson said nothing about a newspaper, but Freneau needed no special skill in reading between lines to discern what the Secretary of State had in mind.) Whereupon Madison went to New York to persuade his old school friend (they were both Princeton men) to reconsider. The "monarchists," he told Freneau, were making rapid strides to power; Freneau must abandon all thought of rustic retreats and pastoral delights: his place was on the firing line in Philadelphia editing a Republican newspaper.

With financial backing provided by Francis Childs, a printer, Freneau came to Philadelphia, where in October, 1791, the *National Gazette* was launched. To help pay expenses, Freneau accepted the position of translating clerk in the State Department.[1]

Freneau's editorship of the *National Gazette* made the Federalists regret that he had not buried himself in New Jersey or confined himself to writing poetry. Seldom has a political party had more cause to lament that the wages of poetry in America were so inadequate. True, the *National Gazette* printed material reflecting all shades of political opinion, and Hamilton took advantage of this indulgence to send several anonymous contributions which Freneau duly printed; but it was Freneau's particular delight to rake Hamilton over the coals and to watch his reputation go up in smoke. In describing the iniquities of Alexander Hamilton, the Poet of the Revolution abused both his poetic and journalistic license. Freneau seemed to have imagined that he was fighting the American Revolution over again, this time with Alexander Hamilton and the Federalist party in the place of George III and the Tories.[2]

Although the *National Gazette* could hardly be said to be Hamilton's favorite newspaper, he read every issue: he could hardly wait to discover what new crimes were being laid at his door by Philip Freneau. Perhaps because he drew so liberally upon his imagination, Freneau never seemed to run out of copy; but he found the English language sadly lacking in adjectives to describe Hamilton's iniquities.[3]

To be hunted down "for the unpardonable sin of having been the steady, invariable and decided friend of broad national principles of government" —such, Hamilton exclaimed, was the unhappy reward of virtue and integrity in the United States. Contrasting the purity of his intentions, his patriotism and his devotion to the public welfare with the vilification to which he was subjected in Congress and the newspapers, Hamilton concluded that he was a much-injured man. "It is a curious phenomenon in political history (not easy to be paralleled)," he observed, "that a measure which has elevated the credit of the country from a state of absolute prostration to a state of exalted pre-eminence, should bring upon the authors of it obloquy and reproach."4

Hamilton was never inclined to turn the other cheek to a journalist, but it might be supposed that long exposure would have toughened him to newspaper scurrility. Instead, he revealed a sensitivity to such abuse that seriously handicapped his career in American politics. "I trust that I shall always be able to bear, as I ought," he wrote Washington in 1792, "imputations of error of judgment; but I acknowledge that I cannot be entirely patient under charges which impeach the integrity of my public motives or conduct. I feel that I merit them *in no degree;* and expressions of indignation sometimes escape me, in spite of every effort to suppress them." He would have been wiser—but less human—had he accepted this denigration as one of the inevitable concomitants of political office. Unfortunately for his peace of mind, he could never forget that he was a man of honor, vigilant in all that affected his good name. He carried into political life the ethics and the punctilio of the military man, and he never fully realized that they were out of place in the nether world of politics in which he had cast his lot.5

Freneau's barbs stung Hamilton the more sharply because they were always accompanied by the most honeyed praise of Thomas Jefferson. If the *National Gazette* ran short of adjectives in describing Hamilton's crimes against republicanism, it experienced a similar difficulty in finding words to convey a proper sense of the transcendent virtues of the Secretary of State. Jefferson was hailed as "that illustrious Patriot, Statesman and Philosopher," "the Colossus of Liberty" who alone prevented monarchy and aristocracy from overwhelming the land. These effusions afforded the Secretary of the Treasury much food for thought; and when he discovered that Freneau was employed in Jefferson's department as a translator, Hamilton concluded that he was being made the victim of a character assassin.6

Lacking proof that Jefferson had deliberately hired Freneau for this purpose, Hamilton could do no more than insinuate in the *Gazette of the United States* that the State Department paid Freneau a salary for publishing lies and abuse of public men in order to "oppose the measures of government, and, by false insinuations, to disturb the public peace." If this were true, it explained a good deal about Freneau's activities: "In common life," Hamilton observed, "it is thought ungrateful for a man to bite the hand that puts bread into his mouth; but if the man is hired to do it, the case is altered."7

Shortly after this veiled and anonymous attack upon Jefferson, Hamilton learned that James Madison had been instrumental in bringing Freneau to Philadelphia. By 1792, Hamilton was certain that when Madison's hand appeared, it was guided by Thomas Jefferson. He ascribed Madison's apostasy to the "French principles" dispensed by Jefferson: here, he exclaimed, was a frightening instance of the results of entertaining "an exalted opinion of the talents, knowledge and virtues of Mr. Jefferson." Hamilton's sense of grievance against Jefferson was stronger than against Madison because he believed that the older man was actuated by personal rancor. Until he had been provoked by the *National Gazette,* Hamilton had never held Jefferson up to contempt, nor had he descended to air their differences in the newspapers.[8]

Whereas Jefferson, he complained, had never attempted to conceal his satisfaction when he found the Secretary of the Treasury in difficulties. He had delivered his opinion on the Bank of the United States "in a style and manner," Hamilton said, "which I felt as pertaining of asperity and ill humor toward me"; and he had censured the funding system in a way which left no doubt in Hamilton's mind that he intended to subvert the entire financial structure. Moreover, Jefferson had applied to the President to remove the Post Office from Hamilton's control and transfer it to the State Department. Although the Post Office eluded him, Jefferson was able to have the Mint put under the jurisdiction of the State Department in spite of Hamilton's protests that it was "a most material link in the money system of the Treasury." Most egregious of all, Hamilton was informed in the summer of 1792 that Jefferson and Madison had met with Robert Livingston and Aaron Burr in Albany to lay plans for his downfall.

Putting everything together, Hamilton concluded that Jefferson nursed an insatiable ambition to dominate the government and that he would not rest until he had installed himself in the Treasury. He himself had incurred the Virginian's hatred, Hamilton concluded, because he was "the steady, invariable, and decided friend of broad national principles of government" and because he stood in the way of Jefferson's overweening ambition. In order to encompass that ambition, he believed that Jefferson would not hesitate to pull down the whole edifice of government.[9]

In this frame of mind, Hamilton had no difficulty in persuading himself that it was his public duty "to confound and put down a man who is continually machinating against the public happiness"—a description that he thought sufficiently identified Thomas Jefferson. Early in August, 1792, writing in the *Gazette of the United States* under the signature "An American," Hamilton returned to the charge against Jefferson—but this time without the equivocation of queries and insinuations. He now flatly asserted that the Secretary of State had put Freneau on the public payroll in order to vilify the Secretary of the Treasury and that government money was being used to underwrite a subversive newspaper. Only one merit was he willing to concede Jefferson—in his choice of a character assassin he had shown rare discernment when he picked Philip Freneau.[10]

While Hamilton gave vent to his anger in the newspapers, Jefferson remained silent, leaving it to Freneau and his other friends to answer the Secretary of the Treasury. Such treatment merely exasperated Hamilton the more: his tone became progressively more shrill and his allegations more extravagant as the dispute went on. Chief Justice John Jay, a cooler head than Hamilton, advised him to justify his reputation by writing his memoirs—preferably to be published posthumously. But Hamilton replied that he could not wait for posterity to do him justice—the national government was in danger of being destroyed, in which event it would matter very little what posterity thought about him.

Hamilton might have strengthened his case had he taken posterity into greater account. Because he made little pretense of consulting accuracy or truth, his tactics encouraged other journalists and politicians to enter the fight with the same weapons, and in the resulting free-for-all some hard—and low—blows were exchanged. Edmund Randolph, the Attorney General, a Virginian and admirer of Thomas Jefferson, writing under the sobriquet of "Aristides," struck at Hamilton in the *National Gazette*. Hamilton answered under the signatures of "Catullus" and "Scourge"; but it is doubtful whether he gave or received the deepest cuts.[11]

Thus the two secretaries began the exhilarating but dangerous sport of hunting each other down with journalistic bloodhounds.

As Hamilton admitted, it was not easy to bring Jefferson to bay: armored as he was in rectitude and republican virtue, he appeared to his countrymen as a "quiet, modest, retiring philosopher; as the simple, unambitious republican"—a wise and good man to whom politics was an unwelcome interlude in his philosophical and scientific pursuits. How, then, Hamilton asked himself, could the toga be ripped off this fraudulent Old Roman in order to reveal him for what he was: a revolutionary, "a man of profound ambition and violent passions," "the most intriguing man in the United States," "the intriguing incendiary, the aspiring turbulent competitor," "the heart and soul of faction"? To prove that Jefferson was all these things, Hamilton reverted to the slam-bang style of "Caesar." He pictured Jefferson and Freneau meeting in some "snug sanctuary" where the former, "seated on his pivot-chair, and involved in all the obscurity of political mystery and deception . . . compounds and, with the aid of his active tools, circulates his poison thro' the medium of the National Gazette." Possibly from whirling too much in the famous pivot chair he had invented, Jefferson appeared to Hamilton to be a badly mixed-up philosopher. His mind was "prone to projects which are incompatible with the principles of stable and systematic government"; "in short," remarked Hamilton, "his opinion appears to have been as versatile as his chair, and as in schools, applications to the breach are said to have a wonderful effect on the head, by driving up learning, so there appears to be such a wonderful connexion between the seat and the head of this great politician, and the motions of the one have such a powerful effect on the operations of the other."[12]

As "proof" of Jefferson's turpitude, Hamilton dug up in the archives of the Continental Congress a letter written by Jefferson in 1787 dealing with the national debt. From this letter the Secretary of the Treasury lifted several sentences which seemed to indicate that Jefferson was willing to defraud Dutch investors in order to make things easier for the French government. One sentence, in particular, appeared to damn Jefferson: "If there be a design that our payments may not be punctual," he had written, "it may be better that the discontents which would then arise, should be transferred from a country [France] of whose goodwill we have so much need, to a private company." Since it was then doubtful, to say the least, if the United States could ever pay this debt, Jefferson seemed to be trying to unload on innocent Dutch capitalists the well-nigh worthless securities of the United States—presumably on the ground that this was proper treatment for speculators. Such "treachery," exclaimed Hamilton, would have indelibly stained American honor and ruined the credit of the government with European capitalists; but this was of small concern to an "intellectual voluptuary" who loved France more than his own country.

This letter struck more alarm among Jefferson's friends than did any of Hamilton's other charges. It placed Jefferson in the invidious light of advocating robbing the Dutch to pay the French; it created the impression that he had been overruled by more honorable men; and it was based upon official documents.

But, as a comparison with the original document quickly revealed, Hamilton had quoted Jefferson out of context and had deliberately garbled his meaning. Omitted altogether from Hamilton's version was the sentence in which Jefferson had expressed his wish that "the honor and credit of the United States may be preserved inviolate, that the French debt may be discharged without discount or loss to that Nation, and the stipulations of the United States be complied with, to all its creditors." Moreover—although Hamilton did not mention it—this proposed transfer of the French debt to Dutch bankers was approved by John Adams, the then Minister to Great Britian, as well as by Jefferson. It was intended as an accommodation to France, at that time sorely in need of money. The plan was rejected by the Treasury Board on the ground that it was better for the United States to have as a creditor the Bourbon monarchy than Dutch speculators who were certain to dun the government unmercifully.[13]

With the Cabinet a scene of contention between the heads of the departments, Hamilton saw his hopes of strong Executive leadership go glimmering. The quarrels of the Cabinet officers, he foresaw, would disunite the country: each would have his following in Congress and his own newspapers with which to marshal public support for his policies and to flay his adversaries in the administration. From such dissension among the leaders of the government, Hamilton feared the prostration of the Executive Branch at the feet of Congress and the vassalage of the federal government to the sovereign states.

Tormented by such dismal apparitions, Hamilton resolved to drive Jefferson from the Cabinet. To that end, he presented to President Washington a bill of complaints against the Secretary of State, alleging, among other things, that Jefferson was a venomous enemy of the funding system; that he had treated the Secretary of the Treasury with gross discourtesy; that he had frequently predicted that the people would not long endure Hamilton's corrupt practices; and that he had sown "the seeds of discord in the executive branch of the government, in the infancy of its existence." All this added up to a picture of Jefferson as an enemy of administration policies, working within the administration itself to defeat the enforcement of measures approved by Congress and the President. While admitting the right of a member of the Cabinet to disagree officially with his colleagues, Hamilton contended that "out of an official line he ought not to interfere *as long as he thinks* fit to continue a part of *the administration.*" After a measure became law it was his duty to acquiesce, especially if the law received the approval of the President. Hamilton rightly observed that this course of action was incumbent upon members of the Cabinet because they were not independent of the Chief Executive: as his appointees they were obliged to submit to his decisions or to resign their offices.

It was this latter course that Hamilton strongly recommended that Jefferson take. It offered the Secretary of State an opportunity to display the republican virtue he was fond of talking about: he could announce that he was unable to continue in office without doing violence to his conscience and that he had quitted it to be at liberty to serve the people's interests. Then, Hamilton sarcastically remarked, Jefferson would be free to set up as many newspapers as he pleased in order to vilify the men at the head of the federal government.

In this dispute Hamilton was careful to point out that the issue was not freedom of the press but the freedom of a member of the Cabinet to use public funds to set up a newspaper to attack the measures agreed upon by the Cabinet, the Congress and the President. Hamilton never denied Freneau's right to criticize the administration, but he did deny Jefferson's right to put a journalist unfriendly to the administration on the public payroll. Had the *National Gazette* supported the government, Hamilton presumably would have raised no objections to the arrangements entered into by Jefferson and Freneau. A close connection existed between Hamilton and Fenno, the editor of the *Gazette of the United States;* but Hamilton always insisted that there was a world of difference between his support of a newspaper dedicated to promote administration policies and Jefferson's patronage of a newspaper that conducted a smear campaign against one of the highest officers of the government.[14]

Hamilton's insistence upon the necessity of party uniformity in the policy-making branch of the government was not shared by Republicans— that is, not until they came into power. Did Hamilton mean to say, indignantly asked Jefferson's friends, that all members of the Cabinet must subordinate their judgment to the will of the majority, thus sacrificing "in the spirit of the corps, the native rights of a freeman?" Such a doctrine, they warned, would make the Cabinet a secret divan "into whose measures the profane eye of the publick should in no instance pry." By standing upon his right to object publicly to the measures of the government while remaining within the administration, Jefferson demonstrated to his admirers that he was a firm and virtuous patriot. For had he kept silent, it was said, Hamilton, "with his royal and sycophantic band of the Treasury at his heels," would have led the country into monarchism.

Although Hamilton professed his willingness to consider a joint resignation, this was to him strictly a last resort. He was not a man to quit under fire—and the *National Gazette* was really pouring it on. Accordingly, he redoubled his efforts to turn President Washington against the Secretary of State. Thus it went: Hamilton complained of Jefferson to the President; Jefferson complained of Hamilton. Both men put themselves in the undignified position of running to the President with tales against each other. It was a case of tittle and tattle; had the President believed everything he heard, he might well have concluded that he was nursing two vipers—one a British monarchist and the other a French democrat—in his official family.[15]

Jefferson's trump card against Hamilton was to warn the President that he himself was in danger of falling victim to the Secretary of the Treasury's "monarchical" ambition. Already, Jefferson exclaimed, his rival had attained so much influence that the Treasury threatened to swallow up the entire Executive Branch. Future Presidents, lacking Washington's popularity and strength of character, would not be able, Jefferson predicted, "to make head against that department."

Harrowing as was this prospect, Washington exhibited no signs of panic: instead of being moved to throw out this archintriguer, he defended Hamilton's conduct. Washington knew the man a great deal more intimately than did Jefferson and, moreover, he had heard Hamilton's allegedly "monarchical" speech in the Constitutional Convention. From a relationship extending over fifteen years, he was aware that his former aide-de-camp spoke his mind honestly—even when it injured him most. Therefore, when Hamilton pledged his best efforts to make the republican government of the United

States a success, Washington knew that he was as good as his word. Secure in the knowledge of Hamilton's loyalty, he told Jefferson that he did not think that there were ten men of any consequence in the United States who seriously contemplated the establishment of a monarchy: only a madman, he declared, could entertain such a thought—and he had observed no signs of insanity in the Secretary of the Treasury.[16]

Nor would the President agree that Hamilton's financial measures had been injurious to the country. It was not true, he said, that the assumption of state debts had increased the debt, "for . . . all of it was honest debt." Whether or not history would vindicate the work of the Secretary of Treasury, he could not say, but he was of the opinion that it was too soon to pass judgment upon Hamilton's labor. For his part, he was inclined to give Hamilton the benefit of every doubt: he himself "had seen our affairs desperate & our credit lost, and that this was in a sudden & extraordinary degree raised to the highest pitch." And, the President made clear, he regarded attacks upon the administration as attacks upon him; "he must be a fool indeed," he told Jefferson, "to swallow a little sugar plumb here & there thrown out to him."[17]

From this interview, Jefferson carried away the unhappy conviction that the President would not throw Hamilton to the lions; if it came to fighting lions, indeed, the Chief Executive seemed disposed to descend into the arena himself and do battle alongside the Secretary of the Treasury. It was only too apparent to Jefferson that Washington identified himself with the measures of his administration, including those conceived by Hamilton. Jefferson could only deplore such shortsightedness on the part of the President: it seemed to him to be the tragic story of a great and good man, sinking into dotage and imposed upon by an unscrupulous adventurer.

Nevertheless, upon both Hamilton and Jefferson, the President's pleas for harmony had a sobering effect. Hamilton admitted that there was a reciprocal duty on the part of Cabinet officers to cultivate good understanding, and that unless the quarrel between himself and Jefferson were settled it would "destroy the energy of government, which will be little enough with the strictest union." While Hamilton was too deeply engaged emotionally to take a wholly objective point of view, on at least one occasion he revealed that he was capable of detaching himself from the quarrel. "One side," he remarked, "appears to believe that there is a serious plot to overturn the general government, and elevate the separate power of the States upon its ruins. Both sides may be equally wrong. . . ." In the same spirit, Jefferson remarked that reason was too fallible to make differences of opinion the decisive line between the honest and the dishonest part of the community: "Integrity of views," he said, "more than their soundness, is the basis of esteem."[18]

And so Hamilton and Jefferson continued to work together in the

Cabinet. It was a triumph of self-restraint on the part of both men, for each regarded himself as the injured party. For Hamilton, in particular, it was difficult to sit across the table from the man he regarded as his inveterate enemy, the instigator of the attacks made upon him in Congress and the patron of his traducers in the newspapers. An open and avowed enemy he could perhaps respect, but Jefferson seemed to delight in accomplishing his ends by stealth and stratagem. Jefferson, on the other hand, looking into the cold blue eyes of the man sitting opposite him, believed that he was in the presence of a deadly schemer against republicanism who ruled by corruption and who would not rest until he had planted the feet of speculators and stockjobbers upon the neck of the American farmer.[19]

Hamilton's situation was rendered the more intolerable by the fact that the attacks in the *National Gazette* showed no signs of abating. His fulminations against Jefferson seemed to have raised up a host of newspaper writers whose particular delight was to execrate the Secretary of the Treasury. He found himself arraigned before the newspaper-reading public as a man of "selfish, narrow, and vain-aspiring heart" who could not be at rest as long as a spark of republicanism remained in the country and as an enemy of virtue who persecuted Jefferson simply because he was an honest man.

Had Hamilton been asked what had been gained by this attack upon Jefferson, he might have answered that the Secretary of State now stood unmasked as the leader of a "faction" bent upon subverting the government. This bookish Virginian who tried to pass himself off as everyone's friend could no longer be regarded, Hamilton imagined, as anything but a consummate hypocrite. Yet it is clear that where his political enemies were concerned, Hamilton too often acted as passion, rather than as reason, dictated. He was too apt to believe that he could overwhelm his enemies with a rhetorical onslaught, forgetting in his anger that it was at least as easy to write himself out of reputation as it was to destroy the good name of his adversary.

In this instance, the venture could be accounted a success only if it had been Hamilton's objective to increase Jefferson's stature among Republicans. Thanks to the publicity he received from Hamilton, he now stood forth as the leading figure of the opposition; henceforth, even James Madison was cast into the shade. And whatever the merits of the controversy between Hamilton and Jefferson, it signally failed to injure Jefferson in the opinion of the voters of the country. The congressional elections of 1792 went against the Hamiltonians: even Fisher Ames, one of Hamilton's chief spokesmen in Congress, was hard pressed in Massachusetts by his Republican rival.[20]

Hamilton could ill afford to see the Republicans increase their strength in Congress: as a result of the defections from federalism, his position was steadily becoming more insecure. The southern wing of the Federalist party was crumbling. The cry that the American farm was in danger tended to unite the farmers and planters of the South in a militant agricultural bloc. By 1793, a Hamiltonian had become a distinctly rare bird in the South outside the Federalist sanctuary in South Carolina, where the merchants and planters continued to feel the happy effects of the assumption of state debts. In Virginia, Federalism was almost wholly confined to the towns of Alexandria and Richmond; and among the leaders of the Virginia bar only Charles Lee, John Marshall and Bushrod Washington supported Hamilton's policies. Those who remained loyal to Hamilton paid the price of social ostracism: south of Mason and Dixon's line, good society was as predominantly Republican as it was predominantly Federalist in the commercial cities of the North. The political consequences in the South of associating with the Secretary of the Treasury were calamitous: John Steele, a North Carolina congressman, was accused of having sold out to the Federalists—and the evidence cited against him was that he had breakfasted with Alexander Hamilton![21]

The proscription of his friends and the moribund state of the Federalist party in the South dismayed Hamilton: he dreaded sectionalism as the bane of the American union; certainly it had never been his intention to give the Federalist party a sectional bias. Moreover, the Virginia and Carolina Federalist were vital to the increasingly precarious Federalist majority in Congress, where enemies to the policies of the Secretary of the Treasury were multiplying alarmingly.[22]

Virginia was not the only state in which Hamilton raised up enemies: largely as a result of his miscalculations, the New York Federalists were divided into hostile factions. Throughout his career, Hamilton demonstrated that he could destroy as well as create—and sometimes it was his own creations that he smashed. By inadvertently alienating powerful groups in New York and Virginia, he prepared the way for a political alliance between these two states that ultimately enabled his enemies to humble him and his party.

Governor Clinton of New York had survived the conservative resurgence that had accompanied the ratification of the Federal Constitution; although the "old sinner" sat a little less securely in the governor's chair, he continued to sin with impunity against the canons of federalism. Nevertheless, the governor's days of power seemed numbered: against him was aligned the whole weight of the Federalist party—which in New York meant the Schuyler and Livingston families and their followers and dependents together with the more prosperous farmers and artisans. Federalism followed trade: the strongholds of the party were New York City, Albany, Lansingburgh and Hudson, the principal commercial centers of the state. While the New York Federalists were led by lawyers, landed patricians and merchants, a large part of its voting strength was derived from the more prosperous farmers living near the cities and from the tradesmen, shopkeepers and artisans of the towns—the men who had hauled the good ship *Alexander Hamilton* through the streets of New York in celebration of the adoption of the Constitution. If Hamilton could hold this coalition together, he might look forward with confidence to the day when the "Great Demogogue" would no longer make life miserable for the good, the wise and the rich.[23]

It was primarily against this alliance of two powerful aristocratic factions that Governor Clinton exhorted the small farmers and tenants of the state to unite. Since "all the great & opulent families were united in one Confederacy," he declared that "his politicks were to keep a constant eye to the measures of their Combination."[24]

Divide and rule was the maxim by which Clinton lived. But not until Alexander Hamilton came to the governor's aid did he meet with any success in dividing the Livingstons and the Schuylers.

In the elections of 1789, Hamilton gave to the New York Federalists the slogan "UNANIMITY AND EXERTION." He was particularly concerned to impress upon the party the necessity of unanimity because, as he said, "we have experienced the happy effects of union among ourselves, and we cannot be too watchful against every thing that may lead to disunion." The Federalists took Hamilton's advice to such good purpose that they gained control of both the state Assembly and the Senate. Having thus laid down the precept that in union there is strength and having it triumphantly vindicated in the election, Hamilton proceeded to violate his maxim and to destroy the unanimity he had been so assiduous in fostering.[25]

Being in command of both branches of the legislature, the New York Federalists were in a position to dictate the choice of United States senators. Since the victory had been won through the joint efforts of the Livingston and Schuyler factions, it was generally supposed that one United States senatorship would go to each of the two families that composed the winning coalition. Indeed, before the election, it had been agreed that such a division of the spoils would take place: the Livingstons would send James Duane to the Senate, while the Schuyler family would be represented by its titular head, General Philip Schuyler himself.[26]

With the victory won, Hamilton gave short shrift to the promises of politicians. Rather than elect James Duane to the United States Senate, Hamilton urged his father-in-law to support the candidacy of Rufus King for the seat. Although by breaking his agreement with the Livingston family General Schuyler jeopardized his own chances of attaining the Senate, he permitted himself to be persuaded by his son-in-law to endorse King rather than Duane. The result seemed to vindicate Hamilton's theory that he could lay down the law to the New York Federalists: both Schuyler and King were elected to the United States Senate. The Livingstons were left out in the cold, Duane insisting to the end upon his "right" to the office of which he had been "defrauded."[27]

It was soon made plain even to Hamilton that in this instance his "bold, imperious temper" had played him false. Only upon the score of ability did Rufus King have a claim to the senatorship. Several years before, Hamilton claimed to have "revolutionized" King's mind, thereby making King a lifelong Hamiltonian. But King had no personal following, no great wealth, no important family connections. Among the New York Federalists, to whom family was hardly less important in politics than in society, he was definitely an interloper. Nor did it help matters that he was a New Englander by birth, a Harvard graduate and a Congregationalist. But at least it could be said of King that he was a Yankee who had seen the light: he had left Boston and settled in New York to practice law.

In preferring ability to availability, Hamilton committed one of the major blunders of his career. The Livingstons, discovering that all the political plums were to go to the Schuyler faction, saw nothing to be gained from continuing the alliance. But instead of merely splitting off from the Schuyler wing of the Federalist party and playing a lone hand—probably the worst that Hamilton anticipated—the Livingstons joined forces with Governor Clinton against the Schuylers. It was more than Clinton had dared hope for—not merely were the aristocrats divided; a considerable body of them now stood shoulder to shoulder with him against the "faction" all good democrats held in abhorrence.* [28]

By achieving this new alignment of parties, Hamilton revealed how little he comprehended the rudiments of the art of holding together a political party based upon an alliance of several factions. He later repeated this process upon a national scale; indeed, the events in New York were a foreshadowing of the later disruption of the Federalist party—an event for which Hamilton bore a large measure of responsibility.

With the Livingstons on his side, Clinton seemed to be beyond Hamilton's reach; for if the governor could not be dislodged by the combined force of the Livingston-Schuyler axis, what chance was there that the Schuylers alone could pull him from his perch? And the case seemed more hopeless still when Aaron Burr, always sedulous to put himself on the winning side, joined forces with Governor Clinton.

Aaron Burr began life with several advantages denied Hamilton: a family tree with no embarrassing gaps—he was descended from a long line of ministers and college presidents—and an unassailable social position. Even more precocious than Hamilton, he applied for admission to Princeton at

* Chancellor Livingston was also angered by his failure to receive the post of Chief Justice of the United States Supreme Court. John Jay, a close friend and collaborator of Hamilton's, was appointed to the Chief Justiceship. To placate the Livingstons, Duane was later appointed, at Hamilton's instigation, a federal judge. But, having lost first prize, the Livingstons were not appeased by this gesture.

the age of eleven. But the college authorities deemed him too young for matriculation, with the result that he did not enter Princeton until he was thirteen. In recognition of his intellectual brilliance, however, he was permitted to skip his freshman year.

In 1775, with an Indian girl to keep him company, Burr marched with Benedict Arnold to Quebec, where, as a reward for gallantry in action, he was awarded his majority. But Burr was not satisfied with this rank. In 1777 he was complaining of his failure to win promotion: he was twenty-one years old and only a major! Even though he was commissioned a lieutenant colonel in 1777, he, like Hamilton, attributed his failure to secure an active command to Washington's obstructionism. From thence he advanced naturally to the proposition that Washington, besides being "an ill-made, nap-kneed man," was a bad general. After the battle of Monmouth, Burr supported General Charles Lee against the Commander in Chief. Twenty years later Washington had neither forgotten nor forgiven this affront.

Extremely attractive to women—he was involved in several amorous escapades in the army that hampered his advancement—when it came to marriage Burr conspicuously failed to make the most of his opportunities. Instead of following Hamilton's example of marrying into wealth and social position, Burr unaccountably fell in love with a physically unattractive woman ten years his senior, the mother of five children and the wife of a British officer. She brought him nothing in the way of a dowry or social prestige, but she did present him with a daughter, Theodosia, upon whom Burr lavished a care and attention that fell to the lot of few girls in the eighteenth century. It was Burr's consuming ambition to make Theodosia the most accomplished woman of her day.

Burr began practice as a lawyer in New York at the same time that Hamilton hung up his shingle. In 1782, however, lawyers were so swamped with business that competition between Hamilton and Burr for briefs was kept at a minimum, despite the fact that each aspired to make his reputation as a coming man in the legal profession. In Burr's case, the necessity was particularly imperative because his style of living was almost princely.

Outside the courtroom—and even here they often served as cocounsel—Hamilton and Burr were on friendly, if not intimate, terms. Hamilton described Burr as a man of honor, influence and ability; and Burr repaid the compliment by giving Hamilton timely notice of the fact that the house he occupied was for sale and could be bought at a bargain price.[29] There was as yet no political rivalry between them: what little part Burr took in the political struggles of the day was often of an equivocal nature. While he worked to emancipate the slaves, he was considered to be hostile to the Loyalists; as regards the Constitution, he was as nearly neutral as it was possible to be.

As long as Hamilton and Burr confined their rivalry to the courtroom, their relations remained amicable. It was not until after the adoption of the Constitution, when Burr began to play an active part in politics, that definite signs of strain appeared. Then, as Burr later said, the world proved to be too small to hold both him and Hamilton.

Superficially, Hamilton and Burr appeared to have many points of similarity. Both were small, well-poised, striking men, possessed of an indefinable magnetism that made them the center of attraction in every company. For sheer gentility of manners, Burr outshone even Hamilton: visiting French and British aristocrats were impressed by his bland, conciliatory and urbane address, spiced with wit and erudition. For handing a lady into a carriage, bowing out a visitor and presiding over a dinner table, Burr had no peer in the United States.

But the resemblance was only skin deep: as personalities, Hamilton and Burr were poles apart. Whereas Hamilton was open, straightforward and impetuous, Burr was subtle, evasive and cautious. Hamilton was a man of principle who acted, sometimes to his detriment, upon ideas strongly held; Burr, on the other hand, made expediency his guide, played fast and loose with all parties and never permitted ideological considerations to stand in the way of his political advancement. While Hamilton directed his energy toward the creation of a great nation, Burr sought political office for the prestige and wealth it would bring him. Zeal he held to be beneath the dignity of a gentleman: coolness, circumspection and an eye to the main chance were the qualities he valued and practiced. Yet there was one cause that Burr served unstintingly—the furtherance of his ambition. In that cause he even permitted himself a little ungentlemanly fervor.

Certainly one political party was too small to contain two such vaulting ambitions. In 1789, Burr supported Hamilton's efforts to elect Yates governor of New York and he served as a member of the federal committee of which Hamilton was chairman. It was soon borne in upon Burr, however, that in the Federalist party he could never hope to be more than the second man, and he was never disposed to play the satrap to Alexander. Probably for that reason he used Yates's defeat as a pretext to abandon the Federalist party; in 1789 he accepted from Governor Clinton an appointment as attorney general.

Despite the fact that he condescended to receive political office from the hands of Governor Clinton, Burr never let it be supposed that his political allegiance had been knocked down at a bargain price. His ambition transcended any office at Clinton's disposal, and he made perfectly clear to all concerned that his services were for sale to the highest bidder. He declared himself to be neither Federalist nor Clintonian—he was, indeed, throughout his career, a Burrite—and settled back to watch, not without disdain, the politicians scramble for his favor.

Hamilton made no effort to win Burr back to the Federalist party by holding out the promise of a substantial ration of loaves and fishes; despite his strong convictions regarding the importance of self-interest, he seemed inclined to act upon the principle that the honor of serving a worthy cause ought to suffice for Colonel Burr. But Burr left no doubt that he was in politics for what it would bring in the form of personal advancement. He continued, therefore, to lean to the Clintonians, and in 1791 his patience was rewarded by the offer of a seat in the United States Senate.

The price tag attached to this political prize might have given pause to a less ambitious man. For no one could fail to see that by accepting a seat in the Senate, Burr was certain to incur the enmity of Alexander Hamilton. Nevertheless, Burr took the prize—and paid the price.

In 1791, General Schuyler came up for re-election as United States senator. Having been "cheated" of the Senate seat they had been promised, the Livingstons were in no mood to return their betrayer to office; accordingly they and their new allies, the Clintonians, put up Burr against Schuyler. The result was a humiliating defeat for the Hamilton-Schuyler forces: the general was returned to private life and Burr went to the Senate.

It was never Burr's practice to burn his bridges behind him; when he crossed the Rubicon he was careful to leave open a line of retreat. In 1792, he let it be known that he was prepared to run against Clinton for the governorship of New York, and he dropped hints to the effect that if the Federalists gave him their support he would declare himself to be one of them. To smooth the way for his re-entry into the Federalist party, he asserted that he approved of Hamilton's policies, and that he felt "a real personal Friendship" for the Secretary of the Treasury and that any reports to the contrary were the work of "meddling interveners." Obviously, Burr expected Hamilton to swallow his resentment and take him on his own terms—for did not the Secretary live for the day when he could drive Clinton from the governorship?

Some New York Federalists, in their eagerness to be rid of Clinton, were prepared to roll out the carpet for Burr and welcome the prodigal into the party in style. But Hamilton would have none of Burr; not for the last time, he slammed the door to party headquarters in the colonel's face.[30]

Only Burr's withdrawal as a candidate for the governorship spared him from an open attack by Hamilton. In renouncing the governorship, however, Burr made clear that he aspired to an even higher prize—the vice-presidency of the United States. From Hamilton's point of view, Burr promised to be even more dangerous as Vice-President than as governor of New York. "Nothing which has hitherto happened so decisively proves the inveteracy of the opposition," he wrote in alarm to Washington. "Should they succeed much would be apprehended."[31] To Burr he would concede no virtues, private or public. Thoroughly unprincipled and corrupt, he was, said Hamilton, "for or against nothing, but as it suits his interest or ambition." He had no principles other than "to mount, at all events, to the full honors of the State," and Hamilton greatly feared that unless Burr were opposed at every step he would ultimately arrive at supreme power. For Burr seemingly had all the qualifications of the successful demogogue: "Embarrassed . . . in his circumstances, with an extravagant family, bold, enterprising and intriguing," willing to play the game of confusion by setting class against class, there seemed to be nothing to which Burr would not stoop—even to putting himself at the head of the so-called "popular party"—in pursuit of his ambition. "In a word," Hamilton concluded, "if we have an embryo Caesar in the United States, it is Burr."[32]

Obviously, Hamilton distrusted Burr as a political turncoat, an opportunist, and as a rival for the leadership of the Federalist party. For Hamilton had already come to look upon Burr as a serious contender for the top place in the party of the good, the wise and the rich. Yet there was more in this than the dislike a politician naturally feels toward a rival. Hamilton removed the controversy to another plane altogether: "I feel it to be a religious duty to oppose his [Burr's] career," he said, and his opposition always partook of the nature of a crusade. In Hamilton's eyes, Burr was evil incarnate: in this elegant little gentleman who looked more like a *grand seigneur* than an American politician were mirrored all the depravity of human nature which had been revealed to Hamilton during the great hurricane of 1772.[33]

Gone—or at least hurriedly swept under the rug—were Hamilton's objections to John Adams. In the election of 1788 he had swung votes away from the New Englander; but with Burr in hot pursuit of the second office, Hamilton went out of his way to praise the New Englander's honesty, firmness, patriotism and independence—"a real friend to genuine liberty, order and stable government." In short, a thoroughgoing Hamiltonian!

Hamilton's alarm proved premature: the Republicans were not yet ready to exalt Burr to the second highest office in the government, nor did Burr himself seriously expect to receive the prize. In the Electoral College, he received only one vote.

If it were vital to Hamilton to keep Burr out of the vice-presidency in 1792, it was even more imperative to keep Washington in the presidency. Here the Secretary was obliged to contend with the President's eagerness to return to his beloved Mount Vernon. When he accepted the presidency in 1789, Washington declared that he intended to remain in office "no longer than when he saw matters fairly set going." By 1792, these conditions seemed to have been fulfilled and Washington was prepared to lay down his burden. He was not made for the storms and stresses of political life, he protested; and riding the whirlwind with Alexander Hamilton was utterly out of the President's element. "His inclination," he said, "would lead him rather to go to his farm, take his spade in his hand, and work for his bread, than remain in his present situation."[34]

But Washington found that he could not strike off the fetters against

Hamilton's determination to rivet them for at least another four years. As was his settled habit when he wished to persuade Washington to adopt a certain course of action, Hamilton directed his appeal to the President's patriotism and sense of duty. Let Washington have no illusions that his work was done, Hamilton exclaimed; the great task of creating a nation had just begun. "In fine," Hamilton concluded, "on public and personal accounts, on patriotic and prudential considerations, the clear path to be pursued by you will be, again to obey the voice of your country, which, it is not doubted, will be as earnest and as unanimous as ever." It seemed that the Father of His Country would never get this troublesome charge off his hands.[35]

PART IV
The Union Against Foreign Aggression

24.

The Proclamation of Neutrality

To an even greater degree than did Hamilton's plans for diversifying the economy of the United States and concentrating power in the federal government, the French Revolution divided Americans and sharpened the lines of demarcation between the rival political parties led by Hamilton and Jefferson. As Jefferson said, the French Revolution "kindled & brought forward the two parties with an ardour which our own interest merely, could never excite."

After 1792, foreign affairs could not be kept out of American politics, for upon the outcome of the struggle being waged upon the European continent Americans believed that their own destiny depended. But whether the course of events in Europe boded good or ill to the United States was a matter of heated debate: whereas some Americans beheld the dawn of a new republican era, others saw the rise of a terrible revolutionary "monster" which, in the name of "Liberty, Equality and Fraternity" threatened to swallow all independent nations that resisted its dominion.

Hamilton took control of the United States Treasury at almost the same time that the Parisian mob stormed the Bastille. These two events symbolized the divergent paths the two countries were entering upon: while the United States stood upon the threshold of a period of order and stability, France was embarking upon an era of revolution, war and dictatorship.

Shortly after the fall of the Bastille, Lafayette sent President Washington the key to the demolished fortress-prison—a gesture by which he intended to signify the solidarity of the French and American peoples in a common love of freedom. Hamilton was at first inclined to receive the gift in that spirit. He told Jefferson that his heart was wholly with the French in their struggle against tyranny and that he felt the same passionate stirrings that had impelled him in 1775 to take up arms against Great Britain. He hoped to see a gradual reform of abuses—order brought into the finances of the government, the economy rehabilitated and representative institutions, preferably upon the model of Great Britain's, introduced. Then, he exclaimed, the revolution might well terminate in the "establishment of free and good government." But Hamilton's emotional transports were of remarkably short duration: late in 1789 he told Lafayette that he observed the progress of events in France "with a mixture of pleasure and apprehension"—pleasure that the French were throwing off oppression, apprehension that they were seeking too much liberty for their own good. The people, he complained, had fallen under the sway of speculative philosophers, who, like all their kind, built castles in the air about the rights of man without paying the slightest heed to the nature of man. An attempt to establish a republic in a nation of twenty million people, nineteen and a half million of whom could neither read nor write, was in his opinion certain to produce a tyranny far worse than anything against which the French were rebelling—a totalitarian democracy which admitted of no restraints upon the power of the people and in which the state was deified into an all in all. Hamilton never ceased to believe that a people who were content with nothing less than absolute liberty would achieve absolute tyranny.

Americans had come relatively unscathed through the fires of revolution, but Hamilton had no hope that the French would have an equally happy deliverance. That there was any connection between the two revolutions he indignantly denied: they had neither a common parentage, a similar upbringing, nor a parallel destiny. One had turned out to be moral, law-abiding and peace-loving, whereas the other, even in its infancy, had a criminal record the compilation of which promised to occupy historians for generations. "Would to Heaven," he exclaimed, "we could discern in the mirror of French affairs the same humanity, the same decorum, the same gravity, the same order, the same dignity, the same solemnity, which distinguished the cause of the American Revolution." None of these were visible to his eyes; any resemblances between the two revolutions seemed to him to be purely coincidental.[1]

Much as Hamilton prided himself upon taking a historical view of events, he did not see the French Revolution for what it was—an effort on the part of the bourgeoisie to free itself from the vestigial remains of feudalism and to redress the balance of power in the state in its favor. He could not see the bourgeoisie for the sans-culottes: from beginning to end the upheaval seemed to be nothing more than a vast outpouring of the slums—"a volcano of atheism, depravity, and absurdity." He never wrote or spoke of the Revolution in France without registering the "horror," "abhorrence" and "revulsion" it excited in him.

Hamilton feared triumphant reaction in Europe much less than he did triumphant democracy: apparently the United States could live with kings and nobles in Europe but not with democrats of the French breed. While he did not imagine that the kings leagued against France would display moderation and magnanimity in victory, he was even less disposed to trust to the good will of the "monster born with teeth."

The Proclamation of Neutrality

As the French Revolution progressed, it became increasingly apparent to a large number of Americans that this was not the American Revolution with French subtitles. The execution of the royal family, the triumph of violence and irreligion and the spread of revolutionary doctrines by means of armed force left no doubt in the minds of conservatives that the established order was menaced everywhere. The fact that the government of France called itself a "republic" did not conceal its true nature from American conservatives; nor did they suppose that the French revolutionaries would balk at devouring the nation France had helped call into being in 1783.

Certainly it was true that no government could afford to overlook the effects of the French Revolution upon its citizens. The storm blowing out of France threatened to demolish all vested interests and established institutions: as Edmund Burke said, it was not merely kings and nobles "but our property, our wives, everything that was dear and sacred" that were endangered by the hurricane. Translated into action, the ideas of the French Revolution threatened to undo all the gains won by conservatives in the United States since 1788. For the French Revolution, at least in the early stages of its development, stood for decentralization of power, a unicameral legislature, a weak executive and universal suffrage. If these principles triumphed in the United States, nothing would be left of Hamiltonianism or, it was to be feared, of the Hamiltonians.[2]

Even though French armies could not easily traverse the Atlantic, French revolutionary principles made the passage without difficulty. Recognizing that ideas were the *avant-garde* of conquest and reposing little faith in the wisdom or self-restraint of the people, Hamilton assumed that those Americans who had been indoctrinated with "French philosophy" were ready to repeat in the United States all the excesses of French revolutionaries. A republic, he believed, was particularly vulnerable to imported revolutionary doctrines: weakened by factionalism and open to the inroads of foreign influence, it offered comparatively little resistance to subversive ideas. Moreover, the people of the United States already seemed infected by the virus of equality—the dreaded herald, according to Hamilton's diagnosis, of the "French disease."

Exposed to these contagions, Americans were advised by Hamilton to count their blessings and render thanks that they were three thousand miles away from "the never to be satiated lovers of innovation and change" in France. Like John Adams, Hamilton considered one revolution to be enough in a lifetime: Americans had no grievances which cried out for redress; they were prosperous beyond their most sanguine expectations; and they already enjoyed as much liberty as they could conveniently digest. Above all, he urged them to stand upon American ground. The "passion for a foreign mistress, as violent as it is irregular," had, he said, produced three parties in the United States—an English party, a French party and an American party, "if the latter can with propriety be called a party." There was no doubt in Hamilton's mind where an American's loyalties lay: the true patriot, he said, "will regard his country as a wife, to whom he is bound to be exclusively faithful and affectionate; and he will watch with a jealous attention every propensity of his heart to wander towards a foreign country, which he will regard as a mistress that may pervert his fidelity, and mar his happiness."[3]

The majority of Americans plainly did not agree with Hamilton either in his assessment of the significance of the French Revolution or in his conviction that the doctrine of "Liberty, Equality and Fraternity" had no place in the United States. John Marshall lamented "the passionate and almost idolatrous devotion of a great majority of the people for the French republic"—devotion which sometimes seemed to surpass the enthusiasm Americans had exhibited for their own revolution. The public pulse beat feverishly for France and even atrocities failed to alienate its devotees—they saw "the monster," said Hamilton, "in all its dreadful transformations, with complacency or toleration." With the dawn of "the glorious and blessed light of the French Revolution," Republicans contrasted the shadows that had begun to fall upon their own country. At the very time that liberty was triumphing in France, the United States seemed to be caught in the throes of a conservative reaction: while the French were "exterminating the monster aristocracy," Alexander Hamilton was erecting the Bank of the United States. The love of freedom, lamented Richard Henry Lee, had flown across the Atlantic and taken refuge in France: outdone by the Gallic cock, the American eagle must take the lower perch.[4]

The Republican leaders made loyalty to France the touchstone of American patriotism: "Those who do not rejoice at the glorious successes of our Gallic brethren," they said, "are no friends to American Liberty." A supporter of Great Britain was not merely the advocate of a mistaken foreign policy but an enemy of the rights of man who presumably wished to establish monarchism and aristocracy in the United States. Grieving over "the murdered Majesty of France" was held to be unworthy of republicans; instead, they ought to be rejoicing that the greatest malefactor of them all had met a deserved end. For if republicanism went down in France, it was feared that it would suffer the same fate in the United States; presumably this country was next on the list of the "bloody despots" arrayed against France. Deprived of its connection with France, the United States would become a "political orphan" at the mercy of that ogre, John Bull. With such a contingency in mind, Jefferson declared that rather than see absolutism restored in France, he would prefer to see half the earth depopulated.[5]

If the United States took the side of France in this war, Hamilton believed that it would be owing mainly to Thomas Jefferson. Almost from the beginning of their relationship in the Cabinet, Hamilton deplored Jeffer-

The Proclamation of Neutrality

son's "womanish attachment to France and a womanish resentment against Great Britain." He had supposed that romantic knight-errantry had been laughed off the stage with Don Quixote—yet here was Jefferson, his head spinning with the same sort of chivalric folly that had addled the brains of the Spanish don when he set spur to Rosinante. But the madness of the Spaniard appeared venial to Hamilton compared with that of Jefferson: Quixote had imagined inns to be castles, but Jefferson deluded himself into acclaiming "a furious despotism, trampling on every right, and sporting with life, as the essence of liberty."

As a sovereign cure for this kind of lunacy, Hamilton recommended a good bath in "Americanism." Had the Secretary of State been exposed to those purifying waters, Hamilton felt certain that he would have approved of the funding system, the Bank of the United States and the Report on Manufactures. But, having laved himself in French philosophy, Jefferson—or so it seemed to Hamilton—was engaged in blowing "fine spun theoretic systems" in the air and trying to counterwork the patriots who were occupied in establishing the national government upon a solid economic bedrock.

In the spring of 1790, Hamilton had even gone to the length of warning the British government against the Francophilism of the Secretary of State. At that time, with war threatening between Great Britain and Spain, Lord Dorchester, the governor of Canada, sent his aide-de-camp, Major Beckwith, to New York to arrange for the passage of British troops across American territory in order to attack Spanish Louisiana. Beckwith discovered that Hamilton was prepared to give the British everything they asked in exchange for assurances of support for American claims to the navigation of the Mississippi. Sensible of the fact that he was dealing with an imperious people not accustomed to take "no" for an answer, Hamilton feared that if the government refused to grant the British permission they would march anyway, damning the Yankees as they went. He therefore advised Washington that no objections be offered the British plan. He made clear, however, that if the government decided to refuse permission and the British marched in despite of this interdiction, he was prepared to go to war as the only way of preserving the honor and territorial integrity of the United States.

In these talks with Major Beckwith, Hamilton confessed that he was speaking only for himself, not for the United States government. But he told Beckwith that as far as the President was concerned, the British had nothing to fear—Washington was almost wholly liberated from anti-British prejudices—yet he regretted to say that the same could not be said of the Secretary of State. While he was careful not to impugn Jefferson's patriotism, Hamilton indicated that his colleague was suffering from an advanced case of Anglophobia accompanied, as might be expected, by an equally pernicious form of Francophilism. Hamilton tried to pass it off as a joke: the Secretary of State, he said, was so far gone in folly that he actually thought that the ferment in France would advance the cause of freedom and would prove to be of inestimable commercial advantage to the United States. Any man that believed such nonsense, he told Beckwith, was not a person to be taken into the confidence of a British Minister. To prevent the Secretary of State from defeating the purposes of men of good will on both sides of the Atlantic, Hamilton urged Beckwith to keep him informed of what went on in his conferences with Jefferson, especially if the State Department raised any objections to a closer Anglo-American understanding. "I should wish to know them," he said, "in order that I may be sure they are clearly understood and candidly examined." In effect, Hamilton was proposing to aid the representative of a foreign power in counteracting the policies of the Secretary of State.

Thus Hamilton helped to establish the conviction in the minds of British officials that Jefferson was their enemy and that the State Department ought to be by-passed when negotiations were undertaken with the United States. From Hamilton's report, Lord Dorchester concluded that Jefferson could not be confided in; and Lord Hawkesbury dismissed him as a mere "Party Man" unworthy of the attention of His Majesty's ministers.

The dispute between Great Britain and Spain was settled amicably in 1790, but there was no armistice in the struggle for power being waged by the Secretary of State and the Secretary of the Treasury. The outbreak of war in January, 1793, between France and Great Britain was the signal for the two men to resume their quarrel. The United States government was now compelled to state its position vis-à-vis the belligerents. While both Hamilton and Jefferson wished to see the United States remain neutral, they were sharply divided as to whether this neutrality ought to be slanted in favor of France or of Great Britain. Jefferson favored giving France the benefit of every doubt; Hamilton, on the other hand, advocated a policy which, while ostensibly more neutral than Jefferson's, would in effect have benefited Great Britain, the dominant sea power.

In this contest, the scale was weighted in favor of Jefferson. The United States was bound to France by a perpetual military alliance and a commercial treaty dating from 1778. By the terms of the alliance, the United States was obliged to aid France if she were attacked by affording protection to the French West Indies. In the commercial treaty, the United States had committed itself to permit French privateers to bring their prizes into American ports and, under certain conditions, to lay in supplies and equipment. Since none of the amenities were extended to the British, the United States was put at the outset in the position of favoring one belligerent over the other.

Lest the United States be forced into war as a result of its treaty commit-

The Proclamation of Neutrality 369

ments, Hamilton urged that the administration adopt a policy of nonrecognition toward the French Republic and declare the treaties suspended. No other government had extended recognition to the men who had presided over the execution of Louis XVI and Marie Antoinette, and Hamilton was unwilling that the United States should be the first to grasp the bloodstained hands.* As for the treaties, he would have preferred to declare them null and void, but, finding no warrant in the law of nations for such action, he fell back upon the policy of pronouncing them suspended until a stable government has been established in France. But here Jefferson vehemently disagreed: the French minister, he insisted, must be received and nothing must be done to impair the Franco-American treaties. Jefferson's counsel prevailed with President Washington: he declared that he would receive Citizen Edmond Genêt as the envoy of the French Republic and that the Franco-American treaties were binding upon both parties.

There was an equally sharp difference of opinion between the two Cabinet officers as to how the government should act to preserve American neutrality. Since Congress was not in session in April, 1793, the question before the Cabinet was whether the Executive was competent to issue a proclamation of neutrality. Hamilton urged the President to "proclaim the neutrality of the nation" forthwith; but Jefferson, taking a much narrower view of the powers of the President, held that such action was the special province of Congress and that therefore the legislature ought to be summoned into special session.

In this instance, the issue was decided in Hamilton's favor. At the Cabinet meeting held on April 19, 1793, President Washington determined to issue a proclamation of neutrality by which the United States would give assurance to foreign powers that it intended to pursue "a conduct friendly and impartial" toward the belligerents. The only concession made to Jefferson was that the word "neutrality" was omitted from the proclamation. Even so, he, too, supported the President's action.[6]

President Washington had made his proclamation—but could he enforce it? In view of the strong partiality felt by many Americans for France and the impatience with which they regarded the restraints imposed by the President upon their freedom of action, it could safely be predicted that Washington's action would encounter stiff resistance, especially since the Neutrality Proclamation was being denounced by the Republicans as an unconstitutional usurpation of power.[7]

This challenge to the constitutionality of the proclamation impelled Hamilton to write in defense of the President's action a series of newspaper

---
* In March, 1793, with President Washington's approval, Jefferson had instructed Gouverneur Morris to present his credentials to the government of the French Republic. Hamilton was apparently trying to reverse this action.

articles under the signature of "Pacificus." If, as Hamilton supposed, the American people needed to be instructed in their duties as well as their rights as a neutral, he was well qualified to serve as preceptor to the nation—no other American of his time was more thoroughly grounded in the rules of international law.

But as usual when Hamilton set himself up as guide and philosopher to the American people, there was considerable doubt whether they would listen to his words of wisdom. Certainly in this instance Hamilton's views ran counter to some cherished popular preconceptions. Most of his countrymen, for example, had supposed that the meaningful decisions in foreign policy would be made by Congress, the branch of the government invested by the Constitution with the warmaking power. They had also assumed that the treaty of alliance with France was an ironclad agreement which bound the United States irrevocably to that country. In the writings of "Pacificus," however, they learned that the President was in effective control of foreign policy and that the treaty with France was riddled with escape clauses.

Under the most disarming of pseudonyms, Hamilton laid down the principle that the Executive clause of the Constitution was a general grant of power which took precedence over the subsequent enumeration of the powers of the President. According to this interpretation, the enumeration simply specified the principal items implied in the larger grant of Executive power. Thus, in effect, the President enjoyed all Executive power not denied him by the Constitution; the provision of the Constitution which made the President the organ of communication with other governments was expanded into a creative control of foreign policy.

While "Pacificus" acknowledged that faith and justice between nations were essential to international comity, gratitude was something else again. He denied that all for love and the world well lost was a fundamental maxim in politics; did not the Republicans know, he asked, that all nations made self-interest their guiding principle and that "the predominant nature of good offices from one nation to another, is the interest or advantage of the nation which performs them"? As a prime example of how self-interest actuated nations, Hamilton cited the case of France in the War of American Independence. If any Americans supposed that the Bourbon monarchy had been impelled by a disinterested and generous ardor to aid a people struggling for liberty, "Pacificus" provided them with an eye opener to the realities of power politics. In joining the Americans, Hamilton asserted, France had been pursuing its national interests: its objectives were to cripple Great Britain and to aggrandize its own commerce by breaking up the British Empire.

"Pacificus" cried peace, but there was no peace on the domestic scene. His views of Executive control of foreign policy and his condemnation of France as an aggressor were far more calculated to agitate than to calm

The Proclamation of Neutrality

the troubled waters. Republicans insisted that such sentiments as gratitude and generosity ought to be taken into account in the determination of foreign policy, particularly, they said, since if the United States abandoned France, Americans were certain to find themselves "in a state as deplorable as galley slaves" with Great Britain again cracking the whip about their ears.

Above all, Jefferson was staggered by the interpretation placed by "Pacificus" upon the President's proclamation: the Virginian regretted that he had not examined it more closely before giving it his approval, but it is doubtful if even the most meticulous reading would have revealed to him what Hamilton discerned in that document. Jefferson's immediate concern was to have Hamilton answered by some Republican writer of higher caliber than the "mere bunglers & brawlers" who had hitherto entered the lists against him. "Nobody answers him," he wrote Madison in extreme agitation of spirit, "& his doctrines will therefore be taken for confessed. For God's sake, my dear Sir, take up your pen, select the most striking heresies and cut him to pieces in the face of the public."

Madison was under no illusion that making mincemeat of Hamilton was as simple as Jefferson made it appear: he knew only too well that Hamilton had carved up some very redoubtable adversaries and would enjoy nothing so much as adding Madison to his list of victims. Moreover, having some acquaintance with Hamilton's "prolixity and pertinacity," he expected the contest to be long and bitterly contested—an ordeal for which Madison declared himself altogether unprepared, his mind having been "perfectly alienated from such things."

Nevertheless, Madison agreed that the Republicans could not afford to let the argument go by default. Regarding the proclamation as "a most unfortunate error"—a violation of the Constitution and an injury to France—he believed that Hamilton was attempting to embroil the United States with France in order to achieve his ambition of an alliance with Great Britain and a "gradual approximation to her Form of Government." And so, under the conviction that he was defending republicanism itself, Madison took the pen name of "Helvidius" and essayed to answer Hamilton in the newspapers. He found himself on the familiar battlefield, contending with Hamilton over the interpretation of the Constitution. From Madison's reading of that document, it appeared that Congress rather than the Executive had been entrusted with the direction and control of American foreign policy. The only power that had been given solely to the President, he asserted, was that of receiving the representatives of foreign nations—but this was a purely ceremonial matter without significant effect upon the determination of policy. As for the interpretation Hamilton placed upon the Executive clause, it seemed to Madison to "strike at the vitals of the Constitution, as well as its honor and true interest."

Although Madison asserted that "Pacificus" made an impression only upon "the foreigners and degenerate citizens among us, who hate our republican government, and the French revolution," the Federalists prized these essays as a much-needed corrective to the pro-French bias of the American people. One of Hamilton's friends told him that the writings of "Pacificus" had brought "Irresistible Conviction to every discerning and Impartial Mind"—of which, it was acknowledged, there was a serious shortage in the United States. But at least it could be said that after "Pacificus" had finished his work, the Federalists did not lack arguments with which to defend the Proclamation of Neutrality both on the score of its constitutionality and its compatability with the terms of the Franco-American alliance.[8]

Upon the Treasury Department devolved most of the work of enforcing the Neutrality Proclamation. Hamilton's agents, by virtue of the fact that they were stationed in all the principal seaports, furnished the most effective means of making the authority of the federal government felt in every part of the country.* It was soon apparent that Hamilton would need the full-time services of all the officers under his jurisdiction to give force to the directives laid down by the President. For Edmond Genêt, the new French minister, was no respecter of American neutrality; indeed, he regarded the President's proclamation as a harmless little pleasantry designed to throw dust in the eyes of the British.

This fiery young revolutionist owed his rapid rise in the diplomatic service to his connections in the Queen's bedchamber (his sister was a lady in waiting) and to his habitual insubordination. Thanks to the Queen's influence, he had been appointed chargé d'affaires at St. Petersburg, where he distinguished himself by criticizing his chief, Count de Montmorin, head of the Foreign Ministry. With the overthrow of the French monarchy and the accession of the Girondists to power, Genêt was rewarded for his contumacy toward the old regime by the offer of several choice diplomatic assignments. "He chose America, as being *the best Harbor during the Storm*," reported Gouverneur Morris. But Genêt had the knack of manufacturing his own storms wherever he went; a few months after his arrival in the United States, he was again looking for a snug harbor.

In April, 1793, Hamilton viewed Genêt as a harbinger of war and revolution. Actually, however, Hamilton had gained a powerful ally for his policies. It was no easy task to destroy the good will the American people felt for France, but Genêt came close to achieving that improbable result.

From the moment of his arrival in the United States, Genêt was treated

---

* Hamilton wished to centralize in the Treasury control of the enforcement machinery. To that end, he suggested that customs officers report violations to the Collectors of the Revenue, who in turn would report to the Secretary of the Treasury. But the President decided that violations must be reported to the United States District Attorneys.

like a conquering hero: his journey to Philadelphia (he deliberately chose the overland route from Charleston, South Carolina, in order to put himself on public display) resembled a triumphal progress. So much adulation was heaped upon him that by the time he reached the capital his head was completely turned. More and more he began to behave like an apostle preaching a crusade against kings, priests and aristocrats—and among the last he included Federalists. Probably he was the only man in the country who believed that he could win a popularity contest against President Washington: "I live in the midst of continual parties," he exulted. "Old man Washington is jealous of my success, and of the enthusiasm with which the whole town flocks to my house."

From Washington and Hamilton, Genêt received a chilly reception, but the Secretary of State, by the warmth of his welcome, let Genêt know that he was not without a friend at court. Indeed, Jefferson took the French Minister into his confidence as trustingly as did Hamilton the British representatives. "It is impossible," Jefferson exclaimed, "for any thing to be more affectionate, more magnanimous, than the purport of his mission. . . . He offers everything & asks nothing." Not surprisingly, therefore, Genêt soon began to talk like a Jeffersonian Republican, declaring that he preferred the company of plain farmers and honest workmen to that of "distinguished personages, who speculate so patriotically on the public funds, in the lands and paper of the state." No doubt, Jefferson alerted the young Frenchman against Hamilton's predilection for British monarchy and his partiality toward speculators to such good purpose that Genêt was soon hinting darkly that the administration was under the influence of "British gold" and that an attempt would be made to restore George III.[9]

The Frenchman's suspicions were confirmed by Hamilton's refusal to permit him to get his hand into the United States Treasury. Pleading the extreme financial necessities of France, Genêt demanded an advance upon the installments that the United States government had pledged itself to pay France. Well aware that Genêt intended to use this money to finance an attack from United States territory upon Spanish Louisiana and Florida (he had already corrupted George Rogers Clark and organized on paper the Armée du Mississippi and the Armée des Florides), Hamilton refused to give him a dollar; whereupon Genêt swore that the Secretary of the Treasury was hand in glove with "the infernal system of the King of England, of the other kings his accomplices, to destroy by famine, the French Republicans and liberty." He carried his grievances to Jefferson, where he found a willing and credulous listener. When Genêt declared that Hamilton had given him to understand that "if he would put the contract into the hands of Mr. Hamilton's friends he could get money," Jefferson set it down in his book as evidence of the corruption that prevailed in the Treasury.

All this time, Genêt was outfitting privateers and selling British prizes in American ports. As a result, it became a question whether the United States could preserve even the fiction of a neutrality, and Hamilton shuddered to think what the British would make of these goings-on. He did not have long to wait for the British Minister to arrive with a glint in his eye he usually reserved for Thomas Jefferson. His Majesty's Government, Hammond informed Hamilton, demanded the return of British ships captured by French cruisers fitted out in American ports and the closing of these ports to French privateers.

As a result of this pressure, the government stopped the outfitting of French privateers, but Jefferson took the position that this action was not retroactive and that therefore the British ships captured by the French belonged to the captors. He even asserted that the ships commissioned by Genêt prior to July, 1793, were free to continue to operate from United States ports—a defiance of the British that Hamilton was certain would lead to war. Fortunately for the cause of Anglo-American harmony, the President sided generally with Hamilton in these disputes. He declared that restitution or compensation must be made the British and that the French privateers commissioned by Genêt could not return to American ports. In only one particular did he deviate from Hamilton's policy: he held that the French were free to sell prizes in American ports—a privilege that was denied the British.

But Genêt was not stopped by these rulings: he screamed that the government was bent upon "bringing the country back under the power of Great Britain" and that he alone could save the people from such "slavery." He soon indicated to what lengths he was prepared to carry his defiance of the government. Among the English ships captured by the French was the brigantine *Little Sarah*. With a keen eye for the potentialities of this smart, fast-sailing ship as a commerce raider, Genêt smuggled fourteen cannon aboard, manned it with a French and American crew, and formally commissioned it in the French service as the *Petit Démocrate*. By so doing, he blandly informed Jefferson, he was merely exercising authority given him by his government and expressly permitted by the Franco-American treaties.

Getting wind of what was going on aboard the *Petit Démocrate*, Governor Mifflin of Pennsylvania sent Alexander Dallas, the secretary of state, to Genêt for assurance that the ship would not put to sea until President Washington had been consulted. Although both Mifflin and Dallas were friendly toward Genêt and his government, the French Minister bluntly told Dallas that he would tolerate no interference in his activities. When Dallas requested a promise that the *Petit Démocrate* would remain at its moorings, Genêt answered with a hysterical outburst, the gist of which seemed to be that, rather than submit to the dictates of Washington, he would publish his correspondence with the administration and appeal to

The Proclamation of Neutrality

the American people over the head of the President. And, he ominously added, "he hoped no attempt to seize her would be made, for, as she belonged to the Republic, she must defend the honor of her Flag, and would certainly repel force by force."

When Genêt's conversation with Dallas was reported to Hamilton, he saw that this challenge to the authority of the federal government must be met forcefully or the United States would sink to the status of a French dependency. "Not to act with decision under such circumstances," Hamilton said, "will be to prostrate the government, to sacrifice the dignity and essential interests of the nation. . . . Nothing is so dangerous to a government as to be wanting either in self-confidence or self-respect."

If the *Petit Démocrate* were to be prevented from putting to sea, quick action on the part of the government was essential: the ship was almost ready to sail and Genêt had left no doubt that she would hoist anchor when she had been made seaworthy. Fortunately for the French Minister, the government was unable to act with celerity: while the heads of the departments were in Philadelphia, President Washington, in whose hands the final decision lay, was at Mount Vernon. This situation worked in Genêt's favor, but, even so, he would never have gotten the *Petit Démocrate* out of port had not Jefferson unwittingly come to his aid.

Without a single frigate at its disposal, the United States government was in no position to contest the passage of the *Petit Démocrate*. But the government was not entirely helpless: between the *Petit Démocrate* and freedom lay a small island called Mud Island. During the War of Independence, American gunners stationed on this island had denied passage to the British fleet and almost forced Sir William Howe to evacuate Philadelphia in 1777. Having once barred the way to British men of war, there was little doubt that Mud Island could hold back a single privateer. True, the cannon had long since been removed and the fortification fallen into decay, but it was a simple matter to place a few guns on the island and to give the *Petit Démocrate* a broadside if she attempted to drop down the river.

With this idea in mind, Hamilton advocated the erection of a battery on Mud Island. But Jefferson, although now persuaded of the necessity of preventing the equipping of French privateers in American ports, could not bring himself to sanction a measure which carried the threat of war between the United States and France. Under the conviction that the *Petit Démocrate* was a mere "feather" when weighed against the incalculable consequences to which an act of aggression would give rise, Jefferson voted against placing cannon on Mud Island.

With at least equal cause, Hamilton feared that if the *Petit Démocrate* were permitted to escape to sea and prey upon British shipping, His Majesty's Government would retaliate with a declaration of war. But this argument carried no weight with the Secretary of State. He had come to the conclusion that Hamilton's idea of neutrality was to scream in anguish at the touch of a feather wielded by France and to present his breech to the kicks of John Bull. In Jefferson's eyes, the Secretary of the Treasury seemed never so happy as when he was groveling at the feet of His Brittanic Majesty, repenting in sackcloth and ashes the independence of the United States. "Some propositions have come from him," Jefferson said, "which would astonish Mr. Pitt himself with their boldness"; apparently even the British Prime Minister took a higher view of American neutral rights than did the American Secretary of the Treasury!

While the Cabinet deliberated, Genêt acted. The *Petit Démocrate* slipped downstream past Mud Island, on which not a single cannon sprouted, anchored at Chester and put to sea a few days later. In the happy hunting grounds off the Delaware, the French privateer bagged one helpless British merchantman after another.[10]

Even Jefferson was compelled to admit that his spectacles had been badly fogged when he first saw Genêt as a pure and perfect patriot without reproach. The more he studied the ebullient young Frenchman, the stronger grew Jefferson's conviction that he was dealing with a madman bent upon dividing the people from their government and France from the United States: "If our citizens have not already been shedding each other's blood," he declared, "it is not owing to the moderation of Mr. Genêt, but to the forbearance of the government." In August, 1793, he told the British Minister that the administration regarded war with France as "neither improbable nor distant," and, he added, it would largely be the work of Genêt.

Nor did Jefferson overlook the fact that the Frenchman's highhanded diplomacy was reacting heavily against the Republicans; in agony of spirit, Jefferson cried out that the French minister would sink the Republican party if he were permitted to go on.

Beholding the Republicans making heavy weather in the tempest stirred up by Genêt, Hamilton tried to send the ship to the bottom for good. With this purpose in mind, he urged the President to order the publication of Genêt's correspondence with the government. Knowing full well that this action would "excite universal indignation" against France and the Republican party, Jefferson vehemently opposed Hamilton's plan. As was his custom in these controversies, Secretary of War Knox jumped—all three hundred pounds of him—"plump into all his [Hamilton's] opinions." But the President did not leap with the Secretary of War: although some of Genêt's correspondence was laid before Congress in December, 1793, the President also included, over Hamilton's objections, the record of British depredations upon American shipping.

In Genêt's apparent madness, Hamilton discerned a method: the French

The Proclamation of Neutrality

envoy had been instructed by his government to precipitate war between the United States and Great Britain. The Secretary of the Treasury was keenly aware of the fund of propaganda Genêt's conduct furnished the enemies of France if the actions of the Minister could be attributed to the policies of his government. But, as usual, the Secretary of State demurred: in his opinion, Genêt ought to be treated as an irresponsible and ungovernable zealot who had permitted his ardor to get the better of his judgment. Despite Hamilton's protests, the administration officially adopted the view that the French government was not accountable for Genêt's aberrations: in his message to Congress of December, 1793, the President declared that Genêt had evidenced "nothing of the friendly spirit of the nation which sent him."

Rebuffed in his efforts to induce the government to identify Genêt with his government, Hamilton published in the newspapers, beginning in July, 1793, a series of articles under the signature "No Jacobin." Here he set forth a full and damning account of Genêt's activities. As the Secretary of the Treasury pictured it, Genêt's purpose was "to drag us into the war, with the humiliation of being plunged into it without even being consulted, and without any volition of our own. . . . It is impossible," he continued, "for a conduct less friendly or less respectful than this to have been observed. . . . It is a novelty reserved for the present day, to display the height of arrogance on one side and the depth of humiliation on the other." The point Hamilton labored to drive home was that Genêt was at all times acting under orders from his superiors at home. In this irrepressible democrat, Hamilton invited Americans to behold the incarnation of revolutionary France, the wild-eyed radical who mistook liberty for license and who sought to uproot order and stability wherever he found them.

In the "No Jacobin" essays, Hamilton stated as a matter of report that Genêt had threatened to appeal to the people over the head of the President. Later, in August, 1793, in a private letter to Rufus King and John Jay, he described in detail the events leading up to Genêt's outburst. But when King and Jay published a denunciation of Genêt in the newspapers, Genêt denied that he had ever spoken of appealing to the people and threatened to sue those responsible for giving currency to this "fabrication."

Jefferson no longer objected to Genêt's recall—in fact, he thought that the preservation of peace depended upon it—but whereas Hamilton wished to demand Genêt's recall in peremptory terms, Jefferson insisted upon the observance of the diplomatic proprieties to the last. In August, 1793, the President decided to request Genêt's recall, but it occasioned Hamilton no little heartburning that Washington used the Secretary of State's draft when addressing the French government for this purpose.

By this time, the authorities in France were as eager to get their hands on Genêt as Hamilton was to be rid of him. Since Genêt had left France, the guillotine had been working overtime, a new revolutionary government had come into power, and Genêt had been proscribed as a dangerous reactionary by the Jacobin rulers of France. The unfortunate Minister found his diplomacy condemned on both sides of the Atlantic. In France, the Minister of Foreign Affairs declared that by attempting to exercise proconsular powers in the United States and by appealing to the people over the head of the government, Genêt had violated his instructions and was guilty of "criminal manoeuvres."

Often as Hamilton had in the past been given cause to complain that Genêt had lost his head, he had no desire to see the Frenchman lose it in earnest. And so, instead of handing the now thoroughly terrified Minister over to the emissaries of the French government, Hamilton recommended that he be given sanctuary in the United States. Genêt took full advantage of this invitation: he became a United States citizen and married the daughter of Governor Clinton. Hamilton hoped that the Frenchman would henceforth confine his talents for creating tumult and confusion to the governor's household, but here Genêt inconsiderately declined to oblige the Federalist leader. Seldom have the sobering effects of marriage been more remarkably exemplified: this stormy petrel, his wings clipped, became a harmless and completely domesticated lovebird.

25.
The War Clouds Gather

It had long been a question whether Hamilton or Jefferson would retire first from the Cabinet. Neither man had spared any effort to make public life as uncomfortable as possible for his rival. But in the autumn of 1793, the issue seemed about to be resolved in favor of the Secretary of State. Hamilton fell dangerously ill of yellow fever; where Jefferson, Madison and Freneau had failed, a mosquito almost succeeded in laying low the "Colossus of Monocrats."[1]

The summer of 1793 was unusually hot and humid in Philadelphia. Near the waterfront—particularly on Water Street, a narrow, filthy lane bordered by houses and high banks—the stagnant pools of water furnished a luxuriant breeding ground for mosquitoes. At the same time, hundreds of refugees were pouring into Philadelphia from San Domingo, where a slave uprising was running its bloody course. The refugee ships probably brought the yellow-fever virus to Philadelphia, and the mosquitoes took over from there.[2]

Yellow fever was nothing new in Hamilton's experience; he had seen enough of that disease in the West Indies to treat it with respect. He therefore moved his family to a house a few miles outside Philadelphia and he himself commuted to the city to attend to his official business. Nevertheless, early in September, shortly after he had incautiously entered a house where a victim of yellow fever was confined (the doctors had warned citizens against such contact), Hamilton and his wife began to exhibit symptoms of the disease.

Political resentments curdled even the milk of human kindness. Thomas Jefferson was not inclined to show Hamilton charity in his illness: he advised the Secretary of the Treasury to pull himself together and act like a man. According to Jefferson's diagnosis, Hamilton was suffering from nothing more serious than a bad case of funk: "He had been miserable several days before," the Virginian noted, "with a firm persuasion he should catch it"; and now he was in danger only of frightening himself to death. It was a marvel to Jefferson how this poor maligner had ever won a reputation for courage on the battlefield: "A man as timid as he is on the water, as timid on horseback, as timid in sickness."[3]

But even Jefferson was soon compelled to admit that the Secretary of the Treasury was suffering from something more serious than hypochondria. His condition rapidly grew worse: headache, languor and nausea ran their course, quickly followed by the high fever and the peculiar yellowness that gave the malady its name.[4]

Perhaps the air of distraction Jefferson observed in Hamilton just before he came down with yellow fever was occasioned not so much by fear of the disease as of the cure. Dr. Kuhn, one of the leading physicians of Philadelphia, prescribed two cold baths a day for yellow-fever victims. Dr. Wister advised his patients to try the salutary effects of cold air. He had the courage of his own remedy: when delirious with pain and fever, he exposed himself to a cold, raw wind—and lived to bear witness either to the efficacy of his cure or the durability of his constitution. But Dr. Benjamin Rush favored even more drastic methods: he combated yellow fever with "mercurial purges" and "heroic bloodletting." Under the impression that the human body contained several more quarts of blood than it actually does, he bled his patients to the limit—and sometimes beyond—of tolerance.*

Instead of trusting himself to the lancet and the emetics of Dr. Rush, Hamilton turned to his boyhood friend, Dr. Edward Stevens. After graduating from King's College, Stevens had done postgraduate work in medicine at the University of Edinburgh. Having had some experience in St. Croix with yellow fever, Stevens prescribed bark, wine, laudanum and baths —a mild regimen compared with the rugged therapy advocated by Dr. Rush.

Of this disease which seemed to take its largest toll among the lower class of citizens, Hamilton was the most distinguished victim. If it did nothing else, his illness served to reveal how precious was his life to the businessmen of the United States: when it was reported in New England that he was dead, the merchants and shipowners took the news as though a major disaster had befallen the country. But, happily, the report was premature. Hamilton pulled through and the businessmen of the country breathed easier. Although it is probable that Hamilton recovered in spite of the doctor, he generously ascribed his deliverance, after allowing due credit to God, to the ministrations of Dr. Stevens. Indeed, so confident was Hamilton that his friend had hit upon a sovereign cure for yellow fever that he published a testimonial letter in the newspapers, sent a clinical report of his case to the Philadelphia College of Physicians, and advised the citizens of Philadelphia to remain in the city and call in Dr. Stevens at the first sign of illness.[5]

* Dr. Benjamin Rush was a signer of the Declaration of Independence, a leader of the reform movement (temperance, prisons, Negro slavery and the care of the insane), and one of the first practitioners in the United States of preventive medicine.

Much as his friends respected Hamilton's knowledge of finance they doubted his right to speak with equal finality about materia medica. Fisher Ames, the valetudinarian Federalist statesman from Massachusetts, whose knowledge of human ills was perhaps more extensive than that of any of his contemporaries—he had had them all—declared that much as he admired the zeal and heroism of the doctors, he prayed to be preserved from their ministrations: "I had rather trust nature," he said. "She would do better contending with one enemy than with two."

Hamilton would have been well advised to leave matters in the hands of the professional, graduated homicides. Neither his expostulations nor the high mortality rate among his patients dissuaded Dr. Rush from bleeding and purging. In some cases he removed as much as eighty ounces of blood "and," he added jubilantly, "in most cases with the happiest effects. I have observed the most speedy convalescence where the bleeding has been most profuse." When treated by his methods, he declared, yellow fever was no more serious than a common cold.

While he did not employ his scalpel and lancet against his critics—he reserved those implements for the unfortunates he treated professionally—Dr. Rush wielded an equally sharp and piercing pen. In the newspapers, he excoriated his enemies, Hamilton among them, as malefactors leagued with the powers of darkness; and he groaned to think how many lives had been "sacrificed to bark and wine" that might have been saved had he gotten to the sickroom in time. He swore that Hamilton was persecuting him because he had presumed to differ with the Secretary politically: had he not been "a decided Democrat and a friend of Madison and Jefferson," he said, Hamilton would not have taken Dr. Stevens' side in the controversy. Adding insult to this injury, Doctor Rush ascribed the epidemic to God's displeasure at the people's avarice and self-seeking—for which, of course, Hamilton bore the chief responsibility.

More because he remained in Philadelphia after most of the other physicians, including Dr. Stevens, had fled than because his methods were effective in curing the disease, Dr. Rush emerged as the hero of the epidemic. The common people of Philadelphia, among whom he labored to the very end, responded by giving him their affection and in many instances paid him the last full measure of devotion.

Hamilton, on the other hand, suffered in popular esteem by reason of his opposition to the heroic Dr. Rush. Here was further evidence that Hamilton was an enemy of the people: he traduced their benefactors and attempted to mislead them with false panaceas. Before the epidemic was over, Dr. Rush reported that the remedies advocated by Hamilton were as unpopular in Philadelphia as was the funding system in Virginia. Although the doctor could not quite put his finger upon it, there seemed to be some connection between Hamilton's physic and his finance.

As soon as Hamilton and his wife were able to travel—their children had happily been spared the disease—they set out for New York City. Everywhere, as potential carriers of yellow fever, they were compelled to submit to the local quarantine laws. When they reached New York, they were bluntly told that there would be no relaxation in their favor of the quarantine laws requiring fourteen days' stay at Governor's Island. Even so, Hamilton was treated no worse than was Secretary of War Knox, who, arriving in New York from Philadelphia a few days later, was also denied permission to enter the city despite his pleas that it was of the utmost importance for him to go to Boston immediately and that he was "too bulky to be *smuggled* through the Country." Hamilton was presented with the hard choice of submitting to quarantine or of leaving New York. Exhausted as he was, Hamilton decided to take his family directly to his father-in-law's house at Albany.

In consequence of these delays and obstructions, by the time Hamilton and his family reached Albany, his nerves were badly frayed and he was in a state of near collapse. But here a new and even more agonizing trial awaited him. Almost within sight of his destination, he was informed by Abraham Yates (brother of Robert Yates, Hamilton's colleague at the Constitutional Convention), the mayor of Albany, that municipal regulations required him and his family to undergo an extended quarantine before entering the city. To this inconvenience Hamilton flatly refused to submit: he had, he told the mayor, taken every precaution since leaving Philadelphia against spreading the disease; all used clothing had been left behind and it was therefore plain that "no particle of infection can remain about us." Having thus given himself and his family a clean bill of health, Hamilton peremptorily demanded passage into the city.

Mayor Yates was not convinced by Hamilton's self-certification. His duty to the citizens of Albany, he told the impatient Secretary, obliged him strictly to enforce the quarantine laws. Whereupon Hamilton declared that he and his wife and children would enter Albany regardless of the mayor and all the other city fathers. The mayor knew that if Hamilton carried out his threat, he and his family would almost certainly be mobbed in the streets of Albany. He therefore hastily summoned the Common Council and appointed a physician to examine the Hamiltons for evidences of yellow fever. They were promptly pronounced to be in good health, and with this assurance the mayor and council gave the Hamilton family special permission to pass through the town. Lest Hamilton suppose that his self-importance entitled him to transgress the laws, the mayor informed him that "those are absolutely mistaken who may conceive that intimidations of this nature and menaces can prevent us from fulfilling our duties."

Illness and fatigue may explain Hamilton's imperious behavior on this occasion, but it is not on record that he ever apologized to the mayor and

The War Clouds Gather

members of the council. It is probable that he regarded himself as the victim of his political enemies or officious functionaries who deliberately closed their eyes to the special nature of his case. In any event, a few days after Hamilton and his family arrived at General Schuyler's house, a visitor reported that the Secretary was recovering his spirits and that the "little vanity he has had not been dimmed."

During Hamilton's absence from Philadelphia, the business of the Treasury was conducted by Oliver Wolcott, the Controller. Wolcott fought a losing battle against yellow fever: with his assistants incapacitated and all government business virtually at a standstill, he stood his ground until he was down to his last clerk. Together they fled the city and established the temporary headquarters of the United States Treasury in an outlying village.

At the end of October, 1793, weak and emaciated from his bout with yellow fever, Hamilton arrived in Germantown, the temporary site of the government, and took up his residence at Fair Hill, a mansion belonging to Robert Morris. When he attempted to resume work at the Treasury, he suffered a relapse; convinced that he had contracted the disease a second time, he sent to New York for Dr. Stevens, in whom his confidence remained unshaken. Despite huge doses of bark and laudanum, he was absent from his offices and Cabinet meetings during most of the month of November. Meanwhile the autumnal frosts put an end to yellow fever and the city gradually returned to normal. But over four thousand Philadelphians were dead.

In 1797, the medical faculty of Columbia University recommended that Dr. Benjamin Rush be appointed to the chair of the practice of medicine. Rather than see a man he regarded as a dangerous quack elevated to a position of such eminence, Hamilton, as one of the trustees of Columbia University, blocked the appointment. Although Dr. John Rodgers of the medical faculty protested against what he called the "old leaven of Bigotry & political resentment," Rush withdrew his name from consideration. It was not until Jefferson became President that Rush came into official favor: he was appointed Director of the United States Mint.

When Hamilton returned to Philadelphia the autumn of 1793, he found that the *National Gazette* had been one of the casualties of the yellow-fever epidemic. Freneau's paper had failed to pay its way and the post of translating clerk in the State Department was no help at all: in fact, toward the end, Freneau was paying out more for translations of foreign documents than he received by way of salary. Furthermore, in 1793, Freneau's financial backers decided to call it quits. The yellow fever proved to be the finishing stroke: Freneau resigned his position in the State Department, closed the *National Gazette* and headed for the rural solitude of New Jersey.

Yet the *Gazette of the United States* triumphantly carried on—thanks in large measure to Hamilton's timely aid. When Fenno got into financial difficulties, the Secretary of the Treasury raised enough money from well-heeled Federalists to tide him over his troubles. But when Fenno asked for a job in the Bank of the United States, Hamilton declined to oblige him: the parallel with Jefferson and Freneau was too close to be risked. The Secretary continued, however, to underwrite Federalist newspapers: in 1794, he assisted Noah Webster to establish the New York *Minerva* and he later helped William Cobbett to launch *Porcupine's Gazette*.

At almost the same time that Freneau left Philadelphia, Jefferson resigned his post as Secretary of State and retired to the seclusion of his beloved Monticello. With Jefferson gone, the Cabinet seemed a tamer and perhaps a lonelier place to Hamilton; he missed the rapierlike exchanges, the sense of contending against an adversary worthy of his steel, and the stimulation of a mind that saw the constitutional, political and social questions of the day in a very different light than did Hamilton himself. However, he could hardly suppose that he had seen the last of Jefferson: he knew only too well the Virginian's penchant for working behind the scenes and moving his followers like puppets against the man he regarded as the archenemy of republicanism.

Jefferson's retirement coincided with the worst crisis in Anglo-American relations since the peace of 1783. That the United States did not wage a second war against Great Britain in 1794-95 was owing primarily to the Washington administration's determination to settle the differences between the two countries by peaceful means. But the issue was long in doubt and Hamilton was obliged to contend against ideas fixed rigidly in the American mind and against men who, without wishing war, advocated measures certain in Hamilton's opinion to precipitate an armed conflict with Great Britain.

Foremost among the factors making for war were the American concept of neutral rights, the hatred felt by many citizens for their late "mother country" and their equally strong adulation of France, and the conviction held by Jefferson and Madison that Great Britain could be brought to terms by economic coercion.

In all the treaties made by the United States with foreign powers, it had sought to include a liberal definition of neutral rights. Because the new republic was possessed of a large merchant marine and expected to be neutral in future European wars, it attached high importance to the doctrine that, except in the case of contraband, free ships made free goods. If this principle were generally adopted by the maritime powers, it would mean that the United States, as a neutral, would become the carrier for European belligerents in time of war. Seldom has a principle of international law promised to confer greater material benefit upon a neutral nation.

In the outbreak of the war between Great Britain and France in 1793, Americans saw their opportunity to grow rich while Europeans went about their business of cutting each others' throats. If Hamilton adopted the position in 1793 that war did not pay, it was partly owing to the fact that peace was paying so handsomely for Americans. As an American newspaper put it, Europe was raining riches upon the United States "and it is as much as we can do to find dishes to catch the golden shower." But Americans were soon diverted from this pleasant occupation by the vexing question of neutral rights.[6]

As the dominant sea power, Great Britain was traditionally no respecter of the "rights" of neutrals. For the most part, the exercise of these rights worked against the interests of Great Britain: by trading freely with the enemy, neutrals tended to nullify the force of British sea power. Therefore the British government generally refused to admit the validity of the principle that free ships make free goods; instead, it put forward the very different doctrine of the Consolato del Mare—that regardless of the flag of the ship in which they were found, enemy goods were liable to seizure.

Shortly after the outbreak of hostilities with France, the British government instructed its Minister in the United States to sound prominent members of the Washington administration upon the subject of neutral rights. As was by now his settled habit, Hammond dropped in upon the Secretary of the Treasury and prepared to listen to the Secretary unbosom himself upon Anglo-American relations. The British Minister was not disappointed: Hamilton was his usual forthright self, ready to talk at length upon the foreign policy of the United States. And, to the even greater gratification of the British Minister, Hamilton took the position that the Consolato del Mare was the accepted rule of international law and that the United States ought to recognize its validity. The right of the British to seize enemy goods in American ships, to confiscate contraband—even though the property of Americans—and to deny American ships the right to enter blockaded ports —upon these points, the Secretary of the Treasury yielded to Great Britain. After this agreeable conference, Hammond informed his government that "in the justice of these principles Mr. Hamilton perfectly coincided and assured me that he would be responsible for the concurrence of all the members of this administration in the admission of their propriety to the fullest extent."[7]

He sought to win the concurrence of the American people as well. In newspaper articles he asserted that the United States must abandon its "historic" position on the freedom of the seas and submit to the hard facts of maritime law as defined by the dominant sea power: "In a war of opinion and passion like the present," he said, "concessions to ill-founded or doubtful pretensions [on the part of neutrals] are not to be expected." As for the principle that free ships make free goods, Hamilton warned that the United States could not "in prudence or good policy insist upon it, unless we are prepared to support it by arms."[8]

In Hamilton's attitude there was a notable indifference to the abstract concept of neutral rights. He was not concerned with what neutral rights ought to be: he thought only in terms of the rights which belligerents—especially the great maritime powers—had traditionally granted neutrals. This attitude was based upon a sound understanding of the American economy and of vital national interests. To American merchants, carrying the goods of belligerents under the protection of a neutral flag was not nearly as important or as profitable as selling dear and buying cheap or, as one of them said, "trading where the market is under supplied with what they sell & overstocked with what they buy." From this point of view, the security of their property on the high seas was of paramount importance. This being the case, they chose to bow to British regulations in return for the protection that the British navy alone could give American shipping.[9]

Had the British government confined itself to seizing French property on board American ships, it might have escaped with little more than a formal protest on the part of the United States government; certainly no responsible official in that government was prepared to go to war over this issue. But in the war with revolutionary France, the old and cherished concepts of the sea were thrown overboard one by one until little remained to the neutral powers except to conform to the will of the dominant sea power.

The first big splash occurred in June, 1793, when the British government, on the grounds that France, by mobilizing its population against Great Britain and its allies, was waging total war, proclaimed its intention of reducing its adversary to "reasonable terms" by means of a blockade. William Pitt contended that it was truly humanitarian to starve the civilian population of France into subjection: harrowing as this expedient was certain to be, it promised to shorten the war and thereby save lives and money.

To accomplish this laudable objective as expeditiously as possible, Great Britain concluded treaties with Russia, Spain and Prussia by which the signatories agreed to stop all shipments of corn (i.e., flour, wheat, barley, etc.) destined for France. On June 16, 1793, orders were issued by the British government to seize all neutral ships carrying these commodities to France. To ease the impact of this blow, it was stipulated that compensation would be made for confiscated cargoes.

Any idea that the British government may have had that Hamilton would accept the Order in Council of June, 1793, by shouting "Rule Britannia! Britannia rules the waves!" was summarily shattered by the results of Hammond's interview with the Secretary of the Treasury in September, 1793. Hammond came primed to justify his government's plan of starving France

The War Clouds Gather

by cutting off neutral trade, but he found Hamilton in anything but a receptive frame of mind. Disposed as he was to acknowledge Britain's maritime supremacy and to accommodate American policy to the rules laid down by the mistress of the seas, he denounced the Order of June 6 as a "very harsh and unprecedented measure" aimed directly at the commerce of the United States. He flatly contradicted the British claim that corn was contraband; only in cases of blockade, siege or investment could it be so considered, he said, and a blockade to be binding must be effective—a requirement which the British blockade of France fell far short of fulfilling.

Despite the strenuous objections made by the Washington administration to the Order in Council of June 6, this was by no means the worst blow that befell the United States. In the autumn of 1793, a British fleet and army were sent to the Caribbean to conquer the French West Indies. Since the success of this operation depended to a large degree upon cutting off the French islands from outside supplies, the British government issued on November 6, 1793, an Order in Council directing the commanders of British ships of war to seize and bring into a British port all neutral ships carrying provisions or other supplies to the enemy's islands or carrying the produce of any enemy colony. This measure was patently aimed at the American merchant marine, the chief carrier of provisions to the French West Indies and of the produce of those islands to the outside world.

To ensure that the bag of American ships should be as large as possible, the publication of this Order in Council was delayed until late in December, 1793. This ruse enabled British cruisers and privateers to capture about 250 unsuspecting American vessels, almost half of which were condemned in British admiralty courts. From the point of view of the officers of His Majesty's Navy, who by long custom shared in the profits of these seizures, the trap had worked perfectly. True, the Yankees were certain to scream, but in the meantime the British navy had never had it so good.

If this were not war, Americans confessed that they did not know the meaning of the word. As for Hamilton, he was both angered and dismayed to find that this was the recompense for his efforts to promote Anglo-American understanding. Jefferson had lamented that Genêt was sinking the Republican interest; with almost equal cause, Hamilton could have said that the British were engaged in scuttling the Federalist party. He had supposed that the British government had learned something from the American Revolution—yet here were British statesmen exhibiting the same shortsightedness that had cost them the American colonies. The capacity of the British for resisting enlightenment never ceased to astonish him.

Even though the actions of the British government hardly admitted of doubt that it was prepared to go to war to enforce its demands upon the neutrals, Hamilton was not inclined to pick up the challenge. Instead, he attempted to put as fair a face as possible upon British policy, picturing the seizures the result of an error that would soon be rectified. Hamilton was playing for time with very little prospect that time would bring anything but disaster.[10]

James Madison's answer to British actions in the West Indies took the form of seven "Commercial Propositions" submitted to Congress in January, 1794. Here he recommended, among other things, that discriminatory duties be levied upon the ships and manufactures of Great Britain in order to free the American economy from "the caprice, the passions, the mistaken calculations of interest, the bankruptcies, and the wars of a single foreign country." In effect, Madison offered northern shipowners and manufacturers a virtual monopoly of the American market: even the payment of the national debt—the cardinal objective of Republican finance—was to be subordinated to the fostering of the "carrying trade, the great resource of our safety and respectability."

Hearing Madison proclaim such views, some Federalists began to wonder whether he was not a Hamiltonian after all. But Hamilton was strangely unwilling to welcome the apostate's return. At another time and under different circumstances he might have received Madison with open arms; but with a war raging between France and Great Britain and the United States trying to steer a neutral course between the belligerent powers, Hamilton could regard Madison's "Commercial Propositions" only as further proof of how lamentably his former friend and colleague had fallen under the influence of the "Frenchified philosopher" from Monticello.

With the ultimate objectives enunciated by his former friend and collaborator Hamilton was in sympathy, but he felt that in this instance the means vitiated the end. He would not consent to build up the economy of the United States by contributing to the ruin of Great Britain, particularly at a time when the warmaking power of that country seemed essential to the safety of the United States. Moreover, strangely enough, considering the importance he attached to self-interest, Hamilton did not share the Republicans' view that John Bull was the personification of Economic Man, forever examining his bread to see upon which side it was buttered and ready to take a full loaf regardless of the cost to national honor and prestige. Instead, Hamilton always allowed a wide margin for the operations of irrationality and folly: particularly in international relations was he prepared to admit the potency of such imponderables as prejudice, pride and long-standing resentments. For this reason, he felt certain that Madison's "Commercial Propositions" would provoke war with Great Britain—a war which would annihilate the revenues of the United States government. Although Jefferson and Madison gave it scant consideration, the fact that nine tenths of the revenue of the United States government was derived from commercial duties and that three fourths of this total came from commerce with Great

The War Clouds Gather

Britain and its colonies was always uppermost in Hamilton's mind. Moreover, he never forgot that the United States was dependent upon British credit; deprived of that resource, the commercial, industrial and agricultural expansion of the United States would wither on the vine.

From war with Great Britain, Hamilton feared even worse consequences than the overthrow of his financial system. Fearful that "French principles" had already seriously undermined the moral fiber of the American people, he anticipated that war, "by putting in motion all the turbulent passions, and promoting a further assimilation of our principles with those of France, may prove to be the threshold of disorganization and anarchy." In short, there was no more effective way of destroying the union and ensuring the triumph of a foreign ideology than by going to war with Great Britain.

True, Madison was not talking about war with Great Britain: his "Commercial Propositions" envisaged nothing more serious than an economic showdown with the former mother country. But as Hamilton perceived, there was as much politics as commerce in these proposals. Madison's objective was to "cultivate the connection and intercourse with the French nation" and to sever the ties with Great Britain. Significantly enough, he said nothing about buying and selling in the most advantageous market; certainly he could not pretend that Americans could buy cheaper and sell dearer in the French market.

Before Americans cast themselves into the arms of France, Hamilton invited them to look at some statistics concerning American shipping and commerce that he had compiled. Priming his Congressman Friday, William Smith, with the rough draft of a speech, he sent him down to the House of Representatives to answer Madison. Through Smith, Hamilton pointed out that the United States had imported from Great Britain goods to the value of $14 million; from France, in the same year, the United States had imported goods valued at $150,000. At the same time, over 75 per cent of the exports of the United States went to Great Britain or its colonies—proof, said Hamilton-Smith, that the trade of this country was following its natural channel. Even the fact that Great Britain re-exported to the European continent a large part of the raw materials it imported from the United States ought not to disturb Americans: in view of the uncertainty of foreign markets, it was advantageous to the United States, Hamilton-Smith pointed out, to have a customer always prepared to absorb our exports. From which it could be seen, Hamilton lamented, that Madison's proposals were the familiar story of a people throwing away their blessings in order to gratify their resentments.[11]

Those resentments were rapidly reaching the boiling point. Even though the British government announced in January, 1794, that the interpretation put upon the Order in Council of November, 1793, by British naval officers and admiralty judges had been erroneous, otherwise the news was as black as a warmonger could have wished. In the Mediterranean, the Barbary corsairs (believed to be under the control of Great Britain) began to pillage American shipping; Lord Dorchester, the Governor General of Canada, told his Indian allies that in the event of war between his country and the United States, "a line must be then drawn by the warriors"; and, acting under orders from Lord Dorchester, Colonel Simcoe erected a fort upon American territory—a step which Washington termed "the most open and daring act of the British agents in America." Had the Washington administration called for a declaration of war upon Great Britain in the spring of 1794, it probably would have met with overwhelming support in Congress. Indeed, the country was swept by a wave of hatred of the former mother country that reminded some observers of 1776: in Philadelphia, a bas-relief of George II that had escaped the Revolution was taken down under the threat of forcible removal by the mob. "Our blood is in a flame," exclaimed an American, "—yea, we are ready to curse the hard hearted Pharaoh, who sits on the British throne —a scourge to his fellow mortals. . . . The avenging arm of America once uplifted, should chastise and pursue a corrupt and base tyrant till his worthless life is terminated upon a scaffold."[12]

In this highly charged atmosphere, Hamilton courted unpopularity by warning his countrymen that bringing their late sovereign to the executioner's block was an undertaking not lightly to be entered upon. Admitting that the United States was a Hercules, it was a Hercules still in the cradle— and Hamilton advised it to conduct itself accordingly. By this he did not mean, as Jefferson supposed, that the republic ought to creep back to Mother Britain, whimpering at every sign of displeasure from that imperious dame. Rather, Hamilton urged his countrymen to remain at peace for at least ten years before they began to flex the sinews of war. Above all, he wanted no war until all sectors of public opinion, particularly that of the business community, were united in a determination to prosecute it to the utmost. It would be fatal to the war effort, he pointed out, if the most influential citizens believed that war had been rashly entered into: "Unanimity among ourselves," he said, ". . . can only be secured by its being made manifest, if war ensues, that it was inevitable by another course of conduct."[13]

Uncertain whether the belligerence of the British or the foolhardiness of the Republicans would precipitate war, Hamilton undertook to strengthen the defenses of the country. Through his spokesmen, he urged Congress to create an army of 25,000 men (later reduced to 15,000), to hold 80,000 militia in readiness for any eventuality, to build a navy, fortify the harbors, impose higher taxes and invest the President with adequate powers to deal with the national emergency.

It was a peculiarity of the Republican leaders that even though they pushed the country to the brink of war, they insisted to the end that they were still a safe distance from the edge; the more belligerent they became toward

The War Clouds Gather

Great Britain, the more optimistic they waxed over the prospects of preserving peace. If by some mischance war should come, it was then sufficient time, they held, to think of measures of defense. In the meantime, they seemed disposed to act upon the comforting assumption that weakness, innocence and purity of motives were a guarantee of peace. Or, if these failed to keep off aggressors, they had no doubt that the militia could dispose of any invader. Secure in these assumptions, they opposed every measure proposed by Hamilton to put the country in a posture of defense. The war talk, said Madison, was manufactured by Hamilton in order to saddle the country with "armies and debts"—the Secretary was up to his "old trick of turning every contingency into a resource for accumulating force in the government."[14]

While the Republicans talked peace, they advocated increasingly severe reprisals against Great Britain. Before Madison's proposals could be acted upon, a new plan was broached in Congress—the sequestration of debts owing by Americans to British subjects.* To the southern planters and to the "agricultural interest" in general, this measure was vastly more attractive than were Madison's propositions. As a debtor nation, the United States was in a particularly advantageous position to coerce its principal creditor, Great Britain, and this without the unwelcome necessity of paying the bills for the aggrandizement of northern commerce and manufactures. Moreover, it held out hope to debt-ridden Southerners of escaping altogether from their debts to British merchants, a prospect significantly absent from Madison's plan.[15]

And yet from Hamilton's point of view the sequestration of debts was more indefensible and more likely to provoke war with Great Britain than were Madison's proposals. "No powers of language at my command," he exclaimed, "can express the abhorrence I feel at the idea of violating the property of individuals ... on account of controversies between nation and nation." If the United States stooped to such perfidy, he said, it would sacrifice its last shred of honor; the courage of its citizens would be frozen "by the cowardly declaration that we have no recourse but in fraud"; and the expunging of all debts, foreign and domestic, would almost certainly follow. Since 1783, he had been preaching to his countrymen that debts were sacred and must be paid in full regardless of wars and revolutions; any other course, he had repeatedly said, was certain to destroy private and public credit, with fatal consequences to the American government and economy. With the adoption of the Constitution and the opening of the federal courts to British and Loyalist creditors, Hamilton had supposed that the victory had been won, but it now appeared that the decisive battle was yet to be fought.

* This measure was proposed by Dayton of New Jersey, a Federalist.

To prevent the adoption of the sequestration bill, Hamilton supplied his supporters in Congress with arguments drawn from the leading authorities on international law. He had no difficulty in showing that the action contemplated by the Republicans was contrary to the accepted law of nations. Upon the same principle that foreign nationals were assumed to be innocent of the wrongdoing of their government and therefore could not justly be punished for its acts, their property was likewise placed beyond the reach of a hostile government.[16]

At no time during this period of crisis did Hamilton deny that the injuries suffered by the United States at the hands of Great Britain were grave and must be redressed. He acknowledged that the policy of the British government toward the United States had been "inexplicably mysterious" and in some instances had "discovered strong tokens of deep-rooted hatred, and hostility towards this country." But he did insist that the resources of diplomacy had not been exhausted; war might yet be averted, he said, if British and American negotiators could sit down together and calmly discuss the differences between the two countries. While he acknowledged that the auguries for a peaceful settlement of the dispute were not propitious, he thought that the experiment ought to be made if for no other reason than that failure would tend to unite the country against its intractable enemy across the Atlantic.[17]

A commercial treaty with Great Britain and the cession of the Northwest posts were not less vital national objectives to Hamilton than they were to Madison and Jefferson. He deplored the failure of the United States to reach an accord with Great Britain upon these points; as long as they remained in dispute, he told the British Minister, peace between the two countries hung precariously in the balance. It was the difference of opinion regarding the methods of achieving these objectives, not the objectives themselves, that divided Hamilton and the Republican leaders.

They were likewise at variance over the question: to which of these two goals of American foreign policy ought priority to be given? Hamilton awarded precedence to the recovery of the Northwest posts. He thereby revealed a sound appreciation of the strength and weakness of his country's economic position. Relaxation of British commercial laws could be safely postponed: the United States was riding the crest of a wave of prosperity which British restrictions did not seriously affect. The policy advocated by Madison and Jefferson of concentrating attention upon the West Indies, while appropriate enough during the period of the Articles of Confederation, when the United States seemed to be gravely injured by British restrictions upon American shipping, did not apply to the very different economic conditions that now prevailed. In the West, on the other hand, the situation had become more critical since the inauguration of the new government: the Indians were on the warpath and being supplied with arms and ammuni-

The War Clouds Gather

tion by British traders, and there was a growing note of menace in the demands of Americans that the British be ousted from the Northwest posts. Obviously, the danger spot was in the interior of the continent, not in the British West Indies; and it was American frontiersmen rather than American merchants and shipowners who were likely to provoke war between the two countries.

Singularly enough, it was Madison and Jefferson who professed to be dedicated to the welfare of the commercial and maritime interests of the country, while Hamilton claimed to be speaking for the farmers, frontiersmen and taxpayers of the country. Possession of the posts, he contended, was of more immediate importance to the United States than was trade with the West Indies because with the posts in American hands the frontier would be secured, the westward advance might be resumed, and the country would be relieved of the heavy expense of an Indian war. Moreover, the United States would then be in a position to secure from Spain an acknowledgment of its right to navigate the Mississippi freely to the sea—a right which Hamilton held to be "of the first moment to our territories to the westward, they *must have that outlet, without it they will be lost to us*."[18]

The result of Hamilton's insistence upon the surrender of the Northwest posts was that he jeopardized his reputation among British officials as a friend of Great Britain. Colonel Simcoe, for example, told his superiors that Hamilton was no better than Jefferson—"Jefferson openly avows, whilst Hamilton tries to disguise it." The trouble with both men, Simcoe decided, was that they were unreconstructed rebels who took a wholly American view of the subjects in dispute.

Since Hamilton admitted that the United States had grievances that called imperiously for redress, it was asked how he proposed to reach an understanding with Great Britain. Hamilton's answer was that the United States must swallow its pride and its sense of injury by sending a minister plenipotentiary to the Court of St. James's. By taking this action, Hamilton told his countrymen, they would not be supplicating the aggressor: limited as the measures of defense undertaken by the United States were, they nevertheless made it appear that the administration was taking the ground of negotiation in the midst of preparations for war, thereby carrying its appeal "to the prudence of the British Cabinet, without wounding its pride and to the justice and interest of the British nation, without exciting feelings of resentment."

On March 10, 1794, a group of worried Federalist senators met in Philadelphia to discuss ways and means of averting war with Great Britain. The result of their deliberations was a request to the President to send a peace emissary to Great Britain. This individual, it was specified, ought to be "a person possessing Talents of the first order, enjoying the confidence of the friends of Peace and of the government, and whose character was unexceptionable in England." To the Federalist senators, this description applied to only one man—Secretary Hamilton; and it was he whom the senators recommended that the President invest with the powers of a minister plenipotentiary.[19]

It is probable that the Secretary himself was the moving spirit in this maneuver; rather than put his case directly before the President, he chose to work through some of the more influential members of the Senate. Certainly it would not have required a second invitation to induce Hamilton to start off for England: with characteristic optimism and self-confidence he believed not only that war could be averted but that he was the man to do it. But the Republicans would have none of Hamilton as a peacemaker. John Nicholas, a representative from Virginia, and James Monroe, a senator from that state, wrote the President expressing vehement opposition to the Secretary's appointment. Among other things, they asserted that Hamilton was eager to go to England in order to revel with dukes and lords, acquaint himself with the latest methods of corrupting legislators and kiss the rod which the "Royal Brute" still kept on hand just in case he had an opportunity to use it upon Americans. Jefferson recorded in his diary the rumor that Hamilton, Rufus King and William Smith were planning to seek political asylum in Great Britain when the United States became too hot to hold them. In that event, Jefferson would not have been surprised if His Majesty's Government had awarded them a pension similar to that given to Benedict Arnold for services rendered to the British Crown.[20]

If Jefferson's suspicions proved correct, bundling Hamilton off to Britain would be an effective way of removing him forever from the American scene; but the Virginian, being firmly of the conviction that the Secretary of the Treasury was guilty of a whole catalogue of crimes against his country, was not disposed to let him off so easily. The Republicans' most persistent fear, however, was not that Hamilton would find sanctuary in England but that he would make a treaty, return home in triumph and carry off the presidency. For this reason, they wished to have James Madison or Thomas Jefferson entrusted with the negotiations: not only would these "true republicans" safeguard the interests of the United States, but if they succeeded in making a treaty, the honor would redound wholly to them.[21]

The outcry raised by the Republicans against Hamilton helped persuade the President that the Secretary of the Treasury was qualified upon every score except that of popularity to conduct the negotiations with Great Britain. A Federalist less intimately identified with the controversial measures of the administration had therefore to be found. Washington was not obliged to go far afield to find his man: John Jay, the Chief Justice of the United States Supreme Court, was called upon to undertake the mission to Great Britain. Hamilton might well have congratulated himself upon having escaped the post of honor: when John Jay left New York on May 12, 1794,

The War Clouds Gather

his effigy was guillotined and blown up with gunpowder. Even so, the demonstrations that marked his departure were nothing compared with those that greeted him upon his return.[22]

Jay's nomination was made barely in time to avert the adoption of measures which Hamilton felt certain would lead to war. The sequestration bill was dropped in April, 1794, but a bill providing for nonintercourse with Great Britain passed the House of Representatives and was defeated in the Senate only by the casting vote of the Vice-President. Had not Jay's appointment already been confirmed by the Senate, the measure would almost certainly have been carried. The only legislation of this nature passed by Congress and approved by the President imposed an embargo upon American ships. Intended to prevent the capture of American ships by British cruisers, the embargo was terminated when it was found that it seriously injured the southern states.[23]

With Jay on his way to England, Hamilton took a brighter view of the future. "There is every prospect," he wrote his wife on June 8, 1794, "that we shall not put on the French yoke." Thomas Jefferson wished that he could be equally sure that the United States would not put on the British yoke.[24]

26.

The Whisky Rebellion

Hamilton had no more than congratulated himself upon having clipped the wings of the Republican warhawks when some birds of exceedingly ill omen appeared in the West. This untoward development stemmed from the adoption in 1791 by the federal government of an excise upon the manufacture of whisky. This tax had been strongly recommended by Hamilton in his first Report on Public Credit in order to pay for the assumption of state debts. When Congress failed to take action, he returned to the subject in a second report. This time Congress was more amenable to Hamilton's request—indeed, it had very little to say in the matter since the assumption of state debts had already been consummated—and the excise became law early in 1791.

As was true of most of the fiscal measures devised by Hamilton, the excise was more than a mere revenue-producing measure. Being a form of taxation shared concurrently by the federal and state governments, the excise represented to Hamilton one of the most objectionable vestiges of state sovereignty that had been allowed to remain in the Constitution. He was determined that it should be possessed wholly by the federal government, not only because the revenue arising from the tonnage and import duties was insufficient to meet the charges upon the foreign and domestic debts, but because if the states were deprived of the excise they would have no other source of revenue except direct taxation. From Hamilton's viewpoint, every concurrent power created by the Constitution was an invitation to the federal and state governments to grapple for supremacy, and he always acted upon the maxim that the first objective of the federal government was to get a deadlock upon the states.

As a means of uniting the country, the excise likewise strongly recommended itself to Hamilton. The funding system and the assumption of state debts were intended to attach men of means to the central government, but Westerners—less fortunate than eastern capitalists—had, it seemed, to be taught to respect the government by being forced to pay taxes to it. If Westerners thought that this arrangement was unfair, Hamilton reminded them that without the army maintained by the federal government they

The Whisky Rebellion

would be at the mercy of the Indians—and any man in his right mind would prefer a tax collector to a redskin at his door.

Although Hamilton enjoyed the gratification of seeing the federal government pre-empt the excise, he soon had occasion to wonder if it were not a Pyrrhic victory. For of all the various forms of taxation, the excise was one of the most unpopular. In *The Federalist*, Hamilton had admitted that "the genius of the people will ill brook the inquisitive and peremptory spirit of excise laws"; only if used in moderation and kept strictly supplementary to more acceptable kinds of taxation, would they be tolerable. Against these counsels of prudence, however, he placed the necessity of increasing the revenue and furthering the solidarity of the country; but from the beginning it was doubtful whether either the cause of revenue or union would be advanced by forcing Westerners to pay a tax popularly regarded as an emblem of slavery.[1]

It would have been truly remarkable if the excise had not been hated in the whisky-producing areas. Against it the Republicans kept up a steady drumfire of propaganda as an unjust and discriminatory tax which had been imposed for the enrichment of speculators. "The fate of the excise law," it was said, "will determine whether the powers of the government of the United States are held by an aristocratic junto or by the people. The free citizens of America will not quietly suffer the *well born few* to trample them under foot." Westerners were told that the excise was part of a deliberate plot conceived in the Treasury to depopulate the West in order that the "moneyed interests" might rule the union. Having taxed whisky, it was predicted that Hamilton would go on burdening other commodities with duties until the day would arrive "when a shirt will not be washed without an excise." During the Revolutionary War, with equal disregard of probability, Hamilton had predicted that the British government, if it had its way, would impose a tax upon kisses between sweethearts.[2]

In the West, whisky was not only a potable but a form of manufacture and a medium of exchange. It was estimated that half the farmers of western Pennsylvania had a still "out back" which they tended with loving care. In some parts of the country, travelers beheld on every side smoke curling from the stillhouses—certainly a cheering sight to the parched and footsore. At the country stores, a gallon of whisky bought a definite amount of feed and dry goods. Even the salaries of ministers were sometimes paid in "Monongahela rye"—a liquid that could hardly be described as sacramental, but which certainly conveyed some idea of hell-fire.

The excise on whisky—levied at the still head—was extremely high. Eight cents a gallon represented about 25 per cent of the net value of the product. Moreover, as was to be expected under Hamilton's stewardship of the Treasury, the tax was efficiently collected. Nor was it any avail to protest against the excise: after studying the complaints that poured into the Treasury,

Hamilton issued a report upholding the excise law in every particular and telling the farmers in effect to stop grumbling and go back to their stills. The tax, he asserted, was not excessive; scarcity of money was "as much an objection to any other tax as the one in question"; and the expenditures of the army in the West provided the inhabitants with the means of paying the excise. When the backwoodsmen pleaded that because they drank more hard liquor than other Americans—the climate and the difficult conditions of life were, they averred, responsible for this consuming thirst—the heavy hand of the excisemen fell disproportionately upon them, Hamilton advised Westerners to taper off on their drinking. After all, he observed, the consumer paid the tax in the long run—and therefore the way to pay less taxes was to drink less whisky.

This was the kind of advice Westerners might have expected from an eastern winebibber; it took a whisky drinker—which Hamilton was not—to sympathize with their predicament. Nor did the Secretary advance his cause among Westerners by summoning morality to his side and enrolling himself under the banner of temperance. The drinking habits of the American people, he declared, ought to be an object of concern to the government: he estimated that the United States, with a population of four million, consumed between ten and eleven million gallons of spirits annually.[3]

Hamilton did not account it an evil that one of the effects of the excise was to squeeze the small distillers out of business and to concentrate the industry in a few larger units. In his opinion, the industry suffered from too much dispersion of labor and capital, stemming from the fact that it was carried on in households rather than in factories. The small operator who, aided by wife and children, operated his still on a part-time basis offended Hamilton's organizational sense and made the collection of the excise more difficult. For these reasons, he would not have been sorry to see the small distillers driven to the wall—the place, indeed, where they were being pushed.[4]

Hamilton's administrative genius was perhaps never better displayed than in the system he devised for the collection of the internal revenue duties. The country was divided into fourteen ditsricts each under the jurisdiction of a supervisor, and the districts in turn were divided into surveys and collectorships. Whereas the states, in their efforts to collect excise duties had relied chiefly upon the integrity of the distillers themselves, and had accepted oaths as evidence of full compliance with the law, Hamilton declined to put his trust in the probity of the distillers. The system adopted by the states had placed a premium upon perjury and fraud—with the result that the honest minority paid the tax while the majority perjured itself and defrauded the government. Accordingly, Hamilton put the responsibility for the enforcement of the law upon the revenue officers themselves, and they were given to understand that the full force of the government was behind

The Whisky Rebellion

them. For the unprecedented success of this method Hamilton took full credit: "The revenue of the government," he said, "were perhaps never collected under a more simple organization, or through a smaller number of channels."[5]

After a flare-up of resistance in 1792—so intense that Hamilton advised the use of military force—the West became quiet: the farmers paid the tax and the revenue officers became a familiar part of the western landscape. But this calm was illusory: Westerners were really boiling and bubbling as fiercely as their own stills and their one thought was to get rid of the hated excise. If they could rid the country of Alexander Hamilton in the process, so much the better![6]

While the whisky distillers bided their time, an increasingly strident chorus of complaint rose from the other victims of the excise. For Hamilton had never intended that internal revenue duties should be confined to whisky alone: according to his plans, when domestic industries attained sufficient strength and maturity to bear taxation they were to be treated in the same way as the whisky distillers. This was the price manufacturers were expected to pay for protection—what the state gave with one hand it took at least a part thereof with the other hand.

The intensive study of American manufactures made by Hamilton to provide material for his Report on Manufactures had established the fact that domestic brands of snuff and loaf sugar had virtually succeeded in capturing the American market. Before the Revolution, there had been only two snuff mills in the colonies; by 1792, protected first by a tariff imposed by the State of Pennsylvania and later by the tariff laws of the United States, twenty-seven snuff and tobacco factories had sprung up in Philadelphia alone, giving employment to over four hundred workers. Almost equally remarkable was the burgeoning of the manufacture of loaf sugar; by 1792, it had become one of the most solidly established of American industries.

Therefore it seemed to Hamilton wholly appropriate that the manufacture of snuff and loaf sugar should be subjected to an excise. In the spring of 1794, faced with the prospect of a heavy deficit as a result of the Indian War and the naval armament program adopted by Congress, Hamilton proposed that the tariff be increased, a stamp duty imposed, and excise duties imposed on carriages, snuff, loaf sugar, sales of spiritous liquors and auction sales. The stamp tax was rejected by Congress, but the other taxes were adopted over the vehement opposition of many southern members.

This policy won Hamilton no popularity among businessmen. The snuff and sugar manufacturers protested that the Secretary was singling out "infant industries" for his unwelcome attentions. In language reminiscent of that commonly used by southern planters and western farmers, these capitalists swore that they were being made the victims of unjust, discriminatory and unconstitutional taxes. Why, they asked, should they be chosen above all others to bear this heavy burden: were they not equally entitled to the privileges of freemen, the Heaven-ordained right to keep their profits inviolate from the grasping hand of government? When Hamilton pointed out that snuff was a luxury and therefore peculiarly eligible to serve as an object of taxation, the snuff manufacturers replied that their product was "a powerful specific against weak eyes and the headache." Having already imposed a duty upon whisky, it could be said of Hamilton that he had taxed both the cause and cure of headaches.

So outraged by this treatment were the Pennsylvania tobacco manufacturers that they drew up a memorial urging the businessmen of America to unite against a measure which they compared to *"famine, pestilence and the sword."* "The freemen of America," they declared, "have early learned to detect and to repel the first approaches of tyranny"; rather than submit tamely to this oppression, they called upon their fellow manufacturers to join them in migrating to the Mississippi, leaving Hamilton and his whole pack of taxes to "yelp in solitude" in the depopulated and impoverished East.

Certainly in 1791 no businessman reading the Report on Manufactures would have supposed that it would be necessary to flee the country to escape from Alexander Hamilton. Nor did it lessen the feeling that the world had been turned upside down when the Virginia Republicans, not hitherto conspicuous for their devotion to the cause of manufactures, came to the defense of businessmen, crying that the freedom of the American entrepreneur depended upon frustrating the plans of that ogre, Alexander Hamilton, "to crush American manufactures in the bud."[7]

Despite this high talk, there was no snuff rebellion, nor did Americans throw sugar into the Bay after the tea. Northern manufacturers discovered that the excise could be loaded upon that patient beast of burden, the consumer; and Southerners found that they had pressing grievances of their own that needed redressing.

Among the taxes levied by Congress in 1794 at Hamilton's recommendation was a tax on carriages. Since it affected only those who kept carriages for pleasure or for hire—vehicles employed in agriculture and transport were exempt—it could be regarded as a luxury tax. As a congressman observed, although not all men who possessed a carriage were rich, none was poor.

If any further evidence was needed of Hamilton's unique ability to infuriate Virginians, the carriage tax provided it. While they talked like democrats, the Virginia planters rode like aristocrats in their carriages, many of which were emblazoned with coats of arms. In their eyes, the carriage tax was "soak the rich" legislation especially aimed at the southern gentry. The fact that it had been recommended by Alexander Hamilton removed all doubt that the measure was inimical to the South. Would Hamilton never rest content, it was asked, until he had reduced the planters of the Old Dominion to walking as well as to famine and nakedness? John Taylor of Caroline, one of the principal spokesmen of the Virginia Republicans, was prepared to contemplate disunion: "A union emphatically and solemnly contracted, is dissolved," he declared; "states which impose unequal taxes, are masters, those which pay them, slaves."[8] But before resorting to this extremity, Taylor decided to take the issue to the federal courts. Hamilton had proposed and Congress had adopted the carriage tax under the assumption that it was an excise rather than a direct tax. As an excise it was authorized by the Constitution, but if it could be shown to be a direct tax, it would almost certainly be pronounced unconstitutional.*

The opponents of the carriage tax contended that it was a direct tax, not an excise. When suit was brought against Daniel Hylton, a Virginian, for evasion of the tax, John Taylor, acting as Hylton's counsel, argued the case on these grounds before the Circuit Court of the United States. Although Hylton lost the suit, the judges of the Circuit Court were divided in their opinions. Accounting this a moral victory for his client, Taylor urged Virginians to refuse to pay the tax when it fell due the following year. Uncertain of its own constitutional position, the government decided to take the case to the Supreme Court. Here, it could be foreseen, not merely Daniel Hylton and the carriage tax would be on trial; the chief defendant would be Alexander Hamilton, and the Virginians would seek to indict the entire Hamiltonian fiscal system.

Fully appreciating the importance of the case, William Bradford, the Attorney General of the United States, called upon Hamilton for aid: "Ought you not to have a little parental concern in this occasion," he asked, "& take care that no injustice be done to your own begetting?" Since the Republicans made no concealment of their determination to strangle the whole brood, taking care of his offspring promised to be a full-time employment for Hamilton. More than pride of parentage, however, entered into Hamilton's decision to come to the defense of the carriage tax: the system upon which he had founded the authority of the federal government was in jeopardy, and Hamilton was always ready to respond to the cry—"the union in danger!"

Before the case came to trial, Attorney General Bradford died and was succeeded by Henry Lee of Virginia. It was with Lee that Hamilton worked in drawing up the government's brief and in arguing the case before the Supreme Court when Hylton's appeal came before it in February, 1796.

The intrinsic significance of the case, together with the fact that Hamilton

* The Constitution states that no direct tax shall be laid unless apportioned among the states "in proportion to the census or enumeration, of the inhabitants of the United States." This stipulation had not been observed in the case of the carriage tax: no attempt had been made to follow the rule of apportionment.

was going to speak, packed the courtroom with high government officials, members of the Philadelphia bar, congressmen and distinguished foreign visitors. Nor did Hamilton disappoint his auditors: although unwell when he rose to speak, his oratorical and reasoning powers were never more brilliantly displayed. For three hours he held the attention of his audience rooted, speaking all this while, according to one eyewitness, "with astonishing ability, and in most pleasing manner."

Hamilton was one of those rare orators who can wring emotion from abstruse constitutional issues with the same facility that a lesser man plays upon the sad fate of widows and orphans; he keyed the argument to an accompanying obbligato of heartstrings. In one passage, in particular, it was agreed that he had attained real pathos: "Having occasion to observe, how proper a subject it was for taxation, since it was an article of *luxury* which a man might either use, or not, as was convenient to him, he added, 'It so happens, that I once had a carriage myself, and found it convenient to dispense with it. But my happiness is not in the least diminished!'" This was the price, he implied, of his devotion to the public: only a rich man could serve his government in public office and keep a carriage too.

But whether Hamilton walked or rode was beside the point: the question at issue was whether or not the tax on carriages was a direct tax. Hamilton, of course, contended that it was not—citing that in Great Britain a duty on carriages was regarded as an excise. "It is fair to seek the meaning of terms," he remarked, "in the statutory language of that country from which our jurisprudence is derived"—a doctrine which conjured up in Republicans' minds visions of a king, lords and commons.

Because the Constitution was admittedly vague in distinguishing between direct and indirect taxes, Hamilton was given an opportunity to apply his now celebrated method of interpreting that document. In doubtful cases, he told the Court, "no construction ought to prevail calculated to defeat the express and necessary authority of the Government. . . . It would be contrary to reason and to every rule of sound construction to adopt a principle for regulating the exercise of a clear constitutional power which would defeat the exercise of the power."

In its decision, the Supreme Court upheld Hamilton even to the extent of giving its sanction to his method of interpreting the Constitution. The validity of the act of Congress was sustained, the Court holding that since the Constitution prescribed that all direct taxes must be apportioned, the evident meaning was that no taxes were direct except those that could be apportioned. The carriage tax could not be apportioned without producing inequitable results; therefore, said the Court, it was not a direct tax.

The day after this triumph, Hamilton, although still unwell, seemed much improved. "He told me," recounted Justice Iredell, "he believed it was a good deal occasioned by his having left his youngest son ill with the measles, and

The Whisky Rebellion

hearing since that he was much better." The Constitution, too, seemed to Hamilton to be much better, but he suspected that before it could be pronounced out of danger it would have to undergo many more such crises.[9]

While Hamilton admitted of no doubt of Congress' competence to levy a tax upon carriages, he took a much more restricted view of its taxing powers when government bonds were in question. Having helped to create a class of moneyed capitalists, Hamilton was resolved to make the United States safe for capitalism—even though it meant curtailing the powers of the federal government.[10]

In 1791, the assessors of Boston, seeking to determine the value of taxable property held by residents of that city, asked Hamilton to direct his agents in Boston to permit them to inspect the Treasury records in order to assess individuals according to the amount of government securities in their possession. This inspection was made necessary, they declared, by the justified discontent of taxpayers who found themselves obliged to shoulder the entire burden while the security holders went tax-free. "Should we be refused this *reasonable* request for the purpose of doing public equity," the assessors informed Hamilton, "it will throw us into the disagreeable necessity of taxing the stock-holders according to their reputed property in the funds, which in very many instances may be greater than they really possess."[11]

Hamilton answered the Boston assessors with a lecture upon the principles of public finance. It was a standing rule at the Treasury, he declared, not to disclose the amount of public securities held by any individual, lest the private affairs of businessmen be exposed to rivals or the prying eyes of other interested parties; nor did it comport with the safety of the United States to spread its financial secrets before foreign powers. For these reasons he took the position that "everything in the nature of a direct tax on property in the funds of the United States, is contrary to the true principles of public credit, and tends to disparage the value of the public stock"; and he strongly advised the assessors to cease their ill-advised attempt to include public securities in their assessments.*[12]

Under the existing tax laws, stockholders largely escaped taxes upon bank dividends, interest received upon public securities, and transfers of public and private securities. In order to equalize the tax burden by tapping new sources of revenue, the Republicans in Congress proposed in 1794 that a tax of five cents per one hundred dollars be imposed upon the transfer of

---

* Here Hamilton was closely following Adam Smith, who in the *Wealth of Nations* had denounced the inquisitorial practices incidental to an income tax. Until 1798, when an income tax was instituted by William Pitt, England had not taxed public securities. When this tax was repealed in 1802 (it was subsequently reinstated in 1804 and again repealed in 1816), Parliament ordered that all documents and records pertaining to it be destroyed on the ground that a disclosure of the amount of income received ought not be required of any citizen.

public securities. Those affected by this measure, it was observed, were citizens who had "acquired fortunes on the easiest terms possible," who paid no taxes on their wealth, and who could hardly complain if the government took back a small part of the riches it had bestowed upon them.[13]

To protect government securities against taxation, Hamilton invoked the law of contract. According to his reading of this law, taxes laid upon securities represented a breach of public faith, since it was not stipulated in the contract made between the creditors and the government that this property was to be subjected to taxation. He argued further that such taxation was as inexpedient as it was unjust: it violated "the true principles of public credit" by depreciating the value of government securities and rendering them suspect in the eyes of investors. With the existence of the government depending upon the aid of men of wealth, everything must be done to foster their confidence in the honesty of government.*[14]

On the other hand, Hamilton did not deny that the government had the right to tax the income derived by individuals from interest paid upon government securities. When this money passed into the hands of citizens it became subject, Hamilton said, "in common with all other similar property, to the right of the government to raise contributions upon it." His only requirement was that the tax be levied upon general income and that the public creditors be placed in no worse position than other taxpayers.

In general, however, Hamilton advocated that the government confine itself to indirect taxation such as import duties and to excises. Taxes upon luxuries were his favorite method of making the rich contribute to the support of the government; incomes and profits he wished to leave as much as possible in the possession of the fortunate recipients, where they might be employed in fructifying the capital resources of the country. If American businessmen were to be persuaded to invest their capital and energy in manufactures, Hamilton knew that it was not enough to paint a rainbow in the sky: he must convince them that there was a pot of gold at its foot and that they could keep the gold after they found it.

Meanwhile the growing disaffection in the West was occupying an increasing share of Hamilton's attention. The comparative calm that in 1793 had followed upon the demonstrations and protests against the excise proved to be short-lived: in 1794, the embattled farmers again prepared to rise in defense of their "right" to manufacture whisky without interference from "revenooers."

Ironically enough, the grievance that caused the western caldron to boil

* Chief Justice Marshall followed Hamilton closely in handing down the decision that a tax upon government securities was "a tax on the contract, a tax on the power to borrow money to the credit of the United States, and consequently . . . repugnant to the Constitution."

The Whisky Rebellion

over was one of the few that Hamilton had thought fit to redress. Westerners had long complained of the fact they were obliged to leave their farms and stills and make a long journey to Philadelphia to stand trial for alleged violations of the internal revenue law. At Hamilton's instigation, Congress had enacted on June 5, 1794, a law which made such cases cognizable by the state courts when the offense took place more than fifty miles from the seat of a United States district court, thereby relieving Westerners of the necessity of attending court in Philadelphia. No doubt it pained Hamilton to award jurisdiction in these cases to the state courts, but the necessity of bringing to speedy trial those accused of violating the law overrode his partiality for the federal courts.

Nevertheless, processes continued to be served in western Pennsylvania under the old law requiring trial in Philadelphia. Hamilton was not directly responsible for this situation: processes were served under the old law because the alleged offense—not reporting stills in operation to the government—went back to the previous year, 1793, and because the writs were issued in May, 1794, before the passage of the act of Congress providing for a change of venue. Yet as it transpired, the writs were issued under one law and served under another law. Most ironical of all, they were later found to be erroneous.[15]

Manifestly, the serving of the processes requiring attendance in Philadelphia provided the pretext rather than the fundamental cause of the insurrection. The distillers knew that this was the last time that they would be required to stand trial in Philadelphia; but they also knew that, thanks to the law of June 1, 1794, they could expect a much stricter enforcement of the law in both the federal and state courts. In relieving them of the necessity of going to Philadelphia, Hamilton had removed a grievance, but at the same time he had aggravated their sense of injury. Finally, to Westerners, jail was no sweeter in Pittsburgh than in Philadelphia.[16]

In 1794, armed demonstrations against the excise began in the four western counties of Pennsylvania. Revenue officers were terrorized—sometimes at gun point—into resigning their offices; United States marshals were forcibly prevented from serving processes upon rioters; and the United States mail was seized by armed bands. Early in August, 1794, a meeting of armed men was held at Braddock's Field and preparations were made to attack Pittsburgh; the assault was averted only when the citizens, realizing that they could not withstand the attackers, marched out to join them.

President Washington immediately summoned his Cabinet, together with high Pennsylvania authorities, to consider the critical situation in the West. The President himself opened the meeting by declaring that the disorders in the West struck at the roots of law and order and that "the most spirited & firm measures were necessary: if such proceedings were tolerated there was an end to our Constitution." But when he asked Governor Mifflin to aid in suppressing the uprising, the governor seemed far more eager to raise objections than to raise troops: he was not sure that the Pennsylvania militia could be depended upon to act against the Whisky Boys; unless an overwhelming force were brought to bear, a full-fledged insurrection might be provoked; and the British were known to be waiting for just such an opportunity to break up the union. For these reasons, Mifflin recommended that the judiciary be given another opportunity to restore order before coercion was resorted to.[17]

In the case of the western farmers who had dared defy a federal law, Hamilton was of the opinion that they especially deserved to feel the heavy hand of government. He dismissed their grievances as unimportant: they resisted the laws, he said, because they were at heart malcontents and tax dodgers with a penchant for listening to "caballers, intriguers, and demagogues." What made their case particularly heinous was that they had resorted to violence at the very time the government was spending vast sums to protect them against the Indians and exerting itself to win for them the navigation of the Mississippi. To his mind, everything indicated that the leaders of the revolt aspired to create an independent state of which they expected to be the rulers.[18]

With the integrity of the union at stake, he was not inclined to mince words—even when they were uttered by Supreme Court justices—with the insurgents. In effect, he took the position that the only language Westerners understood was force. For the government to hold its hand under such provocation would be equivalent, he declared, to giving "a CARTE BLANCHE to ambition, licentiousness and foreign intrigue."[19]

Even after the seriousness of the situation had become manifest, many Republicans, fearful of aggrandizing the powers of the Executive Branch, urged that punitive action against the insurgents be postponed until Congress had convened. But Hamilton would consent neither to delay nor to congressional intervention: if the insurgents were permitted to go on defying the laws until Congress met, he apprehended that they would succeed in solidifying their strength to such a degree that Congress would be compelled to repeal the excise law. He observed with alarm that while the administration stayed its hand, the season for military operations was passing and the spirit of revolt was beginning to spread to other states: in western Maryland, an attempt was made to seize the armory at Fredericktown; and in Kentucky, Georgia and the Carolinas rumblings of discontent were heard on every hand.[20]

Before the President could call out the militia, it was necessary for the government to secure a written statement from a justice of the Supreme Court or from a district judge certifying that the enforcement of the laws had broken down. To Hamilton was assigned the task of drawing up a report purporting to prove that judicial proceedings had failed and that

The Whisky Rebellion

the government was therefore authorized to resort to force. Upon the basis of this report, Justice James Wilson certified to the President that the laws of the United States were opposed by "combinations too powerful to be suppressed by the ordinary course of Judicial proceedings, or by the powers vested in the Marshal of that district." On August 17, 1794, armed with this authority, the government sent orders to the governors of New Jersey, Pennsylvania, Maryland and Virginia to call out 12,500 militiamen and to hold them in readiness for a march to the West.[21]

Since it was doubtful whether the militia would willingly respond to this order, Hamilton undertook to mobilize public opinion on the side of the government. Hamiltonian "energy" was seldom mere action: usually it was accompanied by a vigorous effort to win the support of public opinion—sometimes, however, after the event. In this instance, Hamilton published in the newspapers, under the signature "An American," a defense of the government's policies; and he drew up a report, likewise printed in the newspapers, recounting the efforts of the government to settle the dispute by peaceful means.

Partly as a result of the good face put upon the government's case by Hamilton, there were so many volunteers for the western expedition that enlistment had to be stopped lest the army become unmanageable from sheer size. By September 12, a high government official declared that the administration did not have "the most remote apprehension of difficulty in quelling the infatuation." The Republican leaders dissociated themselves from the uprising and pledged their support to the administration, and a large number of the volunteers were members of that party.

Hamilton was not a man to sit quietly in his office while the authority of the national government was being forcibly resisted. Both his love of glory and his devotion to the union impelled him to take part in the western expedition. Nor did he lack plausible pretexts for joining the army: Secretary of War Knox was absent in New England and Hamilton's knowledge of the workings of the War Department qualified him to act in Knox's place. Moreover, although he did not say so, he hoped to demonstrate the intimacy of his relationship with Washington by accompanying him on the expedition. The French Minister, who knew a master of diplomacy when he saw one, pronounced Hamilton's action "a stroke of genius"—"a step in the profound policy which directs all his steps—a measure dictated by an exact knowledge of the human heart."

On September 30, leaving Oliver Wolcott to manage the Treasury, Hamilton set out with Washington for Carlisle, Pennsylvania, the encampment of the western army. Reaching their destination on October 4, they immediately set about organizing the detachments of militia and in bringing up supplies—the last being Hamilton's particular responsibility.[22]

In part, the army was composed of gentlemen volunteers, "high-toned

Federalists" to a man, in whose eyes the insurgents merited hanging without the formality of a trial. To make matters worse for any Westerners so unfortunate as to fall into their hands, they were inclined to regard anyone who drank whisky as an insurgent. One corps of Philadelphia gentlemen drew up a list of suspected rebels whom they proposed to put to death, and on the march to Carlisle two citizens were killed by the army. But Hamilton and Washington, after they joined the army, put an end to such acts of violence: "It is a very precious and important idea," the Secretary said, "that those who are called out in support & defence of the laws should not give occasion or even pretext to impute to them infractions of the laws."

Although the privates were kept in order, the officers were not always easily controlled. In particular, Governor Mifflin, the commander of the Pennsylvania militia, proved a trial to Hamilton. Mifflin was a Republican and had at first opposed sending troops into western Pennsylvania, but there was no doubt of his loyalty to the union: it was partly owing to his zeal that the quota of the Pennsylvania militia had been filled. However, there was considerable doubt of his sobriety: a notorious toper, the worst was feared when he reached the Promised Land of Whisky.

True to form, Governor Mifflin got roaring drunk and enlivened the expedition by ordering the Philadelphia light horse to fire upon all comers—with the result that the New Jersey militia was shot up by the silk-stocking lads from Philadelphia. For this offense, Mifflin was obliged to apologize publicly and to confess that he had been intoxicated—a fact of such flagrant notoriety that any confession was wholly superfluous.

But if whisky took its toll, the same could not be said for the Whisky Boys. The leaders of the insurrection had sworn that they would fight like demons: men raised upon whisky, they swore, would annihilate the "water gruel troops over the mountains." Hamilton gave full credit to these reports of the Westerners' valor; in these "deserts" beyond the Alleghenies he expected to see the kind of action he had missed during the War of Independence. His presence in the army seemed almost a certain guarantee that the insurgents would fight to the last man—for what greater provocation could be given them than the spectacle of their archenemy at the head of his troops? And yet, despite even this supreme incitement, the Whisky Boys exhibited no eagerness to come to grips with the invaders. Not an insurgent appeared in arms: the army marched through a peaceful countryside inhabited by inoffensive, docile citizens. The overwhelming force brought against them; the desertion of their leaders; and the fundamental loyalty of the people all conspired to bring about the complete collapse of the insurrection.

Although everything seemed quiet along the Monongahela, Hamilton was resolved that the army should cross the mountains—an enterprise that some disgusted soldiers compared with Hannibal's passage of the Alps—and carry

The Whisky Rebellion

the flag into the heart of the enemy's country.[23] Rather than encounter the rigors of the western climate—apparently more to be dreaded than the western insurgents—Washington returned to Philadelphia, leaving Governor Henry Lee of Virginia in ostensible command of the army. The real leader, however, was reputed to be Alexander Hamilton. The little colonel, although outranked by Lee and without official connection with the expedition, seemed to be running the show; he indulged in the airs of a commander in chief and, capitalizing upon his friendship with Washington, made his influence felt in every department of the army. He issued orders in his own name and on one occasion he rebuked General Mifflin. Hamilton's quarters were the envy of officers who, one complained, had "little to eat, only whisky to drink, bad cooks, noisy companions, a wet room, and stinking beds." Beholding Hamilton in his "superb Marque . . . by far more extensive and elegant than that of the commander in chief," it was hard for some to believe that they were in the presence of a mere Secretary of the Treasury.

Relentlessly prodded by Hamilton, the army toiled through the rain and mud. Racked by fevers, agues, fluxes and pleurisies, even some of "the most frolicsome and the most patriotic heroes of the army" began to grumble, but it was observed that "a double allowance of whisky made them as happy as could be." As happy, that is, as could be without anything to do but to march across seemingly endless mountains.[24]

Hamilton had hoped to capture "a sufficient number of proper persons for examples," but of the 150 men brought in by the army few could qualify for this distinction. In obedience to Washington's orders, the army remained in strict subordination to the civil authorities. Suspects were not haled before a military tribunal and no man was condemned without due process of law. Nevertheless, under the common-law right enjoyed by every citizen to seize a traitor, Hamilton sent out scouting parties to round up suspects, who, in some cases, were brought before him for preliminary examination. While he did not succeed in ferreting out many traitors by these methods, his "inquisitorial" activities later provided his political enemies with a rich vein of propaganda.

Of those taken into custody by the army, the most eligible to grace a Roman triumph was Hugh Henry Brackenridge. Constituting himself the spokesman of his fellow Westerners, Brackenridge had urged Hamilton to postpone the collection of the excise until the Mississippi had been opened to Americans. But Brackenridge accompanied his advice with a warning that left no doubt in Hamilton's mind that he was dealing with a traitor: if the federal government sent an army into western Pennsylvania, Brackenridge predicted that it would be promptly thrown out by the hardy Westerners and that the Whisky Boys would parade triumphantly through the streets of Philadelphia.[25]

When a letter allegedly written by Brackenridge to David Bradford, one of the leaders of the revolt, was picked up in a tavern, Hamilton believed that he had an airtight case against the Westerner. "It is proved," he declared, ". . . that he [Brackenridge] has been the worst of all scoundrels." He therefore received Brackenridge at headquarters with the constrained air of a man who might shortly be obliged to order his visitor taken out and hung. But he did not give the impression that he relished the situation: rather he seemed, said Brackenridge, to be torn between humanity and his sense of justice; but the Westerner saw no reason to believe that humanity would triumph in his case.

The interview opened on a note calculated to aggravate Brackenridge's apprehensions. Hamilton suggested that the prisoner make a clean breast of his part in the plot to overthrow the government; when Brackenridge protested that he knew nothing of such a plot, Hamilton was openly incredulous. Complaining that he detected in Brackenridge's attitude "a disposition to excuse the principal actors," he warned his prisoner that he was not within the pale of the amnesty and that "though the government may not be disposed to proceed rigorously, yet it has you in its power, and it will depend upon the candor of your account what your fate will be." But Brackenridge stoutly declared that he would not change a syllable to save his life; far from being a rebel, he claimed, he had saved Pittsburgh from attack by the insurgents. "I saw the Secretary pause at this, and sink into deep reflection," Brackenridge later remarked. "It staggered him." After a short pause, during which Hamilton struggled to regain his composure, he remarked: "My breast begins to ache—we will stop to-night; we will resume to-morrow at nine o'clock."[26]

The next day, when Brackenridge was brought up for interrogation, he expected the worst. Instead, he met with an apology and protestations of good will. "In the course of yesterday," Hamilton said, "I had uneasy feelings, I was concerned for you as a man of talents; my impressions were unfavorable; you may have observed it. I now think it my duty to inform you, that not a single one remains. Had we listened to some people, I know not what we may have done." Giving the Westerner no opportunity to recover from his surprise, Hamilton went on to say that Governor Lee would hear how egregiously Brackenridge's conduct had been misrepresented: "You are in no personal danger," the Secretary concluded. "You will not be troubled even with a simple inquisition by the judge."[27]

What had so dramatically changed Hamilton's mind was new information that Brackenridge had attempted to restrain the hotheads; that he had always advocated the repeal of the excise by constitutional means; and that the letter supposedly written by Brackenridge to David Bradford, the insurgent leader, had actually been addressed to William Bradford, the Attorney General of the United States.

With the collapse of the case against Brackenridge, Hamilton turned his

The Whisky Rebellion

attention to other quarry. He had marked down as the ringleaders of the plot to detach the west from the union two prominent Republican politicians—William Findley and Albert Gallatin. Findley was a former Antifederalist leader of western Pennsylvania who, as a Republican member of the House of Representatives, had distinguished himself by the zeal with which he had promoted a ways and means committee. Albert Gallatin was a follower of Thomas Jefferson who had led the peaceable resistance to the excise in the western country. But despite Hamilton's diligent questioning of witnesses, he was unable to uncover any evidence that would stand up in court linking Findley and Gallatin with the uprising. As a result, he was forced to content himself with observing that Findley was "a vain man, and a dishonest politician, and had a very bad heart" and that Gallatin was a "Swiss-born Incendiary." Since neither of these charges were indictable under the laws of the United States, the two Republicans went free.

The big ones having gotten away, Hamilton had a sorry kettle of fish to show for his efforts. Of these lesser fry, "two poor wretches only," he lamented, "were sentenced to die, one of them little short of an idiot, the other a miserable follower in the hindmost train of rebellion." Both were so utterly insignificant that, as Hamilton said, to have executed them would have been sheer ferocity, and so he approved the President's decision to pardon them.[28]

Notwithstanding the tame ending of the western expedition, Hamilton was far from persuaded that the region had been pacified. Everything he had seen during his tour of the West indicated that opposition had been merely driven underground and that the moment the troops were withdrawn the Whisky Boys would again be up in arms. "The political putrefaction of Pennsylvania is greater than I had any idea of," he remarked. "Without vigor everywhere, our tranquillity is likely to be of very short duration, and the next storm will be infinitely worse than the present one." His idea of vigor was to keep the army stationed in the whisky country until the inhabitants had given incontestable proof of their loyalty to the government. But President Washington, discerning more clearly than did Hamilton the consequences of keeping a "standing army" in the West, negatived the idea, and virtually all the troops were withdrawn and the army disbanded.[29]

Hamilton always contended that the outcome of the Whisky Rebellion demonstrated that republican government was compatible with order and had thereby added immeasurably to the prestige of the United States at home and abroad. But Republicans, conveniently forgetting their own part in the crushing of the revolt, pictured it as a crusade of stockjobbers, bank directors and speculators against the common people: it was another victory over inoffensive farmers scored by the "knights of the funding system" with Hamilton at their head.[30] To such lengths was political partisanship carried that Hamilton was accused of having deliberately stirred up the Whisky

Rebellion in order to furnish a pretext for increasing the national debt and saddling the country with a standing army. Having failed to cement the union with money, he now sought, it was said, to solidify it with blood: stocks and bonds were to be replaced by bullets and bayonets.

To these allegations, Hamilton entered a denial and a countercharge. The real culprits, he asserted, were the Democratic Clubs and the leaders of the Republican party. While Brackenridge, Findley and Gallatin had slipped through his fingers, Hamilton was resolved that Thomas Jefferson and James Madison should not escape the odium of having fomented the rebellion.

When Genêt was cutting a wide swath across the United States, he had left behind him a crop of Democratic Clubs allegedly modeled upon and affiliated with the Revolutionary Clubs in France. Unlike their French counterparts, however, the American Democratic Clubs were not organs of red revolution; their objective was simply to conduct a constitutional opposition to Hamiltonianism in the name of liberty and democracy. Their heroes were the leaders of the Republican party, not Danton, Marat and Robespierre; the Charleston, South Carolina, club called itself the Madisonian Society; and others took the name of Benjamin Franklin, already elevated to the status of a Republican patron saint.[31]

Whether these clubs were Jacobin or Republican made little difference to Hamilton; a Republican, by his definition, was a French sympathizer, and a French sympathizer was an enemy of order, religion and sound finance. Consequently he made little effort to distinguish between the two: the members of the Democratic Clubs, he declared, were at heart Jacobins who were prepared to add treason to the crimes they committed in the name of liberty.

Accordingly Hamilton undertook to show that while Genêt was the man who had "brought the eggs of these venomous reptiles to our shores," the brood had been adopted and nurtured by Madison and Jefferson and had grown up to be little Republicans. As foster parents of these bloodthirsty delinquents, Jefferson and Madison were to be held accountable for the "Parisian horrors" that the Democratic Societies planned to stage in the United States.[32]

Some color of plausibility was given to Hamilton's indictment of the Democratic Societies by the fact that several Democratic Clubs in western Pennsylvania had fallen under the control of the insurgents. But this was the exception rather than the rule: the Democratic Societies pledged their support to the government and it was said that so many members of the Philadelphia Society turned out that a quorum could have been summoned in the expeditionary force that set out to suppress the rebellion.[33]

In November, 1794, after the Whisky Rebellion had been put down, President Washington delivered a message to Congress in which he denounced the "self-created" Democratic Societies as subversive organizations to whose intrigues and disaffection he attributed the troubles in the West. In the President's message, Jefferson believed that he detected the hand of Alexander Hamilton. Who else, he inquired, could have instigated the President to attack freedoms guaranteed by the Bill of Rights and fix the opprobrious epithet of "self-created societies" upon associations of peace-loving citizens?

In actuality, Washington needed no promptings from Hamilton to inflame him against the Democratic Societies. From the first appearance of these societies he had recoiled from them as instruments of the "French faction" to overthrow the government, and to them he attributed the increasing virulence of the attacks upon him and his administration. Indeed, Washington went even beyond Hamilton in execrating the clubs. "I early gave it as my opinion to the confidential characters around me," he said, "that, if these Societies were not counteracted (not by prosecutions, the ready way to make them grow stronger) or did not fall into disesteem from the knowledge of their origin . . . that they would shake the government to its foundation."

The President's denunciation of the Democratic Societies produced an uproar in Congress far beyond anything either he or Hamilton had anticipated. Washington had struck dangerously near the root of freedom of speech and freedom of assembly; the Democratic Societies had contravened no existing law, and in the absence of proof that they had instigated the rebellion it appeared that they were being condemned because they had expressed opinions offensive to the administration. Although this kind of repression was sanctioned by the example of the British government (William Pitt was at this time engaged in enforcing conformity by punitive means), the Republicans marshaled their forces in Congress with the intent of administering a rebuke to the President.

It was of vital importance to the Federalists that the House of Representatives affix its approval to the President's speech. If the President were not supported, a severe blow would be dealt the concept of Executive leadership laboriously built up by Hamilton since 1789; Washington's prestige would be undermined throughout the country; and the Democratic Societies would be vindicated. But the Republicans in Congress stubbornly refused to endorse the President's remarks about the evil of "self-created societies"; and since the Republicans held a majority in the House of Representatives, there seemed a good chance that the President would be left out on a limb.

In order to rescue the President from this predicament, Hamilton persuaded Representative Fitzsimmons of Pennsylvania to introduce into the House a resolve condemning the "self-created societies . . . which by deceiving the ignorant and the weak, may naturally be supposed to have stimulated and urged the insurrection." For the speech with which Fitzsimmons backed up this resolve, Hamilton supplied the arguments. Even so, Fitzsimmons' motion was lost and the best that the Federalists could do was to secure the

House's approval of a statement that substituted the words "combinations of men" for the phrase "self-created societies."

By virtue of his stand against the "Jacobin" clubs, Hamilton won the acclaim of the Federalists as the savior—next to God and President Washington—of the country, the Argus-eyed enemy of disaffection and the upholder of true "Americanism" against "Gallo-Americanism." Of even greater significance, the President had aligned himself with Hamilton more unreservedly than ever before. Washington had never seemed to Republicans more like a Hamiltonian than when he inveighed against the "self-created societies." With the President on Hamilton's side, the Secretary of the Treasury seemed invincible: "the influence and popularity of General Washington played off by the cunning of Hamilton" was a combination against which Jefferson despaired of making head. The inevitable end of this alliance between the Virginia gentleman and the West Indian "renegade," Jefferson predicted, would be the ruin of Washington's reputation and the loss of the confidence of the people of the United States. The Father of his Country led around by a bastard—to such an unhappy pass, Republicans lamented, had the United States arrived.[34]

27.
Jay's Treaty

In the summer of 1794, it was well within the realm of possibility that the United States would find itself involved in a foreign as well as a civil war. True, John Jay was in London, but it was far from certain that he could save the peace against the evident determination of the Republicans to extort concessions from Great Britain and the equally strong determination of the British government to tolerate no neutral rights that interfered with the prosecution of the war against revolutionary France. In part at least, the issue of peace or war depended upon how far the United States was prepared to go toward adjusting its policies to meet the changed world situation. If this country insisted upon asserting its neutral rights as broadly and as uncompromisingly as it had done in its treaties with France, Prussia and Sweden, war with Great Britain was probably unavoidable. And if war came, the British would have the advantage not only of sea power but the possession of the Northwest posts and the alliance of some of the most formidable Indian tribes upon the continent.[1]

The instructions given John Jay by the United States government were therefore of crucial importance. Fortunately for the cause of Anglo-American harmony, these instructions were largely the work of Alexander Hamilton. Hamilton, of course, was not Secretary of State, but that circumstance had never prevented him from determining the course of American foreign policy. Jefferson's retirement in December, 1793, made it easier for Hamilton to play a decisive role in this field: Edmund Randolph, Jefferson's successor in the State Department, prided himself upon being above party, but he succeeded only in offending both parties. Although Randolph drew up the original instructions to Jay, Hamilton deleted everything which might have given umbrage to the British: "Energy, without asperity," Hamilton observed, "seems best to comport with the dignity of national language. . . . We are still in the path of negotiation: let us not plant it with thorns."[2]

In contrast to Jefferson and Madison, who thought that when dealing with Englishmen the proper accouterment of an American diplomat was a chip prominently displayed upon the shoulder, Hamilton never forgot that he was confronted by proud and confident men who looked upon Americans as revolted subjects and who were not impressed by displays of vainglory, self-righteousness and bravado. He had, besides, a healthy appreciation of British naval and military strength; far from supposing Great Britain to be at its last gasp, as Madison and Jefferson fondly imagined, Hamilton thought that the island kingdom would again triumph over France as it had in every war during the previous hundred years. He therefore acted upon the theory that the success of Jay's mission depended upon persuading British statesmen that the good will of the United States was vital to their welfare and, equally important, that it was within their power to fix the United States in its neutrality by making a generous settlement.[3]

Such a settlement, Hamilton knew, must go to the root of the differences between the two countries. In Jay's instructions, Hamilton indicated the points he considered essential to a good understanding. The cession of the western posts, a commercial treaty (here Hamilton overrode Randolph's opposition), reparation for the losses suffered at the hands of British cruisers and admiralty courts, a precise definition of neutral rights, the prohibition of armed forces on the Great Lakes, free trade with the Indian tribes on both sides of the border, and compensation for the slaves carried away by the British army in 1783—when these issues had been satisfactorily disposed of, he was prepared to believe that the two countries could live in amity.[4]

Lest the British draw any wrong conclusions from his efforts to establish manufactures in the United States—certain in the long run to injure British industry and shipping—Hamilton instructed Jay to point out that the rapid increase of population and the consequent increase in the demand for manufactured goods would, for an incalculable period of time, ensure the British of a considerable share of the American market—provided, of course, that they did not forfeit that market altogether by ill-advised disregard of American rights.

Despite his eagerness to effect an accord with Great Britain, Hamilton was not a treaty-at-any-price man. He enjoined Jay to do nothing that would not bear scrutiny by public opinion in the United States and to enter into no engagements contrary to the terms of the existing treaties with France. Nor was Jay authorized to surrender any vital American rights and interests: "Unless an adjustment of the differences with her [Great Britain] could be effected on solid terms," he told Jay, "it would be better to do nothing."[5]

Unlike the Republicans, Hamilton did not assume that all the grievances were on the American side; indeed, few American statesmen have been more willing than he to admit that their country was in the wrong and to make amends for its misdeeds. As regards the debts owing by Americans to British subjects, he was prepared to see them assumed by the United States government; he wished both countries to renounce the right to sequester or confiscate debts; he advocated a prohibition upon the sale of prizes in American

Jay's Treaty

ports; and he thought that the United States was morally obliged to make full compensation for depredations committed upon British shipping by French privateers unlawfully fitted out in American ports.*6

Manifestly, Hamilton did not share the Republicans' conviction that the United States was negotiating from a position of strength. It was, in fact, his awareness of this country's weakness that accounted in part for the conciliatory tone he employed in addressing Great Britain on this occasion. Finally, the possibility that Jay's mission would fail was always present in Hamilton's calculations: in that all-too-likely event, he acknowledged that the United States would have no alternative but to go to war. With that dire prospect in mind, he urged Congress to prepare for war by land and sea "to the utmost extent of our resources."7

Shortly after Jay's departure, George Hammond, anxious to learn the nature of Jay's instructions, called upon Secretary Hamilton, from whom he had no doubt the information would be promptly forthcoming. Rarely had Hamilton failed to give the British Minister satisfaction in such matters, and he was the more confident of being taken into Hamilton's confidence because he carried with him Lord Grenville's "very conciliatory" explanation regarding the Order in Council of November 6 and the text of the Order of January 8. But here Hammond received one of the surprises of his diplomatic career: the Secretary of the Treasury, instead of accepting Grenville's gracious explanation with gratitude and cordiality, "entered into a pretty copious recital of the injuries which the commerce of this Country had suffered from British cruizers, and into a defense of the consequent claim which the American citizens had on their government to vindicate their rights." When Hammond reminded Hamilton of the views he had formerly expressed of the power of Great Britain, the Secretary interrupted him "with some degree of heat and remarked that however the Government of Great Britain might be united against France, he doubted not that when the wrongs which the American Commerce had suffered were known in Great Britain, a powerful party might be raised in that Nation in favor of this country." Whereupon Hammond flatly told him that such discourse bore a close resemblance to the doctrines advanced by the "demagogues" in the House of Representatives and "the uninformed mass of the American community."8

Against this unwonted show of intransigence, the British Minister could set Hamilton's assurances that the United States would not join the armed league of neutrals being formed by the Scandinavian powers against Great

---

* Although after 1789 no legal impediments were placed in the way of the collection of these debts, American juries were notoriously unwilling to respect the claims of creditors, particularly where overdue interest was concerned. In Virginia it was estimated that four fifths of the original debt was still owing, including nineteen years accrued interest.

Britain. Resentful of the highhanded methods with which the mistress of the seas ruled her element, in 1794 Denmark and Sweden signed a convention by which they pledged themselves to uphold neutral rights, by force if necessary. Since the United States was a fellow sufferer under British exactions, it was natural to suppose that it would be invited to join the Armed Neutrality; and, if history afforded any index to American policy, it could be predicted that the United States would sign with alacrity.[9]

Early in March, 1794, Hamilton had intimated to the President that American rights might best be upheld against Great Britain by means of a defensive league of neutral powers. This project, he later explained, was the product of the "reveries" that occupied his mind when conflict with Great Britain seemed inevitable. This was no more than a passing thought: after the arrival of news of the repeal of the Order in Council of November 6, 1793, the defeat of the punitive measures advocated by the Republicans, and the nomination of John Jay as Minister Extraordinary to the Court of St. James's, Hamilton changed his mind about the desirability of an Armed Neutrality.[10]

Having arrived at this decision, Hamilton proceeded to take the British Minister into his confidence: "In the present conjuncture," he told Hammond, "it was the settled policy of this government in every contingency, even in that of an open conflict with Great Britain to avoid entangling itself with European connexions which could only tend to involve this Country in disputes, wherein it might have no possible interest, and commit in a common cause with allies, from whom in the moment of danger, it would derive no succour." Hamilton made plain that these objections to entangling alliances applied with special force to the Armed Neutrality: the United States had no interests in common with Denmark and Sweden; the project was harebrained and certain to come to grief; and the Baltic powers would be utterly unable to aid the United States against the British navy.[11]

Hammond lost no time in acquainting his superiors in London with the good news that the government of the United States had no intention of stepping out of its role as a neutral. This information reached Lord Grenville in September, 1794. Ten days later, on September 30, John Jay submitted to the British Foreign Secretary a draft of a treaty based upon Hamilton's instructions. Grenville rejected it, proposing in turn terms less favorable than Jay had been led to expect. Upon this circumstance has been based the theory that the British Minister, opportunely informed that the United States would not contest British maritime supremacy by joining the Armed Neutrality, decided that he could write the treaty very much on his own terms.

It is noteworthy that in all Hamilton's outpouring of what ordinarily would be regarded as closely guarded diplomatic secrets, he gave Hammond no assurance that the United States would not go to war with Great Britain.

On the contrary, the burden of his remarks was that if it came to war between the two countries—and Hamilton assumed that if Jay's mission failed this would be the probable outcome—the United States would fight alone. And nothing he said against foreign alliances excluded the possibility that the United States would co-operate with the enemies of Great Britain without a formal convention for that purpose or that the French alliance would not be implemented.[12]

While it is true that upon receiving Hammond's dispatch Lord Grenville remarked that Hamilton's sentiments regarding the Armed Neutrality were "very acceptable"—surely a notable instance of British understatement—the British Foreign Secretary did not draw the conclusion that all danger was over. He was keenly aware that the predilection "so evidently prevalent in America towards the principles of French Anarchy," and the equally strong predilection toward kicking an Englishman when he was down, continued to make the policies of the United States government highly unpredictable. Lord Grenville was compelled to admit that Hamilton was not the government of the United States, however authoritatively he presumed to speak in its name. Accordingly, he instructed Hammond to keep a close watch upon developments in the United States and to take prompt action against any attempts to bring that country into the Armed Neutrality.[13]

Had the United States taken such action at this juncture, it is probable that an abrupt end would have been put to the negotiations between Jay and Grenville, and that instead of a treaty Jay would have brought back an Order in Council authorizing the seizure by the British navy of American shipping. Certainly Lord Grenville would never have agreed to surrender the Northwest posts to a nation that was on the point of adhering to the enemies of His Britannic Majesty.

In writing off the Armed Neutrality as a nullity, Hamilton's judgment did not play him false. Even more than the Armed Neutrality of 1780 it proved to be a rope of sand, for it lacked the support of Russia, the only naval power capable of effectually challenging Great Britain at sea. Actually, the project was inspired by France—Sweden was induced to support it by the hope of a French subsidy—and from the French point of view, the Scandinavian powers were expendable in the war against Great Britain. In the end, the combined fleets never put to sea: the Swedish and Danish armadas separated with mutual recriminations in September, 1794, and the whole project collapsed ignominiously.

Probably with no little satisfaction, Hamilton noted that Denmark and Sweden gained nothing by their efforts to coerce Great Britain.. The British government refused to restore Danish and Swedish ships seized while carrying cargoes to France, and the two Scandinavian powers failed to establish the principle that foodstuffs were not contraband. They succeeded only in fixing in the mind of the British Ministry the conviction that they were under French influence and therefore deserved to be treated as enemies.[14]

Hamilton had always insisted upon the subordination of the Cabinet to the policies laid down by the President, and it had been one of his principal grievances against Jefferson that he placed himself in opposition to measures that had received the approval of the Chief Executive. But by summarily rejecting American participation in the proposed Armed Neutrality, Hamilton was in fact practicing what he had so vehemently deprecated in Jefferson's conduct as Secretary of State. For President Washington was far from sharing Hamilton's contempt of the Armed Neutrality and aversion to treaties of alliance with the enemies of Great Britain. Although the President's scruples did not permit him to enter into negotiations with the neutral powers while Jay was still carrying on negotiations in London, he did not rule out the possibility that the United States might find it to its advantage to join Denmark and Sweden. If the British proved unconciliatory, he was prepared to instruct Jay to "prepare the minds of those Powers, through their representatives in London, and give the earliest notice of the fitness of making a more direct and formal application to them." In the meantime, he wished to keep the British guessing regarding the administration's attitude toward the Armed Neutrality.* Yet Hamilton, not for the first or last time, considered himself to be wiser than the President, and when the Secretary of the Treasury was seized by this conviction he acted pretty much as he saw fit. In this instance, although his intervention probably worked to the best interests of the United States, it was impossible for him to justify his actions upon any constitutional ground—unless, of course, he was a prime minister and the President a mere *roi fainéant*.

If John Jay's position in Great Britain had been weakened by Hamilton's assurances that the United States could be counted out of the Armed Neutrality, Jay himself was unaware of it. "I came here in the moment of exultation and triumph on account of Lord Howe's victory," he wrote Hamilton on November 19, 1794; "from that day to this, I have experienced no change in sentiment or conduct relative to the negotiation."[15]

Even if it is assumed that Lord Grenville was less well disposed toward the United States in September than in June, 1794, it was not owing to anything Hamilton said or did but to the singular conduct of James Monroe, the United States Minister to France. While Jay was negotiating in London, Monroe was receiving—and giving—the "fraternal embrace" in

---

* Edmund Randolph, who in this instance saw eye to eye with the President, inserted in Jay's instructions authorization to enter into discussions with the ministers of Russia, Denmark and Sweden in London; "and if an entire view of all our political relations shall, in your judgment," Randolph's instruction read, "permit the step, you will sound those ministers upon the probability of an alliance with their nations to support those principles." It is significant that although Hamilton permitted this discretionary power to stand in Jay's instructions, Jay did not act upon it.

Paris and pledging the solidarity of the two republics against the monarchical world. In Grenville's opinion, Monroe's actions spoke louder than Jay's words: he bluntly informed Jay that the confidence of His Majesty's Government in the sincerity of American professions of good will toward Great Britain was seriously shaken by the behavior of the American Minister in Paris.[16]

Nothing was more certain to terminate the negotiations between Jay and Grenville than the suspicion that the United States, behind the mask of neutrality, was in reality a satellite of France. Had Lord Grenville been persuaded that this was the case, he would have incontinently shown Jay the door. That he did not do so after Monroe's ardently pro-French antics was in part owing to the fact that Hamilton succeeded in persuading the British government that the Federalist administration was determined to follow a truly neutral course despite the efforts of the Republicans to slant American neutrality in France's favor.

The fact that the British were willing to make a treaty with the United States in 1794 was partly owing to their recognition that the strengthening of the "well-intentioned Party in America" led by Hamilton was Great Britain's best hope of stemming the tide of Jacobinism in the United States and upholding neutrality against the "French faction" headed by Jefferson and Madison. Their purpose was to induce Hamilton and his friends "to come forward with more energy and vigour, to maintain those principles of public order, which it is the interest of this Country [Great Britain] to support in every quarter of the Globe." As long as Hamilton and the Federalist party remained in power, the British government welcomed American rearmament: when the United States sought to import from England anchors and copper sheathing for the frigates under construction in the United States, Lord Grenville arranged to supply them, so certain was he that if the United States ceased to be a neutral it would come into the war on the side of Great Britain. Hamilton so far succeeded in demonstrating to Englishmen that Anglophobia was no longer a guiding principle of American foreign policy that even George III was impressed: he acknowledged that there might be some good in Americans after all; although, as John Quincy Adams said, the King could not rejoice wholeheartedly in the rising power and wealth of the United States because "the greater their prosperity may be, the more poignant all his feelings of regret will be at his having lost so fine an estate."[17]

In November, 1794, after four months of negotiations, Jay and Grenville compromised their differences and agreed upon a treaty. In general, Jay succeeded in gaining the main objectives of the United States, but at high cost to its claims as a neutral carrier. While Hamilton had supposed that in his instructions to Jay he had gone as far as possible toward conciliating Great Britain, Jay went even farther: the man on the spot found that the

Secretary of the Treasury had banked too heavily upon British good will to the United States.[18]

By the terms of this treaty, the United States secured the cession of the Northwest posts; a commercial treaty which admitted ships of seventy tons displacement or less to the British West Indies; the legalization of American trade to Great Britain and India, which before had rested on no firmer foundation than sufferance; and the creation of mixed commissions for the adjustment of territorial disputes and the settlement of spoliation claims. In exchange, the United States renounced the "freedom of the seas" at least for the duration of the war; enemy property not contraband was admitted to be subject to capture from American vessels; the contraband list was extended to include foodstuffs under certain conditions; the United States agreed not to export cotton, sugar and other West India products; it was stipulated that there should be no confiscation of bank deposits; the question of prewar debts was handed over for arbitration to a mixed commission; and to guard against a repetition of Citizen Genêt's activities, it was provided that no privateers were to be fitted out in United States ports and that no prizes were to be brought in and sold. Conspicuously absent from the document was any mention of compensation to Southerners for slaves lost during the War of Independence or of the termination of the impressment of American seamen by the British navy.[19]

When Hamilton first read the text of Jay's Treaty, he did not know whether to rejoice that Jay had carried out his mission or to lament that the price of preserving peace with Great Britain had come so high. To several features of the treaty he took immediate and decisive exception: the restriction in Article XII of American ships entering the British West Indies to seventy tons and the self-denying ordinance which bound the United States not to export cotton and Caribbean products were, he declared, wholly inadmissible. Moreover, he was disturbed by the ambiguity of the provisions regarding the status of foodstuffs; if they were held to be contraband under all conditions, it would mean that the principal exports of the United States would be subject to seizure. In these matters, he was inclined to believe that Jay had been too eager to put his country into the good graces of Great Britain.[20] It was therefore "not without full deliberation and some hesitation," he later said, "that I resolved to support it." There was some truth in his sister-in-law's taunt that he undertook to defend "what he never would himself have deigned to submit to."[21]

Hamilton eased his conscience by recommending that Article XII be deleted. The Senate took his advice and on June 24, 1795, the treaty was ratified by a partisan vote. All that remained was the President's signature and the exchange of ratifications. Even though Washington felt little enthusiasm for several clauses and downright repugnance for some parts of

Jay's Treaty

the treaty, he was nonetheless prepared to sign it. In the meanwhile, the Senate voted to keep secret the terms of the treaty it had just ratified. Hamilton did not approve of this decision: it would, he remarked, merely permit the opponents of the treaty to misrepresent it to the people. But his concern proved unnecessary: the text of the treaty was soon "leaked" to the newspapers by a Republican senator.[22]

If Hamilton felt some reservations toward Jay's Treaty, the same could not be said of the Republicans—they damned it without reservations of any kind. By giving Great Britain most-favored-nation status and by placing stocks, credits and bank deposits beyond the reach of reprisal, Jay seemed to have disarmed the United States and bound it Prometheus-like to the rock in order that vultures (flying the Union Jack) might "feed upon her tortured vitals." Madison called it a "ruinous bargain"; the United States could hardly have done worse, he thought, had it suffered utter defeat in war. As for the surrender of the Northwest posts, that seemed to him like buying the same horse twice. Instead of praising George's "Justice and Benevolence," Jay was advised to reread the Declaration of Independence for a truer insight into the character of that "hardened Pharaoh."[23]

Hamilton did not deny that the Declaration of Independence would make wholesome reading for American diplomats; but he thought that they ought to supplement it with some acquaintance with protocol and good manners. There was nothing to be gained, he pointed out, by storming into the presence of George III and flinging down an ultimatum before the "Royal Brute," and it was better to be received graciously by earls and dukes than to be kicked down the stairs by their footmen. As for Jay being "caressed by the Princesses ... and made much of by the maids of honor," he was merely following the footsteps of Ben Franklin, who had found that the paths of diplomacy often lead to the boudoir.[24]

The fact that the Republicans were hostile to the treaty occasioned Hamilton not the slightest surprise—any treaty whatever with Great Britain, he remarked, would have excited their ire—but he was not prepared for the opposition manifested by the merchants toward Jay's handiwork. Upon them, Hamilton could usually rely for support, yet in this instance they seemed far more inclined to condemn it out of hand than to give it a fair hearing. Resistance appeared in its most tumultuous form in the seaport towns, supposedly the chief beneficiaries of the treaty. In Boston, within twenty-four hours of its arrival it was censured; a motion to read the treaty before taking action was defeated.[25]

Boston having set the example, the New York Republicans gave the citizens of Manhattan a similar opportunity to express their detestation of Jay's handiwork. Popular meetings were usually held in New York during the noon hour in order to enable the mechanics and laborers of the city to attend. As a result, Federalists complained, the Republicans gained the support of allies who were "not afraid of a black eye or a broken head" —in contrast to the friends of peace and order, to whom the bruises incurred in street fighting were anything but emblems of valor.

Agreeable to this custom, the meeting summoned to discuss Jay's Treaty was fixed for twelve o'clock. Despite the certainty that the rougher element would be out in force prepared to make short shrift of anyone who ventured to speak in favor of the treaty, Hamilton and his friends decided to attend the meeting. Accompanying them were a large number of "respectable" citizens resolved to prevent the passage of any ill-considered strictures upon Jay's Treaty.[26]

But most of those who turned out for this meeting had not come to hear an orderly debate on Jay's Treaty but to listen to their favorite orators denounce or praise it. Certainly the Republicans had no intention of wasting their noon hour listening to what Hamilton had to say in its defense: they were already persuaded that only a "monarchist" could see anything good in that unparalleled betrayal of American rights. And so, when Hamilton rose to speak, his words were drowned in an earsplitting chorus of boos and catcalls. Despairing of delivering his speech, Hamilton contented himself with making a motion to the effect that the sense of the meeting was that action ought to be deferred "inasmuch as we have full confidence in the wisdom and virtue of the President of the United States, to whom, in conjunction with the Senate, the discussion of the question constitutionally belongs." When the chairman attempted to read this motion, he was stopped so vociferously at the point at which Hamilton expressed confidence that he could proceed no further.[27]

Thus far Hamilton had braved nothing worse than the hooting, jeers and insults of the crowd. A more serious ordeal was in store for him: not content with hurling abuse, some Republicans began to throw rocks at the Federalist champion. Hamilton was struck several times; but just as the Republicans were beginning to find the range, order was restored. A committee of fifteen, all of whom were hostile to the treaty, was elected. A few days later this committee brought in a report stigmatizing the treaty as a covenant with the "eternal enemy" of freedom. This was proclaimed to be the considered opinion of the people of New York City regarding Jay's Treaty.*[28]

These events spoke more eloquently to the Federalists than anything Hamilton might have said had he been permitted to deliver his speech. Here, they exclaimed, was visible evidence that Jacobinism was at work and that the sans-culottes were seeking "to knock out Hamilton's brains to reduce him to an equality with themselves." On his part, Hamilton declared that there could no longer be any doubt that French sympathizers intended

---

* Maturin Livingston later alleged that Hamilton had on this occasion shown "a want of spirit." Hamilton demanded an explanation and for a time the two men were on the point of a duel. Finally Livingston denied having made the remark.

Jay's Treaty

"serious mischief to certain Individuals," himself included; and that since the New York militia could not be depended upon to protect life and property, he urged that the United States troops stationed in the forts near New York City ought to be alerted for action.[29]

If decisions affecting American foreign policy were to be left to mobs and terrorists, Hamilton said, he could see no difference between the "turbulent mobocracy of Athens" and the government of the United States. He had always doubted the competence of the people to decide questions of foreign policy, but how much less qualified to arrive at right answers, he exclaimed, were "the ignorant and violent class of the community"—the class that thought it was a sufficient answer to scream that Hamilton was a hireling of King George and to silence him with brickbats. Was not this violence, he asked himself, the rumblings of the Great Beast that lay concealed beneath the surface of society—the Beast that had devastated France and was extending its sway over Americans?

Disappointing as the terms of the treaty had seemed to conservatives, when it began to appear that the issue was between "the mobbers and the government" they took a second look at Jay's work. Most important of all, the outrages committed by the opponents of the treaty served to confirm President Washington's decision to sign it.

But while Hamilton was preparing to celebrate the triumph of his policy, an untoward event occurred: news reached Philadelphia that the British navy was again seizing on the high seas American ships carrying foodstuffs to France and its allies. According to the interpretation given Jay's Treaty by the British, they were privileged to seize provisions in neutral ships "when the distress of the enemy is such for want of them that it becomes a means of reducing them, or of procuring an advantageous peace." Holding that France was in this state of distress (the harvest of 1794 had been poor) and that the war could be considerably shortened by blockade, they began in the summer of 1795, under a secret Order in Council of April, 1795, to prevent neutrals from carrying provisions to France. The doctrine that a blockade to be binding must be effective was now declared to be superseded by the principle that provisions could be seized anywhere and at any time provided full value was paid for the cargo.

Edmund Randolph, the Secretary of State, advised the President to withhold his signature to Jay's Treaty until assurances had been received from the British that American provision ships would not be seized unless bound for some port legally blockaded or besieged. As for Washington himself, so violent was his anger against the "perfidious" Britons that he was prepared to let the treaty go by default. Yet, as was his wont before taking final action, he asked Hamilton's advice.[30]

Even though Hamilton still believed that the rejection of Jay's handiwork would be the signal for war with Great Britain, he acknowledged that little would remain of American dignity and honor if the government ratified a treaty at the very time it was being violated by the other signatory. The effect of such conduct upon France likewise gave him concern: as regards all matters relating to neutral rights, he said, the United States ought to uphold the privileges conceded France in the Franco-American treaties and to continue to afford that country "in the midst of war a regular and just source of supply through us." For these reasons, Hamilton advised the President to sign the treaty but to withhold an exchange of ratifications until His Majesty's Government had given assurances that it would not seize provisions except when they were bound to a port legally blockaded or besieged. This plan would have the merit, he observed, of dashing the hopes of the Republicans that the President would kill the treaty and at the same time serve notice upon the British Ministry that the United States would reject all unilateral interpretations.[31]

But President Washington was in no frame of mind to follow Hamilton's advice. Instead, he took Secretary of State Randolph's counsel: when the President left Philadelphia for Mount Vernon in July, 1795, it was understood that the revocation of the Order in Council of April, 1795, would be a condition precedent to the President's signature to the treaty.

At this juncture, however, Providence—working, as the Federalists supposed, through one of its favorite agents, the British navy—gave President Washington a compelling reason for signing Jay's Treaty. True, this intervention incidentally brought about the downfall and disgrace of Secretary of State Randolph, but it did not for that reason seem to the Federalists any the less Heaven-inspired.[32]

In 1794, a British man-of-war had captured a French ship carrying dispatches from Citizen Fauchet, the French Minister to the United States, to his home government. These dispatches indicated that during the Whisky Rebellion, Randolph had urged Fauchet to buy from some American politicians or businessmen (here Fauchet's letters were ambiguous) information concerning British intrigues with the western insurgents, and that Randolph himself was open to pecuniary persuasion. The incriminating documents were delivered to Pickering and Wolcott by the British Minister in July, 1795. Hamilton was called upon by Pickering to help with the translation. Although the incident in question had occurred during the previous year, Washington was so alarmed by the evidence it afforded of French influence in the United States that he forced Randolph's resignation and signed Jay's Treaty. The President could no longer doubt that as long as relations between Great Britain and the United States remained unsettled, France would be in a position to exert pressure upon American foreign and domestic policies. By signing the treaty, Washington hoped to counteract French interference in American internal affairs almost as much as he hoped to regularize our relations with Great Britain.[33]

Jay's Treaty

Having surmounted so many hazards, Jay's Treaty, it might be supposed, could at last be laid to rest; the Senate had ratified, the President had signed, and the ratifications were in the process of being exchanged by Great Britain and the United States. But the unquiet spirit that had attended this treaty from its inception was still very much alive. The Republicans, far from being resigned to what they regarded as an unholy alliance with Great Britain, were resolved to use their numerical preponderance in the House of Representatives to make the treaty a nullity.

Because of Hamilton's responsibility for the treaty, the importance he had attached to its ratification and his reputation as the most redoubtable polemicist of the Federalist party, it was incumbent upon him to sell Jay's handiwork to the American people and to outgeneral the Republican strategists in the House of Representatives. He undertook to accomplish these tasks by writing a series of essays, the first of which appeared in July, 1795, under the signature "Camillus."

Like *The Federalist*, "Camillus" started out as a co-operative effort: Hamilton, Jay and Rufus King planned to divide the labor of presenting the case for the treaty to the American public. But Jay again failed to make good his literary promises; he dropped out without having contributed a single article. Nevertheless, he served as a consultant, and from him Hamilton and King derived the inside story of the negotiations and many of the justificatory arguments they used in their own articles. King wrote many of the later articles, but the work as a whole passed as Hamilton's and as such it was praised or damned.*

In these essays, Hamilton's line of argument was that while this was not the best of all possible treaties, it was the best that could be made under the circumstances; and the test to which he subjected Jay's work was not whether it was satisfactory in every respect but whether, upon the whole, it came reasonably close to attaining the objectives set by the United States. Treaties, he reminded Americans, were usually the product of an agreement reached by negotiation: only when victorious in war could a nation dictate the kind of terms which the Republicans wished to impose upon Great Britain. "Nations could never make contracts with one another," he observed, "if each were to require that every part of it should be adjusted by its own standard of right and expediency."[34]

If Jay's Treaty were judged by these standards, Hamilton maintained, it would not be found wanting. The fact that Great Britain had consented to make a commercial treaty and to surrender the Northwest posts augured to

---

* As has been seen, Hamilton did not choose his classical pseudonyms haphazardly. Camillus saved the Capital from the Gauls and, more aptly, he made a practice of "shrinking from no unpopularity" in opposing the wishes of the people. On several critical occasions he so far prevailed over the popular passions that the multitude followed his advice, "but yet hated Camillus." In Hamilton's case, for "Gauls" read "French."

his mind that the republic was beginning to be recognized by the British government as a power whose friendship was worth cultivating. Not only had the United States risen high in the world sine 1789; Hamilton contended that as a result of Jay's Treaty it would rise even higher. From the clause permitting free trade with Canada, for example, he predicted that many blessings would flow: here Jay had opened up "an immense field of future enterprise." With a prescience shared by few of his countrymen, he foresaw that the economy of Canada would be closely linked with that of the United States and that in the course of time American manufactures would displace those of Great Britain. "As to whatever may depend on enterprise," he said, "we need not fear to be outdone by any people on earth. It may almost be said, that enterprise is our element."*

As "Camillus," Hamilton attempted to do for international relations what "Publius" had done for domestic affairs. In these essays he propounded at such length the principles which he believed ought to guide the United States in its relations with foreign powers that Jefferson complained that Hamilton was writing "an Encyclopedia" on international affairs preparatory, presumably, to taking over the direction of the State Department. If the opposition could have been overwhelmed by the sheer weight of legal authority, "Camillus" would no doubt have been accounted Hamilton's most successful effort. For "Camillus" quoted Pufendorf, Grotius and Vattel very much as though he were drawing up a legal brief. Finally, just as "Publius" had sought to wean the American people from their fondness for democracy, so "Camillus" tried to moderate their passion for France and French principles. The Golden Rule of international life as handed down by "Camillus" was to pursue national interests exclusively and to avoid the seductions of foreign "Circes."

To most Americans in 1795, the immediate danger did not consist in succumbing to the wiles of a foreign enchantress so much as falling into the clutches of John Bull. Here "Camillus" had a ready answer: France was the one country to which Americans were drawn by gratitude and sympathy —therefore they must be especially on their guard against permitting their purely emotional bias toward France to divert them from the course of national self-interest. As for Great Britain being an ogre, that, he said, was the product of the imagination of "turbulent demagogues" and "disorganizers" whose objective was to ride to power upon Anglophobia.

Neutral rights being the sorest point of all, Hamilton approached them gingerly in his "Camillus" essays. He could do little more than observe that Americans were no worse off under Jay's Treaty than before: all that Jay had done was to recognize for the duration of the war the binding force of the existing law of nations. From which Hamilton concluded that the United

---

* The enduring result of Jay's Treaty is the undefended boundary between the United States and Canada.

States had in effect yielded nothing: it had merely acknowledged rules which Great Britain would not and which the United States could not persuade or compel her to renounce. "It is not for young and weak nations to attempt to enforce novelties or pretensions of equivocal validity," he added. "In every view, therefore, it was wise to desert the pretension."

According to Hamilton's reconstruction of events, John Jay did not kill the freedom of the seas—it had already been done to death by the belligerents. It was, in fact, the first casualty of the war between Great Britain and France; and, as in other wars between maritime powers, it was struck down by all the parties to the war. Even France, bound as it was by the treaty with the United States, had begun to invade American neutral rights in 1793. Having some knowledge of the way neutral rights had fared in previous wars, Hamilton was not surprised by this development; and he had little hope that he would live to see the day when free ships made free goods in time of war.

While admitting that neutral rights had gone by the board, Hamilton tried to salvage something from the concessions made by John Jay. "Camillus" denied that Jay had agreed to permit the British to seize from American ships provisions destined for France and he reprobated such seizures as "a wicked and impolitic measure." Only in cases of blockade and investment was "Camillus" willing to admit that provisions were contraband. Here, he conceded, the British had the law of nations on their side and the United States could not do otherwise than acquiesce.

Nevertheless, perhaps the most striking feature of these essays is the sympathy and understanding Hamilton revealed of the problems of empire and of sea power. With a force and lucidity that Lord Grenville could hardly have improved upon, "Camillus" justified the ways of Great Britain to Americans. He urged his countrymen, for example, to bear in mind that impressment "to the belligerent party is a question of national *safety*, to the neutral party a question of commercial convenience and individual security." To explain Jay's failure to secure the admission of American vessels to the British West Indies on satisfactory terms, Hamilton pointed out that "the inviolability of the principles of the navigation act had become a kind of axiom incorporated in the habits of thinking of the British government and nation." Moved by the same spirit of understanding, he held the British to be perfectly justified in insisting upon a settlement of the debts owing them by Americans: if His Majesty's Government failed to protect British capital in foreign countries, it would invite the seizure of these assets. On the other hand, he denied that the British owed the United States reparation for the failure to deliver control of the Northwest posts. Whatever loss the United States had sustained by reason of this unauthorized occupation "admitted," he said, "of no satisfactory rule of compensation" and therefore no claims for damages could be submitted. As for the controversy over the abducted slaves, "Camillus" observed that it was not a matter of great moment: some 2,000 slaves worth at the most $400,000 was hardly a matter over which two countries ought to fall out—particularly since a war with Great Britain would cost ten times that amount.

Instead of dwelling upon British infractions of the treaty of peace of 1783, "Camillus" gave his readers a circumstantial account of Americans' derelictions, with special emphasis on the New York Trespass Act and impediments put in the way of the collection of British debts by Virginians. Wrongdoing, he took satisfaction in reminding his countrymen, was not solely the work of Englishmen—when it came to violating international agreements, Americans were equally hardened offenders.

"Camillus" was not the only "old Roman" to ask the people for their ears: among others, Noah Webster and James Kent, writing under the name of "Curtius" came to the defense of Jay's Treaty. Jefferson, supposing that "Curtius" was Hamilton under a different toga, urged his friends to expose the "sophistry" by which Hamilton was undermining Republicans' opposition to the treaty. Hamilton, he wrote in agitation to Madison, was "really a colossus to the anti-republican party. Without numbers, he is an host within himself." But Madison declined to be drawn into a contest against such odds, and so the responsibility for answering Hamilton was left largely to Republican newspaper editors and minor polemicists.

Against the "adder" John Jay had brought into the country, the Republicans held one weapon in reserve. Even though it had been approved by the President and Senate, the treaty could not be carried into execution without an appropriation of money by the House of Representatives, the majority of which was composed of Republicans upon whom the arguments of "Camillus" had made scant impression. The Republican leaders therefore decided to kill the treaty in the House of Representatives.

In March, 1796, the Republican strategy was revealed. Edward Livingston of New York introduced a resolution requesting the President to submit to the inspection of the House of Representatives Jay's instructions, correspondence and other papers relating to the treaty "excepting such of said papers as any existing negotiation may render improper to be disclosed." This resolution was adopted by a large majority. By this maneuver the House of Representatives signalized its determination to assert a concurrent power in the ratification of treaties and thereby implement its claim to share in the making of foreign policy.

The representatives made clear that they were particularly anxious to see the instructions given John Jay. By so doing they brought Hamilton into the picture, for Jay's instructions were largely his handiwork. Yet here Hamilton exhibited a reluctance to display his work not often encountered in authors. He objected that because of the haste with which they were

Jay's Treaty

drawn up they were not sufficiently polished to stand examination by the littérateurs of the House of Representatives. But the literary shortcomings of the instructions were actually of minor moment: what Hamilton really feared was that they would be censured by the Republicans as "altogether deficient in firmness and spirit." Of course, what to the Republicans was firmness and spirit was to Hamilton simply bellicosity and bad manners; but he knew that once they saw Jay's instructions, they would raise the roof of the House of Representatives.[35]

He had little hope that Jay's Treaty would survive the ordeal. It was obvious that the Republican majority was only seeking a pretext to kill the treaty: once its right to pass upon treaties was admitted, Jay's work would probably be torn to shreds.[36]

Therefore Hamilton, when asked for his opinion by Washington, declared that the President was under no obligation to provide the House with papers relating to treaties, and that by making treaties the supreme law of the land the Constitution left Congress no alternative: it could not say whether or not the pledge made in a treaty should be redeemed by legislative enactment because the treaty was binding upon it. By any other interpretation, he pointed out, treaties would become subject to the vicissitudes of the legislative will: a pledge of public faith would have no greater permanence than public opinion tolerated.[37]

Against Hamilton's theory, Madison contended that by the Constitution Congress was left free to appropriate or to refuse to appropriate money essential to the execution of a treaty. By this view, treaties requiring legislation were simply contracts *in future* and incomplete until the enactment of such legislation.

Hamilton argued the case not only upon its constitutional merits but upon the far more explosive issue of peace or war. If Madison's doctrine prevailed and the House threw out the treaty, Hamilton advised the country to prepare for the worst. "*The Constitution and Peace* are in one scale," he exclaimed, "—the overthrow of the *Constitution* and *War* in the other." With this rallying cry, he mobilized the businessmen who, after their initial coolness toward the treaty, were now among its stanchest supporters. Fearful that the benefits promised by the treaty were about to slip through their fingers and dreading an open break with Great Britain as a national calamity, they deluged Congress with petitions and remonstrances—a stratagem which, said Madison, "produced in many places a fever & in New England delirium for the Treaty."[38]

To such heights did the fever mount among the Federalist members of the United States Senate that, rather than give up Jay's Treaty, they were prepared to throw the foreign affairs of the United States into chaos. At this time, treaties with Spain, Algiers and the Indians were awaiting ratification by the Senate. All these treaties were approved by the Republicans, the treaty with Spain by which the navigation of the Mississippi was promised the United States being especially prized. Despite the advantages won by these treaties, the Federalists proposed to make their ratification conditional upon the adoption of Jay's Treaty. Thus all would stand or fall together; and if the United States failed to win the navigation of the Mississippi, it would be the Republicans' fault![39]

Much to the chagrin of the Federalist senators, Hamilton refused to approve this strategy. Instead of stooping to something "altogether wrong and impolitic," he wished to see the President make a solemn appeal to public opinion, trusting to Washington's popularity to work its accustomed magic with the voters. "Let us be right," he exclaimed, "because to do right is intrinsically proper, and I verily believe it is the best means of securing final success. Let our adversaries have the whole glory of sacrificing the interests of the nation."[40]

Hamilton's advice won no favor with the Federalist members of the Senate. To them, such squeamishness savored more of idealism than of practical politics. Accordingly, they continued to talk of tying up the Spanish, Algerian and Indian treaties in the Senate until the House had voted money to carry Jay's Treaty into execution. Their slogan was to "inflexibly adhere for all or none."

While this crisis was coming to a head in Congress, news reached the United States of new British seizures of provision ships. This ill-timed measure led Hamilton to wonder if more was not to be dreaded from the folly of the friends of the United States than from the malignancy of its enemies. "The British ministry are as great fools or as great rascals as our Jacobins," he exploded, "else our commerce would not continue to be distressed as it is by their cruisers." No longer was he disposed to adopt a soft tone with British statesmen: he wished the administration to deliver a strong remonstrance against the wanton impressment of American seamen: "It will be an error to be too tame with this overbearing Cabinet," he declared.* [41]

On this occasion, however, the spectacle of the British trampling upon American rights did not turn the President against Jay's Treaty. Instead, he asked Hamilton to draw up a statement which might serve as a reply to the request of the House of Representatives for papers relating to the treaty. The draft Hamilton sent the President flatly denied the claim of the House of Representatives to a concurrent right to pass upon treaties. Yet, having established the principle, Hamilton was inclined to appease the representatives by granting them out of free will and favor some of the less important papers relating to the negotiations. By thus demonstrating his desire to

* The seizure of provision ships was stopped, but British privateers operating out of Bermuda continued to capture American ships, and the impressment of seamen went on.

cultivate harmony between the two branches, the President—so Hamilton hoped—would sow division among the Republicans in Congress.

The President was in a less conciliatory frame of mind than was Hamilton. Without waiting for a reply—he later explained that he already knew the general tenor of Hamilton's advice—he sent a message to the House firmly refusing to submit any part of Jay's papers to its inspection and explicitly denying its constitutional right to those papers. As proof of his contention that the Constitution invested the President and Senate with the whole treaty-making power, Washington cited the debates of the Constitutional Convention. Since James Madison had been a prominent member of that Convention, the President's reference to its debates was generally interpreted as a rebuke to Madison, to whose "duplicity and insincerity" the Federalists ascribed the untenable ground taken by the House of Representatives.

The firm and masterful tone assumed by the President toward the representatives delighted Hamilton: this was the proper way to address those troublesome politicians who were always grasping for more power than they were entitled to. "Whatever may happen, it is right in itself," he said, "and will elevate the character of the President, and inspire confidence abroad." Only in one respect did Hamilton find fault with the President's message— the mention of the debates in the Constitutional Convention. In his opinion, these were matters better left dead and buried; there were already too many skeletons rattling around in the cupboard. Moreover, Hamilton always took the position that it was immaterial what the framers had said in the Constitutional Convention. The only decisive consideration, to his mind, was what the Constitution meant when it was interpreted in the light of the accepted rules governing such instruments of government.

Despite the deep offense Washington's message gave the Republican members of Congress, late in April, 1796, the pressure of public opinion, skillfully mobilized by Hamilton and other Federalist leaders, finally told: the bill appropriating funds for the execution of Jay's Treaty was passed by a vote of fifty-one to forty-eight. At the same time, however, the House entered upon its journal a resolution to the effect that it enjoyed a constitutional right to sit in judgment upon the merits of treaties and to request the submission to its inspection of documents pertaining to the negotiation of a treaty. And so, while the Executive had won a victory over the legislature, there had been no surrender on the principle at issue.[42]

Jay's Treaty preserved peace with Great Britain, ended the tension in the West, made possible a vast increase in American shipping and trade, and, in general, created the conditions from which a genuine *rapprochement* between the United States and Great Britain began to emerge. Impressment and differences of opinion upon the definition of contraband—matters which Jay's Treaty had not settled—continued to make trouble, but they did not become acute until 1805. Nevertheless, the Federalists were given no reason to suppose that peacemakers were blessed. In fact, they incurred greater obloquy in some quarters than if they had made war in 1795. Among its other untoward effects, Jay's Treaty gravely impaired Washington's popularity and, hardly less than the funding system and creation of the Bank of the United States, alienated the South. Again, by consulting what he regarded as national interests, Hamilton had actually strengthened sectionalism.[43]

28.

The Election of 1796

Since June, 1793, when Hamilton had first expressed an intention of resigning, he had on several occasions contemplated from afar the sweets of private life. Those occasions, it is true, were determined largely by the ebb and flow of his popularity and by the state of the contending political parties in Congress. In the autumn of 1794, with Jay engaged in negotiations with the British, the Whisky Rebellion suppressed and the Republicans lying low, Hamilton decided that if the elections went in favor of the Federalists he would resign his office, giving Congress sufficient notice of his intention to enable it to stage a full investigation of his conduct in the Treasury if it so desired. "I am heartily tired of my situation," he said, "and wait only the opportunity of quitting it with honor and without decisive prejudice to the public affairs."[1]

While the elections did not turn out well for the Federalists, Hamilton decided to resign in spite of—or perhaps because of—this untoward development. For the Secretary had no desire to face a hostile Congress that was certain to attempt to clip his wings even more drastically than had the previous Republican-controlled Congress. And with Albert Gallatin elected to Congress, Hamilton could hardly doubt that the Republicans would succeed.

During his brief term as United States senator from 1793-94, Gallatin had proved himself to be a thorn in Hamilton's flesh. Alone among the Republican leaders, this Swiss-born statesman was capable of meeting Hamilton in the field of finance upon anything like equal terms. Gallatin insisted that the Secretary of the Treasury should be obliged to account fully for every appropriation and should be prepared at all times to give Congress a detailed statement of the state of the federal finances. By holding the Secretary to strict accountability, Gallatin hoped to correct what he held to be the "flagrant vice" of Hamilton's administration—"the total disregard of laws, and application of public moneys by the Department to objects for which they were not appropriated."* [2]

* Appropriations were not usually made by Congress for specific purposes. The appropriation bill consisted of four or more items: for civil expenses, military expenses, payment of the public debt, pensions. It was not until Gallatin was appointed to the Treasury that Congress specified the revenues from which appropriations should be paid.

Hamilton's reply to Gallatin's request for information revealed that the Secretary had not learned from his experience with Giles that Congress was to be treated with the deference of a servant to a master. Instead of giving the Senate the information it asked, Hamilton sent a letter explaining why it was not convenient for him to comply. He was, he said, already so overburdened with work that he had no time for "unexpected, desultory, and distressing calls for lengthy and complicated statements." Moreover, a series of unexpected events occurring in the domestic and foreign relations of the government had made such reports doubly onerous. And so, in place of facts and figures, the Senate received from Hamilton a statement that "the consciousness of devoting myself to the public service to the utmost extent of my faculties, and to the injury of my health, is a tranquillizing consolation."³

Although the Federalists succeeded in disqualifying Gallatin as a United States senator, they could not prevent the Republicans in the House of Representatives from establishing a committee of ways and means. Composed of members of the House, this body was invested with control of the budget, financial planning and the raising of revenue; while the House would continue to resort to the Secretary for information, the Republicans intended to strip him of his powers of determining the financial policies of the government. By means of the committee of ways and means would the "Colossus of Monocrats" be toppled from his "fiscal throne."

Rather than submit to such treatment, Hamilton swore that he would resign: he "would not be fool enough to make pecuniary sacrifices and endure a life of extreme drudgery without opportunity to do material good or to acquire reputation." Yet in spite of Hamilton's threats of immediate resignation, Congress voted to refer to the committee the business that had hitherto been treated as Hamilton's exclusive concern. The Republicans exulted that they had at last broken the Secretary's "unconstitutional" power over Congress and that the reign of "republican" as opposed to "monarchical" finance was about to begin. No longer, they flattered themselves, would the representatives of a free people submit themselves to the tutelage of a corrupt and self-seeking financier. The oracle had been exposed as a sham and Congress was at last master in its own house.⁴

But the Republicans rejoiced too soon. Lacking a financial expert in the House capable of standing up to Hamilton, they found that the committee easily fell under the Secretary's control. Late in 1794, however, Gallatin was elected to the House of Representatives—an event that augured ill for Hamilton's hopes of keeping the committee of ways and means in leading strings to the Treasury. Other considerations, hardly less weighty, counseled Hamilton's retirement to private life. He was not a wealthy man and, despite Republicans' charges that he had made a fortune by peculation and speculation, he had actually grown poor in office. When he made out his will in

1795, he remarked that he went to this trouble solely for the benefit of his creditors; the utmost that he could hope for was that his assets would pay his debts.[5]

For a man who lived for fame as did Hamilton, the post of Secretary of the Treasury no longer held attraction. The heroic days of that post were over; the great decisions had been made and the important policies laid down. What remained was the drudgery of balancing the budget and of paying off the national debt—a duty that Hamilton was content to leave, under proper supervision, to his successor. As for himself, he felt that he had taken more than his share of abuse from his political enemies. He had long since discovered that saving the people from themselves was an unending and thankless task. Those who devoted themselves disinterestedly to the service of the public could be sure, he said, of only one thing—"a large harvest of obloquy."

When he prepared to leave office in 1794, Hamilton was under no illusion that his work was done and that he could safely retire to rest upon his laurels. Despite his ardent love of the union he had not succeeded in imbuing the people with a like affection. In this respect, Jefferson—whom Hamilton regarded as the archenemy of nationalism—was far more successful than was Hamilton himself. Probably Hamilton's failure stemmed from the fact that he associated the national government with no great moral issue capable of capturing the popular imagination; he seemed to stand only for "the natural right of the great fishes to eat up the little ones whenever they can catch them." Of justice and equality he said little, and his plan of coupling the sections by economic ties and stimulating capitalism by concentrating wealth was not calculated to inspire the people with a passionate attachment to Old Glory. It remained for Andrew Jackson, Daniel Webster and Abraham Lincoln to convey Hamilton's ideal of nationalism to the masses.[6]

Nor could Hamilton claim to be a great popular leader: in him the common people did not hear their own thoughts and aspirations made articulate. If it is true that in a democracy a statesman must be "an uncommon man of common opinions," Hamilton did not qualify upon the second score. He had nothing of the common touch. He was a man who spoke to, not for, the people of America: he set himself up as their preceptor rather than as their sounding board. Estranged from the majority of his countrymen by his ideas of democracy, he was almost as far removed from them by his vision of the United States as a centralized and industrialized world power.

No Republican was willing to concede that Hamilton was leaving the finances of the United States "on a good footing." As they saw it, the Treasury was a sink of corruption, extravagance and embezzlement cleverly concealed by Hamilton's bookkeeping. They were right in one respect: during Hamilton's administration of the Treasury, the national debt had increased and was still increasing. Despite the operations of the sinking fund, the raising of the import duties and the addition of new articles to the dutied list, revenue fell behind expenditures; and, although much was done toward retiring the old debt, new indebtedness was incurred.

Hamilton insisted that a nation was not to be judged solely by the size of its debt and that there were more important things than debt reduction —for example, national power, prosperity and honor. Seen in this light, the increase of the debt was the price of "energetic government"—striking down the Indians, suppressing rebellion at home and resisting aggression from abroad. Nevertheless he recognized that the size of the national debt offered a vulnerable target to the Republicans. For this reason he decided to make the reduction of the debt the theme of his Final Report to Congress, delivered in January, 1795—a proper subject, remarked a Republican, for a man who had spent his career adding to the debts of his country.

Knowing that this report would be his last, the Federalists took pains to invest the occasion with proper solemnity. Even the Republicans, so great was their joy at seeing Hamilton retire from office, were willing to see him go with an unwonted show of amenity. In this spirit, Hamilton informed the House that his report was ready when they should be pleased to accept it; whereupon Elias Boudinot, "in the language applied to the President on such occasions," moved that Hamilton be informed that the House was "ready to receive the Report when he pleased."[7]

In his report, Hamilton handed down what might be regarded as his financial testament. Fidelity to engagements; the cherishing of public credit as a source of national strength and security; the avoidance, if possible, of large debts, but when debts must be incurred, the incorporation of the means of extinguishment into the contract; the preservation of peace as long as peace could be maintained with honor—these were some of the injunctions Hamilton laid down for his countrymen.

Above all, he recommended that the existing debt be put in the course of extinguishment. Without so much as a bow to the Republicans who had been saying this all along, Hamilton declared that the progressive accumulation of debt was "the natural disease of all governments; and it is not easy to conceive any thing more likely than this to lead to great and convulsive revolutions of empire." To avoid this disaster, he impressed upon Congress the necessity of providing additional revenue for the sinking fund and the vital importance of keeping this fund inviolate. Not the slightest loophole must be left, he warned, to "tempt the administrators of government to lay hold of this resource rather than resort to taxes." If the government religiously observed these precepts, he estimated that the national debt would be liquidated by 1826.[8]

And so, in the eyes of his admirers, Hamilton quit his office trailing clouds of glory and carrying his Final Report as the visible evidence of his apotheosis. Here, they exclaimed, was his answer—crushing in its finality— to Republicans' sneers that he knew only how to spend money and that he sought to perpetuate the debt as an "irredeemable" fund for corrupting members of Congress and enriching speculators. Thus rejoicing, they passed the Act of March 3, 1795, by which Congress committed several sources of revenue to the sinking fund "until the whole of the present debt of the United States should be reimbursed."* [9]

Although the Republicans pictured Hamilton's retirement as a flight from justice, they made no effort to revive the Giles resolutions or to conduct an official inquiry into his administration of the Treasury—an abstention which Hamilton regarded as a complete vindication. To clear up any doubts on this score, Benjamin Bache in the *Aurora* predicted that posterity would pronounce "an awful sentence of execration" upon Hamilton as an "ambitious Cataline" and then consign him to oblivion.[10]

But oblivion seemed far removed when Hamilton returned to New York as a private citizen and was received by the businessmen of the city. They demonstrated their gratitude to their benefactor with public dinners, panegyrics and legal business. The president and directors of the Bank of the United States sent him a testimonial of their esteem; he was given the freedom of the City of New York; in the newspapers he was compared with Washington; and he was extolled as the pilot who, having brought the ship safely into port, richly deserved surcease from his labors. The climax of this display of admiration for the late Secretary of the Treasury came in New York City, where at the Tontine Coffee House he was the guest of the merchants at "one of the most Superb Dinners, perhaps, that ever was prepared in this city." Over three hundred people turned out on this occasion to do homage to Hamilton; twenty toasts were drunk, and the last—to Alexander Hamilton—was followed by prolonged cheering.[11]

It was not only among businessmen, speculators and college presidents that Hamilton had won renown: the artisans, shopkeepers and workers of the seaport towns likewise acclaimed him as their benefactor. The men who had pulled the good ship *Alexander Hamilton* through the streets of New York and had drunk his health in waterfront taverns found that they had not mistaken their man: they contrasted the depression of those days with the abounding prosperity that the adoption of the Constitution and Hamilton's financial measures had ushered in, and they gave credit where they believed credit was due. They had supported bounties, tariffs and

---

* Gallatin later complained that the sinking fund did not reduce the debt. When he became Secretary of the Treasury under President Jefferson, he instituted changes by which the redemption of the debt was accelerated.

other enouragements to business and they reaped their reward in the form of full employment and higher wages. Some of these workers were so grateful to Hamilton that they offered to build him a house in New York at their own expense. But, poor as he was, Hamilton did not yet regard himself as an object of charity.[12]

Despite his flourishing law business, Hamilton was so remarkably indifferent to money-making that his friends began to make a joke of it, observing half humorously that they would have to bury him at their expense. He declined to join in get-rich-quick schemes: "You will not even pick up money when it lies at your feet," his friends complained, "unless it comes in the form of a fee!" And even his fees were often ridiculously low. Nor was he willing to take advantage of the fact that his father-in-law was a rich man; in order to re-establish his law practice in New York City, he borrowed money from his friends.

Such wanton neglect of his opportunities indicated to Hamilton's admirers that politics was his consuming passion and that law would always be at best a second love. "You were made for a Statesman," they assured him, "& politicks will never be out of your head." Angelica Church, Hamilton's sister-in-law, posed the question: "Can a mind engaged by Glory taste of peace and ease?" To these pleas that his country had first call upon his talents, Hamilton answered that "Public office in this country has few attractions. The pecuniary emolument is so inconsiderable as to amount to a sacrifice to any man who can employ his time with advantage in any liberal profession. The opportunity of doing good, from the jealousy of power and the spirit of faction, is too small in any station to warrant a long continuance of private sacrifices. . . . The prospect was even bad for gratifying in future the love of fame."[13]

But his friends need have given themselves no concern: although Hamilton had retired from political office, he had not retired from politics. When he left the Treasury he simply moved over to take a more comfortable position behind the President's chair. From this vantage point, he proposed to chart the course of government as effectively as he had while at the head of the Treasury.

As his successor in the Treasury, Hamilton chose Oliver Wolcott, an able New Englander who had served under Hamilton as Assistant Secretary. The selection of Wolcott for the secretaryship reveals that Hamilton was not thinking in political terms: Wolcott brought no strength to the administration, he came from a safely Federalist state, and he was only slightly known to the public. On the other hand, he was admirably suited to carry on Hamilton's policies and to lend an attentive ear to the voice of his former superior officer. As might be expected, under Wolcott, the Treasury ceased to be a policy-making department: Wolcott confined himself to the

The Election of 1796

collection of revenue, the settlement of accounts and other matters specifically within the province of the Treasury.[14]

Nevertheless, the course of government did not run wholly smooth for Hamilton. Early in 1796, Congress refused to act upon his recommendations for funding the unsubscribed debt—an affront which Hamilton regarded as a mortal sin against public credit. He became distraught, inveighing against Congress's action as a "capricious and abominable assassination of the national honor." "To see the character of the government and the country so sported with—exposed to so indelible a blot," he exclaimed, "—puts my heart to the torture." Again, in May, 1796, fearful that Congress was about to raid the sinking fund, he declared that "the fabric of public credit is prostrate and the Country and the President are disgraced." Out of office, Hamilton found it easy to believe that everything was going to rack and ruin.[15]

In 1796, Washington made up his mind not to stand for re-election—and this time, he made clear, his decision was irrevocable. In part, this resolution was owing to the abuse he had experienced at the hands of Republican journalists. "I desire to be buffeted no longer in the public prints," he said, "by a set of infamous scribblers." And, indeed, a man less sensitive than Washington might well have been revolted by American politics as reflected in the newspapers of the time. John Beckley, the clerk of the House of Representatives, writing under the sobriquet of "A Calm Observer," charged that, among other heinous offenses, Washington had stolen public funds and that he richly deserved impeachment. It is not on record that Beckley's good friends Jefferson and Madison thought any less of him after this "exposure" of Washington's crimes and misdemeanors; certainly Beckley continued to function as one of the master strategists of the Republican party.

No one had better reason than Hamilton to deplore these libels upon the President, for no one had capitalized more upon his prestige. Whenever he picked up a Republican newspaper Hamilton shared vicariously in the President's agony of spirit, but there was little that could be done (except, of course, to spread equally damaging and equally false reports about Jefferson), for the Republicans were as industrious in manufacturing as they were in propagating these canards. But in 1795, shortly after he resigned as Secretary of the Treasury, Hamilton was called upon to refute a particularly insidious charge against the President.

When he accepted the presidency in 1789, Washington had stipulated that in lieu of the authorized salary of $25,000 a year, he expected to be reimbursed only for the expenses incurred in the discharge of his official duties. At the time, everyone applauded the President's patriotic self-denial, supposing, of course, that his expenses would be much less than his salary. In 1795, however, an antiadministration newspaper declared that Washington was actually drawing more than his salary. As the custodian of the Treasury records during the period in question, Hamilton published a financial statement designed to prove that Washington had received less than his salary during his first five years in office. American taxpayers breathed easier when they learned that they were getting the services of the Father of His Country at a bargain rate. But what Hamilton omitted to point out was that for several years Washington had actually drawn more from the Treasury for expenses, chiefly for purposes of entertainment, than he would have been entitled to had he been on a straight salary basis.

To Hamilton, the President's decision to retire in March, 1797, was not unexpected: in 1792, Washington had been on the point of declining a second term and had been persuaded to run again only by the entreaties of his close friends. Yet the parting with Washington, however long anticipated, was not for Hamilton a sweet sorrow: it was altogether too much like divesting himself of his armor and going defenseless among his enemies.

When he left the splendid misery of the presidency, Washington intended to give the American people his political testament. In 1792, he had drawn up a valedictory, and when he decided in 1796 to leave office forever, he brought out his earlier draft, together with one submitted by James Madison in 1792, and he and Hamilton began to put it into the form of a Farewell Address.

Since 1792, several important changes had occurred in the United States that could not be ignored in the President's valedictory. Political parties had sprung up in the country and a European war had broken out. Although this war brought prosperity to the United States, it carried in its train the constant threat of involvement. Furthermore, it had by now been demonstrated that the kind of foreign interference in the domestic concerns of the republic, so much dreaded by Hamilton during the period of the Articles of Confederation, had become a reality. The task imposed upon Washington and Hamilton was therefore to devise a policy capable of guiding the United States through the foreign and domestic perils which had opened up on every side.

The two men were agreed that the power which most immediately threatened the sovereign rights of the United States was France. It was France that had intervened in the domestic affairs of its ally; that sought to widen the breach between Great Britain and the United States; and that, on occasion, had violated American neutral rights even more egregiously than had the British themselves. Above all, what made France dangerous in Hamilton's and Washington's eyes was the partiality felt by most Americans for the French republic in its war with Great Britain. As a result of this "love sickness," said Hamilton, there existed in the United States a powerful "French faction" composed of men who had exchanged "the pure and holy love of their own country for a meretricious foreign amour," and who had already laid their heads in the lap of a "french harlot."[16]

To keep Americans' affections on this side of the Atlantic, Washington and Hamilton made the Farewell Address a paean of praise—Hamilton hoped it would not prove to be a dirge—of the union. Upon the preservation of the union, the American people were told, their hope of felicity wholly depended: their independence, tranquillity at home, peace abroad, security, prosperity and liberty could not be dissociated from the union. The people were urged to glory in the name of America and to count it among their blessings that religion, manners, political ideals and the memories of a common struggle for freedom had bound them together. Hamilton likewise made sure that the economic basis of union received more than passing attention: in the Farewell Address he restated his conviction that the country was an economic whole in which each section complemented and strengthened the others.

In the political parties that had sprung up in the United States, Washington and Hamilton discerned the most formidable enemy of union. The catalogue of evils imputed to parties in the Farewell Address is overwhelming: they "distract the public councils and enfeeble the public administration"; they agitate the community with "ill founded jealousies and false alarms"; they foment riotous insurrections; they create prejudice in the popular mind against the national government; and they open the door to foreign influence and intrigue. These pernicious effects, it is stated, are rendered doubly dire by parties founded upon geographical distinctions—then the party spirit really comes into its own and national feeling is utterly extinguished. Even so, Washington and Hamilton acknowledged that parties must be regarded as the price of freedom. Parties free men will always have with them: the best that can be hoped is that party spirit will be confined within the bounds of moderation.

At least two thirds of the Farewell Address was given over to a discussion of the internal concerns of the United States; only in the concluding paragraphs was the subject of foreign policy touched upon. And even here it was treated largely from the point of view of how foreign entanglements would affect the union: the injunction against "permanent, inveterate antipathies against particular nations and passionate attachments for them," which for posterity came to form the heart of Washington's Address, was in reality part of the plea for a national character free from the "insidious wiles of foreign influence."

Washington and Hamilton undertook to persuade their countrymen that they had everything to lose and nothing to gain by becoming involved in "the toils of European ambition, rivalship, interest, humor, or caprice." Already blessed with peace, prosperity, freedom, sound finance and a position happily isolated from the turmoil of Europe, the people of the United

States were in possession, if ever a people were, of the ingredients of happiness. Why, therefore, it was asked, should they abandon their felicity and rush into the bloody rivalries of Europe or, even worse, permit European powers to turn the American continent into another Europe? No people, Washington and Hamilton averred, could be guilty of greater folly. Europe, from their viewpoint, had a "set of primary interests" in which Americans had at most only a remote concern. It followed that the part of wisdom for Americans was to keep out of Europe's affairs as rigorously as they excluded European influences from the affairs of the United States. The ideal, it was inferred, was to limit the contacts between the two spheres to commercial intercourse.

But the President and his adviser were under no illusion that this ideal was attainable. In the first place, the United States already had a "perpetual" alliance with France, and the President was not the man to say that the United States ought to be unfaithful to its obligations under that treaty. Secondly, Washington and Hamilton did not suppose that Americans could enjoy security simply by pretending that Europe did not exist: they knew from experience that Europe had an unpleasant way of intruding upon Americans when they wanted most to be left alone. To guard against such interference, it was essential, the Farewell Address asserted, that the United States hold itself free to make alliances with European powers; such alliances might be necessary to keep unwelcome visitors on the other side of the Atlantic. The only qualification laid down by the Address was that these alliances be of short duration: "temporary alliances for extraordinary engagements." As for perpetual or long-term connections with European powers, Washington and Hamilton expected that the French alliance would serve as an effective warning against such commitments.

Washington wished to publish his Farewell Address early in the summer of 1796, thereby removing "doubts from the minds of *all,* and leaving the field clear for *all.*" But Hamilton was not to be hurried: his health, he complained, was not good that summer and he was burdened with legal work. In actuality, however, Hamilton was seeking pretexts for delay: since there always remained the possibility that events might compel Washington to change his mind about retirement, Hamilton tried, in his own words, to *"hold the thing undecided to the last moment."* By Hamilton's reckoning, the deadline for publication was two months before the meeting of the Electoral College. Since the electors did not meet until December, this meant that Washington would not make his announcement until October.*

---

* Diffident—sometimes unduly so—of his literary ability, Washington sent the drafts of the addresses upon which he and Madison had worked in 1792 to Hamilton for correction, amplification and polishing. Hamilton rewrote the address and returned it to Washington, whereupon the President made his own emendations and additions and sent it back to

The Election of 1796

The President was aware that such an eleventh-hour avowal of his intention would bring down from the Republicans the charge that the Federalists were trying to steal the presidency from Jefferson by denying him an opportunity to marshal his forces for the election. Perhaps this is what Hamilton had in mind; in any event, he tried to postpone the President's announcement almost until the last possible moment. But the President had his draft completed ahead of the schedule set by Hamilton and the Farewell Address was given to the world in September, 1796.[17]

If, after his retirement as Secretary of the Treasury, Hamilton declined to run for elective office in the expectation that he was thereby keeping himself available for the presidency, he was grievously disappointed. In 1796, a group of Federalist leaders passed over Hamilton's claims to the post of honor; instead, it was agreed that John Adams and Thomas Pinckney should be the party's candidates. Although it was understood that John Adams was the choice for President, the caucus pledged itself to support Adams and Pinckney equally. By this arrangement it was hoped to ensure that the southern Federalists would vote for Adams, a New Englander, and that the northern Federalists would cast their ballots for Pinckney, a South Carolinian. Better a tie in the Electoral College, the Federalists reasoned, than to risk the loss of either the presidency or the vice-presidency as a result of rivalry between the two Federalist candidates.*

There was good reason for the Federalists' circumspection. Everything pointed to a close election; the Republicans were bending every effort to bring in Jefferson and Aaron Burr, their candidates for the Presidency and Vice-Presidency; and the Republican newspapers were putting the election upon the plane of a contest between "King" Adams and plain "Mister" Jefferson.

Hamilton characteristically viewed the election as a struggle between good and evil—with the evil, of course, on the other side. "We have every thing to fear if this man [Jefferson] comes in," he said. ". . . All personal and partial considerations must be discarded, and every thing must give way to the great object of excluding Jefferson," the head and front of the "French faction" in the United States. Suiting the action to the word, Hamilton and his Congressman friend William Smith, of South Carolina, collaborated in writing a pamphlet entitled *The Pretensions of Thomas Jeffer-*

Hamilton. Thereupon Hamilton called in John Jay and together they produced a state paper for the President's consideration. But Washington preferred the first draft to this second effort and he accordingly returned it to Hamilton for a final overhaul. When it was returned to Washington, he made a few minor changes and gave it to the printer in September, 1796.

* At this time, votes were not cast in the Electoral College for President and Vice-President. Instead, the candidate receiving the most votes above a majority became President; the candidate receiving the second largest total became Vice-President.

son to the Presidency Examined. Here Hamilton and Smith rang the familiar changes that Jefferson was a Deist, a friend of Tom Paine, an enemy of national good faith and public credit, an incompetent and cowardly governor of Virginia—withal, a man certain to bring upon his country *"national disunion, insignificance, disorder* and *discredit."* But it was chiefly as a philosopher and—worse still—a philosophical politician that the two Federalists tried to damn the Virginian in the eyes of his countrymen.[18]

Hamilton and Smith were willing to concede that Jefferson might make an acceptable college president, but they recommended that he be strictly confined to the academic halls where only undergraduates and faculty members would be exposed to his passion for playing politics, his subversive doctrines and his craving for popularity. They much preferred, however, that he employ his talents in such pursuits as "impaling butterflies and insects, and contriving turn-about chairs, *for the benefit of his fellow citizens and mankind in general."*[19]

If this were a true picture of Thomas Jefferson, it was reasonable to suppose that Hamilton would bend every effort to elect John Adams. And yet, contrary to this expectation, the former Secretary of the Treasury did almost as much toward keeping Adams out of that office as toward defeating the aspirations of Jefferson. One of the most remarkable things about *The Pretensions of Thomas Jefferson to the Presidency Examined* was that it made no favorable mention whatever of the pretensions of John Adams. Plainly, Hamilton's strategy was to damn Jefferson but to speak no good of Adams.[20]

Baldly stated, Hamilton's objections to Adams were that he was not a good Hamiltonian and that he was much too stubborn and opinionated to admit of hope that he would ever be converted to the true faith. Toward banking and the funding system, the Vice-President was almost as hostile as was Thomas Jefferson, and he never hesitated to express his disapprobation of measures which Hamilton regarded as fundamental to the welfare of the country. Adams prided himself upon his independence: he was under obligations to no man and he made clear that he would never submit his judgment to party dictates. If he were elected, Hamilton's chances of dominating the administration would be slight indeed: the former Secretary of the Treasury would then learn for the first time that in retiring from the government he had given up his voice in policy making.[21]

In Thomas Pinckney, on the other hand, Hamilton beheld a much more estimable character. Although relatively unknown to the electorate, as a South Carolinian he could be counted upon to divide the electoral vote of the South with Jefferson, which, together with the certain votes he stood to receive in the strongly Federalist North, would ensure his victory. Hamil-

The Election of 1796

ton thought that Pinckney might even carry Pennsylvania, a state some Federalists had given up for lost.

Yet Hamilton was attracted to Pinckney for even more compelling reasons than those he thought it prudent to avow. It was reasonable to believe that if Pinckney were elected he would be amenable to advice—something that Adams would never willingly accept from Hamilton. Moreover, if elected, Pinckney would owe everything to Hamilton: as Robert Troup said, "we have Mr. Pinckney completely in our power," and the Hamiltonians had no intention of permitting him to escape. Thus, as a President maker, Hamilton would be in a position to console himself for having failed to win the office for himself, and the reality of power was more important in him than were the trappings of office.[22]

Naturally, Hamilton always insisted that his only reason for preferring Pinckney to Adams was pure, disinterested patriotism: Pinckney was the best man and Hamilton was simply trying to make sure that the best man won. Several years later, he observed that "to every essential qualification for the office [Pinckney] added a temper far more discreet and conciliatory than that of Mr. Adams"; and these excellent qualities were accompanied by "an habitual discretion and self-command, which has often occasioned a parallel between him and the venerated Washington." It is only fair to say that few observers besides Hamilton detected this parallel.[23]

Even though Pinckney possessed all the praiseworthy qualities with which Hamilton invested him, the fact remained that the former Secretary was attempting to circumvent the popular will by taking advantage of a defect in the Constitution. True, there had been no formal nominations by an organized political party; nonetheless, Adams, not Pinckney, was regarded as the Federalist candidate for the presidency. Adams was one of the most eminent patriots of the Revolution and had served for seven years as Vice-President, whereas Pinckney, except as the negotiator of the Treaty of 1796 with Spain, was scarcely known outside his own state. From this effort to impose Pinckney upon the country Hamilton had nothing to fear so much as success: it is doubtful if the Federalist party could have survived the "victory."

In the plan of the Federalist leaders to give Adams and Pinckney equal support, Hamilton saw the means of encompassing his objective of making Pinckney President. South Carolina was the state upon which Hamilton's hopes were chiefly fixed: although the Federalists of that state were pledged to support Adams and Pinckney equally, it was rumored that they would abandon Adams at the last moment in favor of Jefferson. Thus the electoral vote of South Carolina would go to Pinckney and Jefferson; Pinckney would be President and Adams would be kept in the vice-presidency, the only office with which Hamilton was willing to accommodate the New Englander.[24]

Not content with the probability that South Carolina would swing the election to Pinckney, Hamilton and William Smith took active steps to ensure that this would indeed be the outcome. Pinckney was told that "the intention of bringing him forward was to make him President," and certain members of the South Carolina legislature (which elected the electors) were instructed to violate the agreement reached in the Philadelphia caucus by throwing away the ballots that were pledged to Adams.[25]

Throughout these events, Hamilton displayed the coolness of a gambler accustomed to play for high stakes. Luck had smiled upon him too often for him to doubt that it would fail him here. And yet, few Federalists shared either his imperturbability or his conviction that Pinckney must be brought in over Adams at almost any cost to honor and party unity. While Hamilton put the existence of the party to the hazard, these cautious souls wrung their hands and predicted the worst of evils—the election of Thomas Jefferson as President.

And indeed, Hamilton's artifice was too shallow to be successful: few were deceived by his ostensible devotion to the principle of equal support of Adams and Pinckney. Moreover, since among his confidential friends Hamilton made no concealment of his preference for Pinckney over Adams, some of Adams' supporters were let into the secret. As a result, Hamilton succeeded only in producing a schism within his own party; confidence between northern and southern Federalists was destroyed and the followers of Pinckney and Adams began to look upon each other as rivals. In order to forestall any effort on the part of the South Carolina Federalists to make Pinckney President, the New England Federalists resolved to throw away votes upon favorite sons.[26]

Hamilton's strategy came within a hairbreadth of making Thomas Jefferson President. Although Adams won, it was by an uncomfortably narrow margin—seventy-two votes to sixty-nine. Close as it was, Adams' victory was owing to the fact that Adams himself, presiding over the Electoral College as President of the Senate, voted to validate the four electoral votes of Vermont that had been cast in his favor. Moreover, North Carolina and Virginia, two strongly Republican states, unexpectedly gave one vote each to Adams. These votes were, as Hamilton acknowledged, "so extraordinary as to have been contrary to all probable calculation." Nothing less than "a sort of miracle" had been required to seat Adams in the President's chair.[27]

In the working of this miracle the French government played an important part. The most flagrant attempt since 1793 to interfere in the domestic affairs of the United States occurred immediately after the promulgation of the Farewell Address. And, with his usual skill at such things, Hamilton succeeded in turning the resentment of a large number of Ameri-

The Election of 1796

cans against the Republican party by making it appear to be the tool of French "Jacobins."

In 1795, Citizen Adet had succeeded Fauchet as the French Minister to the United States. Hamilton watched the new Minister narrowly, persuaded that he was a more circumspect and crafty—and therefore more dangerous—intriguer than Genêt. In actuality, however, Hamilton had little cause to fear Adet's subtlety—he proved to be almost as indiscreet as Genêt himself.

Resentful that the United States had made a treaty with Great Britain, the French government decided to revolutionize the United States—the usual treatment meted out to smaller powers that resisted the Directory's authority. But James Monroe, the American Minister in Paris, persuaded the government to hold its hand pending the outcome of the presidential election of 1796, when, he intimated, a Chief Executive favorable to France would be installed in office. To make sure that the election turned out as Monroe predicted, the Directory instructed Adet to promote the candidacy of Thomas Jefferson, to announce new French decrees affecting neutral commerce and to return forthwith to Paris.[28]

Adet did all these things in the *Appeal to the American People* that he issued on the eve of the election. Here the French Minister laid his cards upon the table with a fine flourish: unless American voters elected a President acceptable to France, they would suffer the displeasure of the French republic—with all that connoted in the way of war and revolutionary upheaval. And yet it was possible for Americans to escape this visitation of wrath—they had only to elect Thomas Jefferson President of the United States to restore themselves to French favor.

Never has a foreign government more wholeheartedly endorsed the election of a presidential candidate than did the Directory in the case of Thomas Jefferson in 1796. As Hamilton said, it was "by far the most bold attempt to govern the country." Coming on top of attempts by French ministers to block the ratification of Jay's Treaty and to divide the people from their government, it reminded Hamilton of the fate of Poland—"a melancholy example of the dangers of foreign influence in the election of a chief magistrate."[29]

Now the United States was not Poland, and Hamilton had no intention of permitting the French to confuse the two countries. A man as versed as he in the art of thrust and counterthrust could hardly fail to perceive that Adet had laid himself open to a finishing stroke. Nevertheless, he advised the President to adopt a moderate tone toward Adet and to confine the dispute to the regular diplomatic channels. Rather than pick a quarrel with France, Hamilton chose to use Adet's *Appeal* to destroy the "French Faction" in the United States. Mindful that the native-born Jacobins were the more deadly of the species, he believed that more good would be accomplished by directing the anger of the American people against the Republican party than against France.[30]

Before Hamilton's letter containing this advice reached Philadelphia, Washington approved Secretary of State Pickering's answer to Adet and permitted its publication in the newspapers. Hamilton was chagrined by this turn of events. He found the Secretary's language "too epigrammatical and sharp" for diplomatic intercourse: where it ought to have been calm and majestic, he detected a belligerency and acerbity wholly out of keeping with the high office of the presidency. As for the publication of Pickering's state paper in the newspapers, Hamilton observed that "the sooner the Executive gets out of the newspapers the better."[31]

And yet Hamilton made sure that Adet did not get out of the newspapers unscathed. The French minister's ill-advised *Appeal* enabled Hamilton and his fellow Federalists to make "French influence" the hottest issue of the campaign. Jefferson was depicted as the leader of a faction that had sold itself body and soul to France. No wonder, Hamilton exclaimed, that the Directory intervened in Jefferson's behalf: he was the agent upon whom they depended to effect their conquest of the United States.* In actuality, however, the Republican leaders deplored the French Minister's indiscretion and tried to dissociate themselves from his actions. And well they might: John Quincy Adams estimated that Adet cost Jefferson at least thirteen votes in the Electoral College—more than enough to have elected him President.†[32]

* Adet gave his government a very different picture of Jefferson. The Virginian was well disposed toward France, Adet reported, "because he detests England; he wishes to draw near to us [France] because he fears us less than England; but tomorrow he might change his opinion about us if England should cease to inspire his fear. . . . He is an American, and as such, he cannot sincerely be our friend. An American is the born enemy of all the peoples of Europe."

† Stephen Kurtz (*The Presidency of John Adams,* New York, 1957) asserts that Adet's strategy contributed to the Republican victory in Pennsylvania. This was not the opinion of contemporaries.

29.
The Mission to France

Hamilton was not so much mortified at having lost Pinckney—in 1800 he found another Pinckney to take Thomas' place—as at seeing Thomas Jefferson step into the vice-presidency. From this vantage point Jefferson would presumably disseminate "Jacobinism" through the federal government and counterwork the policies of President Adams. But the Vice-President-elect had something very different in mind: by exposing Hamilton's part in the election he hoped to turn Adams against the former Secretary of the Treasury.[1] After all, Hamilton had been caught redhanded on the political backstairs trying to trip up John Adams, and the fact was as notorious as the Republican newspapers could make it. "When a *little Alexander* dreams himself to be ALEXANDER THE GREAT," said a Republican journalist, ". . . he is very apt to fall into miserable intrigues."[2]

Adams was slow to credit these stories of Hamilton's treachery. But when he was finally brought to see the truth, his anger flamed fiercely against the "Creole." In Adams' opinion, the plot to smuggle Pinckney into the presidency disclosed how badly Hamilton and his friends had mistaken the character of the American people: "That must be a sordid people, indeed," he exclaimed, "a people destitute of a sense of honor, equity, and character, that could submit to be governed, by a Pinckney, under an elective government."[3]

An open break between Adams and Hamilton was averted in 1797 largely because of the sudden deterioration in our relations with France. Adams had pledged himself to heal the wounds of party strife and, as a result of the threatening attitude of France, union at home became more essential than ever before. In consequence, Hamilton escaped paying the penalty that otherwise would have been exacted of him for his temerity. But, as the future revealed, it was a payment deferred, not canceled.[4]

In 1796, the tide of victory having decisively turned in France's favor, the Directory embarked upon a supreme effort to crush its sole remaining antagonist, Great Britain, by barring British merchandise from the European continent. The execution of this plan—an adumbration of the later

"Continental System" of Napoleon—necessitated almost as strict repressive measures against neutral ships as against those flying the Union Jack: the neutral powers must be compelled to aid France in starving to death the great "sea serpent." Nor was the French government in a mood to show special consideration to the United States. The recall in 1796 of James Monroe, the United States Minister to France; the election of John Adams, regarded in France as the leader of the pro-British faction; and the evident determination of the administration to stand upon Jay's Treaty—these, to the Directory, were intolerable grievances which required immediate and unconditional redress.[5]

The French were soon taking a heavy toll of defenseless American ships. By the spring of 1797, "picaroons" were cruising off the Capes of the Delaware and capturing American merchantmen as they entered American ports. A schooner armed with a gun or two and manned by a handful of cutthroats was able to make prize of richly laden ships which by law were not permitted to carry armament even for defensive purposes. French authorities in the West Indies freely granted to all comers the papers by which this armed robbery was given official sanction by the government. No wonder, therefore, that by June, 1797, over three hundred merchantmen flying the flag of the United States had been sunk or captured; insurance rates had skyrocketed; and American shippers were beginning to transfer their cargoes to the safer, because armed and convoyed, British merchant ships.[6]

To impress further upon Americans how deeply they had offended the "great nation," the Directory refused to recognize Charles Cotesworth Pinckney, the newly appointed Minister to France. Although the Directory did not wholly sever diplomatic relations between the two countries—it was understood that the United States might restore itself to France's good graces by renouncing its commerce with Great Britain—war seemed very close at hand in the spring of 1797.[7]

Hamilton viewed this crisis in Franco-American relations not simply as an invasion of neutral rights but in its larger implications as an integral part of the struggle between France and Great Britain for mastery. He knew that if the United States acquiesced in French exactions it would suffer heavy financial loss and forfeit all pretense to neutrality, but he also recognized that the objective of the French government was to make the United States contribute to the downfall of Great Britain by destroying its trade and markets.[8]

If France triumphed in Europe, Hamilton expected that the next act in the drama would find the United States, having helped to strike down the one power capable of defending the Western Hemisphere against attack, fighting for its own life. Under the guise of liberating mankind from the oppression of kings, priests and nobles, France aimed at world domination— and the Atlantic would not stop the "terrible republic" in its career of conquest.

The Mission to France

Under the conviction that the survival of the United States was at stake, Hamilton urged Americans to look to their defenses. And, indeed, they had to look closely to find them: the United States Army consisted of 3,500 men; except for three frigates under construction, the navy was nonexistent; and the fortifications of American seaports, built during the War of Independence, were in an advanced state of decay. To close these gaps, Hamilton urged that the army be increased to 25,000 men; that a strong force of artillery and cavalry be raised; that the frigates be rushed to completion; that the defenses of American harbors be restored; that American merchantmen be armed; and that a system of naval convoys in the West Indies be instituted.[9]

Belligerent toward Great Britain, the Republicans in Congress were the soul of pacifism wherever France was concerned. Nevertheless, in Republican policy there was one consistent note: whether advocating peace or measures almost certain to precipitate war, they opposed everything that tended to strengthen the armed forces of the United States. Not surprisingly, therefore, in Hamilton's plan of putting the country in a posture of defense they saw the cloven hoof of the militarist. Albert Gallatin declared that there was no danger of war—unless the army or navy of the United States made one, and he pointed out that every regiment struck off the rolls of the United States saved the country $100,000 a year. In 1797, peace seemed to him to be so imminent that he was willing to risk the security of the United States upon this contingency. William Branch Giles of Virginia remarked that "Government would be better without an army, as it was always better for Governments to rest upon the affections of the people than to be supported by terror," and he argued that an army raised for a term of three years was unconstitutional. One Republican congressman was heard to remark that "if the navy was on fire, and he could extinguish the fire by spitting, he would not spit."[10]

Thomas Jefferson not only scoffed at Hamilton's warnings that the British fleet might not forever afford a shield behind which Americans could pursue happiness in peace and security—he denied that the British fleet was in any way necessary to Americans' felicity. At this time, Jefferson's hopes were centered upon a French conquest of Great Britain—a devoutly wished-for event which, he supposed, would greatly benefit the United States. When "the great corsair of the seas" had been scuttled, he predicted that the United States would be emancipated from its commercial and financial "vassalage" to Great Britain and that the seas would be open to the ships of all nations. Resolutely shutting their eyes to the dangers that hung over the United States, Jefferson and Madison emptied their glasses to "the brilliant successes of that wonderful man Bonaparte" and waited impatiently for the day when his standard would be planted over Westminster. Some Republicans were already celebrating the end of that "fallen bully, Britain" and urging that the United States aid France in sending "with ignominy and sorrow, to the grave, those hairs which have grown gray in wickedness and strife."

The warmongering and Caesarian ambition of Alexander Hamilton provided some lively after-dinner conversation at Monticello. So firmly persuaded was Jefferson that Hamilton would plunge the country into war if the national finances admitted of it that the Virginian advocated a constitutional amendment that would have deprived the federal government of the power of borrowing. He supposed that the spectacle of the United States with its hands bound would excite in the French only sentiments of philanthropy and fraternity.

The Republicans in Congress shared these ideas—and so, while the legislature struck an exemplary attitude of defiance toward aggressors, it did little to prepare for war. A small appropriation for fortifications, a slight increase in taxes, an act for the completion of the three frigates and authorization of a loan of $800,000—this was the total of Congress's achievement in 1797. The bill for the creation of a provisional army was lost; in its place, Congress adopted a substitute measure directing that the militia be held in readiness for an emergency. These measures were accompanied by warlike speeches calculated to make the French tremble in their boots, but Hamilton was not impressed. "*Hard words,*" he said, "are rarely useful in public proceedings. *Real firmness* is good for everything. *Strut* is good for nothing."[11]

While Hamilton was of the opinion that the conduct of France had been "very violent, insulting and injurious" and the treatment of Pinckney had reached "the utmost limit of what is tolerable," he had no desire to go to war in 1797. For one thing, he saw no profit in war with France: "Trade she has none," he remarked, "and as to territory, if we could make acquisitions they are not desirable." But of even more decisive importance was the fact that war with France seemed certain to divide Americans and to produce slave rebellions in the South. "The aggregate of these considerations is little less than awful," he declared; war under such conditions would prove to be "a more unmanageable business than war with Great Britain."[12]

Faced by such a sobering prospect, Hamilton advised the United States to reach for its diplomatic pouch rather than for its gun. From the beginning to the end of this dispute, he strove to effect a settlement by diplomacy rather than by war. Even the measures of preparedness he advocated in 1796-97 had as their ulterior objective the furthering of the diplomatic offensive upon which he wished to see the United States embark.[13]

It was a matter of doubt, however, whether the French had left any avenue of diplomacy open to the United States. In rejecting Pinckney, the Directory had declared that it would not receive an American Minister before redress of grievances. Despite the apparent finality of this statement, Hamilton believed that the door remained open for negotiations: the

The Mission to France

Directory had not said, he pointed out, that it would refuse to receive a commission of ministers plenipotentiary invested with the highest rank and powers and attended with all the solemnity of a last effort to preserve peace. And if that commission included a prominent Republican, he thought that the French would warmly welcome the American negotiators.[14]

Hamilton's choice for this assignment was breathtaking in its audacity: either Thomas Jefferson or James Madison, he said, was eminently qualified to carry the olive branch to Paris. With Jefferson or Madison, Hamilton wished to join Charles Cotesworth Pinckney, the American Minister to France, and George Cabot, a Massachusetts Federalist. Outnumbered and closely watched by their Federalist chaperons, it seemed unlikely that Jefferson or Madison would be able to intrigue with the French; but if the Republican member tried any tricks, "a counter game may be played," Hamilton said, "& such a complexion may be given to the thing as may put both him and France entirely in the wrong."[15]

The one thing upon which Hamilton insisted as an absolute condition of any settlement with France was the ending of spoliations upon American shipping. If the Directory refused to renounce this practice, "open war," he declared, "will be preferable. . . . By whatever name treachery or pusillanimity may attempt to disguise it, 'tis in fact war of the worst kind, *war on one side.*"[16] The worst consequence to be apprehended from a continuation of these depredations was not, in Hamilton's opinion, the material losses, great as they would be, but the effect upon the people's morale: "The humiliation of the American mind would be a lasting and mortal disease. Mental debasement is the greatest misfortune that can befall a people. . . . The honor of a nation is its life: Deliberately to abandon it, is to commit an act of political suicide. . . . The nation, which can prefer disgrace to danger is prepared for a *Master* and deserves one."[17]

Despite these strong convictions, Hamilton did not advocate war if the negotiations in Paris failed: "A truly vigorous defensive plan, with the continuance of a readiness still to negotiate," he said, ought to be the answer of the United States to French threats and insults. In addressing France, the President, said Hamilton, ought to adopt "a stile cautious, calm, grave, but free from asperity or insult . . . manly, but calm and sedate, firmness without strut. . . . There ought to be much cool calculation united with much cool fortitude. The government ought to be all intellect while the people ought to be all feeling." If the government pursued this course, Hamilton was sure that the peace mission, whether a success or a failure, would redound to the advantage of the United States. "Suppose the worst," he said, "it will tend to the most precious of all things, Union at *home.* . . . To unite the opinions of all good citizens of whatever political denomination is with me a mighty object." And, finally, by making "the necessity of resistance to the violence of France palpable to every good citizen," the mission to France might "beget the noble resolution to die in the last ditch."[18]

Upon this plan most of Hamilton's friends looked askance. Accustomed as they were to regard him as an oracle and to submit to his superior judgment, they could not share his enthusiasm for sending another mission to the "Cut-throat Directory." A Federalist politician told Hamilton that he preferred that the country be sunk "and an Asphaltic Lake rise, where once stood the States—rather than subject ourselves to that nest of Assassins [France]." In the opinion of these stout haters of France, the inclusion of Jefferson or Madison among the plenipotentiaries damned Hamilton's plan beyond redemption. Had Hamilton forgotten, it was asked, that the Republican leaders were eager to prostrate their country "at the feet of the most ambitious and terrible tyrants that ever cursed the earth" and that, masters of the art of subverting government that they were, they might still profit from the advanced courses taught in Parisian "seminaries of sedition"? It was an interesting question whether Jefferson and Madison could overthrow the government of the United States more quickly at home or from the vantage point of Paris, but few Federalists were inclined to make the experiment.[19]

By way of answer to these objections, Hamilton reminded his fellow Federalists of a fact they were prone to forget—that in 1794, when war with Great Britain had impended, the Federalists had proclaimed themselves to be the defenders of the peace and, by sending John Jay to England, had averted a conflict. If there was any consistency in Federalist policy and any validity in its claim to be the party of peace, it must seek, said Hamilton, "to avoid war with every power, if it could be done without the sacrifice of essential interests or absolute humiliation." The cause of conflict, he did not fail to observe, was the same in 1797 as in 1794: the seizure and confiscation of American shipping by a foreign power. War against Great Britain had then seemed as inevitable as it now seemed against France, yet the timely intervention of diplomacy had averted a conflict. "The idea is a plausible one," he remarked, "that as we sent an Envoy Extraordinary to Britain, so we ought to send one to France. And plausible ideas are always enough for the multitude." That it might not be enough for France he freely admitted, but he was willing "to go to greater lengths to avoid rupture with France than with Great Britain; to make greater sacrifices for reconciliation with the former than with the latter." He acknowledged that the Directory had legitimate grievances against the United States. Particularly in the matter of impressment of American seamen by Great Britain, he said, France had "good ground of inquiry, demanding candid explanation. . . . 'Tis not a matter of indifference to our friend, what conduct of its enemy we permit towards ourselves."[20]

Properly to solemnize the occasion, Hamilton urged the President to

The Mission to France

make an appeal to Heaven when the commissioners set out for Paris. The religious feelings, Hamilton observed, ought to be enlisted on the side of law and order, and all Christians ought to be made to see that they were waging a struggle against Antichrist in the form of the French Revolution. But this revelation seems to have come to Hamilton from Machiavelli rather than from on high. "The politician," he told William Smith, "will consider this an important means of influencing opinion, and will think it a valuable resource in a contest with France to set the Religious Ideas of his Countrymen in active Competition with the Atheistical tenets of their enemies. This is an advantage which we shall be very unskilful if we do not improve to the utmost."[21]

Much to the Federalists' relief, Jefferson and Madison declined appointment to the commission. Freed of the incubus of a Republican member, the commission became tolerable to Hamilton's friends: now, it was said, the ministers plenipotentiary might actually do some of the good Hamilton predicted. But the personnel of the commission still left something to be desired: although Charles C. Pinckney and John Marshall were stalwart-enough Federalists, Elbridge Gerry, the third peacemaker, was suspected of being one of the weaker vessels of the party.[22]

Elbridge Gerry was President Adams', not Hamilton's, choice. The late Secretary of the Treasury was not inclined to risk the security of the United States in the hands of halfway Federalists, and so exacting were his standards that he feared that even Charles Cotesworth Pinckney was a little too soft on Jacobins to be entirely reliable. Had Hamilton had his way, Gerry would never have made the team; but the point is that Hamilton was no longer in a position to have his way.[23]

With President Adams, Hamilton of course did not maintain the intimate and cordial relations that he had enjoyed with President Washington. The New Englander, priding himself upon his independence, made it a point not to consult Hamilton upon matters of state: he treated the former Secretary of the Treasury quite as though he were what he seemed to be—a private citizen. It never occurred to Adams that he should solicit advice from a New York attorney.

But with the Cabinet of President Adams, Hamilton preserved as close a connection as he had with President Washington's Cabinet. Since Adams took over the entire personnel of his predecessor's Cabinet, it was easy for Hamilton to continue to play the part of mentor and father confessor to the heads of the departments. Those gentlemen were eager to continue the relationship: the New York-Philadelphia stage frequently carried letters from them beseeching Hamilton's advice, and Hamilton devoted many hours to giving them detailed instructions, which, of course, were ultimately laid before the President. In January, 1798, when Adams raised the question in the Cabinet what should be done in the event of the failure of negotiations, most of the members promptly wrote Hamilton to learn his pleasure. Oliver Wolcott, the Secretary of the Treasury, who habitually relied upon his former chief for advice in financial matters, virtually yielded his conscience to Hamilton's safekeeping. Pickering, the Secretary of State, wrote Hamilton: "I wish you were in a situation not only 'to see all the cards,' but to play them. With all my soul I would give you *my* hand." McHenry, the Secretary of War, approached the great man with a deference bordering upon humility: "My dear Hamilton," he wrote, "will you assist me, or rather your country, with such suggestions and opinions as may occur to you on the subject of the within paper?"[24]

Ultimately the subservience of the Cabinet to Hamilton produced a violent paroxysm in the administration; but in 1797 there was little evidence of the trouble that was brewing beneath the surface. During the first two years of Adams' term of office, the President and Hamilton were in essential agreement upon foreign policy and, in general, Hamilton's advice to the Cabinet coincided with Adams' views. As the British Minister observed, John Adams was the last man in the country to be "bullied into measures which he does not approve." But from Hamilton's point of view, it appeared that his advice was being followed implicitly and that the President was a weakling who could be easily dominated through his Cabinet. As events were to prove, this was one of the worst miscalculations of Hamilton's career.

In 1796, the prospect, ephemeral though it was, of Hamilton as President had sent a shudder through the Republicans; once he was invested with the "federal diadem," it was predicted, the country would be saddled with a king and nobility, a British alliance and a French war. To blast his chances for the presidency, fabricated letters were circulated in which Hamilton was made to say that he was convinced that "mankind could not be governed but with a rod of iron" and that the dollars he had pilfered "while handling the Government's Cash will not be without their use." But the Republicans were not yet satisfied: something had to be proved against Hamilton that would place the presidency forever beyond his reach and destroy his influence as the plumed knight of the Federalist party.[25]

When he resigned as Secretary of the Treasury, Hamilton said that he yearned to taste the long-deferred sweets of domestic happiness and tranquillity. "It is impossible to be happier than I am in a wife," he said in 1797. And indeed, his cup was almost running over; besides this jewel among wives, he had five children and, while not wealthy, his situation was "extremely comfortable": a fine house on Broadway, an income of about $10,000 a year from his law practice and a seemingly unassailable social position.

Upon this domestic felicity, the Reynolds affair cast hardly a shadow. Hamilton assumed that his secret was safe in the hands of the three con-

The Mission to France

gressmen. Even though they were his political enemies, they were also gentlemen who presumably placed honor above political advantage.

In actuality, however, Hamilton had no grounds for complacency. Besides Oliver Wolcott and the three Republican congressmen, Hamilton's relations with Mrs. Reynolds were known to Thomas Jefferson and John Beckley, clerk of the House of Representatives. Jefferson learned of Hamilton's secret as early as December, 1792, when Monroe, breaking his oath of secrecy, sent him the copies of the documents that had fallen into the congressman's hands. More importantly, John Beckley, one of Hamilton's most rancorous enemies, had known from the beginning of Hamilton's involvement in the sordid affair, Beckley's secretary having transcribed the entire correspondence for the self-constituted "committee's" records.

Early in 1797, outraged by Beckley's flagrantly partisan political activities, the Federalists succeeded in removing him as clerk of the House of Representatives. Indignant at this treatment, some of Beckley's friends predicted that his dismissal would result in the publication of some sensational memoirs, for in his retirement he would, "like Sully, find leisure to write an history of the abominations to which he has been a witness."

Beckley was capable of outdoing Sully in retailing the scandals of the day. He did not hold himself bound by the oath of secrecy taken by the three congressmen: according to his lights, he was free to divulge the facts as he knew them whenever political expediency warranted. He now decided that the time had come to expose Hamilton as a defalcator of public money, for Beckley was certain that Hamilton, while guilty enough of debauching Maria Reynolds, had also used for his corrupt financial purposes the innocent and long-suffering husband.

To exhibit Hamilton's "crimes" to the American people, Beckley employed the services of James T. Callender, a Scottish radical who had been obliged to flee to America for his trenchant criticisms of the British government. In an age when journalism was an euphemism for scurrility and vilification, Callender occupied a peculiar eminence among the practitioners of the craft. Now, in 1797, this vindictive and unscrupulous man was presented with one of the juiciest bits of scandal that has ever fallen to the lot of an American journalist. A keyhole correspondent could not have hoped for a bigger scoop: to reveal the former Secretary of the Treasury in undress, disporting himself in ways frowned upon in the highly moral society of eighteenth-century America—this was the opportunity presented to Callender by his good friend John Beckley. And the glory would be entirely Callender's: no Republican, not even Beckley, wished his name to appear in the business.

Resolved to wring the last drop of political advantage from these documents, Callender made of the Reynolds affair not a simple case of adultery and blackmail but a corrupt bargain between Reynolds and Hamilton for splitting the profits of their speculations. The fact that the three congressmen had explicitly absolved Hamilton of any wrongdoing he brushed aside on the ground that congressmen habitually lied for each other. Callender considered it probable that Reynolds had been merely one among many: although he graciously admitted that it had not yet been proved, he was inclined to believe that Hamilton had had twenty or more agents like Reynolds in the field, all engaged in speculating with government money.*[26]

These charges, supported by the "evidence" gathered by the three congressmen in 1792, appeared in Callender's book, *The History of the United States for the Year 1796*, published early in 1797. When Hamilton saw that the secret of his relations with the Reynoldses was out, his first thought was to secure attestations of innocence from the three congressmen. Accordingly, he wrote Muhlenberg, Venable and Monroe, assuming, as he later said, "from the appearances on their part at closing our former interview on the subject, that their answers would have been both cordial and explicit." And so they were—from Muhlenberg and Venable. But no answer whatever was forthcoming from James Monroe.

There was good reason for Monroe's silence. The Virginian had never been wholly satisfied of Hamilton's innocence of the charge of speculating with Reynolds and Clingman; in January, 1793, unknown to Hamilton, he had had a second interview with Clingman and had attested a statement by that worthy to the effect that Hamilton was guilty as charged. This paper —the existence of which Hamilton did not suspect until he saw it printed in the *History for the Year 1796*—seemed to indicate that Monroe had signed the document certifying to Hamilton's innocence with considerable mental reservation. And, as Hamilton learned in 1797, Monroe, alone of the three congressmen, kept a transcription of the interview that had taken place at Hamilton's house.

Now, for the first time, the suspicion struck Hamilton that Monroe was responsible for the leak. Of the three congressmen, he remembered, Monroe had been the least generous in his expressions of regret for having subjected him to the humiliation of explaining his relations with Mrs. Reynolds: there had been a certain coolness and reserve in Monroe's manner upon that occasion which Hamilton, in recalling it, found disquieting.[27]

This was very much in Hamilton's mind when in a second letter to Monroe he demanded that the Virginian repudiate his apparent endorsement of Clingman's accusations. "And I shall rely upon your delicacy," he told Monroe, "that the manner of doing it will be such as one gentleman

---

* Callender prided himself upon being an impartial historian. With characteristic effrontery, his next literary labor, he told Hamilton, was to be a history of Hamilton's administration as Secretary of the Treasury. For this task he claimed unusual qualifications: objectivity, a passionate devotion to truth, the reputation of being "the hireling of none" and a profound admiration of Hamilton's talents. Therefore he requested Hamilton to submit his papers to inspection "in order that," Callender said, "I may judge what credit is due to them."

The Mission to France

has a right to expect from another." To Hamilton, this meant an unequivocal statement by Monroe to the effect that he placed no credence in the charges made by Clingman.[28]

Hamilton seemed to have presumed too much upon Monroe's gentility, for the Virginian still did not deign to answer. Learning that Monroe was in New York, Hamilton called upon him at his lodgings in Wall Street. After a stormy interview which seemed at one point likely to terminate in a duel, Monroe stoutly protested his innocence of any part in the publication of the *History for the Year 1796* and agreed to confer with Venable and Muhlenberg in drawing up a statement acquitting Hamilton of Clingman's charges.[29]

But when Monroe returned to Philadelphia, Muhlenberg and Venable had already left town. Undecided how to act, he took counsel with his good friends Jefferson and Madison. At this time, Madison and Giles were holding frequent meetings with a former Treasury clerk in the hope of persuading him to accuse Hamilton of speculating in government securities during his tenure of the Secretaryship of the Treasury; and "altho' he repeatedly assur'd them that it was not true, yet they were dispos'd to go every Length for the Purpose." Under these circumstances, it is not probable that Monroe received any encouragement from his friends to give Hamilton a testimonial of good character.[30]

This may have been sound political strategy, but it almost cost Monroe a duel with Hamilton. Through his second, Major William Jackson, Hamilton sent letters to Monroe couched in terms calculated to force the Virginian into a duel. "It was incumbent upon you, as a man of honor and sensibility," he told Monroe, "to have come forward in a manner that would have shielded me completely from the unpleasant effect brought upon me by your agency.... You have been and are actuated by motives towards me malignant and dishonorable."

As a Virginia gentleman, Monroe could not ignore the gauntlet Hamilton flung before him. He therefore named Aaron Burr as his second and sent Burr to Hamilton to learn if he intended to make a formal challenge. No doubt, it was within Burr's power to have precipitated a duel at this time and thus, perhaps, to have relieved himself of the necessity of killing Hamilton a few years later. Instead, Burr tried to effect a reconciliation; on the reverse side of Hamilton's letter to Monroe of August 9, 1797, is a notation in Hamilton's hand to the effect that the letter had been shown Burr, "who advised a revision and alteration as best adapted to some eventual course which might obviate the necessity of publication."*[31]

* In December, 1797, Monroe wrote a belligerent letter to Hamilton which he enclosed in a letter to Burr, to whose discretion he left its transmission to Hamilton. This letter was certain to have precipitated a duel, for in it Monroe declared that by insisting upon an affidavit clearing his character Hamilton in effect confessed his guilt. Again Burr saved the situation: without sending the letter to Hamilton, he found means of placating Monroe.

Having forced Monroe to the verge of a duel, Hamilton declined to take the final step. Perhaps this was owing to Burr's intervention; perhaps to Hamilton's reluctance to make Monroe a Republican martyr; perhaps to his conviction that it was Beckley rather than Monroe who had collaborated with Callender. For several of Hamilton's friends assured him that Beckley was the culprit and warned him against shooting the wrong man. Indeed, Beckley was so widely regarded as the author of the *History for the Year 1796* that Callender—no shrinking violet in such matters—felt obliged to lay claims to the authorship.[32]

Monroe's refusal to testify in Hamilton's behalf compelled him to make a clean breast of his affair with Mrs. Reynolds. His impulse was to make as a last resort an appeal to the good opinion of "respectable men of whatever political party in whose delicacy reliance may be placed." As Hamilton ought to have known, it would have been impossible to confine his confession to such an admittedly narrow circle; and, since Callender's *History* had become a best seller, Hamilton's answer, to be effective, had to receive comparable publicity. Therefore, when it became evident during the summer of 1797 that Monroe was committed to silence, Hamilton decided to give his confession to the world.[33]

Certainly this method had obvious advantages over the kind of vindication he might have won by killing Monroe. Nevertheless, it was not without its drawbacks: it necessitated a public acknowledgment of his marital infidelity and—what was almost equally hard to endure—of the fact that he had fallen, like any greenhorn, into a blackmailer's plot. Worst of all, however, was that in saving his reputation as an honest man he might lose his wife. But here he need not have given himself much concern: Elizabeth Hamilton showed him the perfect understanding and forgiveness he found nowhere else. Upon her, Hamilton's brother-in-law assured him, Callender's charges made "not the least impression, only that she considers the whole knot of those opposed to you to be villains." Hamilton was grateful for such a refuge against the storm: "You are my good genius," he told her. ". . . . You are all that is charming in my estimation and the more I see of your sex the more I become convinced of the judiciousness of my choice." This might seem temperate commendation in comparison with the passionate avowals he had made to Maria, but Mrs. Hamilton wisely refrained from drawing comparisons between herself and the Other Woman.[34]

In electing to answer Callender's *History*, Hamilton was departing from the maxim by which he had hitherto been guided: "to leave the evidence of my conduct and character to answer the calumnies which party spirit is so incessantly busied in heaping upon me." Moreover, he took this decision against the advice of his friends, most of whom pointed out that while confession was good for the soul, it was generally bad politics. Even though Monroe had refused to give Hamilton a clean record, they tried to persuade

The Mission to France

him that there was no real doubt of his innocence. Venable, Muhlenberg and Monroe had acquitted him of any wrongdoing in December, 1792. Under these circumstances, to engage in a controversy with Callender, one of Hamilton's friends observed, would merely "furnish fresh *pabulum* for the virulent invective and abuse of faction to feed on" and provide "the Presbyterian pulpits with subject matter of declamation, however irrelevant, against the best political interests of our country." He would degrade himself, scandalize his family and injure his party—and all to clear his reputation of charges which no honest man believed.[35]

Hamilton brushed aside these objections and in the autumn of 1797 published a pamphlet entitled *Observations of Certain Documents contained in . . . The History of the United States for the Year 1796*. Acting upon the aphorism that the best defense is the offense, Hamilton began by attacking the "spirit of Jacobinism" which, he asserted, had deeply infected the Republican party and which had inspired Callender's publication. These preliminaries out of the way, he got down to the heart of the matter—that he was guilty of an "irregular and indelicate amour," a folly, for which, he said, he had already paid heavily and which he could never recollect "without disgust and self-condemnation." "I can never cease," he said, "to condemn myself for the pang which it may inflict in a bosom eminently entitled to all my fidelity and love." But he denied, with proper scorn and indignation, the charge that he had been guilty of corrupt dealings with Reynolds. "It is necessary to suppose me, not only meanly unprincipled but a fool to imagine that I would not have found better means of gratifying a criminal avarice, and could have stooped to employ such *vile instruments* for such *insignificant* ends."[36]

Hamilton's confession proved to be a literary success comparable, for a brief moment, to Samuel Richardson's *Pamela,* a tale of seduction. Had Hamilton been disposed to collect royalties from this titillating fragment of his autobiography, he no doubt could have added considerably to his income. Never before had the American people had the opportunity of sharing vicariously in the love life of one of their leading statesmen, reading his "love-sick epistles" and watching him grovel in repentance.[37]

As his friends had feared, he played into the hands of his enemies. In Republican newspapers, he was portrayed as a lecherous monster, the nation's greatest menace to female virtue. "Even the frosts of America are incapable of cooling your blood," a Republican told Hamilton, "and the eternal snow of Nova Zembla would hardly reduce you to the standard of common propriety." A man who had made his own home "the rendezvous of his whoredom; taking advantage of the absence of his wife and children to introduce a prostitute to those sacred abodes of conjugal, and filial retirement, to gratify his wicked purposes" could claim no merit except, perhaps, that of virility.[38]

As for Mrs. Reynolds, she bade fair, in the hands of Republican journalists, to become one of the heroines of American history—"an amiable and virtuous wife, seduced from the affections of her husband by artifice and intrigue." And from the number of stones cast at Hamilton, it might be supposed that American politicians were reverting to the austere and rigid code of morals of the Puritan Fathers and that an unblemished private life had become the prerequisite to officeholding in the republic. In truth, however, the righteousness of the Republicans was reserved exclusively for Federalists: a politician like Governor Mifflin of Pennsylvania—profligate and adulterer that he was—enjoyed high repute in his party because his politics were right.[39]

By confessing his adultery, Hamilton persuaded few Republicans that he was innocent of financial wrongdoing. As Jefferson dryly observed, pleading guilty to one crime was not a convincing way to establish innocence of another crime. Madison put an equally uncharitable construction upon Hamilton's action. Moreover, hardly a Republican but rejoiced in Hamilton's discomfiture: few besides Venable protested that Callender's publication was dirty politics unworthy of the party leaders who countenanced it.[40]

It was the opinion of some of Hamilton's enemies that, having fascinated the public with his account of his illicit relations with Mrs. Reynolds, he ought to have been equally frank in describing his "affair" with Mrs. Church. In this instance, the scandal struck very close to home. Angelica Schuyler Church, the wife of John Barker Church, was Hamilton's sister-in-law. She was the cleverest, wittiest and most fashionable of the Schuyler girls. Margaret, the most beautiful of the trio, was fond of flaunting her attractions without regard to the jealous pangs she occasioned in others of her sex—from which it was observed that she would never be popular until she learned to "please the men less and the ladies more." In the case of Angelica Church, it was apparent from the beginning that her objective was to please one man—her brother-in-law, Alexander.[41]

Compared with John Church—and it was a comparison Angelica could hardly avoid making—Hamilton might well have seemed fascinating to an intelligent woman. Church was a heavy, goutish businessman whose conversation ran largely to stocks and bonds. Hamilton, on the other hand, possessed a lightness of touch that made John Church appear to be duller than he really was. Never in all her acquaintance with the great and near-great of England and America had Angelica Church met a man who combined talent and ambition with the capacity of putting people completely at their ease with his agreeable *nonsense* and "little chit-chat."[42]

It was perhaps fortunate for Hamilton's marriage that the Churches returned to England to live after the Revolution. There they cut something of a figure in society, especially among the exiled New York Loyalists who

The Mission to France

had taken up residence. But Angelica was never reconciled to wasting her vivacity upon "dull, gloomy Englishmen," and after a few years of this tedium, they returned to make their home in the United States.

Thenceforth, Hamilton's problem was to keep Angelica Church from compromising him by revealing that her feeling for him was more tender than was proper in a sister-in-law. Fortunately for Hamilton, Betsy was not of a jealous disposition: she accepted her sister's affection for Alexander as a matter of course; in her eyes, it was perfectly natural for every woman to fall at least a little in love with her husband, and it was not to be expected that Angelica could resist his charm.

Mrs. Hamilton—a paragon among wives—seemingly was always aware of her husband's greatness. Not for a moment did she forget what was due his genius. Hamilton attained the rare felicity of being a hero to his own wife. Moreover, Angelica's admiration of Alexander was disarmingly frank and ingenious: "Ah! Bess!" she exclaimed, "you were a lucky girl to get so clever and so good a companion. . . . If you were as generous as the old Romans, you would lend him to me for a little while, but do not be jealous, my dear Eliza, since I am more solicitous to promote his laudable ambition, than any person in the world, and there is no summit of true glory which I do not desire he may attain." She worried lest Hamilton overwork and become a fat, dull, heavy fellow, as incapable of flirting as Robert Morris, the famous American financier, whose conversation consisted chiefly of platitudes and accounts of his business deals.[43]

She also might properly have given some concern to the way people were talking about her and Alexander. At a dinner party, for example, Angelica dropped her shoe bow, whereupon Miss Margaret Schuyler ("a young wild flirt from Albany") picked it up and put it in Hamilton's buttonhole, saying, "there brother I have made you a Knight." "But of what order," asked Angelica, "he can't be a Knight of the Garter in this country." "True, sister," replied Miss Schuyler, "but *he would be if you would let him.*" It was suspected that she would be only too happy to make him Lord of the Bedchamber.[44]

Luckily for what little remained of Hamilton's reputation, he felt no overmastering passion for Angelica Church. Although he enjoyed playing Sir Lancelot to her Lady of Shalott, it is improbable that he ever overstepped the bounds of propriety. But, for a man circumstanced as was Hamilton after the revelation of his affair with Maria, the slightest indiscretion was apt to be magnified into another Market Street love nest, and every woman that looked at him with more than passing interest was in danger of being written down as the successor of Mrs. Reynolds.

30.

Second in Command of the United States Army

Hamilton was spared the full consequences of the exposure of his relations with Mrs. Reynolds by an even greater sensation in the news—the announcement by the French government of new regulations affecting American shipping and the breakdown in Paris of negotiations between the two countries. In January, 1796, the Directory decreed that every neutral vessel laden wholly or in part with articles of British produce or manufacture, regardless of ownership, would be liable to capture and confiscation. And contrary to Hamilton's predictions that the French would receive the three American plenipotentiaries, they fared no better than had Charles C. Pinckney when he was sole United States Minister. Undeniably, Marshall, Gerry and Pinckney arrived in Paris at an unpropitious moment. The Directory had just been purged of its moderate members (they were condemned to the "dry guillotine," i.e., transportation to Guiana); French armies were on the point of forcing Austria to accept the humiliating peace of Campo Formio; and, as John Marshall said, Spain, Portugal, Tuscany, Naples and the Pope stood upon melting ice.

The footing of the American envoys was far from solid; they waited vainly in the anterooms of the Directors for recognition while trophies of victory piled up in Paris. With every batch of good news from the fighting fronts, the attitude of the French government became progressively less conciliatory, until finally, late in October, 1797, the American diplomats were approached by agents of Talleyrand, the Minister of Foreign Affairs. These agents (later designated by President Adams as X, Y, and Z) informed the envoys that unless they were prepared to pay the Directors a $250,000 bribe and to make a large loan to France—$12,800,000 was the figure suggested—they might as well go home. Although the Americans declared that they were prepared to consider a *pourboire* for Talleyrand after a treaty had been signed, and to confer with their home government regarding a loan if the Directory would cease to pillage American commerce, they declined to do business with X, Y, and Z. Their defiance became immortalized by the slogan "Millions for defense, but not one cent for tribute."¹

The news that France had stepped up its seizures of American ships and had tried to extort money from the United States as the price of a treaty aroused Americans to a pitch of anger and resentment against France that Hamilton had supposed they were capable of feeling only against Great Britain. To fan the warlike spirit, thousands of copies of the X, Y, Z correspondence were printed by well-to-do Federalists as anti-French propaganda. For once, the Federalist leaders had no objections to taking the people into their confidence upon a matter of foreign policy.²

The publication of the X, Y, Z dispatches electrified the country: Talleyrand seemed to have made more converts to federalism than had Hamilton himself. The good sense and property of the country had always, the Federalists supposed, been on their side, but now, as the champions of American rights against foreign aggression, they reaped—in the form of unprecedented popularity—the reward for their long crusade against revolutionary France.

Hamilton's response to these events was to urge that the United States get under arms without delay. A French invasion appeared to him wholly possible; he trusted neither the Atlantic Ocean nor the British navy to keep the French from these shores. A new age had opened in history, he declared, and in consequence Americans must revise the ideas that had served them in the past: "Wise men . . . look for prodigies, and prepare for them with foresight and energy." A few years before, no one would have imagined that Great Britain would stand in danger of invasion by France and yet, "when the wonders achieved by the arms of France are duly considered," Hamilton remarked, "the possibility of the overthrow of Great Britain seems not to be chimerical." Nevertheless, if the people resolutely faced this grim reality and took proper precautions to meet the danger when it came, Hamilton did not doubt that the United States would surmount every peril. "The people of the United States," he said, "from their number, situation, and resources, are invincible, if they are provident and faithful to themselves." This, he acknowledged, was a very big "if"; they seemed much too disposed to consider themselves invincible without the necessity of taking precautions.

Believing war to be imminent, Hamilton proposed to prepare for it with energy and dispatch. He called for a regular army of 50,000 men; the creation of a provisional army of the same size; and the construction or purchase of six ships of the line, twelve frigates and twenty smaller vessels. Much as he disparaged the militia as a fighting force, he recognized that it was essential to national defense; if it came to actual invasion, the regular army would be too small to cope successfully with the enemy. He therefore drew up for consideration by Congress a bill providing that any militiaman who refused to serve should be imprisoned or compelled to labor on public works. There were to be no halfway measures in this war!

Less inclined than Hamilton to ignore the cost of putting the country upon a war footing, Congress pared down his army of 50,000 to a mere 10,000 men. This so-called "additional army" was enlisted "for and during the continuance of the existing differences between the United States and the French Republic, unless sooner discharged." Besides these troops, there was organized on paper a provisional army of 50,000 men to be called into the field in case of actual or threatened invasion, and the President was authorized to call 80,000 militia to the colors. Additional ships of the United States Navy were ordered rushed to completion and a Department of the Navy was created in 1798.[3]

If Hamilton was amazed by the popular response to the X, Y, Z dispatches, he was no less astonished by the change that had come over President Adams. Energy, resourcefulness, decision—all the qualities Hamilton most prized in a statesman—were revealed in unexpected plenitude by the President. As Hamilton said, Adams met the crisis with "a manly and courageous lead," doing "all in his power to rouse the pride of the nation . . . and to dispose it to a firm and magnanimous resistance." The rotund little man from Braintree was transformed into a warrior-President who summoned the people to a "holy war" and called down the wrath of an avenging Heaven upon the French "infidels."

In his public statements, Adams led the country to believe that war with France was inevitable; further negotiations he pronounced to be "not only nugatory, but disgraceful and ruinous"; and he declared that he saw no salvation short of girding the country for a long and bloody fight. No Minister would again be sent to France, he promised the country, "without assurances that he will be received, respected and honored, as the representative of a great, free, powerful and independent nation."[4]

If the President was disposed to lead the country into war with France, he was sure of the support of a considerable number of high-ranking Federalists who foresaw advantages to their party as well as to their country from a declared war with France. Among its other blessings, war would cut up by the roots the hope of a settlement with the Directory which threatened to weaken Americans' martial spirit; it would place the United States "beyond the dreaded stroke of French coaxing"; it would put French principles and French sympathizers under the ban of treason; and it might pave the way for a British alliance. As for public opinion, the war hawks saw no difficulties there, provided a bold and energetic leader such as Hamilton placed himself at the head of the war party: then, it was predicted, the people would "mount their zeal up to the old revolutionary pitch."[5]

Here, then, was Hamilton's opportunity to unite the people of the United States, end forever the menace of "Jacobinism" and win for himself the kind of military glory of which he had always dreamed. And yet Hamilton backed away: in the critical days of 1798, he tried to restrain the warlike ardor of the President and the militant Federalists. So far was he from being swept up by the martial spirit that he expressed the fear that the rash old man's "intemperate and revolutionary" statements would plunge the country into war. "It is not for us," he said, "particularly for the government, to breathe an irregular or violent spirit. . . . I wish to see a temperate, but grave, solemn, and firm communication from the President."[6]

Hamilton did not deny that the Directory had given the United States ample provocation for a declaration of war—"the despots of France are waging war against us," he exclaimed in 1798—but even so he did not advocate a final and irremediable rupture. "Our true policy," he said, "is in the attitude of calm defiance, to meet the aggressions upon us by proportionate resistance, and to prepare vigorously for further resistance." Throughout this period, the words he used most frequently were "defense" and "resistance"; even the additional army he pronounced to be "the best of all precautions to prevent, as well as to repel, invasion."[7]

There was good reason for Hamilton's reluctance to sound the drums for offensive war against France. As a result of the failure to take Hamilton's advice in 1797, the United States, when the X, Y, Z crisis burst upon the country, was armed chiefly with rectitude, good intentions and a sense of injury; of the material means of waging war, it was lamentably deficient. There was an army of 3,500 men; a navy hardly a ship of which was ready for action; and a woeful shortage of cannon and small arms. The only fort capable of resistance was at Philadelphia; the forts at New York and Baltimore had been stripped of their guns in order to provide armament for the three frigates launched in 1797 but not yet ready for action.

As Hamilton well knew, despite the aggressions and insults of France, Jefferson still clung to his conviction that the United States stood in no danger of attack and that a French victory in Europe would best serve the interests of this country. Nothing had occurred to alter his opinion that republicanism—he still thought of France as a republic—must triumph abroad or go down to ruin in the United States. So ardent were his sympathies for France that in 1795 he expressed the hope that he would soon be able to go to London to drink tea with the victorious French generals.[8]

Since many Americans shared Jefferson's views, a declaration of war upon France in the spring and summer of 1798 would almost certainly have divided the country. Confronted by this dilemma, Hamilton unhesitatingly chose the course that promised most effectually to unite the people. Many times in the past he had pronounced the creation of union at home to be "a mighty object," "a paramount consideration"; now, in 1798, when his policy was put to the test, he urged that the administration subordinate everything to uniting "the opinions of all good citizens of whatever political denomination." Manifestly, Hamilton prized unity above the problematical benefits of offensive war.

Hamilton sometimes gave the impression that he held public opinion in utter disdain and that he was never more sure that he was right than when he was opposing some popular wish. In 1794, for example, he said: "It is long since I have learned to hold popular opinion of no value. I hope to derive from the esteem of the discerning, and an internal consciousness of zealous endeavors for the public good, the reward of those endeavors." Certainly Hamilton's political odyssey did not consist of floating gently down the stream of public opinion; few American statesmen have breasted that current more consistently than did Hamilton. And yet he did not relish the public disfavor that often fell to his lot; he loved approbation and esteem as much as any man. If he seemed to despise public opinion, it was largely because he found himself so often on the unpopular side of the controversy.[9]

In 1798, Hamilton acted upon the principle that public opinion was "the ultimate arbiter of every measure of government" and that before resorting to war the people must be persuaded that every possibility of a peaceful settlement had been exhausted. Since the government had refused to go to war with Great Britain in 1794 for what Hamilton called the "fine philosophical theory" that free ships make free goods, he knew that the people would not quarrel with France for "pins and needles. The public temper would not bear any umbrage taken," he said, "where a trifling concession might have averted it."

It would be a mistake, however, to imagine that in 1798 Hamilton's objective was to make peace with France. He wanted war and to bring it about he was prepared to risk a showdown with France despite the unpreparedness of the United States. But, as a concession to the popular aversion to waging offensive war upon France, Hamilton wished to see the initiative come from France itself. If the Directory declared war upon the United States, he expected that Americans would become more, not less, united and that they would fight with a fierceness and determination that would teach the French there was at least one people who were not overawed by that dazzling young general, Napoleon Bonaparte.[10]

But would the French oblige by declaring war? In the summer of 1798, Hamilton had little doubt that the Directory had committed itself to war with the United States. It was not reasonable to suppose that the conqueror of half of Europe, the "terrible republic" made more terrible still by the military genius of Bonaparte, would tamely submit to have its extortionate practices exposed by a second-rate power. The American envoys themselves supported this opinion. On June 17, 1798, John Marshall reached New York from Bordeaux on the crack merchantman *Alexander Hamilton*. To the crowds who gathered to welcome him home, Marshall declared that the United States must fight to preserve its freedom; the Directory, he said,

Second in Command of the United States Army

would sooner sacrifice one hundred thousand men than recede a single step. Charles C. Pinckney, who arrived a few months later, gave it as his opinion that peace could be obtained "not by negotiation, but by the sword"; France, he said, was bent upon world conquest and would permit no treaties, friendships or alliances to stand in its path.[11]

With peace hanging by a thread which the Directory apparently was determined to cut forthwith, Hamilton seemed wholly justified in supposing that he could have both war and unity at home. Secure in this comforting belief, Hamilton placed himself in the company of those moderate Federalists, such as John Jay and Rufus King, who sought to curb the more impetuous and warlike wing of the party. As might be expected, the effect of Hamilton's pacific counsel was immediately discernible in the proceedings of the cabinet. Not one member recommended that the President call upon Congress for a declaration of war. Even Timothy Pickering preserved an unwonted silence, although his own predilections ran toward hurling manifestoes, followed by shot and shell, at the French. It is significant that the most bellicose member of the Cabinet, Henry Lee, the Attorney General, was not a Hamiltonian.[12]

Nevertheless, Hamilton did not succeed in persuading all the members of his party that the course of wisdom was to wait for the French to declare war. The war hawks were eager to be at the French; delay seemed to them to be a waste of time that might more profitably be spent in killing Frenchmen. When Hamilton failed them they looked to President Adams for leadership. Although the President had given the impression that he could not wait to be off to the wars, he, too, was disposed to put the onus of declaring it upon the French. Bereft of the strong leadership they required, the Federalists were obliged to make the fateful decision for themselves. A caucus of senators and representatives was summoned in Philadelphia and the question was put to a vote. The war hawks, reported the British Minister, "were mortified to find that the question was still likely to be carried against them by a small majority." They therefore determined not to bring on a debate in Congress, where they were certain to be opposed by the whole body of Republicans. For better or for worse, therefore, Hamilton's policy of preparing for defensive war in the hope that the French would force hostilities upon the United States prevailed.[13]

One of the reasons why Hamilton was reluctant to precipitate war with France in 1798 was the unfavorable military situation of Great Britain. In a war with France, Hamilton knew that, without the protection of British sea power, the United States would not be secure against invasion. Therefore, throughout this period of crisis, a factor which contributed materially to the shaping of Hamilton's attitude toward the question of war or peace with France was the state of the British navy. If it rode the seas in triumph, he was inclined to consider the possibility of war; if, on the other hand, it fell upon adversity, he was disposed to contemplate the advantages of peace.

In the spring of 1798, this indicator pointed steadily to peace. The spectacle of British crews mutinying at the Nore; the Bank of England forced to suspend specie payments; and British influence on the Continent reduced to the vanishing point were not calculated to inspire confidence in Britain's chances of surviving the expected French onslaught upon the British Isles. A French army—the "Army of England"—was actually poised on the Channel and Ireland was seething with revolt. Englishmen were preparing to fight upon the beaches with muskets, pikes and staves. During the X, Y, Z crisis, so far as anyone in the United States knew, France might already have dictated peace on the Thames and the British fleet been placed at the disposal of the Directory.[14]

Extreme as was Great Britain's peril, Hamilton did not advocate that the United States go to war to rescue its old mother country. His enthusiasm for co-operation with Great Britain waxed and waned with the fortunes of war. Certainly he was never disposed to lash the United States to a sinking British navy and go down with all hands while the band played "God Save the King." His zeal for monarchy and his admiration of Great Britain stopped short of immolation; when the island kingdom seemed in desperate straits, Hamilton saw no alternative but to let the war take its course and trust to the ability of the United States to defend itself against French aggression. He was determined to incur no risks that might leave the United States alone "to contend with the Conquerors of Europe."

Rather than make a formal treaty of alliance with Great Britain, Hamilton preferred to trust to the self-interest of Englishmen—always, in his opinion, a firmer bond than written compacts. "Mutual interest," he declared, "will command as much from her [Great Britain] as a treaty. If she can maintain her own ground, she will not see us fall a prey—if she cannot, a treaty will be a public bond. Should we make a Treaty with her & observe it, we take all the chances of her fall." In this spirit, he recommended in the spring of 1798 that the British Minister in Philadelphia be empowered by his government to conclude whatever arrangements the exigencies of the situation required and the state of public opinion permitted. In the meantime, if the British government was disposed to be helpful, he pointed out that the United States could put to good use a dozen or so frigates on lend-lease from the British navy.[15]

Coming from the leader of the so-called "British faction," the man who, according to John Taylor, acted as though the United States were "the truly begotten of John Bull," this attitude seemed sadly lacking in the magnanimity and self-sacrifice expected of every friend of England. To walk out on England when its need was greatest; to come to its aid only when it was winning and when its support could benefit the United States—if this were

Second in Command of the United States Army

the best that the transatlantic friends of England could offer, Englishmen might well conclude that if they were saved no thanks would be owing American republicans.[16]

Hamilton never pretended that his foreign policy was based upon anything other than the national interests of the United States. If he advised his countrymen to hold Great Britain in esteem, it was not because he wished them to love, honor and obey George III but because he regarded it as a plain dictate of policy to cling to Great Britain as a bulwark against revolutionary upheaval and foreign aggression.

He likewise regarded it as a plain dictate of policy for Great Britain to foster closer relations with the United States. It was Hamilton's practice in his interviews with Englishmen to dwell upon the future grandeur and power of the United States—good and sufficient reason, he exclaimed, for Great Britain to prize the friendship of this country. The rapidly increasing population, the vast untouched natural resources, the expanding wealth and commerce of the United States made it, he said, "an act of wisdom in the Minister of Great Britain to attach and connect the States upon political as well as commercial considerations." "We have still much to do," he added, "but the foundation is laid and our difficulties are chiefly owing to ourselves, it will require time, but in the course of things we must become a very considerable people." One Englishman, listening with mounting impatience to these vauntings, interrupted the Secretary of the Treasury by reminding him of the *present* strength and grandeur of Great Britain.

Despite the perilous state of Great Britain in 1798, American ships continued to be seized and American seamen continued to be impressed without regard to the susceptibilities of the United States government. The West Indian admiralty courts were as highhanded as ever—it was said that one admiralty judge condemned American ships "with the rapacity of a shark"— and in November, 1798, a boarding party from a British man-of-war removed by force fifty-five men from the American warship *Baltimore* and impressed five of them. In February, 1799, Secretary of State Pickering admitted that in the preceding six months a Philadelphia insurance company had paid more for losses sustained at the hands of British than French cruisers.[17]

Why British statesmen should insist upon trampling the tender shoots of Anglo-American accord remained always to Hamilton an enigma of the British mind. "By what fatality," he asked, "has the British Cabinet been led to spring any new mine, by new regulations, at such a crisis of affairs? . . . Why are weapons to be furnished to our Jacobins?" Strive as he might to clear away the prejudices and animosities born of the struggle for independence, he found his work undone by men on both sides of the Atlantic. But it was primarily the pride and disdain with which England frequently treated the United States that cast a pall upon his spirit. In 1798, he told General Wilkinson that "he had no doubt that the haughty spirit of that nation would involve us in a war with her in less than seven years and that therefore, we should prepare for that eventuality."[18]

The fact that the United States was dependent upon the protection of the British navy did not strike Hamilton as a wholly happy solution to the problem of national defense. Certain in his own mind that one day the United States would be obliged to contend alone against powerful warring nations, his objective was to make this country sufficiently strong to withstand the coming ordeal. He feared that if Americans were taught to look to Great Britain for succor, they might become as dependent upon that country as they were upon France during the later stages of the War of Independence. Moreover, he saw that such dependence discouraged the building of a navy by the United States—a navy which alone could give American commerce security in all eventualities.

To sail in the wake of a British man-of-war was not the course Hamilton had marked out for the United States. "Regarding the overthrow of Europe at large as a matter not entirely chimerical," he said in December, 1798, "it will be our prudence to cultivate a spirit of self-dependence and to endeavor by unanimity, vigilance, and exertion, under the blessings of Providence, to hold the scales of our destiny in our own hands. Standing as it were in the midst of ailing empires, it should be our aim to assume a state and attitude which will preserve us from being overwhelmed in their ruins."

To foster this precious nationalism, Hamilton recommended that the government adopt a strong tone against Great Britain as well as against France. He envisaged a truly American patriotism that would defend American interests from attack from every quarter: "In my opinion," he observed, "our country is now to act in every direction with spirit. . . . This conduct will unite and animate." More specifically, it would demonstrate to that doubting Thomas—Jefferson—that the Federalists were not a pro-British party which gladly accepted insult and aggression at the hands of His Britannic Majesty but could not endure the least pinprick from France. For that purpose, he advised that a ship be dispatched to Charleston to protect American commerce against the depredations of H.M.S. *Thetis*.[19]

So firmly was he resolved not to play favorites between Great Britain and France that he told Pickering he "would mete the same measures to both of them, though it should even furnish the extraordinary spectacle of a nation at war with two nations at war with each other." Despite the palpable hazards of such a policy, it would have the effect, he said, of proving to the world that "we are neither *Greeks* nor *Trojans*," Frenchmen nor Englishmen, but Americans. Thus, at the very time that Jefferson was accusing him of knuckling under to every British demand, Hamilton was advocating a vigorous protest against British seizures and trying to mobilize public opinion in support of the government's stand.[20]

In 1798, with the high excitement of war in the air, it was unthinkable that Hamilton would remain in the obscurity of a New York law office. Thanks to the Directory, he was provided with an opportunity to return to public life, and his friends proposed to make it a triumphal return. Robert G. Harper, a South Carolina congressman, urged him to take the post of Secretary of War (characteristically, Harper did not take President Adams' wishes in this matter into account), and John Jay advised Hamilton to declare his candidacy for the United States Senate. But Hamilton dreamed of more valorous deeds than were possible for a Secretary of War or a United States senator. As one of his more discerning friends remarked, during the War of Independence Hamilton had "devoted his talents to enhance another's [Washington's] glory"; now he was free to gather laurels for himself. And where did laurels grow more luxuriantly than on the field of battle?[21]

Timothy Pickering, the Secretary of State, was not merely of the opinion that Hamilton ought to be in the army—he thought that the Little Colonel ought to be Commander in Chief. Shortly after the passage of the act of Congress by which the army was strengthened by 10,000 men, President Adams asked Pickering: "Whom shall we appoint Commander in Chief?" Without hesitation, Pickering answered: "Colonel Hamilton." The President could hardly have been more startled had a snake crawled from under the sofa. With ill-concealed agitation, he exclaimed: "Oh no! it is not his turn by a great deal. I would sooner appoint Gates, or Lincoln, or Morgan." This, as Pickering pointed out, was scraping the bottom of the barrel indeed: Gates was no better than an "old woman," Lincoln was in his dotage, and Morgan's health was shattered. How, he asked, could these superannuated veterans be compared to a man of such transcendent military and administrative ability as Alexander Hamilton?[22]

But the President cut short the conversation; the times would have to be critical indeed before he would trust the defenses of the United States to the "Creole." As though to dispel as quickly as possible the painful vision of Hamilton in the gold braid of the Commander in Chief, Adams—without consulting his Cabinet and without waiting for a reply from Mount Vernon—sent Washington's name to the Senate for confirmation as Commander in Chief. Had the French army been on its way to the United States, the President could hardly have acted with greater precipitancy.[23]

Washington was offended by the President's haste, but Hamilton urged him to overlook Adams' bad manners and to accept the proffered command. Well aware that his own qualifications for the post could not stand in competition with Washington's, Hamilton saw advantages both to himself and to the country if Washington could be prevailed upon to serve. Washington's name, he well knew, still had the power of inducing Americans to close ranks against a foreign enemy. Shortly after the publication of the X, Y, Z dispatches, Hamilton recommended that Washington undertake a trip through North Carolina and Virginia, ostensibly to restore his health but actually to solidify American resistance to France. Such an excursion, Hamilton predicted, would "call forth addresses, public dinners &c. which would give you an opportunity of expressing sentiments in answering Toasts &c. which would throw the weight of your Character into the scale of Government, and revive an enthusiasm for your person that may be turned into the right channel." But Washington declined to put himself on display: his health, he informed Hamilton, had never been better and he did not want to do anything that might be interpreted to mean that he expected open war with France.

Nevertheless, Washington accepted the command of the United States Army on condition that he be allowed to designate his immediate subordinates. Since it was understood that Washington would not actively take part unless a French invasion became imminent, the question who was to serve as second in command became of crucial importance. Encouraged by his friends in the cabinet, Hamilton set his sights upon this post. But to his consternation, Washington favored the appointment of Charles Cotesworth Pinckney as his immediate subordinate.

The primacy given Charles Cotesworth Pinckney was mainly owing to the fact that he was a Southerner. If the French came, they were expected to strike at that part of the union where a large slave population might be incited to revolt by the slogan of "Liberty, Equality and Fraternity." But Pickering, Wolcott and McHenry assiduously plied Washington with arguments in favor of Hamilton's pretensions and Hamilton himself threatened to withdraw altogether unless he were awarded the coveted post—with the result that the Commander in Chief finally gave in. Yet no amount of entreaty on the part of the Hamiltonian members of the Cabinet could budge President Adams; a confirmed civilian, he profoundly distrusted the flashy, glory-hunting type of adventurer he conceived Hamilton to be. Not content with relegating Hamilton to an inferior post, the President made the tactical mistake of putting forward his own candidate for the post of second in command—his fellow New Englander, General Henry Knox. Although Knox and Hamilton had been fast friends while they served together in Washington's Cabinet—Knox might have been called Hamilton's shadow had not his vast bulk dwarfed the West Indian—Knox could not demean himself by serving under a mere colonel of the Revolutionary Army. He now declared that he had egregiously mistaken the character of his late colleague: Hamilton seemed to be driven by an "insatiable ambition" against which neither past friendship nor respect for superior rank could stand.

Despite the high esteem in which Washington held Knox's ability as an artillery officer, he was unwilling to accept the New Englander as second in command. Since President Adams, on his part, was adamant in his determination to award the post of honor to Knox, the Commander in Chief was obliged to make his wishes known to the President in no uncertain language. In September, 1798, he delivered to the President a virtual ultimatum: to end this bickering and appoint Hamilton second in command or he would resign his commission as Commander in Chief.[24]

To ease the sting of this dressing down, Washington disclaimed any intention of depreciating the powers of the presidency: his sole purpose, he told Adams, was to secure the aid of an able colleague. He concluded his letter with a brief character study of Alexander Hamilton. "By some," he said, "he [Hamilton] is considered as an ambitious man, and therefore a dangerous one. That he is ambitious I shall readily grant, but it is of that laudable kind which prompts a man to excel in whatever he takes in hand. He is enterprising, quick in his perceptions, and his judgment intuitively great; qualities essential to a Military character. . . . His loss will be irreparable."[25]

Adams salvaged what dignity he could from this humiliation by signing the commissions of the three major generals on the same day, declaring as he did so that the order in which they were signed would determine the respective rank of the officers. And, he told Washington, the Constitution endowed the President with authority to determine questions of rank; while he yielded in this instance, he wished to make clear that he reserved his constitutional rights. But even so, the lacerations inflicted upon the pride of the President never healed. As he said years later, he had been compelled to appoint "the most restless, impatient, artful, indefatigable and unprincipled intriguer in the United States, if not in the world, to be second in command." "You crammed Hamilton down my throat," he cried out in anguish.[26]

Of the three major generals, the only one who made no trouble was Charles Pinckney. At sea while most of these events were transpiring, Pinckney declared upon his arrival in the United States that he saw Hamilton's name at the head of the list of major generals "with the greatest pleasure . . . and applauded the discernment which had placed him there," and that he welcomed the opportunity of serving under such a distinguished officer—thereby setting, said George Cabot, a proper example for all military men.[27]

It is undeniable that Pickering, McHenry and Wolcott were doing, in a more aggravated form, what Hamilton had pronounced reprehensible in Thomas Jefferson when the latter was serving as Secretary of State in Washington's Cabinet: acting contrary to the wishes of the President and counter-working his policies. By condoning this practice, Hamilton was in effect pitting the Cabinet against the Chief Executive and encouraging an internecine struggle that might well have terminated with the President being dragged off at the wheels of the chariot of his advisers. Here Hamilton was striking a far more damaging blow at the prestige and authority of the presidency than Jefferson ever inflicted upon that office; the knight-errant of Executive powers seemed bent upon shattering the Grail which he had been at such toil and trouble to obtain. And all for rank in an army that might never be called upon to fight a battle!

31.

The War That Refused to Come to a Boil

While the generals and the President wrangled, the war effort ground to a halt. Until the question of the rank of the major generals was settled in Hamilton's favor, the Federalist majority of the Senate served notice upon President Adams that it would hold up indefinitely the formation of the additional army of 10,000 men, and of course no steps were taken to appoint the officers of the provisional army of 50,000 men. It was becoming a matter of doubt whether there would be any army—other than the 3,500 regulars—for Hamilton, Washington and Pinckney to command.

As a result of these manifold delays, the work of organizing the additional army did not begin until November 10, 1798, when Washington and Hamilton arrived in Philadelphia. A few days later they were joined by Pinckney, whereupon the Triumvirate, as John Adams dubbed the three generals, buckled down to the task of sifting the applications for officers' commissions that had already begun to pour into Philadelphia. Upon this work the generals were engaged for almost five weeks, sitting from ten until three every day and from seven to half-past nine every evening. Each applicant was scrutinized from the point of view of merit, former services, residence (each state was assigned a certain quota of officers) and political opinions.

The last operation consisted of separating the Federalist wheat from the Republican chaff. Washington, in particular, was intent upon preventing Republicans from infiltrating the higher echelons of the army: "You would as soon scrub the blackamore white," he said, "as to change the principles of a profest Democrat." President Adams likewise made politics the touchstone: he refused to approve higher rank for an officer who, the President said, had "said things which would have damned me and all my children and Grand children."[1]

Among those denied commissions on political grounds was Hamilton's old rival, Aaron Burr. Many years after these events, John Adams remarked that had Hamilton been content to intrigue against the President, he might have lived to an old age—for he ran no risk of being challenged to a duel by John Adams. But when Hamilton began to intrigue against Aaron Burr, Adams pointed out, the matter became more serious, for Burr was a notorious duelist and quick to resent an injury. Had not Hamilton in 1798 refused Burr a commission in the army, the President was of the opinion that the duel at Weehawken would never have taken place.

As Adams remembered the event, he proposed to the Triumvirate that Burr (who held the rank of colonel during the War of Independence) be elevated to brigadier general. This recommendation the three generals rejected on the ground that Burr, although admittedly brave and able, was a Republican of unsavory reputation. According to Adams' account, when Hamilton asked Burr what he thought of Washington and whether he would loyally support the Commander in Chief, Burr replied that "he despised Washington as a Man of no Talents, and one who could not spell a sentence of common English." Later, when Burr informed Adams of this incident, the President said: "I reproved Burr for this sally and said his Prejudice made him very unreasonable, for to my certain knowledge Washington was not so illiterate."

Washington's literacy aside, it is clear that Hamilton was not responsible for the decision to exclude Burr. In June, 1798, when Hamilton learned that Burr was coming to Philadelphia to seek a brigadiership, he wrote Wolcott that he had "some reasons for wishing that the administration may manifest a cordiality to him. It is not impossible he will be found a useful cooperator—I am aware there are different judges but the case is worth the experiment." It was Burr's indiscretion and Washington's well-founded distrust of Burr that prevented Hamilton from carrying out an experiment that might have changed the political history of the United States.[2]

As might be expected from a man who put union above all, Hamilton wished to avoid giving the army too partisan a complexion. Young Republicans, he observed, if caught young enough by the army, might be converted into true-blue Americans. He therefore recommended, particularly in the inferior grades of officers, that appointments be made irrespective of political affiliation. But he was not equally charitable toward college presidents. About this time the presidency of Columbia fell vacant and Hamilton, as a trustee, was asked to pass upon the candidates. His requirements were that the new president be "a gentleman in his manners, as well as a sound and polite scholar . . . and that his politics be of the right sort"—meaning, of course, of the Federalist sort.

The organization of the army completed, Washington returned to Mount Vernon, leaving Hamilton in actual command of the troops. The new major general lost no time in making his authority felt. Harrison Gray Otis, the chairman of the House Committee on Defense, begged to know Hamilton's wishes if, he said, "you can without inconvenience devote an hour to my instruction." Hamilton devoted a good many hours to that task and Otis dutifully laid before Congress the measures suggested by his mentor. In the spring of 1799, the Secretary of War submitted a report to Congress which was little more than a transcription of Hamilton's letters. On March 3, 1799, an Act for the Better Organization for the Troops of the United States Army passed Congress in almost precisely the form in which it had been drawn by Hamilton.

The President seemed to be the forgotten man of the war effort—a treatment he invited, it is true, by his protracted absences from the seat of government. Adams grumbled that all the forts constructed during this period were named after Pickering, McHenry and Hamilton, but "not one of them had been called ADAMS, except perhaps a diminutive work at Rhode Island." With mounting exasperation, he watched Hamilton solidify his influence over Congress and the Cabinet: all Adams' forebodings that Hamilton would make himself the master of the government seemed about to be realized.

And yet, despite the alacrity with which Cabinet officers and members of Congress carried out his orders, Hamilton complained constantly of the "amazing dilatoriness" that he encountered elsewhere in the administration. He was a man for whom all things must move swiftly: sure in his own mind what had to be done, he always acted with vigor and dispatch. But his celebrated "energy" availed him little in 1798-99. At the beginning of the crisis he had estimated that the United States would have less than a year in which to prepare for war. When that year was up, the country had hardly begun to get under arms.

For these delays and deficiencies, Hamilton disclaimed all responsibility. Early in 1799, he gave up his law practice altogether in order to devote his attention exclusively to the army. He set an example of austerity that left no room for heartburnings even among the privates. At first, the government provided him with neither quarters, fuel nor servants; and for much of the time he was his own secretary, toiling far into the night over his military correspondence.

In part, Hamilton's difficulties sprang from the fact that he took upon himself too much responsibility. Probably no man could have accomplished all that Hamilton set out to do. As Inspector General, he prepared a system of tactics and discipline, superintended the recruiting service and attempted to raise the army to the standard attained by the French army, its potential enemy. He studied avidly the organization, tactics and equipment of the leading nations of Europe with a view to "comparing them with each other and selecting the best." No regulation was too minute to escape Hamilton's attention: he prescribed the number and size of rooms and the amount of fuel allotted to each commissioned officer; he handled bounty money; he drew up codes of tactics, plans for maneuvers, drills and field exercises; and he worked out a method for the prompt delivery of arms, clothing and supplies—in short, an entire system of military administration.[3]

Although the Republicans accused Hamilton of trying to establish a monarchy by means of a standing army, in actuality he was attempting at this time to devise a way of providing for the security of the United States without the necessity of a large permanent army. If this country were to avoid war—or to win when war was forced upon it—it must have, Hamilton declared, "either a respectable force prepared for service, or the means of preparing such a force with expedition. The latter is most agreeable to the Genius of our government and Nation." Agreeable to this opinion, in the winter of 1798-99 he drafted two bills creating a School of Engineers and Artillerists, a School of Cavalry and Infantry, and a School of the Navy. Both bills were submitted to a congressional committee which rejected them as too advanced for public opinion. As a result, the honor of establishing the United States Military Academy at West Point in 1802 fell to President Jefferson.

But it was in the administration itself that Hamilton discovered the immediate causes of the delays and shortages which plagued the country's military effort. Although James McHenry, the Secretary of War, was his close friend, Hamilton did not hesitate to blame him for much of the trouble. As long as McHenry presided over the War Department, Hamilton lamented, the generals in command were far more likely to suffer disgrace than to win laurels. Never had he encountered a man who raised dilatoriness and inefficiency to the dignity of a system as did McHenry. Such a tyro richly deserved dismissal. But the President made no move to rid himself of McHenry; indeed, the louder Hamilton complained, the more fondly Adams clung to his Secretary of War.[4]

Washington and Hamilton had proved that the President could be forced against his will to accept a general of the United States Army, but it remained to be seen whether the President could be compelled to support that general. It was observed that after Hamilton had been crammed down Adams' throat, the President lost much of his enthusiasm for waging war. From the outset, his affections had belonged to the navy rather than to the army: "The trident of Neptune is the sceptre of the world," he was fond of saying, and he longed to see his country wield it against would-be aggressors. As early as October, 1798, he deplored the expense occasioned by the army: "There is not a democrat in the world," he exclaimed, "who affects more horror I really feel, at the prospect of that frightful system of debts and taxes into which imperious necessity seems to be precipitating us." Hamilton could look a huge national debt in the face without a tremor, but Adams was too good a New Englander not to recoil from the horrid

The War That Refused to Come to a Boil

spectacle. At the same time, Adams ridiculed the war hysteria which a few months previously he had helped to fan to white heat. He now declared that there was "no more prospect of seeing a French army here, than there is in heaven."[5]

Even many of Hamilton's admirers seemed more eager to make political capital out of the undeclared war than to engage in actual combat with the "Jacobins." One of their first acts during the X, Y, Z crisis was to put French sympathizers, French nationals and members of the Republican party in general under the ban of the Alien, Naturalization and Sedition Acts. Enacted in the name of national security, these measures ordered the removal of dangerous aliens from the United States, raised the probationary period for naturalization from five to sixteen years and imposed drastic restrictions upon the freedom of the press and of speech.

These laws were not the result of Hamilton's initiative. Apparently it did not occur to him in the spring of 1798 that it was necessary to take repressive action at home in order to fight a war with France; at that time he was congratulating himself that Americans were on the road to achieving "national unanimity" insofar as "that idea can ever exist." But the Federalist leaders in Congress were resolved to enforce unanimity by law; and, indeed, the kind of unanimity at which they aimed could be attained—and then only superficially—by coercion.

Nevertheless, it could never be said of Hamilton that he was guilty of underestimating the menace of "Jacobinism" at home or of extending charity to Republicans. In 1795, fearing that French sympathizers intended to assassinate some leading New York Federalists, Hamilton urged that United States troops be moved into the forts near the city; and in January, 1797, alarmed by rumors of plots to burn the city, he stood night watch for several weeks until he fell and injured his leg. (Was his fall accidental or did some malignant Jacobin trip him up in the dark?) As for Jefferson, Hamilton left no doubt that he suspected the Virginian of treachery against the independence of his country: "To be the proconsul of a despotic Directory over the United States, degraded to the condition of a province," he exclaimed, "can alone be the criminal, the ignoble aim of so seditious, so prostitute a character."

By thus whipping up hysteria, Hamilton contributed toward the creation of the poisonous atmosphere of party rancor and fear in which the Alien and Sedition Acts were conceived. Nevertheless, when he learned that the Senate was considering the enactment of a sedition law, he vigorously protested: "Let us not establish a tyranny," he wrote Oliver Wolcott in June, 1798. "Energy is a very different thing from violence. If we make no false step, we shall be essentially united, but if we push things to an extreme, we shall then give to faction *body* and solidity." He made plain that he wanted a nation of warriors, not of witch-hunters, and that unity was not to be achieved by dragooning Americans.[6]

The bill that drew Hamilton's ire had been introduced by Senator James Lloyd of Maryland. It was a measure calculated to arouse fears that tyranny was afoot: one section of the bill provided that anyone who, by speech or print, justified the conduct of France or defamed the government of the United States should be punished by fine or imprisonment. It was too strong for even the Federalist Senate: before Hamilton wrote, it had been dropped in favor of a less rigorous definition of sedition.

While the Sedition Act was under discussion in the Senate and House, Hamilton came to Philadelphia. It is probable that he had a hand in giving the legislation its final form. He was resolved not to establish a tyranny, yet he admitted the necessity of taking repressive measures against the "licentiousness" of the press. The Sedition Act as passed by Congress and signed by the President in July, 1798, seemed to Hamilton to give the country security without going the length of infringing upon basic liberties. Indeed, inasmuch as it effected three reforms in the law of libel he had long advocated, Hamilton was prepared to pronounce the Sedition Act an exemplary law. Under the common law, truth was not a defense, malicious intent need not be proved and it was given to the judge to decide whether the matter was libelous. Because the Sedition Act corrected these faults— no punishment could be inflicted until a jury had been satisfied that the publication was false and that the accused, knowing it to be false, had published it with an evil purpose—Hamilton concluded that it was designed to punish only malicious falsehoods published with intent to destroy the government and to give aid and comfort to the enemy.* [7]

Warmly as Hamilton endorsed the Sedition Act, he found the theory upon which it was based even more gratifying. According to this theory, the Constitution of the United States was erected upon a pre-existing common law by which the federal government was endowed with far wider jurisdiction over criminal and civil matters than the Constitution itself indicated. Anything that extended the powers of the federal government, and especially the powers of the federal courts, was likely to receive Hamilton's enthusiastic approval. Jefferson said that if the common law were in force in the United States, the general government would have "all the powers of the state governments and reduce the country to a single consolidated government." On these grounds, Hamilton could justly acclaim the Sedition Act as the entering wedge for a theory of government that would accomplish a[11] his objectives painlessly and constitutionally.

Contrary to Hamilton's expectations, the Sedition Act did not become a

---

* It is significant that these ameliorations of the common law were written into the Sedition Act by the House of Representatives and that they were proposed by Harrison Gray Otis, a congressman through whom Hamilton frequently communicated his ideas to Congress.

monument to the moderation and magnanimity of the Federalist party. The safeguards it held out to the individual proved in practice to be largely illusory. The truth is that the Federalist lawmakers and judges forgot that the purpose of the Constitution is to reconcile order with freedom, not to establish order at all costs.[8]

At this time there were in the United States a considerable number of French citizens who had taken refuge from the Terror in France and the racial war in San Domingo, and a lesser number of British radicals who had crossed the Atlantic to escape the sedition and libel laws of Great Britain. Some of the French emigrees were suspected of being spies in the pay of the Directory; many of the British refugees, particularly the journalists among them, attacked the Washington administration as furiously as they had once assailed the government of William Pitt. In order to bring these troublemakers within the purview of the national government, the Federalist leaders introduced into Congress in June, 1798, the Alien Friends Bill, by the terms of which all aliens in the United States were made liable to arrest and deportation without the formality of trial upon orders from the President.

Hamilton was concerned not about the rightness or necessity of this law but about the extent to which it would be enforced by President Adams. In this matter, as in others, he did not altogether trust the President's judgment. Knowing Adams' irascibility and his hot anger against "foreign incendiaries," Hamilton feared that the President might take it into his head to order all aliens out of the country in the interests of national security. On his part, Hamilton admitted that in general the British citizens living in the United States were undesirables and ought to be compelled to leave, and he was not disposed to take chances with the French residents. Nevertheless, he warned his party against adopting cruel or violent measures. Exceptions ought to be made, he believed, in the case of British and French merchants—he always had a soft heart for businessmen—and for some other "characters [chiefly French] whose situations would expose them too much if sent away and whose demeanor among us has been unexceptionable." But his misgivings, as far as Adams was concerned, proved unfounded: instead of enforcing the Alien Act too rigorously, Adams did not enforce it at all. In consequence, in 1799 Hamilton was heard complaining that the President was much too lenient: why, he asked querulously, were not the alien enemies of the administration deported? It did not greatly disturb him that if the British journalists in the United States were turned over to William Pitt, they were likely to land in Botany Bay.

James Callender—to whom tightening the screws upon Hamilton was rare and exhilarating sport—gave them still another turn in 1798. It did not require much probing to discover that, apart from his connection with the Reynoldses, he was most vulnerable in his relations with Washington. Rumor had long depicted Hamilton as secretly holding the Commander in Chief in contempt, and Reynolds erected upon this innuendo a sensational charge against the former Secretary of the Treasury. He accused Hamilton of having called Washington an "OLD DAMNED FOOL." But even for some Republicans this was difficult to swallow. As one pointed out, Hamilton drew a nice distinction in these matters: while he set down John Adams as an old damned fool, he did not consider Washington to be necessarily damned.

Yet expert as Callender was in the use of instruments of torture, he did not get under Hamilton's skin as did the Widow Bache. Benjamin Bache—sometimes called "Lightning Rod Junior" because of his descent from Benjamin Franklin and the high-voltage shocks he administered to Federalists in the pages of his newspaper, the Philadelphia *Aurora*—had died in 1798, leaving his newspaper to his widow. Mrs. Bache carried on in the spirit of her departed husband and she secured in William Duane, whom she later married, an editor and helpmate as vitriolic as the one she had lost.

In 1799, the *Aurora* printed a story to the effect that Hamilton had attempted to buy it from the Widow Bache with a view of suppressing that scourge of Federalists. Hamilton was alleged to have offered her $6,000 for the newspaper, whereupon Mrs. Bache replied that "she would not dishonor her husband's memory, nor her children's future by such baseness. When she parted with the paper, it should be to republicans only." The baffled Federalist was supposed to have slunk away, grinding his teeth and swearing that he would yet have the widow's newspaper.

There was nothing particularly defamatory in the statement that Hamilton had attempted to buy an opposition newspaper: not a Federalist but would have rejoiced to see the offices of the *Aurora* padlocked and the Widow Bache and William Duane put on the street. But the *Aurora* went on to say that the $6,000 with which Hamilton proposed to buy out the widow was secret-service money furnished him by the British Minister. Nor were the familiar canards lacking that Hamilton was a monarchist and that he had corruptly used public money while Secretary of the Treasury.

Having long served as a whipping boy for Republicans, Hamilton, it might be supposed, had developed a toughness of hide that permitted him to shrug off this kind of calumny. Up to this time he had endured the ordeal by slander in silence, "repaying," he said, "hatred with contempt." But the attack in the *Aurora* was more than he could endure: the "faction," he declared, had made perfectly clear its intention of subverting the government and, even more alarming, it was making long strides toward that objective, chiefly by destroying the confidence of the people in the "friends of government." Moreover, as a major general in the United States Army,

The War That Refused to Come to a Boil

Hamilton could not let this calumny pass unheeded—for how could the people of the United States or the officers and men of the army repose any confidence in a man who was believed to be in British pay and who had been guilty as Secretary of the Treasury of helping himself at the public till?

The *Aurora*'s story was picked up by several out-of-town newspapers, among them the New York *Argus*, where Hamilton first encountered it. His momentary impulse was to bring action against the *Aurora*, but Mrs. Bache had powerful friends in Pennsylvania, a Republican state, and, being a comely woman, might be expected to distract the attention of susceptible jurymen from the finer points of the law. Hamilton was a brave man, but he knew when he had met his match.

For these reasons, Hamilton decided to bring action against the New York *Argus*. Yet this course was open to the same objection that had dissuaded him from prosecuting the *Aurora*—the proprietress, Mrs. Greenleaf, was also a widow. Fortunately for Hamilton, Mrs. Greenleaf denied responsibility for the publication of the libel. This would not have saved her from standing trial, however, had not David Frothingham, a journeyman printer employed by the *Argus* at $8 a week, volunteered to assume responsibility.

Hamilton's predilections ran strongly toward federal laws and federal courts as distinguished from state laws and state courts. But when he came to defend himself against the aspersions of Republican journalists, he found the federal laws wanting: as a major general of the United States Army, he was not covered by the Sedition Act. Only the President and members of Congress were given protection by this law. The Frothingham and kindred libels thereby brought home to Hamilton the necessity of broadening the scope of the Sedition Act. It was necessary, he now declared, to throw the mantle of that law over all officeholders in the United States government, to include all writings which were seditions at common law, and to make these offenses cognizable in the federal courts. "To preserve confidence in the officers of the general government, by preserving their reputations from malicious and unfounded slanders," he said late in 1799, "is essential to enable them to fulfill the ends of their appointments. It is, therefore, both constitutional and politic to place their reputations under the guardianship of the courts of the United States. They ought not to be left to the cold and reluctant protection of State courts, always temporizing, and sometimes disaffected." But Congress did not respond to his exhortations and Hamilton was left to the cold comfort of the state courts.[9]

Instead of bringing a civil suit against Frothingham, Hamilton placed the case in the hands of the State of New York in order to indicate the public nature of the offense. The attorney general, a Federalist and a friend of Hamilton's, was resolved to make an example of Frothingham. Less than a month after the publication of the alleged libel, the printer was brought to trial in the court of Judge Ratcliffe.*

If it were true, as his enemies alleged, that Hamilton feared to have the truth known, he took unusual means to conceal it. The case of *The State of New York* v. *Frothingham* was tried under common-law procedures, which meant, among other things, that truth was not a defense. Nevertheless, Hamilton tried to bring the question of truth before the court by offering, as a witness in his own defense, "to explain some of the innuendoes in the indictment to prove that every part of it was false." The court, however, ruled that Hamilton was out of order: the truth or falsity of the libel was immaterial and could not be given in evidence by either side; the jury's only function was to consider whether the libel had exposed Hamilton to the contempt of his fellow citizens and whether the defendant had published it. This ruling was not protested by the defense: Brockholst Livingston, Frothingham's counsel, admitted that he had no proof of the accusations made by the *Argus* and, moreover, he believed them to be false.

The trial lasted only from eleven o'clock in the morning until four in the afternoon, when the jury brought in a verdict of guilty with a recommendation of mercy. Little evidence of that quality was displayed by the court: Frothingham was sentenced by Judge Ratcliffe to pay a fine of $100 and to serve four months in jail—an exceptionally severe punishment, exclaimed the Republicans, for a man who had gallantly shouldered the blame to save a lady in distress.

If Hamilton hoped to silence his traducers by putting Frothingham behind bars, he was grievously disappointed. Nor did it avail him when the Widow Greenleaf, indicted for another offense under the Sedition Act, sold the *Argus*. The whole tribe of Republican journalists was after him in full cry, screaming that he was a merciless persecutor of virtue and innocence.

Above this uproar, Hamilton was heard protesting that he was a friend of the freedom of the press. Republicans, he said, had to be taught the lesson that a free press was a responsible press and that there was a distinction between democratic dissent and the indiscriminate vilification of men who were trying to serve their country in public office. But it was not until 1804, when a Federalist journalist ran foul of the libel laws, that Hamilton really exerted himself to maintain the freedom of the press upon which he professed to set such high store.[10]

The hardening of Hamilton's attitude toward Republican libelers and malcontents was owing in a large degree to the efforts of the Republican

* In the eyes of the law, a libel is considered to be a public as well as a private injury. The libeler is therefore not only liable to a private suit but is answerable to the state by indictment, as guilty of an offense tending to a breach of the public peace.

The War That Refused to Come to a Boil

leaders to nullify the Alien and Sedition Acts. Above all, it was the threat of armed resistance by Virginia to these laws that led Hamilton to insist that they be enforced to the letter and, if necessary, by the United States Army.

In *The Federalist,* Hamilton and Madison had argued that the states would sound the alarm against all attempts by the federal government to invade their constitutional rights and that, since the state governments had first claim upon the loyalty and affections of the people, they would easily defeat all "schemes of usurpation." Hamilton had even gone so far as to describe the states as "bodies of perpetual observation . . . capable of forming and conducting plans of regular opposition" if the federal government exceeded its powers.

In 1798-99, faced with the threat of the Alien and Sedition Acts, Madison and Jefferson determined to act upon this principle. In resolutions adopted by the Virginia and Kentucky legislatures in 1798-99, they put forward the theory that the Constitution was a compact between sovereign states which was binding upon them in a moral rather than a legal sense. From this premise they deduced that the states were qualified to act as mediators between the people and the national government, that when Congress overstepped the bounds of its authority its acts were void, and that the states were, in the last analysis, the judges of the constitutional powers of the federal government.

To Hamilton, the doctrines set forth in the Virginia and Kentucky resolutions were the kind of rank heresy that might be expected from Antifederalists, Jacobins and other disorganizers. The federal government, he asserted, was the creation of the people of the United States, not of the states; the states had no authority to interpose their authority to prevent the execution of a federal law; and the federal judiciary was the judge of the powers delegated to the federal government.[11]

Satisfied in his own mind that the effect of the Virginia and Kentucky resolutions would be to destroy the Constitution, Hamilton advised his friends in Congress to make several minor amendments in the Alien and Sedition Acts, to issue a declaration supporting the constitutionality and expediency of the acts, to print this justificatory report and to conduct a pamphlet raid upon Virginia so thoroughgoing that no house in the state would be without a copy. He believed that a distinction ought to be made between the people of the Old Dominion and their government; but if they insisted upon identifying themselves with its acts, he was prepared to point the United States Army toward Virginia as a reminder of the necessity of loyalty to the national government. "This plan," he observed, "will give time for the fervor of the moment to subside, for reason to resume the reins, and, by dividing its enemies, will enable the government to triumph with ease."[12]

A few weeks later, however, Hamilton was not so sure that Virginians could be restored to sanity by threatening them with the United States Army. Early in 1799, reports began to reach the North that Virginia was preparing to raise the militia en masse to resist the enforcement of the Alien and Sedition Acts. Even though this step was not taken, an armory was ordered to be constructed at Richmond, ostensibly for defense against the French and Indians.* But in view of the fact that few Virginians believed there was the slightest danger that the French would invade the United States, Hamilton suspected that the enemy the leaders of the Old Dominion had in mind carried not the tricolor but the Stars and Stripes.[13]

Although there was a "respectable minority" in the Virginia legislature pledged to the support of the federal government, Hamilton was not disposed to dismiss the manifestations of defiance as mere "Virginia froth" certain to vanish when the people took a second look at the consequences of defying federal authority. On the contrary, he was certain that the "Jacobins" were preparing for revolt: the tocsin had sounded and the Virginia gentry would soon be riding forth at the head of their retainers to prevent the execution of federal laws. He suspected that the Alien and Sedition Acts were no more than the pretext for the impending uprising: the source of trouble was the old leaven of state rights fermenting these many years in the minds of Southerners. More fundamentally still, he recognized the tracks of his old enemy, human nature. He was not deceived by the protean forms it assumed: he saw through all its disguises and penetrated all the changes of name by which it sought to conceal itself. "It is only to know the vanity and vindictiveness of human nature," he said in 1795, "to be convinced, that while this generation lasts there will always exist among us men irreconcilable to our present national Constitution; embittered in their animosity in proportion to the success of its operations, and the disappointment of their inauspicious predictions."[14]

Hamilton responded as he generally did when he believed that the authority of the government was seriously challenged—call out the army. He was reported to have exclaimed that "a standing army was necessary, that the aspect of Virginia was threatening, and that he had the most correct and authentic information that the ferment in the western counties of Pennsylvania was greater than previous to the insurrection of 1794." Whisky Boys and Virginia grandees—they were, he thought, brothers under the skin bent upon subverting the national government at any cost. It would

---

* William Branch Giles and John Randolph later asserted that the purpose of Virginia's military preparations in 1798-99 was to resist a possible effort by federal troops to enforce the Alien and Sedition Acts. Even though the Richmond armory was projected before the Alien and Sedition Acts were passed, the timing of the actual construction was calculated to arouse fears of Virginia's ulterior purposes. The Alien and Sedition Acts were only a small part of Virginia's grievances against the federal government, and there was much talk of disunion in the Old Dominion during 1798-99.

The War That Refused to Come to a Boil

have given him peculiar satisfaction to have served the Virginia planters as he had served the whisky distillers of western Pennsylvania.[15]

Had it come to war between the federal government and Virginia, and had the planters gone down to defeat, Hamilton would doubtless have pressed his plan of carving up the Old Dominion into several small states. The events of 1798-99 reinforced his conviction that there was an irrepressible conflict between the large states and the central government. He therefore tried to impress upon his friends in Congress that the subdivision of the large states into smaller and more manageable jurisdictions ought to be made "a cardinal point in the Federal policy" because it was "indispensable to the security of the general government, and with it of the Union." But, perhaps not a little to Hamilton's chagrin, the conflict between Virginia and the federal government that seemed so certain in 1799 did not materialize. All was quiet along the Potomac; Madison and Jefferson continued to lead a loyal opposition; and the fate of the Sedition Act was left to the outcome of the presidential election of 1800. By way of answer to the Virginia and Kentucky resolutions, seven northern states (where the Federalists were in a majority) put themselves on record to the effect that the Alien and Sedition Acts were necessary and that the states had no right to pass upon the constitutionality of laws enacted by Congress—that was the province of the federal judiciary. Thus, for what it was worth, victory in the constitutional debate generated by the Alien and Sedition Acts went to Hamilton. But victory in debate, he shortly learned, did not necessarily lead to victory in an election.[16]

If the Federalists were obliged to beat the bushes for men, it was partly their own fault. Because of the Alien and Sedition Acts, the Irish and Germans who normally could have been counted upon to furnish the rank and file of the army were alienated from the administration and from the army itself. Most of the officers belonged to the party whose spokesmen were fulminating against the "wild Irish" and other foreigners who contaminated the purity of the older stock; it was hardly to be expected therefore that these same Irish would leap at the opportunity to place themselves under the military authority of their contemners. It was made only too clear to the Irish and Germans that they were expendable.[17]

When Hamilton first laid claim to the post of second in command, he little realized upon what a sea of troubles he was embarking. He had expected it to be a simple business of organizing an army and fighting Frenchmen. Certainly he had not reckoned upon the hostility of the President to the army and to the rapid cooling of his ardor for war. It soon began to dawn upon Hamilton that the prize for which he contended so spiritedly was hardly worth the effort. As Washington said, "Our military Theatre affords but a gloomy prospect to those who are to perform the principal parts in the Drama." Indeed, it seemed probable in the winter of 1798-99 that they would be hooted off the stage.

With the catcalls already beginning to be heard from the Republican galleries, Hamilton was in an agony of impatience and bafflement: everywhere, he fretted, he met with "terrible delays" and miscarriages. "In our affairs," he exclaimed, "till a thing is actually begun, there is no calculating the delays which may ensue." Occasionally, he gave way to despair. "I discover more and more that I am spoiled for a military man," he wrote his wife in November, 1798. "My health and comfort both require that I should be at home." For once, Hamilton and Adams were in agreement.[18]

But it was not all toil and trouble: from the ladies, Hamilton received the full measure of adulation and hero worship. "Our gallant general" won no triumphs upon the battlefield, but his successes in the drawing room have been equaled by few American military men. "Though not yet in the field of Mars," wrote his friend Robert Troup, "he maintains an unequalled reputation for gallantry. Such at least is the opinion entertained of him by the Ladies." In his uniform he made a dashing and handsome figure; he looked every inch the general, particularly since Napoleon had set a new fashion of small men in the military profession.

The one thing that would get Hamilton out of the ballroom and onto the battlefield was a declaration of war by France. But by the end of 1798 it had become painfully clear to Hamilton that the Directory would not extricate him from his predicament by declaring war. Caught redhanded in an effort to extort money from the American envoys, Talleyrand struck an attitude of outraged innocence, branded X, Y, and Z as imposters, and disclaimed all responsibility for the depredations committed by French corsairs upon American shipping. Having found, in William Smith's phrase, that he had "taken the wrong *sow* by the Ear," Talleyrand hastened to let go such an unmanageable animal, loudly protesting that it was all a mistake.

Although John Marshall and Charles C. Pinckney lost no time in leaving France, Talleyrand induced Elbridge Gerry to remain under the plea that his continued presence in Paris alone could prevent war. By so doing, Gerry cast a fatal blight upon the warlike plans of the Federalists: reports that he was negotiating with Talleyrand kept alive hopes of a reconciliation. Most ominous of all from the Federalist standpoint was the fact that after his return to the United States it was observed that the President paid him special attention. As well he might, for Gerry brought news that Talleyrand was eager for peace and would go to almost any lengths to resume diplomatic relations with the United States. This message, likewise conveyed to Adams through diplomatic channels, led the President to re-examine the possibility of making another approach to France.

32.

The Effort to Avert Peace

On February 18, 1799, President Adams sent to the Senate a message nominating William Vans Murray as Minister to France. It was one of the most stunning surprises in the history of American foreign policy: the Cabinet, Congress and the country were taken completely unawares. Although Adams had suggested to the heads of the departments the possibility of sending a Minister to France on the strength of the Directory's assurances that he would be properly received, he had not informed them that he had made up his mind to act. He later defended his secretiveness by saying that if he had taken counsel with his cabinet, the members were certain to have opposed the step: "If I had asked their reasons," he remarked, "they would have given such arguments as Hamilton has recorded; for he, it seems, was their recording angel."[1]

Hamilton and his friends could hardly have received a nastier shock had President Adams draped himself in the tricolor and burst into the Marseilles. To see "Jacobinism" rearing its head in the presidency itself—there was a spectacle calculated to curl the hair of the rich, the wise and the good. Some outraged Federalists ascribed Adams' aberration to insanity, dotage or a desire to play for the applause of the Republican galleries; Hamilton, having already set down Adams as a man of "freakish humors," was inclined to believe that vanity, jealousy and spite had led the old man astray—"passion wrests the helm from reason."[2]

The Federalist senators, finding that the President was not to be dissuaded from opening negotiations with France, finally prevailed upon him to send a commission of three members rather than a single Minister to Paris. Hamilton sanctioned this compromise: in a case of this kind, he thought, there was safety in numbers—safety, that is, for those who opposed peace with France. For Hamilton had no intention of permitting the envoys to go to France. What to John Adams were peace feelers were to Hamilton the tentacles of "the monster" reaching out for yet another victim. Had Adams forgotten, he asked, that these assurances of peace and good will issued from the mouth of Talleyrand, whose name had become a byword for treachery and double-dealing?[3]

Throwing all pretense of consistency to the winds, the great exponent of Executive powers now protested against President Adams' "dangerous and degrading system of not consulting ministers." There was sound reason, of course, for Hamilton's insistence that the President consult with his Cabinet—the former Secretary had the Cabinet securely in his pocket. To a man, the Hamiltonian members remained faithful to the gentleman from New York; if John Adams made peace, it would be in spite of the majority of the heads of departments. None was more hostile to the President's policy than was Timothy Pickering. This harsh and dogmatic New Englander needed no promptings from Hamilton to induce him to contravene the President's wishes; from the outset, he took the position that to negotiate with France was to submit to the embrace of a "Tyger" in the hope that it would prove gentle and humane. In language reminiscent of the Mathers, he railed against John Adams as "a degraded and mischievous vessel" leagued with the "Antichrist" on the other side of the Atlantic.[4]

Nothwithstanding the anger they harbored against the President, the Hamiltonians tried to preserve a semblance of unity in the party by treating Adams with what they supposed was delicacy and respect—although they admitted that Adams might have read reproof in their countenances. Had the President looked into their private correspondence, he would have found even more unequivocal expressions of disapprobation: here Hamilton and his friends really let themselves go, rending their hair and beating their breasts over the "folly" and "madness" of the President. For the most part, however, their anger was kept under cover: it did not comport with their high notions of presidential dignity publicly to call the Chief Executive a fool and a madman. Robert G. Harper, Hamilton's spokesman in the House of Representatives, well illustrated the ambivalence of the Hamiltonian Federalists toward the President. While Harper declared that he considered the mission to be a mistake, he added that "the policy and dignity of the Government equally require that it should be supported in a spirit of fairness and liberal good faith." In private, on the other hand, he said that "he prayed to God that his [Adams'] horses might run away with him or some other accident happen to break his neck before he reached Braintree."[5]

Apparently the President's horses were not of the true Federalist breed, for instead of depositing him in the ditch they carried him safely to Braintree. The cheated Federalists exclaimed that they would have war, with or without the President. "Let us then proclaim our rights from the mouths of our Cannon," they exclaimed. "Let us treat with Frenchmen only at the points of our bayonets." In 1798, they had advocated war as the only means of saving the country from "internal faction and french intrigues"; in 1799, they clamored for war to save the country from the "folly" of the President. Hamilton, who in 1798 had tried to restrain the belligerence of his

The Effort to Avert Peace

followers, now admitted that war would have been preferable to peace under a President who dashed cold water upon Americans' ardor to defend the national honor against France and who clutched at the first straw that seemed to promise peace.

And, indeed, it was difficult to recognize in President Adams the onetime apostle of a crusade against revolutionary France. Instead of unleashing the dogs of war, the President seemed determined to kennel those unlovely beasts and to occupy himself exclusively with the care and feeding of doves of peace. But if Hamilton's appetite for martial glory were to be satisfied and his plans for the territorial expansion of the United States brought to fruition, it was essential that somehow or other the country be involved in open and declared war with France. As Hamilton learned to his dismay, this was one of the rare occasions in history when Mars was playing at being coy and elusive.

Even though the French did not invade the United States, Hamilton had work cut out for the American army. He had not helped create this force and struggled for the post of second in command merely for the pleasure of parading the troops and of making a dashing appearance in his uniform. Hamilton was a man who dreamed dreams, and in his imagination he was already leading his army into Louisiana, the Floridas and points south. "We ought," he said, "to squint at South America."[6]

It was Spain rather than France that was to be the victim of Hamilton's empire building. In 1796, having suffered a succession of defeats as an ally of Great Britain in the war against France, His Catholic Majesty joined forces with the executioners of His Christian Majesty. This alliance between Spain and France provided Hamilton with a compelling reason for going to war with France: the decrepit Spanish Empire, certain to be involved in such a war, offered rich pickings to the United States. But if the harvest were to be gathered, no time could be lost: the Directory was known to be trying to secure from Spain the retrocession of Louisiana and to plant the formidable military power of France in the heart of the American West.

Hamilton had long since come to the conclusion that the United States must have Louisiana and the Floridas to round out its "empire." Characteristically, he justified this desire for more territory on the ground that it was "essential to the permanency of the Union." Unless Louisiana and the Floridas were annexed by the United States, he warned, they would continue to serve as bases for Spanish and French intrigues with the western settlers and the Indians. In that event, Hamilton feared that the area between the Appalachians and the Mississippi would be lost to the United States; instead of providing a source of strength to the republic, the interior of the continent would be divided into mutually antagonistic confederacies, each under the domination of a European "protector."[7]

In 1799, Louisiana was to be had almost for the taking. The Spanish garrison was inconsequential: not more than one thousand men guarded the thousands of miles of frontier that separated Louisiana from the United States. Against this weak and isolated force, the United States could bring to bear thousands of frontiersmen as well as its newly enlarged regular army. Louisiana was like ripe fruit, but it remained to be seen who would do the plucking—France or the United States.

Resolved to forestall France in the race to Louisiana, Hamilton looked to Great Britain for aid. He found the British government in a receptive frame of mind: the war with France had taken a decided turn for the better and it was felt in London that the United States might be useful in polishing off the beaten "Jacobins." In fact, so confident of victory was the British government that in 1799 it was contemplating the possibility of breaking up the Spanish Empire.[8]

This project was the brain child of an imaginative Creole, Francisco Miranda. A fervid apostle of Spanish American freedom, Miranda had first come to the United States from his native Venezuela immediately after the War of Independence. To Hamilton he had disclosed his plans for the liberation of the Spanish colonies, and the Federalist leader had listened with the enthusiasm of a romantic and the calculation of a businessman. The two conspirators—perhaps with the aid of a bottle or two—had reached what Miranda described as an exalted state of mind. But it was froth with very little substance. Although Hamilton did supply Miranda with a list of military officers in the United States who might be interested in the scheme, nothing came of it: the United States was in no position to lead a crusade for the liberation of Spanish America, Great Britain was not interested and, while Hamilton would never have suspected it from listening to Miranda, the attitude of the Spanish colonials themselves was doubtful.[9]

After several years spent in drifting about Europe attempting to sell his scheme to France or any other interested power, Miranda succeeded in 1796 in getting an audience with William Pitt. To the British Prime Minister, Miranda proposed a triple alliance of the United States, Great Britain and Spanish America. Pitt did not consider this scheme fantastic. He was eager to redress the balance of power in Europe by calling in the support of the New World, and the prospect of penetrating the rich markets and exploiting the natural resources of Spanish America was enough to turn the head of any British statesman.[10]

Thus it happened that the British government was cocking its eye upon Spanish America at the very time that Hamilton was squinting in the same direction. Rufus King, the American Minister at the Court of St. James's, kept Hamilton informed of developments in England, and Miranda wrote in high excitement that all Spanish America awaited only a signal to throw

The Effort to Avert Peace

off the yoke. He was prepared to acclaim Hamilton as "a benefactor of the human race" who had helped save "the entire World which staggers on the edge of an abyss."[11]

Surprisingly enough, it was at this moment that Hamilton decided to write off Miranda as a liability to the enterprise. All the devotion that the Venezuelan had poured into the cause apparently counted for nothing with Hamilton; upon the back of Miranda's letter, the West Indian made the notation: "I shall not answer because I consider him as an intriguing adventurer." As one Creole to another, Hamilton saw through Miranda's vainglory, impracticability and ingenious idealism. Perhaps more importantly, he recognized Miranda as a rival in fame. When the glory for the liberation of Spanish America was dealt out, Hamilton was resolved to garner the full measure. Miranda, on the other hand, seems to have envisaged Hamilton not as the leader of a victorious army but as an adviser on constitutional questions to the emancipated people of Spanish America. With this in mind, he urged Hamilton to draw up a constitution for the liberated regions—"Your Greek predecessor Solon," he assured Hamilton, "would have given much for such an opportunity." How little he knew Hamilton! For a man who aspired to play the role of Alexander, Solon was hardly more than a bit part.[12]

For Hamilton's horizon, once limited to Louisiana and the Floridas, had expanded under the genial influence of Miranda and the British Foreign Office to include all of Spanish America. As he said in 1799, "If we are to engage in war, our game will be to attack where we can. France is not to be considered as separated from her ally [Spain]. Tempting objects will be within our grasp." Chief among these tempting objects were the commercial possibilities afforded by the Spanish colonial empire. Hitherto closed to all interlopers by mercantilist laws, this market was one of the richest prizes in the world. If the walls could be overthrown, a continent and a half would be open to the ships and manufactures of the United States. Here, then, was the capstone to the Report on Manufactures: the United States was to become the commercial entrepôt and the workshop of the Western Hemisphere.* [13]

By associating the United States with Great Britain in this adventure, Hamilton expected that the republic would signalize its coming of age as a world power: its majority would be attained upon the battlefields of Latin America. As Great Britain's ally, the United States, moreover, would be entitled to take part in the peace conference and to make its views felt in the final settlement. And finally, the Western Hemisphere would be

---

* As early as 1787, Hamilton had urged Americans to assume the hegemony of this hemisphere. With a small but efficient navy, he remarked in *The Federalist*, the United States might become "the arbiter of Europe in America, and to be able to incline the balance of European competitions in this part of the world as our interest may dictate."

safeguarded against the introduction of French revolutionary doctrines and their inevitable concomitant, French revolutionary armies. "If universal empire is still to be the pursuit of France," he asked in January, 1799, "what can tend to defeat the purpose better than to detach South America from Spain, which is only the channel through which the riches of *Mexico* and *Peru* are conveyed to France?"[14]

Playing for such high stakes, Hamilton was resolved that the United States should take a dominant part in the emancipation of Spanish America. The attack upon the Spanish Empire ought to be undertaken, he said, by a joint Anglo-American force. Responsibility for the entire army of this land-sea force Hamilton assigned to the United States: the British contribution was to be confined exclusively to ships and seamen for the armada. As Hamilton knew, this meant that the United States would bear the principal part in the expedition and, he candidly admitted, "The command . . . would very naturally fall upon me." The United States as the dominant power in the coalition and Alexander Hamilton as the dominant leader in the Western Hemisphere—Hamilton's ambition for himself and for his country could hardly vault higher than this.[15]

As its share of the spoils, the United States, according to Hamilton's plans, was to receive Louisiana and the Floridas, thus gaining undisputed control of both banks of the Mississippi and a commanding position in the Caribbean. To this arrangement, the British offered no objections, but the rest of Hamilton's project did not sit well with the British Foreign Office. Lord Grenville had no intention of permitting the United States to play a major part in the enterprise. As he visualized it, Britannia would rule the land as well as the sea. The contribution of the United States was to consist chiefly of sailors for His Majesty's Navy. The Americans were not even to have the satisfaction of sailing in a cockboat behind the British man-of-war—they were to be *aboard* the British man-of-war and, if Lord Grenville's ideas were carried out, taking orders from a British admiral.[16]

While Hamilton impatiently awaited the raising of the tricolor over Louisiana and the Floridas—the signal that would put the American army in motion—he made his military dispositions for the event. Early in 1799, he summoned to Philadelphia General James Wilkinson, the commander of the western army. On the agenda of this interview was "the best mode (in the event of a rupture with Spain) of attacking the two Floridas."[17]

General Wilkinson was left in no doubt that military action was close at hand. Hamilton ordered Wilkinson to ascertain the attitude of the western settlers and Indians toward the projected attack upon the Spanish possessions; the disposition of Spanish troops and the location of their fortifications; and the means of supplying an army in the field with provisions, ammunition and forage. Wilkinson was directed to stockpile ammunition

The Effort to Avert Peace

and weapons, particularly heavy cannon and mortars for use in siege warfare, and a plan was worked out by the two generals for transporting three thousand men down the Mississippi.[18] Nor did Hamilton neglect to alert John Adams to the necessity of preparing for war in the Southwest: he urged the President to appoint as officers in the provisional army men of distinction from Natchez and other western settlements: "It is obviously a powerful means of conciliating the inhabitants," he told Adams, in what might prove to be the most important theater of the war.[19]

If Hamilton had any ideas of "jumping the gun" by invading Spanish Louisiana and the Floridas before they had been ceded to France, they were quickly dissipated by General Washington. The Commander in Chief would hear of no offensive operations against Spanish territory prior to a declaration of war. He even disapproved of Wilkinson's plan of stationing a detachment at Natchez, on the ground that it might alarm the Spaniards and lead them to reinforce their troops in Louisiana, thereby bringing war between the two countries measurably closer.[20]

Despite his vigilance against admitting Republican subversives into the army, Hamilton failed to detect a real traitor when he saw one. In a long career of duplicity and treachery, James Wilkinson deceived many others besides Hamilton, but probably his greatest triumph was in hoodwinking the West Indian. And this even though Hamilton was repeatedly warned of Wilkinson's double-dealing. "I recommend it to you, most earnestly," McHenry wrote Hamilton in June, 1799, "to avoid saying any thing to him [Wilkinson] which would induce him to imagine government had in view any hostile project, however remote, or dependent on events, against any of the possessions of Spain." But Hamilton ignored this advice: he took Wilkinson unreservedly into his confidence and recommended his appointment as a major general as "a man of more than ordinary talent, of courage and enterprise."*

If Hamilton's grand design for Spanish America were to be achieved, it was necessary to win the consent of John Adams to a closer connection with Great Britain. But by 1799 it had become clear that if there were to be a marriage between the United States and Great Britain, President Adams would have to be dragged to the altar. Indeed, he now regarded the project as a plot concocted by Hamilton to wreck the peace mission to France and to bind the United States to Great Britain as a vassal. Furthermore, he held Miranda to be a "knight errant, as delirious as his immortal countryman, the ancient hero of La Manche"—a fit collaborator, he thought, for Hamilton. He neither believed that Spanish America was ready to receive the blessing of freedom nor that Hamilton was the man to bestow it. Rather than serve the ambition of this "Creole," Adams declared that

---

* For many years, Wilkinson drew a pension from the Spanish government at the same time that he was on the payroll of the United States Army.

he would resign the presidency, retire to Braintree, follow his plow and "leave the nation to follow its own wisdom." He saw little chance for wisdom if Hamilton held the reins.[21]

Eager to convert the tepid conflict with France into a hot war, Hamilton urged in 1799 that the President be empowered by Congress to demand of the Directory reparation for past injuries and security against further acts of spoliation. According to Hamilton's plan, if France did not signify by August 1, 1799, its willingness to enter into negotiations, or if negotiations failed to produce a satisfactory settlement, the President was authorized, at his own discretion, to declare that a state of war existed. Such a course of action, Hamilton said, would offer "a further proof of moderation in the government, and would tend to reconcile our citizens to the last extremity . . . gradually accustoming their minds to look forward to it." As Hamilton probably expected, his plan would accelerate the approach of the last extremity, for it could hardly be supposed that France would enter into negotiations with the United States under a threat of duress.

During the summer of 1799, the course of events in Europe raised Hamilton's hopes that peace could be averted. France suffered defeats upon several fronts; Talleyrand was purged from the government; and an entire French army was immured in Egypt. On the strength of these reverses, Hamilton concluded that another Reign of Terror was imminent, that the republic would be crushed by the allied army and that the Bourbons would be restored. Manifestly, if this fate was in store for France, the United States ought not attempt to make peace at the eleventh hour with the doomed republic. By so doing, the United States would surrender all right to participate in the forthcoming peace conference; instead of ranking as a cobelligerent of the victorious allies, the American republic would find itself despised as a weakling and turncoat that had failed to stay the distance in the conflict with "the monstrous, bloody, cannibal Republic."

In June, 1799, while President Adams was at Braintree, from whence he conducted the affairs of government through the United States mails— he pronounced it to be a very convenient and satisfactory method—Hamilton urged the Cabinet to seize control of the government. As matters stood, he pointed out, the administration had no policy worthy of the name and the President was clearly incapable of formulating one. In view of the President's virtual abdication—he seemed resolved never to stir from Braintree—Hamilton saw no alternative but for the Cabinet to assume the direction of affairs. He did not doubt that this would be a happy arrangement for all concerned: the President could enjoy to the full the joys of retirement, while those who were capable of making a wise use of power would be in a position of authority. Of course Hamilton had no intention of remaining a mere spectator of this palace revolution: "If there was everywhere a disposition, without prejudice and nonsense, to concert a rational plan," he told McHenry, "I would cheerfully come to Philadelphia and assist in it; nor can I doubt that success may be insured."[22]

In spite of Hamilton's eagerness to save the country from a doddering President, the President himself proved unco-operative. Adams insisted that he not only had a policy but that it was proving its worth with every budget of news that arrived from France. The Directory, much to Hamilton's chagrin, responded to Adams' advances with further acts of propitiation. Definite assurance was given the United States that its envoys would be received; the demand for redress of grievances as a condition preliminary to negotiations was dropped; and restrictions upon the movements of American ships were relaxed. It could no longer be denied that the Directory had fulfilled all the requirements laid down by the President.

The Cabinet having failed to dissuade Adams from embarking upon negotiations with France, Hamilton resolved in August, 1799, to make a personal appeal to the President. At this time Hamilton's division was stationed at Newark, where, the President later sarcastically remarked, he ought to have remained, "disciplining, and teaching tactics to his troops, if he had been capable of it." Instead, without leave from the President, Hamilton left his troops under the command of a subordinate and took the road to Trenton.

This journey was a measure of Hamilton's desperation. For several months, the President had not even deigned to answer the letters written by the heads of departments protesting against the mission to France. Pickering, in particular, had been made to feel that he had fallen into disfavor; but the treatment meted out to the Secretary of State seemed to be nothing in comparison with the reception that awaited Hamilton at Trenton.

Nevertheless, the old dragon proved surprisingly genial: instead of belching smoke and flame, he greeted Hamilton affably and listened patiently while the general stated his case. "I received him," Adams later said, "with great civility, as I always had done from my first knowledge of him. I was fortunately in a very happy temper, and very good humor." But Hamilton was very mistaken if he supposed that the President's graciousness indicated any weakening of his resolution. It was the geniality of a man who had made up his mind and could not be swerved by any arguments from the course of action he had decided upon.[23]

During this interview, Hamilton made a supreme effort to convince Adams that the war in Europe was about to end in victory for the allies and that the days of the "sans-culotte Republic" were numbered. He spoke, said Adams, in a "style of dogmatical confidence" as though the future had been revealed to him by a special dispensation. He seemed to have had a special revelation regarding British policy as well, for he argued that if the United States embarked upon peace negotiations with France, the British would be so resentful that they would declare war upon the United States. John Adams was not frightened by this bugbear. He declared that he had met the British too often in peace and war to be worried by anything they might do: "*Great Britain could not hurt us!*" he exclaimed, adding that "in a just and righteous cause I shall hold all her policy and power in total contempt."[24]

According to his own account, Adams heard Hamilton out more in pity than in anger. "His eloquence and vehemence wrought up the little man to a degree of heat and effervescence" that reminded Adams of Hamilton's excitement at the battle of Monmouth. The President's patience was the more remarkable because, he remarked, "never in my life did I hear a man talk more like a fool." Every time he heard people speak of the imminent downfall of France, he later remarked, he was tempted to laugh in their faces. Quite as dogmatically as Hamilton, he asserted that the French Revolution would last at least seven years more and in the meantime it was more probable that Great Britain than France would sue for peace. As for continuing hostilities against France in the hope of currying favor with Great Britain, Adams would have none of it; for twenty-five years, he said, George III and his ministers had "entertained a particular resentment towards him" and he saw no reason to believe that they were still not pursuing him rancorously.[25]

After several hours of these unsatisfactory exchanges, Hamilton took his leave, convinced that New England granite was not more unyielding than was this hard-bitten son of the Bay State. He marveled at the pertinacity with which the old man persisted in error and resisted enlightenment. He gave up Adams for lost—and he was inclined to think that the country was in equally bad state. His mind a prey to the gloomiest apprehensions, he returned to his troops who, he now feared, would never meet a Frenchman in battle. His only solace was the assurance of his friends that "equally in vain would have been the remonstrances of Pericles, of Phocion and Demosthenes."[26]

On his part, Adams parted from Hamilton under the strong conviction that this so-called "Colossus" was in reality a ridiculous little gamecock notable chiefly for his conceit and ignorance. "I could not help reflecting in my own mind," Adams observed, "on the total ignorance of everything in Europe, in France, England, and elsewhere" that Hamilton revealed. Nor could he help reflecting upon the presumption of this upstart who, although he had never been abroad, set himself above a seasoned diplomat like John Adams. In fact, as far as dogmatism was concerned, Hamilton had met his match. It was a conflict of strong-willed, incisive and imperious personalities who laid down the law and predicted future events with Olympian

The Effort to Avert Peace

assurance. Of course, neither succeeded in shaking the other's convictions in the slightest.[27]

In actuality, Hamilton was much too sanguine in his expectations of a speedy restoration of the Bourbons; he did not live to see the day when Louis XVIII ascended the throne of his ancestors. At the very moment that Hamilton was prophesying the downfall of France, the armies of the republic were winning victories over the Russians, Austrians and British that eventuated in the collapse of the Second Coalition. In October, 1799, Suvorov, the Russian general whose earlier successes against the French had made him the white hope of the allies, was recalled to Russia. In November, 1799, Bonaparte, abandoning his army in Egypt and Syria, returned to France, overthrew the Directory and established the Consulate, with himself as First Consul. Hamilton may have divined Europe, but he did not divine Bonaparte. But then, of course, the Corsican upset the calculations of most of the statesmen of Europe.

This unexpected turn in the fortunes of war revealed how unfounded was Hamilton's assumption that the United States stood to gain by refusing to treat with France. As the event proved, the United States could have made peace upon much more advantageous terms in 1799, when French armies were on the retreat and Bonaparte was marooned in the Near East, than in 1800, when, as a result of Hamilton's delaying tactics, the American envoys arrived in France to find that nation in the full flush of military victory.

As a last resort to prevent the departure of the envoys, Hamilton pleaded with Ellsworth to refuse to embark for France. The Chief Justice, who made no effort to conceal his aversion to the mission, agreed to advise the President to postpone the envoys' departure indefinitely, but Ellsworth did not dare to decline outright to go under any circumstances lest Madison or Burr be put in his place. With this compromise Hamilton had to be content: at least the commission would be composed of "safe persons to be intrusted with the execution of a bad measure."[28]

And so, in October, 1799, at the President's orders, the envoys—or "Suppliants" as the Hamiltonians called them—set sail for France, while "the champions of the faith, in moody, sullen despair, retired from the field" and took their stations at the wailing wall, lamenting "the ruin, to which ignorance, self-sufficiency, and most blind and criminal pertinacity" had brought the country. Seldom have the leaders of an American political party more doggedly fought peace.

John Adams' decision to send a mission to France was an act of rare courage and statesmanship. Toward the end of his life, Adams told his friends that he wanted no other inscription upon his gravestone than the simple words: "Here lies John Adams, who took upon himself the responsibility of the peace with France in the year 1800." Alexander Hamilton would have composed a very different epitaph for John Adams—and no doubt he would have found pleasure in 1799 in writing it. But with the leaders quarreling among themselves, the real question was: who would write the epitaph for the Federalist party and who would be held accountable for its untimely end?[29]

With the sailing of the envoys, Hamilton knew that, barring a miracle, the dream of leading his troops into battle in Mexico, Venezuela and Peru, and of adding Louisiana and the Floridas to the territory of the United States, had been shattered. Apparently "the Chapter of extraordinary events which," he said, "characterize the present wonderful epoch" was not to include the name of Alexander Hamilton writ large across the history of Latin America. The succession of magnificent possibilities that had once unfolded before him had now to be put away with his other unrealized ambitions. Between President Adams and the French Directory, the war that had begun so promisingly had fizzled out like a damp squib. And now, thanks to the peacemongers, there was hardly a spark left in the poor paltry thing that Hamilton had hoped would carry him to glory.[30]

And indeed, the days of the army that had been raised in 1799 were numbered. President Adams began to fear that the troops, with time hanging heavy on their hands, would resort to "pillage and plunder, in debauching wives and seducing daughters"—a work for which he believed Hamilton to be specially qualified. In the meantime, the troops remained in camp waiting a call to action that never came. They became so restive under this inactivity that General Wilkinson reported that some of his officers at Natchez were ready to resign and "commit matrimony, in the course of the Winter, if not prohibited by Authority."[31]

Of all the "crimes" of which the Federalist stood accused, none was more damning than the charge of having needlessly saddled the country with a "standing army."[32] As a Federalist journalist said, "this touches the purse, and of consequence the more tender feelings of vast numbers. And of how many is the simple reasoning this: if the government tax us, it must be wrong: we will have other men to rule over us." Comparatively few Americans felt the weight of the Alien and Sedition Acts—that was reserved, said the Federalists, for the incorrigibly seditious and licentious—but virtually everyone had to pay the war taxes imposed by the government. In 1798, Congress laid a tax on dwelling houses, land and slaves—the first direct taxes imposed by the federal government. To supplement this revenue, additional duties were laid on imports; the tax on carriages was increased 50 per cent; and, at the risk of provoking cries of "tyranny," a stamp duty was imposed.* All told, the revenue of the government was raised to $7,500,000.

* In 1799, Hamilton advocated the issuance by the government of Treasury notes. Had his advice been followed, the federal government would, in effect, have resorted to paper money.

The Effort to Avert Peace

But even this was not sufficient: in 1799, the government was obliged to borrow $5 million at 8 per cent interest—an ironical commentary upon Hamilton's conviction that the interest rate was bound to decline.[33]

The financial difficulties of the government reinforced President Adams' conviction that peace was essential. He swore that "this damned army will be the ruin of this country": within a year, he predicted in 1800, the government would be bankrupt. The fact that Hamilton was clamoring for a larger army indicated to the President that the "Creole" "knew no more of the sentiments and feeling of the people of America, than he did of those of the inhabitants of one of the planets." Had Hamilton forgotten, he asked, that high taxes had produced three rebellions in recent American history?[34]

The President's forebodings were soon borne out: in 1799, armed resistance to the collection of taxes occurred in Pennsylvania. The land and house taxes were the immediate cause of the trouble. Among the German-speaking Pennsylvania "Dutch," hitherto Federalist in their political sympathies, the Republicans spread reports that Congress had empowered the President to mortgage all the real property in the United States and that John Adams planned to marry his son to a daughter of King George III. It was for these nefarious purposes, the farmers were told, that an army was being raised and taxes levied upon houses and land. Terrified by these specters—against which no hex was apparently of any avail—the farmers of Montgomery, Northampton and Bucks counties refused to pay taxes to the federal collectors. When some of the more obstreperous were put in jail, John Fries, a Bucks County auctioneer, at the head of a party of armed men, forced the United States marshal at Bethlehem to release his prisoners from the tavern where they were being detained. Not a shot was fired; the only "dead soldiers" in this fray were the kind that require corking.[35]

Ever since the adoption of the Virginia and Kentucky resolutions, Hamilton had expected a "Jacobinical" uprising in the United States. He had no doubt therefore that the "insurrection" in Pennsylvania was the beginning of red revolution; he was surprised only that it had manifested itself in a predominantly Federalist part of Pennsylvania rather than in Virginia. His consuming fear was that the government would not act with sufficient vigor. "Beware, my dear Sir," he enjoined McHenry, "of magnifying a riot into an insurrection, by employing in the first instance an inadequate force. 'Tis better far to err on the other side. Whenever the government appears in arms, it ought to appear like Hercules, and inspire respect by the display of strength. The consideration of expense is of no moment compared with the advantages of energy."

No doubt, Hercules ought to carry a big stick, but it was also true that Hercules might make himself ridiculous by arming himself to the teeth against a pygmy. Hamilton was misinformed of the magnitude of the danger and, because he was disposed to see Jacobins behind every bush, he made little effort to ascertain the truth. In actuality, the "rebels" were a mob less than one hundred strong whose actions might properly be attributed to the fact that the German-speaking citizens of this area were inclined to believe everything they read in the Republican newspapers.

Hamilton's fears that the government would not act decisively against the rioters were quickly set at rest. President Adams was of Hamilton's opinion that the occasion called for a display of overwhelming force. Besides dispatching a sizable part of the regular army to the scene, Adams called out two Philadelphia volunteer companies. Over this formidable force, Brigadier General Macpherson was placed in command.

As in 1794, the army encountered no resistance and no one was found who admitted to the description of a rebel. By the time Macpherson's troops reached Reading, Fries had quietly resumed his trade as an auctioneer. But it could not be said of Macpherson that he ran unnecessary risks: four companies of cavalry were sent to capture Fries. He was apprehended in the midst of an auction. The rest of the army was deployed against "rebels" who were engaged in their farm chores. The only casualty of these forays was a bull.[36]

The contrast between the mighty preparations of the government and the insignificance of the results achieved exposed the army and the administration to the gibes of Republican journalists. They pictured the troops maltreating the sick, driving pregnant women and children into the streets and loading innocent civilians with chains. The fact that Hamilton did not personally supervise these operations did not save him from being held responsible for all the outrages allegedly committed by the army. Hamilton was beginning to find that his unpopularity as Secretary of the Treasury was exceeded only by his unpopularity as a major general of the United States Army.[37]

In actuality, for Hamilton, the Northampton "rebellion" was a poor substitute for the kind of action for which he pined. He had not maneuvered himself into the post of second in command in order to round up yokels accused of terrorizing federal officials; if he had to combat insurrection at home, he much preferred to take the field against the Virginia gentry with Jefferson and Madison at their head. Nor had he, contrary to the allegations of the Republicans, raised this army in order to enforce the Sedition Act. He was prepared to use the troops to maintain "a proper respect & confidence in the Government," but he never made this the main business of the army.[38]

Even though it could no longer be doubted that the most formidable danger the troops were likely to encounter in eastern Pennsylvania was black looks from the countrypeople, the army remained in the Northampton area for the entire summer of 1799. This was not done at Hamilton's behest: as early as May, 1799, he was prepared to withdraw the troops, not only

The Effort to Avert Peace

because the pacification had been completed, but because he feared that the men might be corrupted by the "Jacobinical" principles endemic in the area. But he allowed himself to be persuaded by McHenry that immediate withdrawal would be dangerous. In consequence, the troops remained long beyond the period required by military necessity, if, indeed, such necessity had ever existed.[39]

With the federal courts presided over by judges whose rancor against "Jacobins" left nothing to be desired by the friends of government, there could be little doubt that summary "justice" would be meted out to Fries and his fellow prisoners. About thirty were found guilty of conspiracy and misdemeanors, and were imprisoned or fined. Fries and two other participants in the disorders were convicted of treason and sentenced to death. The case was appealed but the verdict was upheld at the second trial.

In order to secure Fries's conviction, it was necessary for the court to define treason as resistance to the execution of a law, despite the fact that the Sedition Act declared it to be a misdemeanor only. Although he had been among the first to demand that Fries be punished, John Adams was also among the first to admit that he had been mistaken. Accordingly, in May, 1800, against the advice of his Cabinet and without consulting the federal bench, the President pardoned Fries and all other persons involved in the riot. "What good, what example would have been exhibited to the nation," Adams asked, "by the execution of three or four obscure, miserable Germans, as ignorant of our language as they were of our laws, and the nature and definition of treason?"[40]

John Adams' decision to follow the precepts of mercy and humanity struck no chord in Alexander Hamilton. He thought only of the necessity of upholding the authority of the state and the sanctity of the laws: "The general opinion of the friends of the government," he said, "demanded an example, as indispensable to its security." The fact that the "insurrection" had occurred in Pennsylvania seemed to him to preclude leniency: the seeds of disaffection had taken such deep root in that state that they must be eradicated before they produced anarchy. He believed that this could be accomplished only by executing Fries and his companions: the blood of these martyrs would water the seed of the commonwealth by inspiring the well-disposed with confidence in the government and striking terror among the factious.[41]

Later, Hamilton used Adams' leniency toward Fries as evidence of the President's unfitness to occupy high office, hoping thereby to drive another nail into the New Englander's political coffin. But all he succeeded in doing was to give his enemies an opportunity to inveigh against his "bloodthirsty vindictiveness." Had Hamilton had his way, it was said, he would have loaded the gibbets in Pennsylvania in a manner that would have appalled even Jeffreys.[42]

Contemplating this unheroic army and calculating the cost of its maintenance, Americans too easily forgot the good it had done by discouraging French aggression and in what need they might have stood of its services if Louisiana had passed under French control. With the danger of invasion— if it had ever existed—at an end, Republicans inveighed against the troops as a "handful of ragamuffins," "men the most abject and worthless in the community," "loungers who live upon the public, who consume the fruits of their honest industry under the pretext of protecting them from a foreign yoke." The *Aurora* groaned that "we who have virtuously struggled, and obtained our INDEPENDENCE should be eat up, plundered and bullied by the very dregs and refuse of mankind, who are too lazy to apply themselves for an honest livelihood."[43]

The army held up to contempt and its commander reviled—was it any wonder Hamilton exclaimed that "it is very certain that the military career in this country offers too few inducements and it is equally certain my *present* Station in the Army *cannot* very long continue under the plan which seems to govern?" The people seemed intent, not upon the glory and conquests Hamilton offered them, but upon getting the boys out of uniform as quickly as possible. It made no difference that peace had not yet been made with France—the fact that peace envoys had been sent was enough to start a move to disband the army.[44]

Surveying the American people in their present mood, Hamilton concluded that "America, if she attains to greatness, must creep to it." But, he added, "slow and sure is no bad maxim. Snails are a wise generation." His most persistent fear was that Americans would back away from greatness, as, indeed, they seemed to be doing in 1800. Even so, he took heart from the fact that the republic was young and vigorous: perhaps, he said, the United States could survive mistakes that would have ruined any other country. He was occasionally so optimistic as to believe that his own policies would be vindicated by future events: "I stand on ground which, sooner or later will ensure me a triumph over my enemies." Already he could see posterity, that refuge of disappointed statesmen, generals and authors, paying him honor.[45]

Recognizing that the game was up, the Federalists vied with the Republicans in getting rid of this now useless force. The Federalists' first impulse was to leave the reduction of the additional army to the discretion of the President, but they hastily dropped this idea when Adams declared that "if it were left to his choice, the [additional] army should not exist a fortnight." Rather than leave the army to the mercies of the President, Robert G. Harper moved in Congress that the troops should be discharged on or before June 15, 1800, and that they should be given three months' severance pay. Thus the army at whose head Hamilton had hoped to ride into Louisiana, the Floridas and South America was reduced to its peacetime strength of 3,500 men. The dream of glory was over.[46]

33.
The Election of 1800

From presiding over the dissolution of the army, Hamilton turned with relief to the political scene. Although the war had stubbornly refused to come to a boil, the same could not be said of politics—there the pressure was rising fast in preparation for the presidential election of 1800. The abortive war with France was now to be fought over by the politicians, and this time neither side would fight under wraps.

The Federalists went into this struggle with high hopes of victory. In the congressional elections of 1799, they had scored impressive gains. If there was discontent over the Alien and Sedition Acts, the undeclared war with France, or the "standing army" commanded by Hamilton, it was not manifested at the polls. On the contrary, the voters seemed so eager to stamp their approval upon Federalist policies that the party attained the largest majority it had ever held in Congress. Rather than be outvoted by this majority, some Republicans, James Madison among them, made a strategic retreat to the state legislatures, hoping thereby to hold back the Federalist tide in these last strongholds of Republicanism.[1]

Decisive as this victory was for Federalism, it could not be accounted a triumph for Hamiltonianism. By no means all the new Federalists elected to Congress were devoted to the policies of the former Secretary of the Treasury: "We have heretofore experienced that there were shades of Federalism," said Theodore Sedgwick, "and we know that there are infinite degrees as well of firmness as of nerve, as of mental comprehension." On these counts, many of the new members were tried and found wanting: in Fisher Ames's words, they stacked up as "so-called" Federalists who bore little resemblance to the tough-fibered New England breed. These newcomers looked to President Adams rather than to Hamilton for leadership and were more disposed to make peace with France than to fight either a declared or an undeclared war.

In the presidential election of 1800, it might almost be said that as New York went, so went the nation. Not only were the elections held early in New York but so evenly balanced nationally were the Republican and

Federalist parties that it seemed likely the vote of New York would prove decisive. In the election of 1796, New York had given John Adams twelve electoral votes, yet Adams had been elected by a majority of only three votes. If New York could not be held in the Federalist column, John Adams' chance of re-election was doubtful in the extreme.[2]

The decision was to be made in May, 1800, when the voters were to go to the polls to elect members for the New York legislature. Since the legislature chose New York's electors in the coming presidential election, the balloting in May would determine whether New York cast its votes for the Federalist or Republican candidates.

Had Hamilton at this time drawn up a balance sheet as he had done in 1787, when the adoption of the Federal Constitution was in doubt, he would have listed on the credit side of the ledger the war prosperity, the rapid increase in the number of freeholders and the heavy immigration from New England into western New York by which the political complexion of that area was being changed from radicalism to conservatism. On the debit side, however, he would have placed the growing strength of the Republicans in the towns, particularly New York City. Having already undermined the Federalists' following among the farmers, Jefferson now threatened to deprive the good, the wise and the rich of their urban allies. Although these new recruits toiled in factories, shipyards and workshops instead of pursuing the ennobling occupation of agriculture, the Virginian did not spurn them.[3]

Fundamentally, the trouble with federalism was that it no longer appealed, as it had in the brave days of '88 and '89, to the urban population by holding up a picture of a bright new America of teeming cities, busy factories and a higher standard of living—the America of peace, plenty and prosperity without limit. Instead, it now sought to perpetuate itself in power by playing upon the people's fears of foreign and domestic "Jacobins." It had ceased to be the party of progress: federalism offered the people the *status quo* or—what some of the party leaders really preferred— reaction. More and more, the Federalists tended to rely upon property qualifications on the franchise and other undemocratic devices to maintain themselves in office.[4]

Among the Federalists' principal liabilities as they went into this election, Hamilton would have included Aaron Burr. And rightly so, for Burr was determined to make 1800 memorable by attaining the vice-presidency of the United States. To his practiced political eye, the Federalists were rushing upon destruction, piling up debts and taxes as they went. "Six million per annum for a fleet & as much for an Army," he observed in 1799, "begin to excite examination to which the land tax gives impulse. Considerable changes will probably take place in this State [New York] within two years."[5]

The Election of 1800

True, the Federalists had soundly whipped Burr in the election of 1799. On that occasion, they had made political capital out of Burr's connection with the Manhattan Company to such good effect that his popularity in New York City had plummeted disastrously. The Manhattan Company had been organized by Burr in 1799 ostensibly in order to supply New York City with water. Soon after receiving its charter, the company branched out into banking; New Yorkers awoke one morning to find another bank in town, but the water supply very much as before. Although the Manhattan Company did sink a few wells, the Federalists raised the cry of fraud—a cry in which Hamilton had special reason to join. For he had been badly outgeneraled by Burr: finding that the city of New York was planning to build a municipal water works, Hamilton had joined Burr in urging that this undertaking be left to private enterprise. Burr had repaid this kindness by establishing a Republican bank that ultimately overshadowed the Bank of New York.* [6]

Unlike his fellow Federalists, Hamilton did not regard the victory of 1799 as a deliverance from "democratic fetters." He was of the opinion that the "Monster," Jacobinism, was not dead but merely wounded, and he suspected that Burr was never so dangerous as in the moment of defeat. He therefore tried to stimulate his party to new efforts by sounding the the alarm against "Antifederalism." Late in 1799, he recommended to the Speaker of the House of Representatives that the Federalist majority make a concerted effort to expand the influence and promote the popularity of the federal government by increasing the powers of the federal judiciary, committing the government to a policy of turnpike and canal construction, and encouraging manufactures and agriculture. He was especially concerned to demonstrate to the farmers—a class of men "to whom the benefits derived from the government have been heretofore the least manifest"—that the government had their welfare at heart.[7]

But nothing came of these proposals except, early in 1801, a reorganization of the federal judiciary. As a result, the Federalists went into the election of 1800 on their record—with whatever that implied to the voters of the United States.

In the winter and spring of 1800, Burr set about mending his political fences. Being a practical politician rather than a mob orator and disposed to attain his ends by subterfuge rather than by force, Burr undertook to enlist the aid of the town workers to overthrow the Federalists in New York City. Equally important, the Bank of Manhattan demonstrated that it was a political power in its own right: many well-to-do New Yorkers swung their votes to Burr in exchange for favors granted by the Republican bank. The

---

* In 1801, Hamilton said that Burr had contended against banks with the same arguments that Jefferson used—"yet he has lately, by a trick, established a bank—a perfect monster in its principles but a very convenient instrument of *profit* and *influence*."

truth is, the more energetic and ambitious members of the New York business community believed that the city required another bank; in their eyes, the Federalists were seeking to maintain repressive controls upon business expansion by granting credit facilities only to long-established and conservative businessmen.[8]

At the same time, Hamilton was obliged to combat the propensity among his fellow Federalists to savor the fruits of prosperity. For them, private life had irresistible charms: after all, large profits were to be made in business and the professions—so why, it was asked, bother with politics? The privations and discomforts incidental to public life were so deeply impressed upon the Federalists that few volunteered to stand as candidates: of the thirteen Federalists who represented New York City in the state legislature, eleven declined in 1800 to seek re-election. So hard pressed were the Federalists for candidates that the ticket for New York City consisted of a ship chandler, a baker, a potter, two booksellers, a grocer, a shoemaker, a mason, several lawyers and a bankrupt. As a Federalist said, "Gentlemen are not worth their salt in a political struggle. . . . They are in kid gloves, and cannot shake hands with an honest man who is poor."[9]

Hamilton, for one, peeled off his kid gloves and he did not disdain to shake hands with a laboring man. Unlike Jefferson, he drew no invidious distinctions between the workingmen of the cities and the "virtuous" farmers, the chosen people of God. Hamilton was essentially a city man to whom farmers were no better than ordinary mortals, and he no doubt would have been dismayed to find Heaven peopled with farmers. Had he discovered it to be tenanted with Virginia planters, he probably would have requested a change of address.

But Heaven could wait: in the meantime politics must be served. Hamilton went out of his way to declare his esteem for the "leading mechanics" of New York City and he reiterated the well-worn argument that rich and poor alike belonged in the Federalist party. At meetings of the faithful, reported a Republican newspaper, "Hamilton harangues the astonished group; every day he is seen in the street hurrying this way, and darting that; here he buttons a heavy hearted fed, and preaches up courage, there he meets a group, and he simpers in unanimity, again to the heavy headed and hearted, he talks of perseverance, and (God bless the mark) of virtue!"[10]

All Hamilton's energy could not compensate for the lethargy of his colleagues and the tireless activity of Aaron Burr. A Federalist newspaper declared that Burr "travels every night from one meeting of Republicans to another, haranguing and spiriting them to the most zealous exertions. Many people wonder that the ex-Senator and the would-be Vice-President, can stoop so low as to visit every low tavern that may happen to be crowded with his dear fellow-citizens. But the prize of *success to him* is well worth all this dirty work." He compiled lists of voters; every ward was thoroughly canvassed; on election day, he was at the poll of the Seventh Ward ten hours without respite. Never before had New York seen anything quite like Aaron Burr in action; almost singlehanded he created a party "united, diligent, and unsparing of Time, Trouble or Expence."*

Burr's reward was a victory over the Federalists which ensured that New York would cast its electoral votes in the Republican column. The entire Republican slate from New York City to the state legislature was elected (but only by a margin of 250 votes) and the swing to Republicanism upstate was even more impressive. So remarkable was this triumph that some Republicans could account for it only "from the intervention of a Supreme Power and friend Burr the agent." While Hamilton did not doubt that "God moves in a mysterious way His wonders to perform," he was not yet prepared to regard Burr as one of the chosen instruments of the Deity.[11]

It was bitter for Hamilton to have lost the election, but to have lost it to Burr was an insupportable humiliation. In dealing with this dapper little man, he now lamented, he had been too intent upon observing the rules of decency and decorum; forgetting the nature of his antagonist, he had treated him like a gentleman. Burr and his kind, Hamilton declared, put republicanism to its supreme test: could popular government endure in a country where one party called to its aid all the vice and depravity in the community, whereas the other party, possessing all the virtue and most of the property, depended upon its own rectitude and merit to win elections? The election of May, 1800, seemed to have provided a conclusive answer.[12]

Although Hamilton ascribed his defeat to demagoguery, Burr's methods were less those of a demagogue than a machine politician. " 'So,' says an aristocrat to Mr. Burr, '. . . you democrats have beat us in the election.' 'Yes,' replied Mr. Burr, '. . . we have beat you by superior *Management.*' " He had taught his party how to conquer: the secret of success consisted in getting out the vote. As an organizer of victory, he seemed to have put all other politicians in the shade: he was "far superior to your Hambletonians," remarked a Republican, "as much so as a man is to a boy."

Before the results of the New York election were known, a Republican had predicted that if the Federalists lost they would "endeavour to move heaven & hell, rather than give up the loaves & fishes."[13] Considering that the presidency itself was among the loaves and fishes, it did not seem improbable that this prophecy would be borne out. And, sure enough, Hamilton broached a plan which, the Republicans asserted, had been fished up from Hell. Rather than submit to having Republican electors chosen by the state legislature, Hamilton urged Governor John Jay to summon the

---

* Robert Troup was not guilty of sitting back while Hamilton carried the fight to Burr. Just before the election, Troup declared that he had not eaten dinner for three days, so intense was the pressure of electioneering.

legislature into special session in order to change the method of choosing presidential electors from election by the state legislature to popular election on a district basis. Anticipating Jay's objections to this procedure, Hamilton pointed out that "in times like these in which we live, it will not do to be over-scrupulous. *It is easy to sacrifice the substantial interests of Society by a strict adherence to ordinary rules.*" Surely, he continued, in "the great cause of social order" it was permissible to take "a *legal* and *constitutional* step to prevent an atheist in religion, and a fanatic in politics from getting possession of the helm of state."[14]

Stripped of its rhetoric and self-righteousness, Hamilton's argument was simply that to save the country from "the fangs of Jefferson," guile, sophistry and fraud were lawful. To this suggestion Jay made no written reply other than a brief notation to the effect that Hamilton's letter proposed "a measure for party purposes which it would not become me to adopt." Hamilton did not again raise the issue. Presumably, second thought revealed to him its impracticability, if not its immorality.[15]

When the results of the New York election were known, such gloom and despondency settled upon the Federalists in Philadelphia that it was said that fashionable people were wearing their faces long that season. The United States Senate had to be adjourned while the Federalist members huddled in the lobby to consider the fate of their women and children in the impending cataclysm. For few doubted that Hamilton was right when he said that the Republican party was composed of malcontents and incendiaries some of whom were bent upon "the OVERTHROW OF THE GOVERNMENT, by stripping it of its due energies; others of them, to a Revolution, after the manner of BONAPARTE."[16]

In their imagination, the "friends of government" heard the tumbrils creaking through the streets of American cities accompanied by the cries of the American canaille. But they looked in vain to Alexander Hamilton to save them from these horrors. For, instead of leading the embattled forces of law and order against Thomas Jefferson, Hamilton concentrated his attention upon keeping John Adams out of the presidency. The barbarians were at the gates, and Hamilton was playing politics![17]

Since February, 1799, when President Adams announced his intention of sending a peace mission to France, Hamilton had given much thought to how this crotchety old man could be eased out of the Presidency. His first impulse was to draft Washington for a third term, but the sage of Mount Vernon refused again to "become a mark for the shafts of envenomed malice, and the basest calumny to fire at." Nor was the former President flattered by Hamilton's practice of looking to him for succor in every emergency. When, he asked bitingly, would the Federalist party be strong enough to stand of its own accord? "If principles, instead of men, are not the steady pursuit of the Federalists," he declared, "their cause will soon be at an end."[18]

A few months later, Washington was dead. It was the blackest news that reached Hamilton in a year marked by frustration and disappointment. His first reaction was an expression less of personal bereavement than of political loss. As his anguished cry makes clear—Washington was "an aegis very necessary to me"—he was acutely aware that Washington's protective mantle had been removed at a time when President Adams' intractability made it more essential to Hamilton than ever before. "Perhaps no friend of his," Hamilton said, "has more cause to lament on personal account than myself."

With Washington gone, the Federalists seemingly had no alternative but to resign themselves to suffering John Adams for another four years. But Hamilton and his close friends accepted their fate with bitter lamentations: these "friends of religion and good Government" believed that Adams had fallen utterly from grace and was deserving of long and painful punishment in the party purgatory. "We shall never find ourselves in the straight road of Federalism while Mr. Adams is President," said Oliver Wolcott; the only guide along that increasingly tortuous highway was Alexander Hamilton.[19]

Early in 1800, the Federalist caucus nominated John Adams and, with him, Charles Cotesworth Pinckney, the hero of the X, Y, Z negotiations and, since 1798, a major general in the United States Army. Being a South Carolinian, Pinckney was expected to strengthen the Federalist ticket in the South. Ostensibly in order to make doubly sure of the adherence of the South to the Federalist ticket, the party leaders pledged themselves to work equally for the election of Adams and Pinckney. There was to be no question of a presidential and vice-presidential candidate: in the eyes of the party, each was the equal of the other. Thus the Federalists would ride two horses across the torrent in the hope that one or the other would carry them to safety.

John Adams could not fail to remember how this strategy had worked in 1796—how Hamilton had tried to switch horses in midstream, leaving Adams to founder. Nor was the President wrong in concluding that Hamilton was planning to try the trick again. After the Federalist caucus had announced that Adams and Pinckney were to be supported equally, Hamilton undertook to juggle the votes in the Electoral College in such a way that Pinckney rather than Adams would carry off the prize. As in 1796, Hamilton's efforts were directed toward inducing Massachusetts and other New England states to cast their votes equally in the Electoral College for Adams and Pinckney, while South Carolina, which voted last, was to give the presidency to Pinckney by withholding a few votes from Adams.[20]

In dealing with Thomas Jefferson, Aaron Burr and John Adams, Hamilton obviously acted upon the maxim that the end justified the means. And, since the end was the preservation of the American government from a "Frenchified, visionary philosopher" in Jefferson's case, an unscrupulous demagogue in Burr's case and a refractory old fool in the case of John Adams, he easily convinced himself that he had the loftiest sanction for what he did. But there were other factors that entered into his decision to resort to the most palpable kind of chicanery to keep Adams out of the presidency. The New Englander was about as malleable as flint; Charles Cotesworth Pinckney, on the other hand, was of a more pliable temperament. Had not Pinckney graciously yielded to Hamilton when the question of the primacy of the major generals was in controversy? With Pinckney in the presidency, Hamilton could hope to guide the foreign and domestic policies of the United States. He might even yet lead the American army into Louisiana.[21]

Hamilton took his gamble in the face of ever-mounting evidence that the Federalists were losing their fighting spirit. Some of the most redoubtable paladins of the party had stacked their lances and retired to the relative peace and quiet of the diplomatic service: Rufus King had left the Senate to serve as Minister to the Court of St. James's; William Smith of South Carolina had accepted appointment as Minister to Portugal; and Robert G. Harper, John Jay and Harrison Gray Otis had announced their intention of abandoning politics. William Duer and Robert Morris were behind bars and James Wilson was in the custody of the sheriff—"a victim to misfortune and liquor." Thus, by one means or another, the wise, the rich and the good were forsaking their followers.[22]

Equally portentous, the old cries of "Jacobinism" and "the Constitution in danger" no longer had quite the same effect in bringing out the voters. The device of piling horror upon horror in order to frighten the voters away from Jefferson tended to defeat its purpose: since it was impossible that the Republicans could be as bad as Hamilton pictured them to be, many people began to wonder if the Republicans were bad at all. As a result, they became indifferent about the election: if Jefferson were elected, it began to be said, things would go on much as before—"the political ship will change her pilot but not her course."[23]

Despondingly, the Federalists contrasted their own weakness and disorganization with the zeal, unity and discipline of the Republicans. Despite the Sedition Act, scores of newspapers were established to promote the candidacy of Thomas Jefferson and to denigrate Adams and Hamilton. Keeping watch and ward over the American press proved to be too heavy a responsibility for the Federalists, particularly since the Sedition Act seemed to have had no other effect than to make two libels sprout where only one grew before. In 1800, had the law been rigorously enforced, the courts would have been jammed with sedition cases and the jails filled with journalists.[24]

Whatever illusions President Adams may once have possessed regarding the loyalty of his Cabinet, it was now manifest to him that he walked a slippery quarterdeck and that "all the officers and half the crew" were ready to pitch him overboard. His only hope seemed to lie in striking hard against the mutineers and making examples of the ringleaders. With characteristic energy and decision he undertook to purge his Cabinet of Hamiltonians: a few days after the New York elections, he demanded the resignations of Secretary of State Pickering and Secretary of War McHenry; and when Pickering refused to resign, he was peremptorily dismissed. This action Adams later described as "the most deliberate, virtuous and disinterested" of his career: he had rid himself of two "idolators of Hamilton" who had plagued his administration from the beginning and who had done everything in their power to destroy him politically.[25]

Adams removed Pickering and McHenry for much the same reasons, although in an aggravated form, that had led Hamilton in 1792-93 to demand the resignation of Thomas Jefferson as Secretary of State. At that time, Hamilton had laid down the principle that, he then said, ought to govern the conduct of members of the Cabinet—implicit obedience to the President or resignation. Unity, energy and responsibility were impossible, he asserted, without the subordination of the heads of the departments to the Chief Executive. If Hamilton put any value upon consistency, therefore, he could not deny Adams the right to rid himself of such notorious malcontents as Pickering and McHenry. Moreover, Hamilton had pronounced McHenry to be utterly incompetent and, before Pickering came over to his side, he had warned his friends not to trust the Secretary of State. Pickering, he said, was "a very worthy man" but with "some thing warm and angular in his temper, and will require much a vigilant, moderating eye." Not being a Puritan himself, Hamilton had no love for Puritans.[26]

Nevertheless, Hamilton took the dismissal of this incompetent Secretary of War and this shifty Secretary of State as a personal affront. By doing no little violence to the facts, he made it appear that Pickering and McHenry were martyrs to the caprice of a willful master. In working this metamorphosis, Hamilton was aided by a conveniently short memory: McHenry he now described as a "sensible, judicious, well informed" public servant; and he justified Pickering's insubordination on the ground that it was not "in the disposition of this respectable man [Pickering], justly tenacious of his own dignity and independence, to practice condescension towards an imperious chief."[27]

In the spring of 1800, Hamilton set out on a tour of New England to take leave of the troops who were about to be disbanded. Dispiriting as the occasion was, it proved to be something of a personal triumph. At Providence, Rhode Island, for example, the soldiers were moved to tears, "not merely on account of this last interview with their General, but by the impressive sentiments which fell from his lips, enforced by the most charming eloquence and pointed diction." The burden of his remarks was that the soldiers, even though they were about to become civilians, ought to hold themselves in readiness for future emergencies: there were far too many Jacobins in the world for any man to allow his gun to grow rusty. At Boston he was welcomed like a conqueror come to be crowned with laurels. By the time the toasts were over, the stiffness and reserve characteristic of Boston social gatherings had been completely washed away, and the magistrates and ministers embraced a man from whom their ancestors would have recoiled as a bastard and adulterer. For Hamilton had won his Scarlet Letter—and it was not from Harvard![28]

It was soon apparent that Hamilton's New England tour was not wholly given over to sad farewells and patriotic toasts: the general was playing politics on the side with a view to making Pinckney President. In New Hampshire for example, Hamilton informed the leading Federalists "of the errors and defects of Mr. Adams," pointing out, among other things, that Adams was "a very unfit and incapable character, excessively *vain* and *jealous* and *ignobly* attached to *place*." Everywhere he spoke without reserve —"you know," said Fisher Ames, "he is the most frank of men."[29]

From the adulation heaped upon Hamilton in Boston by the defenders of the good old ways and good old principles, it was clear that in their eyes he, rather than President Adams, was the chief bulwark against Jacobinism in the United States. But the Essex Junto was not the Federalist party—and least of all was it representative of the opinion of the rank and file of that party. Hamilton's New England tour satisfied him that John Adams was still a power to be reckoned with. So strong was the popular attachment for Adams that Hamilton feared that New Englanders would repeat the game they had played in 1796—promise to support Adams and Pinckney equally and then, in the final vote, divert enough votes from Pinckney to secure Adams' election as President.[30]

As was to be expected, reports of Hamilton's activities in New England reached the President. In contrast to his attitude under similar conditions in 1796, Adams gave ready credence to these stories. He railed against Hamilton as "a bastard, and as much an alien as Gallatin"; as the leader of a "damned faction" of "British partisans"—"a set of men more inimical to the Country than the worst Democrats or Jacobins"; and as the moving spirit of the faction that was trying to produce an open rupture with France. Even those to whom the spectacle of John Adams in eruption was familiar had never seen anything quite like this. In his agitation of spirit, the President exclaimed that "Mr. Jefferson is an infinitely better man than [Hamilton], a wiser one I am sure; and if President, will act wisely. I know it, and would sooner be Vice-President under him, or even Minister Resident at the Hague, than be indebted to such a being as Hamilton for the Presidency."[31]

Not to be outdone, Hamilton declared that he preferred Jefferson to Adams as President. "If we must have an enemy at the head of the government," he asserted, "let it be one whom we can oppose, and for whom we are not responsible, who will not involve our party in the disgrace of his foolish and bad measures."

The charge of heading a "British faction" was throwing down the gauntlet to Hamilton in earnest. True, he was accustomed to hearing this from Republicans, but coming from John Adams, himself accused of being pro-British, it became a much more serious matter. It might be construed to mean that Adams was prepared to turn state's evidence against his accomplice. With the President's testimony entered on the record, the American people could no longer doubt that there were traitors in their midst.[32]

Alive to this danger, Hamilton wrote two letters to President Adams demanding an explanation of the remarks attributed to him. When Adams refused even to answer these communications, Hamilton resolved to speak out against the weaknesses and follies of the President. His decision made, he set about gathering evidence against Adams somewhat in the manner of a prosecuting attorney seeking to convict a prisoner in the dock. Nothing was too small or inconsequential to escape his scrutiny; not even Thomas Jefferson, jotting down in his little black book the latest scandal about Hamilton, was more painstaking. At Hamilton's request, the Cabinet members had kept records of the President's conversation "with a view," it was said, "to sink him into contempt and to deprive him of his remaining partisans." Pickering and McHenry, to whom this was a labor of love, had likewise made copies of all documents which might be used against Adams; especially prized was "a very curious journal" kept by Adams while he was in Europe and which was thought to bring into sharp relief all his "weakness and vanity."[33]

Among Hamilton's research assistants in this work, none was more valuable than Oliver Wolcott, who, after the dismissal of Pickering and McHenry, remained in the Cabinet as Secretary of the Treasury. Although otherwise an honorable man, Wolcott thought nothing of playing the part of a spy and informer against a man who trusted him.[34]

Strongly impressed with the idea that the Federalists had been altogether too lenient with Adams and had not sufficiently carried their case against the President to the people, Hamilton intended to give as much publicity as possible to his attack upon John Adams. The people, he reasoned, had a right to know with what kind of President they were afflicted and how cruelly he had maligned Hamilton. "This," he said, "seems to me the most authentic way of conveying the information, and best suited to the plain dealing of my character."[35]

Except, however, for Timothy Pickering, who pronounced Adams to be "blind, stone blind, to his own faults and failings," none of Hamilton's friends relished the prospect of seeing the President dragged publicly through the mud. Most took the position that much as Adams deserved this treatment, too much ordure was bound to splatter upon the Federalist party—with fatal consequences to the slim hope that remained of winning the election. But John Jay stoutly declared that he still confided in the President's "Integrity and Patriotism"—a sentiment that placed him completely outside the pale of the Hamiltonians.[36]

It is probable that Washington, had he been alive in 1800, would have kept Hamilton's resentment against Adams within bounds. Almost certainly the Virginian would have been among those who counseled Hamilton against writing an exposé of the President's character, and the fear of offending Washington might have deterred Hamilton. But Hamilton was now free of the overshadowing presence of the late Commander in Chief and he celebrated his liberation by destroying the Federalist party. No more convincing evidence could have been given that Washington was the man who held together the diverse elements of that party by his wisdom and prestige.

Deferring to no man except his now-departed "aegis," Hamilton could not be dissuaded from writing a philippic against John Adams. Only by exhibiting the meanness, folly and vindictiveness of the President, Hamilton declared, could he refute the calumnies propagated against him by the President and his adherents. He would show that Adams was the evil genius of the Federalist party, the fomenter of dissension and the implacable enemy of innocence and rectitude. "We fight Adams on very unequal grounds," he told his friends, "because we do not declare the motives of our dislike. . . . We have the air of mere caballers, and shall be completely run down in the public opinion." Nevertheless, Hamilton did make a concession to the more cautious members of his party: he agreed that whatever he wrote against Adams should be circulated only among a few party leaders.[37]

In October, 1800, after three months spent in sifting the evidence, Hamilton brought forth his *Letter from Alexander Hamilton concerning the Public Conduct and Character of John Adams*. Here he treated the favored few of the Federalist party to the spectacle of "the disgusting egotism, the distempered jealousy, and the ungovernable indiscretion of Mr. Adams's temper." It was the case history, he exclaimed, of a man obsessed by "Vanity without bounds, and a jealousy capable of discoloring every object"—an unhappy tale of mental unbalance and human frailty that would provoke pity were it not for the fact that the repository of these deplorable idiosyncrasies was the President of the United States!

"It is a fact," Hamilton assured the party elders, "that he [Adams] is often liable to paroxysms of anger, which deprive him of self-command and produce very outrageous behavior to those who approach him." Of the

The Election of 1800

provocations that occasioned these outbursts, Hamilton gave no hint. Indeed, he seldom saw fit to descend to particulars—and wisely so, for most of the aberrations of which he accused the President were the most popular measures of his administration.

No doubt, much of what Hamilton said about Adams was true: the President was not a good administrator; he lacked tact and discretion; and he was certainly guilty of violent outbursts of temper. He was jealous of Franklin and Washington and he understood little of the art of getting along with people. But Adams' foibles were not the sum total of his character: he was, besides, a man of rare courage and independence of mind, and, as he demonstrated repeatedly during his long career, he was capable of striking out on a course which he believed to be right, regardless of popularity.

In taxing Adams with instability and vacillation, Hamilton could not truthfully say that the President had been feeble and wavering when it came to opposing the policies recommended by Hamilton himself. Had Adams actually been as weak as Hamilton made him appear, the New Yorker would not have found it necessary to write against the President. With a better appreciation of the strength of character of this rock-ribbed New Englander, the British Minister remarked that Adams was chiefly remarkable "for a perseverance in sentiments adopted, and for an extreme impatience when contradicted." Even as hostile an observer as McHenry never found Adams weak: "With talents of a very different and inferior cast from those of the Great Frederick," McHenry said, "like him he [Adams] would be every thing and do every thing himself." William Smith, after dining at the President's, offered no more serious criticism than that the wine was mediocre.[38]

The force of Hamilton's strictures was appreciably weakened, moreover, by his admission that Adams was a man of patriotism and integrity and that he even possessed "talents of a certain kind." The former Secretary conceded that his quarrel with the President was not wholly over questions of public policy: he had, he said, "causes of personal dissatisfaction with Mr. Adams." And, finally, he made no claim that his own character was without fault. His quickness to resent injury was not, he remarked in another place, an altogether happy characteristic. "Perhaps," he said, "my sensibility is the effect of an exaggerated estimate of my services to the United States; but on such a subject a man will judge for himself; and if he is misled by his vanity, he must be content with the mortifications to which it exposes him."[39]

In spite of the appalling infirmities Hamilton discovered in John Adams' character, he concluded that Adams must be supported equally with Pinckney in accord with the agreement reached at Philadelphia. To this lame ending had Hamilton's researches into human depravity brought him. And yet few could fail to see that Hamilton's purpose in writing his pamphlet was not to reinforce the pledge of equal support but to swing the vote to Pinckney.

To the rabid enemies of the President, Hamilton's philippic, particularly his stunning anticlimax, was a sad disappointment. Having been led to expect a revelation of turpitude upon which articles of impeachment might be drawn, they found nothing more than a clinical report upon a neurotic personality. In a sense, Hamilton's character study absolved John Adams of the charges of corruption and misconduct so freely leveled against him: if his worst enemy, after the most assiduous probing, had been unable to uncover any offenses worse than those enumerated by Hamilton, the President could safely stand upon his record. The Federalists had set a high standard of honesty in government—none of the leaders of the party was ever proved guilty of fraud or misconduct in office—yet it almost broke the hearts of some of the stanchest pillars of the party that a Federalist President could not be proved guilty of crimes which would have disgraced the reign of a Roman emperor of the decadence.

While the party elders were pondering the implications of Hamilton's diatribe against the President, Aaron Burr took an unexpected hand in the proceedings. Procuring a copy of the pamphlet, Burr gave it to the newspapers. Although Hamilton did not make a practice of forgiving Burr his transgressions, in this instance he had only charity for his enemy. When Robert Troup expressed apprehensions that the publication would do harm, Hamilton replied that he "had no doubt it would be productive of good." The pride of authorship together with the conviction that the country needed to be told the "truth" about John Adams helped persuade him that Burr had unwittingly done him a good turn. To guard against unauthorized publication in the newspapers, Hamilton took out a copyright. This, together with the copyright he had procured for his pamphlet dealing with the Reynolds scandal, promised to make him one of the leading authors in the "true confession" field. However, he was no longer confessing his own sins but—a vastly more congenial subject—the sins of John Adams.[40]

To Hamilton's chagrin, even after the publication of the Authorized Version of *The Letter from Alexander Hamilton*, there was no rush to abandon Adams for Pinckney. In the eyes of the people, he remained a plain, old-fashioned, forthright patriot, learned in diplomacy and law, who had grown gray in the service of his country and who, as President, had carried on "the same line of politics adopted by the illustrious WASHINGTON." Granted that he was short-tempered and impetuous, for all that, it was observed, "he is a good husband, a good Father, a good Citizen, and a good Man." Furthermore, he was now engaged in trying to make peace with France, and the American people were not easily persuaded that to make peace was a crime.[41]

Instead of joining Hamilton in heaping coals upon the head of the Presi-

The Election of 1800

dent, the moderate Federalist leaders ranged themselves alongside Adams. John Marshall took the position that the party must follow the President's leadership in foreign policy or "be lost in a labyrinth of perplexities," and even Harrison Gray Otis, the erstwhile war hawk, praised Adams' devotion to the cause of peace. Tench Coxe, Hamilton's former assistant in the Treasury, defected to the Republicans, swearing that Hamilton had confessed to him that he was a monarchist. Noah Webster, hitherto one of Hamilton's warmest admirers, published a pamphlet accusing Hamilton of Caesarian ambition. Subjecting the Federalist leader to the same kind of psychological analysis that Hamilton himself had used so painstakingly upon Adams, Webster concluded that the root of the trouble was an insatiable thirst for glory. "Your ambition, pride and overbearing temper," he thundered, "have destined you to be the evil genius of the country!" Webster was not alone in detecting in Hamilton's pamphlet more self-revelation than portraiture of his adversary. The egotism, vanity, jealousy and impetuosity with which he taxed John Adams seemed to be blazoned forth on every page of the *Letter from Alexander Hamilton*.[42]

So downcast was Hamilton by the reception accorded his profile of John Adams that he told his friends that if Adams or Jefferson were elected, he would retire from public life. As though to prepare for this only-too-likely contingency, it was observed that he began to devote himself much more seriously to the bar. "My spirits, in spite of all my philosophy," said his friend Robert Troup at about this time, "cannot maintain the accustomed level. For the present they have sunk me into an apathy for public concerns. Shadows, clouds, and darkness rest on our future prospects." But black as things seemed to Robert Troup, he remarked that Hamilton "thinks worse of the state of our affairs than I do."

As is the happy privilege of those who manage to outlive most of their contemporaries, John Adams had the last word in this controversy with Alexander Hamilton. In his later years, the old statesman, himself an amateur psychologist, pondered deeply the strange quirks of character revealed by that "bastard brat of a Scotch pedlar." He came to the conclusion that Hamilton's ambition, his restlessness, and his preoccupation with grandiose schemes of conquest sprang from "a superabundance of secretions which he [Hamilton] could not find whores enough to draw off." If the ex-President's diagnosis were correct, American history might have had a different and happier course had Hamilton not been interrupted in his pleasures with Mrs. Reynolds.[43]

One swallow does not make a summer, nor does one amorous adventure, particularly if it is with a woman of such easy virtue as Mrs. Reynolds, make a Great Lover. Hamilton confessed to no other transgressions against the moral code and there is no evidence that he was a hardened libertine. When Adams described Hamilton's debaucheries in New York and Philadelphia—"his audacious and unblushing attempts upon ladies of the highest rank and purest virtue"—the ex-President was patently drawing upon an imagination inflamed with resentment toward the man he held responsible for wrecking his political career.

By calumniating the President, Hamilton was in effect competing with the Republicans in a field where they had expected to enjoy a monopoly. Indeed, Hamilton's pamphlet raised the question whether "the most deadly hostility against the constituted authorities" was to be found among Republicans or Federalists. "Who," it was now asked, "are the real disorganizers and enemies of government? . . . What party are chargeable with the most indictable libels and seditions against the president?"

Republican editors had been fined and imprisoned for expressing less derogatory opinions of President Adams than those Hamilton had set his name to. Manifestly, he was as guilty of violating the Sedition Act as were the Republicans—unless, of course, the act applied only to Republicans. Thomas Cooper, a Republican editor who had just served six months' imprisonment for libeling President Adams, was resolved to bring Hamilton, "this conspicuous offender of the Sedition Law—this Arch-defender of our first magistrate," to justice. For that purpose, Cooper wrote Hamilton to inquire if he were actually the author of the *Letter from Alexander Hamilton.* If Hamilton acknowledged the authorship, Cooper was prepared to institute suit against him under the Sedition Act. But instead of replying to Cooper's letter, Hamilton turned it over to the newspapers.[44]

Hamilton was in no danger of suffering the pains and penalties of the Sedition Act. Despite his wrath against Hamilton, President Adams was sick of the Sedition Act and, besides, he was beginning to wonder if he did not have more well-wishers among Republicans than Federalists. And so the country was never treated to the truly astonishing sight of Alexander Hamilton in the dock to answer charges of having written seditious and defamatory statements against the President of the United States.

As thought to separate themselves wholly from the "monarchical" Hamiltonians, Adams' friends attempted to form a third party called "The Constitutionalists." Nothing more was needed to reveal the extent of the schism which had rent the Federalist party. There were now two factions, each claiming to be the "friends of government" and denouncing the other as apostates. It was entirely superfluous for the Republicans to talk of dividing and conquering—the Federalists had obligingly divided themselves.

As many Federalists had feared, Hamilton succeeded in electing neither the manageable Charles Cotesworth Pinckney nor the unmanageable John Adams. In the Electoral College, Jefferson and Burr received seventy-three electoral votes, Adams sixty-five and Pinckney sixty-four. Ironically enough, it was the Republicans who, by supporting Jefferson and Burr equally, produced a tie between their two candidates in the Electoral College. As a

The Election of 1800

result, the election was transferred to the House of Representatives, where, indeed, the framers of the Constitution had expected that the election of the President and Vice-President would generally be decided.*

Thus embarrassed by a wealth of electoral votes, the Republicans were exposed to the hazard of a struggle between Burr and Jefferson for the presidency. In actuality, there ought to have been no doubt of the outcome: Jefferson was obviously the choice of the people for the presidency; Burr was a secondary, almost a local, figure. Nevertheless, Burr was believed to be an ambitious man, not averse to trying to steal the presidency from Jefferson if he thought he could get away with it.

In the drawn vote in the Electoral College, Hamilton saw an opportunity to divide the victorious Republicans. On December 16, 1800, he wrote Wolcott that it might be "well enough to throw out a lure for him [Burr], in order to tempt him to start for the plate, and then lay the foundation of dissention between the two camps." Not without reason, the Republicans called Hamilton a Machiavellian.

Seldom, however, did Hamilton have more reason for regretting a Machiavellian tactic. For the Federalists were not only inclined to tempt Burr to start for the plate—they were prepared to give him the plate with all the honors and emoluments thrown in. Instead of dividing the victors, Hamilton's strategy proved to be the means of spreading dissension among the already broken ranks of the Federalists. For many Federalists, Burr possessed strong attractions—and never more so than when he was compared with Jefferson. This elegant, urbane and aristocratic New Yorker, they now perceived, might make a wholly acceptable Federalist: he was not a democrat, not a revolutionist, not an atheist and not a "philosopher" in the pernicious sense of that word. Nor was he an enemy of the navy, army or Executive powers. These were negative virtues, it is true, but the Federalists were hardly in a position to insist upon a paragon. Indeed, so low had they fallen that they were willing to take Burr, vices and all. Admitting that he had no principles, that his ambition would not stop short of the very pinnacle of power, that he was dissolute and a spendthrift—none of these things stood in the way of his admission to the party of the wise, the good and the rich. It was sufficient for them that if they made Burr President, his election would be "a mortal stab to them [the Republicans], breed an invincible hatred to him, and compel him to lean on the Federalists."[45]

Not all the Federalist leaders were prepared to embrace Burr in preference to Jefferson. John Jay, James McHenry, Gouverneur Morris, Fisher Ames,

* This notable instance of party discipline was owing to the fact that Burr, having been overreached in the election of 1796 (the promise of equal support to each candidate had then been honored chiefly in the breach), agreed to run in 1800 only upon the condition that the party pledge itself to give him equal support with Jefferson. The Republican victory was made possible by the fact that the vote of South Carolina went to Jefferson and Burr.

Thomas Willing, John Marshall, William Bingham and James A. Bayard regarded Burr, for Federalists, as an untouchable. But the strength of the Federalist opposition to Burr lay outside Congress: in the Senate and House of Representatives there was hardly a member of that party who did not prefer Burr to Jefferson.

To choose between Jefferson and Burr was for Hamilton like choosing between two rotten apples. Nevertheless, he unhesitatingly picked Jefferson over Burr. To dissuade the Federalists from entering into a compact with Burr, Hamilton composed a character study of his rival calculated to make them think twice before doing business with this "Catiline." Character studies were becoming a specialty with Hamilton. If, when drawing his portrait of John Adams, he had dipped his pen in gall and wormwood, for Burr nothing less than vitriol would do. He pronounced Burr to be "the most unfit and dangerous man of the community"; inordinately ambitious, daring to the point of recklessness, utterly unprincipled, and withal a demagogue who, despising the people, used them for his own purposes. Burr, said Hamilton, was "not very far from being a visionary: I have myself heard him speak with applause of the French system, as unshackling the mind and leaving it to its natural energies." "In a word," Hamilton exclaimed, "if we have an embryo Caesar in the United States, 'tis Burr."

By bracketing themselves with Burr, Hamilton warned his fellow Federalists, they would make themselves responsible for all his misdeeds. Yoked to the chariot of a Caesar, they would still be as accountable to the country as though they were holding the reins. If Hamilton's predictions were borne out, this would be a responsibility that no party—least of all the self-styled "friends of government"—would care to assume. For, he was persuaded, Burr would attempt to rule by appealing to the worst passions of human nature and, having "the boldness and daring necessary to give success to the Jacobin system," he would "employ the rogues of all parties to overrule the good men of all parties, and to prosecute projects which wise men of every description will disapprove." A Francophile at heart, he would precipitate war with Great Britain within six months of taking office. In short, said Hamilton, everything the Federalists held most dear would be sacrificed to the Napoleonic ambition of Burr: "Adieu to the Federal Troy," he exclaimed, "if they once introduce this Grecian horse into their citadel."[46]

While Burr was portrayed as an example of total depravity, Jefferson came off comparatively unscathed. Without discounting the Virginian's full share of original sin, Hamilton discerned some redeeming qualities in Jefferson which made him seem, at least in comparison with Burr, almost estimable. Preoccupied as he was in currying popularity with the masses and playing the demagogue, Jefferson, Hamilton admitted, possessed certain "pretensions to character." Among these was an indeterminate amount of integrity and devotion to principle—in contrast to Burr, who could lay claim to integrity and no principles whatever. Moreover, Jefferson's very lack of daring could be cited in his favor; in Hamilton's opinion, it augured that Jefferson would be much less likely to overturn the Federalist system than was an adventurer like Burr. No longer the errant Jacobin of earlier days, Jefferson was not likely to introduce French principles into the United States; and Hamilton was not without hope that Jefferson would respect the Executive authority that the Federalists had been at such pains to build up—"viewing himself as the reversioner, he was solicitous to come into the possession of a good estate."[47]

Hamilton, it is true, never suggested that the Federalists accept Jefferson without nailing him down to certain conditions. Essentially his advice was that the party strike a bargain with the Virginian by which, in exchange for the presidency, he would bind himself not to interfere with Hamiltonian finance, foreign policy and the navy, and make no removals from office except those of Cabinet rank. With the Republican President thus manacled, Hamilton was hopeful that the country could survive a Republican administration.

In preferring Jefferson to Burr, Hamilton professed to have only the public welfare at heart. "If there be a man in the world I ought to hate, it is Jefferson," he said. "With Burr I have always been personally well. But the public good must be paramount to every private consideration." Nevertheless, there is little doubt that Hamilton was here translating his jealousy and dislike of Burr into the more exalted language of statesmanship. True, by his subsequent conduct, Burr did much to confirm the darker shades of the portrait painted by Hamilton in 1800-1801. And yet had Burr not been driven to desperation by political disappointments—to which Hamilton contributed—and by financial reverses, he might never have exhibited this side of his character to the world.

When Hamilton counseled Federalist congressmen against the *"impolitic and impure* idea" of making Burr President, he did not stand before his party with wholly clean hands. In the presidential elections of 1796 and 1800, Hamilton himself had advocated measures that would have done hardly less violence to the spirit of popular government than those contemplated by the Federalist members of Congress. With some justice, his party might have retorted that it was following his example, and that although he had failed to defeat the will of the people by putting Pinckney over Adams, it might succeed by greater boldness and pertinacity in making Burr President over Jefferson.[48]

Certainly the Federalist congressmen did not take kindly to Hamilton's advice. The good he said of Jefferson was as offensive to their ears as the hard things he said of Burr. Robert G. Harper—usually the first to follow Hamilton's lead—now declared that he was ready to accept Burr without reservations: "Burr's temper and disposition," he said, "give an ample security for a conduct hostile to the democratic spirit." Corrupt as they acknowledged Burr to be, the Federalists were ready to acclaim him as their Sir Galahad if he would save them from the dragon Jefferson.[49]

In a sense, the Federalists were the prisoners of their own propaganda: they could not accept the man they had been vilifying for years as a Jacobin without repudiating the reason for their existence as a party. During the campaign of 1800, they had predicted that if Jefferson were elected, the wise, the good and the rich would be proscribed; the churches and the clergy would be involved in a common ruin; the morals of "Jacobinical" Paris would be established in this country; "some infamous prostitute, under the title of the Goddess of Reason will preside in the Sanctuaries now devoted to the most High"; and the United States would present the horrid scene of "dwellings in flames, hoary hairs bathed in blood, female chastity violated . . . children writhing on the pike and halbert." Jefferson himself was pictured as "a ravening wolf, preparing to enter your peaceful fold, and glut his deadly appetite on the vitals of your country."[50]

It is a significant commentary upon the state of mind of the Federalist party that when Hamilton advocated a statesmanlike course of action, as he did in the Jefferson-Burr controversy, the congressional leaders of the party declined to follow him; whereas when he attempted to deprive John Adams of the presidency by trickery, they were his willing abettors. Certainly, by commending Jefferson to the Federalists, Hamilton sank his own prestige, already much reduced by the outcome of the election of 1800. He was no longer the hero of the Essex Junto: true, he had freed them of John Adams, but they did not regard Thomas Jefferson as a fair exchange.[51]

For the second time within six months Hamilton threatened to bolt the Federalist party. During the presidential campaign he had said that he would withdraw if Adams were re-elected. Now, in 1801, he told his friends that he would leave the party if Burr were elevated to the presidency by Federalist votes. In that event, however, his disillusionment would have gone deeper than discouragement with political action: "I shall see no longer," he said, "any anchor for the hopes of good men." The spectacle of the good, the wise and the rich falling victim to their passions placed Hamilton in "the awkward situation of a man who continues sober after the company are drunk."[52]

Despite Hamilton's expostulations, it was plain by February, 1801, when the balloting in the House of Representatives began, that it would only be owing to the fact that the Federalists lacked sufficient strength to elect Burr that he would fail of the presidency. Since the voting was by states, the Federalists were not able to dictate a choice, but, on the other hand, they were strong enough to prevent a choice. This last some of them were willing to do—even at the risk of producing an interregnum that would have shaken the federal government to its foundations.

The Election of 1800

Of the handful of Federalists who shared Hamilton's views of Burr, by far the most important was James A. Bayard, the representative from Delaware. In Bayard's eyes, Hamilton was something more than a mere politician: "You have the reputation of being our father confessor in politics," he told him, "and I have therefore made to you a frank confession. My sins, I hope will be remitted." But Bayard's importance at this critical moment was not owing merely to his veneration for Hamilton. By virtue of his control of the vote of Delaware (the state sent only one representative to Congress), it was in his power to elect Jefferson by changing his vote from Burr to Jefferson.*

From the first ballot, Bayard had declared his intention of switching his vote when it became apparent that Burr could not win. On February 16, after thirty-five ballots had been taken, Bayard decided to break the deadlock. He took this action not because of Hamilton's adjurations but because he was convinced that Burr had lost the contest and because he had been given reason to believe that Jefferson would observe the conditions Hamilton had laid down for the Virginian's election.

The Federalist phalanx had cracked and there was no alternative for the "friends of government" but to submit to the inevitable. As was now characteristic of the party, they yielded with as bad grace as possible. "The jigg is up," exclaimed a Federalist. "In no situation, however," he added, "will I degrade myself by voting for such a wretch as Jefferson." The entire party acted upon this maxim: not a single Federalist, not even Bayard, gave his vote to Jefferson. The party of the good, the wise and the rich went down with its prejudices nailed triumphantly to the masthead.[53]

* Altogether, there were six Federalist members of Congress, the vote of any one of whom would have decided the election in Jefferson's favor. The Maryland delegation, for example, was divided equally between Federalists and Republicans; if one of the Federalist members joined the Republicans or abstained from voting, Jefferson would be elected.

PART V
The Union Above All

34.
A Prophet of Woe

Having stood sponsor to Jefferson in 1801, Hamilton felt a certain measure of responsibility for the President's good behavior. In commending Jefferson to the Federalist members of Congress, Hamilton had banked heavily upon the sobering effects of political power; there was nothing like responsibility, he argued, to put a damper upon radicalism and innovation. While he never supposed that a popularity seeker like Burr would change his ways, Hamilton ventured to hope that Jefferson would learn that being President was not simply a matter of flattering the people and playing for their votes.

The moderate and conciliatory tone of Jefferson's inaugural address seemed to vindicate Hamilton's hopes that the statesman would emerge from the "Jacobin." The President's statement that "We are all Republicans, we are all Federalists" was taken to mean by the Federalists that there would be no revolutionary changes in the government. Hamilton went so far as to say that it represented a virtual "retraction of past misapprehensions, and a pledge to the community, that the new President will not lend himself to dangerous innovations, but in essential points will tread in the steps of his predecessors." If Jefferson wished—as some of his remarks inclined Hamilton to believe—to turn Federalist, he was prepared to welcome the prodigal to the true faith. "In the talents, the patriotism, and the firmness of the Federalists," Hamilton exclaimed, "he [Jefferson] will find more than an equivalent for all that he shall lose" by forsaking his own party.[1]

But instead of accepting Hamilton's warm invitation to join the Federalists, Jefferson set out to absorb the opposition within the Republican party. Hamilton had predicted that Burr would enter the Federal Troy in a Grecian horse, but in actuality it was Jefferson who rode in on his old mare, quietly hitched it to a post and proceeded to take over most of the Federalist party.

In holding out the olive branch to the Federalists, President Jefferson had no intention of including Hamilton within the amnesty. The Virginian's charity was reserved exclusively for what he called "the honest part of those who were called federalists"—no "monocrats" need apply. These last, he suggested, ought to be consigned to madhouses until pronounced cured of Anglomanism. The President was inclined to believe that no more implacable enemy of republicanism than Hamilton existed in the United States. One of his first acts as President was to direct Secretary of the Treasury Albert Gallatin to ransack the Treasury records in search of evidence of Hamilton's turpitude. The fact that Gallatin found none struck Jefferson not as proof of the innocence of the former Secretary of the Treasury but of his skill in concealing the evidences of his wrongdoing.

Meanwhile, Hamilton was seeking an issue with which to reanimate the moribund Federalist party. When President Jefferson removed a few Federalist officeholders, Hamilton raised the cry that a democratic "reign of terror" had begun. But these dismissals raised hardly more than a flurry: as a Federalist lamented, "the great body of the people appear not to care whether A or B be in this or that office." Equally disappointing, from Hamilton's point of view, was the effect of the repeal of the excise, including the tax on whisky. Although Hamilton charged that "the culpable desire of gaining or securing popularity" had led Jefferson to sacrifice the financial stability of the government for the votes of western farmers, the dismal fact remained that the President won the votes, whereas Hamilton won only unpopularity by opposing a tax cut.

This turn of events demonstrated to Hamilton that Jefferson was still lost in the clouds of philosophy—from whence he apparently proposed to preside over the dissolution of the Federalist system. A year after the new President had taken office, Hamilton was saying that the great "Jacobin" in Washington had done more evil than his moderate opponents had feared, more than "the most wrongheaded of his own sect dared to hope; infinitely more than any one who had read the fair professions in his inaugural speech could have suspected." The only consolation remaining to Hamilton was that the federal judiciary was at last in a position to stop the "Revolution of 1800" in its tracks.[2]

In *The Federalist*, Hamilton had held out the prospect of combining the federal and state courts into "ONE WHOLE." To strengthen the state courts, "Publius" assured his readers, was to strengthen the federal government: Hamilton's antipathy to the states did not extend to the state judiciaries.

It did not take long for Hamilton to discover that his dream of federal and state courts composing one big happy family of judges was wholly insubstantial. The federal and state justices, he found, were not brothers under their judicial robes: too often, the state judges partook of the jealousy and rancor toward the national government that seemed to possess all state officials, high and low. Unfortunately for the national government, the state judges were in a position to make their antagonism felt; and the dearth of federal courts meant that the central government was obliged in many instances to depend upon the state courts to give force to the laws.³

Whereas Hamilton had envisaged the Supreme Court of the United States magisterially presiding over the federal and state governments, in actuality the justices were much too busy riding circuit to give their best efforts to expounding the Constitution. By the terms of the Judiciary Act of 1789, the six judges of the Supreme Court were compelled to travel a circuit twice a year besides holding court in Philadelphia—a schedule which necessitated, said Gouverneur Morris, the erudition of a judge combined with the agility and hardihood of a jockey. As for litigants in the United States circuit courts, they were obliged to have the patience of Job, and prisoners held for trial underwent long periods of imprisonment waiting for the judge to arrive. Under this expensive and time-consuming system, appeals from the state courts to the United States Supreme Court were so infrequent that during the twelve years the Federalists were in power only three cases were heard.* ⁴

In 1799, alarmed by the growth of subversive ideas in the United States, the "cold and reluctant protection" afforded by the state courts to the reputations of federal officeholders, and the spectacle of United States Supreme Court justices running from one end of the continent to the other to preside over circuit courts, Hamilton presented to the Federalist leaders in Congress a plan for the reorganization of the federal judiciary. This plan called for the creation of small judicial districts, each presided over by a federal judge, and a corps of justices of the peace entrusted with the responsibility of enforcing federal laws. At the same time, the United States circuit and district courts would be given jurisdiction over all cases arising under common law.⁵

Obviously influenced by Hamilton's ideas, a committee of the House of Representatives reported in March, 1800, a plan which provided for the division of the United States into twenty-nine districts which studiously avoided all reference to state names and boundaries. Republicans immediately detected the fine West Indian hand of Alexander Hamilton, seeking, as always, the annihilation of the states and the consolidation of the powers of government. Perhaps because it was feared that the bill would have an adverse effect upon the election, the Federalists postponed action upon it until February, 1801.⁶

When he drew up his plan for the reorganization of the judiciary, Hamilton had not foreseen the loss of the presidency and of Congress by the Federalist party. In 1799, the Federalists were riding the crest of power; the Republicans, on the other hand, were seeking refuge in the states against

* In *The Federalist*, he depicted the Supreme Court as "a court paramount to the rest, possessing a general superintendence, and authorized to settle and decide in the last resort a uniform rule of civil justice." He left no doubt in the minds of his readers that the Supreme Court would pervade the whole union, establishing the uniformity which he believed essential to its welfare.

the Federalist "reign of terror." But in February, 1801, when the question of strengthening the powers of the judiciary was brought before Congress, the political situation had changed radically. It was now the Federalists who looked for shelter against the impending storm and prayed to be delivered from the triumphant "Jacobins."

This objective was achieved in the Judiciary Act of 1801. By the provisions of this act, the jurisdiction of the federal courts was expanded, six circuit courts consisting of three judges for each court (one court had only one judge) were created, and the Supreme Court was reduced to five members. At long last, the judges of the highest court in the land were relieved of the necessity of riding post the length and breadth of the United States; they could now settle down and enjoy the amenities—such as they were—of Washington.[7]

With the federal judiciary converted into a bulwark against Republicanism, Hamilton did not retreat, as did many Federalists, to the privileged sanctuary of the states; instead, he executed a withdrawal to the Supreme Court. Essentially, it was a retreat to a previously prepared position, for in *The Federalist* he had provided a constitutional defense against the very situation in which he and his party found themselves in 1801. Against the power of a Republican President and a Republican Congress, Hamilton interposed the authority of the Federalist Supreme Court armed with the doctrine of judicial review.

The Republicans had no intention of leaving the Federalists in undisturbed possession of this bastion. In 1802, confronted by a monstrous regiment of thirty-eight Federalist judges, they moved to repeal the Judiciary Act of 1801.

Had the Republicans attacked the Constitution itself, Hamilton would hardly have been more horror-stricken. That document declares that judges are to be appointed during good behavior—a provision which *The Federalist* had pronounced to be "an excellent barrier to the encroachments and oppressions of the representative body." Hamilton saw little difference between taking the office from a judge and removing a judge from the office; it did not palliate the crime, he exclaimed, to enter the holy temple of justice and pluck from their seats the venerable personages on the ground that their seats had just been abolished. If such enormities were condoned, he gave the Constitution little chance of survival. "Probably before these remarks shall be read," he said in 1802, "that Constitution will be no more! It will be numbered among the numerous victims of Democratic frenzy."[8]

In effect, Hamilton was saying that Congress, having established courts and created judges, could not undo its work. "The proposition that a power to do includes, virtually, a power to undo, as applied to a legislative body," he asserted, "is generally but not universally true; all vested rights form an exception to the rule." Since judges' commissions were, by Hamilton's definition, vested rights, they were beyond congressional interference.[9]

During this clash of argument with the Republicans, Hamilton spoke as though the Federalist incumbents of the bench were models of impartiality and disinterestedness whose judicial decisions were untainted by party feeling. Actually, however, it was the very partisanship of the judges that endeared them to Hamilton. Had they handed down decisions favorable to the Republicans, it is improbable that he would have acclaimed their purity, their integrity and their wisdom. Hamilton acted upon the premise that his —and the judges'—interpretation of the Constitution was the only version a right-minded man could hold. A judge who interpreted that instrument of government in accord with Jefferson's ideas would have been cast out as a corrupt and prostituted defiler of the temple of justice.

Hamilton may have had the better of the constitutional argument, but, as he wryly observed, the Republicans had something better—a majority in Congress. In 1802 the Judiciary Act was repealed, Aaron Burr, as Vice-President, casting the decisive vote in the Senate. Nevertheless, the heavens remained in place and the Constitution did not crumble into dust. The federal courts went on as before and the justices of the Supreme Court resumed their weary rounds, back in the saddle again.[10]

That, figuratively speaking, was precisely where Chief Justice Marshall wanted to be—in the saddle, riding herd on President Jefferson and the Republican party.

Hamilton had no reason to think kindly of the Old Dominion, and yet without the aid of three Virginians he probably would have failed to achieve his purposes. James Madison, George Washington and John Marshall were indispensable to Hamilton as collaborators in the work of creating a strong central government. While Madison turned against Hamilton, the other two great Virginians remained loyal to the end. And just as Washington was all-important to the success of Hamilton's economic and financial plans, so John Marshall was essential to the final triumph—the embodying of Hamiltonian principles in the Constitution of the United States.

In 1803, John Marshall, who under happier circumstances might have been proud to call Thomas Jefferson "cousin," deliberately undertook to assert the primacy of the Supreme Court as the interpreter of the Constitution. A suit brought by Marbury, one of the justices of the peace appointed by John Adams in the final hours of his administration, to compel James Madison, the Secretary of State, to deliver the commission which had been withheld by the Republicans provided Marshall with an opportunity to read a lecture to President Jefferson on the duties of his office and to declare unconstitutional an act of Congress.

Thus the black-robed justices, the high priests of the Hamiltonian dispensation, resolutely placed themselves in the path of the Jeffersonian "revolution." But Hamilton rejoiced with fear and trembling: for all he knew, the decision in *Marbury* v. *Madison* might prove to be the last shriek of John Marshall before he was pulled off the bench by a vengeful President and Congress. And, in fact, in the last year of Hamilton's life, as the Republicans moved to impeach Justice Samuel Chase, it seemed likely that the Chief Justice himself would not survive the Republican purge of the Supreme Court.

While Hamilton was lamenting that the country was far gone in "Jacobinism," Jefferson was complaining that he was a prisoner of the circumstances created by Hamilton and the Federalist party. After Hamilton had done his work, the President said in 1801, the government of the United States could never be the same: "When this government was first established, it was possible to have kept it going on true principles but the contracted, English, half-lettered ideas of Hamilton destroyed that hope in the bud. We can pay off his debts in fifteen years: but we can never get rid of his financial system."

And so, although it cut Jefferson to the quick to leave this system untouched, he did not, except in the case of the excise, radically alter the handiwork of his defeated enemy. After threatening for years to pull down the temple and drive out the money-changers, the temple was permitted to remain virtually intact and the money-changers continued to do business at the old stand. Even the Bank of the United States was undisturbed as long as Jefferson remained President, although the government did dispose of all of its stock in the institution. Jefferson, pledged to the "honest payment of our debts and sacred preservation of the public faith," found it impossible to dispense with the Bank of the United States.[11] On several occasions he borrowed money from it.

Indeed, Hamilton could have wished that Jefferson was a little more devoted to theory and a little less the practical politician. The Republican President and his advisers deliberately adopted Hamilton's policy of using government funds for the purpose of aiding banks and winning the support of capitalists—only now the banks were Republican and the capitalists were in many instances former Federalists who discovered that the good, the wise and the rich had nothing to fear from a Republican President and Congress.

As regards the Executive power, Hamilton might have set his fears of Jefferson at rest. His first surmise proved correct: Jefferson was no enemy of the Executive Department provided that it was in the right hands. If, as an opposition leader, he had talked as though he could not wait to make Congress the supreme branch of the government, he acted upon very different principles after he had been installed in the presidency. Having observed the effects of Hamilton's leadership of Congress, Jefferson took upon himself as President to give that body the benefit of his guidance. In 1810, he remarked that the people of the United States were "looking to the executive to give the proper direction to their affairs, with a confidence as auspicious as it is well founded."

Thus, although Hamilton never realized it, President Jefferson's real "crime" against the Federalists consisted in stealing their political principles. By the end of his second term as President, he had left them little more than their fear of democracy, their penchant for suppressing dissent and their fondness for settling the dispute with France by force. These he gladly consigned to his political enemies, and they apparently did not ask for more. In effect, however, Jefferson sealed the doom of the Federalist party by appropriating its nationalism and its belief in strong, energetic government, for herein the Federalists surrendered everything that had justified their existence as a party and that had given them influence with the American people.

As a result, the Federalist party slipped rapidly into political limbo. As John Quincy Adams said in 1802, to attempt the restoration of federalism "would be as absurd as to undertake the resurrection of a carcass seven years in its grave." In the South, the party was withering on the vine: although a few sprouts were still to be seen, it was, said Fisher Ames, "such a sickly, yellow vegetation as the potatoes show in winter, in a too warm cellar." Even New York had become to the Federalists a horrible example of Jacobinism Triumphant—a preview of what Ames called "that awful futurity to which we are hastening." In this benighted region, it was lamented, "malignant democrats" did not lurk in dark places—instead, they occupied the highest offices in the government and even presumed to crash the best society. True, the guillotine had not yet been erected in Wall Street, but that, some jittery conservatives feared, was on the democrats' building program.

The Federalists took their defeat in the spirit, one of them remarked, of the Austrian general who lost the battle of Marengo. In this struggle, however, they did not have the consolation, usually vouchsafed defeated generals and politicians, that it would be different next time. Indeed, they doubted if there ever would be a next time; as they said, the sun of federalism seemed to have set forever and they "viewed with horror the awful night that would follow." In that Stygian gloom, they saw the lurid light of burning cities and heard the shrieks of violated women. They had no doubt that after 1800 the course of events in the United States would bear out Edward Gibbon's dictum that history was the record of the crimes, follies and misfortunes of mankind.[12]

Hamilton saw in Jeffersonian democracy the awful realization of all his predictions that the people, urged on by demagogues, would override every constitutional obstacle that stood in the way of the gratification of their desires. Once a country had set out on "the mad career of democracy, experience, sad experience," he exclaimed, "warns us to dread every extremity—

to be prepared for the worst catastrophe that can happen." For Hamilton, the worst was the breakup of the union and the establishment of foreign domination—and apparently the United States was not to be spared even these calamities. He told Gouverneur Morris that he expected the government would grow weaker with every election until it became completely enervated, and then "the minions of faction would sell themselves and their country as foreign powers should think it worth while to make the purchase."[13]

Having once, as he believed, saved the country from "democratic license," Hamilton now found that the work had to be done all over again. This was beginning to bear a disquieting resemblance to the labor of Sisyphus; whenever he reached the top, a horde of democrats were waiting to undo his work. More and more, Hamilton wondered if a people could be saved against their will. If Americans were determined to go to Hell in a democratic hack, Hamilton said that to Hell they must go.

Rather than continue to wage a struggle on such unequal terms, Hamilton decided in the autumn of 1801 to retire altogether from politics: he would remain a mere spectator of the "excesses" of democracy, observing with philosophical detachment the awful fulfillment of his prophecies. Let things take their course, he now said: "nothing short of a general convulsion" would again call him into public life. He took comfort in the thought that the crisis could not be far off. According to Hamilton's prognosis, democracy worked its own cure: as the people sought increasingly to free themselves from the restraints of law and government in order to attain the millennium promised by the demagogues, everything fell into anarchy until finally Nemesis descended upon the folly-ridden people in the form of dictatorship. Then, with democracy having run its predestined course, "the virtuous and the prudent of every description" would be acclaimed as saviors; and the people, chastened by suffering and weary of running after false gods, would listen eagerly to the "truths" they had once rejected as unrepublican.

The hazard of permitting democracy to sink into anarchy was that there might be no one left to save society in its last extremity. As Gouverneur Morris said, "the worst of it is those who perceive the multitude going to the devil, cannot avoid being drawn into the gulf along with them." Fisher Ames, swinging from a gibbet, was in no position to rescue his country from democracy, yet Fisher Ames gave himself little chance of escaping that fate. Nor did Hamilton relish the prospect of perishing nobly in the ruins of his country, and he wryly admitted that a dead vindicated prophet is as dead as any other prophet.

Amid this gloom and despondency, the Federalists took solace in the idea that "the talent, the virtue, and the wealth" of the United States were arrayed against all that was vicious, base and reprehensible. In their eyes, it was a struggle of "Vice against Virtue, and poverty against property." But they

A Prophet of Woe

had no confidence that truth and goodness would triumph in the end; to be right in a democracy, they lamented, was almost a certain guarantee of losing an election. In the world of Thomas Jefferson, truth and virtue seemed to be crushed to earth, never to rise again. There was no place for them to hide: sooner or later the sans-culottes would drag them screaming from their last refuge.

As Jefferson's popularity in the country grew apace, the sense of doom weighed increasingly upon Hamilton. In 1802 he told a meeting of the New York bar that he would give every drop of his blood "to arrest the present destructive system of public measures," but he did not believe that even this sacrifice would be of any avail. The progress of democracy, he was persuaded, was from bad to worse, and whatever the future held, it was almost certain not to be good. "He has said all along, and still maintains the opinion," said his friend Robert Troup, "that Jefferson and his party had not talents or virtue sufficient to administer the government well; and he entertains no doubt that they will finally ruin our affairs and finally plunge us into serious commotions."[14]

Somber as was Hamilton's mood, it was less funereal than that of the other leaders of the party. They saw the "imps of democracy" everywhere and, indeed, they were plagued most unmercifully by these creatures of darkness. As though their own fears of the wrath to come were not sufficient, the Federalists fed each other's apprehensions until they reached a state of mind bordering upon panic. George Cabot, for example, wrote his friend Timothy Pickering: "I have lately read your *gloomy* letter to Ames, and his *desponding answer*. It was a melancholy pleasure *to me*." For sheer lugubriousness it was impossible to improve upon Fisher Ames. "Our days are made heavy with the pressure of anxiety, and our nights restless with visions of horror," Ames said of himself and his friends. "We listen to the clank of chains, and overhear the whispers of assassins. . . . We see the dismal glare of their burnings and scent the loathsome steam of human victims offered in sacrifice." Infirm as was his constitution, Ames expected that if the Jacobins hurried, he would yet live to be hanged.[15]

With such apocalyptic visions of "blood and ashes," rapine and massacre, the Federalists braced themselves against the coming holocaust. They seem to have derived a mordant kind of satisfaction from contemplating these horrors from the comfortable security of their clubs and drawing rooms. In January, 1804, for example, at a small private dinner attended, among others, by Hamilton, Rufus King and Gouverneur Morris, the conversation turned, as it usually did, to the miseries that Jeffersonianism was bringing upon the country. Hamilton and King agreed that the Constitution was about to be destroyed, but Gouverneur Morris argued that it had already suffered that fate. When Hamilton and King predicted, however, that a "bloody anarchy" would be visited upon the United States, Gouverneur

Morris rather spoiled the effect by contending that in the impending upheaval, property rather than human life would be the object of the "Jacobins."[16]

This, then, was the best advice Hamilton could offer his stricken party: to wait the inevitable debacle and pray that out of anarchy a strong, stable and "energetic" government would emerge. He held out no prospects of speedy salvation; the consolations he offered seemed almost as remote as those of the next world. It was the counsel of despair, not to say of defeatism. Even though such a state of mind had been warranted by the state of the country, it afforded no foundation upon which to build a political party. It was as though Hamilton expected to hold the Federalists together with tears and lamentations: here all the downhearted, the alarmists and the chronic croakers could be sure of finding kindred spirits.

Since their leaders had little to offer by way of a program of action except "grief and terror," it was no wonder that many Federalists abandoned the party. They were weary of the struggle: "They seem to pant so much for repose," said Robert Troup, "that they are ready to submit to any state of things short of Parisian Massacres." Even Paris had ceased to figure as the place bad Americans went when they died. The bugbear of "Jacobinism," having long done service for the Federalists, no longer terrorized the electorate. When Hamilton paraded this poor, battered and no longer frightening scarecrow, he was exposing himself to ridicule as the upholder, not only of a lost cause, but of a discredited bogey.

In playing Cassandra, Hamilton had only his forebodings, insubstantial and illusory as they might be, to draw upon—the facts were all against him. Even Hamilton and his friends were compelled to admit that the country was flourishing under Jefferson as much as under the Federalists: "Go where you will," reported Robert Troup, "you behold nothing but the smiling face of improvements and prosperity. . . . Broadway now presents one of the most delightful spectacles in all probability in the world!" John Quincy Adams, returning to the United States in 1801 after an absence of seven years, observed "those splendid and costly mansions which since my departure seem to have shot up from the earth by enchantment." Even Pickering acknowledged that "our lands yield their increase, our commerce flourishes, we are marrying and given in marriage"—quite as though the lands would not soon be declared common property, commerce destroyed and the marriage sacrament abolished.[17]

Even the businessmen—the mainstay of Hamiltonianism—began to ignore these croakings of disaster. Too often they had been told that massacre and pillage were just round the corner—only to find that it was really prosperity that awaited them. They now learned that it was much pleasanter—and certainly more profitable—to take advantage of the good times than to join the Federalist leaders at the wailing wall. Thus the business spirit, upon

A Prophet of Woe

which Hamilton had principally relied to hold the union together, rose up to confound his preachments. The merchants and manufacturers, lamented a Federalist journalist, "rest in security, trusting that things are not yet so bad, as has been pretended, and that all will yet come right"; and an English traveler described the United States at this time as "a land of liberty, and vulgar aristocracy, seated on her bags of dollars." No doubt they would have defended their bags of dollars to the last ditch had Jefferson made a move to dispossess them, but the President seemed to respect the rights of property no less than did Hamilton himself.

To believe that the horrors confidently predicted by the Federalists could occur in the United States under President Jefferson required a morbidity of imagination which seems to have been confined to the good, the wise and the rich. Certainly negation and despair were not the mood of the American people, and by giving way to these emotions Hamilton cut himself off from the vital currents of American life. Here Hamilton exhibited the triumph of his philosophy over the facts. He was never more doctrinaire, never farther removed from reality, than when he cried havoc in the midst of the greatest prosperity, stability and democratic advance the United States had ever known.[18]

The irony of his lot increasingly preoccupied Hamilton: that he, the expositor and defender of the Constitution, the prophet of national power through finance and industrialization, the devoted public servant who had brought order and stability out of financial chaos, the organizer of his country's armed defenses, should be held up to the people as their oppressor, the advocate of tyranny and the archenemy of republicanism, seemed to him a bizarre twist of fate. "Mine is an odd destiny," he said in 1802. "Perhaps no man in the United States has sacrificed or done more for the present Constitution than myself; and contrary to all my anticipations of its fate . . . I am still laboring to prop the frail and worthless fabric. Yet I have the murmurs of its friends no less than the curses of its foes for my reward. . . . Every day proves to me more and more, that this American world was not made for me."[19]

The fact that this American world seemed created for Thomas Jefferson rendered his pain even more acute. His own work went unhonored and unsung while that of his rival, destructive to the best interests of the country as Hamilton believed it to be, was applauded and admired. If Jeffersonianism was what the people of the United States wanted, then, Hamilton admitted, he stood on alien ground indeed. It was perhaps owing in part to his growing conviction that he was out of his element that in 1804 he was prepared to exchange this world for the next at the hands of Aaron Burr.

35.

Defender of the Freedom of the Press

Had Hamilton acted upon the ideas he was expressing in newspapers, speeches and private letters, he no doubt would have sold his property, gathered his wife and children about him and taken ship for England, where, Jefferson always maintained, he properly belonged. Or he might have gone West, where his chances of surviving among the savages would be vastly better than among the "Jacobins."

In actuality, however, Hamilton was in no hurry to put either the Atlantic Ocean or the American wilderness between himself and Jefferson. Indeed, for a man who presumably believed that the country was headed for a smash, Hamilton's behavior was truly extraordinary. He built an expensive house in the country and plunged into speculation on a large scale quite as though he expected prosperity to continue forever.

Early in 1801, to the distress of his friends, who warned him against the expense of maintaining a country house, Hamilton began the construction of a house on Manhattan Island several miles outside New York City. Here, on seventeen acres, Hamilton proposed to live the life of a country gentleman commuting to the city only to conduct his practice. "To men who have been so much harassed in the base world as myself," he remarked, "it is natural to look forward to a comfortable retirement. . . . A garden is a very useful refuge for a disappointed politician." "Experience more and more convinces me," he added, "that true happiness is only to be found in the bosom of one's own family." As befitted a man descended from Scottish lords, he called his country seat "The Grange" after the ancestral home in Scotland. On what is now 144th Street, he built his house, fondly imagining, no doubt, that it would shelter future generations of Hamiltons in rural seclusion.[1]

As his friends had predicted, country living proved to be costly beyond all expectations. To his consternation, Hamilton discovered that instead of enjoying the leisure and repose of semiretirement, he had to work harder than ever to keep "The Grange" going. Moreover, he found it necessary to maintain a town house as well: a confirmed theatergoer and man about town, Hamilton was unable to immure himself in the country. At consider-

Defender of the Freedom of the Press

able cost he learned that the country never appears so attractive as when one is in town. Nevertheless, he persisted in the hope that he could find happiness in retirement, that he could renounce politics and that he would be satisfied pottering around a garden.[2]

Despite his burgeoning law practice—"his powers," said Robert Troup, "are now enormous; and the only chance we have of success is now and then when he happens to be on the weaker side"—Hamilton was in financial difficulties during the last years of his life. Ruinously expensive as was the life of a country gentleman, it was not "The Grange" that brought Hamilton to these straits. The source of his woes was speculation in—of all things—land.

As the apostle of commerce and manufacturing to a nation of farmers, it was to be expected that Hamilton would set his countrymen an example by investing his capital in machinery and ships. The S.U.M., although moribund, might have been revived by a transfusion of capital and there were scores of other manufactures in the United States that were desperately in need of this kind of lifeblood. Nevertheless, Hamilton chose to invest his money in land, thereby tacitly admitting the defeat of his plans for building up American manufactures with the aid of domestic capital. Despite all that he had done to encourage industrialism, the shortest way to wealth in the United States still lay in land and commerce rather than in manufactures.

As Hamilton well knew, it was also a highroad to ruin, lined with *memento mori*. For scores of speculators had gone over the edge and had landed in prison or the potter's field. Some of Hamilton's best friends were jailbirds: James Wilson and Robert Morris had been imprisoned for debts incurred in unlucky land speculation.*[3]

In 1802, giving free rein to an exuberant optimism that completely belied his political gloom, Hamilton proposed to Oliver Wolcott and two other friends that they form a company for land speculation, banking, factoring and engaging in "speculative enterprises in navigation and commerce." Hamilton was prepared to invest from five to ten thousand dollars in the company, "confident that when it should be known in Europe that certain characters were of the Company it would attract a good portion of profitable employment." Apparently no one was struck by the incongruity between Hamilton's predictions that the bottom was about to fall out of everything and the boldness with which he risked his capital in business ventures.[4]

Although nothing came of this particular project, Hamilton bought heavily in lands near Oswego and settled down to wait for the price to go up

---

* In investing his capital in western lands, Hamilton was following the example of most of his professional and business associates. William Bingham of Philadelphia owned over one million acres in Pennsylvania and several million acres in Maine; Washington had extensive land holdings in the Ohio Valley; William Duer held stock in a company which claimed title to three and a half million acres; and John Jay, James Duane, James Kent, Alexander Macomb and James Wilson were among the leading land speculators of the day.

as immigrants and capital poured into the country. But the European war kept the immigrants and much of the capital at home—with the result that Hamilton was faced with the disquieting possibility that the sheriff would get his lands before the settlers arrived. As for his friends, they began to wonder if they would not have to pay his funeral expenses after all.

At this critical juncture, he secured a loan from the Merchants' Bank of New York City, which he had helped to found in 1803. The Merchants' Bank advanced him credit even beyond the market price of his lands. Yet this unprecedented generosity merely postponed the day of reckoning. In 1804, he estimated his estate to be worth $75,000, but he acknowledged that in case of a forced sale, his assets would probably not cover his debts. This assessment of his financial worth proved to be correct: although he paid his own way on his funeral, his friends were obliged to reach deep into their pockets to provide for his widow.

Not only was Hamilton himself a land speculator; he actively aided other speculators in their efforts to engross the public domain. Indeed, it may be questioned whether Hamilton did not actually do more during his lifetime for land speculation than for American manufactures. Compared with his failure at Paterson, his efforts in behalf of land speculators were a notable triumph and involved a far greater outlay of capital than was expended by the S.U.M.

In the 1790's, one of the largest land companies operating in the United States was the Holland Land Company, organized in 1791 by the Dutch speculators who had profited from the adoption of Hamilton's funding system. Within a few years, the company owned or held options upon over five million acres in western New York and Pennsylvania. In New York, however, the company found its activities brought to a standstill by a law restraining alien land ownership. The repeal of this law therefore became a primary objective of the Holland Land Company, and to that end Alexander Hamilton was retained in 1795 as an attorney.

It was upon Hamilton's skill as a lobbyist rather than his sagacity as a lawyer that the Holland Company relied to clear the obstructions from its path. Here Hamilton disappointed his employers: the best he could do was to secure the passage of a law permitting alien land ownership for a period of seven years. Since this was unacceptable to the company, it turned to General Philip Schuyler, who promised to procure the desired change in the law in exchange for a loan of $250,000 to the Western Inland Lock Navigation Company, of which he was the president. But the Dutchmen deemed Schuyler's demands excessive; and when Aaron Burr promised to do the job at a cheaper price, he was hired. Burr was as good as his word: thanks to the judicious expenditure of money in the right places, the New York legislature passed a law confirming the right of aliens to hold land in perpetuity. For his services, Burr received a "loan" from the Holland Company which he never repaid.[5]

Hamilton, Schuyler and John Church were indignant that Burr should have made off with the prize—and by methods which they had disdained to employ. Church, in particular, denounced Burr's corrupt practices so vehemently that Burr challenged him to a duel. The two men met on the field of honor at Hoboken, where, on the first fire, Burr received a ball through his coat while Church escaped unscathed. While the seconds were reloading the pistols, Church admitted that he had been mistaken and apologized to Burr. It was a wise decision, for Burr did not often miss his target twice running.

Hamilton's failure to satisfy the Holland Land Company was not owing to any lack of good will on his part toward land speculators; it was scruples, he said, that had gotten in his way—scruples that Burr apparently brushed aside with the greatest ease. But in 1796, Hamilton was prepared to condone the very methods that Burr had employed in New York in behalf of the Holland Land Company, and on a scale that made Burr's transgressions seem insignificant.

In 1795, having bribed virtually the entire legislature of Georgia (it is said that one member was honest), four companies were granted title to an area (the so-called Yazoo country) comprising a large part of the present states of Alabama and Mississippi. The theft was so barefaced, however, that public opinion was aroused and in 1796 the legislature, now composed of new men, repudiated the cession to the Yazoo land companies. The companies, in the meantime, had begun to dispose of their lands to speculators and settlers. And so the land companies and those who had bought land from them in good faith raised the cry that property rights were being invaded and the sanctity of contract violated.

The following year, the purchasers from the Yazoo land companies applied to Hamilton for an opinion regarding the validity of their titles and of the rescinding act of the Georgia legislature. Hamilton's answer was to the effect that the legislature had no right to revoke the grant under the allegation of corruption; according to his reading of the federal Constitution, the states were debarred from "revoking, invalidating, or altering a contract." Therefore, if Georgia had held title to the lands in question and if that title had passed to the Yazoo land companies, the deed could not be invalidated by any subsequent act of the Georgia legislature.

Up to this time, it had been generally supposed that the contract clause of the Constitution applied only to private grants and conveyances. Hamilton, however, held that contracts and grants made by a state were equally within the reach of the prohibition: when a legislature made a grant, that grant became irrevocable and could not be impaired by succeeding legislatures.

This principle, he said, was in accord with "the first principles of natural justice and social policy."

Hamilton's critics were not slow to point out that this opinion revealed that he was no enemy of the powers of the state legislatures so long as these powers were exercised for the benefit of favored individuals or corporations. It seemed, they said, that when a state legislature was guilty of wrongdoing, it won his support; but when it attempted to right the wrong, it was held guilty of violating the Constitution. This doctrine, said John Taylor, put liberty and property "at the feet of a legislature. They may parcel out public property and public rights, which are the only wares they deal in, until none worth having remain."

Hamilton predicted that his opinion would be upheld by the federal courts if the Yazoo land question ever came before them. He was not mistaken: in 1810, in the case of *Fletcher* v. *Peck,* Chief Justice John Marshall sustained the Yazoo claimants in a decision that did little more than restate Hamilton's earlier opinion. "When a law is in its nature a contract, when absolute rights have been vested under that contract," Marshall declared, "a repeal of the law cannot divest those rights." Marshall thereby made the doctrine of vested rights one of the fundamental doctrines of American constitutional law. The contract clause, together with "the immutables of right and justice," became one of the principal bulwarks of the rights of property.[6]

Hamilton had hoped to find in his family the happiness and contentment that had been denied him in politics; but it was here that fate dealt him the cruelest blow he experienced during his life. In 1801, his oldest son, Philip, was killed in a duel.

On July 4, 1801, George Eacker, a young lawyer and "a violent and bitter democrat," as the Federalist newspapers described him, delivered an oration in which he accused Hamilton, among other things, of having raised a large army not to resist foreign aggression but to suppress the Republican party—a canard by this time so familiar as to have become commonplace. Several months later, Philip Hamilton and a friend encountered Eacker at the theater, where, with the deliberate intention of baiting the Republican orator, they began to make invidious remarks about his politics, person and qualifications to frequent the company of gentlemen. Whereupon Eacker, who was sitting in the next box, called young Hamilton and his friend into the hall. Seizing Philip Hamilton by the collar, he exclaimed, "I will not be insulted by a set of rascals." To leave no doubt of his intentions, he declared that "he should treat them as blackguards." The young men assured Eacker that they were acquainted with the code of gentlemen, and the next day Philip Hamilton formally challenged him to a duel.

John Church, having learned of this ugly turn of events, attempted to make peace between Philip Hamilton and Eacker. His efforts were chiefly directed toward inducing Eacker to disavow the use of the word "rascal." But this the offended Republican refused to do: "The expressions I made use of towards Mr. Hamilton at the Theatre on Friday night last," he informed Church, "were produced by his conduct on that occasion; I thought them applicable then, AND I THINK SO STILL."

Without informing Eacker of his intention, Philip Hamilton decided not to fire at his adversary. Whether this signal act of self-denial was designed to demonstrate his disapproval of dueling or his contempt of Eacker, he did not say. In any event, when the two young men met on the field of honor at Weehawken, Eacker's ball struck Philip, who, as he fell, discharged his pistol. Eacker's seconds declared that young Hamilton had fired deliberately, but Philip's seconds were convinced that his gun had gone off accidentally. Young Hamilton could throw no light upon the matter: he had been wounded mortally.*

They bore the dying boy home where, for the first time, Alexander Hamilton learned of the quarrel with Eacker and the duel. The loss of Philip Hamilton was to Hamilton more than an ordinary bereavement. "Never did I see a man so completely overwhelmed with grief as Hamilton has been," said his friend Robert Troup; months after the event, his face was "strongly stamped with grief." Hamilton himself described it as "an event, beyond comparison, the most afflicting of my life"; "the brightest, as well as the ablest, hope of my family has been taken from me. . . . He was truly a fine youth." Of all the Hamilton children, Philip promised to be the most like his father; to him was given something of Alexander's charm, magnetism and love of adventure. For this reason, Hamilton had taken particular pains with Philip's education, drawing up a set of rules intended to guide him in his career. Graduated from Columbia at the age of twenty, Philip had turned to the study of law; no doubt Hamilton hoped one day to make his son his partner.

True, Philip Hamilton had sown his share of wild oats: Robert Troup set him down as "a sad rake" whose fondness for the less seemly diversions left some doubt whether he would have brought honor to his family. But these shortcomings were generally forgotten in the tragic circumstances of his death: for Hamilton, his eldest son always remained a pure and noble young man, a victim of a gentlemanly sense of honor joined with a Christian aversion to shedding human blood.

After Philip Hamilton's death, the note of futility and despair swelled almost to a dirge. It was his consolation that his dead son was "out of the reach of the seductions and calamities of a world, full of folly, full of vice,

* The New York *Evening Post*, Hamilton's newspaper, reported that Philip Hamilton, "aware that the origin of the controversy lay with him, and averse to shedding blood, decided to reserve his fire, receive that of his antagonist, and then discharge his pistol in the air."

full of danger, of least value in proportion as it is best known." From this mood of disenchantment, Hamilton never wholly escaped; the shadow of tragedy lay darkly across the remaining years of his life.[7]

Hamilton was not meant to be a mere croaker of doom and destruction: his ambition, ardor and dedication to the cause of union had nothing in common with the pessimism he preached. Yet if Hamilton belied his political despondency in the conduct of his private affairs, he was no less inconsistent in the zeal he displayed in combating Jefferson through the newspapers and churches and in upholding the freedom of the press. Events in the United States lent gloomy confirmation to his fears that democracy was running its foreordained course, but Hamilton was resolved to go down—if go down he must—fighting.

The Federalist press had declined with the fortunes of the party. William Cobbett, "Peter Porcupine," shot his last quill and fled across the Atlantic, and John Fenno died in 1798, leaving the *Gazette of the United States* to his son, who sold it three years later. As a result, said Fisher Ames, "uneducated printers, shop-boys, and raw schoolmasters" were left to carry the Federalist party's message to the people.

None was more alarmed by this turn of events than was Hamilton. He believed that the struggle against Jeffersonianism must be fought in the press: "It is the *Press*," his newspaper said a few years later, "which has corrupted our political morals—and it is to the *Press* we must look for the means of our political regeneration." But in the low state of the Federalist party, the establishment of a newspaper was no easy matter. Morale had been badly shaken by defeat and, as Hamilton had learned to his chagrin, money could not be readily extracted from Federalist merchants, bankers and professional men. Despite these obstacles, Hamilton succeeded in 1801 in raising sufficient money to finance a daily newspaper called the New York *Evening Post*. Hamilton himself gave $100 and, under a promise of reimbursement from future earnings, prominent Federalists were persuaded to contribute to its support.[8]

In its first issue, the *Evening Post* struck a note of high-mindedness and dedication to principle which, in general, it succeeded in maintaining over its long career. Matching the spirit of Jefferson's inaugural address, the editor's prospectus announced that although the *Evening Post* was a Federalist newspaper, it acted upon the conviction that "honest and virtuous men" were to be found in both parties and that it appealed to reason rather than to partisan passion. In keeping with this policy, it promised to avoid invective and scurrility when commenting upon political affairs; let the Republican newspapers rage—the *Evening Post* would cleave to a *"line of temperate discussion and impartial regard to truth."*

For the post of editor of the *Evening Post,* Hamilton chose William Cole-

Defender of the Freedom of the Press

man, a New Englander of very different background from that of his employers, the Federalist patricians of New York. Coleman was born in the Boston poorhouse and, like Hamilton, he had known from experience poverty and adversity. More importantly, Hamilton and Coleman were drawn together by an affinity of mind: Coleman understood Hamilton's thought process so implicitly and sympathized so deeply with his purposes that the newspaper, to all intents and purposes, was Hamilton's. Coleman sat at the feet of the man he called "the great & good Hamilton," firmly persuaded that he was the greatest man in the world. Although Hamilton contributed some articles to the *Evening Post,* for the most part he was content to let Coleman do the actual labor of composition. When important decisions were to be made, Coleman dropped in at Hamilton's house, usually late at night, and took down in shorthand Hamilton's dictation. From these midnight meetings he returned home with the lead article for the next day's edition.

As a result, the *Evening Post,* under Coleman's direction, became a mirror of Hamilton's mind: here his ideals and policies were laid before the American people—or, rather, that small and dwindling part of the people that was inclined to look at a Federalist newspaper. Whatever cohesion the party possessed after its defeat by Jefferson came largely from the *Evening Post* and its weekly edition, called the *Herald,* which was sent to subscribers all over the United States. Enjoying a larger circulation than the *Evening Post* itself, the *Herald* served to keep alive the Federalist pretensions to be a national party.

In one instance, at least, the understanding between Hamilton and Coleman fell short of being a perfect meeting of minds. In 1802, the *Evening Post* printed James Callender's libelous attack upon the morals of President Jefferson—certainly a departure from the editorial policy proclaimed by Coleman when the newspaper was launched. Hamilton was so roundly blamed for this lapse that in September, 1802, he felt obliged to publish a statement in the *Evening Post* to the effect that he had not been consulted regarding the printing of the offending article. Hamilton took this occasion to reiterate his aversion to discussing "all personalities, not immediately connected with public considerations."[9]

At first, he undertook to fight Jeffersonianism with the well-worn "truths" he had been preaching for many years to the American people: that they were their own worst enemies, that they were a prey to mass emotions and that they were afflicted with a fatal weakness for demagoguery. But these "truths" had not become more palatable with the passage of time and they were now obliged to compete with the "half-truths" and "fallacies" purveyed by President Jefferson and his party. As a result, Hamilton's methods of influencing the people never seemed more wanting than they did after 1801.

Mordantly observing the success of his rival, Hamilton decided that there was a law of politics by which the base and spurious drove the genuine article out of circulation. While nothing had shaken his conviction that popularity-seeking was the bane of good government, he was now prepared to admit that unpopularity was worse. Indeed, when he surveyed the thinning ranks of the Federalists, he saw no alterative but to fight Jefferson with his own weapons. Without stooping to emulate the Republicans' electioneering methods, there were, he contended, many "fair and justifiable expedients" for getting out the vote as yet untried by the Federalists.

First of all, Hamilton pointed out, the party would have to get over the idea that it was born to rule. When the people asked for the Federalists' credentials for holding the highest offices in the land, it was not enough to bring out their genealogies. Moreover, he remarked, much as they hated it, the Federalists would have to go to school under Jefferson in the "paltry science of courting and winning popular favor." Instead of depending upon reasoned arguments to set the people right, Hamilton was of the opinion that their emotions would have to be appealed to: "Unless we can contrive to take hold of, and carry along with us some strong feelings of the mind," he said, "we shall in vain calculate upon any substantial or durable results."[10]

Hamilton disdained to address himself to the baser passions and instincts of mankind—there, he acknowledged, Jefferson had no peer. Nevertheless, the Federalist leader observed that in one important area of the "feelings of the mind" he had the field virtually to himself. Religion was an emotional force which Jefferson, a suspected Deist, had signally failed to exploit. Here, then, was an opportunity for the Federalists to move in with all their forces: let the preachers become politicians and the politicians become preachers and the truth would soon be manifest that the way to make good citizens was to make them good Christians. To that end, he urged that an association to be known as "the Christian Constitutional Society" be organized to support the Christian religion and the United States Constitution. The members of this Society would pledge themselves to vote for Federalist candidates and to provide charitable institutions for the relief of immigrants and the training of artisans where, presumably, the worthy poor would be indoctrinated with Federalist principles as well as with Holy Writ.[11]

Despite the religious garb, it is plain that Hamilton's "Christian Constitutional Society" was the wise, the good and rich with their collars reversed. A more telling objection to Hamilton's plan, however, was that in essentials it had already been tried. In many areas—and nowhere was this more true than in New England—the churches were bulwarks of federalism. The faithful had long been summoned to the polls by beating the drum ecclesiastic; without prompting from Hamilton, the clergy had raised the cry that religion was in danger and had preached a crusade against the Republican "infidel" in Washington. Under his auspices, it was predicted,

Defender of the Freedom of the Press

the altars would be desecrated, the churches burned and the clergy strung up in their own pulpits or, in case of invasion, put in the front lines "as those who, in his opinion, may be most easily spared." In anticipation of these dire events, nervous New England farmers hung their Bibles down their well and oiled their flintlocks. Credulity and bigotry could hardly do more for the Federalist party than they had already done—and yet they had failed to bring it victory.[12]

During the so-called "Reign of Terror", the Republicans had proclaimed themselves the champions of the freedom of the press. After they came into power, however, they began to institute prosecutions for libel against Federalist editors accused of aspersing President Jefferson. True, no Sedition Law was enacted by the Republicans, nor did the federal government throw a dragnet over the country in order to round up subversives. But state officials, including judges, entered into the work of suppressing Federalist newspapers so wholeheartedly that the ideals proclaimed by the Republicans in opposition seemed destined to become one of the casualties of their victory at the polls.

Among the Federalist editors thus arraigned in the state courts was Harry Croswell, printer of the *Wasp*, a small New York country newspaper. Croswell was charged with having "wickedly and seditiously disturbed the peace and tranquillity" by printing a statement to the effect that President Jefferson had paid James Callender for writing *The Prospect Before Us*, a pamphlet in which Washington had been held up to scorn as a traitor, thief and perjurer and President Adams had been characterized as a "hoary-headed incendiary." Since this allegation had appeared frequently in the Federalist press, it is probable that Croswell was selected as a test case because of his obscurity and straitened circumstances.[13]

This attack upon the *Wasp* brought out the whole Federalist hive. No less than eight Federalist lawyers served as counsel for the indicted journalist. Their efforts proved unavailing: when they attempted to call James Callender as a material witness to prove the truth of the charges made in the *Wasp* against President Jefferson, Judge Lewis held that truth was no defense. Had he ruled otherwise, the case might have taken a turn embarrassing to the President, for James Callender was eager to bear testimony against his former patron, whom he now accused of dishonesty, cowardice and immoral relations with the slave women on his plantation. Thus deprived of his only effective line of defense, Croswell was convicted in July, 1802, of libeling the President.[14]

By their conduct toward Harry Croswell and other Federalist newspaper editors, the Republicans gave their adversaries an opportunity to come forward as the defenders of the freedom of the press. Perhaps it was not as obvious an opportunity as the Federalists, by the enactment of the Sedition

Law, had given the Republicans; nevertheless, without turning a hair, the former exponents of the Sedition Act rose to the occasion by proclaiming themselves to be the guardians of American liberty.[15]

The Republicans revealed to Hamilton a truth that Jefferson had learned during the days of the Alien and Sedition Acts—that judges might bend the law to suit the purposes of the party in power, even to the extent of invading the fundamental liberties of the people. "Dependent judges," Hamilton now said, could destroy the constitutional safeguards of the freedom of the press and by "judicial mandates" stifle the voices of critics of the administration. As one of those critics, Hamilton inveighed against the "high toned" doctrines advanced by Republican judges. "No man can think more highly of judges," he declared. ". . . But I must forget what human nature is, and what history has taught us," before he could believe that they were infallible.*[16]

This fear of partisan judges was typical of Hamilton's attitude, now that Jefferson was in the presidency, toward all men in positions of authority. "Men are not to be trusted implicitly in elevated States," he declared, "for humble lovers of the People by Hypocrisy & cant, very often *change* when they arrive at Power, & become deadly Enemies & Persecutors of the People." This was precisely the burden of Jefferson's complaint against Hamilton when he was in power, although the Virginian had never accused Hamilton of pretending to love the people.

Croswell's attorneys immediately asked for a new trial on the ground that the case ought to have been postponed in order to give the defendant an opportunity to summon material witnesses. Persuaded that the editor of the *Wasp* was "the first victim marked out by the hand of power," Hamilton joined the battery of Federalist legal talent that had volunteered its services to Croswell. In January, 1804, he went to Albany to argue a motion before the Court of Errors for a new trial for the Federalist editor.

Here he delivered a memorable speech in defense of freedom of the press. In the crowded courtroom, he launched into "a pathetic, impassioned & most eloquent address on the Danger to our Liberties" and a penetrating analysis of the principles of free government. Hamilton made the case of this obscure "village printer" part of the long struggle of the English-speaking peoples for liberty. "If this right [that of criticizing those in office] was not permitted to exist in vigor and in exercise," he exclaimed, "good men would become silent, corruption and tyranny would go on, step by step, in usurpation, until, at last, nothing that was worth speaking, or writing, or

---

* "The real danger to our liberties," Hamilton said, "was not from a few provisional troops. The road to tyranny will be opened by making dependent judges, by packing juries, by stifling the press, by silencing leaders and patriots. His apprehensions were not from single acts of open violence. Murder rouses to vengeance. . . . But the most dangerous, the most sure, the most fatal of tyrannies, was, by selecting and sacrificing single individuals, under the mask and forms of law, by dependent and partial tribunals."

Defender of the Freedom of the Press

acting for, would be left in our country." Never, said Judge Kent, one of the presiding judges, had Hamilton exhibited more convincing evidence of greatness: "His whole Soul was enlisted in the Cause." And the cause was that of human freedom against oppression by government—the same that had moved Jefferson and Madison to protest against the Alien and Sedition Acts.

Flatly contradicting the prosecution's interpretation of the common law, Hamilton insisted that it permitted the defendant to prove the truth of an alleged libel. "I never did think truth was a crime," he declared. ". . . My soul has ever abhorred the thought, that a free man dared not speak the truth." His definition of tyranny was a law that held "in the very teeth of justice and common sense that a man is equally guilty of having maliciously and wickedly published a *falsehood,* although every syllable is strictly *true.*"

Hamilton was of course aware of the immense partisan advantage he stood to gain from the acceptance of the principle that truth was a defense. True, Callender was now dead, having fallen from a ferry and drowned "in congenial mud"; but even without his testimony, Hamilton had little doubt of being able to prove that Jefferson had contributed financially to Callender's support—as in fact he had. Therefore, said Hamilton, "it ought to be distinctly known whether Mr. Jefferson be guilty or not of so foul an act as the one charged. It is in every view interesting." Had he said it was explosive, he would have been nearer the truth.

Hamilton recognized no inconsistency between the views he advanced as defense counsel for Harry Croswell and those he had expressed in 1798-99. As he saw it, his fundamental principles had remained unaltered despite the changes that had taken place in his own and his party's position. At no time, he pointed out to the jury, had he contended for a press wholly freed of restraint and responsibility. "The novel, the visionary, the pestilential Doctrine of an unchecked Press," he said, could find acceptance only among Jacobins and demagogues; no friend of liberty and order could possibly believe that the press was wholly free. Nor did he think that truth was always an ironclad defense. A malicious intent might, he observed, constitute a libel, even though the charge was true; under certain circumstances, he conceded, the printing of texts of Scripture might be libelous and even treasonable, even though the texts were in themselves laudable. It was the intent, he insisted, that constituted the crime of libel—"this is a fundamental principle of jurisprudence."

Wherein then did the freedom, as distinguished from the license, of the press consist? Hamilton answered that the press ought to be as free as the juries of the land were disposed to permit it to be. When this power was deposited in the courts or in magistrates, the danger of tyranny was always present; when it resided in "an occasionally and fluctuating Body, the Jury," liberty was secure. The jury must therefore be free to determine the intent, the truth and the law. Because the Sedition Act had given these powers to the jury, he pronounced it to have been "an honorable, a worthy and glorious effort in favor of public liberty."[17]

From a strictly legal point of view, much of Hamilton's eloquence, however "impassioned" and "sublime," was beside the point. Nor did his arguments impress the Republican members of the bench; their object was to punish the vilifiers of President Jefferson, not to permit the jury to probe into the truth or falsity of the charges leveled against him. As a result, on the question of granting Croswell a new trial, the judges divided two against two on purely partisan lines. The tie vote meant that Croswell's suit was denied.

Nevertheless, Hamilton did not plead the cause of freedom of the press in vain. A few years after his unsuccessful attempt to win Croswell a new trial, the legislature of New York enacted a law conceding substantially everything that Hamilton had contended for in 1804. Other states followed suit and Hamilton's definition of libel was incorporated into several new state constitutions.*

Thus, in the last important speech of his career, Hamilton resumed the ground he had taken during the American Revolution. Deprivation of office may sometimes be good for the soul of a politician. In the case of Alexander Hamilton it had the effect of reinvigorating the liberalism that his fear of Jacobinism had gravely impaired. In 1804, as in 1775, he asserted the "inalienable rights of man" against government. His was no longer a counsel of despair, of patiently waiting the deluge: "We ought to resist, resist, resist," he exclaimed in the crowded courtroom in Albany, "till we hurl the Demagogues & Tyrants from their imaginary Thrones."[18]

* Hamilton's definition was as follows: "The liberty of the press consists in the right to publish with impunity Truth with good motives for justifiable ends though reflecting on Government, magistracy or Individuals."

36.

The Duel with Burr

In 1798-99, the signal for which Hamilton had waited before turning the American army against Louisiana and the Floridas was the transfer of this region to France. He had supposed that Spain, weakened by defeat and internal dissension, could not long resist France's demands that Louisiana be retroceded—hence his conviction that war was not far away. But Hamilton underestimated the cunning and resourcefulness of Spanish diplomacy. As a result of the delaying tactics of Florida Blanca, the wily Spanish Minister, the surrender of Louisiana was postponed until after the Federalists had fallen from power.

In the meantime, the United States had made peace with France. After six months of fruitless negotiations, the American envoys discarded their instructions and made the best terms they could for ending the undeclared war. Napoleon drove a hard bargain. The United States was obliged to pay a higher price for peace than would have been necessary had negotiations been entered into in 1798-99.[1]

When they read the terms of the Convention of 1800, a groan went up from the Federalist leaders: not since John Adams first broached the idea of a mission to France had they received a ruder jolt. Rather than accept the cup of humiliation from Napoleon, some advocated throwing it back in his face. "There is no condition of disgrace below it," exclaimed Fisher Ames; "without being vanquished we agree to pass under the yoke." The yoke of the First Consul promised to be no less galling than that of the Jacobins.[2]

But again Hamilton stood out against the party leaders: disappointing as the terms of the Convention were, he advised ratification. It had been finally borne in upon him that the people were weary of this bootless war. He himself had long since renounced all hope of reparations from France—they were "rather to be wished for than expected," he remarked, "while France is laying the world under contribution." But it was chiefly in the interests of the unity and prestige of the Federalist party that he advised his friends to vote for ratification. If the Federalists bore the responsibility for the defeat of the treaty, he predicted that the party would

557

be divided and ruined. "It will be of consequence to the federal cause in future," he said, "to be able to say the federal administration steered the vessel through all the storms raised by the contentions of Europe into a peaceful and safe port." Thus, tacitly at least, Hamilton admitted that President Adams' foreign policy had been right and that his own policy had been wrong.*³

But the vessel was still far from port and some fancy steering was required before the haven finally hove into view. Like the Directory before him, Napoleon was bent upon restoring the French Empire in the Western Hemisphere. Having made peace with both the United States and Great Britain, Napoleon felt free to turn his attention to the Mississippi and the Caribbean—the nexus of his projected empire. The first step toward the realization of this dream was taken while Americans were preoccupied with the election of 1800 and in the process of disbanding their army. By the secret Treaty of San Ildefonso, Spain retroceded Louisiana to France.

Few Americans had ever heard of San Ildefonso, but, not for the last time, an obscure place in a faraway country became of vital importance in American history. Although the treaty signed by Napoleon and Charles IV of Spain was intended to be secret, rumors of its existence reached the United States as early as 1801. The prospect, so unexpectedly revived, of the most formidable military power in the world as a neighbor of the United States had no terrors for Federalists like George Cabot and Fisher Ames. On the contrary, they expected that the proximity of the French legions would prove a blessing in disguise: confronted by this peril, Americans would presumably forsake the Pied Piper of democracy in Washington and look for safety to the Federalists, those unimpeachable patriots who had lately led the resistance to the "devouring monster."⁴

Hamilton did not share his friends' confidence that the presence of French troops in Louisiana would overthrow the demagogues and reinstate the good, the wise and rich in the affections of the people. In Napoleon's "hideous despotism" he saw the awful consummation of democracy, the foreordained fulfillment of all the prophecies of bloodshed, violence and anarchy that he had predicted for the French Revolution. The man on horseback had at last arrived. But Hamilton was not inclined to invite him to come to North America in order to unite Americans behind the leadership of the Federalist party.⁵

Rather than permit the French to take possession of Louisiana, Hamilton wished to fight them on land and sea. Let the United States get under arms, he told his friends, call in the aid of British sea power, seize Louisiana before

* In actuality, the Senate modified the terms of the Convention signed by the American representatives in Paris. Ultimately, the two countries agreed that in exchange for the abrogation of the Franco-American alliance (which had been declared void by Congress in 1798), the United States government would assume the bill for the depredations committed upon American commerce by French ships.

The Duel with Burr

the French could get there and then offer to negotiate with Napoleon. "Such measures," he declared, "would astonish and disconcert Buonaparte himself . . . and all Europe would be taught to respect us." There was, however, one small matter which Hamilton seems to have overlooked—he left Napoleon nothing to negotiate about.[6]

If President Jefferson followed this advice, Hamilton was willing to forgive him all his transgressions and even to concede him a respectable place in history. "He [Jefferson] might yet retrieve his character," Hamilton observed; "induce the best part of the community to look favorably upon his political career, exalt himself in the eyes of Europe, save the country, and secure a permanent fame. But for this, alas! Jefferson is not destined." Apparently Jefferson's destiny was to court popularity by flattering the people until the tricolor was within sight of Washington. When history took note of Jefferson, Hamilton feared that it would be only to point the moral that a demagogue, next to a foreign master, is the greatest calamity a country can suffer.

And, indeed, in 1801 there was little to indicate that President Jefferson appreciated the gravity of the danger that threatened the United States. He had no patience with those who, like Hamilton, sounded the warning that the French were seeking to re-establish their empire in the Western Hemisphere. Instead, by his policy in the West Indies, Jefferson unwittingly abetted the French plans.

Rather than permit the French to regain control of the revolted island of San Domingo, Hamilton had recommended and President Adams had adopted in 1799 a policy of aid for the black republic established by Toussaint L'Ouverture. By assisting the French colonies in the Caribbean to achieve independence, Hamilton and Adams believed that they were acting in the interest of American commerce and security. Although promoting insurrections abroad was regarded by the Federalists as one of the most heinous practices of French Jacobins, when the necessity arose, Hamilton did not hesitate, even though it meant the domination of whites by blacks and the aggrandizement of the power of Toussaint L'Ouverture, "the black Napoleon of the Antilles." As a neighbor, Hamilton much preferred the black to the white Napoleon.[7]

Thomas Jefferson, the avowed champion of the rights of man, drew the color line in human freedom to a much greater degree than did Hamilton: as a Southerner and slaveholder, he could not welcome the prospect of a black republic in the Caribbean. And so Jefferson reversed the policy of Adams and Hamilton toward San Domingo. He gladly abetted Napoleon's efforts to coerce and starve the blacks into subjection, thereby demonstrating how completely he missed the point that French ambitions in Louisiana and San Domingo were closely connected. That the French failed to reconquer San Domingo was not owing to any lack of effort on President Jefferson's part; but when L'Ouverture died in a European prison, the United States lost a good ally against French designs in the Western Hemisphere.

Although Hamilton thought that Jefferson was certain to miss the boat to Louisiana—indeed, a man who was as eager as Jefferson to lay up the navy seemed likely to have no boat at all—in point of fact the President was anxiously consulting the timetables. In 1802, he no longer spoke of having tea with conquering French generals in London; it seemed all too likely that the French intended to take their tea in Washington. Fortunately for the United States, the British had a fleet; and Jefferson, despite his aversion to navies and British monarchism, was prepared to marry the United States to the British fleet and nation rather than see Napoleon seize Louisiana and the Floridas. This went far beyond anything advocated by Hamilton, but Jefferson was confident that an Anglo-American alliance initiated by Republicans would be a very different thing from the "monarchical" connection which he suspected Hamilton had set his heart upon. In *his* offer of marriage to the British fleet and nation, Jefferson said nothing about taking George III along on the honeymoon.*

Before entering into an alliance with Great Britain, Jefferson decided to try the effect of negotiations with France. The utmost that he expected from these *pourparlers* was that Napoleon might be persuaded to sell New Orleans and the Floridas. Hamilton and Jefferson were agreed that the possession of this territory, conveying as it did in unrestricted right to the use of the Mississippi and control of the northern approaches to the Gulf of Mexico, was essential to the security and prosperity of the United States. But Hamilton ridiculed the notion that it could be gained by methods short of war: of the success of any negotiations, he said, there was not "the most distant probability. . . . Its acquisition is of immense importance to France, and has long been an object of her extreme solicitude."

Yet, as Hamilton learned, the surprises of diplomacy are infinite. To everyone's astonishment, including Jefferson's, Napoleon offered to cede the United States not only New Orleans but the entire province of Louisiana, extending from the Rockies to the Mississippi and from Canada to the Gulf of Mexico. Discouraged by French losses in San Domingo and resolved to renew the war against Great Britain, Napoleon preferred to sell this territory to the United States rather than see it pass by conquest to "perfidious Albion."[8]

Thus it fell to President Jefferson and Napoleon to demonstrate that the victories of peace could be no less renowned than those of war. But the Federalist leaders were not inclined to thank the President or Napoleon for

---

* Nothing Hamilton ever said about the importance to the United States of the friendship of Great Britain exceeded Jefferson, who in his old age declared that "Great Britain is the nation which can do us the most harm of any one, of all on earth; and with her on our side we need not fear the whole world."

The Duel with Burr

the verification of this aphorism. Certainly they had expected better things of Napoleon; who could have predicted, they asked plaintively, that the victor of Lodi and Marengo would have surrendered to President Jefferson without firing a shot? Having made abundantly clear that they preferred hostilities to negotiations, they could not but regret that the administration had permitted such a splendid opportunity for war to slip through its fingers. And yet, as the advocates of territorial annexation, they were unable consistently to oppose the purchase of Louisiana. Neither could they approve, without doing violence to their most cherished prejudices, anything done by a Republican President. In this struggle between consistency and prejudice, there never was any doubt which would triumph.

Fisher Ames, whose appetite for foreign territory—provided it was acquired by Alexander Hamilton at the head of a conquering army—knew no bounds, had little desire for additional soil if bought by a Repubican administration. "The acquiring of territory with money is mean and despicable," he remarked, and "as to the territory, the less of it the better." He remained firmly of the opinion that the United States could have gotten everything it asked merely by rattling its saber—a much more eligible method, he thought, than opening its purse. "The least show of spirit, the least array of force," he said, ". . . would certainly have brought the Consul to terms—to any terms."[9]

Hamilton was too ardent a partisan not to feel the force of these objections and he was too human not to show his chagrin when his rival carried off the prize. He was perforce driven to cry down in the *Evening Post* the importance of Louisiana and to belittle Jefferson's part in its acquisition. When he contemplated "this new, immense, unbounded world" so unexpectedly added to the United States and pondered the difficulties of administering this territory under a republican form of government, the qualms and misgivings that he had experienced at the Constitutional Convention returned upon him. He feared that Jefferson had inadvertently hastened "the dismemberment of a large portion of our country, or a dissolution of the Government" by enlarging too rapidly the sphere of its activity. But he took pains to make clear that his forebodings did not apply to New Orleans and the adjacent area. From every point of view he found the acquisition of this territory beneficial. Indeed, to have done otherwise would have involved him in contradictions and inconsistencies beyond the portion usually allowed politicians.[10]

Unlike many members of his party, Hamilton had never been fearful of the growing power of the Old West. He said of himself: "No one has been more uniformly nor more entirely than myself in favor of the system of giving a free course to the population and settlement of our interior country." As a stockholder in the Ohio Company, he had a direct financial interest in seeing Americans go west. Nevertheless, he vigorously opposed any efforts on the part of government to stimulate emigration to the back country. In this regard, he was a wholehearted advocate of laissez faire.[11]

For the Louisiana Purchase, Hamilton declined to give Jefferson any credit other than that of having his hand out when Napoleon decided to let the region drop. While Jefferson had palliated and temporized, said Hamilton, the deadly climate of San Domingo, the courage of the blacks led by L'Ouverture and the imminence of a resumption of the war in Europe had impelled the First Consul to relinquish Louisiana. From this fortuitous chain of events Hamilton inferred that Providence, having repeatedly intervened to save the United States from the consequences of its own folly, was still on the job. But he thought that it was too much to expect of Providence that it counteract forever the "feebleness and pusillanimity" of the Jeffersonian administration.

With more justice, Hamilton might have contended that had it not been for his reorganization of the nation's finances, the United States could have commanded neither the cash nor the credit necessary to take advantage of Napoleon's offer. In order to purchase Louisiana, the United States Treasury sold $13 million in certificates and $2 million was taken from current revenues—a total greater than the foreign debt when Hamilton took over the Treasury. By 1803 the credit of the United States government was so firmly established that it was able to take this debt in its stride; and Republicans—the traditional opponents of government expenditures—were able to speak of a debt of $15 million as "a trifling sum." In consequence of the Louisiana Purchase the national debt reached its highest point before the Civil War; but since Albert Gallatin rather than Alexander Hamilton occupied the office of the Secretary of the Treasury, President Jefferson no longer trembled for the national solvency.[12]

As might be expected, Hamilton did not credit the Republicans with sufficient wisdom and integrity to cope with this debt. Louisiana, he predicted, would be paid for—if it were paid at all—"not by luxury and wealth and whisky, but by increasing the taxes on the necessaries of life." Apparently the North was to be compelled to bear the cost of Louisiana while the South received most of the political benefits.

Above all, it was this last point that agitated the Federalists. Allied with the West, the South seemed destined after the Louisiana Purchase to establish a perpetual ascendancy over the national government. To the conservators of the old order, the economic consequences of the Louisiana Purchase seemed no less dismal: the depopulation of the older states as a result of the emigration of hundreds of thousands of land-hungry Easterners; the crippling of eastern manufactures, with the loss of the labor force necessary to man the factories; and the triumph of the agrarians over the "moneyed interest."

Without denying that the relative importance of New England in the

The Duel with Burr

national councils would be diminished as a result of the Louisiana Purchase, Hamilton saw what few of the other Federalist leaders discerned—that New England was the section most likely to benefit economically from the acquisition of western territory. Its shipping, he pointed out, would expand; its merchants would find new customers; and its manufacturers would be blessed with new markets. But above all, he reminded his party, the acquisition of Louisiana would extend the "national power and security" and advance the cause of peace. "From a formidable and ambitious neighbor, she [France]," he said, "would be turned . . . into a natural ally."[13]

By 1804, the Federalists were everywhere in retreat. Even New England, the citadel of Federalist principles, had been penetrated by the Republicans: Rhode Island and Vermont had fallen; Connecticut, famed for its steady habits, and Massachusetts, "the Head Quarters of good Principles," were tottering. The "friends of government" were not only surrounded; they were thoroughly infiltrated by the enemy.

The Federalist leaders could endure adversity no better than they had stood success; victory and defeat went to their heads with equally disastrous results. In prosperity they had been overbearing and vindictive; in defeat they revealed themselves to be prone to hysteria and panic.

Both states of mind were exemplified by Timothy Pickering, the late Secretary of State. Distinguished by a choleric temper, an imperious bearing and an abounding sense of righteousness, Pickering was described, not unjustly, by Mrs. John Adams as a man "whose manners are forbidding, whose temper is sour and whose resentments are implacable." Pickering dignified these traits under the names of "honesty," "plain speaking" and a hyperactive New England "conscience," and he prided himself upon being, in Pope's words, "an old prig who never changed his principles or his wig." He never changed his wig for the sufficient reason that he did not wear one: rather than conform to the fashion of the day, Pickering wore his own hair or, rather, what remained of it. "While all sorts of people are greased with pomatum, and whitened with powder," he said, "my bald head and lank locks remain in *status quo*." That was where he thought everything ought to remain.[14]

Convinced that the Constitution afforded no protection to the minority of good men "when Jacobinism comes to rob or slay," Timothy Pickering began to calculate the value of the union. The rapidly increasing population of the South and West decreed, he decided, that they would become the dominant sections of the country and, to ensure that their victory would be complete and final, the three-fifths rule condemned the United States to a never-ending succession of "Negro Presidents and Negro Congresses." Although he shed no tears over the defeat of John Adams in 1800, Pickering could not forbear pointing out that without the three fifths rule, Jefferson would not have won the presidency.[15]

Pickering and his fellow Federalists had not created a strong central government in order to enable Thomas Jefferson to liquidate the wise, the good and the rich. Happily, these Federalists thought, Jefferson had provided an antidote against his own "poison." In the Kentucky resolutions, Jefferson had asserted that the states were the ultimate arbiters of the Constitution and that they interposed a protective shield between the individual and the federal government. After 1801, the Federalists felt quite as much in need of protection from the federal government as had Jefferson and Madison in 1798. Like the Republicans before them, they therefore beat a retreat to the states, resolved to defend the sovereign powers of these jurisdictions against the "consolidated" government headed by President Jefferson.

But with the states falling one by one to the Republicans, Timothy Pickering came to the conclusion that nothing short of disunion would save the godly remnant from the encroaching flood. He proposed to draw a geographical line between the righteous and wicked; on one side, the "baleful powers of hell and democracy" would rage in all their fury; on the other side, the virtuous would revel in an earthly paradise hermetically sealed against Jacobins.[16]

From such a division of the union, Pickering anticipated many advantages. Among other things, he remarked, it would permit New Englanders to govern themselves, which, it was hardly necessary for him to point out, they could do a great deal better than could Virginians; and it would "unite congenial characters," although it was hard to suppose that a nation of Pickerings was a guarantee of felicity. But above all, it would free the virtuous part of the community from the scourge of Jefferson. "The cowardly wretch at the head," Pickering said of the President, "while, like a Parisian revolutionary prating about humanity would feel an infernal pleasure in the utter destruction of his opponents. . . . Virtue and worth are his enemies, and therefore he would overwhelm them."[17]

In the proposed Northern Confederation, Pickering included New York as well as the New England states and, never one to deny salvation to those disposed to receive it, he held the door open to Pennsylvania, Nova Scotia and other British dominions. But these larger considerations, he acknowledged, could wait: the immediate task was to bring New York into the fold. Once that key state had been redeemed, the work of empire building might begin in earnest.[18]

Despite the low esteem in which he held Virginians, Pickering expected that the separation, when it came, would not be resisted: the erring sisters would let the chaste sisters go in peace. Nevertheless, by way of providing against all contingencies, he asked Alexander Hamilton to lead the military forces of the Northern Confederacy. With this "military genius" at the head

The Duel with Burr

of the Northern Army, Pickering almost wished that the Virginians would try to make trouble when the North seceded—it would give Hamilton an opportunity, which the French had inconsiderately denied him, of exhibiting his generalship in the field.

For Hamilton, Pickering's offer meant a military command free from the overshadowing presence of George Washington and the meddling of John Adams, an active career after years of enforced idleness, and perhaps an opportunity to draw up a constitution for the Northern Confederacy more in accord with his ideas of "energetic government." And yet, although Hamilton had always predicted that a more perfect system of government was likely to come only as the aftermath of anarchy and civil war, he had no desire to hasten the advent of these evils. When he said that he was prepared to shed his "heart's blood in the opposition," he meant that he was ready to die for his principles, not that he was prepared to kill other Americans who disagreed with him. Galling as was the rule of the "Virginia oligarchs," he was determined to stand his ground in the United States rather than retreat behind a geographical line.[19]

While he fully shared Pickering's hatred of democrats, Hamilton doubted whether anything short of a wall of brass—and this was not in Pickering's specifications for the Northern Confederacy—would be of any avail. It was futile, he knew, to tell democracy "thus far and no farther." Nor did he think that it was possible to run away from democracy; after all, the democrats were everywhere, spreading subversive ideas even in the households of the happy few. Finally, even admitting the feasibility of Pickering's plan, he did not consider it wise to attempt to segregate the democrats in a separate country in order that they might stew in their own turpitude. To dismember the union, he said, was to ensure that the poison of democracy would be only "the more concentrated in each part, and consequently the more virulent."[20]

Thus, if Hamilton's prescription were correct, union, while not precisely the cure for democracy, at least tended to alleviate the worst pangs of that "disease." By diffusing the evil over a wide area, the parts were in less danger of becoming gangrened. His advice, therefore, to Timothy Pickering was to dismiss all thought of breaking up the union and to concentrate his attention upon strengthening the loyal opposition to Jeffersonianism.

In Pickering's state of mind, this was equivalent to asking him to form a loyal opposition to Antichrist. Ignoring Hamilton's exhortations, the New Englander summoned the Federalist leaders to meet in Boston in the autumn of 1804 in order to put the finishing touches to his plans for the Northern Confederacy. Hamilton agreed to attend, but he made clear that he would go not as a conspirator but as an observer and, he hoped, a restraining influence upon the hotheads. His recent experience, however, afforded him little reason to suppose that he could dissuade the Essex Junto from a course of action upon which it was resolved.[21]

Since so much hinged upon New York's adhesion to the Northern Confederacy, Pickering was obliged to find an ally capable of delivering New York by subterfuge—for it was apparent that it could be delivered in no other way—into the hands of the Essex Junto. Ironically enough, the fact that New York was no longer controlled by the Federalists afforded the best security that it would not be detached from the union. In fact, the state was so strongly Republican in tone that it was obvious that only a Republican could win the governorship of the state in 1804.

When Pickering thought of craft, guile and duplicity, his thoughts turned naturally to Aaron Burr. While he held Burr's morals in abhorrence, Pickering had no objection to making use of the New Yorker in order to save the Federalist remnant from "the fangs of Jefferson." Here was one Puritan who did not disdain to do business with a man he regarded as a blackleg. On his part, Burr was willing to play the Federalists' game because, having been discarded by the Republicans after he had served their purpose in the election of 1800, he had nothing to hope from his party. From Vice-President to whipping boy—such was the political progress of Aaron Burr.[22] Nevertheless, with characteristic caution, Burr declined to commit himself to breaking up the union; during his negotiations with Pickering, he remained as enigmatic and unpredictable as ever.[23]

Pickering was acting upon the time-honored maxim that when rogues fell out, honest men came into their own. Even though Hamilton agreed that the Federalists ought to do everything in their power to widen the breach between the "rogues"—it was said that Jefferson hated Burr "as much as one demagogue can possibly hate another who is to rival him"—he did not think that one of the chief rogues ought to be invited to join the Federalist party. As a castoff from the Republican party, Burr had even less merit in Hamilton's eyes than when the Vice-President stood high in the graces of President Jefferson. Hamilton thought that Burr was in the party where he belonged—the abandoned characters, "Jacobins" and other miscreants who called themselves Republicans. No "union of honest men," he said, could tolerate Burr without suffering contamination; not only would the Federalists destroy their reputation as men of honor and principle—worse, they would acquire a master who would prostitute them to his personal ambition. Admitting that the fortunes of the Federalist party were at a low ebb, Hamilton did not agree that it ought to sink to the level of Aaron Burr.[24]

With Burr's election as the Republican Vice-President in 1801, Hamilton had hoped he had heard the last of his rival as a Federalist. He had expended every argument—and almost every epithet—to keep Burr out of the Federalist party: the Trojan horse had received no advance billing such as Hamilton gave Burr. Nevertheless, the Federalists seemed to have profited not a whit from these warnings; at the very mention of Burr's name, they rolled

The Duel with Burr

over and begged to be stroked by this elegant little gentleman with the flowery waistcoats and the manners of a born aristocrat.

Closely as Burr guarded his cards, Hamilton believed that he had seen enough of his rival's hand to predict his next play. On one occasion, Hamilton said, Burr told him that "our Constitution is a miserable paper machine. You have it in your power to demolish it, and give us a proper one, and you owe it to your friends and the country to do it." According to his own version of this conversation, Hamilton replied that the army was incapable of effecting a *coup d'état* and that he was "too much troubled with that thing called morality to make the attempt." To which Burr answered: "General, all things are moral to great souls!"[25]

Burr's near miss of the presidency in 1801 opened Hamilton's eyes—as his own actions had never done—to the hazard of permitting electors to cast their ballots in the Electoral College without designating their choice of President and Vice-President. Under this method, he now perceived, the presidency was made the sport of "intriguers" and it seemed far more likely to elevate to the office of Chief Magistrate a "demagogue" like Aaron Burr than a sterling patriot like Charles C. Pinckney. From such a system, the Federalists had nothing to gain, for, as Hamilton said in 1802, "in everything which gives opportunity for juggling arts our adversaries will nine times out of ten excel us." Accordingly, Hamilton warmly endorsed a proposed constitutional amendment by which it was made mandatory for electors to specify the President and Vice-President. He even recommended that electors be chosen by the people rather than by the state legislatures, on the ground that popular elections strengthened the connection between the President and the people. The Twelfth Amendment (1804) ordained the first but not the second of Hamilton's recommendations.

Once before, in 1801, Hamilton had given the party leaders a choice between himself and Burr—if Burr were elected President, Hamilton had made plain, he would withdraw from the party. With few exceptions, the Federalists in Congress had clung to Burr to the last. It could therefore be safely predicted that if the Federalists succeeded in making Burr governor of New York, he would become the leader of the party. In that event, Hamilton, discredited by his failure to carry the election for Pinckney in 1800 and by the reverses suffered by the party since that fateful election, would be obliged either to accept demotion in the party hierarchy or to leave the Federalists altogether. But where, if he chose the second alternative, would he go? Certainly he was not yet prepared to embrace Thomas Jefferson.

And so, instead of grooming Burr as a Federalist dark horse, Hamilton went out of his way to hobble the steed upon which Pickering hoped to ride to victory. At a meeting of Federalists held in Albany early in 1804 to decide the party's attitude toward Burr's candidacy as governor of New York, Hamilton spoke emphatically and without reserve against Burr. Again he warned his party of the lamentable fate of the Trojans and predicted a similar end for the Federalists once Burr had been admitted into the party. If it were the intention of the New York Federalists to destroy the Constitution, break up the union and bury themselves in the ruins, he told his audience, they could do no better than elect Burr—the most adroit, able, daring, ambitious and unscrupulous Jacobin in the country. Rather than bring disaster upon themselves and their country, Hamilton urged the Federalists to vote for Morgan Lewis, the Republican candidate favored by the Clinton-Livingston wing of the Republican party.[26]

Yet, as Hamilton ruefully admitted, his party was fascinated "by the enterprising and adventurous character of this man [Burr], and hope to soar with him to power." Roger Griswold, a Federalist member of Congress from New York, published a campaign document in favor of Burr in which he accused Hamilton of being actuated by "personal resentment towards Burr." Even granting that Burr was everything that Hamilton said—a man fit only for stratagems and spoils—these were precisely what the Federalists had in mind. When Jacobins were about to take over the country, it was no time, these worried gentlemen exclaimed, to subject the man who carried the seals of salvation to a catechism regarding his moral qualifications.[27]

For once, the weakness of the Federalists stood Hamilton in good stead. Burr could no longer work his old magic: the "miracle" of 1800 was not repeated. Despite the fact that approximately five sixths of the Federalists voted for Burr, he was defeated by Morgan Lewis. It was the most crushing reverse sustained up to that time by a candidate for the governorship of New York.[28]

The size of the vote piled up by Lewis indicated that Hamilton's opposition to Burr was not a decisive factor in the election. Burr was defeated by the Clinton-Livingston combination, a union of forces against which no aspirant to the governorship could make headway. In all probability, therefore, Hamilton might have spared himself the effort—not to mention the hazard—of actively opposing Burr. This, of course, is hindsight, but Hamilton cannot be wholly absolved of the charge of rashness: before undertaking to ruin Burr politically, he made no cool appraisal of the Vice-President's chances of winning the election.

It had long since been impressed upon Hamilton that he was not a popular leader, yet he had always taken a certain consolation in the thought that he was above the low arts to which, in his opinion, Thomas Jefferson owed his popularity. But now even the illusion that he was important in the party councils was being taken from him. As John Quincy Adams said, the Federalist vote for Burr in the New York election of 1804 and the decision of the Essex Junto to go ahead with its plans for a Northern Confederation revealed that the Federalist party was a minority, and "of that minority, only a minority were admirers and partisans of Mr. Hamilton."[29]

The Duel with Burr

It is not customary for two disappointed politicians to try to kill each other; and, immediately after the election, neither Burr nor Hamilton gave any indication of seeking each other's blood. Burr appeared to accept his defeat and the vilification to which he had been subjected in good spirit: he wrote his daughter Theodosia that "some new and amusing libels against the vice-president" had appeared and that "the election is lost by a great majority: *tant mieux*."[30]

"*Tant mieux*" indeed! Burr did not take his defeat as lightly as his letter to his daughter implied. No man who had risen as high as Burr, and who had so narrowly missed the highest office of all, could view with equanimity the wreck of his political career. Burr was fond of striking the pose of a philosopher in politics who observed his own conduct with ironical detachment, but in the spring of 1804 the shaft had penetrated too deeply for him to maintain his air of aloof indifference. Heavily in debt, his standing in the Republican party all but gone and his enemies openly exulting in his downfall, Aaron Burr seemed to have attained, politically speaking, the point of no return.

If, in 1804, Burr had to shoot someone to square accounts, his victim might properly have been Thomas Jefferson. Had Burr been so inclined, he could have made a strong case against the President as the prime mover who, behind the scenes, had deprived him of patronage, egged on his enemies in New York and, finally, excluded him from the higher councils of the Republican party. But Burr's resentment was not so overmastering as to blind him to the fact that nothing was to be gained by picking a quarrel with the President: no matter how flagrant the provocation, Jefferson would not accept a challenge to a duel.

The same could not be said of Hamilton: being a gentleman and an officer, he would not refuse a challenge. Equally important, Burr nursed a deep and abiding sense of injury against this fine-feathered West Indian. Had not Burr maintained tight rein upon his temper, it is probable that Hamilton would have been called upon to give satisfaction long before 1804. Why Hamilton pursued him with such vindictiveness passed Burr's understanding: did the little lawyer really imagine, Burr asked himself, that politics was a struggle between good and evil and that the good was wholly on Hamilton's side? In Burr's estimation, of course, politics was a game in which the prizes went to the astute, the most resourceful and the most adroit in manipulating public opinion and the party machinery.

Perhaps Burr would have ignored the aspersions cast upon him by Hamilton in 1804 had not a newspaper story virtually compelled him to take action. In April of that year an account appeared in an Albany newspaper of a dinner party held at the home of Judge John Taylor at which Hamilton had been present. The notice was not inserted in the society column, however; the author, Charles D. Cooper, Taylor's son-in-law, had quite another object in view than purveying social chitchat. Cooper declared that he could prove that Hamilton had declared in Judge Taylor's house that he "looked upon Mr. Burr to be a dangerous man, and one who ought not to be trusted with the reins of government." And, Cooper added portentously, he could cite instances in which Hamilton had expressed "a still more despicable opinion of Burr."

These statements obliged Burr to call Hamilton to account or to appear before the world as a man lacking sufficient courage to defend his own honor. With such an alternative before him, Burr acted quickly and decisively: in a curt note, accompanied by a copy of Cooper's letter, he demanded of Hamilton "a prompt, unqualified acknowledgment or denial of the use of any expressions which would warrant the assertions of Dr. Cooper," including the "still more despicable" opinions which Cooper alleged that he had heard Hamilton express on other occasions.

The tone of Burr's letter struck Hamilton as "unnecessarily peremptory and menacing," particularly since it was delivered by William Van Ness, Burr's friend who usually acted as his second in his duels. Hamilton's immediate reaction was that Burr was more intent upon provoking a duel than in receiving an explanation. Nor was Hamilton averse to giving him that kind of satisfaction: in his reply, he declared that if Burr insisted upon an inclusive disavowal of all the disparaging remarks allegedly made against him, he was free to take such action as he deemed expedient. Although Hamilton crossed out these words before he sent the letter, it was clear from the outset that he was not going to evade a challenge.[31]

Even in its amended form, Hamilton's reply was couched in language quite as testy, terse and uncompromising as was Burr's. Instead of avowing or disavowing the remarks imputed to him by Dr. Cooper, Hamilton flatly asserted that Burr had no right to question him upon such matters because there was no specific conversation alluded to in Cooper's letter and because the entire charge was based upon inferences drawn by Cooper from remarks he allegedly overheard. Hamilton offered to admit or deny explicitly any "precise or definite opinion" of which he stood accused, but, he said, his honor forbade him from answering vague and uncircumstantial charges. As for Dr. Cooper's statement that he could enumerate instances in which Hamilton had expressed a "still more despicable opinion" of Burr, Hamilton dismissed this as a mere play upon words: " 'Tis evident," he told Burr, "that the phrase 'still more despicable' admits of infinite shades, from very light to very dark. . . . Between gentlemen, *despicable* and *more despicable* are not worth the pains of distinction. . . . I trust, on mature reflection," he concluded, "you will see the matter in the same light with me. If not, I can only regret the circumstance, and must abide the consequences."[32]

This letter impressed Burr as mere quibbling—the kind of thing he might expect from a man with a guilty conscience. Burr therefore returned

The Duel with Burr

to the charge with a demand for a retraction, denial or avowal of any statements tending "to impeach the character of Col. Burr without reference to time or place." Instead of obliging the colonel, Hamilton declared that he would not submit to "an inquisition into his most confidential as well as other conversations through the whole period of his acquaintance with Col. Burr."

No doubt, by the rigid etiquette governing dueling in the early nineteenth century, Burr was demanding more of Hamilton than he had a right to ask. A blanket disavowal of alleged remarks covering a long period of time, without reference to a designated time and place, Hamilton was not required by the code to give; only specific remarks, usually defined as to time and place, could be made the subject of controversy. Moreover, the lapse of such a long period of time between the alleged statements and Burr's notice of them, and the fact that Burr spoke openly to his friends of his intention of challenging before he actually called out Hamilton, showed that Burr was more eager to get Hamilton within the sights of a pistol than to secure the kind of retraction to which he was entitled.

On the ground that Hamilton's equivocation called imperiously "for the last appeal," Burr sent Van Ness to Hamilton with a challenge. The exchange of letters had convinced the Vice-President that Hamilton was not quite a gentleman—and therefore he felt less compunction about shooting him. More important, "he was sure," he later told Jeremy Bentham, "of being able to kill him [Hamilton]."[33]

Why did not Hamilton apologize to Burr, promise to make no more derogatory remarks behind his back and live happily ever after? Apparently Hamilton did not for a moment contemplate such an escape from his predicament: he believed that his opposition to the Vice-President proceeded from "pure and upright motives" and he was persuaded that Burr was a demagogue whose insatiable ambition would never cease to menace the union. Furthermore, Hamilton knew that the harsh things he had said about Burr could not be palliated or explained away. By traducing Burr as he had—and he had not left Burr a shred of honor or repute—Hamilton was aware that he might have to answer for it. He took the risk and, as the event proved, he lost.

As a man of honor, Hamilton was obliged to go through with the duel. His reputation as a gentleman, his influence as a political leader (he did not forget the forthcoming meeting with Pickering, where the fate of the union might be decided), his self-esteem and the respect of his friends would be forfeited if he declined Burr's challenge. As Oliver Wolcott said, Hamilton "reasoned himself into a belief, that though the custom was the highest degree criminal, yet there were peculiar reasons which rendered it proper for *him,* to expose *himself* to Col. Burr in particular." Without hesitation, therefore, he instructed his second to arrange the time, the place and the weapons, asking only that he be allowed sufficient time to clear up some legal business pending in the courts.

While deferring outwardly to the code of honor, Hamilton had come to a momentous decision—he would withhold his first fire in the impending duel, and, he added, "I have thoughts even of reserving my second fire, and thus giving a double opportunity to Col. Burr to pause and reflect." To only one "judicious friend" did Hamilton confide this resolution. Rufus King was horrified by his friend's decision: "any man of ordinary understanding," he exclaimed, could see that Hamilton "owed it to his family and the rights of self-defense to fire at his antagonist"; it was as fatal to rely upon Burr's poor marksmanship as upon his magnanimity. Hamilton paid no heed to King's expostulations. For several years, his religious convictions had been undergoing a marked revival. No doubt, this spiritual reawakening was owing in part to his realization that, in a chaotic world of revolution, religion offered social stability as well as hope of a better future. But he did not return to the religious views that had found expression in his "Hurricane" letter: he now thought less of God's wrath and more of His mercy and benignity. Moreover, as a Christian, he had conceived scruples about taking human life. In his speech defending Harry Croswell he had laid down the proposition that "no man shall be the avenger of his own wrongs, especially by a deed, alike interdicted by the laws of God and of man." And in the last letter he wrote, he told his wife that "the scruples of a Christian have determined me to expose my own life to any extent rather than subject myself to the guilt of taking the life of another."

The death of his son in 1801 had reinforced Hamilton's abhorrence of dueling. As his quarrel with Burr approached its climax, the memory of his son Philip was much in Hamilton's mind. Philip, too, had not believed in dueling, yet he had accepted Eacker's challenge rather than suffer dishonor; and Philip, too, had resolved not to fire at his antagonist. Philip had gone to his death and Hamilton was prepared to follow his son. Weehawken was a name engraved upon his heart.

Manifestly, if dueling were to be stopped, someone must take a stand against it and reveal the practice for what it was—a senseless killing for trivial affronts, a relic of the "ignorance, superstition and Gothic barbarism," a false romanticism that taught the "sight of human blood can alone promote satisfaction." Hamilton could not bring himself to bear testimony against dueling to the extent of refusing Burr's challenge; but he could indicate his disapproval of the custom by refusing to fire at Burr.[34]

It was an audacious challenge of death—the supreme gamble of a life in which boldness, courage and self-confidence had repeatedly proved their worth. It was a fitting end, if end it proved to be, for a man who had always wished to die with a flourish, with a gesture of disdain for death. Not,

The Duel with Burr

however, that it was quite the way Hamilton had planned to go; but at least it could be said that stopping Aaron Burr's bullet was no ordinary death.

Hamilton spent the two weeks' grace granted him by Burr in winding up his affairs, making his will and settling as many of his legal cases as time allowed. Outwardly, he gave no sign of agitation; at parties he appeared his usual self: witty and lighthearted with the ladies, properly grave and apprehensive when he discussed public affairs over port with the gentlemen. To his wife, he gave no hint of what he planned to do; perhaps she might have observed that he was a little more tender than usual to the children.

The last day of his life Hamilton devoted to writing a letter to his wife and a statement of the reasons that impelled him to meet Burr upon the field of honor. This apologia was dictated, his friend Pendleton said, "by the excessive sensibility which kept him tremblingly alive to every thing which might have the appearance of being a ground of censure." He was more tender of his reputation than of his life; for him, a duel was the last infirmity of a noble mind.[35]

The duel was to take place on the heights of Weehawken on the New Jersey side of the river, the very spot on which Philip Hamilton had met his death. This was not wholly coincidental, however, for Weehawken was the favorite dueling ground of New Yorkers who wished to settle their affairs of honor without running foul of the strict laws of their own state. Partly as a result of Hamilton's efforts, dueling had been outlawed in New York. Any person giving or receiving a challenge was held to be guilty of a misdemeanor; if convicted, he was disqualified for holding any office of honor, profit or confidence in the state for a period of twenty years.

Burr and his second were the first to arrive at Weehawken and they were clearing brush from the ground when Hamilton, Pendleton and Dr. David Hosack, the attending physician, came up. The paces were stepped off, the positions were marked and the seconds chose lots to determine where the principals should stand and by whom the command to fire should be given. Pendleton won both counts. The final instructions were then given, among them the rule governing unexpended chances: "If one of the parties fire," it was stated, "and the other hath not fired, the opposite second shall say one, two, three, fire, and he shall then fire or lose his shot. A snap or flash is a fire."

As the two men took their positions on the field and their seconds handed them the pistols, Hamilton raised and lowered his gun several times as if to try the position. "I beg pardon for delaying you," he said to Burr, "but the direction of the light renders it necessary." Whereupon he put on his spectacles and said that he was ready to begin.[36]

At the given signal, both men presented their weapons. Apparently

Hamilton was resolved to carry through to the end the mimicry of a duel; certainly there was nothing in his posture to indicate to Burr that his adversary had made up his mind not to fire. For Burr, this was the real thing: his only thought was to kill or disable before he himself was cut down. No religious scruples about the taking of human life marred his aim. Burr's first bullet struck Hamilton in the abdomen. As he fell, Hamilton's pistol went off, probably as a result of involuntary reflex action. This rather spoiled the effect that Hamilton had hoped to achieve, but he was not immediately aware of what had happened. When his second reached him, he managed to gasp: "Take care of that pistol; it is undischarged and still cocked; it may go off and do harm. . . . Pendleton knows . . . that I did not intend to fire at him." But, on the other hand, it completed a parallel which Hamilton had striven for from the beginning—with his son's death four years before. When Philip fell, he, too, had fired his gun involuntarily.*

When Burr saw that his bullet had taken effect, he started toward the wounded man to learn how seriously he was hurt, but his second hurried him away lest he be observed on the field by witnesses who might later be called upon to testify in court. As he made his way to the river, Burr kept repeating, "I must go and speak to him." There was no doubt, however, about the gravity of Hamilton's condition; for a few moments, his agonized second feared that he would die on the spot. But he rallied from the shock and Pendleton and Dr. Hosack carried him through the woods and down the bank to a boat waiting to take him across the river to New York.

From "ye tragic shores of Hoboken, crimsoned with the richest blood," Hamilton was borne to the house of William Bayard on Manhattan Island. Mrs. Hamilton was immediately summoned to his side, but, to spare her the sudden shock of finding her husband mortally wounded, she was told that he was suffering from "spasms." Hamilton was in such extremity, however, that the true nature of his condition could not be long concealed from her. Burr's bullet had penetrated Hamilton's liver and lodged in his vertebrae; surgeons from the French frigate then in New York Harbor were called in, but they pronounced the case hopeless. Despite the administration of laudanum, Hamilton remained in extreme pain.[37]

* Van Ness, Burr's second, asserted that Hamilton had fired first. But it is obvious that the two shots must have followed so closely as to make it almost impossible to determine whether Burr or Hamilton was the first to fire. Both Hamilton's and Burr's seconds agreed, however, that it was improper to say that "both parties agreeably to the word of command took aim": they merely presented. Burr took aim.

By immediately leaving the scene, Burr and his seconds were accused by Hamilton's friends of refusing to lend assistance to a wounded man. It is evident, however, that Burr was greatly disturbed by what had occurred. Shortly after the duel, Burr directed his second, Van Ness, to write Nathaniel Pendleton to learn Hamilton's condition: "I sincerely hope," wrote Van Ness, "that his wound is not, as has been stated to me, pronounced mortal." The next day, Burr himself wrote Dr. Hosack, Hamilton's attending physician.

The Duel with Burr

As he lay dying, Hamilton expressed to the Reverend Dr. Mason of the Dutch Church, "HIS FIRM BELIEF IN CHRISTIANITY, and fervent hope of forgiveness, THROUGH THE MERITS AND MEDIATION OF OUR BLESSED REDEEMER." At a time when many public men were noted for their indifference to revealed religion, it was something for a statesman to face his Maker with the name of Jesus Christ on his lips. When the Reverend Dr. Mason asked him if he would bear testimony against the practice of dueling—"a crowning service to those, which he had already rendered to his country"— Hamilton replied that "no man more abhorred the practice, and at his death it would be discovered, he had left a solemn Protest against a custom so ferocious and unprincipled." He again asserted that he had not intended to fire, that he bore no malice to Burr, that he was dying at peace with all men, and that "he was perfectly reconciled to death, though he knew his friends would deplore its manner, which he did himself."[38]

Before the end came, Hamilton asked to be accepted into the Episcopal Church and to receive the sacrament, but so strong was the prejudice against dueling that none of the available clergymen would administer it. Finally, Bishop Moore was prevailed upon to give the sacrament to the dying man. Shortly afterward, on the morning of July 12, 1804, he died. He was buried in Trinity Churchyard with all the panoply of the Society of the Cincinnati.

The Federalists mourned Hamilton as a Hercules "treacherously slain in the midst of his unfinished labors, leaving the world overrun with monsters." And well they might lament—for the only hope of keeping the party out of the pitfall of a narrow provincialism, and ultimately of secessionism, had died with Hamilton. But even had he lived and held the Federalists true to their earlier nationalism, it is doubtful whether the party would have been restored to the people's confidence. As for Hamilton himself, his achievements were behind him; his great days had been lived. In a larger sense, however, Hamilton belonged to the future: to that united, strong, self-reliant nation which had captured his imagination.[39]

In death, the "Little Lion" no longer seemed fearsome to those who had dreaded lest he destroy singlehanded the Constitution and establish a monarchy. Since he was no longer capable of doing evil, some of the good he had accomplished began to be remembered. It was now said that he was a man "who lived for glory, not for power, who was ready at all times to devote himself to his country's service, but disdained the practices of unworthy artifices to obtain its favours." His unremitting labor for the consolidation of the union; the financial stability his policies had created; the prosperity and well-being of the American people to which he had so largely contributed—all these achievements were now brought to mind. At last Hamilton seemed to have attained the kind of renown that he had envied in Washington and that had eluded him during his lifetime. Yet irony did not cease to pursue him even in death: much of the Republicans' acclaim of Hamilton was owing to their desire to blacken Burr's reputation.

With Hamilton's death, a power passed from the earth. But the American union, his noblest work, endured and the great nation of which he dreamed became in the fullness of time a reality that far transcended even his vision.

Notes

Abbreviations

AAS   American Antiquarian Society
APS   American Philosophical Society
CHS   Connecticut Historical Society
HSP   Historical Society of Pennsylvania
LC   Library of Congress
LCP   Library Company of Philadelphia
NYHS New-York Historical Society
NYPL New York Public Library
PRO, FO Public Record Office, Foreign Office

Chapter 1. The Making of a Revolutionary

1. *The United States Magazine*, I (Philadelphia, 1779), 81-83; W. C. Westergaard, *The Danish West Indies Under Company Rule* (New York, 1917), pp. 222, 227, 236, 250, 253; F.W. Pitman, *The Development of the British West Indies* (New Haven, 1917), pp. 280-282, 313, 316; Bryan Edwards, *The History, Civil and Commercial, of the British Colonies in the West Indies* (Philadelphia, 1805), II, 184, footnote.
2. H. U. Ramsing, *Alexander Hamilton og hans modrene slaegt*, Tidsbilleder fra Dansk Vest-Indiens Barndom, Personalhistorisk Tidskrift, 59 de Aargang, 10 Rekke, 6 Bind (1939), pp. 229-231. (Translated by Fleming Higard.)
3. *The American Genealogist*, XXI (1945), 166; *American Heritage* (June, 1955), p. 7.
4. *Virginia Quarterly Review* (Autumn, 1953), pp. 598-599; Gertrude Atherton, *A Few of Hamilton's Letters* (New York, 1903), pp. 266-267; Alexander Hamilton to Nicholas Cruger, November 27, 1771, Hamilton MSS., LC.
5. Dorothy R. Dillon, *The New York Triumvirate* (New York, 1949), pp. 39-40, 47; *William and Mary Quarterly* (April, 1947), p. 212; Michael J. O'Brien, *Hercules Mulligan* (New York, 1937), pp. 42-44; Poem Written by Hamilton When Residing in New Jersey on the Death of a Child of Mr. Boudinot, Hamilton MSS., LC; John C. Hamilton, *The Life of Alexander Hamilton* (New York, 1834), II, 10.
6. Thomas Jones, *The History of New York During the Revolutionary War* (New York, 1879), I, 3-5; Bower Ally, *The Rhetoric of Alexander Hamilton* (New York, 1941), pp. 53-54; *William and Mary Quarterly* (April, 1947), pp. 209, 213-214; *An Alarm to the Legislature of the Province of New York* (1775), p. 12; E. E. Beardsley, *The Life and Correspondence of Samuel Seabury* (Boston, 1881), pp. 38, 41, 46-47.
7. Hamilton, *Works*, ed. H. C. Lodge (New York, 1904), I, 120, 124-125, 146-147, 169, 176-177.
8. Charles F. Mullett, *Fundamental Law and the American Revolution* (New York, 1933), pp. 189-190; Hamilton, *Works* (Lodge), I, 18, 119, 124; *New York Journal or General Advertiser*, December 1, 1774; January 5, 1775.
9. Hamilton, *Works* (Lodge), I, 113.
10. Jones, *History of New York*, I, 36-37.

Chapter 2. Aide-de-Camp to Washington

1. E E. Beardsley, *The Life and Correspondence of Samuel Seabury* (Boston, 1881), pp. 38, 41, 46-47; *William and Mary Quarterly* (April, 1946), p. 211; T. J. Wertenbaker, *Father Knickerbocker Rebels* (New York, 1948), p. 64.
2. A. McLane Hamilton, *Intimate Life of Alexander Hamilton* (New York, 1910), pp. 25-26.
3. *Ibid.;* Hamilton, *Works* (Lodge), I, 38, 181, 186, 194-196.
4. Hamilton, *Works* (Lodge), I, 38, 194-196.
5. *William and Mary Quarterly* (April, 1947), p. 215; Washington, *Writings*, ed. John C. Fitzpatrick, VI, 167, 186; Emily Stone Whiteley, *Washington and his Aides de Camp* (Washington, 1936), pp. 27, 133; Broadus Mitchell, *Alexander Hamilton, From Youth to Maturity* (New York, 1957), pp. 168-169.
6. Hamilton, *Works* (Lodge), IX, 103-111; John C. Fitzpatrick (ed.), *The Writings of George Washington* (Washington, 1940-41), IX, 468.
7. Washington, *Writings* (Fitzpatrick), XII, 113-115, 121-122; Sir Henry Clinton, *The American Rebellion* (New Haven, 1954), pp. 90-91; W. S. Stryker, *The Battle of Monmouth*, ed. William S. Myers (Princeton, 1927), pp. 75-76; Charles Lee, *The Lee Papers* (New York, NYHS Collections, 1871-74), II, 417-418, 467.
8. Stryker, *Battle of Monmouth*, Appendix IV, pp. 180-181, 282-289; *Proceedings of a General Court Martial for Trial of Major General Lee* (1778), pp. 69, 71-72, 146, 229-230, 233; *Lee Papers*, II, 381-382, 393-394, 435, 467-468, 472-473; Narrative of an Affair of Honor Between General Lee and Colonel Laurens, Hamilton MSS., LC; James McHenry to Elias Boudinot, July 2, 1778, Emmet MSS., NYPL; Stan V. Henkels (ed.), *The Confidential Correspondence of Robert Morris* (Philadelphia, 1917), pp. 141-142; Hamilton, *Works* (Lodge), IX, 156.
9. Hamilton, *Works* (Lodge), IX, 122-124, 131, 134, 206, 227.
10. Edward C. Burnett (ed.), *Letters of Members of the Continental Congress* (Washington, 1921-38), IV, 168, 181, 260; *American Historical Review*, I (1896), 509; Francis Dana to Hamilton, July 25, 1779, Hamilton MSS., LC; Hamilton, *Works* (Lodge), IX, 175; Hamilton to Colonel Brookes, August 6, 1779, Hamilton MSS., LC.
11. Hamilton, *Works* (Lodge), IX, 175, 195; A. McLane Hamilton, *Intimate Life*, p. 360; Massachusetts Historical Society, *Proceedings*, LXIII (1931), 425-26; Douglas S. Freeman, *George Washington* (New York, 1952), V, 505-509.
12. Hamilton, *Works*, ed. John C. Hamilton (New York, 1850-51), I, 136, 183-185; Burnett, *Letters of the Continental Congress*, V, 205, and *The Continental Congress* (New York, 1941), pp. 458-460, 465, 472.
13. Hamilton, *Works* (Lodge), IX, 159-162; Nathan Schachner, *Alexander Hamilton* (New York, 1946), pp. 79-80; Hamilton, *Works* (J. C. Hamilton), I, 204, 215.

Chapter 3. The Struggle Against Inflation

1. Hamilton, *Works* (Lodge), I, 200.
2. *Ibid.*, I, 203-206, 208-209.
3. Hamilton to ?, February 26, 1781, Hamilton MSS., LC.
4. *Pennsylvania Gazette*, August 26, 1779; Allan Nevins, *The American States During and After the Revolution* (New York, 1920), pp. 568-569; *American Historical Review*, XXXV (1930), 5; *Journals of the Continental Congress* (Washington, 1907), III, 458; Burnett, *Continental Congress*, pp. 80-81, 102; Henry Hollingsworth to Colonel John Coxe, April 30, 1779, Greene MSS., APS; James Lovell to Horatio Gates, June 10, 1779, Gates MSS., NYHS.
5. Washington, *Writings* (Fitzpatrick), VIII, 112; XVII, 52; Jeremy Belknap, *History of New Hampshire* (Boston, 1791-92), II, 326-327; *American Historical Review*, XXXV (1930), 53-54; Charles Pettit to Nathanael Greene, May 11, 1779, Greene MSS., APS; *Journals of the Continental Congress*, VII, 45-46.
6. David Ramsay, *The American Revolution* (Charleston, 1789), pp. 177-178; Massachusetts Historical Society, *Proceedings*, Second Series (Boston, 1907), XVII, 319-320;

Notes

William Irvine to Anthony Wayne, August 26, 1781, Wayne MSS., HSP; *Pennsylvania Magazine*, XXIX (1905), 234; William Gordon to Benjamin Rush, April 4, 1780, Rush MSS., LCP; *Pennsylvania Archives* (Philadelphia, 1853), IV, 742-743; *Pennsylvania Packet*, March 27, 1779; *Documents Relating to the Revolutionary History of New Jersey* (Trenton, 1914), IV, 27; A. H. Smyth (ed.), *Writings of Benjamin Franklin* (New York, 1905-1907), VII, 293; Hamilton to Alexander McDougall, November 3, 1779, Hamilton MSS., LC.
7. Burnett, *Continental Congress*, p. 421; Burnett, *Letters*, III, 486.
8. Hamilton, *Works* (Lodge), IX, 71-72; I, 206.
9. *Documents Relating to the Revolutionary History of New Jersey*, IV, 335; Elkanah Watson, *Men and Times of the Revolution* (New York, 1856), 382; *Journals of the Continental Congress*, XVI, 13-18; Burnett, *Letters*, IV, 529; V, 71.
10. Hamilton, *Works* (Lodge), III, 336, footnote, 338-339, 341; I, 236-237.
11. Hamilton, *Works* (Lodge), III, 333; Hamilton, *Works* (J. C. Hamilton), I, 150-168.
12. Hamilton, *Works* (Lodge), I, 214-215, 257-258, 266.
13. Burnett, *Continental Congress*, pp. 489-490; J. Franklin Jameson, *Essays on the Constitutional History of the United States* (Boston, 1889), pp. 147-149, 150-151; J. B. Sanders, *The Evolution of the Executive Departments of the Continental Congress* (Chapel Hill, 1939), pp. 150-151.
14. Hamilton, *Works* (Lodge), I, 219-220, 226.
15. Washington, *Writings* (Fitzpatrick), XXI, 183, footnote; Otis G. Hammond (ed.), *Letters and Papers of General John Sullivan* (Concord, N. H., 1930-31), III, 279, 292.
16. Clarence ver Steeg, *Robert Morris* (Philadelphia, 1954), pp. 58-62; William Clajon to Horatio Gates, March 3, 1781, Gates MSS., NYHS; E. P. Oberholtzer, *Robert Morris, Patriot and Financier* (New York, 1903), pp. 67-68, 70-78; Hamilton, *Works* (Lodge), III, 344, 372; I, 229, 233-234.

Chapter 4. The Quarrel with Washington

1. Hamilton to Miss Livingston, April 11, 1777; May, 1777, Hamilton MSS., LC; Hamilton, *Works* (Lodge), IX, 187.
2. Hamilton, *Works* (Lodge), II, 206-223; IX, 184-188; A. M. Hamilton, *Intimate Life*, pp. 95-99, 127-128, 134; Hamilton, *Works* (J. C. Hamilton), I, 53, 186-187; Colonel Fleury to Hamilton, October 20, 1780; John Jay to Hamilton, September 28, 1783; Hamilton to John Laurens, June 30, 1780; Hamilton MSS., LC; Gertrude Atherton, *A Few of Hamilton's Letters*, pp. 76-77.
3. Whiteley, *Washington and his Aides-de-Camp*, 139-140; Octavius Pickering and C. W. Upham, *The Life of Timothy Pickering* (Boston, 1867-73), II, 98-99; W. C. Rives, *History of the Life and Times of James Madison* (New York, 1868-73), III, 275-276; A. M. Hamilton, *Intimate Life*, pp. 123-124; Massachusetts Historical Society, *Proceedings*, LVIII (1925), 221; Louis Gottschalk (ed.), *Letters of Lafayette to Washington* (New York, 1924), pp. 78-79; Lafayette to Hamilton, January 7, 1781, Hamilton MSS., LC; Hamilton, *Works* (Lodge), IX, 184, 225; IX, 208; H. E. Wildes, *Anthony Wayne* (New York, 1941), pp. 366-368.
4. Carl Van Doren, *Secret History of the American Revolution* (New York, 1941), pp. 346-347, 366-368; Hamilton, *Works* (Lodge), IX, 208-209; 215-216, 222, 225, 257; Hamilton to Clinton, September 30, 1780, Clements Library MSS.; James T. Flexner, *The Traitor and the Spy* (New York, 1953), pp. 253-259.
5. Hamilton, *Works* (Lodge), IX, 232-236; Schuyler to Hamilton, February 25, 1781, Hamilton MSS., LC.
6. Samuel Eliot Morison, *By Land and by Sea* (New York, 1955), p. 162.
7. *Letters of Lafayette to Washington*, p. 184; Washington, *Writings* (Fitzpatrick), XXI, 491; Mitchell, *Alexander Hamilton*, pp. 242-243.
8. *A Military Journal kept by Major Ebenezer Denny* (Philadelphia, 1860), pp. 242-243; *Pennsylvania Archives*, Second Series, IV, 747-748; James McHenry to Nathanael Greene, September 4, October 7, 1781, J. P. Morgan Library MSS., New York; Anthony Wayne to Joseph Reed, September 3, 1781, Morgan MSS.

9. Hamilton, *Works* (Lodge), III, 393-394; IX, 245-247; Henry Lee, *Memoirs of the War in the Southern Department of the United States* (New York, 1869), p. 501; Isaac Q. Leake, *Memoirs of the Life and Times of John Lamb* (Albany, 1850), pp. 278-279; James Thacher, *A Military Journal during the American Revolutionary War* (Boston, 1825), p. 285; Douglas S. Freeman, *George Washington* (New York, 1954), V, 269.

Chapter 5. Congress and the Army

1. A. M. Hamilton, *Intimate Life*, pp. 148-149.
2. Clarence ver Steeg, *Robert Morris* (Philadelphia, 1954), pp. 99-100; E. P. Oberholtzer, *Robert Morris* (New York, 1903), pp. 141-143.
3. Hamilton, *Works* (J. C. Hamilton), I, 280; Thomas Sickels to Greene, January 11, 1780, Greene MSS., LC; Hamilton to Robert Morris, August 13, 1782, Henkels MSS.
4. *New York Journal and Weekly Register*, March 1, 1787; Hamilton, *Works* (Lodge), IV, 264; Morris to Hamilton, October 28, 1782, Hamilton MSS, LC; Hamilton to the County Treasurers, September 7, 1782, Hamilton MSS., LC; E. Wilder Spaulding, *New York in the Critical Period* (New York, 1932), pp. 167-168.
5. Ver Steeg, *Robert Morris*, pp. 136-137; Hamilton, *Works* (Lodge), IX, 280-281.
6. *Journals of the Continental Congress*, XVII, 758; XXIII, 798-799; XXV, 904; *Letters of Members of the Continental Congress*, V, 563-564; Francis Wharton (ed.), *The Revolutionary Diplomatic Correspondence of the United States* (Washington, 1889), IV, 609; Burnett, *Continental Congress*, p. 480; Hamilton, *Works* (Lodge) I, 283-284; II, 190, 213; *Pennsylvania Packet*, December 5, 1782; Notes of April 18, 1782, Hamilton MSS., LC.
7. *Journals of the Continental Congress*, XXV, 896-897, 910; Massachusetts Historical Society, *Proceedings*, LXIII (1931), 487-488; *Independent Chronicle and Universal Advertiser*, September 4, 1783.
8. Hamilton, *Works* (Lodge), I, 277.
9. *Journals of the Continental Congress*, XXIII, 798; D. R. Dewey, *Financial History of the United States* (New York, 1931), p. 50; *Journals of the Continental Congress*, XXIII, 770-772.
10. *Journals of the Continental Congress*, XXV, 868, 886; *Freeman's Journal*, December 4, 1782, March 26, 1783; W. C. Ford (ed.), *Letters of Joseph Jones* (Washington, 1889), pp. 114, 117; *Historical Magazine*, Second Series, II (Morrisania, N.Y., 1867), 226; Dewey, *Financial History*, p. 50; *Letters of Members of the Continental Congress*, VI, 445-446; *Independent Chronicle*, December 12, 1782.
11. David Howell to Benjamin Rush, February 8, 1783, Rush MSS., LCP; William R. Staples, *Rhode Island in the Continental Congress* (Providence, 1870), pp. 413-415, 447-448; *Journals of the Continental Congress*, XXIII, 792, 816, 822, 863-864, 867-868; XXIV, 32-33; XXV, 582, 607, 845; Irving Brant, *James Madison, The Nationalist* (Indianapolis, 1950), p. 220; Washington, *Writings* (Fitzpatrick), XI, 237-240, 307; *Pennsylvania Magazine of History and Biography*, XXIV (1905), 17; *Letters of Members of the Continental Congress*, III, 32, 83, 176, 262, 270; Frederick Kirkland (ed.), *Letters on the American Revolution* (Philadelphia, 1941), p. 64.
12. Madison, *Writings* (Hunt), I, 386; *Letters of Members of the Continental Congress*, VII, 280; *Journals of the Continental Congress*, XXV, 207-209, 911; *Independent Chronicle and Universal Advertiser*, September 25, 1783; Wayne to Colonel Delany, May 21, 1778, Wayne MSS., HSP; G. W. Greene, *The Life of Nathanael Greene* (New York, 1867-71), II, 84; *Papers of Noah Webster* (New York, 1843), p. 318.
13. *Journals of the Continental Congress*, XXV, 852-853, 864, 889; Madison, *Writings* (Hunt), I, 306-307, 310-312, 386; Wharton, *Diplomatic Correspondence*, V, 828; *Pennsylvania Packet*, December 7, 1782; *Letters of Members of the Continental Congress*, VI, 398; McDougall to Loudon, July 19, 1783, McDougall MSS., NYHS; Jared Sparks, *Life of Gouverneur Morris* (Boston, 1832), I, 177; Hamilton, *Works* (Lodge), IV, 328-329.
14. Brant, *James Madison, The Nationalist*, pp. 224-225; W. C. Ford (ed.), *Letters and Correspondence of S. B. Webb* (New York, 1893), III, 14.

15. Ver Steeg, *Robert Morris*, pp. 169-170; Hamilton, *Works* (Lodge), I, 284-285; IX, 325, 332-333; *Journals of the Continental Congress*, XXIII, 784; XXIV, 383; George Bancroft, *History of the Formation of the Constitution* (New York, 1882), I, 295; Hamilton, *Works* (Lodge), IX, 309, 330-331; I, 302-303.
16. Hamilton, *Works* (Lodge), I, 226-227.
17. Washington, *Writings* (Fitzpatrick), XXVI, 292-293; Conversation with William Duer, October 12, 1788, Rufus King MSS., NYHS; Sparks, *Gouverneur Morris*, I, 249-251.
18. John Armstrong to Gates, April 18, 1783, Gates MSS., NYHS; Webb, *Letters and Correspondence*, III, 6, footnote; Bancroft, *History of the Constitution*, I, 318; Hamilton, *Works* (Lodge), IX, 323, 331; Knox to McDougall, February 23, 1783, McDougall MSS., NYHS.
19. Washington, *Writings* (Fitzpatrick), XXVI, 187, 213-214, 285-286, 292-293, 323-325, 352; *Journals of the Continental Congress*, XXIV, 295-297; XXV, 906-907; Hamilton, *Works* (Lodge), IX, 310-312, 323-325, 331; McDougall to Knox, February 8, 1783; Knox to McDougall, March 13, 1783, McDougall MSS., NYHS; St. Clair to Irvine, May 6, 1783, Irvine MSS., HSP; John Armstrong to Gates, April 18, 23, 1783, Gates MSS., NYHS; Bancroft, *History of the Constitution*, I, 296-297; W. H. Smith (ed.), *Papers of General Arthur St. Clair* (New York, 1882), I, 584; Conversation with William Duer, October 12, 1783, Rufus King MSS., NYHS; Ver Steeg, *Robert Morris*, p. 172; Brant, *James Madison, The Nationalist*, p. 235; *Pennsylvania Magazine of History and Biography*, XLIV (1920), 243; H. P. Johnston (ed.), *Correspondence and Public Papers of John Jay* (New York, 1890-93), p. 93; Webb, *Letters and Journals*, III, 56-57.
20. *Journals of the Continental Congress*, XXIV, 103-104, 258, 261, 279, 198-200; XXV, 870, 896-897, 937; Burnett, *Letters*, VII, 124, 147-148; Hamilton, *Works* (Lodge), II, 185; X, 340-341; Spaulding, *New York in the Critical Period*, pp. 171-172; V. L Collins, *The Continental Congress at Princeton* (Princeton, 1908), pp. 6-7; Brant, *James Madison, The Nationalist*, p. 291; Gaillard Hunt (ed.), *The Writings of James Madison* (New York, 1900-1910), I, 335-336, 373-374; Francis Wharton, *Revolutionary Diplomatic Correspondence of the United States* (Washington, 1889), IV, 608; VI, 279.

Chapter 6. Law and the Loyalists

1. Hamilton to Robert R. Livingston, August 13, 1783, Livingston MSS., NYHS; Livingston to Hamilton, August 30, 1783, *ibid.*
2. *Rutgers v. Waddington*, Hamilton MSS., LC.
3. *Arguments and Judgments of . . . the Mayor's Court . . . in a Cause Between . . . Rutgers and Waddington* (New York, 1784), pp. 5-8; Henry B. Dawson (ed.), *The Case of Elizabeth Rutgers* (New York, 1886), p. 35.
4. William Crosskey, *Politics and the Constitution* (Chicago, 1953), II, 964-965; *Selected Essays in Constitutional Law* (Chicago, 1938), I, 169; *American Historical Review*, XXX (1925), 524-525, 531; *Michigan Law Review*, X (1910), 115-117.
5. Stephen J. De Lancey to Hamilton, September 12, 1785, Hamilton MSS., LC; Harry B. Yoshee, *The Disposition of Loyalist Estates in Southern New York* (New York, 1938), pp. 103-104; Alexander McDougall to Mrs. Catherine Leonard, May 10, 1784, McDougall MSS., NYHS; Nathaniel Hazard to Hamilton, April 21, 1786, Hamilton MSS., LC; Hamilton to Hazard, April 22, 1786, Hamilton MSS., LC; Spaulding, *New York in the Critical Period*, pp. 118-120, 130-132; C. E. Miner, *Ratification of the Federal Constitution in New York* (New York, 1921), pp. 46-47.

Chapter 7. "A Rage for Liberty"

1. Massachusetts Historical Society, *Collections*, Fifth Series (Boston, 1877), V, 207; *Freeman's Journal*, March 28, October 22, 29, 1783.
2. Hamilton, *Works* (Lodge), I, 217-19, 312.
3. *Ibid.*, I, 217, 246, 248-249, 254; II, 191.
4. Crosskey, *Politics and the Constitution*, I, 42, 375; *The Federalist* (New York, 1937), pp. 94, 97-98, 126; Hamilton, *Works* (Lodge), I, 238, 256; II, 200-201; C. J. Friedrich, *Constitutional Government and Democracy* (Boston, 1941), p. 398; Brant, *James Madison, The*

Nationalist, pp. 109-110, 129, 378; Journals of the Continental Congress, XX, 469-470; XXV, 874; Theophilus Parsons, Memoir of Theophilus Parsons (Boston, 1859), p. 469.
5. Federalist, pp. 143, 183; Jonathan Elliot, Debates in the State Conventions on Adoption of the Federal Constitution (Washington, 1836-45), II, 566.
6. Elliot, Debates, II, 500; Hamilton, Works (Lodge), I, 214-216.
7. Hamilton to Washington, February 24, 1783, Columbia University MSS.; Federalist, 130; J. R. Strayer (ed.), The Delegate from New York (Princeton, 1939), pp. 64-65; Hamilton, Works (Lodge), I, 217, 246, 252-253; IX, 309, 313-316, 319-321, 323; Journals of the Continental Congress, XXIV, 112-115; XXV, 848, 854-855, 886-887; XXVI, 192; Franklin, Works (Sparks), X, 323, 345; Crosskey, Politics and the Constitution, II, 1188-1189; Burnett, Letters, VII, 406, 415, 553, 563, 595, 598; Brant, James Madison, The Nationalist, pp. 227-229; Jonathan Arnold to William Arnold, February 11, 1788, Gratz Collection, HSP; The Political Establishments of the United States (Philadelphia, 1784), p. 13; A. S. Bolles, The Financial History of the United States from 1789 to 1860 (New York, 1894), I, 327, 334, 337-340.
8. Hamilton, Works (Lodge), I, 250; II, 209; IX, 393.
9. Ibid., I, 223-224; III, 378-379.
10. Washington, Writings (Fitzpatrick), XXIV, 49-51, 276-277, 298, 486; XXVII, 305-306, 244.
11. Sparks, Gouverneur Morris, I, 266.

Chapter 8. Democracy and Banking

1. Jefferson, Papers (Boyd), VIII, 645; G. J. McRee, The Life and Correspondence of James Iredell (New York, 1857-58), II, 162; Elliot, Debates, III, 179; Schoepf, Travels in the Confederation, II, 61; Bancroft, History of the Constitution, I, 438; Pennsylvania Gazette, February 6, 1782; Pennsylvania Packet, March 24, 1781; John Quincy Adams, Life in a New England Town (Boston, 1903), p. 174; Francis W. Coker, Democracy, Liberty and Property (New York, 1942), p. 465; Richard Hildreth, History of the United States (New York, 1849-56), IV, 34-35; Bancroft, History of the Constitution, I, 428, 491; Schoepf, Travels, II, 61; Essays on Money, By a Citizen of the United States (Philadelphia, 1786), pp. 34, 39, 43, 59; Harvard Law Review, XLI (1928), 495; Thomas Hartley to Yeates, July 19, 1789, Yeates MSS., PHS.
2. New York Daily Advertiser, July 7, 1786; American Museum, IX (Philadelphia, 1798), 9-10; Pennsylvania Magazine of History and Biography, IX (1885), 189.
3. M. D. Conway, Omitted Chapters of History, Disclosed in the Life and Papers of Edmund Randolph (New York, 1888), p. 72; Massachusetts Historical Society, Proceedings, Second Series (1903), XXVII, 458-459; John Jay, Writings (Johnston), III, 373; Hildreth, History, IV, 34-35; Continental Journal and Weekly Advertiser, September 19, 1782.
4. New York Journal and Weekly Advertiser, May 3, 1787.
5. Hamilton, Works (Lodge), VII, 266; VIII, 448; Washington, Writings (Fitzpatrick), XXVIII, 502; Massachusetts Historical Society, Proceedings (1931), LXVI, 531.
6. Hamilton, Works (Lodge), III, 14; Elliot, Debates, II, 303.
7. Ibid.
8. Lord Acton, Essays on Freedom and Power (Boston, 1949), pp. 136-137; Hamilton, Works (Lodge), I, 246-247.
9. John Church to Hamilton, February 17, 1784; May 2, 1784, Hamilton MSS., LC.
10. Hamilton, Works (Lodge), IX, 396-398; Henry W. Domett, A History of the Bank of New York (Cambridge, 1884), pp. 4-5; Independent Journal or General Advertiser, March 13, 1784; New York Independent Gazette, March 11, 1784; New York Journal and State Gazette, March 18, 1784; New York Daily Advertiser, January 2, 1686; Robert A. East, American Business Enterprise in the American Revolutionary Era (New York, 1938), pp. 293-294; Joseph S. Davis, Essays in the Early History of American Corporations (Cambridge, 1917), II, 45, 90; J. Wadsworth to Hamilton, November 11, 1785; Plan for the Incorporation of a Bank, Hamilton MSS., LC; Allen Nevins, History of the Bank of New York (New York, 1934), 9, 17, 20; M. Carey (ed.), Debates and Proceedings of the General Assembly of Pennsylvania (Philadelphia, 1785), p. 93.

Notes

Chapter 9. "More Power to Congress"

1. Sparks, *Gouverneur Morris*, I, 212-213; E. P. Alexander, *A Revolutionary Conservative* (New York, 1938), pp. 168-169; D. R. Fox, *Yankees and Yorkers* (New York, 1940), pp. 172-174; New York *Journal and Weekly Register*, May 29, 1787; James Kent to Elizabeth Hamilton, December 10, 1833, Kent MSS., LC; Hamilton, *Works* (Lodge), VIII, 44-48; IX, 309, 450; Kent, *Commentaries on American Law*, I, 179; Chilton Williamson, *Vermont in Quandary* (Montpelier, 1949), pp. 174-176; Daniel Chipman, *Life of Nathaniel Chipman* (Boston, 1846), pp. 31, 74-75; *Federalist*, pp. 36-37; *Public Papers of George Clinton* (New York, 1890-1914), IV, 846-847, 859; V, 64, 68; VI, 347; Howard Swiggett, *War Out of Niagara* (New York, 1933), p. 235; B. F. Stevens, *The Clinton-Cornwallis Controversy* (London, 1888), I, 469; Frederick F. van de Water, *The Reluctant Republic*, p. 309; Washington, *Writings* (Fitzpatrick), XXVI, 122-123; *Letters to Washington* (Sparks), IV, 545-547; Madison, *Writings* (Hunt), I, 174-175; Burnett, *The Continental Congress*, pp. 543-544; Bancroft, *History of the Constitution*, I, 373; *Journals of the Continental Congress*, XXIII, 7631; *Historical Magazine*, VII, 1863, 53.
2. Joseph Story, *Commentaries on the Constitution*, abridged (Boston, 1833), pp. 99-101; *Federalist*, pp. 131-132; Crosskey, *Politics and the Constitution*, II, 1192-1196; Elliot, *Debates*, II, 59.
3. Bancroft, *History of the Constitution*, I, 487, 499; Hárold U. Faulkner, *American Economic History* (New York, 1949), pp. 178-179; *Gazette of the United States*, April 24, 1790; Nathan Dane to Sedgwick and Dwight, February 11, 1786, Nathan Dane MSS., LC; New York *Daily Advertiser*, March 23, April 13, 27, May 2, July 4, 1786; New York *Journal or Weekly Register*, February 25, 1785.
4. Massachusetts Historical Society, *Proceedings* (1916), XLIX, 89; *Journal of Economic History*, November, 1946, p. 210; Hamilton, *Works* (Lodge), I, 337-338; II, 157.
5. Brant, *James Madison, The Father of the Constitution* (Indianapolis, 1950), p. 15; *American Historical Association, Report for 1896* (Washington, 1897), I, 745.
6. Charles A. Beard, *The Supreme Court and the Constitution* (New York, 1922), pp. 84-85; Brant, *James Madison, The Nationalist*, pp. 385-387; Bancroft, *History of the Constitution*, II, 401; Hamilton, *Works* (Lodge), I, 335-339.
7. James Kent to Elizabeth Hamilton, December 10, 1832, Hamilton MSS., LC.
8. Cash Book, Hamilton MSS., LC; Spaulding, *New York in the Critical Period*, p. 184; Hamilton, *Works* (Lodge), II, 158.
9. Washington, *Writings* (Fitzpatrick), XXIX, 123; J. M. Palmer, *General von Steuben* (Princeton, 1927), pp. 336-337.
10. Richard B. Morris (ed.), *America in Crisis* (New York, 1956), p. 40.
11. *American Historical Association, Report for 1896* (Washington, 1897), II, 734; Elliot, *Debates*, III, 89, 180.
12. *Federalist*, pp. 29, 127; Washington, *Writings* (Fitzpatrick), XXIX, 123; Elliot, *Debates*, II, 521; Bancroft, *History of the Constitution*, II, 417.
13. *Federalist*, p. 33; Washington, *Writings* (Fitzpatrick), XXIX, 123-124; Franklin, *Writings* (Smyth), IX, 564; Edmund Randolph to Edward Carrington, April 11, 1787, Emmet MSS., NYPL; Ridley to Joseph Johnson, June 20, 1787, Ridley MSS., MHS.
14. Jay, *Writings* (Johnston), III, 244; John Quincy Adams, *Life in a New England Town*, p. 119, footnote; Fisher Ames, *Works*, II, 106-107; James Sullivan to Duane, April 16, 1787, Duane MSS., NYHS.
15. *Federalist*, pp. 157-158; Ames, *Works*, II, 103.
16. *American Historical Review*, XXX (1925), 535; Ames, *Works*, II, 97; Elliot, *Debates*, II, 521; Jay, *Writings* (Johnston), III, 212-213; Washington, *Writings* (Fitzpatrick), XXV, 126.
17. Dewey, *Financial History*, p. 51; *Pennsylvania Magazine of History and Biography*, XLVI (1920), 245; Massachusetts Historical Society, *Proceedings*, Second Series, VIII (1894), 177-179; *Letters of Members of the Continental Congress*, VII, 425; B. C. Steiner, *The Life and Correspondence of James McHenry* (Cleveland, 1907), p. 90; L. B. Walker (ed.), *Bland Papers* (Philadelphia, 1897), II, 112.

18. *Era of the American Revolution*, p. 381.
19. V. L. Parrington (ed.), *The Connecticut Wits* (New York, 1926), p. 456.
20. Spaulding, *New York in the Critical Period*, 22-25; M. Carey (ed.), *Debates and Proceedings of the General Assembly of Pennsylvania* (Philadelphia, 1786), pp. 82, 89; Washington, *Writings* (Fitzpatrick), XXVIII, 503-506, 523; Elliot, *Debates*, II, 56, 136, 229; New York *Daily Advertiser*, July 7, 1785.
21. *Era of the American Revolution*, pp. 373-375; Bancroft, *History of the Constitution*, I, 446-447.
22. John Adams, *Works* (Adams), VIII, 211, 219-221; Jefferson, *Writings* (Ford), I, 115-117; *American State Papers*, VIII, *Finance*, I, 12-13 (Boston, 1817); *Letters of Members of the Continental Congress*, VIII (February 6, 1788).

Chapter 10. The Constitutional Convention (1)

1. C. E. Miner, *Ratification of the Federal Constitution in New York* (New York, 1951), pp. 51-52; New York *Journal and Weekly Register*, March 15, 1787; Spaulding, *New York in the Critical Period*, pp. 186-187.
2. New York *Journal and Weekly Register*, May 3, 1787; Spaulding, *New York in the Critical Period*, p. 180.
3. E. H. Scott, *The Federalist and Other Papers* (Brooklyn, 1892), II, 652-653.
4. Madison, *Writings* (Hunt), II, 341.
5. C. C. Tansill (ed.), *Documents Illustrative of the Formation of the Union of the American States* (Washington, 1927), p. 282.
6. J. R. Strayer (ed.), *The Delegate from New York* (Princeton, 1939), pp. 61-62; Tansill, *Documents*, pp. 776-777; Crosskey, *Politics and the Constitution*, II, 1192-1193.
7. *American Political Science Review*, II (1908), 532-534, 544; Thomas Cooper, *Consolidation, An Account of Parties in the United States* (Charleston, 1824), pp. 2-4; Charles A. Beard, *The Supreme Court and the Constitution* (New York, 1922), p. 86.
8. Strayer, *The Delegate from New York*, pp. 62-63; Tansill, *Documents*, pp. 216, 776-777; P. L. Ford (ed.), *Pamphlets on the Constitution of the United States* (Brooklyn, 1888), pp. 100-101.
9. Tansill, *Documents*, p. 787; *Federalist*, pp. 251-252; Strayer, *The Delegate from New York*, pp. 77-78.
10. E. S. Corwin, *The Doctrine of American Judicial Review* (Princeton, 1914), pp. 84, 90-91; Washington, *Writings* (Fitzpatrick), XXIX, 526; Brant, *James Madison, Father of the Constitution*, p. 16; A. C. McLaughlin, *Constitutional History of the United States* (New York, 1935), p. 149.
11. Washington, *Writings* (Fitzpatrick), XXIX, 526; Brant, *James Madison, Father of the Constitution*, p. 16; Tansill, *Documents*, pp. 748-749.
12. Tansill, *Documents*, p. 219.
13. *Ibid.*, pp. 221, 915; Strayer, *The Delegate from New York*, pp. 60, 67, 77; *Federalist*, p. 140; Max Farrand (ed.), *Records of the Federal Convention of 1787* (New Haven, 1911-37), III, 409-410; George Shea, *The Life and Epoch of Alexander Hamilton* (New York, 1881), p. 85.
14. Edward C. Mason, *The Veto Power* (Boston, 1931), p. 17; McLaughlin, *Constitutional History*, pp. 154, 163-166; Hamilton, *Works* (Lodge), I, 216; B. J. Lossing, *Philip Schuyler* (New York, 1873), II, 439; Strayer, *The Delegate from New York*, pp. 63-64; Tansill, *Documents*, pp. 99, 783.
15. Tansill, *Documents*, pp. 90, 219, 979; Madison, *Writings* (Hunt), III, 183-184; *Selected Essays on Constitutional Law*, II, 913-914.
16. Strayer, *The Delegate from New York*, pp. 63-64, 122; Tansill, *Documents*, pp. 216, 219, 778-779, 786; *The Review of Politics*, II (1940), 108; K. C. Wheare, *Federal Government* (Oxford, 1947), p. 15; Schuyler, *The Constitution of the United States*, p. 46; *Federalist*, p. 194; James Wilkinson, *Memoirs of My Own Times* (Philadelphia, 1816), I, 464.
17. C. H. McIlwain, *Constitutionalism and the Changing World* (Cambridge, Eng., 1939), pp 69-70; R. G. Adams, *Selected Political Essays of James Wilson* (New York, 1930),

Notes 585

p. 173; Roscoe Pound et al., *Federalism as a Democratic Process* (New Brunswick, N. J., 1942), p. 23.
18. Tansill, *Documents*, 812; Hamilton, *Works* (Lodge), II, 462; X, September 18, 1803; *Federalist*, pp. 137-138.
19. J. L. De Lolme, *The Constitution of England* (London, 1775), pp. 13, 36; Wright, *Growth of American Constitutional Law*, pp. 24-25.
20. *Federalist*, p. 137.
21. *Ibid.*, pp. 137-138.
22. Tansill, *Documents*, pp. 782, 913; Strayer, *The Delegate from New York*, p. 67.
23. Tansill, *Documents*, p. 290.
24. *Ibid.*, p. 221.
25. Elliot, *Debates*, III, 164; Friedrich, *Constitutional Government and Democracy*, pp. 27-28; Lord Acton, *Essays on Freedom and Power*, p. 200; A. F. Pollard, *Factors in American History* (New York, 1925), pp. 68-69.

Chapter 11   The Constitutional Convention (2)

1. W. C. Ford (ed.), *Correspondence and Journals of Samuel B. Webb* (New York, 1894), III, 108, 169; Tansill, *Documents*, pp. 98-99, 220, 785-786, 830, 834, 837, 854, 859; Bancroft, *History of the Constitution*, I, 491; Jay, *Writings* (Johnston), III, 244; Charles Warren, *The Making of the Constitution* (Boston, 1937), pp. 443-444; *Annals of Congress*, II, 800-801; *Papers of Noah Webster*, pp. 330-331; *General Advertiser*, January 13, 1798; November 15, 1799; Beard, *The Supreme Court and the Constitution*, pp. 88, 91, 96; *Port Folio*, July 21, 1804; Strayer, *The Delegate from New York*, p. 38.
2. Tansill, *Documents*, pp. 785-786.
3. Scott, *The Federalist*, p. 670.
4. Brant, *James Madison, Father of the Constitution*, pp. 40, 105-106.
5. William Thompson Read, *The Life and Correspondence of George Read* (Philadelphia, 1870), pp. 453-454; Tansill, *Documents*, p. 851; Brant, *James Madison, Father of the Constitution*, pp. 52, 64.
6. Strayer, *The Delegate from New York*, p. 83.
7. Tansill, *Documents*, pp. 102-103.
8. *Ibid.*, pp. 787-788.
9. *Ibid.*, pp. 296-297.
10. *Ibid.*, p. 847; Brant, *James Madison, Father of the Constitution*, p. 106.
11. E. S. Corwin, *The President, Office and Powers* (New York, 1948), p. 11.
12. Tansill, *Documents*, pp. 675-676.
13. *Ibid.*, p. 649; Brant, *James Madison, Father of the Constitution*, p. 72.
14. *American Political Science Review*, XXXII (1938), 4; Elliot, *Debates*, III, 28; R. L. Schuyler, *The Constitution of the United States* (Boston, 1923), p. 152; Oster, *John Marshall*, p. 311.
15. Warren, *Making of the Constitution*, pp. 610, 684; Schuyler, *The Constitution*, 152; *Essays in the Constitutional History of the United States*, p. 48; *American Political Science Review*, XXXII (1938), 4; Mitchell, *Alexander Hamilton*, pp. 412-413; *Federalist*, 141, 570; Tansill, *Documents*, p. 812.

Chapter 12.   The Federalist

1. Hamilton, *Works* (Lodge), I, 424; E. H. Scott (ed.), *The Federalist and Other Papers* (Brooklyn, 1892), II, 616-618, 643, 645-646.
2. Washington, *Writings* (Fitzpatrick), XXIX, 290-291; Hamilton, *Works* (Lodge), I, 424, 429; *Letters of Richard Henry Lee*, II, 475-476.
3. Monaghan, *Jay*, p. 288; *Federalist*, pp. 5, 437-438, 440-441, 568-569.
4. *Federalist*, pp. 226, 437-438, 440-441, 457, 568-569; *University of Chicago Law Review*, XXI (1953), 79, 84; Pound, *Federalism as a Democratic Process*, p. 79.
5. *Federalist*, pp. 140, 226, 396.
6. Ernest Barker, *Essays on Government* (Oxford, 1951), p. 127.
7. Madison, *Writings* (Hunt), V, 66-67, 81; Monaghan, *Jay*, p. 283.

8. *William and Mary Quarterly*, Third Series, III (1946), 565; *Federalist*, p. 241.
9. *William and Mary Quarterly*, IV (1947), pp. 219-220; Monaghan, *Jay*, pp. 289-290; *American Historical Review*, II (1897), 685.
10. Edward Gaylord Bourne (ed.), *The Federalist* (Washington, 1901), pp. vii-viii; *William and Mary Quarterly*, Third Series, I (1944), 244.

Chapter 13. The Rule of Law

1. Charles A. Beard, *The Enduring Federalist* (New York, 1948), pp. 1, 7; A. N. Holcombe, *Our More Perfect Union* (Cambridge, 1950), p. 192; *Federalist*, pp. 248-249.
2. *Federalist*, p. 3.
3. *Ibid.*, pp. 87-88, 94-95.
4. *Ibid.*, pp. 40, 46, 42-44, 65-66.
5. *Ibid.*, pp. 29-31, 47, 49-50, 206; *William and Mary Quarterly*, Third Series, IV (1947), 237-238.
6. *Federalist*, pp. 62-63, 388.
7. *Ibid.*, pp. 145-146, 186, 188, 205, 214.
8. *Ibid.*, pp. 191-192; *American Historical Review*, LX (1955), 334.
9. *Federalist*, pp. 495-496.
10. *Ibid.*, pp. 163-164, 170-171, 202, 209, 249, 255.
11. James Kent to Elizabeth Hamilton, December 10, 1832, James Kent MSS., LC.
12. *Ethics*, LIX (1949), 10-11; *Federalist*, pp. 30, 364-365, 409-410, 495-496.
13. *Federalist*, p. 464; *Ethics*, LIX (1949), 12, 27-28; Beard, *The Enduring Federalist*, 13-15; John Laird, *Hume's Philosophy of Human Nature* (London, 1932), p. 188; *Federalist*, 32-33, 464; Tansill, *Documents*, p. 273; Adams, *James Wilson*, p. 165.
14. *Ethics*, LIX (1949), 16-17.
15. *Federalist*, pp. 4, 47; *American Historical Review*, LX (1955), 332-333.
16. *Cornell Law Quarterly*, XII (1927), 546-547; Benjamin Cardozo, *The Nature of the Judicial Process* (New Haven, 1921), p. 48; Charles G. Haines, *The American Doctrine of Judicial Supremacy* (New York, 1914), p. 140; A. Lawrence Lowell, *Essays on Government* (Boston, 1892), p. 40; Joseph Story, *Commentaries*, abridged (Boston, 1858), pp. 117-118; *Texas Law Review*, XXII (1944), 253; *American Political Science Review*, XXII (1928), 277-278; *Michigan Law Review*, IX (1910), 109; *Federalist*, pp. 505-506.
17. W. W. Buckland, *Some Reflections on Jurisprudence* (Cambridge, 1945), p. 9; Haines, *Judicial Supremacy*, p. 18; *New York Journal and Weekly Register*, May 3, 1787; James M. Varnum, *The Case Trevett against Weeden* (Providence, 1787), pp. 23-29, 35-36; *Michigan Law Review*, IX (1910), 191, 316 footnote.
18. *Michigan Law Review*, IX (1910), 113-114; *Ethics*, LIX, 14-15; Benjamin F. Wright, *The Growth of American Constitutional Law* (New York, 1946), pp. 14, 17-18, 21-22; E. S. Corwin, *The Doctrine of Judicial Review* (Princeton, 1914), pp. 28-30; *Selected Essays on Constitutional Law*, I, 39-43, 164; James Bryce, *The American Commonwealth* (New York, 1888), I, 218; Fred Rodell, *Fifty-Five Men* (New York, 1936), p. 112; Tansill, *Documents*, 44; Holcombe, *Our More Perfect Union*, 40-41; *Harvard Law Review*, LXVII (1954), 1481-1482; *Federalist*, p. 508.
19. A. C. McLaughlin, *The Foundations of American Constitutionalism* (New York, 1932), p. 78; W. S. Carpenter, *The Development of American Political Thought* (Princeton, 1930), p. 73; *Federalist*, pp. 505-506, 510-511, 526; Haines, *Judicial Supremacy*, pp. 178-179; Percy T. Finn, *The Development of the Constitution* (New York, 1948), pp. 3-4; Story, *Commentaries*, pp. 117-119; *Ethics*, LIX (1949), 14, 16; *American Historical Review*, XXX (1925), 525; *Selected Essays on Constitutional Law*, I, 162 footnote; Holcombe, *Our More Perfect Union*, 40; *American Political Science Review*, XXII (1928), 276-278; Cardozo, *The Nature of the Judicial Process*, pp. 14-15, 16-17; E. S. Corwin, *Twilight of the Supreme Court* (New Haven, 1934), p. 181; *Harvard Law Review*, XLI (1928), 125.
20. Finn, *The Development of the Constitution*, pp. 6, 55; *Harvard Law Review*, XLI (1928), 125; *Cornell Law Review*, XII, 548; Cardozo, *The Nature of the Judicial Process*, pp. 14-16; Wright, *Growth of American Constitutional Law*, pp. 8, 25, 37, 244; *Ethics*, LIX

(1949), 16-17; Corwin, *Twilight of the Supreme Court*, p. 155; *Michigan Law Review*, IX (1910), 109-110; Pound, *Federalism as a Democratic Process*, p. 27; Haines, *The American Doctrine of Judicial Supremacy*, pp. 198-199.

Chapter 14. A More Perfect Union

1. Washington, *Writings* (Fitzpatrick), XXIX, 324, 331, 346; XXX, 66; *Harvard Law Review*, LXVII, 1, 1443-1445.
2. R. A. Rutland, *The Birth of the Bill of Rights* (Chapel Hill, 1955), p. 150.
3. Rufus King to Wadsworth, December 23, 1787, Jeremiah Wadsworth MSS., LC; New York *Evening Post*, February 5, 1802.
4. *Federalist*, pp. 3-4.
5. Scott, *The Federalist*, 910; John T. Horton, *James Kent* (New York, 1939), p. 55; *William and Mary Quarterly*, Third Series (1944), pp. 235, 236, footnote; *Harvard Law Review*, LXVII, 1443-1445; E. K. Bauer, *Commentaries on the Constitution* (New York, 1952), pp. 344-345.
6. Jared Sparks (ed.), *Correspondence of the American Revolution* (Boston, 1853), IV, 173; *Pennsylvania Gazette*, April 30, 1788; Warren, *Making of the Constitution*, p. 767; Octavius Pickering and Charles W. Upham, *Life of Timothy Pickering* (Boston, 1867-1873), II, 340-341.
7. Strayer, *The Delegate from New York*, p. 92.
8. Spaulding, *New York in the Critical Period*, pp. 70, 74, 76-77, 80; Elliot, *Debates*, II, 19-20, 38-40.
9. Madison, *Writings* (Hunt), V, 81; F. S. Oliver, *Alexander Hamilton, An Essay on American Union* (London, 1915), p. 169; Monaghan, *Jay*, p. 283.
10. Massachusetts Historical Society, *Collections*, Fifth Series (Boston, 1877), III, 48; Spaulding, *New York in the Critical Period*, pp. 151-152, 199-200, 225.
11. *Pennsylvania Gazette*, June 25, 1788; Hamilton, *Works* (Lodge), IX, p. 434.
12. Miner, *New York Ratification*, p. 98.
13. Elliot, *Debates*, II, 301, 304, 353, 355.
14. *Ibid.*, II, 255, 259.
15. *Ibid.*, II, 322, 358, 360, 366, 370-371; James Kent to Elizabeth Hamilton, December 10, 1832, Kent MSS., LC; New York *Daily Advertiser*, July 16, 1788; Miner, *New York Ratification*, p. 111.
16. Minutes of Proceedings, June 19, 1788, McKesson MSS., NYHS; Bancroft, *History of the Constitution*, II, 472; Hamilton, *Works* (Lodge), IX, 435; Hamilton's Notes of Debates in the New York Convention, Hamilton MSS., LC; Elliot, *Debates*, II, 404, 406; Isaac Q. Leake, *Memoirs of General John Lamb* (Albany, 1850), p. 315; Strayer, *The Delegate from New York*, p. 66.
17. Elliot, *Debates*, II, 312, 376; Tansill, *Documents*, 786; Schuyler to Stephen van Rensselaer, November 26, 1787, Schuyler MSS., LC; *Federalist* (Ford), pp. xxi, 664-665; New York *Daily Advertiser*, July 4, 1788; Miner, *New York Ratification*, p. 103; Leake, *General John Lamb*, 315.
18. Elliot, *Debates*, II, 370; Hamilton, *Works* (Lodge), IX, 432; Joshua Atherton to John Lamb, June 11, 1788, Lamb MSS., LC; Rufus King to John Langdon, June 4, 1788, King MSS., NYHS; Sullivan, *Letters and Papers*, III, 591.
19. New York *Daily Advertiser*, July 16, 1788; Schuyler to Van Rensselaer, July 14, 1788, Schuyler MSS., LC.
20. New York *Daily Advertiser*, July 26, 1788; *Historical Magazine*, Second Series, VI (1869), 349.
21. Daniel Chipman, *Life of Nathaniel Chipman* (Boston, 1846), pp. 71-72.
22. Elliot, *Debates*, II, 236; John Marshall, *The Life of George Washington* (Philadelphia, 1804-7), V, 177; *Pennsylvania Gazette*, January 18, 1788; Rufus King to Wadsworth, December 23, 1787, Jeremiah Wadsworth MSS., LC; *Essays on the Constitutional History of the United States*, p. 87.

Chapter 15. The First Secretary of the Treasury

1. Washington, *Writings* (Fitzpatrick), XXX, 110-111, 119, 121, 148, 171, 185-186, 268; Marshall, *Washington*, V, 135; Hamilton, *Writings* (Lodge), IX, 441, 444-445.
2. *Federalist*, pp. 441-443.
3. Hamilton, *Writings* (Lodge), VIII, 311; IX, 452-454; Madison, *Writings* (Hunt), V, 270.
4. Channing, *History*, IV, 170-171; Hamilton, *Writings* (Lodge), VIII, 315-316; R. L. Brunhouse, *The Counter-Revolution in Pennsylvania* (Harrisburg, 1942), p. 218.
5. *Letters to Washington* (Sparks), IV, 266; *Pennsylvania Magazine of History and Biography*, XXXVIII (1914), 54; *Annals of Congress*, III, 210-211; Madison, *Writings* (Hunt), V, 371; *Pennsylvania Gazette*, May 13, 1785.
6. *Federalist*, pp. 63-64.
7. *Report on Canadian Archives, 1890* (Ottawa, 1891), pp. 121-122.
8. Morgan Lewis to Robert Troup, April, 1789, Hamilton MSS., LC; Hamilton, *Works* (Lodge), IX, 457-458; E. P. Panagapoulos, "Hamilton's Notes in His Pay Book of the New York State Artillery Company," *American Historical Review*, LXII (January, 1957), 310-325.
9. Henry C. Adams, *Public Debts* (New York, 1890), p. 262.
10. W. G. Sumner, *Finances and Financiers of the American Revolution* (New York, 1891), II, 208-210; E. P. Oberholtzer, *Robert Morris* (New York, 1903), pp. 214-215; Conversation with William Duer, October 12, 1789, Rufus King MSS., NYHS; Brant, *Madison, The Nationalist*, pp. 130-131; Warren, *Making of the Constitution*, p. 647; Monaghan, *Jay*, p. 301; Christopher Gore to King, September 13, 1789, Rufus King MSS., NYHS; Charles F. Dunbar, *Economic Essays* (New York, 1904), p. 72 footnote.
11. Kenneth and Anna M. Roberts (eds.), *Moreau de St. Méry's American Journey* (New York, 1947), p. 138; *William and Mary Quarterly*, Third Series, XI (October 1954), 599.
12. Seth Ames (ed.), *The Works of Fisher Ames* (Boston, 1854), II, 258-260, 262.
13. Oliver, *Alexander Hamilton*, p. 431.
14. Morris, *Gouverneur Morris*, II, 524.
15. Hamilton, *Works* (J. C. Hamilton), I, 431; Marshall, *Washington*, V, 212-213; Fisher Ames, *Works*, II, 258; Obituary Notice, Pendleton MSS., NYHS; Lodge, *Alexander Hamilton*, p. 272.

Chapter 16. The Report on Public Credit

1. *Federalist*, pp. 101-102, 105, 192-193, 200, 534; Massachusetts Historical Society, *Proceedings*, Second Series, XVI (1902), 129; Madison, *Writings* (Hunt), V, 336; Marshall, *Life of Washington*, V, 178, 353; Hamilton, *Works* (Lodge), I, 422.
2. Matthew McConnell, *An Essay on the Domestic Debts of the United States* (Philadelphia, 1787), pp. 7-8.
3. Warren, *The Making of the Constitution*, pp. 469-470; *Letters Addressed to the Yeomanry of the United States, By an American Farmer* (Philadelphia, 1793), p. 7; *Herald of Freedom and Federal Advertiser*, February 16, July 23, 1790; *Columbian Centinel*, August 7, 1790; *General Advertiser*, April 24, 1792; *Gazette of the United States*, February 22, 1792.
4. Hamilton, *Works* (Lodge), VIII, 421, 448; Dunbar, *Economic Essays*, p. 81.
5. John H. Morison, *The Life of Jeremiah Smith* (Boston, 1845), p. 57; *Federalist*, pp. 22-23.
6. Joseph S. Davis, *American Corporations* (Cambridge, 1917), I, 181-182; Tansill, *Documents*, p. 605; Peletiah Webster, *A Seventh Essay on Free Trade and Finance* (Philadelphia, 1785), pp. 20-22; R. L. Brunhouse, *The Counter-Revolution in Pennsylvania* (Philadelphia, 1942), p. 169; *Journals of the Continental Congress*, XXV, 905; Dewey, *Financial History*, p. 46; Burnett, *Letters*, VIII, 223-224, 293, 313; Webb, *Correspondence and Journals*, III, 69; Charles P. Noyes (ed.), *A Family History in Letters and Documents* (St. Paul, Minn., 1914), p. 152; Studenski and Krooss, *Financial History*, p. 56; McLaughlin, *Constitutional History*, pp. 194, 195 footnote.
7. Hamilton, *Works* (Lodge), II, 436, 442; VIII, 38, 455; IX, 17; William Bradford to

Elias Boudinot, January 21, 1790, Bradford to ?, January 5, 1790, Wallace MSS., PHS; Benjamin Rush to John Montgomery, March 27, 1789, Rush MSS., LCP; "Foreigner" to Madison, February 17, 1790, Madison MSS., NYPL; Edward Carrington to Madison, March 27, 1790, Madison MSS., NYPL; McConnell, *An Essay on the Domestic Debt of the United States*, p. 23; Dorfman, *Economic*, I, 293; *Annals of Congress*, II, 1250-1251; *Documents Relating to the Revolutionary History of New Jersey* (Trenton, 1914), III, 29, 31, 311; Burnett, *Continental Congress*, p. 408; William Gordon to Gates, June 17, 1779, Gates MSS., NYHS.
8. New York *Daily Advertiser*, February 18, 1790; Hamilton, *Works* (Lodge), VIII, 13-14.
9. Samuel McKee, Jr. (ed.), *Papers on Public Credit, Commerce and Finance* (New York, 1957), pp. 5-6; Craigie to Daniel Parker, October 2, 1789, Craigie MSS., AAS.
10. Davis, *American Corporations*, I, 182.
11. Peletiah Webster, *A Seventh Essay on Free Trade and Finance* (Philadelphia, 1785), pp. 4, 6; Webb, *Correspondence and Journals*, III, 55; New York *Daily Advertiser*, February 14, 1786; William Gordon to Benjamin Rush, July 27, 1792, Rush MSS., LCP; Bancroft, *History of the Constitution*, II, 411; Washington, *Writings* (Fitzpatrick) 29, 260; *American State Papers, Finance*, I, 82; Hamilton, *Works* (Lodge), IX, 539; *Life, Letters and Journals of George Ticknor* (Boston, 1876), II, 113; *Federal Gazette and Philadelphia Evening Post*, February 5, 1790; *Remarks Occasioned by the Late Conduct of Mr. Washington* (Philadelphia, 1797), p. 63; Theodore Sedgwick, Notes of a Speech delivered on February 12, 1790, Hamilton MSS., LC; James Blanchard to Hamilton, May 3, 1790, Hamilton MSS., LC.
12. Washington, *Writings* (Fitzpatrick), XXIX, 57; Madison (Rives), III, 84; Davis, *American Corporations*, I, 142-143; Richard B. Morris (ed.), *American Business Enterprise in the American Revolutionary Era* (New York, 1938), pp. 279-280; Salem *Gazette*, July 20, 1798; Sparks, *Gouverneur Morris*, III, 4.
13. G. S. Hillard (ed.), *Life, Letters and Journals of George Ticknor* (Boston, 1876), II, p. 113.
14. Tansill, *Documents*, pp. 565-567; *Annals of Congress* II, 1313, 1608; Brant, *James Madison, Father of the Constitution*, pp. 134, 565; McKee, *Papers on Public Credit*, p. 17; Hamilton, *Writings* (Lodge), IX, 5, 19, 30-31; Scott, *Federalist*, pp. 513, 525-526; Burnett, *Letters*, VIII, 703; Gorham to Knox, January 20, 1790, Knox MSS., MHS; Craigie to Parker, November 5, 1789, Craigie MSS., AAS; Warren, *Making of the Constitution*, p. 466; William Irvine to His Wife, February 5, 1789, Irvine MSS., PHS; Madison, *Works* (Hunt), V, 48; Elliot, *Debates*, II, 132; Gibbs, *Memoirs*, I, 24-25.
15. Hamilton, *Works* (Lodge), VIII, 479-481; IX, 14, 16-17, 28, 460; *Federalist*, pp. 204, 207, 221; New York *Journal and Weekly Register*, April 5, 1787; Marshall, *Washington*, V, 250-251.
16. McKee, *Papers on Public Credit*, pp. 35, 45-46; Hamilton, *Works* (Lodge), VIII, 450-451, 457.
17. E. A. J. Johnson, *Predecessors of Adam Smith* (New York, 1937), pp. 170-171.
18. John Watts Kearney, *Sketch of American Finances* (New York, 1877), p. 13; McKee, *Papers on Public Credit*, p. 25; Hildreth, *History*, IV, 155-156.
19. Richard Price, *Additional Observations on the Nature and Value of Civil Liberty* (London, 1777), pp. 181-182; *Journal of Business and Economic History* (1946), III, 673; Hargreaves, *The National Debt*, pp. 64, 80, 86; *The Works of . . . Sir James Steuart* (London, 1805), III, 144; *Pennsylvania Gazette*, November 18, 1789; *A Plan for the Payment of the National Debt* (New York, 1785), p. 6; *American State Papers*, VII, *Finance*, I, 78; Hamilton, *Works* (Lodge), VIII, 438; *Annals of Congress*, I, 792-795.

Chapter 17. "Speculators" vs. "Patriots"

1. James Hart, *The American Presidency in Action*, 1789 (New York, 1948), pp. 227-228, 230-232.
2. Colonial Society of Massachusetts, *Publications*, XXXV (1943), 33; *Pennsylvania Gazette*, March 11, 1789; William W. Crosskey, *Politics and the Constitution* (Chicago, 1953), I, 332-334; Madison (Rives), III, 84, 85, 88; Davis, *American Corporations*, I,

186-188; Paul D. Evans, *The Holland Land Company* (Buffalo, 1924), pp. 3-7; W. W. Bond, Jr. (ed.), *Correspondence of John Cleves Symmes* (New York, 1926), pp. 239-240; Madison to Rush, March 7, 1790, Madison MSS., LC; *Journals of the Continental Congress*, XXIV, 250, 283.
3. Peletiah Webster, *A Seventh Essay*, p. 16; Dorfman, *Economic Mind*, I, 293; *Gazette of the United States*, May 5, 1792; *Independent Chronicle*, July 31, 1794; John Taylor, *An Enquiry* (Philadelphia, 1794), p. 44; *Pennsylvania Gazette*, February 14, 1790; Abraham Bishop, *An Oration* (Philadelphia, 1800), p. 33; James Humbert, *Thoughts on the Nature of Civil Government* (New York, 1797), p. 34; *A Definition of Parties* (Philadelphia, 1794), p. 14; *Answer to Alexander Hamilton's Letter* (New York, 1800), pp. 4-5; Hamilton, *Works* (Lodge), VIII, 466; Madison (Rives), III, 177-178 footnote.
4. Jefferson, *Writings* (Boyd), 263 footnote, 266, 270-271.
5. *Mississippi Valley Historical Review* (December, 1951), pp. 406-408; *Remarks on the Report of the Secretary of the Treasury, By a Friend to the Public* (Philadelphia, 1790), pp. 18-19; Benjamin Foster to Craigie, April 7, May 6, 1790, Craigie MSS., AAS; *Essex Institute Historical Collections* (April, 1948), p. 152; Richard Henry Lee, *Letters*, II, 536; William Heth to Hamilton, February 21, 1790, Hamilton MSS., LC; *Gazette of the United States*, February 15, 1792; *A Review of the Revenue System* (Philadelphia, 1794), p. 16.
6. John Crawford to William Irvine, May 3, 1790, Irvine MSS., PHS.
7. Alexander Macomb to Wadsworth, September 21, 1790, Wadsworth MSS., CHS; *Independent Chronicle*, May 6, 1790; Hamilton, *Works* (Lodge), III, 20-21.
8. Hamilton, *Works* (Lodge), IX, 465.
9. Hamilton, *Works* (Lodge), I, 58; IX, 460, 465-466; Tansill, *Documents*, 722; Sumner, *Finances and Financiers*, II, 18-19; T. P. Abernethy, *Western Lands and the American Revolution* (New York, 1937), pp. 173, 210.
10. Davis, *American Corporations*, I, 184; William H. Hill, *History of Washington County, New York* (Fort Edward, N.Y., 1933), p. 185; Madison, *Writings* (Hunt), V, 460; Hamilton to Samuel Osgood, September 14, 1789, Livingston MSS., NYHS.
11. Davis, *American Corporations*, I, 124, 130, 134-135, 139, 159, 166; Channing, *History*, IV, 98.
12. Sidney J. Pomerantz, *New York* (New York, 1938), pp. 181, 183 footnote; Craigie to Daniel Parker, October 30, 1789, Craigie MSS., AAS; G. A. Corner (ed.), *Benjamin Rush* (Princeton, 1948), pp. 268-269; *Remarks on the Report of the Secretary of the Treasury*, pp. 18-19.
13. *Journal of Business and Economic History*, III (1946), 671; Benjamin Foster to Craigie, May 6, 1790, Craigie MSS., AAS.
14. *Essex Institute Historical Collections* (April, 1948), p. 158; Hamilton, *Works* (Lodge), IX, 442-443.
15. William Bradford to Elias Boudinot, September 6, 1789, Wallace MSS., PHS; Burnett, *Letters*, VII, 347, 349; Maclay, *Journal*, 220, 263; Thomas Hartley to Yeates, July 29, August 28, September 6, 1789; January 24, 1790, Yeates MSS., HSP; *Pennsylvania Gazette*, September 16, 1789; *An Essay on the Seat of the Federal Government, By a Citizen of Philadelphia* (Philadelphia, 1789), pp. 25-27.
16. Dorfman, *Economic Mind*, I, 434, 445; Bolles, *Financial History*, I, 356; Jefferson, *Papers* (Boyd), VI, 364-365; *American Political Science Review*, XIII (1914), 383.
17. Saul K. Padover, *Thomas Jefferson and the National Capital* (Washington, 1946), p. 14; Jefferson, *Papers* (Boyd), VIII, 331; Jefferson, *Writings* (Ford), I, 162; Harold Hutcheson, *Tench Coxe* (Philadelphia, 1938), p. 25; Thomas Hartley to Yeates, March 14, 1790; July 29, August 28, September 6, 1789, Yeates MSS., HSP; *Pennsylvania Gazette*, September 16, 1789; Maclay, *Journal*, p. 263.
18. R. H. Lee, *Letters*, II, 526; *Pennsylvania Magazine of History and Biography*, LXX (1946), 102; Benjamin Rush to Madison, July 17, 1790, Madison MSS., LC; Thomas Hartley to Yeates, June 9, 1790, Yeates MSS., HSP; Webb, *Correspondence and Journals*, III, 161; Fisher Ames, *Works*, II, 79-80.
19. Jefferson, *Writings* (Ford), I, 62-63; Jefferson, *Writings* (Boyd), VI, 364-365, 371; Rush, *Commonplace Book* (Corner), p. 181; Padover, *Jefferson and the National Capital*,

Notes

p. 14; W. P. and J. P. Cutler, *The Life Journals and Correspondence of the Reverend Manasseh Cutler* (Cincinnati, 1888), I, 237; I. N. P. Stokes, *Iconography of Manhattan Island* (New York, 1915-28), V, 1267-1268; *The Alexander Biddle Papers* (New York, Parke-Bernet Galleries, 1943), pp. 50-51; R. H. Lee, *Letters*, II, 532; *Historical Collections of the Essex Institute* (April, 1948), p. 159.

20. Jefferson, *Writings* (Ford) I, 162, 164, 215; Lewis Burd Walker (ed.), *The Burd Papers* (Philadelphia, 1897), p. 162; *Pennsylvania Magazine of History and Biography*, XXXVIII (1914), 204; Stokes, *Iconography*, V, 1268; *The Politicks and Views of a Certain Party Displayed* (Philadelphia, 1792), pp. 13-14; Jefferson, *Writings* (Boyd), VI, 365-366, 371; Madison, *Writings* (Hunt), VI, 16; *Essex Institute Historical Collections* (April, 1948), p. 159; McRee, *Iredell*, II, 301; S. M. Hamilton (ed.), *Writings of James Monroe* (New York, 1898-1903), I, 209; Edward Carrington to Madison, April 7, 1790, Madison MSS., NYPL.

21. John P. Branch *Historical Papers* (Richmond, 1905), II, 253-254, 258-259; *Independent Chronicle*, October 10, 1793; Fisher Ames, *Works*, I, 404; *A Review of the Funding System*, pp. 125-126, 130; Washington, *Writings* (Fitzpatrick), XXXI, 28; XXXII, 95, 98; Henry Lee to Madison, April 3, 1790, Madison MSS., LC; Theodore Sedgwick to Williams, December 20, 1790; January 10, 1791, Sedgwick MSS., MHS; *Columbian Centinel*, December 4, 1790; Hamilton, *Works* (Lodge), VIII, 442.

22. Ibid., VIII, 430-435; *Federalist*, pp. 70-71; Seymour E. Harris, *The National Debt and the New Economics* (New York, 1947), p. 276.

23. Harris, *The National Debt and the New Economics*, p. 68; Jared Sparks, *The Life of Gouverneur Morris* (Boston, 1832), III, September 17, 1790.

Chapter 18. The Bank of the United States

1. Gaillard Hunt (ed.), *Disunion Sentiment in Congress in 1794* (Washington, 1905), p. 21; *Annals of Congress*, III, 1040, 1106-1107; John P. Branch *Historical Papers*, II, 252-254, 258-259; Massachusetts Historical Society, *Collections*, Fifth Series (1878), III, 266.

2. Elliot, *Debates*, III, 171; *Annals of Congress*, II, 1313; Maclay, *Journal*, p. 286; William Wirt Henry, *Patrick Henry* (New York, 1891), III, 405; John Page, *An Address* (Philadelphia, 1794), pp. 22, 27-28; *A Review of the Revenue System* (Philadelphia, 1794), pp. 27, 36; *An Examination of the Conduct of the Executive of the United States* (Philadelphia, 1797), pp. 40-41; *General Advertiser*, June 16, 1794.

3. Edward Carrington to Madison, April 7, 1790, Madison MSS., NYPL; McRee, *Iredell*, II, 301; Monroe, *Writings* (Hamilton), I, 209; Henry Lee to Madison, April 3, 1790, Madison MSS., LC; Washington, *Writings* (Fitzpatrick), XXXI, 28; XXXII, 45, 48.

4. Theodore Sedgwick to Williams, December 20, 1790; January 10, 1791, Sedgwick MSS., MHS; *Columbian Centinel*, December 4, 1790.

5. H. P. Johnston (ed.), *Correspondence and Public Papers of John Jay* (New York, 1890-93), III, 410.

6. Madison, *Works* (Hunt), VI, 19-20; R. H. Lee, *Letters*, II, 534; *A Review of the Revenue System*, p. 24; Channing, *History*, IV, 79; Hamilton, *Works* (Lodge), II, 436-440; IX, 32-33, 473-474; Studenski and Krooss, *Financial History*, p. 53; Henry M. Wagstaff (ed.), *The Papers of John Steele* (Raleigh, 1924), I, 83; *American State Papers, Finance*, I, 150; Henry C. van Schaack, *Life of Peter van Schaack* (New York, 1892), p. 437; Gallatin, *Writings* (Adams), III, 133; *Annals of Congress*, XIII, 933; *National Gazette*, January 26, 1792; *General Advertiser*, May 11, 1792; *Gazette of the United States*, February 19, 1791.

7. *Scots' Magazine* (1785), p. 453; Richard Price, *Additional Observations on the Nature and Value of Civil Liberty* (London, 1777), pp. 64-65; Joseph Priestley, *Lectures on History and General Policy* (Birmingham, 1785), p. 513; Hargreaves, *The National Debt*, pp. 75-77; Adam Smith, *Wealth of Nations* (New York, 1937), p. 27; *Independent Chronicle*, February 24, 1794; Washington, *Writings* (Fitzpatrick), pp. 29, 476.

8. Dunbar, *Economic Essays*, p. 86; Hamilton, *Works* (Lodge), II, 411-412; Studenski and Krooss, *Financial History*, 53.

9. McKee, *Papers on Public Credit*, p. 47; Davis, *American Corporations*, I, 208-209; Channing, *History*, IV, 82; Hargreaves, *The National Debt*, pp. 1-2, 13, 104, 112; Maclay, *Journal*, pp. 354-355; Hamilton, *Works* (Lodge), VIII, 445; Steuart, *Works*, III, 141, 191; *Annals of Congress*, X, 394; Price, *Additional Observations*, p. 153; Seymour E. Harris, *The National Debt and the New Economics* (New York, 1947), pp. 65-66; Studenski and Krooss, *Financial History*, p. 53.
10. *Federalist*, p. 182.
11. McKee, *Papers on Public Credit*, pp. 145-146.
12. *Ibid.*, p. 72.
13. *Pennsylvania Magazine of History and Biography*, LXI (1915), 282; McKee, *Papers on Public Credit*, pp. 55, 66, 92; *Annals of Congress*, VII, 748; *Gazette of the United States*, March 10, 1792; Heckscher, *Mercantilism*, II, 234-235; Hildreth, *History*, I, 266.
14. Malachy Postlethwayt, *Great Britain's True System* (London, 1757), pp. 66, 90, 273; Dunbar, *Economic Essays*, p. 304; Smith, *Wealth of Nations*, p. 304; Sir J. H. Clapham, *The Bank of England* (Cambridge, Eng., 1945), I, 151, 193, 212, 226; Steuart, *Works*, II, 409; Thornton, *An Enquiry*, pp. 185-186; Hargreaves, *The National Debt*, p. 9; *Journal of Economic History*, VI (May, 1946), 84.
15. Hildreth, *History*, IV, 264-265; Clapham, *Bank of England*, I, 226; Thornton, *An Enquiry*, 109-110.
16. *Dunlap's American Daily Advertiser*, January 31, August 19, 1791; *Gazette of the United States*, February 19, 1791; *General Advertiser*, February 18, 1793.
17. Bray Hammond, *Banks and Politics in Early American History* (Princeton, 1957), p. 133; Redlich, *The Molding of American Banking*, pp. 12-13; McKee, *Papers on Public Credit*, pp. 73, 83-84.
18. J. T. Holdsworth and D. R. Dewey, *The First and Second Banks of the United States* (Washington, 1910), p. 32; Dunbar, *Economic Essays*, pp. 92-93; Samuel Paterson to Hamilton, February 15, 1791, Hamilton MSS., LC; Hildreth, *History*, IV, 25; *Gazette of the United States*, March 10, 1792; Miller, *Banking Theories*, 30-31; E. R. Taus, *Central Banking Functions of the United States Treasury* (New York, 1943), pp. 14, 16-17; McKee, *Papers on Public Credit*, pp. 32, 55, 66; *Pennsylvania Magazine of History and Biography*, XVI (1892), 282; *New York Evening Post*, April 14, 1802; Studenski and Krooss, *Financial History*, p. 63.
19. *American Historical Review*, XXX (1925), 529.
20. Channing, *History*, IV, 162; Crosskey, *Politics and the Constitution*, I, 206, 213-214.
21. B. F. Wright, *The Growth of American Constitutional Law* (New York, 1946), p. 47; *Harvard Law Review*, XLII (1928), pp. 41, 130-131.
22. *Harvard Law Review*, XII (1899), 414-420; *University of Chicago Law Review*, XXI (August, 1953), 40; McKee, *Papers on Public Credit*, pp. 101-103, 109, 128, 133, 135; Sir William Blackstone, *Commentaries* (Oxford, 1765-69), I, 41; *Selected Essays on Constitutional Law*, IV, 256-257; Story, *Commentaries*, 138-140, 143-144, 147-148; E. S. Corwin, *The Constitution* (Princeton, 1927), p. 34, and *The Twilight of the Supreme Court* (New Haven, 1934), pp. 2-3; Crosskey, *Politics and the Constitution*, I, 374; *Federalist*, p. 199; Oster, *Marshall*, pp. 282-283; Bauer, *Commentaries on the Constitution*, p. 322; Warren, *Making of the Constitution*, p. 485.
23. *Harvard Law School Bulletin*, II (October, 1951), 11; Marshall, *Washington*, V, 212-213; *William and Mary Quarterly*, Third Series, XII (January, 1955), 176.
24. Massachusetts Historical Society, *Proceedings* (Boston, 1914), pp. 42-43, 47.
25. *Ibid.*, pp. 42-43; Oster, *Marshall*, p. 313; *Selected Essays on Constitutional Law*, III, 42-43; Hildreth, *History*, I, 265; McKee, *Papers on Public Credit*, pp. 79-80; Madison, *Writings* (Hunt), VI, 43.
26. James Sullivan, *The Path to Riches* (Boston, 1792), p. 39; *General Advertiser*, June 25, 1791; Massachusetts Historical Society, *Collections*, Fifth Series (1877), III, 265; *Gazette of the United States*, July 2, 1791.
27. Madison, *Writings* (Hunt), V, 5; VI, 55; *A Review of the Revenue System*, pp. 79-80; *Dunlap's American Daily Advertiser*, July 12, 1791; Rush, *Autobiography* (Corner), pp. 203, 205-206; William Bradford to Boudinot, June 16, 1791, Wallace MSS., HSP; *General Advertiser*, May 29, 1792.

Notes 593

28. *Pennsylvania Gazette*, August 17, 1791; *General Advertiser*, July 11, 1791; Anthony Wayne to John Houston, August 29, 1791, Wayne MSS., HSP; William Morris to Duer, April 11, 1791, Duer MSS., NYHS; Hamilton to George Picet, John Graham, etc., August 27, 1791, Hamilton MSS., LC; *Dunlap's American Daily Advertiser*, July 8, 1791; *Pennsylvania Magazine of History and Biography*, LXI (1915), 273-274.
29. *Gazette of the United States*, August 13, 1791; *Pennsylvania Gazette*, July 20, 1791; Hamilton, *Works* (J. C. Hamilton), V, 473.
30. Hamilton, *Works* (Lodge), IX, 493-494; McKee, *Papers on Public Credit*, p. 21; Davis, *American Corporations*, I, 202-204; *National Gazette*, January 16, March 22, 1792; *Pennsylvania Gazette*, August 17, 1791; *A Review of the Revenue System*, p. 74; Nicholas Roosevelt to Duer, March 23, 1791, William Duer MSS., NYHS.
31. Hamilton, *Works* (Lodge), IX, 486.
32. *Burd Papers* (Walker), p. 173; Rush, *Autobiography* (Corner), pp. 205-207; *General Advertiser*, August 10, 1791; Davis, *American Corporations*, I, 205-207; Hamilton, *Works* (Lodge), IX, 490-491.
33. Talleyrand, *Memoirs*, I, 179-180; Redlich, *The Molding of American Banking*, pp. 12-13.
34. Holdsworth and Dewey, *The First and Second Banks of the United States*, p. 32; Agreement Between Alexander Hamilton and the President, Directors and Company of the Bank of the United States, Etting Papers, HSP; Hildreth, *History*, I, 399.
35. Hamilton to William Bingham, April 10, 1793, Gratz Coll., HSP., McKee, *Papers on Public Credit*, p. 127; Gallatin, *Writings* (Adams), III, 143; Esther R. Taus, *Central Banking Functions of the United States Treasury, 1789-1941* (New York, 1943), pp. 19-20.
36. Peletiah Webster, *To the Stockholders of the Bank of North America* (Philadelphia, 1786), p. 9.
37. Hamilton, *Works* (J. C. Hamilton), V, 474; Davis, *Essays*, pp. 55-56; Christopher Gore to King, April 1, 1792, King MSS., NYHS; Stephen Higginson to Hamilton, February 23, 1791, Hamilton MSS., LC.; Hamilton, *Works* (J. C. Hamilton), V, 509; Davis, *Essays*, pp. 94-95; William Seton to Hamilton, August 6, 1792, Hamilton MSS., LC.
38. Hamilton, *Works* (J. C. Hamilton), IX, 498; Allan Nevins, *History of the Bank of New York* (New York, 1934), p. 23.
39. Hamilton, *Works* (Lodge), II, 459; McKee, *Papers on Public Credit*, pp. 58, 73; *Journal of Economic History*, II (1945), 87; Gallatin to Thomas Willing, March 29, 1802, Etting MSS., HSP; *Annals of Congress*, VII, 799.

Chapter 19. The Report on Manufactures

1. Hutcheson, *Tench Coxe*, pp. 36, 99; Tench Coxe, *A View of the United States* (Philadelphia, 1794), pp. 50, 54-55; Dorfman, *Economic Mind*, I, 290.
2. Washington, *Writings* (Fitzpatrick), XXX, 218; Mathew Carey, *The American Museum* (Philadelphia, 1798), VI, 236-237; Robert A. East, *Business Enterprise in the American Revolutionary Period* (New York, 1938), p. 7; *Gazette of the United States*, June 18, 1791; Coxe, *View*, 228; McKee, *Papers on Public Credit*, p. 220; Cutler and Cutler, *Manasseh Cutler*, I, 205; Noah Webster, *Papers*, p. 260; *American Historical Review*, I (1896), 631-633.
3. Ralph H. Brown, *Mirror for Americans* (New York, 1943), pp. 43-44, 50; *General Advertiser*, March 8, May 7, June 8, 1792; *Pennsylvania Gazette*, October 29, 1798; A. S. P. Gras, *Business and Capitalism* (New York, 1939), p. 177; Davis, *Essays*, 283; Dorfman, *Economic Mind*, I, 27; *American State Papers*, VII, *Finance*, I, 5; Channing, *History*, IV, 62-63.
4. McKee, *Papers on Public Credit*, p. 233.
5. *Ibid.*, p. 77.
6. *Ibid.*, p. 193.
7. *Ibid.*, p. 173; *Gazette of the United States*, January 25, 1792; Henry Cabot Lodge, *Life and Letters of George Cabot* (Boston, 1877), p. 46; Adam Smith, *Wealth of Nations* (New York, Modern Library, 1937), pp. 5-6, 11, 249.

8. Coxe, *View*, pp. 54-55; Hutcheson, *Tench Coxe*, 152; Jefferson, *Writings* (Ford), VII, May 14, 1799.
9. *Gazette of the United States*, June 22, 1791; Smith, *Wealth of Nations*, p. 70; Henry Warfel, *Noah Webster, Schoolmaster to America* (New York, 1936), p. 209; Webb, *Correspondence and Journals*, III, 144; Washington, *Writings* (Fitzpatrick), XXX, 186; J. C. Fitzpatrick (ed.), *George Washington Diaries 1748-1777* (Boston, 1925), IV, 38; Kirkland, *History of American Economic Life*, pp. 341-342.
10. McKee, *Papers on Public Credit*, p. 206; Smith, *Wealth of Nations*, pp. 242-243.
11. McKee, *Papers on Public Credit*, p. 253; Robbins, *American Commercial Policy*, p. 126; *Federalist*, p. 210.
12. McKee, *Papers on Public Credit*, p. 224; Smith, *Wealth of Nations*, p. 91.
13. McKee, *Papers on Public Credit*, pp. 244-245.
14. *Ibid.*, pp. 66, 239; *Journal of Political Economy*, XXXVI (December, 1928), 424; Walton Hamilton and Douglas Adair, *The Power to Govern* (New York, 1937), pp. 68, 75, 90, 101; Charles A. Beard, *The Republic* (New York, 1943), p. 124; Heckscher, *Mercantilism*, II, 116-119, 164, 261, 293, 296, 318; Whittaker, *History of Economic Ideas*, pp. 284-285; Johnson, *Predecessors of Adam Smith*, p. 88; Hamilton, *Works* (Lodge), I, 267-268, 309; Miller, *Banking Theories*, pp. 23, 51; Ugo Robbins, *American Commercial Policy*, pp. 310, 313.
15. Herbert W. Schneider, *A History of American Philosophy* (New York, 1946), pp. 98-99.
16. Smith, *Wealth of Nations*, pp. 313, 325, 419, 433, 460-461, 863-865, 867, 880-881; Whittaker, *History of Economic Ideas*, p. 247; Eli Ginzberg, *The House of Adam Smith* (New York, 1934), pp. 17-18, 21, 46, 156-157; Lionel Robbins, *The Theory of Economic Policy* (London, 1952), pp. 21-22, 57-58, 66-73, 104; D. H. Macgregor, *Economic Thought and Policy* (Oxford, 1949), pp. 72, 78-79; John Maynard Keynes, *Laissez Faire and Communism* (New York, 1926), p. 14; *Quarterly Journal of Economics*, XLIV (1930), 240-241.
17. Basil Willey, *The Eighteenth Century Background* (New York, 1956), p. 95; Smith, *Wealth of Nations*, pp. 325, 421, 423, 431-435, 627-628; Ginzberg, *The House of Adam Smith*, pp. 156-158; Lionel Robbins, *Theory of Economic Policy*, pp. 12, 18; F. J. C. Hearnshaw, *The Social and Political Ideas of Some Representative Thinkers of the Revolutionary Era* (London, 1931), pp. 173-174, 177; Robert M. MacIver, *The Web of Government* (New York, 1947), p. 335; Whittaker, *History of Economic Ideas*, p. 316; *Journal of Political Economy*, XXXVI (1928), 432; Dunbar, *Economic Essays*, p. 47.

Chapter 20. The Effort to Transform the American Economy

1. Hamilton, *Works* (Lodge), II, 458-459; Fisher Ames, *Works*, I, 114-115.
2. Corwin, *The Constitution*, p. 20.
3. Bauer, *Commentaries on the Constitution*, p. 324; Crosskey, *Politics and the Constitution*, I, 367-368, 370-371; Warren, *Making of the Constitution*, p. 476.
4. K. C. Wheare, *Federal Government* (Oxford, 1953), p. 234; Warren, *Making of the Constitution*, pp. 473-476.
5. Beard, *The Republic*, iii; McKee, *Papers on Public Credit*, pp. 131, 239-240; Crosskey, *Politics and the Constitution*, I, 93, 375; *Texas Law Review*, XXXII (1952), 251; Hamilton, *Works* (Lodge), II, 454, 458; Henry Adams, *Documents Relating to New England Federalism, 1800-1815* (Boston, 1877), p. 6; James Bryce, *The American Commonwealth* (New York, 1888), I, 337-339; R. H. Lee, *Letters*, II, 445; Taylor, *An Enquiry*, p. 5; *William and Mary Quarterly*, Third Series, III (1946), 567-568; *Independent Chronicle*, September 15, 18, 1792; Channing, *History*, IV, 162; Tansill, *Documents*, p. 759; Rives, *Madison*, III, 106.
6. Brant, *James Madison, Father of the Constitution*, pp. 128, 180; Elliot, *Debates*, II, 503; Warren, *Making of the Constitution*, pp. 473-476; *Annals of Congress*, III, 385-386; Wheare, *Federal Government*, 234; *Selected Essays on Constitutional Law*, III, 568.
7. Washington, *Writings* (Fitzpatrick), XXX, 299-300; Corwin, *Twilight of the Supreme Court*, pp. 156-157.
8. Edward C. Kirkland, *A History of American Economic Life* (New York, 1933), pp.

Notes

341-342; *Gazette of the United States*, September 10, 1791; McKee, *Papers on Public Credit*, p. 241.
9. Davis, *American Corporations*, I, 368; Hutcheson, *Tench Coxe*, p. 158.
10. Davis, *American Corporations*, II, 95; Hamilton, *Works* (Lodge), IX, 512-513.
11. F. B. Tolles, *George Logan of Philadelphia* (New York, 1953), p. 122.
12. Nevins, *Bank of New York*, pp. 24-25; Davis, *Essays*, 83-87, 90; Stokes, *Iconography*, V, 1285; Henry W. Domett, *History of the Bank of New York* (Cambridge, 1884), pp. 40-42; Davis, *American Corporations*, II, 40.
13. *General Advertiser*, March 8, June 8, 1792; B. J. Lossing, *Life and Times of Philip Schuyler* (New York, 1873), II, 465-470; Elkanah Watson, *Men and Times of the Revolution* (New York, 1856), pp. 360-366.
14. Davis, *American Corporations*, I, 279-281; Channing, *History*, IV, 102; Seth Johnson to Craigie, January 8, 1792, Craigie MSS., AAS.
15. Rives, *Madison*, III, 244; *Burd Papers*, p. 174; Davis, *American Corporations*, I, 295.
16. Hamilton, *Works* (Lodge), IX, 502, 507; *Gazette of the United States*, April 21, 1792; Hamilton to P. Livingston, March 2, 1792, Livingston MSS., NYPL.
17. Channing, *History*, IV, 102.
18. William Seton to Hamilton, April 6, 1792, Hamilton MSS., LC; Hamilton, *Works* (Lodge), IX, 503-505; Schuyler to Hamilton, March 29, 1792, Hamilton MSS., LC; Hamilton, *Works* (J. C. Hamilton), V, 505; Davis, *American Corporations*, I, 295.
19. William Duer to Hamilton, March 18, 1792, Hamilton MSS., LC.
20. Charles S. Hall, *Benjamin Tallmadge* (New York, 1943), p. 127; Davis, *American Corporations*, I, 311-312.
21. Hamilton, *Works* (Lodge), IX, 503.
22. Rives, *Madison*, III, 245; Rush, *Autobiography*, p. 218; *General Advertiser*, April 17, 1792; Davis, *American Corporations*, I, 303-308; Seth Johnson to Craigie, April 10. 1792, Craigie MSS., AAS; Webb, *Journals and Correspondence*, III, 180; *A Review of the Revenue System*, p. 34; Hall, *Tallmadge*, p. 129.
23. *Gazette of the United States*, May 5, 1792; *Burd Papers*, 175; James Sullivan, *The Path to Riches* (Boston, 1792), Preface; Madison to Pendleton, April 15, 1792, Madison MSS., NYPL; W. B. Smith and A. H. Cole, *Fluctuations in American Business, 1790-1860* (Cambridge, 1935), p. 13; Allan McLane Hamilton, *Intimate Life of Alexander Hamilton* (New York, 1910), p. 273; Davis, *Essays*, pp. 88-89; William Seton to Hamilton, April 6, December 20, 1792, Hamilton MSS., LC.
24. Davis, *American Corporations* II, 91-93; Miller, *Banking Theories*, pp. 56-57.
25. Archibald Mercer to Hamilton, April 30, 1792, Hamilton MSS., LC; Nicholas Low to Hamilton, April 10, 1792, Hamilton MSS., LC; Rush, *Autobiography*, p. 218; Hamilton, *Works* (Lodge), IX, 510.
26. Davis, *American Corporations*, I, 318-319; A. H. Cole, *Industrial and Commercial Correspondence of Alexander Hamilton* (Chicago, 1928), p. 193.
27. Archibald Mercer to Hamilton, April 6, 1792, Hamilton MSS., LC.
28. Henry Wansey, *An Excursion to the United States of North America in 1794* (Salisbury, Eng., 1798), pp. 69-70; Davis, *American Corporations*, I, 400, 417, 499-500.
29. *Journal of Economic History* (1946), III, p. 217; Samuel L. Mitchell, *The Picture of New York* (New York, 1807), p. 181.
30. Kirkland, *History of American Economic Life*, pp. 305, 390.

Chapter 21. The Opposition Emerges

1. Bishop, *An Oration*, pp. 40-41.
2. Dorfman, *Economic Mind*, I, 438; John Taylor, *An Enquiry* (Philadelphia, 1794), pp. 71, 74-76; *National Gazette*, September 21, 1793; *A Review of the Revenue System*, pp. 33-34; Peletiah Webster, *To the Stockholders of the Bank of North America* (Philadelphia, 1791), p. 8; Marshall, *Washington*, V, 347; *Dunlap's American Daily Advertiser*, March 28, 1792; Maclay, *Journal*, p. 372; Jefferson to Volney, December 9, 1795, Jefferson MSS., LC.

3. George Turberville to Madison, January 28, 1793, Madison MSS., LC; Wilfred E. Binkley, *American Political Parties* (New York, 1943), p. 44.
4. John Williams, *Life of Alexander Hamilton* (Boston, 1804), p. 24; Tom Callender, *Letters to Alexander Hamilton, King of the Feds* (New York, 1802), pp. 31-32; *National Gazette*, August 14, 1793; Weld, *Travels*, p. 187; *Annals of Congress*, III, 547; Madison, *Writings* (Hunt), VI, 60; John Davis, *Travels* (New York, 1902), pp. 388-389.
5. *Virginia Magazine of History and Biography*, XLVI (1938), 289; Hamilton, *Works* (Lodge), VIII, 214.
6. Jefferson, *Writings* (Ford), VI, 145; *Virginia Magazine of History and Biography*, XLVI (1938), 288-289.
7. Jefferson, *Writings* (Ford), IX, 425; *Papers of Noah Webster*, 35; C. M. Wiltse, *The Jeffersonian Tradition in American Democracy* (Chapel Hill, 1935), p. 81.
8. William Dunlop, *History of the Province of New York* (New York, 1840), II, 265.
9. Richar Hofstadter, *The American Political Tradition and the Men Who Made It* (New York, 1948), p. 37; *American Political Science Review*, XIII (1915), 303; Wiltse, *Jeffersonian Tradition*, pp. 81, 84, 175-177; Jefferson, *Writings* (Ford), VII, August 13, 1800.
10. Jefferson, *Writings* (Ford), I, 115, 165; Roscoe Pound et al., *Federalism as a Democratic Process* (New Brunswick, N. J., 1942), pp. 51-52, 89.
11. Merle Fainsod, *Government and the American Economy* (New York, 1941), p. 84; B. J. Hendrick, *Bulwark of the Republic* (Boston, 1937), p. 112.
12. Jefferson, *Writings* (Ford), VII, December 15, 1800; American Philosophical Society, *Proceedings*, LXXXVII, No. 3 (July, 1943), 207.
13. Fisher Ames, *Works*, II, 159; James Hart, *The American Presidency in Action* (New York, 1948), pp. 28-29, 31, 34, 45-46; *Gazette of the United States*, November 24, 1794; Lyon G. Tyler, *Letters and Times of the Tylers* (Richmond, 1884-96), I, 170; Adams, *Gallatin*, p. 197; Massachusetts Historical Society, *Proceedings*, LVII (1924), 129.
14. Jefferson, *Writings* (Ford), I, 169; IX, 269, 295-296; *Gazette of the United States*, August 28, 1800; Fragment, Vol. 23, p. 3254, Fragment, Hamilton MSS., LC; Hamilton, *Works* (Lodge), VII, 287.
15. Conversation Between Judge Purdy and General Hamilton, February 25, 1804, Nathaniel Pendleton MSS., NYHS; Anonymous to Hamilton, August 30, 1793, Hamilton MSS., LC; *National Gazette*, August 14, 1793; Robert Slender (pseud.), *Letters on Various Interesting and Important Subjects* (Philadelphia, 1799), p. 42; *A Roaster; or, a Check to the Progress of Political Blasphemy* (Philadelphia, 1796), p. 4; *General Advertiser*, December 2, 1800; *Answer to A. Hamilton's Letter* (New York, 1800), p. 6; Marshall, *Washington*, V, 590; John Williams, *Life of Alexander Hamilton* (New York, 1805), pp. 17, 48; *University of Illinois Studies in the Social Sciences*, X (1920), 125.
16. *Independent Chronicle*, July 7, 1794; Hamilton, *Works* (Lodge), VII, 243.
17. Hamilton, *Works* (Lodge), IX, 532-533; James Wilkinson, *Memoirs of My Own Times* (Philadelphia, 1816), I, 469.
18. Louise Dunbar, *A Study of Monarchical Tendencies in the United States, 1776-1801* (New York, 1923), pp. 83-86; *William and Mary Quarterly*, Third Series (1946), p. 221; A. C. Morris (ed.), Gouverneur Morris, *Diary and Letters* (New York, 1888), II, 525; *Dunlap's American Daily Advertiser*, February 20, 1792; Jefferson, *Writings* (Ford) VI, 78.
19. Marshall, *Washington*, V, 610; Tansill, *Documents*, p. 948.
20. Hamilton, *Works* (Lodge), II, 454-455; IX, 534.
21. *Federalist*, p. 458; Washington, *Writings* (Fitzpatrick), XXXI, 48, 51; Holcombe, *Our More Perfect Union*, p. 401; *Gazette of the United States*, March 24, 1795; Elliot, *Debates*, II, 320; Hamilton MSS., LC; XXIII, 3255; Friedrich, *Constitutional Government and Democracy*, p. 304; Binkley, *American Political Parties*, pp. 61-62; *National Gazette*, September 26, 1792; Channing, *History*, IV, 169; Jefferson, *Writings* (Ford), I, 204, 215; Fisher Ames, *Works*, I, 142; *American Historical Review*, XIV (1909), 738, 787, 798.
22. *Papers of Noah Webster*, p. 332; *Letters of Franklin* (Philadelphia 1795), p. 28; Hamilton, *Works* (Lodge), III, 3; Weld, *Travels*, pp. 124-125.

Notes 597

Chapter 22. The Attack upon Hamilton

1. Mary L. Hinsdale, *A History of the President's Cabinet* (New York, 1911), pp. 19-20; Hamilton to Jay, December 10, 1792, Jay MSS., Columbia University.
2. Leonard D. White, *The Jeffersonians* (New York, 1951), p. 46, and *The Federalists* (New York, 1948), p. 58; Channing, *History*, IV, 150-151; Adams, *Gallatin*, p. 268.
3. *A Review of the Revenue System*, pp. 20, 85.
4. R. V. Harlow, *A History of Legislative Methods* (New York, 1917), pp. 149-150; Jefferson, *Writings* (Ford), I, 204; *National Gazette*, August 25, 1792; Maclay, *Journal*, pp. 373-374, 376; Findley, *History of the Insurrection*, p. 259; Gallatin, *Writings* (Adams), I, 67; *Five Letters Addressed to the Yeomanry of the United States, By a Farmer* (Philadelphia, 1792), p. 10; *General Advertiser*, April 18, 1792; White, *Jeffersonians*, p. 68.
5. White, *Jeffersonians*, pp. 71-72.
6. Hamilton, *Works* (Lodge), IX, 521-522; *General Advertiser*, April 18, 1792; *Gazette of the United States*, April 18, 1792; Rives, *Madison*, III, 274-275.
7. White, *Federalists*, p. 69.
8. Hamilton, *Works* (Lodge), VIII, 101; IX, 522; *Independent Chronicle*, December 9, 1793; *General Advertiser*, March 6, 1794.
9. Gallatin, *Writings* (Adams), III, 100-101, 111-112; *Dunlap's Daily American Advertiser*, March 9, 1793.
10. John Page, *An Address to the Citizens of the District of York* (Richmond, 1794), pp. 35-36; *Gazette of the United States*, January 13, 1793; *General Advertiser*, February 18, 1793; *A Review of the Revenue System*, p. 99; D. R. Anderson, *William Branch Giles* (Wisconsin, 1914), p. 20; Holdsworth and Dewey, *First and Second Banks of the United States*, pp. 60-61; Rives, *Madison*, III, 279-280.
11. *Gazette of the United States*, January 13, February 23, 1793; *National Gazette*, July 24, August 14, 1793; Rives, *Madison*, III, 292; *Political Truth* (Philadelphia, 1796), p. 13; Page, *An Address*, p. 35.
12. Dewey, *Financial History*, pp. 110, 116; Adams, *Gallatin*, pp. 114-115; *National Gazette*, July 24, 1793; *Gazette of the United States*, February 20, March 27, April 20, 1793; *General Advertiser*, February 18, 1793; Hamilton, *Works* (Lodge), VII, 374; Gibbs, *Memoirs of the Administrations of Washington and Adams*, I, 132-133.
13. Maclay, *Journal*, p. 374; *Annals of Congress*, III, 919.
14. *Gazette of the United States*, March 27, 1793; Rives, *Madison*, III, 282, 292; Joseph Jones to Madison, February 7, 1793, Madison MSS., LC; Page, *An Address*, p. 35; *National Gazette*, February 20, 27, July 24, August 14, 1793; *Political Truth* (Philadelphia, 1796), p. 11.
15. *Gazette of the United States*, February 20, 1793; Hildreth, *History*, IV, 396; Massachusetts Historical Society, *Collections*, Belknap Papers, Fifth Series, III (1877), 323.
16. Hamilton, *Works* (Lodge), VII, 373; Marshall, *Washington*, V, 386; Washington, *Writings* (Fitzpatrick), XXXVI, 190; Adams, *Gallatin*, pp. 114-115.
17. Hamilton, *Works* (Lodge), III, 63-64, 107, 124, 152-153; Holdsworth and Dewey, *First and Second Banks of the United States*, p. 61.
18. *Dunlap's American Daily Advertiser*, March 7, 1793; *National Gazette*, February 20, 1793; *General Advertiser*, February 18, 1793.
19. *The Nation*, LXI (1895), 163-164.
20. White, *Federalists*, pp. 68-69.
21. Jefferson, *Writings* (Ford), I, 222; Hildreth, *History*, IV, 409; Marshall, *Washington*, V, 385-387; Rives, *Madison*, III, 286; Robert Armstrong to Gates, March 14, 1793, Gates MSS., NYHS.
22. *Dunlap's American Daily Advertiser*, March 4, 1793; Hammond to Grenville, February 4, 1793, Hammond MSS., Henry Adams Trans., LC; Hildreth, *History*, IV, 393; *A Review of the Revenue System*, pp. 83-84.
23. Rives, *Madison*, III, 286 footnote; Hildreth, *History*, IV, 403; Anderson, *Giles*, pp. 21-22; Hammond to Grenville, March 7, 1793, Hammond Corr., LC.

24. Madison to Jefferson, April 12, 1793, Madison MSS., LC; Robert Armstrong to Gates, March 14, 1793, Gates MSS., NYHS; Madison, *Writings* (Hunt), VI, 210-211; *The Nation*, LXI (1895), 164.
25. Hamilton, *Works* (Lodge), III, 84, 190-193; V, 596; M. D. Conway, *Edmund Randolph* (New York, 1888), p. 217; Washington, *Writings* (Fitzpatrick), XXXIII, 318; *The Nation*, LXI (September 1895), 164; Hamilton, *Works* (J. C. Hamilton), V, 596; Manlius, *Boston, 1794*, p. 41; Gallatin, *Writings* (Adams), III, 111; Madison, *Writings* (Hunt), VI, 201-211; Taylor, *An Enquiry*, p. 3; *Independent Chronicle*, November 21, 1793; Massachusetts Historical Society, *Proceedings*, Second Series, XV (1902), 141; Marshall, *Washington*, V, 367.
26. Edward Carrington to Hamilton, July 2, 1793, Hamilton MSS., LC; Hamilton, *Works* (J. C. Hamilton), V, 598; *The Nation*, LXI (1895), 164-165.
27. Sarah Mumford to Hamilton, September 24, 1792, Hamilton and McLane MSS., LC.
28. Hamilton, *Works* (Lodge), VII, 391, 423-424, 427, 431, 438.
29. Hamilton, *Works* (Lodge), VII, 388-389, 396-397, 446; J. D. Schoepf, *Travels Through the Middle and Southern States of the United States* (Philadelphia, 1911), I, 100; Oliver Wolcott to Hamilton, July 3, 1797, Hamilton MSS., LC.
30. Hamilton, *Works* (Lodge), VII, 406-407.
31. P. A. W. Wallace, *The Muhlenbergs of Pennsylvania* (Philadelphia, 1950), pp. 282-283; Gustave B. Wallace tc Madison, April 20, 1790, Wallace MSS., LC.
32. John Beckley to James Monroe, June 22, 1793, Hamilton MSS., NYPL, photostat.
33. Jefferson, *Writings* (Ford), I, 226; John Beckley to James Monroe, June 22, 1793, Hamilton MSS., NYPL, photostat.
34. J. Clingman to John Beckley, June 27, 1793, Hamilton MSS., NYPL, photostat.
35. Andrew G. Fraunces, *An Appeal* (Philadelphia, 1793), pp. 17-18; *Independent Chronicle*, December 30, 1793, January 9, 1794.
36. Deposition of William Bayly, 1792, Hamilton MSS., LC; Washington, *Writings* (Fitzpatrick), XXXII, 194; Hamilton to Colonel Mercer, September 4, December 4, 1792; March 14, 1793; Mercer to Hamilton, October 16, 1792; March 5, 1793, Hamilton MSS., LC; *John P. Branch Historical Papers*, II, 283; Hamilton, *Works* (Lodge), X, 29-30.
37. Hamilton, *Works* (Lodge), X, 29-30.

Chapter 23. Hamilton's Quarrel with Jefferson and Burr

1. Dumas Malone, *Jefferson and the Rights of Man* (Boston, 1951), p. 424; Lewis Leary, *That Rascal Freneau* (New Brunswick, 1941), p. 191.
2. Leary, *Freneau*, pp. 187-188; Madison, *Writings* (Hunt), VI, 55.
3. *National Gazette*, October 31, 1791; January 16, September 19, 1792; *Gazette of the United States*, June 6, 1792.
4. Hamilton, *Works* (Lodge), III, 9; VII, 230-232, 236, 271.
5. *Ibid.*, II, 304, 427.
6. *National Gazette*, September 8, October 24, 1792; January 12, 1793.
7. Hamilton, *Works* (Lodge), VII, 229, 241-242; *Gazette of the United States*, July 25, 1792.
8. *The Politicks and Views of a Certain Party Displayed* (Philadelphia, 1792), pp. 22, 25; *Gazette of the United States*, April 17, 1790; *New England Quarterly*, XVIII (1945), p. 243 footnote; Hamilton, *Works* (Lodge), IX, 529.
9. Hamilton, *Works* (Lodge), VII, 285-286, 304; IX, 529-531; John Adams, *Works* (Adams), VIII, 503-504; *Gazette of the United States*, September 22, 27, 1793; *The Pretensions of Thomas Jefferson to the Presidency Examined, Part II* (Philadelphia, 1796), p. 2; Conway, *Randolph*, p. 188.
10. John Beckley to Madison, September 2, 1793, Madison MSS., NYPL; *The Nation*, LX (1895), 148; Leary, *Freneau*, pp. 186-188, 212; Hamilton, *Works* (Lodge), VII, 236-237, 241-242, 251, 304; IX, 516, 529; *Gazette of the United States*, September, 15, 22, 1792; *The Politicks and Views of a Certain Party Displayed*, pp. 2-3.
11. *Gazette of the United States*, September 15, 1792; Mott, *Jefferson and the Press*, p. 18.

Notes

12. Edmund Randolph to Madison, August 12, 1793, Madison MSS., LC; *National Gazette*, September 8, 1792; *Pennsylvania Magazine of History and Biography* (1948), p. 547.
13. Hamilton, *Works* (Lodge), VII, 233, 271, 273; IX, 518, 535; *Gazette of the United States*, September 22, 1792; Hamilton, *Works* (J. C. Hamilton), IV, 7-9; *Pretensions of Jefferson*, pp. 3-4; Americanus, *Address to the People of the United States* (Philadelphia, 1800), pp. 15-16; Hamilton, *Works* (Lodge), VII, 304.
14. *Gazette of the United States*, September 22, 1792; Hamilton, *Works* (Lodge), VII, 264, 287-288.
15. Mary L. Hinsdale, *A History of the President's Cabinet* (New York, 1911), pp. 22, 25; Washington, *Writings* (Fitzpatrick), XXXIV, 315; *Dunlap's American Daily Advertiser*, October 10, 1792; Rives, *Madison*, III, 381; *National Gazette*, September 8, 1792; January 12, 1793; *American Daily Advertiser*, October 10, 1793; Jefferson, *Writings* (Ford), I, 204.
16. Washington, *Writings* (Fitzpatrick), XXXII, 48, 130, 137, 186; XXXIV, 252; XXXV, 119; Jefferson, *Writings* (Ford), VII, 235-236; *Gazette of the United States*, September 19, 1792; Mott, *Jefferson and the Press*, 16-17.
17. Jefferson, *Writings* (Ford), I, 174, 177, 199, 205, 225.
18. Madison, *Writings* (Hunt), VI, 117-118; Leary, *Freneau*, pp. 186-188; *An Examination of the President's Policy* (New York, 1801), p. 21.
19. Hamilton, *Works* (Lodge), VII, 300.
20. *Ibid.*, VII, 264; *National Gazette*, January 12, 1793; *Pennsylvania Magazine of History and Biography* (1948), LXXII, p. 247; *Dunlap's American Daily Advertiser*, October 12, 1792; *National Gazette*, September 8, 1792; January 12, 1793.
21. Singer, *South Carolina in the Confederacy*, p. 313; William Heth to Hamilton, June 28, 1792, Hamilton MSS., LC; Steele, *Papers* (Wagstaff), I, 105-106, 442-452, 453; *North Carolina Historical Review*, XXV (1948), p. 442.
22. *North Carolina Historical Review*, XXV (1948), 442; Hamilton, *Works* (Lodge), II, 1792.
23. James Kent to Elizabeth Hamilton, December 10, 1836, Kent MSS., LC; Wilkinson, *Memoirs*, I, 464; E. W. Spaulding, *His Excellency, Governor George Clinton* (New York, 1938), pp. 222-223.
24. Monaghan, *Jay*, 325; Conversation with Governor Clinton, June 12, 1789, Rufus King MSS., NYHS.
25. New York *Daily Advertiser*, March 3, 1789.
26. *Ibid.*
27. Edward P. Alexander, *A Revolutionary Conservative* (New York, 1938), pp. 260-261; Hamilton, *Works* (Lodge), IX, 458 footnote; Morgan Lewis to Hamilton, June 24, 1789, Hamilton MSS., LC; Philip Schuyler to John B. Schuyler, January 26, 1791, Schuyler MSS., NYPL; Hamilton to Robert R. Livingston, March 13, 1789, Livingston MSS., NYHS.
28. Edwin Brockholst Livingston, *The Livingstons of Livingston Manor* (New York, 1910), p. 333.
29. Hamilton to Hugh Seton, January 1, 1785; Hamilton to Mrs. Hamilton, March 12, 1785, Hamilton MSS., LC.
30. Hamilton, *Works* (J. C. Hamilton), V, 493-495.
31. Hamilton to Washington, September 23, 1792, Gratz Collection, HSP; Raymond Walters, Jr., *Alexander James Dallas* (Philadelphia, 1943), p. 41.
32. Hamilton, *Works* (Lodge), X, 22.
33. *Ibid.*, X, 20; James Cheetham, *A View of the Political Conduct of Aaron Burr* (New York, 1802), p. 15, and *Nine Letters on the Subject of Aaron Burr's Political Defection* (New York, 1803), p. 14; James Kent to T. Bailey, January 27, 1791, Kent MSS., LC.
34. James Kent to Moses Kent, October 15, 1792, Kent MSS., LC; Hamilton, *Works* (J. C. Hamilton), V, 494-496; Maclay, *Journal*, p. 85; Madison, *Writings* (Hunt), VI, 106.
35. Hamilton, *Works* (Lodge), X, 7-8; Madison, *Writings* (Hunt), VI, 106; Washington, *Writings* (Fitzpatrick), XXXII, 46-47, 310; *Annals of Congress*, III, 13; Hammond, *Political Parties in the State of New York*, I, 55-56; James Hillary to Hamilton, January 4, 1793; Hamilton MSS., LC; Monaghan, *Jay*, 329-331; Webb, *Journals and Correspondence*, III, 177; *General Advertiser*, July 15, 1792.

Chapter 24. The Proclamation of Neutrality

1. F. J. C. Hearnshaw (ed.), *The Social and Political Ideas of Some Representative Thinkers of the Revolutionary Era* (London, 1931), pp. 93-94; *American Historical Review*, XLVI (1941), 43; Russell Kirk, *The Conservative Mind* (Chicago, 1953), pp. 15, 18, 32-34; *The Works of Edmund Burke* (12 vols., Boston, 1880), III, 106; *Gazette of the United States*, May 14, 1790; Hamilton, *Works* (Lodge), IV, April 1793; VII, 266; Madison, *Writings* (Hunt), VI, 321.

2. Hamilton, *Works* (Lodge), V, April 4, 1798; VII, 361; Jefferson, *Writings* (Ford), I, 268; James Kent to Moses Kent, September 25, 1793, James Kent MSS., LC; *American Historical Review*, II (1897), 295; *Parliamentary History* (London, 1816), XXX, 53.

3. *Gazette of the United States*, December 7, 1795; *Papers of Noah Webster*, p. 40; Hamilton to *Gazette of the United States*, 1793, Hamilton MSS., LC.

4. R. H. Lee, *Letters*, II, 501; *National Gazette*, April 5, December 15, 1792; *General Advertiser*, January 28, March 26, 1793; Marshall, *Washington*, V, 541; Alexander Graydon, *Memoirs of My Life* (Harrisburg, 1811), p. 357; *Gazette of the United States*, January 26, 1796.

5. Monroe, *Writings*, III, 112 footnote, 113; *General Advertiser*, March 15, 1793; *Gazette of the United States*, January 6, 1799; *Independent Chronicle*, August 15, 1793; Hammond to Grenville, March 7, 1793, Hammond Corr., LC; *Works of William Cobbett* (London, 1835), I, 46-47; *Historical Magazine*, VIII (New York, 1864), 19; *A Rub for the Snub* (Philadelphia, 1795), pp. 70-71.

6. Jefferson, *Writings* (Ford), I, 267; Madison, *Works* (Hunt), V, 276; C. M. Thomas, *American Neutrality in 1793* (New York, 1931), p. 14; C. D. Hazen, *Contemporary American Opinion of the French Revolution* (Baltimore, 1897), p. 11.

7. Marshall, *Washington*, V, 541; *General Advertiser*, January 28, 1793; Hamilton to Henry Lee, June 22, 1793, American Art Association; Hammond to Grenville, April 14, 1794, Hammond MSS., LC; Hamilton to the *Gazette of the United States*, 1793, Hamilton MSS., LC.

8. Thomas, *American Neutrality*, pp. 70-76; S. von Pufendorf, *Of the Law of Nature and Nations* (Oxford, 1703), pp. 1356-1358; Kent, *Commentaries*, I, 49-50; Hamilton to the *Gazette of the United States*, 1793, Hamilton MSS., LC; Observations of Mr. Dunlop by A. H., 1793, Hamilton MSS, LC; A. C. McLaughlin, *A Constitutional History of the United States* (New York, 1935), pp. 251, 253-254; Edmund Randolph to Washington, May 6, 1793, Washington MSS., LC; Jefferson, *Writings* (Ford), I, 226; *National Gazette*, June 5, July 27, 1793; Monroe, *Writings* (Hamilton), I, 262; Hamilton, *Works* (Lodge), IV, 439, 443-444; Madison, *Writings* (Hunt), I, 542, 634; E. C. Corwin, *The President, Office and Powers* (New York, 1948), pp. 252-253; Quincy Wright, *The Control of American Foreign Relations* (New York, 1922), p. 5.

9. Corwin, *The President*, 209-212, 252-253, *The Constitution and World Organization* (Princeton, 1944), pp. 22-23, and *The President's Removal Powers* (New York, 1927), p. 26; McLaughlin, *Constitutional History*, pp. 253-254; Thomas, *American Neutrality*, p. 39; Hamilton, *Works* (Lodge), IV, 456, 458-459, 462-463, 475; Hamilton to *Gazette of the United States*, 1793, Hamilton MSS., LC; *National Gazette*, June 1, 5, July 6, August 31, 1793; *Independent Chronicle*, September 22, November 8, 1793; December 1, 1794; Stokes, *Iconography*, V, 1299; Marshall, *Washington*, V, 591; *General Advertiser*, May 21, June 1, 1793; *An Examination of the Conduct of the Executive of the United States* (Philadelphia, 1797), p. 40; Monroe, *Writings* (Hamilton), I, 262; Madison, *Writings* (Hunt), I, 633, 640, 650-651; VI, 135-138, 174; Jefferson, *Writings* (Ford), I, 217, 268; VI, April 25, 1792, June, 1793; Rives, *Madison*, III, 335, 354; C. F. Jenkins (ed.), *Jefferson's Germantown Letters* (Philadelphia, 1906), pp. 135-136; Wright, *Control of American Foreign Relations*, p. 147; Hamilton, *Works* (J. C. Hamilton), V, 571; C. R. King, *The Life and Correspondence of Rufus King* (New York, 1894-1900), August 4, 1793; John Bard to Hamilton, August 24, 1793, Hamilton MSS., LC; Hamilton to Henry Lee, June 22, 1793, American Art Association; William Heath to Hamilton, June 14, 1793, Hamilton MSS., LC; H. Higginson to Hamilton, April 10, 1793, Hamilton

MSS., LC; *Federalist*, pp. 64-65; Conway, *Randolph*, p. 203; Morris (ed.), *Diary and Letters of Gouverneur Morris*, II, 594; Timothy Pickering, *A Review of the Correspondence Between John Adams and William Cunningham* (Salem, 1824), pp. 35-36; *A Message of the President, December 5, 1793*, p. 90; *Papers of Noah Webster*, 370; Hammond to Grenville, August 10, 1793, Hammond MSS., LC.

10. *Independent Chronicle*, August 8, 28, 1793; January 2, 6, 1794; September 23, 1795; *The Windham Papers* (London, 1913), I, 128; *American Historical Review*, II (1897), 475-476; III (1898), 669-670; Channing, *History*, IV, 130-131; Joseph Fauchet, *A Sketch of the Present State of our Political Relations* (Philadelphia, 1797), p. 12; Lodge, *George Cabot*, p. 75; Dorfman, *Economic Mind*, I, 466; Cabinet Meeting Minutes, March 10, 1794, Washington MSS., LC; Emeric de Vattel, *Law of Nations* (London, 1760), pp. 293, 331-332, 334-335; Washington, *Writings* (Fitzpatrick), XXXIII, 172; Kent, *Commentaries*, I, 49-51; Henry Lee to Hamilton, June 15, 1793, Hamilton MSS., LC; Edmund Randolph to Washington, June 11, 1793, Washington MSS., LC; Bond to Grenville, June 4, 1793, PRO, FO; William Bradford to Boudinot, July 14, 1793, Wallace MSS., HSP; Massachusetts Historical Society, *Proceedings*, XLIV (1911), 394; Thomas, *American Neutrality*, pp. 94-95, 112, 197-200, 227, 229-231; *A Message of the President, December, 1793*, pp. 45, 93; Walters, *Dallas*, pp. 46-48; Hamilton, *Works* (Lodge), V, 35, 49, July 8, 1793; *National Gazette*, July 10, 1793; Jefferson, *Writings* (Ford), I, 228, 242, 247, 252, 259-260, 265-267; Phineas Bond to Grenville, August 5, 1793, PRO, FO; John Hamilton to Grenville, August 1, 1793, PRO, FO; Hammond to Grenville, March 7, April 3, May 17, July 7, August 10, 1793; Historical Manuscripts Commission, *Report on the MSS of J. B. Fortescue* (London, 1899), III, 524-525, 528; William Bradford to Boudinot, July 10, 1793, Wallace MSS., HSP; Adams, *Gallatin*, p. 111; *Jefferson's Germantown Letters*, pp. 121, 138-139, 148; *Pennsylvania Gazette*, December 18, 1793.

Chapter 25. The War Clouds Gather

1. Weld, *Travels*, I, 6; Massachusetts Historical Society, *Collections*, Fifth Series, III (1877), 333.
2. Gibbs, *Memoirs of the Administrations of Washington and Adams*, I, 110.
3. Jefferson, *Writings* (Ford), VI, 173.
4. John Powell, *Bring Out Your Dead* (Philadelphia, 1949), p. 74; Rush, *Letters*, II, 750; *Independent Chronicle*, October 10, 1793; *General Advertiser*, August 30, 1793; Rush, *Autobiography* (Corner), p. 365; C. F. Volney, *A View of the Soil and Climate of the United States* (Philadelphia, 1804), pp. 241-242.
5. Tobias Lear to Hamilton, October 19, Hamilton MSS., LC.
6. W. B. Smith and A. H. Cole, *Fluctuations in American Business* (Cambridge, 1935), pp. 13-14.
7. John Adams, *Works* (Adams), IX, 86; George Cabot to Rufus King, June 3, 1801, King MSS., NYHS; *Address to the House of Representatives* (Philadelphia, 1796), p. 36; Bernard Mayo, *Instructions to British Ministers* (Washington, 1941), pp. 37-38; Kulsrud, *Maritime Neutrality*, pp. 142-143, 153, 336-337; *Political Science Quarterly*, XLVI (1931), 508; Sir A. W. Ward and G. P. Gooch, *The Cambridge History of British Foreign Policy* (Cambridge, Eng., 1922-23), I, 238; Hammond to Grenville, May 17, 1793, LC; *Annals of Congress*, III, 208; Hamilton, *Works* (Lodge), V, 36; Kent, *Commentaries*, I, 141.
8. Hamilton, *Works* (Lodge), V, 37-38.
9. King, *Rufus King*, III, George Cabot, January 28, 1801.
10. Ward and Gooch, *Cambridge History of British Foreign Policy*, I, 238; Mayo, *Instructions to British Ministers*, p. 42 footnote; Historical Manuscripts Commission, *Report on the MSS. of J. B. Fortescue*, II, 24; Hunt, *Political History of England*, V, 349; *American Historical Review*, XXIV, 27; King, *Rufus King*, III, 549; Thomas, *American Neutrality*, pp. 253-257; Hammond to Grenville, September 13, 1793, LC; Copy of a Letter from Philadelphia, 1793, PRO, FO; *Annals of Congress*, III, 155-157, 221, 347, 369-370, 437-438; John Taylor, *A Definition of Parties* (Philadelphia, 1794), p. 5; Lee,

Letters, II, 581-582; General Advertiser, March 17, April 3, 1794; Independent Chronicle, February 20, November 10, 1794; Madison, Writings (Hunt), VI, 209; Hamilton, Works (Lodge), V, 97-115.

11. Hamilton, Works (Lodge), V, April 14, 1794; Gazette of the United States, February 12, 1794; Manlius, Boston, 1794, pp. 22, 24; Annals of Congress, III, 337-338, 347, 518-520; Taylor, A Definition of Parties, p. 5; An Address from William Smith of South Carolina to his Constituents (Philadelphia, 1794), p. 5; Sir James Bland Bury, Selections from Letters and Correspondence of James Hutton (London, 1885), pp. 247-248; James Sprunt Historical Magazine, III (Chapel Hill, 1902), 99; John H. Morison, Life of Jeremiah Smith (Boston, 1845), pp. 61-62; Papers of Noah Webster, pp. 322-323.
12. J. Thomas Sharf and Thompson Wescott, History of Philadelphia (Philadelphia, 1884), I, 478; D. B. Read, Life and Times of General John G. Simcoe (Toronto, 1890), pp. 207-208; General Advertiser, April 13, 1794; Independent Chronicle, May 29, 1794; South Carolina Historical and Genealogical Magazine, XLI (1940), 36; Marshall, Washington, V, 541; Washington, Writings (Fitzpatrick), XXXVI, 177; Christopher Greenup to Nathaniel Pendleton, March 26, 1794, Pendleton MSS., NYHS; Mayo, Instructions to British Ministers, pp. 74, 75 footnote; Annals of Congress, III, 738.
13. Hamilton, Works (Lodge), V, April 14, 1794.
14. Hugh Williamson to Hamilton, May 27, 1794, Hamilton MSS., LC; Independent Chronicle, June 21, 1794, June 2, 3, 1794; Madison to Jefferson, March 14, 1794, Madison MSS., LC; William Henderson to Nicholson, March 16, 1794, Joseph H. Nicholson MSS., LC; Sedgwick to Williams, March 29, 1794, Sedgwick MSS., MHS; Duke de la Rochefoucault-Liancourt, Travels (London, 1799), I, 403; General Advertiser, February 12, March 18, May 21, 1794; Annals of Congress, III, 736; Monroe, Writings (Hamilton), I, 286-288.
15. Annals of Congress, III, 549; General Advertiser, March 17, 1799; Manlius, Boston, 1794, p. 26; American Historical Association, Report for 1898 (Washington, 1899), pp. 548-549; An Address from Robert Goodloe Harper (Boston, 1896), p. 13; Rives, Madison, III, 507-508; William Hindman to Nicholson, March 9, 1794, Nicholson MSS., LC; Christopher Greenup to Nathaniel Pendleton, March 26, 1794, Pendleton MSS., NYHS; Madison to Jefferson, March 2, 1799, Madison MSS., LC; Independent Chronicle, December 23, 1793.
16. Hamilton, Works (Lodge), V, April 14, 1794; Annals of Congress, III, 537; B. R. Curtis, Reports of Decisions in the Supreme Court of the United States (Boston, 1855), I, 225; McKee, Papers on Public Credit, p. 173; Arthur Nussbaum, A Concise History of the Law of Nations (New York, 1950), pp. 159-161; Gazette of the United States, March 29, 1794; Kent, Commentaries, I, 57, 60, 63-64.
17. Fisher Ames, Works, I, 139; South Carolina Historical and Genealogical Magazine, XLI, 1940, 36.
18. Report on Canadian Archives, 1890, 125-126.
19. C. R. King, Rufus King, I, March 10, 1794.
20. John Nicholas to Washington, April 6, 1794, Washington MSS., LC; Madison to Jefferson, April 14, 1794, Madison MSS., LC; Jefferson, Writings (Ford), I, 186, 231-232; II, 231-232; James Monroe to Washington, April 8, 1794, Washington MSS., LC; Washington, Writings (Fitzpatrick), XXXIII, 320; Madison to Jefferson, January 11, 1795, Madison MSS., LC; S. F. Bemis (ed.), American Secretaries of State, II, 114; Randolph to Washington, April 9, 1794, Washington MSS., LC; Madison, Writings (Hunt), VI, 220.
21. Madison to Jefferson, April 14, 1794, Madison MSS., LC.
22. Scharf and Wescott, History of Philadelphia, I, 478; General Advertiser, April 28, 1794; Independent Chronicle, May 25, 1794; Bemis, American Secretaries of State, II, 115; Monaghan, Jay, 366; Monroe, Writings (Hamilton), I, 250; Monroe, A View of the Conduct of the Executive, p. vi; Franklin, Letters, pp. 32-35.
23. Hammond to Grenville, April 4, May 28, 1794, LC; Madison to Jefferson, April 14, 1794, Madison MSS., LC; Sedgwick to Williams, April 22, May 4, December 6, 1794, Sedgwick MSS., MHS; Madison, Writings (Hunt), VI, 211; Annals of Congress, III, 675, 677, 680, 682; Monroe, Writings (Hamilton), II, 6; Marshall, Washington, V, 544.

24. Hamilton to His Wife, June 8, 1794, Hamilton MSS., LC; Madison to Jefferson, May 11, 1794, Madison MSS., LC.

Chapter 26. The Whisky Rebellion

1. *Independent Chronicle*, December 21, 1789; *Herald of Freedom and the Federalist Advertiser*, February 4, 1790.
2. *A Short History of the Excise Laws* (Philadelphia, 1795), pp. 22-27, 118; *Annals of Congress*, III, 636.
3. *Five Letters Addressed to the Yeomanry of the United States, By a Farmer*, p. 9; *Gazette of the United States*, May 9, 1792; *The Politicks and Views of a Certain Party Displayed*, pp. 14-15; *Daily Advertiser*, March 12, 1792; *National Gazette*, May 7, 1792, February 9, 1792; Leland D. Baldwin, *Whisky Rebels* (Pittsburgh, 1939), pp. 57, 65; Frederick B. Tolles, *George Logan of Philadelphia* (New York, 1953), p. 131.
4. *Gazette of the United States*, May 15, 1792; *General Advertiser*, April 29, 1792; Fisher Ames, *Works*, I, 89; Jonathan Trumbull to William Wrax, June 7, 1790, Trumbull MSS., CHS; *Columbian Centinel*, February 16, 1791; James Kent to T. Bailey, January 27, 1791, James Kent MSS., LC; Gibbs, *Memoirs of the Administrations of Washington and Adams*, I, 65; Hugh H. Brackenridge, *History of the Western Insurrection* (Philadelphia, 1795), I, 144-145.
5. Baldwin, *Whisky Rebels*, p. 66; *General Advertiser*, January 18, 1791; *Gazette of the United States*, February 12, 1791; Tench Coxe, *Views*, p. 15.
6. Gibbs, *Memoirs*, I, 295; Hamilton, *Works* (Lodge), VIII, 301; Jasper Dwight, *A Letter to Washington* (Philadelphia, 1796), p. 15; John Page, *An Address* (Richmond, 1794), p. 31; Maclay, *Journal*, p. 387; Baldwin, *Whisky Rebels*, p. 67; *General Advertiser*, January 20, 1791; Washington, *Writings* (Ford), XXXII, 235-236; Gaillard Hunt, *Disunion Sentiment in Congress in 1794* (Washington, 1905), pp. 22-23; Bennett Milton Rich, *The Presidents and Civil Disorder* (Washington, 1941), pp. 4-6; Hamilton to Edward Carrington, July 22, 1792, Hamilton MSS., LC; Fisher Ames, *Works*, I, 122; *A Short History of the Excise*, pp. 11, 20, 62, 111, 116.
7. *A Short History of the Excise*, pp. 62, 111, 118; *Annals of Congress*, III, 625, 636, 1182, 1191.
8. John Taylor, *An Argument Respecting the Constitutionality of the Carriage Tax* (Richmond, 1795), pp. 5, 17; *Manlius, Boston, 1794*, pp. 38-39.
9. Charles Warren, *The Supreme Court in United States History* (Boston, 1935), I, 147; Taylor, *An Argument*, p. 16; William Bradford to Hamilton, July 2, 1795, Hamilton MSS., LC; *Gazette of the United States*, February 26, 1796; H. E. Scudder (ed.), *Recollections of Samuel Breck* (Philadelphia, 1877), p. 210; McRee, *Iredell*, II, 461-462; Hamilton, *Works* (Lodge), VIII, 381-382; Alexander J. Dallas, *Writings* (Philadelphia, 1799), III, 178-179, 181, 184; Notes of the Carriage Tax, Hamilton MSS., LC; Corwin, *Judicial Review*, pp. 5, 51.
10. *Federalist*, 75-76; McKee, *Papers on Public Credit*, pp. 247-248.
11. *Columbian Centinel*, August 20, 1791.
12. Arthur Hope Jones, *Income Tax in the Napoleonic Wars* (Cambridge, 1939), pp. 5, 13-14; Hunt, *Political History of England*, X, 347-348; *Columbian Centinel*, August 20, 1791.
13. *Annals of Congress*, III, 617; *Independent Chronicle*, December 19, 1793; *A Review of the Revenue System*, p. 13
14. Hamilton, *Works* (Lodge), II, July 27, 1791; McKee, *Papers on Public Credit*, pp. 162-163.
15. Findley, *History of the Insurrection*, pp. 63, 73-74, 224-225, 295, 300, 304; Baldwin, *Whisky Rebels*, p. 110; James T. Callender, *American Annual Register* (Philadelphia, 1796), p. 115.
16. *Pennsylvania Archives*, Second Series, IV, 350-351.
17. Hamilton, *Works* (Lodge), VIII, 301; John Neville to George Clymer, August 23, September 15, 1794, Wolcott MSS., CHS; *Pennsylvania Archives*, Second Series, IV, 81, 105-118; Alexander Graydon, *Memoirs* (Harrisburg, 1811), p. 372; John Williams to

Irvine, August 12, 1794, William Irvine MSS., HSP; Boudinot, *Journal*, II, 87; William Bradford to Washington, August ?, 1794, Washington MSS., LC.
18. *Federalist*, pp. 170-171.
19. *Ibid.*, p. 171; Hamilton, *Works* (Lodge), X, 71.
20. *Gazette of the United States*, August 28, 1794; C. M. Newlin, *The Life and Writings of H. H. Brackenridge* (Princeton, 1932), p. 160 footnote; Hamilton, *Works* (Lodge), VI, August 28, 1794.
21. *Pennsylvania Archives*, Second Series, IV, 145-146; Edmund Randolph to Washington, August 5, 1794, Washington MSS., LC; William Bradford to Boudinot, August 1, 1794, Wallace MSS., HSP; *A Translation of Citizen Fauchet's Intercepted Letter* (Philadelphia, 1795), p. 5; *Gazette of the United States*, September 13, 1794; William Findley, *History of the Insurrection* (Philadelphia, 1796), p. 178; Hammond to Grenville, September 28, 1794, LC.
22. Rich, *The Presidents and Civil Disorder*, pp. 7-9.
23. *Pennsylvania Archives*, Second Series, IV, 166, 234; Gibbs, *Memoirs*, I, 159.
24. Hamilton to Mifflin, October 10, 1794, Wolcott MSS., CHS.; Findley, *History of the Insurrection*, 157, 181; Boudinot, *Journal*, II, 87; Adams, *Gallatin*, 143; *Pennsylvania Archives*, Second Series, IV, 433; Washington, *Diaries*, IV, 212, 215; Baldwin, *Whisky Rebels*, pp. 228-229.
25. *Pennsylvania Archives*, Second Series, IV, 143; Brackenridge, *History of the Western Insurrection*, pp. 144-145; Newlin, *Brackenridge*, p. 129.
26. Brackenridge, *History*, pp. 305-306.
27. *Ibid.*, p. 305.
28. Hamilton, *Works* (Lodge), VII, 352; Rich, *The Presidents and Civil Disorder*, p. 13; Adams, *Gallatin*, p. 149; Madison to ? July 21, 1791, Madison MSS., LC.
29. Hamilton, *Works* (Lodge), VII, 353; X, October 30, 1794; Walters, *Dallas*, p. 61; Dallas, *Life and Writings*, p. 30; Gallatin, *Writings* (Adams), III, 104; Findley, *History of the Insurrection*, pp. 82-83.
30. A. M. Hamilton, *Intimate Life of Alexander Hamilton*, p. 231.
31. *An Examination of the Conduct of the Executive of the United States*, p. 41; Findley *History of the Insurrection*, p. 224; Madison, *Writings* (Hunt), VI, 220; *Independent Chronicle*, August 25, September 15, November 24, 1794; *President II* (Newark, 1799), p. 12; *Gazette of the United States*, June 21, July 24, August 20, December 22, 1794; Baldwin, *Whisky Rebels*, p. 110; Hammond to Grenville, July 7, 1793, LC; Walters, *Dallas*, p. 45; Tolles, *Logan*, p. 141; Eugene P. Link, *Democratic Societies from 1790 to 1800* (New York, 1942), p. 20; *Annals of Congress*, III, 909, 925, 929-930, 938; *National Gazette*, June 8, July 20, 1793; Washington, *Writings* (Fitzpatrick), XXXIII, 475-476.
32. *Annals of Congress*, III, 925-928, 930, 935; Gibbs, *Memoirs of the Administrations of Washington and Adams*, I, 175; Morison, *Jeremiah Smith*, pp. 67-68; Peter Porcupine, *A Little Plain English* (Philadelphia, 1795), p. 70; *Gazette of the United States*, February 21, March 7, August 24, November 24, 1794; Madison, *Writings* (Hunt), VI, 222-223; Link, *Democratic Societies*, pp. 103, 124.
33. Tolles, *Logan*, p. 131; *Gazette of the United States*, September 27, December 30, 1794; Hamilton, *Works* (Lodge), X, November 27, 1794; *Annals of Congress*, III, 908, 921, 935; *Pennsylvania Magazine of History and Biography*, LXII (1938), 324-327; Findley, *History of the Insurrection*, p. 168; *Pennsylvania Archives*, Second Series, IV, 356; Baldwin, *Whisky Rebels*, p. 108; John Hamilton to Grenville, August 15, September 7, December 1, 1794, PRO, FO; *Letters of Germanicus* (Philadelphia, 1794), p. 13; Rives, *Madison*, III, 464, 469.
34. William Duane, *A Letter to George Washington* (Philadelphia, 1796), p. 18; *General Advertiser*, June 10, 1794; *Gazette of the United States*, September 17, November 24, 1795; C. F. Adams (ed.), *Letters of Mrs. Adams* (Boston, 1846), p. 361; Washington, *Writings* (Fitzpatrick) XXXIII, 23; XXXV, 102-3; XXXVI, October 15, 1797; Jasper Dwight, *A Letter to George Washington* (Philadelphia, 1795), pp. 47-48; *National Gazette*, June 12, 1793; *Remarks Occasioned by the Late Conduct of Mr. Washington*

Notes 605

(Philadelphia, 1797), p. 65; Jefferson, *Writings* (Ford), I, 245; Hamilton, *Works* (Lodge), VIII, 123, 152-153; Hamilton to Wolcott, October 26, 1795, Wolcott MSS., CHS; Stephen Decatur, Jr., *Public Affairs of George Washington* (Boston, 1933), pp. 328-332.

Chapter 27. Jay's Treaty

1. Kent, *Commentaries*, I, 127-128.
2. Hamilton, *Works* (Lodge), VII, 121; Bemis, *American Secretaries of State*, II, 116; Conway, *Randolph*, p. 220; Callender, *American Annual Register*, pp. 262-263.
3. Hamilton, *Works* (Lodge), V, 126.
4. *Ibid.*, V, 125, 127-128.
5. *Ibid.*, VII, 369.
6. A Brief State of the Case of the British Merchants Trading to North America previous to the Year 1776, March 20, 1794, PRO, FO; Points upon which the Right Honourable William Pitt wished to have Information from Messrs. Hamilton and Findley of Glasgow, July 8, 1794, PRO, FO; Extract of a Letter from Virginia, December 10, 1793, PRO, FO.
7. Hamilton, *Works* (Lodge), VII, 358; X, June 4, 1794; Huth and Pugh, *Talleyrand in America* (Washington, 1942), p. 37; American Historical Association, *Report for 1898*, pp. 492-493; Jonathan Trumbull, *Autobiography, Reminiscences and Letters* (New York, 1841), p. 136; John Jay to Washington, November 14, 1794, Washington MSS., LC; C. F. Adams (ed.), *Memoirs of John Quincy Adams* (Philadelphia, 1874-77), I, 49-50; Hammond to Grenville, April 28, 1794, LC; Grenville to Jay, September 3, November 21, 1794, PRO, FO; *Parliamentary History*, XXXI, 638; Robert J. Eden (ed.), *The Journal and Correspondence of William, Lord Auckland* (London, 1862), III, 217; Fortescue, *British Statesmen of the Great War*, p. 191.
8. Hammond to Grenville, April 14, 1794, LC; Mayo, *Instructions to British Ministers*, pp. 71-73.
9. D. Hailes to Grenville, April 29, 1794, PRO, FO; James Crawford to Grenville, November 18, 1794; January 3, 1795, PRO, FO.
10. Hamilton, *Works* (Lodge), X, 65.
11. Hammond to Grenville, August 3, 1794, LC; Kulsrud, *Maritime Neutrality*, pp. 242, 292; Kent, *Commentaries*, I, 127-128.
12. Jared Sparks (ed.), *Correspondence of the American Revolution* (Boston, 1853), V, 454-455; *American Historical Review*, XXXIV, 36.
13. Mayo, *Instructions to British Ministers*, pp. 67-68; D. Hailes to Grenville, April 5, 22, 1794; Henry Spencer to Grenville, April 18, 1794, PRO, FO; *Lord Auckland* (Eden), III, 197, 202, 204.
14. John Adams, *Works* (Adams), IX, 86-87; *American Historical Review*, XXIV, 35-43; D. Hailes to Grenville, April 24, June 14, June 21, June 28, July 26, August 1, August 16, September 16, November 8, 1794, PRO, FO; James Crawford to Grenville, October 11, November 4, May 15, 22, 1795, PRO, FO.
15. John Jay to Hamilton, July 18, 1794, Hamilton MSS., LC.
16. Mayo, *Instructions to British Ministers*, pp. 61, 63-64, 66, 72; Jay to Hamilton, September 11, 1794, Jay MSS., Columbia University.
17. Hammond to Grenville, April 19, 1794, LC; Project of Heads of Proposals to be made to Mr. Jay, August, 1794; Grenville to Jay, August 30, 1794, November 21, 1794, PRO, FO; Jay, *Writings* (Johnston), IV, 27, 33-34, 114-115; Jay to Grenville, September 1, September 7, 1794; Jay to Hamilton, September 11, 1794, Hamilton MSS., LC; C. C. Pinckney, *Life of General Thomas Pinckney* (Boston, 1905), pp. 139-141; *Parliamentary History*, XXX, 1432; John Quincy Adams, *Memoirs*, I, 137; James Greig (ed.), *The Farington Diary* (London, 1922-24), I, 278-279.
18. Jay to Grenville, July 30, 1794; Grenville to Jay, August 1, 1794, PRO, FO; James F. Zimmerman, *Impressment of American Seamen* (New York, 1925), pp. 45-46.
19. S. F. Bemis, *John Quincy Adams and the Foundations of American Foreign Policy* (New York, 1949), p. 46; Jay to Washington, March 6, 1795, Washington MSS., LC;

Hammond to Grenville, June 27, August 3, 1794, LC; King, *Rufus King*, III, 547-548; Gibbs, *Memoirs of the Administrations of Washington and Adams*, I, 228; Historical Manuscripts Commission, *Report on the MSS. of J. B. Fortescue*, II, 613, 620-621; John Adolphus, *History of England* (London, 1817), VI, 25-26, 29-30, 32-33; Ward and Gooch, *History of British Foreign Policy*, I, 247, 252-254; *Lord Auckland* (Eden), II, 261, 275, 284, 293; *Parliamentary History*, XXI, 1036-1037, 1052-1053, 1153; Paul Frischauer, *England's Years of Danger* (New York, 1938), p. xiv; *Sketches of French and English Politicks in America. By a Member of the Old Congress* (Charleston, 1797), pp. 23, 27. Cato (Robert R. Livingston), *Examination of the Treaty* (Philadelphia, 1795), p. 4; *An Address to the House of Representatives* (Philadelphia, 1796), pp. 31, 34-35; *A Rub from Snub*, p. 67; *Remarks Occasioned by the Late Conduct of Mr. Washington*, p. 46; *Papers of Noah Webster*, p. 221; *Letters of Franklin* (Philadelphia, 1795), p. 27; *An Address from Robert Goodloe Harper* (Boston, 1796), p. 7; E. D. Adams, *The Influence of Grenville on Pitt's Foreign Policy* (Washington, 1904), p. 54; Jay, *Writings* (Johnston), IV, 164; Monaghan, *Jay*, pp. 380-381; Washington, *Writings* (Fitzpatrick), XXXIV, 16-17; Jay to Grenville, August 16, 1794, PRO, FO.

20. Kulsrud, *Maritime Neutrality*, p. 294; Hamilton, *Works* (Lodge), VII, 359; Bemis, *John Quincy Adams*, p. 46.
21. Jay to Washington, March 1, 1794, Washington MSS., LC; John Quincy Adams, *Memoirs*, I, 49; Hamilton, *Works* (Lodge), VII, 359; Madison to Jefferson, February 15, 1795, Madison MSS., LC.
22. *Parliamentary History*, XXXI, 1306; Jay, *Writings* (Johnston), IV, 132-133, 164; Mayo, *Instructions to British Ministers*, pp. 69, 92; John Quincy Adams, *Memoirs*, I, 45.
23. John Hamilton to Grenville, July 8, 1795, PRO, FO; Gibbs, *Memoirs of the Administrations of Washington and Adams*, I, 218; *Gazette of the United States*, December 11, 1795; Mary Elizabeth Clark, *Peter Porcupine in America* (Philadelphia, 1939), p. 48; Corwin, *The President*, p. 331; Thornton, *An Enquiry*, p. 27; Hammond to Grenville, July 27, 1795, LC; John B. McMaster, *Stephen Girard* (Philadelphia, 1918), I, 294; Madison, *Writings* (Hunt), VI, 260.
24. Jefferson to Edward Rutledge, November 30, 1795, Jefferson MSS., LC; Edward Rutledge to Jefferson, October 12, 1795, Jefferson MSS., LC; Dallas, *Life and Writings*, p. 161; *Letters of Franklin*, pp. 11, 201; Monroe, *Writings* (Hamilton), II, 341, 347-348; Page, *An Address*, p. 13; *Features of Mr. Jay's Treaty* (Philadelphia, 1795), pp. 20-21; *The Treaty's Merits and Demerits Fairly Examined and Explained* (Philadelphia, 1795), pp. 30-31; McRee, *Iredell*, II, 450; Alexander Martin to Smith, June 27, 1795, William L. Smith MSS., LC; Hamilton, *Works* (Lodge), V, 117; *Independent Chronicle*, November 13, 1794; *A Rub from Snub*, p. 67; Edmund Randolph to Washington, October 22, 1794, Washington MSS., LC; Stan V. Henkels, *Washington-Madison Letters* (Philadelphia, 1897), p. 79; *Remarks Occasioned By the Late Conduct of Mr. Washington*, p. 46; *President II*, p. 13; Peter Porcupine, *A Little Plain English* (Philadelphia, 1795), p. 105.
25. Washington, *Writings* (Fitzpatrick), XXXIV, 262; Fisher Ames, *Works*, I, 174; *Gazette of the United States*, December 11, 1794; Octavius Pickering and C. W. Upham, *The Life of Timothy Pickering* (Boston, 1867-73), III, 178; Aaron Burr to Monroe, July 5, 1795, Monroe MSS., LC; Peter Porcupine, *A Little Plain English*, p. 109.
26. Webb, *Journals and Correspondence*, III, 197.
27. *Gazette of the United States*, July 23, 1795.
28. Webb, *Journals and Correspondence*, III, 198; Pickering and Upham, *Pickering*, III, 202; Hamilton to Maturin Livingston, January 18, 1796, Hamilton MSS., LC; Maturin Livingston to Hamilton, January 20, 1796, Hamilton MSS., LC.
29. Hamilton to Oliver Wolcott, July 23, 1795, Wolcott MSS., CHS; Gibbs, *Memoirs of the Administrations of Washington and Adams*, I, 217, 229; C. R. King, *Rufus King*, July 27, 1795; Peter Porcupine, *A Little Plain English* (Philadelphia, 1795), pp. 107, 109.
30. Hamilton, *Works* (J. C. Hamilton), VI, 31; Hamilton, *Works* (Lodge), VII, 360.
31. Conway, *Randolph*, pp. 268-269; Bemis, *John Quincy Adams*, p. 67; Edmund Randolph to Monroe, July 2, July 14, 1795, Randolph MSS., LC.
32. Washington, *Writings* (Fitzpatrick), XXXIV, 244.

Notes 607

33. *Political Truth* (Philadelphia, 1796), p. 14; Rives, *Madison*, III, 511; *Gazette of the United States*, September 11, 1795; Bradford Perkins, *The First Rapprochement* (Philadelphia, 1955), p. 37.
34. Warfel, *Noah Webster, Schoolmaster to America*, p. 233; Jefferson, *Writings* (Ford), VII, September 10, 1795.
35. Leary, *That Rascal Freneau*, p. 255; Hammond, *Political Parties*, I, 98; *Independent Chronicle*, May 8, May 22, 1794; *Letters of Franklin*, pp. 16, 24, 27; Callender, *American Annual Register*, p. 266; Titus Wortman, *An Address to the Republican Citizens of New York* (New York, 1801), pp. 18-19; Gibbs, *Memoirs of the Administrations of Washington and Adams*, I, 332; Hamilton, *Works* (Lodge), March 28, 1796; Stan V. Henkels, *Washington-Madison Papers* (Philadelphia, 1892), p. 76; *William and Mary Quarterly*, Third Series, III (1946), 593-594.
36. David Redlick to Gallatin, April 20, 1796, Gallatin MSS., NYHS; Oliver Wolcott to Washington, March 26, 1796, Washington MSS., LC.
37. Corwin, *The President*, p. 206; Draft of a Speech for Washington, March 29, 1796, Hamilton MSS., LC., *Federalist*, p. 488; Kent, *Commentaries*, I, 106.
38. To the Citizens Who Shall Be Convened This Day in the Fields, 1796, Hamilton MSS., LC; Madison to Jefferson, December 13, 1796, Madison MSS., LC; *General Advertiser*, April 17, 1796; Adams, *Gallatin*, pp. 164-165; Madison, *Writings* (Hunt), VI, 300-301; Washington, *Writings* (Fitzpatrick), XXXV, 62.
39. Gibbs, *Memoirs of the Administrations of Washington and Adams*, I, 331; Gallatin to Alexander Addison, May 13, 1796, Gallatin MSS., NYHS; Rufus King to Hamilton, April 17, 1796, King MSS., NYHS.
40. Hamilton, *Works* (Lodge), X, 160.
41. Hamilton, *Works* (Lodge), X, 161-162; Washington, *Writings* (Fitzpatrick), XXXIV, 293, 295, 398; Bemis, *John Quincy Adams*, p. 67; Mayo, *Instructions to British Ministers*, p. 93; Historical Manuscripts Commission, *Report on the MSS. of J. B. Fortescue*, III, 59, 77.
42. Madison, *Writings* (Hunt), VI, 413; Adams, *Gallatin*, pp. 165-166; Morison, *Jeremiah Smith*, pp. 95-96; Gibbs, *Memoirs of the Administrations of Washington and Adams*, I, 335; McRee, *Iredell*, II, 475; Jasper Dwight, *A Letter to President Washington* (Philadelphia, 1796), p. 11; Corwin, *The President*, pp. 214-216; Holcombe, *Our More Perfect Union*, p. 196.
43. *Selected Essays on Constitutional Law*, III, 412; Wright, *Control of American Foreign Relations*, pp. 353-354; Kent, *Commentaries*, I, 106; Jefferson, *Writings* (Ford), I, 169; Dwight, *A Letter to George Washington*, pp. 10-11; Henkels, *Washington-Madison Letters*, p. 76; Joseph Charles, *The Origins of the American Party System* (Williamsburg, 1956), pp. 47-48; Perkins, *The First Rapprochement*, pp. i, 70-73, 76.

Chapter 28. *The Election of 1796*

1. Hamilton, *Works* (Lodge), VII, 375-376; Hammond to Grenville, January 5, February 23, 1794, LC.
2. Gallatin, *Writings* (Adams), I, 68; Dewey, *Financial History*, p. 115.
3. Adams, *Gallatin*, p. 113.
4. Hammond to Grenville, February 27, 1794, LC; Harlow, *History of Legislative Methods*, pp. 129-130.
5. Steele, *Papers*, I, 114; *Gazette of the United States*, April 11, 1794; White, *Federalists*, pp. 68-69; Findley, *History of the Insurrection*, p. 261; Harlow, *History of Legislative Methods*, pp. 130, 160-162; Raymond Walters, Jr., *Albert Gallatin, Jeffersonian Financier and Diplomat* (New York, 1957), pp. 88-89.
6. *American Economic Review*, XXXVII (May, 1947), 151-152; Madison to Jefferson, April 14, 1794; February 11, 1795, Madison MSS., LC; Adams, *Gallatin*, p. 172; Hamilton, *Works* (Lodge), X, July 25, 1795; VII, 339; *General Advertiser*, February 11, November 21, 1795; William Giles to Jefferson, December 7, 1794, Jefferson MSS., LC; American Historical Association, *Report for 1896* (Washington, 1897), I, 777.
7. Madison, *Writings* (Hunt), VI, 232.

8. McKee, *Papers on Public Credit*, p. 151; Kearny, *Sketch of the Finances of the United States*, pp. 35-37, 43-44; Harris, *The National Debt and the New Economics*, p. 64.
9. Chien Tsing Mei, *The Fiscal Policies of Albert Gallatin* (New York, 1937), p. 53; Fisher Ames, *Works*, I, 167; Adams, *Gallatin*, 296; *Annals of Congress*, II, 834; III, 1176-1177; X, 394; *Gazette of the United States*, March 4, 1795; Massachusetts Historical Society, *Proceedings*, LX, 1927, 380; Sedgwick to van Schaack, February 7, 1795, Sedgwick MSS., MHS; Taylor, *An Enquiry*, pp. 44-46, 61; Madison to Jefferson, February 15, 1795, Madison MSS., LC; Dewey, *Financial History*, 113; A. S. Bolles, *The Financial History of the United States from 1789 to 1860* (New York, 1894), II, 65.
10. John Adams, *Works* (Adams), X, 127; Hamilton, *Works* (Lodge), VII, 375-376; A. M. Hamilton, *Intimate Life*, p. 164; *Gazette of the United States*, September 11, 1795; *General Advertiser*, February 11, November 21, 1795; Henkels, *Washington-Madison Papers*, p. 208; John Ward Fenno, *Desultory Reflections* (New York, 1800), p. 4.
11. *Gazette of the United States*, March 2, February 11, 1795; Hamilton to Richard Varick, April 13, 1795, Hamilton MSS., LC; *General Advertiser*, February 11, 1795; President and Directors of the Bank of the United States to Hamilton, February 3, 1795, Hamilton MSS., LC.
12. James Humbert, *Thoughts on the Nature of Civil Government* (New York, 1797), pp. 39-40; McRee, *Iredell*, I, 442-443.
13. William Bradford to Hamilton, July 2, 21, 1795, Hamilton MSS., LC; A. M. Hamilton, *Intimate Life*, p. 231; James A. Hamilton, *Reminiscences* (New York, 1869), p. 5; Hammond to Grenville, January 5, 1795, LC; American Historical Association, *Report for 1903* (Washington, 1904), II, 537; James Cheetham, *A View of the Political Conduct of Aaron Burr* (New York, 1802), I, 88; Morison, *Jeremiah Smith*, p. 83; David Campbell to Hamilton, January 27, 1795, Hamilton MSS., LC; Madison to Jefferson, February 15, 1795, Madison MSS., LC; J. D. Hammond, *The History of Political Parties in the State of New York* (New York, 1852), I, 88.
14. White, *Jeffersonians*, p. 134.
15. Hamilton, *Works* (Lodge) X, 89-90; Hamilton to Wolcott, May 30, 1795, Wolcott MSS., CHS.
16. Washington, *Writings* (Fitzpatrick), XXXVII, 67; *American Historical Review*, XXIX (1924), 262-263; Robert Morris to Gustavus Scott, October 16, 1797, R. Morris Letter Book, LC; A. M. Hamilton, *Intimate Life*, p. 286; Hamilton, *Works* (Lodge), V, May, 1795 (Horatio); *Mississippi Valley Historical Review* (March, 1957), pp. 641-643.
17. V. H. Paltsits, *Washington's Farewell Address* (New York, 1935), pp. 42, 44, 49-50; Robert Liston to Grenville, October 13, 1796, LC; *Pennsylvania Magazine of History and Biography*, LX (1936), 384; Gibbs, *Memoirs of the Administrations of Washington and Adams*, I, 332.
18. *The Pretensions of Thomas Jefferson to the Presidency* (Philadelphia, 1796), pp. 14-16, 34, 57, 59-60.
19. *Pretensions of Jefferson*, p. 4.
20. *Gazette of the United States*, November 4, 1796; John Adams, *Works* (Adams), VIII, 521; *Political Science Quarterly*, LVI (1941), 567.
21. *Gazette of the United States*, November 30, 1796; Hamilton, *Works* (J. C. Hamilton), VI, 191; H. E. Miller, *Banking Theories*, p. 20.
22. *General Advertiser*, October 30, 1800; Hamilton, *Works* (Lodge), VII, 320; R. Troup to King, November 16, 1796, King MSS., NYHS.
23. Hamilton, *Works* (Lodge), VII, 320.
24. Dayton to Sedgwick, November 12, 1796, Hamilton MSS., LC; Hamilton, *Works* (Lodge), VII, 319; Liston to Grenville, December, 1796, LC.
25. Charles C. Pinckney, *Life of General Thomas Pinckney* (Boston, 1895), p. 157; Hamilton, *Works* (J. C. Hamilton), VI, 113.
26. Sedgwick to Dayton, November 19, 1796, Hamilton MSS., LC; Gibbs, *Memoirs of the Administrations of Washington and Adams*, I, 408-409; *Brief Consideration of Mr. Adams* (Boston, 1796), p. 31; Steiner, *McHenry*, pp. 200-203.
27. Hamilton, *Works* (Lodge), VII, 320; Hammond, *Political Parties*, I, 101-102; *Pennsylvania Magazine of History and Biography*, LX (1936), 386; Walters, *Dallas*, p. 73;

Channing, *History*, IV, 173; C. F. Adams, *John Adams*, II, 205-206; *Gazette of the United States*, December 26, 1796; Massachusetts Historical Society, *Proceedings*, XLIV (1911), 395, 407.
28. Massachusetts Historical Society, *Proceedings*, LXVII (1945), 374-375; *American Historical Review*, XXXIX (1934), pp. 256-257; Gibbs, *Memoirs of the Administrations of Washington and Adams*, I, 491-492; Monroe, *Writings* (Hamilton), II, 459, 461; III, 49; Bemis, *John Quincy Adams*, pp. 60-61.
29. Washington, *Writings* (Fitzpatrick), XXXV, 385; Clark, *Peter Porcupine in America*, p. 85; Massachusetts Historical Society, *Proceedings*, LXVII (1945), 375; Lodge, *Cabot*, p. 111; Hamilton, *Works* (Lodge), VI, December 5, 1796.
30. Hamilton to Wolcott, June 15, 1796, Wolcott MSS., CHS.
31. Hamilton, *Works* (Lodge), IX, 200-201.
32. *Gazette of the United States*, December 26, 1796; *American Historical Review*, (XXXIX), 1934, 267; Rives, *Madison*, III, 586-587, 596; Steiner, *McHenry*, pp. 202-203; Gibbs, *Memoirs of the Administrations of Washington and Adams*, I, 413.

Chapter 29. The Mission to France

1. Madison, *Writings* (Hunt), VI, 300-301, 303, 305; Jefferson to John Adams, December 28, 1796, Emmet MSS., NYPL.
2. *General Advertiser*, March 20, 1797; Caius, *A Few Remarks on Mr. Hamilton's Last Letter* (Boston, 1800), pp. 5, 6, 11.
3. Massachusetts Historical Society, *Proceedings*, LVII (1924), 500; John Adams, *Works* (Adams), VIII, 524.
4. *Men and Times of the Revolution, or Memoirs of Elkanah Watson* (New York, 1856), p. 399; Hamilton, *Works* (Lodge), VII, 321-322.
5. John Adams, *Works* (Adams), VIII, 535; C. F. Adams, *John Adams*, II, 207-209; McRee, *Iredell*, II, 491-495; Henkels, *Washington-Madison Papers*, p. 77; *General Advertiser*, March 20, 1797.
6. Joseph Fauchet, *A Short Sketch of the Present State of our Political Relations* (Philadelphia, 1797), p. 26; Monroe, *Writings* (Hamilton), II, 305, 459; *American State Papers*, I, 578; Massachusetts Historical Society, *Proceedings*, XLIV (1911), 395.
7. Washington, *Writings* (Fitzpatrick), XXXV, 359; Joseph Hopkinson, *What Is Our Situation? By an American* (Philadelphia, 1798), p. 14.
8. Hamilton, *Works* (Lodge), VI, January 27, 1797; Lodge, *Cabot*, p. 121.
9. Steiner, *McHenry*, pp. 292-293; Hamilton to William L. Smith, April, 1797, Smith MSS., LC.
10. Madison, *Writings* (Hunt), VI, 307; Jefferson, *Writings* (Ford), I, 274; VII, September 1, 1797; John Dawson to Madison, June 4, 1797, Madison MSS., LC; *John P. Branch Historical Papers*, II, 282-283; *Annals of Congress*, III, 1123, 1164-1166; *Papers of Noah Webster*, p. 333.
11. Callender, *History of the United States for 1796*, pp. 26-27; Adams, *Gallatin*, pp. 185-187, 195-196, 300; *Gazette of the United States*, May 26, 1798; *Sketches of French and English Politicks in America, By a Member of the Old Congress* (Charleston, 1797), pp. 20, 29, 38, 49-50; Jefferson, *Writings* (Ford), I, 274; Hamilton, *Works* (Lodge), X, 267-270.
12. Fisher Ames, *Works*, I, 217; Hamilton to W. L. Smith, April, 1797, Smith MSS., LC; Hamilton, *Works* (Lodge), VII, 361; X, June 6, 1797; Steiner, *McHenry*, p. 217; Robert G. Harper, *Observations on the Dispute Between the United States and France* (London, 1798), pp. 99-100; Gibbs, *Memoirs of the Administrations of Washington and Adams,* I, April 24, 1797.
13. Hamilton, *Works* (J. C. Hamilton), VI, 216-217.
14. Hamilton to W. L. Smith, April, 1797, Smith MSS., LC.
15. Hamilton to W. L. Smith, April, 1797, Smith MSS., LC; J. C. Hamilton, *Alexander Hamilton*, VII, 23; Steiner, *McHenry*, pp. 217, 293-294; Hamilton, *Works* (Lodge), X, 165-170, 243-246, 253-254; Hamilton, *Works* (J. C. Hamilton), VI, 174; Hamilton to Wolcott, June 15, 1796, Hamilton MSS., LC.

16. Hamilton to McHenry, April, 1797, Hamilton MSS., LC; Hamilton to W. L. Smith, April, 1797, Smith MSS., LC.
17. J. C. Hamilton, *Alexander Hamilton*, VII, 21; Hamilton, *Works* (Lodge), X, 243-257, 275-279.
18. Hamilton to McHenry, April, 1797, Hamilton MSS., LC; Hamilton, *Works* (J. C. Hamilton), VI, 216-217; VII, 330; Hamilton to W. L. Smith, April, 1797, Smith MSS., LC; *What Is Our Situation?* p. 15; Gibbs, *Memoirs of the Administrations of Washington and Adams*, I, 478, 493; Lodge, *Cabot*, pp. 119, 133; Uriah Tracy to Hamilton, March 23, 1797, Hamilton MSS., LC.
19. Hamilton, *Works* (J. C. Hamilton), VI, 220; J. C. Hamilton, *Alexander Hamilton*, VII, 21-22; Steiner, *McHenry*, p. 225; Lodge, *Cabot*, pp. 11, 19, 131, 133, 137-138; Morison, *Jeremiah Smith*, p. 129; A. M. Hamilton, *Intimate Life*, p. 319.
20. Hamilton, *Works* (Lodge), X, 224-230.
21. Hamilton to W. L. Smith, April, 1797, Smith MSS., LC.
22. John Adams, *Works* (Adams), VIII, 536-539, 540; Hamilton, *Works* (J. C. Hamilton), VI, 242.
23. J. C. Hamilton, *Alexander Hamilton*, VII, 380; John Dawson to Madison, June 22, 1797, Madison MSS., LC.
24. McHenry to Hamilton, January 24, 1793, Hamilton MSS., LC; C. F. Adams, *John Adams*, II, 239; Steiner, *McHenry*, pp. 213-216, 291; Hamilton, *Works* (J. C. Hamilton), VI, 282-283, 307, 353; Timothy Pickering to S. Higginson, December 23, 1799, Pickering MSS., MHS; Gibbs, *Memoirs of the Administrations of Washington and Adams*, I, March 31, 1797.
25. Hamilton, *Works* (Lodge), VII, 23; J. C. Hamilton, *Alexander Hamilton*, VIII, 23; Liston to Grenville, December 7, 1796; February 13, 1797; May 29, 1800, LC; Pickering to W. L. Smith, June 7, 1800, Pickering MSS., MHS; Callender, *American Annual Register*, pp. 173-174; *President II*, pp. 10, 11; David Ross to Hamilton, November 16, 1797; Hamilton to Robert Cooper, March 3, 1796 (fabricated); William E. Van Allen to Dr. Stephen Gordon, February 6, 1796 (fabricated), Hamilton MSS., LC; *A Roaster; or a Check to the Progress of Political Blasphemy* (Philadelphia, 1796), pp. 3-4; C. F. Adams, *John Adams*, II, 197.
26. Callender, *History of the United States for 1796*, p. 117; *Pennsylvania Magazine of History and Biography*, LX (1936), 382; American Historical Association, *Report for 1912* (Washington, 1913), p. 356; John Beckley to James Monroe, June 22, 1793, Monroe MSS., LC.
27. Callender, *History of the United States for 1796*, pp. viii, 205, 219, 222, 228, 231; Hamilton, *Works* (Lodge), VII, 401; *General Advertiser*, July 19, 1796; Hamilton to Monroe, July 8, 1797; Venable to Hamilton, July 10, 1797; Oliver Wolcott to Hamilton, July 3, 8, 1797, Hamilton MSS., LC; *Mississippi Valley Historical Review*, XXXVI (1947), p. 460.
28. Hamilton, *Works* (Lodge), July 5, 1797.
29. Monroe to Hamilton, July 10, 1797, Hamilton MSS., LC.
30. John B. Church to Hamilton, July 13, 1797, Hamilton MSS., LC; Hamilton, *Works* (J. C. Hamilton), VII, 261.
31. Hamilton, *Works* (Lodge), VII, 472-473, 477-478; *Mississippi Valley Historical Review*, XXXVI (1947), 445-447, 462; William Jackson to Hamilton, July 24, August 7, 11, 1797, Hamilton MSS., LC; Hamilton, *Works* (J. C. Hamilton), VI, 261; Hamilton to Monroe, August 9, 1797, Hamilton MSS., LC.
32. *Mississippi Valley Historical Review*, XXXVI (1947), 467; Edward Jackson to Hamilton, August 13, 1797; Venable to Hamilton, July 10, 1797; Wolcott to Hamilton, July 3, 1797, Hamilton MSS., LC.
33. William Jackson to Hamilton, July 31, 1797, Hamilton MSS., LC; *General Advertiser*, July 19, 1797; Pickering and Upham, *Timothy Pickering*, III, 422.
34. A. M. Hamilton, *Intimate Life*, pp. 43-44; John B. Church to Hamilton, July 13, 1797, Hamilton MSS., LC.
35. Hamilton to John Fenno, July ?, 1797; William Jackson to Hamilton, July 14, July 24, 1797, Hamilton MSS., LC; Noah Webster, *A Letter to General Hamilton* (New York, 1800), p. 6.

Notes

36. Hamilton, *Works* (Lodge), VII, 379-380; Hamilton to John Fenno, July ?, 1797, Hamilton MSS., LC.
37. *General Advertiser*, July 19, 1797.
38. *Answer to Alexander Hamilton's Letter* (New York, 1800), pp. 28-29; *General Advertiser*, July 19, 27, October 18, 1797; January 19, 1798; October 31, 1800; Webster, *Letter to Hamilton*, p. 6.
39. John Wood, *A Correct Statement* (New York, 1802), p. 4; Rush, *Autobiography* (Corner), p. 190.
40. Massachusetts Historical Society, *Collections*, Seventh Series (Jefferson Papers), I, 59; James Madison to Jefferson, October 20, 1797, Madison MSS., LC; *John P. Branch Historical Papers*, II, 283; Callender, *History of the United States for the Year 1796*, p. 206; *General Advertiser*, October 31, 1800; Richmond *Examiner*, June 21, 1797.
41. A. M. Hamilton, *Intimate Life*, p. 147.
42. S. E. Morison, *Harrison Gray Otis*, I, 143; H. C. van Schaack, *Life of Peter van Schaack* (New York, 1892), pp. 357-358.
43. A. M. Hamilton, *Intimate Life*, pp. 13, 243, 259-260.
44. Morison, *Otis*, I, 143.

Chapter 30. Second in Command of the United States Army

1. Elbridge Gerry to William Vans Murray, October 31, 1797; Gerry to Adams, July 5, 1799, Gerry MSS., LC; W. C. Ford (ed.), *The Writings of John Quincy Adams* (New York, 1913), II, 316; Massachusetts Historical Society, *Proceedings*, XLIV (1911), 398-399; C. C. Pinckney to King, December 24, 1797, Rufus King MSS., LC; John Marshall to Rufus King, December 24, 1797, King MSS., LC; John Marshall to Pickering, October 22, 1798, Marshall MSS., LC; Pickering, *A Review of the Adams-Cunningham Correspondence*, pp. 82-83.
2. Liston to Grenville, April 12, 1795, LC; Madison to Jefferson, May 5, 1798, Madison MSS., LC; John Dawson to Madison, April 5, 1798, Madison MSS., LC; John Quincy Adams to W. L. Smith, July 18, 1798, W. L. Smith MSS., LC; Timothy Pickering to Hamilton, March 25, 1798, Hamilton MSS., LC; Hamilton, *Works* (Lodge), VI, 277-279; Lodge, *Cabot*, p. 154; C. F. Adams, *John Adams*, II, 239.
3. Hamilton, *Works* (Lodge), VI, April 17, 19, 1798, VII, 180; Hamilton to W. L. Smith, April, 1797, Hamilton MSS., LC; Hamilton to the Secretary of War, November 23, 1799, Hamilton MSS., LC.
4. Hamilton, *Works* (Lodge), VII, 331; John Adams, *Works* (Adams), VIII, 622; IX, 203-205, 210, 219-220, 222; X, 10-11; Jefferson, *Writings* (Ford), IX, 296; J. C. Hamilton, *Alexander Hamilton*, VII, 168; Albany *Centinel*, August 17, 1798; *Gazette of the United States*, June 20, 30, July 16, 1798; December 6, 1799; Liston to Grenville, May 21, 1798, LC; *New Hampshire Gazette*, July 17, 1798.
5. Pickering and Upham, *Pickering*, III, 411; Salem *Gazette*, July 17, 1796; *New Hampshire Gazette*, July 26, 1798; *The Alarm* (New York, 1799), p. 6; *Gazette of the United States*, June 18, 1799; John Adams, *Works* (Adams), IX, 217, 220; Stewart Mitchell (ed.), *New Letters of Abigail Adams* (Boston, 1947), p. 104; Stokes, *Iconography*, V, 1354-1355.
6. Hamilton, *Works* (Lodge), VI, April 19, 1798.
7. J. C. Hamilton, *Alexander Hamilton*, VII, 21; Hamilton, *Works* (Lodge), VII, 179.
8. Madison, *Writings* (Hunt), VI, 322-325; Madison to Jefferson, February 12, 1795, May 5, 1798, Madison MSS., LC; Fisher Ames, *Works*, I, 232; J. C. Hamilton, *Alexander Hamilton*, VII, 236-237.
9. J. C. Hamilton, *Alexander Hamilton*, VII, 21; Hamilton, *Works* (Lodge), VI, March 10, 1798.
10. Hamilton, *Works* (Lodge), VII, 330; *Gazette of the United States*, May 22, 1798.
11. *Gazette of the United States*, June 15, 20, November 3, 1798; Hamilton, *Works* (J. C. Hamilton), VI, 321; Liston to Grenville, April 27, September 27, 1798, LC.
12. John Adams, *Works* (Adams), IX, 220-221, 304-305.
13. Gibbs, *Memoirs of the Administrations of Washington and Adams*, II, 68-71; John Adams, *Works* (Adams), IX, 235; Mitchell, *New Letters of Abigail Adams*, pp. 148, 207;

Hamilton, *Works* (J. C. Hamilton), VI, 273; Jefferson, *Writings* (Ford), I, 282-283; Fisher Ames, *Works*, I, 232-233, 237; Lodge, *Cabot*, p. 165; Fenno, *Desultory Reflections*, pp. 15, 55; *Gazette of the United States*, November 20,1798; American Historical Association, *Report for 1898* (Washington, 1899), I, 808; Liston to Grenville, June 12, 1798, LC.

14. E. D. Adams, *Influence of Grenville on Pitt's Foreign Policy*, pp. 48, 50, 52, 53-55, 57, 61; A. P. Primrose (ed.), *The Windham Papers* (London, 1913), II, 18; J. C. Hamilton, *Alexander Hamilton*, VII, 22; *American Historical Review* (1897), II, 303-304; Ward and Gooch, *Cambridge History of British Foreign Policy*, I, 279-281; Hamilton to W. L. Smith, April, 1797, Smith MSS., LC.

15. J. C. Hamilton, *Alexander Hamilton*, VII, 106-107; Pickering to Hamilton, March 28, 1798, Hamilton MSS., LC; Steiner, *McHenry*, p. 294; C. F. Adams, *John Adams*, II, 234-236.

16. Fisher Ames, *Works*, II, 159; John Taylor, *An Enquiry into the Principles and Policy of the Government of the United States* (Philadelphia, 1794), p. 47; *An Examination of the Conduct of the Executive of the United States* (Philadelphia, 1797), p. 65.

17. Timothy Pickering to King, February 8, 1795, Rufus King MSS., LC; Liston to Grenville, May 2, 1798, LC; Fisher Ames, *Works*, I, 263-264.

18. Hamilton, *Works* (Lodge), X, May 17, 1798, 294; Wilkinson, *Memoirs*, pp. 464-465.

19. Hamilton, *Works* (Lodge), X, 294.

20. *Ibid.*, VI, 156; X, 254; Steiner, *McHenry*, p. 217; Hamilton to William L. Smith, April 10, 1797, Smith MSS., LC; J. C. Hamilton, *Alexander Hamilton*, VII, 26; *Annals of Congress*, VII, March, 1798.

21. Hamilton, *Works* (J. C. Hamilton), VI, 330.

22. Charles Biddle, *Autobiography* (Philadelphia, 1883), pp. 276-278; *New Hampshire Gazette*, June 5, 1798; Timothy Pickering, *Review of the Adams-Cunningham Correspondence* (Salem, 1824), p. 112; Henry B. Ashmead (ed.), *Letters to John Langdon* (Philadelphia, 1880), p. 16; N. W. Stephenson and W. H. Dunn, *George Washington* (New York, 1940), II, 457-459.

23. Timothy Pickering to Washington, September 13, 1798, Washington MSS., LC.

24. Pickering, *Review of the Adams-Cunningham Correspondence*, p. 114; Hamilton, *Works* (J. C. Hamilton), VI, 352, 369; Hamilton, *Works* (Lodge), X, 297; John Adams, *Works* (Adams), VIII, 602-604; Washington, *Writings* (Fitzpatrick), XXXVI, 323-324; Pickering to Hamilton, July 16, 1798, Hamilton MSS., LC; Lodge, *Cabot*, p. 61; Henry Knox to Pickering, August 8, 1798, Hamilton MSS., LC; Steiner, *McHenry*, pp. 164-165; McHenry to Washington, September 14, 1798, Washington MSS., LC; J. Hillhouse to Trumbull, July 18, 1798, Trumbull MSS., CHS; George Cabot to John Adams, September 29, 1798, Hamilton MSS., LC; Oliver Wolcott to William L. Smith, November 29, 1798, Smith MSS., LC; J. C. Hamilton, *Alexander Hamilton*, VII, 193; John Adams to McHenry, August 19, 1798, Hamilton MSS., LC; McHenry (Hamilton) to Henry Knox, August 22, 1798, Hamilton MSS., LC; McHenry to Washington, August 25, 1798, Hamilton MSS., LC; Pickering to Washington, September 13, 1798, Hamilton MSS., LC; A. M. Hamilton, *Intimate Life*, p. 322; Hamilton to Knox, March 14, 1799, Knox MSS., MHS; John Jay to Pickering, July 10, 1798, Hamilton MSS., LC; McHenry to Hamilton, October 5, 1798; Adams to Washington, October 9, 1798, Hamilton MSS., LC; Stephenson and Dunn, *George Washington*, II, 459-460.

25. Washington, *Writings* (Fitzpatrick), XXXVI, 340, 460-461.

26. John Adams, *Works* (Adams), X, 124; Henry Adams, *New England Federalism*, p. 335.

27. George Cabot to Pickering, October 31, 1798, Pickering MSS., MHS; C. C. Pinckney to McHenry, October 31, 1798, Washington MSS., LC.

Chapter 31. The War That Refused to Come to a Boil

1. Benjamin Goodhue to Pickering, October 12, 1798, Pickering MSS., MHS; John Adams to McHenry, August 14, 1798, Hamilton MSS., LC; Washington, *Writings* (Fitzpatrick), XXXVI, 462, 474; Hamilton to ?, September 9, 1798; Hamilton to Washington, March 27, 1799, Hamilton MSS., LC; Hamilton, *Works* (J. C. Hamilton), VI, 193; Hamilton,

Notes

Works (Lodge), VII, 63; McHenry to William L. Smith, November 30, 1798, Smith MSS., LC; *Gazette of the United States*, November 10, 1798; John Adams, *Works* (Adams), X, 119, 124; Gibbs, *Memoirs*, II, 71; Alexander Biddle, *Old Family Letters* (Philadelphia, 1892), p. 71.

2. Cheetham, *View of the Political Conduct of Aaron Burr*, pp. 28-29; Washington, *Writings* (Fitzpatrick), XXXVII, 160-161; Hamilton, *Works* (Lodge), VII, 63.
3. Washington, *Writings* (Fitzpatrick), XXXVII, 271; J. C. Hamilton, *Alexander Hamilton*, VII, 246-247; *Annals of Congress*, V, 267; Steiner, *McHenry*, p. 295; Hamilton, *Works* (J. C. Hamilton), VI, 480.
4. Hamilton, *Works* (Lodge), VII, 100, 103-105, 116, 145-146, 160, 194; J. C. Hamilton, *Alexander Hamilton*, VII, 225; Hamilton, *Works* (J. C. Hamilton), V, 239, 248-249, 291, 306-309, 403; VI, 336, 374; McHenry to Hamilton, September 6, November 16, 1799; March 19, 1800, Hamilton MSS., LC; Robert Troup to King, June 5, 1799, King MSS., NYHS; Hamilton to General Duportail, July 23, 1798; Hamilton to Washington, July 9, 1798, Hamilton MSS., LC; Steiner, *McHenry*, pp. 168, 291, 295, 450-451; Gibbs, *Memoirs*, II, 315; White, *Jeffersonians*, pp. 224, 251-252, 259; Washington, *Writings* (Fitzpatrick), XXXVI, 162-164, 473; Leonidas, *A Reply to Lucius Junius Brutus* (New York, 1801), p. 7; *Greenleaf's New York Daily Advertiser*, July 6, 1799; *General Advertiser*, January 11, November 14, 1799; *The Oracle of Dauphine and Pittsburgh Advertiser*, August 8, 1798; John Beckley to Irvine, July 20, 1798, William Irvine MSS., HSP; Marshall, *Washington*, V, 746.
5. Channing, *History*, IV, 199; McHenry to Hamilton, February 8, 1799, Hamilton MSS., LC; John Adams, *Works* (Adams), VIII, 613, 622; IX, 586-587, 596; X, 127-128; Washington, *Writings* (Fitzpatrick), XXXVI, 425-426; XXXVII, 190 footnote; Webster, *Letter to General Hamilton*, p. 7.
6. Hamilton, *Works* (J. C. Hamilton), VI, 307; Hamilton, *Works* (Lodge), X, 295; James Morton Smith, *Freedom's Fetters* (Ithaca, N. Y., 1956), pp. 150-156; John C. Miller, *Crisis in Freedom* (Boston, 1951), p. 71; *Gazette of the United States*, June 20, July 2, 1798; Allan Nevins, *American Press Opinion, Washington to Coolidge* (Boston, 1928), pp. 27-28; American Historical Association, *Report for 1896*, I, 808; *Porcupine's Gazette*, May 7, 1798; Clark, *Peter Porcupine in America*, pp. 132-133; James Hillhouse to Jonathan Trumbull, June 21, 1798, Trumbull MSS., CHS; Henry Knox to Oliver Wolcott, May 27, 1798, Knox MSS., MHS; J. Eugene Smith, *One Hundred Years of Hartford's Courant* (New Haven, 1947), pp. 68, 73.
7. A. M. Hamilton, *Intimate Life*, p. 325; Kent, *Commentaries*, II, 16-18.
8. Pound, *Spirit of the Common Law*, p. 27; Crosskey, *Politics and the Constitution*, I, 1346, 1357; *Debates in Congress* (abridged) (Washington, 1861), II, 616; Felix Frankfurter (ed.), *Mr. Justice Brandeis* (New Haven, 1933), pp. 109-110.
9. Hamilton, *Works* (Lodge), X, 335-336; *Greenleaf's New Daily Advertiser*, November 6, 1799; Kent, *Commentaries*, II, 16-18; *General Advertiser*, March 19, November 7, 1800; *Albany Centinel*, November 29, 1799; *New York Journal and Patriotic Register*, December 11, 1799; Francis Wharton, *State Trials* (Washington, 1849), pp. 649-651.
10. *New York Journal and Patriotic Register*, December 14, 1799; Milton W. Hamilton, *The Country Printer in New York State, 1785-1930* (New York, 1946), p. 45; F. L. Mott, *American Journalism* (New York, 1950), p. 150; A. M. Hamilton, *Intimate Life*, pp. 68-69; Dumas Malone, *Public Life of Thomas Cooper, 1783-1839* (New Haven, 1926), p. 140 footnote; *Claypoole's American Daily Advertiser*, December 4, 1799; *Greenleaf's New Daily Advertiser*, December 4, 1799; *General Advertiser*, November 7, 1800.
11. McLaughlin, *Constitutional History*, pp. 267-277; *Selected Cases of Constitutional Law*, II, 571-572; *Federalist*, pp. 200, 308-309, 311-312; Corwin, *Twilight of the Supreme Court*, p. 48; A. Lawrence Lowell, *Essays on Government* (Boston, 1892), p. 58; *William and Mary Quarterly* (April, 1948), p. 147 footnote; Sobei Magi, *The Problem of Federalism* (New York, 1951), I, 76-77, 82-83; Corwin, *Judicial Review*, pp. 55-56.
12. Hamilton, *Works* (Lodge), X, 341-342.
13. Edward Thornton to ?, February 4, 1799, PRO, FO; Winchester (Virginia) *Gazette*, May 29, 1799; February 19, 1800; Crosskey, *Politics and the Constitution*, II, 1345; *Annals of Congress*, XXX, 795, 805.

14. McRee, *Iredell*, II, 543; Hamilton, *Works* (Lodge), VII, 56; X, 329-336; Theodore Sedgwick to ?, February 18, 1799, Sedgwick MSS., MHS.
15. Adams, *Gallatin*, p. 233; Notes of a Conversation with General Dayton in 1799, Hamilton MSS., LC; *William and Mary Quarterly* (April, 1948), pp. 147, 158 footnotes.
16. Corwin, *Judicial Review*, pp. 55-56.
17. *Annals of Congress*, X, 399; *Greenleaf's New Daily Advertiser*, July 11, 1799; *Porcupine's Gazette*, July 27, 1798; Albany *Centinel*, December 28, 1798; C. C. Pinckney to Harper, June 13, 1799, R. G. Harper MSS., LC; J. C. Hamilton, *Alexander Hamilton*, VII, 247.
18. Hamilton to His Wife, November, 1798, Hamilton MSS., LC.

Chapter 32. The Effort to Avert Peace

1. John Adams, *Works* (Adams), X, 127.
2. Charles Warren, *Jacobin and Junto* (Cambridge, 1931), p. 149; Hamilton, *Works* (J. C. Hamilton), VI, 396, 399; Lodge, *Cabot*, p. 217; Sedgwick to Hamilton, February 22, 1797, Hamilton MSS., LC; Fenno, *Desultory Reflections*, p. 10; Liston to Grenville, March 4, 1799, LC.
3. Hamilton, *Works* (Lodge), VII, 341; X, 346, February 21, 1799; October 21, 1799; Pickering and Upham, *Timothy Pickering*, III, 440-441; Lodge, *Cabot*, pp. 224, 236-237; John Adams, *Works* (Adams), IX, 248-250; C. F. Adams, *John Adams*, II, 280-281, 286; Richard Peters to Pickering, August 30, 1798, Pickering MSS., MHS; American Historical Association, *Report for 1912* (Washington, 1913), pp. 602, 612; *New Hampshire Gazette*, June 5, 1798; Albany *Centinel*, May 3, 1799; Gibbs, *Memoirs of the Administrations of Washington and Adams*, II, 169-170; Fenno, *Desultory Reflections*, p. 13; Liston to Grenville, March 4, 1799, LC; *William and Mary Quarterly*, Third Series, IX (1954), 623; William Smith to Pickering, September 5, 1798; George Cabot to Pickering, October 21, 1798; B. Goodhue to Pickering, September 1, 1798, Pickering MSS., MHS; John Quincy Adams to W. L. Smith, November 1, 1796, Smith MSS., LC; Philadelphia *Gazette*, March 15, 1799; *Federalist*, p. 43.
4. Hamilton, *Works* (J. C. Hamilton), VI, 399; Lodge, *Cabot*, p. 216; C. R. King, *Rufus King*, II, March 6, 1799; *Correspondence Between John Adams and William Cunningham*, p. 46.
5. *Greenleaf's New Daily Advertiser*, March 7, 1799; Jefferson, *Writings* (Ford), I, 284; R. G. Harper to the Secretary of War, August 2, 1799, Harper MSS., LC; John Lowell, *An Oration* (Boston, 1799), pp. 25-26; *Country Porcupine*, July 11, 12, 1799; Pickering to S. Higginson, August 14, 1799, Pickering MSS., MHS; Hamilton, *Works* (Lodge), VII, 332; American Historical Association, *Report for 1896*, I, 814.
6. J. C. Hamilton, *Alexander Hamilton*, VII, 243; Hamilton, *Works* (Lodge), VII, 97.
7. *American Historical Review*, XLIII, 524-525; Hamilton, *Works* (Lodge), January 29, 1799; Fauchet, *A Sketch of the Present State of our Political Relations*, p. 28; *Mississippi Valley Historical Review*, XXXVI (1947), pp. 429, 432, 442; Albany *Centinel*, January 2, 1798; E. W. Lyon, *Louisiana in French Diplomacy* (Norman, Okla., 1934), pp. 89-90.
8. Fenno, *Desultory Reflections*, pp. 55-56.
9. William Spence Robertson, *Life of Francisco Miranda* (Chapel Hill, N.C., 1929), I, 110, 127, 176-177; John Adams, *Works* (Adams), X, 134-135; *American Historical Review*, VII (1902), 713.
10. *Edinburgh Review*, XIII (1809), 290-291; *American Historical Review*, VII (1902), 709, 713.
11. Robertson, *Miranda*, I, 185.
12. Miranda to Hamilton, April 6, 1798, Hamilton MSS., LC; Robertson, *Miranda*, I, 176-177.
13. C. C. Tansill, *The United States and Santo Domingo* (Baltimore, 1938), pp. 47-48.
14. Hamilton, *Works* (Lodge), X, January 26, 1799.
15. Robertson, *Miranda*, I, 180; *Federalist*, pp. 64-65; Hamilton, *Works* (Lodge), X, August 22, 1798; *Edinburgh Review*, XIII (1809), 290-292.
16. Mayo, *Instructions to British Ministers*, p. 159.

Notes

17. Hamilton, *Works* (Lodge), VII, 76.
18. Walters, *Dallas*, pp. 108-110; Albany *Centinel*, January 2, 1798; Liston to Grenville, March 16, 1797, LC; Hamilton to Adams, September 7, 1799, Adams MSS., MHS; Hamilton, *Works* (J. C. Hamilton), V, 360; Hamilton, *Works* (Lodge), VII, 123-124; McHenry to Hamilton, November 20, 1799, Hamilton MSS., LC.
19. J. C. Hamilton, *Alexander Hamilton*, VII, 334; James R. Jacobs, *Tarnished Warrior* (New York, 1933), pp. 190-191; McHenry to Hamilton, March 3, 1799, Hamilton MSS., LC.
20. Hamilton, *Works* (Lodge), X, June 15, 1799; VII, 43; Hamilton, *Works* (J. C. Hamilton), V, 283; Hamilton to John Adams, September 7, 1799, Adams MSS., MHS; John Adams, *Works* (Adams), VIII, 584 footnote.
21. John Adams, *Works* (Adams), X, 144-151; Tansill, *United States and Santo Domingo*, pp. 35, 36 footnote.
22. Hamilton, *Works* (J. C. Hamilton), V, 183, 195, 274-275; Hamilton, *Works* (Lodge), X, January 26, 1799; Wolcott to Hamilton, August 9, 1799, Hamilton MSS., LC.
23. Pickering to S. Higginson, August 14, 1799, Pickering MSS., MHS; Gibbs, *Memoirs of the Administrations of Washington and Adams*, II, 189; Washington, *Writings* (Fitzpatrick), XXXVII, 428 footnote; John Adams, *Works* (Adams), VIII, 629; IX, 254; Liston to Grenville, March 11, 1799, LC.
24. Morison, *Otis*, I, 175; John Adams, *Works* (Adams), IX, 11, 254; X, 70, 113; *Correspondence Between John Adams and William Cunningham*, p. 48.
25. American Historical Association, *Report for 1896*, I, 822; Lodge, *Cabot*, pp. 234-235, 239; *Correspondence Between John Adams and William Cunningham*, pp. 47, 49; Morison, *Otis*, I, 175; John Adams, *Works* (Adams), IX, 32-33, 70, 254.
26. J. C. Hamilton, *Alexander Hamilton*, VII, 335; Fenno, *Desultory Reflections*, p. 11.
27. John Adams, *Works* (Adams), IX, 254, 289-290.
28. C. R. King, *Rufus King*, III, November 6, 1799; Gibbs, *Memoirs of the Administrations of Washington and Adams*, II, 274; Fenno, *Desultory Reflections*, p. 11.
29. John Adams, *Works* (Adams), X, 113.
30. Hamilton to Knox, March 14, 1799, Knox MSS., MHS.
31. James Wilkinson to McHenry, December 6, 1799, Hamilton MSS., LC.
32. Hamilton, *Works* (Lodge), VII, 356-357.
33. John Williams, *Life of Alexander Hamilton* (Boston, 1804), p. 12; Caius, *A Few Remarks on Mr. Hamilton's Late Letter* (Baltimore, 1800), p. 21; *Political Science Quarterly*, XVIII (1903), 99.
34. *General Advertiser*, July 10, 1799; *To the Republican Citizens of the State of Pennsylvania* (Lancaster, Pa., 1800), pp. 3-4.
35. John Adams, *Works* (Adams), IX, 290; X, 127-129; Hamilton, *Works* (J. C. Hamilton), VI, 393-394.
36. General Macpherson to Hamilton, March 25, 1799, Hamilton MSS., LC; McHenry to Hamilton, March 15, 1799, Hamilton MSS., LC; McRee, *Iredell*, II, 549; Hamilton to General Dayton, March 18, 1799, Hamilton MSS., LC; Hamilton, *Works* (Lodge), VII, 69; Rich, *The Presidents and Civil Disorder*, pp. 25-26; Tolles, *Logan*, pp. 208-209.
37. Albany *Centinel*, May 25, 1798; Callender, *The Prospect Before Us*, I, 84; Gallatin, Greene County Address, September, 1798, Gallatin MSS., NYHS; *Greenleaf's New Daily Advertiser*, February 22, 1799; New York *Evening Post*, July 15, 1803; Adams, *Gallatin*, p. 223; Leonidas, *A Reply to Lucius Junius Brutus* (New York, 1801), p. 8.
38. Southern Historical Association, *Publications*, IX (Washington, 1935), W. B. Grove to McHenry, August 20, 1798; John Quincy Adams, *Writings* (Ford), II, 495.
39. Hamilton, *Works* (J. C. Hamilton), V, 260; John Alden to Hamilton, July 22, 1795, Hamilton MSS., LC; Steiner, *McHenry*, p. 437.
40. John Adams, *Works* (Adams), X, 153; Hamilton, *Works* (Lodge), VII, 353-354; Liston to Grenville, May 30, 1800, LC; Timothy Pickering to John Pickering, June 7, 1800, Pickering MSS., MHS; Steiner, *McHenry*, p. 415.
41. Hamilton, *Works* (Lodge), VII, 354-355; IX, 381-382; Pickering to Cabot, June 16, 1800, Pickering MSS., MHS; Steiner, *McHenry*, p. 436; *Porcupine's Gazette*, March 30, 1795; John Adams, *Works* (Adams), VIII, 644; IX, 59.

42. Williams, *Alexander Hamilton*, pp. 21-22; John Adams, *Works* (Adams), IX, 60; Timothy Pickering to John Pickering, June 7, 1800, Pickering MSS., MHS; Liston to Grenville, May 30, 1800, LC.
43. Graydon, *Memoirs*, p. 392; Hamilton, *Works* (Lodge), VII, 355.
44. Pickering, *Review of the Adams-Cunningham Correspondence*, pp. 67-68; *General Advertiser*, November 14, 29, 1799; St. George Tucker to Monroe, December 29, 1799, Monroe MSS., LC; John Adams, *Works* (Adams), X, 118; *Annals of Congress*, X, 268, 283-284, 298; McHenry to Hamilton, February 18, 1800, Hamilton MSS., LC; Liston to Grenville, February 2, 1800, LC; Hamilton, *Works* (J. C. Hamilton), VI, 400; Burr to Jefferson, February 3, 1799, Jefferson MSS., LC.
45. Hamilton to Captain G. Izard, February 27, 1800, Hamilton MSS., LC.
46. Hamilton, *Works* (Lodge), X, February 17, 1800; Liston to Grenville, May 28, 1800, LC; Simeon Baldwin, *Life and Letters* (New York, 1919), pp. 415-416.

Chapter 33. The Election of 1800

1. *Gazette of the United States*, May 7, 1799; *Porcupine's Gazette*, May 7, 1799.
2. *Gazette of the United States*, August 23, 1800; Adams, *Gallatin*, p. 240.
3. *Essays in American History Dedicated to F. J. Turner* (New York, 1910), pp. 120-121; *New England Quarterly*, XVII (1944), 351-352.
4. Edward Livingston to Gallatin, May 6, 1798, Gallatin MSS., NYHS; Gallatin, *Works* (Adams), I, 50-51; Pickering to Rufus King, May 5, 1799, Pickering MSS., MHS.
5. Burr to Jefferson, February 3, 1799, Jefferson MSS., LC.
6. Hammond, *Political Parties*, I, 95, 115; Cheetham, *View of the Political Conduct of Aaron Burr*, pp. 19, 23-25; Monaghan, *Jay*, p. 418.
7. *Porcupine's Gazette*, May 7, 1799; Monaghan, *Jay*, p. 417; Gouverneur Morris, *Letters and Diaries*, II, 379.
8. Hammond, *Political Parties*, I, 134-136; Spaulding, *Clinton*, p. 230; Adams, *Gallatin*, pp. 233-234; Rochefoucault-Liancourt, *Travels*, II, 439; *Political Science Quarterly*, XXXII (1919), 252-255; Charles Biddle, *Autobiography*, pp. 289-290; Bray Hammond, *Banks and Politics in Early America* (Princeton, 1957), pp. 153-155, 160.
9. William Vans Murray, *Letters*, p. 494; Jay to King, March 29, June 16, 1800, King MSS., NYHS; M. L. Davis to Gallatin, March 29, 1800, Gallatin MSS., NYHS.
10. *General Advertiser*, April 3, 1800.
11. *Albany Centinel*, May 6, 1800; Liston to Grenville, May 8, 18, October 8, 1800, LC; John Rutledge to Oliver Wolcott, October 15, 1800, Wolcott MSS., CHS.
12. Hamilton, *Works* (Lodge), X, May 7, 1800.
13. Adams, *Gallatin*, pp. 241-242; John Dawson to Madison, May 4, 1800, Madison MSS., LC.
14. Hamilton, *Works* (Lodge), May 7, 1800; Jay, *Writings*, IV, 275; Monaghan, *Jay*, p. 419.
15. Schachner, *Aaron Burr*, p. 178; Hammond, *Political Parties*, I, 144-145; Monaghan, *Jay*, p. 417; Pickering and Upham, *Pickering*, III, 327; Gallatin, *Works* (Adams), I, 51; Morison, *Otis*, I, 136; John B. Weston to Pickering, January 19, 1800, Pickering MSS., MHS; *Gazette of the United States*, November 10, 1800.
16. Nathaniel Macon to Nicholson, May 9, 1800, Joseph H. Nicholson MSS., LC; Adams, *Gallatin*, p. 240; Hamilton, *Works* (Lodge), X, May 7, 1800.
17. Hamilton, *Works* (Lodge), X, 376.
18. Washington, *Writings* (Fitzpatrick), XXXVII, July 21, 1795; Adams, *New England Federalism*, p. 149.
19. Lodge, *Cabot*, p. 279.
20. Massachusetts Historical Society, *Collections*, Seventh Series, I (1902), 77; Morison, *Otis*, I, 105; Adams, *Gallatin*, p. 241; Gabriel Duval to Madison, June 8, 1800, Madison MSS., LC; Pickering to W. L. Smith, May 7, 1800, W. L. Smith MSS., LC; William Bingham to Hamilton, August 24, 1800, Hamilton MSS., LC; Fisher Ames to R. King, August 26, 1800, King MSS., NYHS; George Cabot to King, May 19, 1800, King MSS., NYHS; Gibbs, *Memoirs of the Administrations of Washington and Adams*, II, 347, 387; Fisher Ames, *Works*, I, 280; Liston to Grenville, May 29, 1800, LC.
21. Hamilton, *Works* (J. C. Hamilton), VI, 454.

Notes

22. Stephen Higginson to Pickering, January 12, 1800, Pickering MSS., MHS; R. G. Harper to Hamilton, June 9, 1800, Hamilton MSS., LC; Henry W. Saursure to Pickering, August 12, 1800, Pickering MSS., MHS; Adams, *Gallatin*, p. 241; Gibbs, *Memoirs of the Administrations of Washington and Adams*, II, 387-388; Massachusetts Historical Society, *Collections*, Seventh Series, I (1902), 78; *Independent Chronicle*, June 19, 1800; Albany *Centinel*, December 16, 1800.
23. Philadelphia *Gazette*, October 25, 1800.
24. Fisher Ames, *Works*, II, 115; Pickering to Samuel Gardner, June 25, 1800, Pickering MSS., MHS.
25. *Alexander Biddle Papers*, p. 7; John Adams, *Works* (Adams), IX, 301.
26. Hamilton, *Works* (Lodge), X, November 5, 1796.
27. White, *Federalists*, pp. 45-46; Hamilton, *Works* (Lodge), VII, 348-349.
28. White, *Federalists*, pp. 44-45; Gibbs, *Memoirs of the Administrations of Washington and Adams*, II, 348; Pickering and Upham, *Pickering*, III, 487-488; *Correspondence Between John Adams and William Cunningham*, pp. 39-40; *Massachusetts Mercury*, June 20, 1800; *Gazette of the United States*, July 3, 13, 1800; *Columbian Centinel*, June 21, 1800.
29. Hamilton, *Works* (Lodge), X, May 10, 1800; C. R. King, *Rufus King*, III, July 18, 1800.
30. *Columbian Centinel*, July 5, 1800; Fisher Ames to King, August 26, 1800, King MSS., NYHS; R. Troup to King, June 24, 1800, King MSS., NYHS; Hamilton, *Works* (Lodge), VII, 362; Lodge, *Cabot*, pp. 281-282; John Adams, *Works* (Adams), IX, 278; Gibbs, *Memoirs of the Administrations of Washington and Adams*, II, 223; C. F. Adams, *John Adams*, II, 158; *Correspondence Between John Adams and William Cunningham*, p. 107; Pickering to King, June 26, 1800, King MSS., NYHS; C. R. King, *Rufus King*, III, June 26, July 19, August 19, 1800.
31. Hamilton, *Works* (Lodge), May 10, 1800.
32. John Adams, *Works* (Adams), X, 274; Lodge, *Cabot*, p. 274; Liston to Grenville, July 5, 1800, LC; Gibbs, *Memoirs of the Administrations of Washington and Adams*, II, 447; McHenry to Hamilton, December 1, 1800, Hamilton MSS., LC; *Gazette of the United States*, August 23, 1800.
33. Hamilton, *Works* (J. C. Hamilton), VI, 447.
34. Liston to Grenville, July 5, 1800, LC; Pickering to Christopher Gore, June 9, 1800; Pickering to Herman Stump, May 30, 1800; Pickering to Timothy Williams, May 19, 1800; Pickering to J. Pickering, June 7, 1800, Pickering MSS., MHS; C. R. Brown, *The Northern Confederacy* (New York, 1915), p. 18; Hamilton to Pickering, May 15, 1800, Pickering MSS., MHS.
35. Lodge, *Cabot*, pp. 286-288; John Rutledge, Jr., to Hamilton, July 17, 1800, Hamilton MSS., LC; R. Troup to King, September 4, 1800, King MSS., NYHS; *Columbian Centinel*, March 15, 1800; John Jay to Pickering, June 19, 1800, Pickering MSS., MHS; Lodge, *Cabot*, pp. 286-288; Gibbs, *Memoirs of the Administrations of Washington and Adams*, II, 368-370, 407.
36. C. F. Adams, *Adams*, II, 328; Hamilton, *Works* (J. C. Hamilton), VI, 479; Gibbs, *Memoirs of the Administrations of Washington and Adams*, II, 407, 416, 384-385; Hamilton, *Works* (Lodge), X, August 3, 27, 1800.
37. Hamilton, *Works* (Lodge) VII, 320, 348; Gibbs, *Memoirs of the Administrations of Washington and Adams*, II, 419.
38. Liston to Grenville, May 29, 1800, LC; McHenry to Wolcott, July 22, 1800, Hamilton MSS., LC; Webster, *A Letter to General Hamilton*, p. 8.
39. Irving Brant, *James Madison, Secretary of State* (Indianapolis, 1953), p. 21; McHenry to Hamilton, November 9, December 1, 1800, Hamilton MSS., LC; Hamilton, *Works* (Lodge), VII, 356; X, March 7, 1800.
40. *Gazette of the United States*, August 23, 1800; C. R. King, *Rufus King*, November 9, 1800; *General Advertiser*, October 31, 1800; *The Political Magazine for November, 1800* (Ballston, N. Y., 1800), p. 61.
41. *Gazette of the United States*, August 9, 1800; Fisher Ames to King, September 24, 1800, G. Cabot to King, November 13, 1800, King MSS., NYHS; William Bingham to Hamilton, August 24, 1800, Hamilton MSS., LC; Arthur Campbell to Pickering, December 23, 1798, Pickering MSS., MHS; *American Historical Review*, XIV, 700;

The Political Magazine for November, 1800, pp. 54, 56; General Advertiser, August 7, 8, September 3, November 17, 1800; Gibbs, Memoirs of the Administrations of Washington and Adams, II, 414; Liston to Grenville, November 6, 1800, LC.
42. Tom Callender, Letter to A. Hamilton, King of the Feds, p. 22; Gibbs, Memoirs of the Administrations of Washington and Adams, II, 449; Gazette of the United States, June 14, November 24, 1800; Hamilton, Works (J. C. Hamilton), VI, 482; A Letter to General Hamilton (Philadelphia, 1800), pp. 1, 7, 8; Noah Webster, Works, I, 494, 501, 504-505; Philadelphia Gazette, December 5, 1800; American Historical Association, Report for 1896, I, 833; John Adams, Works (Adams), VIII, 627-628.
43. C. R. King, Rufus King, III, October 1, 1800; Gibbs, Memoirs of the Administrations of Washington and Adams, I, 381, 433; G. Cabot to King, December 23, 1800, King MSS., NYHS; Biddle, Old Family Letters, pp. 92, 118; John Adams, Works (Adams), IX, 277; General Advertiser, December 31, 1800.
44. Brown, Northern Confederacy, p. 27; Lodge, Cabot, p. 284.
45. Theodore Sedgwick to Theodore Sedgwick, Jr., January 11, 1800, Sedgwick MSS., MHS; John Hillhouse to Jeremiah Wadsworth, January 1, 1801, Trumbull MSS., CHS; Edward Thornton to Grenville, December 27, 1800, Thornton Correspondence. Henry Adams transcript, LC; Hamilton, Works (J. C. Hamilton), V, 512-513; Albany Centinel, January 2, 1801.
46. Hamilton, Works (Lodge), X. August 10, December 16, 1800.
47. Hamilton, Works (Lodge), X, December 16, 1800; January 16, 1801.
48. Steiner, McHenry, pp. 463-465; Hamilton, Works (Lodge), X, December 24, 1800; C. R. King, Rufus King, III, December 31, 1800; A. M. Hamilton, Intimate Life, p. 385.
49. Uriah Tracy to J. Wadsworth, January 8, 1801, Trumbull MSS., CHS; Hamilton, Works (J. C. Hamilton), VI, 513; Gouverneur Morris, Diary and Letters, II, 397.
50. Charles Warren, Odd Byways in American History (Cambridge, 1942), pp. 127-128. Philadelphia Gazette, October 27, 1800; Smith, One Hundred Years of Hartford's Courant, p. 77; Mott, American Journalism, p. 169.
51. Fisher Ames, Works, I, 288-289; R. Troup to King, February 18, 1801, King MSS., NYHS.
52. Baldwin, Life and Letters, p. 427; John Beckley to Gallatin, February 15, 1801, Gallatin MSS., NYHS; St. George Tucker to Madison, January 23, 27, 1801, Madison MSS., LC.
53. Morten Borden, The Federalism of James A. Bayard (New York, 1954), pp. 80-81, 90-93; Hamilton, Works (J. C. Hamilton), VI, 458, 524; Channing, History, IV, 242; Brant, Madison, Secretary of State, pp. 29-33; Documents Relating to the Presidential Election in the Year 1801 (Philadelphia, 1831), p. 7; Pickering to King, February 7, 1801, King MSS., NYHS; William and Mary College Quarterly, I (1892), p. 103; John Beckley to Gallatin, February 4, 1801; Gallatin to James Nicholson, February 14, 1801, Gallatin MSS., NYHS; Massachusetts Historical Society, Collections, Seventh Series, I, 88; Jefferson, Writings (Ford), VII, February 15, 1801; Remarks in the Senate Vindicating James A. Bayard (Wilmington, 1907), pp. 16-18; Brant, Madison, Secretary of State, p. 33; Schachner, Burr, pp. 206-209; Gallatin to John Nicholson, February 16, 1800, Gallatin MSS., MHS; William Eustis to Gallatin, March 6, 1801, Gallatin MSS., NYHS; George W. Ewing to Monroe, February 17, 1801, Monroe MSS., LC; Edward Thornton to Grenville, February 28, 1801, Adams MSS., LC; Adams, Gallatin, p. 263; John P. Branch Historical Papers, III, 32-33, June, 1909; Documents Relating to the Presidential Election, pp. 9-10; Theodore Sedgwick to Theodore Sedgwick, Jr., February 16, 1801, Sedgwick MSS., MHS; Hamilton, Works (J. C. Hamilton), VI, 523; New York History, XXVI (1945), 449-450; Uriah Tracy to J. Wadsworth, February 17, 1801, Trumbull MSS., CHS; Noble E. Cunningham, Jr., The Jeffersonian Republicans (Chapel Hill, 1958), pp. 245-247.

Chapter 34. A Prophet of Woe

1. Hamilton, Works (Lodge), VIII, 240-241.
2. Harvard Law Review, XLI (1928), 488-489; Federalist, pp. 103, 556; Crosskey, Politics and the Constitution, II, 74; Strayer, The Delegate from New York, p. 63; Story, Commentaries, pp. 584, 637; Selected Cases on Constitutional Law, II, 1243.

3. *Selected Cases on Constitutional Law*, II, 1249; *Harvard Law Review*, XLI (1928), 495-497, 500; *Cornell Law Review*, XII, 499-500, 515.
4. *Annals of Congress*, II, 38; Walters, *Dallas*, p. 125; Warren, *Supreme Court*, I, 11-12, 85; Crosskey, *Politics and the Constitution*, II, 756-758; Percy T. Finn, *The Development of the Constitution* (New York, 1940), p. 55; *Selected Essays on Constitutional Law*, III, 16; McLaughlin, *Constitutional History*, p. 302; Holcombe, *Our More Perfect Union*, p. 363; Wright, *Growth of American Constitutional Law*, p. 28; Corwin, *Twilight of the Supreme Court*, p. 4.
5. Hamilton, *Works* (Lodge), VIII, 331-332; Gibbs, *Memoirs of the Administrations of Washington and Adams*, II, 316.
6. Warren, *Supreme Court*, I, 185-186.
7. *Ibid.*, I, 185-188; Morison, *Otis*, I, 202; *Journal of Economic History*, III (1946), p. 212; *Cornell Law Quarterly*, XII (1927), 507-508; Crosskey, *Politics and the Constitution*, II, 759.
8. Hamilton, *Works* (Lodge), VIII, 313-314, 332; Adams, *New England Federalism*, p. 348.
9. Dorfman, *Economic Mind*, I, 416; Warren, *Supreme Court*, I, 206-207.
10. Warren, *Supreme Court*, I, 208, 231; Schachner, *Burr*, p. 222.
11. Studenski and Krooss, *Financial History*, pp. 71-72.
12. Fisher Ames, *Works*, I, 313-314, II, 205; J. Q. Adams to King, October 8, 1802, King MSS., NYHS; Troup to King, May 27, December 5, 1801, King MSS., NYHS; Fisher Ames, *Works*, I, 292-293; II, 401; Adams, *New England Federalism*, p. 338; Philip S. Foner (ed.), *The Complete Writings of Thomas Paine* (New York, 1945), II, 949; *Annals of Congress*, X, 917; Massachusetts Historical Society, *Proceedings*, LIV (1926), 259; B. Tallmadge to Jeremiah Wadsworth, January 5, 1801, Trumbull MSS., CHS; Uriah Tracy to Jeremiah Wadsworth, December 10, 1800, Trumbull MSS., CHS.
13. Gouverneur Morris, *Diary and Letters*, II, 522, 530-531; Hamilton, *Works* (Lodge), VIII, 225, 322.
14. John Rutledge to Harper, August 3, 1803, R. G. Harper MSS., LC; Adams, *New England Federalism*, p. 364; Hamilton, *Works* (Lodge), VIII, 225, 245, 364; *American Historical Review*, XLII (1937), 78; Fisher Ames, *Works*, II, 205; American Historical Association, *Report for 1896*, I, 838-839; John Nicholson to Hamilton, August 4, 1803, Hamilton MSS., LC.
15. C. R. King, *Rufus King*, III, August 8, 1801; New York *Evening Post*, February 15, 1802.
16. Fisher Ames, *Works*, II, 354; Gouverneur Morris, *Diary and Letters*, II, 454; Stokes, *Iconography*, V, 1428.
17. C. R. King, *Rufus King*, III, May 27, October 14, 31, 1801; Washington, *Writings* (Fitzpatrick), XXXVII, 88; Morison, *Jeremiah Smith*, p. 99; Adams, *New England Federalism*, p. 338; *Port Folio*, May 9, September 5, 1801.
18. *Gazette of the United States*, August 1, 1795; Hamilton, *Works* (J. C. Hamilton), V, 571; Gibbs, *Memoirs of the Administrations of Washington and Adams*, I, 127-128, 130, 264; Lodge, *Cabot*, pp. 318-319; Fisher Ames, *Works*, I, 182; II, 166, 441.
19. Henry Adams, *History of the United States During the Administrations of Thomas Jefferson and James Madison* (New York, 1930), II, 180, and *New England Federalism*, p. 388; Hamilton, *Works* (Lodge), VIII, 225, 231, 240-242; 245, 286, 290, 292; X, 425-426, February 22, April 10, December 29, 1802; *Correspondence Between John Adams and William Cunningham*, pp. 3, 5; James Kent to Elizabeth Hamilton, December 10, 1832, Kent MSS., LC; *Port Folio*, January 19, 30, 1802; March 3, 1804; George Franklin, *The Legislative History of Naturalization in the United States* (Chicago, 1906), pp. 100-101; New York *Evening Post*, January 9, 1802; *Annals of Congress*, II, 616; Studenski and Krooss, *Financial History*, pp. 71-72; White, *Jeffersonians*, pp. 135-136.

Chapter 35. Defender of the Freedom of the Press

1. A. M. Hamilton, *Intimate Life*, p. 354; Hamilton, *Works* (Lodge), X, 444-446.
2. A. M. Hamilton, *Intimate Life*, pp. 235, 415; R. Troup to King, December 31, 1800, May 27, December 8, 1801; December 12, 15, 1802, King MSS., NYHS.
3. Dorfman, *Economic Mind*, I, 461; Weld, *Travels*, I, 21; Washington, *Writings* (Fitzpatrick), XXXI, 60-61, 71, 175; Channing, *History*, IV, 111-112; John Hamilton to

Grenville, July 28, 1795, PRO, FO; J. D. Forbes, *Israel Thorndike, Federalist Financier* (New York, 1953), pp. 89, 93; *New York History*, XXV (1944), 37-38; New York Historical Association, *Proceedings*, XL (1942), 166-167.
4. Hamilton to Wolcott, August 14, 1803, Wolcott MSS., CHS; *New York History*, XXV (1944), 39-41; R. Troup to King, September 2, 1799; May 27, 1801; January 8, 1803, King MSS., NYHS; A. M. Hamilton, *Intimate Life*, p. 419; Hamilton to Merchants' Bank, 1803, Wolcott MSS., CHS; Spaulding, *George Clinton*, p. 233; Ralph Brown, *A Mirror for Americans* (New York, 1943), pp. 160-161, 166, 175; Channing, *History*, IV, 96; Horton, *Kent*, pp. 98-101; Paul D. Evans, *The Holland Land Company* (Buffalo, 1924), pp. 9-10, 25, 32, 207-210; Mathew L. Davis, *Memoirs of Aaron Burr* (New York, 1836), I, 417.
5. Evans, *Holland Land Company*, pp. 207-210.
6. B. F. Wright, *The Contract Clause of the Constitution* (Cambridge, 1938), pp. 21-23, 41-42, and *Growth of American Constitutional Law*, pp. 30-31, 41-43; Gibbs, *Memoirs of the Administrations of Washington and Adams*, I, 305; Taylor, *An Enquiry*, pp. 62-63; R. G. Harper, *The Case of the Georgia Lands on the Mississippi Considered* (Philadelphia, 1799), pp. 37-38, 84, 89; Scott, *The Federalist*, p. 560; Roscoe Pound, *The Spirit of the Common Law* (Boston, 1921), p. 97; Francis W. Coker, *Democracy, Liberty and Property* (New York, 1942), p. 489; Story, *Commentaries*, pp. 505-506.
7. Nathan Schachner, *Alexander Hamilton* (New York, 1946), pp. 406-408; J. C. Hamilton, *Alexander Hamilton*, VII, 500, 503; C. R. King, *Rufus King*, IV, December 5, 1801; New York *Evening Post*, November 28, 1801; R. Troup to King, December 8, May 22, 1801, King MSS., NYHS.
8. Nevins, *Evening Post*, p. 12; Fisher Ames, *Works*, I, 314; New York *Evening Post*, November 16, 1801; January 9, 1802.
9. Nevins, *Evening Post*, pp. 20, 24, 36; *Memorials and Correspondence of Jeremiah Mason*, (Cambridge, 1872), p. 32.
10. Gouverneur Morris, *Diary and Letters*, II, 450-451, 472-473; Hamilton, *Works* (Lodge), VIII, 373; X, 429-434.
11. Jay, *Correspondence* (Johnston), III, 404; G. A. Koch, *Republican Religion* (New York, 1933), pp. 294-295; *Gazette of the United States*, November 27, 1795.
12. *Port Folio*, August 1, 1801; *Annals of Congress*, XI, 616; William Plumer, *Memorandum of Proceedings in the Senate, 1803-1807*, ed. E. S. Brown (New York, 1923), p. 454.
13. William Johnson, *Reports of Cases Adjudged in the Supreme Court of Judicature of the State of New York* (Philadelphia, 1834-36), III, 337-358; M. W. Hamilton, *The Country Printer*, pp. 175-176.
14. New York *Evening Post*, July 19, 1803; *Speeches . . . in the Great Cause of the People against Harry Croswell* (New York, 1804), pp. 3-5.
15. *Speeches . . . in the Great Cause*, p. 64; Johnson, *Reports*, III, 353, 358; James Kent, The Case of Harry Croswell, Kent MSS., NYPL.
16. James Kent, The Case of Harry Croswell, Kent MSS., NYPL; *Speeches . . . in the Great Cause*, p. 77.
17. James Kent, The Case of Harry Croswell, Kent MSS., NYPL; *Speeches . . . in the Great Cause*, pp. 71-73, 78; Johnson, *Reports*, III, 338-342, 350, 355; Hamilton, *Works* (Lodge), VIII, 383-384; New York *Evening Post*, July 19, 1803.
18. James Kent, The Case of Harry Croswell, Kent MSS., NYPL; New York *Evening Post*, January 9, July 19, 1804; Johnson, *Reports*, III, 411-413; Kent, *Commentaries*, II, 20 footnote; M. W. Hamilton, *The Country Printer*, pp. 197-198.

Chapter 36. The Duel with Burr

1. Forbes, *Thorndike*, p. 44; Massachusetts Historical Society, *Proceedings*, XLIV (1911), 406; Bemis, *American Secretaries of State*, II, 242; Edward Thornton to Grenville, January 16, 1801, Adams MSS., LC.
2. Fisher Ames, *Works*, II, 158; C. R. King, *Rufus King*, III, December 28, 1800; S.

Notes 621

Higginson to Pickering, April 16, 1800, Pickering MSS., MHS; Hamilton, *Works* (J. C. Hamilton), V, 441, 492, 511.

3. Hamilton, *Works* (Lodge), X, December 22, 1800; Philadelphia *Gazette*, November 26, 1800; Fisher Ames to King, August 18, 1800, King MSS., NYHS.
4. C. A. King, *Rufus King*, IV, April 12, 13, 1802; Cabot to King, September 21, 1802, King MSS., NYHS; John Quincy Adams, *Works* (Ford), II, April 25, 1801.
5. New York *Evening Post*, March 12, 1802; *Annals of Congress*, XII, 186-187, 197.
6. Richard Peters to Pickering, November 8, 1803, Pickering MSS., NYHS.
7. Gibbs, *Memoirs of the Administrations of Washington and Adams*, II, 50-51; Pickering to Hamilton, February 4, 1799, Hamilton MSS., LC; Ralph Korngold, *Citizen Toussaint* (Boston, 1945), p. 221; John Adams, *Works* (Adams), VIII, 634; Pickering to Edward Stevens, July 13, 1799, Pickering MSS., MHS; American Historical Association, *Report for 1896*, I, 829; Liston to Grenville, January 31, 1799, Adams MSS., LC.
8. *Annals of Congress*, IX, 2572; Tansill, *United States and Santo Domingo*, pp. 47-48; Mayo, *Instructions to British Ministers*, pp. 169-170.
9. Tansill, *United States and Santo Domingo*, p. 48; John Quincy Adams, *Memoirs* (Adams), I, 314; Korngold, *Citizen Toussaint*, p. 246.
10. *Annals of Congress*, I, 323-324; XV; 73, 456; Plumer, *Memorandum of Proceedings in the Senate; 1803-1807*, p. 6; Richard Peters to Pickering, November 5, 1803, Pickering MSS., MHS; *William and Mary Quarterly*, XII (April, 1955), 274-275; Hamilton, *Works* (Lodge), X, 26.
11. Hamilton, *Works* (Lodge), IX, 26-27.
12. Studenski and Krooss, *Financial History*, 63; *American Economic Review*, XXXVII (1947), 131-132.
13. Adams, *New England Federalism*, pp. 52-53, 147-148; Nevins, *Evening Post*, p. 37; *Annals of Congress*, XII, 193-195; XIII, 454, 457, 545-546, 1960; Plumer, *Memorandum*, pp. 27, 136-138; American Historical Association, *Report for 1896*, I, 837; *Pennsylvania Magazine of History and Biography*, XLVI (1920), 329; McLaughlin, *Constitutional History*, 296-297; White, *Jeffersonians*, p. 14.
14. Mitchell, *New Letters of Abigail Adams*, p. 221; Pickering and Upham, *Pickering*, III, 301; Cooper, *Consolidation*, p. 85; Bemis, *American Secretaries of State*, II, 170-171; Pickering, *Review of the Adams-Cunningham Correspondence*, p. 124.
15. Fisher Ames, *Works*, I, 321; Theodore Roosevelt, *Gouverneur Morris* (Boston, 1888), p. 135; Adams, *New England Federalism*, p. 340.
16. William Plumer, Jr., *The Life of William Plumer* (Boston, 1856), pp. 287-289; Lodge, *Cabot*, pp. 338-340; *Country Porcupine*, March 30, April 1, 1799; *Port Folio*, August 15, 1801; Adams, *New England Federalism*, p. 328.
17. C. R. King, *Rufus King*, IV, March 4, 1800.
18. Henry Adams, *History of the United States* (New York, 1930), II, 160, 166, 170; Brown, *The Northern Confederacy*, pp. 36-37; Adams, *New England Federalism*, p. 340.
19. *Annals of Congress*, XI, 874.
20. Hamilton, *Works* (Lodge), X, July 10, 1804.
21. Adams, *History*, II, 182-183.
22. Hammond, *Political Parties*, I, 172-173, 185-186; Gallatin, *Works* (Adams), I, 51-52; New York *Evening Post*, June 9, 1802; Plumer, *Memorandum*, pp. 256-257; Adams, *Gallatin*, pp. 282, 286-287, 289; *New York History*, XXVI (1945), 450; A. J. Beveridge, *The Life of John Marshall* (Boston, 1916), II, 379-380.
23. Adams, *History*, II, 179, 182.
24. Hamilton, *Works* (Lodge), VIII, 303-304; R. Troup to King, October 24, 1801, King MSS., NYHS.
25. *William and Mary Quarterly* (April, 1947), pp. 216-217.
26. Schachner, *Burr*, p. 242.
27. Hammond, *Political Parties*, I, 207-208; *Port Folio*, August 7, 1802; Plumer, *Memorandum*, pp. 256-257; Schachner, *Burr*, pp. 243-244.
28. Spaulding, *Clinton*, pp. 264-266, 273-274; Fisher Ames, *Works*, II, 347.
29. Adams, *History*, II, 184-185, and *New England Federalism*, p. 167.
30. Davis, *Memoirs of Aaron Burr*, II, 281, 285.

31. *New York History,* XXVII (1946), 493-494; James Parton, *The Life and Times of Aaron Burr* (New York, 1863), pp. 339-340.
32. Hamilton, *Works* (Lodge), X, 461-463.
33. *New York History,* XXVIII (1947), 67; Schachner, *Burr,* pp. 249-251.
34. Plumer, *Memorandum,* p. 451; William Coleman, *A Collection of the Facts and Documents Relating to the Death of Major General Alexander Hamilton* (New York, 1804), p. 11; John Quincy Adams, *Writings* (Ford), IV, 42; Adams, *New England Federalism,* pp. 166, 169; W. C. Bruce, *John Randolph of Roanoke* (New York, 1922), I, 298-299; Lorenzo Sabine, *Notes on Duels and Duelling* (New York, 1855), p. 212; *New York History,* XXVII (1946), 497-498; XXVIII (1947), 71; Hamilton, *Works* (Lodge), X, 467, 470, 474; *Port Folio,* May 19, July 14, August 18, 1804; Louis B. Wright, *The First Gentlemen of Virginia* (San Marino, Calif., 1940), p. 10; Stokes, *Iconography,* V, 1425; John Williams, *Life of Alexander Hamilton* (New York, 1805), pp. 52-53; New York *Evening Post,* June 9, 1802; *Gazette of the United States,* November 8, 1800; A. M. Hamilton, *Intimate Life,* pp. 72, 78, 394, 405-406; Edmund Quincy, *Life of Josiah Quincy* (Boston, 1868), p. 81; *Speeches . . . in the Great Cause,* pp. 66-67; James Abercrombie, *A Sermon Occasioned by the Death of Major General Alexander Hamilton* (Philadelphia, 1804), pp. 26-27, 35; Frederick Oliver, *Alexander Hamilton* (London, 1915), pp. 420-421.
35. A. M. Hamilton, *Intimate Life,* p. 407; *William and Mary Quarterly,* IV (April, 1947), p. 218; Hamilton to Nathaniel Pendleton, July 4, 1804, Pendleton MSS., NYHS; Hamilton, Financial Statement, Pendleton MSS., NYHS; Nathaniel Pendleton to Oliver Wolcott, July 28, 1804, Pendleton MSS., NYHS; M. L. Weems, *George Washington* (New York, 1927), pp. 224-225.
36. *New York History,* XXVII (1947), 72; Statement of Nathaniel Pendleton, Pendleton MSS., NYHS.
37. *The New York Times,* August 1, 1954; Koch, *Republican Religion,* p. 126; Elizabeth Hamilton to Nathaniel Pendleton, September 20, 1804, Pendleton MSS., NYHS.
38. *Port Folio,* July 14, August 18, 1804; Fisher Ames, *Works,* II, 259, 263-264.
39. *Port Folio,* August 18, 1804; *The Balance and Columbian Repository,* July 24, 1804.

Bibliography

MANUSCRIPTS

Adams, Henry, Transcripts, Library of Congress
Adams, John, MSS., Massachusetts Historical Society
Craigie, Andrew, MSS., American Antiquarian Society
Duer, William, MSS., New York Historical Society
Emmet MSS., New York Public Library
Etting MSS., Historical Society of Pennsylvania
Gallatin, Albert, MSS., New York Historical Society
Gates, Horatio, MSS., New York Historical Society
Gerry, Elbridge, MSS., Library of Congress
Greene, Nathanael, MSS., American Philosophical Society
Hamilton, Alexander, MSS., Library of Congress
Harper, Robert Goodloe, MSS., Library of Congress
Irvine, William, MSS., Historical Society of Pennsylvania
Jay, John, MSS., Columbia University Library
Jefferson, Thomas, MSS., Library of Congress
Kent, James, MSS., Library of Congress
King, Rufus, MSS., New York Public Library
Knox, Henry, MSS., Massachusetts Historical Society
Lamb, John, MSS., New York Public Library
Livingston, Edward, MSS., New York Historical Society
McDougall, Alexander, MSS., New York Historical Society
McHenry, James, MSS., Library of Congress
Madison, James, MSS., Library of Congress
Marshall, John, MSS., Library of Congress
Monroe, James, MSS., Library of Congress
Nicholson, Joseph H., MSS., Library of Congress
Pendleton, Nathaniel, MSS., New York Historical Society
Peters, Richard, MSS., Historical Society of Pennsylvania
Pickering, Timothy, MSS., Massachusetts Historical Society
Rush, Benjamin, MSS., Library Company of Philadelphia
Sedgwick, Theodore, MSS., Massachusetts Historical Society
Smith, W. L., MSS., Library of Congress
Trumbull, Jonathan, MSS., Connecticut Historical Society

Wadsworth, Jeremiah, MSS., Connecticut Historical Society
Wallace, MSS., Historical Society of Pennsylvania
Washington, George, MSS., Library of Congress
Wayne, Anthony, MSS., Historical Society of Pennsylvania
Wilson, James, MSS., Historical Society of Pennsylvania
Wolcott, Oliver, MSS., Connecticut Historical Society
Yeates, Jasper, MSS., Historical Society of Pennsylvania

NEWSPAPERS

Albany *Centinel*
The Balance and Columbian Repository
Claypoole's American Daily Advertiser
Columbian Centinel
Federal Gazette and Philadelphia Evening Post
Freeman's Journal
Gazette of the United States
General Advertiser
Greenleaf's New Daily Advertiser
Herald of Freedom and Federal Advertiser
Independent Chronicle
Massachusetts Mercury
National Gazette
New Hamsphire Gazette
New Jersey Journal and Weekly Advertiser
New York *Daily Advertiser*
New York *Evening Post*
New York *Journal and Patriotic Advertiser*
New York *Packet*
Pennsylvania Gazette
Philadelphia *Gazette*
Porcupine's Gazette
Salem *Gazette*

CONTEMPORARY PAMPHLETS

Abercrombie, James, *A Sermon Occasioned by the Death of Major General Alexander Hamilton* (Philadelphia, 1804).
An Address to the House of Representatives (Philadelphia, 1796).
An Address to the Legislature of the Province of New York (New York, 1775).
The Alarm (New York, 1799).
Americanus, *Address to the People of the United States* (Philadelphia, 1800).
Bache, Benjamin, *Remarks Occasioned by the late Conduct of Mr. Washington* (Philadelphia, 1797).
———, *Truth Will Out* (Philadelphia, 1798).
Bayard, James A., *Documents Relating to the Presidential Election in the Year 1801* (Philadelphia, 1831).
Bishop, Abraham, *An Oration* (Philadelphia, 1800).

Bibliography

Brief Consideration of Mr. Adams (Boston, 1796).
Callender, James T., *The History of the United States for 1796* (Philadelphia, 1797).
———, *The American Annual Register* (Philadelphia, 1796).
———, *The Prospect Before Us* (Philadelphia, 1797).
Callender, Tom, *A Letter to Alexander Hamilton, King of the Feds* (New York, 1800).
Cheetham, James, *A View of the Political Conduct of Aaron Burr* (New York, 1804).
———, *Nine Letters on the Subject of Aaron Burr* (New York, 1802).
Cobbett, William (Peter Porcupine), *A Little Plain English* (Philadelphia, 1797).
Coleman, William, *A Collection of the Facts and Documents Relating to the Death of Major General Hamilton* (New York, 1804).
Cooper, Thomas, *Consolidation* (Columbia, S. C., 1824).
———, *Political Essays* (Northumberland, Pa., 1799).
Coxe, Tench, *A View of the United States of America* (Philadelphia, 1794).
Duane, William, *A Letter to George Washington* (Philadelphia, 1796).
Dwight, Jasper, *A Letter to President Washington* (Philadelphia, 1796).
Fauchet, Joseph, *A Sketch of the Present State of our Political Relations* (Philadelphia, 1797).
———, *An Examination of the Conduct of the Executive of the United States* (Philadelphia, 1797).
———, *Features of Mr. Jay's Treaty* (Philadelphia, 1795).
Fenno, John Ward, *Desultory Reflections* (Philadelphia, 1800).
Fraunces, Andrew G., *An Appeal* (Philadelphia, 1793).
———, *Letters of Germanicus* (Philadelphia, 1794).
Harper, Robert Goodloe, *The Case of the Georgia Lands on the Mississippi Considered* (Philadelphia, 1799).
———, *Observations on the Dispute Between the United States and France* (London, 1798).
———, *An Address from Robert Goodloe Harper* (Boston, 1796).
Hopkinson, Joseph, *What Is Our Situation? By an American* (Philadelphia, 1798).
Humbert, Jasper, *Thoughts on the Nature of Civil Government* (New York, 1797).
Leonidas, *A Reply to Lucius Junius Brutus* (New York, 1801).
Letters of Franklin (Philadelphia, 1795).
Livingston, Robert R. (Cato), *An Examination of the Treaty* (Philadelphia, 1795).
Logan, George, *Letters Addressed to the Yeomanry of the United States By an American Farmer* (Philadelphia, 1793).
Lowell, John, *An Oration* (Boston, 1799).
McConnell, Matthew, *An Essay on the Domestic Debts of the United States* (Philadelphia, 1787).
Page, John, *An Address to the Citizens of the District of York* (Richmond, 1794).
Pickering, Timothy, *A Review of the Correspondence between John Adams and William Cunningham* (Salem, 1824).
Political Truth (Philadelphia, 1796).
The Politicks and Views of a Certain Party Displayed (Philadelphia, 1792).
President II (Newark, 1799).
Price, Richard, *Additional Observations on the Nature and Value of Civil Liberty* (London, 1777).

Priestly, Joseph, *Lectures on History and General Policy* (Birmingham, Eng., 1785).
Remarks on the Report of the Secretary of the Treasury, By a Friend to the Public (Philadelphia, 1790).
A Review of the Revenue System (Philadelphia, 1794).
A Roaster: or a Check to the Progress of Political Blasphemy (Philadelphia, 1796).
A Rub from Snub (Philadelphia, 1795).
Seabury, Samuel, *Free Thoughts on the Proceedings of the Continental Congress* (New York, 1774).
———, *A View of the Controversy between Great Britain and Her Colonies* (New York, 1775).
A Short History of the Excise Laws (Philadelphia, 1795).
Sketches of French and English Politics in America. By a Member of the Old Congress (Charleston, 1797).
Smith, William L., *The Pretensions of Thomas Jefferson to the Presidency Examined* (Philadelphia, 1796).
———, *An Address from William Smith of South Carolina to his Constituents* (Philadelphia, 1794).
The Speeches . . . in the Great Cause of the People against Harry Croswell (New York, 1804).
Strictures on a Pamphlet entitled "A Friendly Address to all Reasonable Americans" (Philadelphia, 1774).
Taylor, John, *A Definition of Parties* (Philadelphia, 1794).
———, *An Inquiry into the Principles and Policy of the Government of the United States* (Philadelphia, 1794).
———, *An Argument Respecting the Constitutionality of the Carriage Tax* (Richmond, 1795).
To the Republican Citizens of the State of Pennsylvania, (Lancaster, Pa., 1800).
The Treaty's Merits and Demerits Fairly Examined and Explained (Philadelphia, 1795).
Varnum, James M., *The Case Trevett against Weeden* (Providence, 1787).
Webster, Noah, *A Letter to General Hamilton* (Philadelphia, 1800).
Webster, Peletiah, *A Seventh Essay on Trade and Finance* (Philadelphia, 1787).
———, *A Plea for the Poor Soldiers* (Philadelphia, 1790).
———, *Political Essays on the Nature and Operation of Money, Public Finances, and other Subjects* (Philadelphia, 1791).
Wortman, Tunis, *An Address to the Republican Citizens of New York* (New York, 1801).
———, *A Solemn Address to Christians and Patriots, upon the Approaching Election* (New York, 1800).

MAGAZINES

American Economic Review
American Heritage
American Historical Review
American Museum (edited by Mathew Carey)
American Political Science Review
Chicago, University of, Law Review

Bibliography

Columbia Law Review
Edinburgh Review
Harvard Law Review
Harvard Law School Bulletin
Historical Magazine
Journal of Business and Economic History
Journal of Economic History
Journal of Political Economy
Magazine of American History
Michigan Law Review
Mississippi Valley Historical Review
New England Quarterly
New York History
North Carolina Historical Review
Pennsylvania Magazine of History and Biography
Political Science Quarterly
Port Folio (1801-4).
Quarterly Journal of Economics
South Carolina Historical and Genealogical Magazine
Texas Law Review
The United States Magazine (1779)
Virginia Magazine of History and Biography
Virginia Quarterly Review
William and Mary Quarterly

TRAVELERS' ACCOUNTS

Brissot de Warville, J. P., *New Travels in the United States of America* (Dublin, 1792).
Brown, Ralph H., *Mirror for Americans* (New York, 1943).
Davis, John, *Travels of Four Years and a Half in the United States of America during 1798, 1799, 1800, 1801, and 1802* . . . (Bristol, Eng., 1803).
Drayton, John, *Letters Written During a Tour of America* (Charleston, 1794).
Mitchell, Samuel L., *The Picture of New York* (New York, 1807).
Porter, Kenneth and Anna M. (eds.), *Moreau de St. Méry's American Journal* (Boston, 1948).
Rochefoucault-Liancourt, Duke de la, *Travels Through the United States of North America* (2 vols., London, 1799).
Schoepf, J. D., *Travels Through the Middle and Southern States of the United States* (2 vols., Philadelphia, 1911).
Volney, C. F., *A View of the Soil and Climate of the United States* (Philadelphia, 1804).
Wansey, Henry, *An Excursion to the United States of North America in 1794* (Salisbury, Eng., 1798).
Weld, Isaac, Jr., *Travels Through the States of North America* (2 vols., London, 1807).

HISTORIES

Adams, Henry, *History of the United States During the Administrations of Thomas Jefferson and James Madison* (4 vols., New York, 1930).
Bailey, Thomas, *The American Pageant* (Boston, 1956).
———, *A Diplomatic History of the American People* (Boston, 1956).
Channing, Edward, *History of the United States* (6 vols., New York, 1928).
Hildreth, Richard, *History of the United States* (6 vols., New York, 1871).
Jones, Thomas, *The History of New York During the Revolutionary War* (2 vols., New York, 1879).
McMaster, John B., *A History of the People of the United States from the Revolution to the Civil War* (8 vols., New York, 1883-1913).
Morison, Samuel Eliot, and Commager, Henry Steele, *The Growth of the American Republic* (2 vols., New York, 1957).
Ramsay, David, *The American Revolution* (Charleston, 1789).
Ward, Sir A. W., and Gooch, G. P., *The Cambridge History of British Foreign Policy, 1783-1919* (3 vols., Cambridge, Eng., 1922-23).

COLLECTIONS OF DOCUMENTS

Adams, Henry, *Documents Relating to New England Federalism, 1800-1815* (Boston, 1877).
American Historical Association, *Reports*.
Annals of Congress.
Burnett, Edmund C. (ed.), *Letters of Members of the Continental Congress* (8 vols., Washington, 1921-36).
Clinton, George, *Public Papers of George Clinton* (New York, 1890-1914).
Colonial Society of Massachusetts, *Publications*.
Documents Relating to the Revolutionary History of New Jersey (Trenton).
Essex Institute Historical Collections.
Journals of the Continental Congress.
The Lee Papers, General Charles Lee, New-York Historical Society, *Collections* (1871-74).
Massachusetts Historical Society, *Collections* and *Proceedings*.
Mayo, Bernard (ed.), *Instructions to British Ministers to the United States, 1791-1812* (Washington, 1941).
Moore, Frank, *Diary of the American Revolution* (2 vols., New York, 1859-60).
Morris, Richard B. (ed.), *Alexander Hamilton and the Founding of the Nation* (New York, 1957).
New York Historical Society, *Collections*.
Pennsylvania Archives (Harrisburg, Pa.).
Report on Canadian Archives (Ottawa, 1890-92).
Wharton, Francis, *The Revolutionary Diplomatic Correspondence of the United States* (6 vols., Washington, 1889).

CONSTITUTION

Acton, Lord, *Essays on Freedom and Power* (Boston, 1948).
Bancroft, George, *History of the Formation of the Constitution of the United States* (2 vols., New York, 1882).

Bibliography

Bauer, E. K., *Commentaries on the Constitution, 1790-1860* (New York, 1952).
Beard, Charles A., *The Supreme Court and the Constitution* (New York, 1922).
———, *The Republic; Conversations on Fundamentals* (New York, 1943).
———, *The Enduring Federalist* (New York, 1948).
———, *Economic Origins of Jeffersonian Democracy* (New York, 1915).
———, *An Economic Interpretation of the Constitution* (New York, 1935).
Blackstone, Sir William, *Commentaries on the Laws of England* (4 vols., Oxford, 1765-1769).
Brown, E. S. (ed.), *William Plumer's Memorandum of Proceedings in the United States Senate, 1803-1807* (New York, 1923).
Brown, Robert E., *Charles Beard and the Constitution* (Princeton, 1956).
Bryce, James, *The American Commonwealth* (2 vols., New York, 1888).
Buckland, W. W., *Some Reflections on Jurisprudence* (Cambridge, Eng., 1945)
Cardozo, Benjamin, *The Nature of the Judicial Process* (New Haven, 1921).
Carpenter, W. S., *The Development of American Political Thought* (Princeton, 1930).
Corwin, Edwin S., *Court over Constitution* (Princeton, 1938).
———, *The Twilight of the Supreme Court* (New Haven, 1934).
———, *The President, Office and Powers* (New York, 1940).
———, *The President's Removal Power* (New York, 1927).
———, *The Constitution and World Organization* (Princeton, 1944).
———, *The Constitution and What It Means Today* (Princeton, 1930).
Croker, Francis W., *Democracy, Liberty and Property* (New York, 1942).
Crosskey, William, *Politics and the Constitution* (2 vols., Chicago, 1952).
Curtis, Charles P., *Lions Under the Throne* (Boston, 1947).
Dawson, H. B. (ed.), *Arguments and Judgment of the Mayor's Court . . . in a Cause between . . . Rutgers and Waddington* (Morrisania, N. Y., 1866).
Earle, Edward Meade (ed.), *The Federalist* (New York, 1937).
Elliot, Jonathan (ed.), *Debates in . . . the State Conventions on Adoption of the Federal Constitution* (5 vols., Washington, 1836-45).
Farrand, Max (ed.), *Records of the Federal Convention of 1787* (3 vols., New Haven, 1911).
Finn, Percy T., *The Development of the Constitution* (New York, 1940).
Ford, P. L., *Essays on the Constitution . . . Published during its Discussion by the People* (Brooklyn, 1892).
———, *Pamphlets on the Constitution* (Brooklyn, 1888).
Frankfurter, Felix (ed.), *Mr. Justice Brandeis* (New Haven, 1933).
Friedrich, Carl J., *Constitutional Government and Democracy* (Boston, 1941).
Haines, Charles G., *The American Doctrine of Judicial Supremacy* (New York, 1914).
Hamilton, Walton, and Adair, Douglas, *The Power to Govern* (New York, 1914).
Hand, Learned, *The Bill of Rights* (Cambridge, 1958).
———, *The Spirit of Liberty* (New York, 1953).
Hearnshaw, F. J. C. (ed.), *The Social and Political Ideas of Some Representative Thinkers of the Revolutionary Era* (London, 1931).
Holcombe, A. N., *Our More Perfect Union* (Cambridge, 1950).
Jameson, J. Franklin (ed.), *Essays on the Constitutional History of the United States* (Boston, 1889).

Johnson, William, *Reports of Cases Adjudged in the Supreme Court of Judicature of the State of New York* (7 vols., Philadelphia, 1834-36).
Jones, W. Melville, *Chief Justice John Marshall, a Reappraisal* (Ithaca, N.Y., 1956).
Kelly, A. H., and Harbison, W. A., *The American Constitution, Its Origins and Development* (New York, 1948).
Kent, James, *Commentaries on American Law* (2 vols., Boston, 1826-30).
Kirk, Russell, *The Conservative Mind* (Chicago, 1953).
Lowell, A. Lawrence, *Essays on Government* (Boston, 1892).
McDonald, Forrest, *We the People* (Chicago, 1958).
McIlwain, C. H., *Constitutionalism and the Changing World* (Cambridge, Eng., 1939).
McLaughlin, Andrew C., *The Confederation and the Constitution* (New York, 1905).
———, *A Constitutional History of the United States* (New York, 1935).
Magi, Sobei, *The Problem of Federalism* (New York, 1951).
Miner, C. E., *Ratification of the Federal Constitution in New York* (New York, 1921).
Mullett, Charles F., *Fundamental Law and the American Revolution* (New York, 1933).
Oster, J. E., *The Political and Economic Doctrines of John Marshall* (New York, 1914).
Pound, Roscoe, *Federalism as a Democratic Process* (New Brunswick, 1942).
——— et al., *The Spirit of the Common Law* (Boston, 1921).
Pufendorf, S. von, *Of the Law of Nature and Nations* (Oxford, 1703).
Read, Conyears (ed.), *The Constitution Reconsidered* (New York, 1938).
Rodell, Fred, *Fifty-Five Men* (New York, 1936).
———, *Nine Men: A Political History of the Supreme Court* (New York, 1955).
Rutland, R. A., *The Birth of the Bill of Rights* (Chapel Hill, N.C., 1955).
Schuyler, R. L., *The Constitution of the United States* (New York, 1923).
Scott, E. H. (ed.), *The Federalist and Other Constitutional Papers* (2 vols., Chicago, 1894).
Selected Essays on Constitutional Law (5 vols., Chicago, 1938).
Smith, H. F. Russell, *Harrington and His Oceana* (Cambridge, 1914).
Story, Joseph, *Commentaries on the Constitution of the United States* (2 vols., Boston, 1858).
Strayer, J. R. (ed.), *The Delegate from New York, or, Proceedings of the Federal Convention from the Notes of John Lansing, Jr.* (Princeton, 1939).
Tansill, C. C. (ed.), *Documents Illustrative of the Formation of the Union of the American States* (Washington, 1927).
Warren, Charles, *The Making of the Constitution* (Boston, 1937).
Wheare, K. C., *Federal Government* (Oxford, 1953).
Wright, Benjamin F., *The Contract Clause of the Constitution* (Cambridge, 1938).
———, *The Growth of American Constitutional Law* (New York, 1946).
Wright, Quincy, *The Control of American Foreign Relations* (New York, 1922).

FINANCIAL AND ECONOMIC

Adams, Henry C., *Public Debts; an Essay in the Science of Finance* (New York, 1890).
Bezanson, A., *Prices and Inflation During the American Revolution* (Philadelphia, 1951).

Bibliography

Bolles, Albert Sidney, *The Financial History of the United States from 1789 to 1860* (New York, 1894).
Breck, Samuel, *Historical Sketch of Continental Paper Money* (Philadelphia, 1843).
Clapham, Sir John Harold, *The Bank of England* (Cambridge, Eng., 1945).
Clark, Victor S., *History of Manufactures in the United States, 1607-1860* (Washington, 1916).
Cole, A. H., *Industrial and Commercial Correspondence of Alexander Hamilton* (Chicago, 1928).
Coxe, Tench, *A View of the United States of America* (Philadelphia, 1794).
Davis, Joseph S., *Essays in the Earlier History of American Corporations* (2 vols., Cambridge, 1917).
Dewey, D. R., *Financial History of the United States* (New York, 1931).
Domett, Henry W., *History of the Bank of New York* (Cambridge, 1884).
Dorfman, Joseph, *The Economic Mind in American Civilization* (2 vols., New York, 1946-49).
Dunbar, Charles, *Economic Essays* (New York, 1904).
East, Robert A., *Business Enterprise in the American Revolutionary Period* (New York, 1938).
Ginzberg, Eli, *The House of Adam Smith* (New York, 1934).
Gras, N. S. B., *Business and Capitalism* (New York, 1939).
Hammond, Bray, *Banks and Politics in Early America* (Princeton, 1957).
Harris, Seymour, *The National Debt and the New Economics* (New York, 1947).
Heckscher, Eli, *Mercantilism* (2 vols., London, 1935).
Higgs, Henry, *The Physiocrats* (New York, 1897).
Hirst, Francis W., *The Credit of Nations* (Washington, 1910).
Holdsworth, J. T., and Dewey, D. R., *The First and Second Banks of the United States* (Washington, 1910).
Hume, David, *Essays Moral, Political and Literary* (New York, 1889).
Johnson, E. A. J., *Predecessors of Adam Smith; The Growth of British Economic Thought* (New York, 1937).
Keynes, John Maynard, *Laissez Faire and Communism* (New York, 1926).
Kirkland, Edward C., *A History of American Economic Life* (New York, 1933).
Larkin, Paschal, *Property in the Eighteenth Century* (New York, 1930).
McConnell, Matthew, *An Essay on the Domestic Debt of the United States* (Philadelphia, 1787).
Macgregor, D. H., *Economic Thought and Policy* (Oxford, 1949).
McKee, Samuel (ed.), *Papers on Public Credit, Commerce and Finance* (New York, 1957).
Messner, Ernest Campbell, *The Life of David Hume* (London, 1954).
Miller, H. E., *Banking Theories in the United States before 1860* (Cambridge, 1927).
Nevins, Allan, *History of the Bank of New York* (New York, 1934).
Postlethwayt, Malachy, *Great Britain's Commercial Interest* (London, 1759).
———, *Great Britain's True System* (London, 1757).
Ratner, Sidney, *American Taxation, Its History as a Social Force in Democracy* (New York, 1942).
Redlich, Fritz, *The Molding of American Banking* (2 vols., New York, 1951).

Robbins, Lionel, *The Theory of Economic Policy in English Classical Political Economy* (London, 1952).
Rotwein, Eugene, *Hume's Writings on Economics* (London, 1955).
Smith, Adam, *Wealth of Nations* (New York, 1942).
Smith, W. B., and Cole, A. H., *Fluctuations in American Business, 1790-1860* (Cambridge, 1935).
Steuart, Sir James, *The Works, Political, Metaphysical, and Chronological of the late Sir James Steuart* (6 vols., London, 1805).
Studenski, Paul, and Krooss, Herman E., *Financial History of the United States* (New York, 1952).
Sumner, William Graham, *Finances and Financiers of the American Revolution* (2 vols., New York, 1891).
Taus, E. R., *Central Banking Functions of the United States Treasury* (New York, 1943).
Webster, Peletiah, *An Essay on Free Trade and Commerce* (Philadelphia, 1779).
———, *A Seventh Essay on Free Trade and Finance* (Philadelphia, 1785).
Wetterau, James O., "New Light on the First Bank of the United States," *Pennsylvania Magazine of History and Biography*, LXI (1939).

MONOGRAPHS

Abernethy, T. P., *Western Lands and the American Revolution* (New York, 1937).
Adams, E. D., *The Influence of Grenville on Pitt's Foreign Policy* (Washington, 1904).
Ally, Bower, *The Rhetoric of Alexander Hamilton* (New York, 1941).
Baldwin, Leland D., *Whisky Rebels: The Story of a Frontier Uprising* (Pittsburgh, 1939).
Bemis, Samuel F. (ed.), *American Secretaries of State* (10 vols., New York, 1927-29).
———, *Jay's Treaty, A Study in Commerce and Diplomacy* (New York, 1923).
Binkley, Wilfred E., *American Political Parties* (New York, 1943).
Brown, C. R., *The Northern Confederacy* (New York, 1915).
Brunhouse, R. L., *The Counter-Revolution in Pennsylvania 1776-1790* (Philadelphia, 1942).
Burnett, Edmund C., *The Continental Congress* (New York, 1941).
Caldwell, L. K., *The Administrative Theories of Hamilton and Jefferson* (Chicago, 1944).
Charles, Joseph, *The Origins of the American Party System* (Williamsburg, 1956).
Clinton, Sir Henry, *The American Rebellion* (New Haven, 1954).
Collins, V. L., *The Continental Congress at Princeton* (Princeton, 1908).
Dauer, Manning J., *The Adams Federalists* (Baltimore, 1953).
Decatur, Stephen, Jr., *Public Affairs of George Washington* (Boston, 1933).
Dillon, Dorothy R., *The New York Triumvirate* (New York, 1949).
Dunbar, Louise, *A Study of Monarchical Tendencies in the United States, 1776-1801* (New York, 1923).
Dunlop, William, *History of the Province of New York* (New York, 1840).
Edwards, Bryan, *The History, Civil and Commercial, of the British Colonies in the West Indies* (2 vols., Philadelphia, 1805).
Evans, Paul D., *The Holland Land Company* (Buffalo, 1924).

Bibliography

633

Fiske, John, *The Critical Period of American History* (Boston, 1888).
Flick, A. C., *Loyalism in New York* (New York, 1901).
Ford, W. C., *The United States and Spain in 1790* (Brooklyn, 1890).
Fox, Dixon Ryan, *Yankees and Yorkers* (New York, 1940).
Franklin, George, *The Legislative History of Naturalization in the United States* (Chicago, 1906).
Hacker, Louis M., *Alexander Hamilton in the American Tradition* (New York, 1957).
Hamilton, Milton W., *The Country Printer in New York State, 1785-1930* (New York, 1948).
Hammond, J. D., *The History of Political Parties in the State of New York* (New York, 1852).
Harlow, R. V., *History of Legislative Methods before 1825* (New York, 1917).
Hart, James, *The American Presidency in Action* (New York, 1948).
Hazen, Charles D., *Contemporary American Opinion of the French Revolution* (Baltimore, 1897).
Hinsdale, Mary L., *A History of the President's Cabinet* (New York, 1911).
Hofstadter, Richard, *The American Political Tradition and the Men Who Made It* (New York, 1948).
Hunt, Gaillard, *Disunion Sentiment in Congress* (Washington, 1905).
Jensen, Merrill, *The New Nation* (New York, 1950).
Koch, Adolph, *Republican Religion* (New York, 1933).
Kulsrud, Carl J., *Maritime Neutrality to 1780* (Boston, 1936).
Kurtz, Stephen G., *The Presidency of John Adams: The Collapse of Federalism, 1795-1800* (Philadelphia, 1957).
Laird, John, *Hume's Philosophy of Human Nature* (London, 1932).
Link, Eugene, *Democratic-Republican Societies, 1790-1800* (New York, 1942).
Lyon, E. Wilson, *Louisiana in French Diplomacy 1759-1804* (Norman, Okla., 1934).
———, "The Directory and the United States," *American Historical Review*, XLIII (1938).
Miller, John C., *Crisis in Freedom* (Boston, 1951).
———, *Origins of the American Revolution* (Boston, 1943).
———, *Triumph of Freedom* (Boston, 1948).
Morison, Samuel Eliot, *By Land and By Sea* (New York, 1955).
Mott, Frank Luther, *American Journalism* (New York, 1950).
Myers, W. S., *The Battle of Monmouth*, ed. W. S. Stryker (Princeton, 1927).
Nevins, Allan, *American Press Opinion, Washington to Coolidge* (Boston, 1928).
———, *The New York Evening Post* (New York, 1922).
———, *The American States During and After the Revolution* (New York, 1924).
Padover, Saul K. (ed.), *Thomas Jefferson and the National Capital* (Washington, 1946).
Paltsits, Victor H., *Washington's Farewell Address* (New York, 1935).
Perkins, Bradford, *The First Rapprochement* (Philadelphia, 1955).
Pitman, F. W., *The Development of the British West Indies* (New Haven, 1917).
Pomerantz, Sidney I., *New York: an American City* (New York, 1938).
Powell, John, *Bring Out Your Dead* (Philadelphia, 1952).
Rich, Bennett Milton, *The Presidents and Civil Disorder* (Washington, 1941).

Sabine, Lorenzo, *Notes on Duels and Duelling* (New York, 1855).
Sanders, J. B., *The Evolution of the Executive Departments of the Continental Congress* (Chapel Hill, 1939).
Scharf, J. Thomas, and Wescott, Thompson, *History of Philadelphia* (3 vols., Philadelphia, 1884).
Schneider, H. W., *A History of American Philosophy* (New York, 1946).
Smith, J. Eugene, *One Hundred Years of Hartford's History* (New York, 1947).
Smith, James Morton, *Freedom's Fetters* (Ithaca, N.Y., 1956).
Spaulding, E. Wilder, *New York in the Critical Period* (New York, 1932).
Stokes, I. N., *Iconography of Manhattan Island* (6 vols., New York, 1915-28).
Swiggett, Howard, *War Out of Niagara* (New York, 1933).
Tansill, Charles C., *The United States and Santo Domingo, 1798-1873* (Baltimore, 1938).
Thomas, Charles M., *American Neutrality in 1793: A Study in Cabinet Government* (New York, 1931).
Van Doren, Carl, *Secret History of the American Revolution* (New York, 1941).
Warren, Charles, *Odd Byways in American History* (Cambridge, 1942).
Wertenbaker, T. J., *Father Knickerbocker Rebels* (New York, 1948).
Westergaard, W. C., *The Danish West Indies under Company Rule* (New York, 1917).
White, Leonard D., *The Federalists* (New York, 1948).
Whiteley, Emily Stone, *Washington and his Aides-de-Camp* (Washington, 1936).
Willey, Basil, *The Eighteenth Century Background* (New York, 1956).
Williamson, Charlton, *Vermont in Quandary* (Montpelier, 1949).
Wiltse, Charles M., *The Jeffersonian Tradition in American Democracy* (Chapel Hill, 1935).
Wright, Louis B., *The First Gentlemen of Virginia* (San Marino, Calif., 1940).
Yoshee, Harry B., *The Disposition of Loyalist Estates in Southern New York* (New York, 1938).
Zimmerman, James F., *Impressment of American Seamen* (New York, 1925).

MEMOIRS, LETTERS, DIARIES AND COLLECTED WORKS

Adams, Charles Francis (ed.), *The Works of John Adams* (10 vols., Boston, 1850-56).
———, *Letters of John Adams Addressed to His Wife* (2 vols., Boston, 1841).
———, *Letters of Mrs. Adams, Wife of John Adams* (Boston, 1848).
———, *Memoirs of John Quincy Adams* (12 vols., Philadelphia, 1874-77).
Correspondence between the Honorable John Adams . . . and William Cunningham (Boston, 1823).
Adams, Henry (ed.), *Writings of Albert Gallatin* (3 vols., Philadelphia, 1879).
Adams, Randolph G. (ed.), *Selected Political Essays of James Wilson* (New York, 1930).
Ames, Seth (ed.), *The Works of Fisher Ames* (2 vols., Boston, 1854).
Ashmead, Henry B. (ed.), *Letters to John Langdon* (Philadelphia, 1880).
Atherton, Gertrude (ed.), *A Few of Hamilton's Letters* (New York, 1903).
Ballagh, J. C. (ed.), *Letters of Richard Henry Lee* (2 vols., New York, 1911-14).
Biddle, Alexander, *Old Family Letters* (Philadelphia, 1892).
Biddle, Charles, *Autobiography* (Philadelphia, 1883).

Bibliography

Bond, W. W., Jr. (ed.), *The Correspondence of John Cleves Symmes* (New York, 1926).

Boudinot, Elias, *Journal or Historical Recollections of American Events during the Revolutionary War* (2 vols., Philadelphia, 1894).

Boudinot, Jane J. (ed.), *The Life, Public Services, Addresses and Letters of Elias Boudinot* (Boston, 1896).

Boyd, Julian (ed.), *Papers of Thomas Jefferson* (11 vols., Princeton, New Jersey, 1950——).

Butterfield, Lyman H. (ed.), *The Letters of Benjamin Rush* (2 vols., Princeton, 1951).

Corner, G. A. (ed.), *Autobiography of Dr. Benjamin Rush, Together with His Commonplace Book for 1789-1813* (Princeton, 1948).

Dexter, Franklin B. (ed.), *The Literary Diary of Ezra Stiles* (3 vols., New York, 1901).

Dodd, William E. (ed.), *Letters of John Taylor* (John P. Branch Historical Papers, Vol. 2, Richmond, 1903).

Donnan, Elizabeth (ed.), *Papers of James A. Bayard* (American Historical Association Annual Report for 1914, Washington, 1915).

Fitzpatrick, John C. (ed.), *The Diaries of George Washington* (4 vols., Boston and New York, 1925).

——, *The Writings of George Washington* (39 vols., Washington, 1931-44).

Foner, Philip S. (ed.), *The Complete Writings of Thomas Paine* (2 vols., New York, 1945).

Ford, Paul Leicester (ed.), *Writings of Thomas Jefferson* (10 vols., New York, 1892-99).

Ford, Worthington Chauncey (ed.), *Correspondence and Journals of Samuel B. Webb* (3 vols., New York, 1894).

——, *Letters of William Vans Murray to John Quincy Adams, 1797-1803* (American Historical Association Annual Report for 1912, Washington, 1914).

——, *Some Letters of Elbridge Gerry* (Brooklyn, 1896).

——, *Writings of John Quincy Adams* (7 vols., New York, 1913-17).

Gibbs, George, *Memoirs of the Administrations of Washington and John Adams, Edited from the Papers of Oliver Wolcott* (2 vols., New York, 1846).

Graydon, Alexander, *Memoirs of a Life Chiefly Passed in Pennsylvania Within the Last Sixty Years* (Harrisburg, 1811).

Greene, G. W., *The Life of Nathanael Greene* (3 vols., New York, 1867-71).

Greig, James (ed.), *The Farington Diary* (London, 1923).

Hamilton, John Church, *Works of Alexander Hamilton* (7 vols., New York, 1850-51).

Hamilton, Stanislaus Murray (ed.), *Writings of James Monroe* (7 vols., New York, 1898-1903).

Hammond, O. G., *Letters and Papers of General John Sullivan* (3 vols., Concord, N.H., 1930-31).

Henkels, Stan V. (ed.), *The Confidential Correspondence of Robert Morris* (Philadelphia, 1917).

——, *Washington-Madison Papers* (Philadelphia, 1899).

Hunt, Gaillard (ed.), *The Writings of James Madison* (9 vols., New York, 1900-1910).

Jameson, J. Franklin (ed.), *Letters of Phineas Bond* (American Historical Association Annual Report for 1897, Washington, 1898).

Jenkins, C. F. (ed.), *Jefferson's Germantown Letters* (Philadelphia, 1906).

Johnston, Henry P. (ed.), *The Correspondence and Public Papers of John Jay* (4 vols., New York, 1890-93).
Kent, William (ed.), *Memorials and Letters of James Kent* (New York, 1869).
King, Charles R., *The Life and Correspondence of Rufus King* (6 vols., New York, 1895).
Kirkland, Frederick (ed.), *Letters on the American Revolution* (Philadelphia, 1941).
Lodge, Henry Cabot (ed.), *The Works of Alexander Hamilton* (12 vols., New York, 1904).
Maclay, Edgar (ed.), *The Journal of William Maclay* (New York, 1927).
Mason, Jeremiah, *Memorials and Correspondence of Jeremiah Mason* (Cambridge, 1872).
Mitchell, Stewart (ed.), *New Letters of Abigail Adams* (Boston, 1947).
Morris, Anne C. (ed.), *Diary and Letters of Gouverneur Morris* (2 vols., New York, 1888).
Pickering, Timothy, *A Review of the Correspondence between John Adams and William Cunningham* (Salem, 1824).
Primrose, Archibald P. (ed.), *The Windham Papers: Life and Correspondence of the Right Honorable William Windham, 1750-1810* (London, 1913).
Simms, William G. (ed.), *The Army Correspondence of John Laurens* (New York, 1867).
Sizer, Theodore (ed.), *The Autobiography of Colonel John Trumbull* (New Haven, 1953).
Smith, William H. (ed.), *The St. Clair Papers; Life and Public Services of Arthur St. Clair* (2 vols., Cincinnati, 1882).
Sparks, Jared (ed.), *Correspondence of the American Revolution* (4 vols., Boston, 1853).
———, *The Works of Benjamin Franklin* (10 vols., Boston, 1840).
Turner, Frederick Jackson (ed.), *Correspondence of the French Ministers to the United States, 1791-1797* (American Historical Association Annual Report for 1903, II, Washington, 1904).
Vance, Clarence H. (ed.), *Letters of a Westchester Farmer (1774-1775) by the Reverend Samuel Seabury* (White Plains, N.Y., 1930).
Wagstaff, Henry M. (ed.), *The Papers of John Steele* (2 vols., Raleigh, 1924).
Warren, Charles, *Jacobin and Juno; or Early American Politics as Viewed in the Diary of Dr. Nathaniel Ames, 1758-1822* (Cambridge, 1931).
Watson, Winslow C. (ed.), *Men and Times of the Revolution; Memoirs of Elkanah Watson* (New York, 1856).
Webster, Noah, *A Collection of Papers on Political, Literary and Moral Subjects* (New York, 1843).
Wilkinson, James, *Memoirs of My Own Times* (3 vols., Philadelphia, 1816).

BIOGRAPHIES

Adams, Charles Francis, *The Life of John Adams* (2 vols., Boston, 1874).
Adams, Henry, *The Life of Albert Gallatin* (Philadelphia, 1879).
Alden, John Richard, *General Charles Lee, Traitor or Patriot?* (Baton Rouge, 1951).
Amory, Thomas C., *The Life of James Sullivan* (2 vols., Boston, 1859).

Bibliography

Anderson, Dice R., *William Branch Giles* (Menasha, Wis., 1914).
Austin, James T., *The Life of Elbridge Gerry* (2 vols., Boston, 1827-29).
Baldwin, S. E., *Life and Letters of Simeon Baldwin* (New York, 1919).
Beardsley, E. E., *Life and Correspondence of Samuel Seabury* (Boston, 1881).
Bemis, Samuel Flagg, *John Quincy Adams and the Foundations of American Foreign Policy* (New York, 1949).
Beveridge, Albert J., *The Life of John Marshall* (4 vols., Boston, 1916-19).
Borden, Morton, *The Federalism of James A. Bayard* (New York, 1954).
Boudinot, J. J., *Life of Elias Boudinot* (2 vols., Boston and New York, 1896).
Boutel, Lewis H., *Roger Sherman* (Chicago, 1896).
Bowers, Claude G., *Jefferson and Hamilton: The Struggle for Democracy in America* (Boston, 1925).
Boyd, George Adams, *Elias Boudinot, Patriot and Statesman, 1740-1821* (Princeton, 1952).
Brant, Irving, *James Madison* (3 vols., Indianapolis, 1941——).
Bruce, William C., *John Randolph of Roanoke* (2 vols., New York, 1922).
Chinard, Gilbert, *Honest John Adams* (Boston, 1933).
Chipman, Daniel, *Life of Nathaniel Chipman* (Boston, 1846).
Clark, Mary E., *Peter Porcupine in America: The Career of William Cobbett, 1792-1800* (Philadelphia, 1939).
Conway, Moncure D., *Omitted Chapters of History . . . Edmund Randolph* (New York, 1888).
Cresson, William P., *James Monroe* (Chapel Hill, 1946).
Cutler, W. P. and J. P., *The Life Journals and Correspondence of the Reverend Manasseh Cutler* (2 vols., Cincinnati, 1888).
Dallas, George Mifflin, *Life and Writings of Alexander James Dallas* (Philadelphia, 1871).
Davis, Matthew L., *Memoirs of Aaron Burr* (2 vols., New York, 1836).
Drake, Francis S., *Life and Correspondence of Henry Knox* (Boston, 1873).
Forbes, J. D., *Israel Thorndike, Federalist Financier* (New York, 1953).
Ford, Emily E. F., and Skeel, E. E. F., *Notes on the Life of Noah Webster* (2 vols., New York, 1912).
Ford, Paul Leicester, *The True George Washington* (Philadelphia, 1896).
Forman, Samuel E., *The Political Activities of Philip Freneau* (Baltimore, 1902).
Freeman, Douglas Southall, *George Washington: A Biography* (6 vols., New York, 1948-54).
Hall, Charles S., *Benjamin Tallmadge* (New York, 1943).
Hamilton, A. McLane, *The Intimate Life of Alexander Hamilton* (New York, 1911).
Hamilton, John Church, *History of the Republic of the United States, as Traced in the Writings of Alexander Hamilton and His Contemporaries* (New York, 1857-64).
Henry, William Wirt, *Patrick Henry: Life, Correspondence and Speeches* (3 vols., New York, 1891).
Horton, James T., *James Kent, A Study in Conservatism* (New York, 1934).
Howard, Leon, *The Connecticut Wits* (Chicago, 1943).
Humphreys, David, *Life of Israel Putnam* (Philadelphia, 1811).

Hutcheson, Harold, *Tench Coxe* (Philadelphia, 1938).
Jacobs, James R., *Tarnished Warrior: Major General James Wilkinson* (New York, 1938).
King, Charles R., *The Life and Correspondence of Rufus King* (6 vols., New York, 1895).
Koch, Adrienne, *Jefferson and Madison: The Great Collaboration* (New York, 1950).
Korngold, Ralph, *Citizen Toussaint* (Boston, 1945).
Leake, Isaac Q., *Memoir of the Life and Times of John Lamb* (Albany, 1850).
Leary, Lewis, *That Rascal Freneau* (New Brunswick, N.J., 1941).
Livingston, Edwin Brockholst, *The Livingstons of Livingston Manor* (New York, 1910).
Lodge, Henry Cabot, *Alexander Hamilton* (Boston, 1909).
———, *Life and Letters of George Cabot* (Boston, 1877).
Lossing, B. J., *Life and Times of Philip Schuyler* (2 vols., New York, 1873).
McLaughlin, J. F., *Mathew Lyon* (New York, 1900).
McMaster, John B., *The Life and Times of Stephen Girard* (2 vols., Philadelphia, 1918).
McRee, G. J., *Life and Correspondence of James Iredell* (2 vols., New York, 1857).
Malone, Dumas, *The Public Life of Thomas Cooper* (New Haven, 1926).
———, *Jefferson and the Rights of Man* (Boston, 1951).
Marshall, John, *Life of George Washington* (5 vols., Philadelphia, 1804-07).
Minnegerode, Meade, *Jefferson, Friend of France* (New York, 1928).
Mitchell, Broadus, *Alexander Hamilton, Youth to Maturity* (New York, 1957).
Monaghan, Frank, *John Jay, Defender of Liberty* (Indianapolis, 1935).
Morison, John H., *Life of Jeremiah Smith* (Boston, 1845).
Morison, Samuel Eliot, *Life and Letters of Harrison Gray Otis, Federalist, 1765-1848* (2 vols., Boston, 1913).
———, "Elbridge Gerry, Gentleman Diplomat," *New England Quarterly*, II, (1929).
Newlin, Claude M., *The Life and Writings of Hugh Henry Brackenridge* (Princeton, 1932).
Oberholtzer, E. P., *Robert Morris* (New York, 1903).
O'Brien, Michael, Jr., *Hercules Mulligan* (New York, 1937).
Oliver, F. S., *Alexander Hamilton: An Essay on American Union* (London, 1915).
Palmer, J. M., *General von Steuben* (Princeton, 1927).
Parsons, Theophilus, *Memoir of Theophilus Parsons* (Boston, 1859).
Parton, James, *The Life and Times of Aaron Burr* (2 vols., New York, 1864).
Patterson, S. W., *Horatio Gates* (New York, 1941).
Pickering, Octavius, and Upham, Charles W., *Life of Timothy Pickering* (4 vols., Boston, 1867-73).
Pinckney, Charles C., *The Life of General Thomas Pinckney* (Boston, 1895).
Plumer, William, *Life of William Plumer* (Boston, 1856).
Quincy, Edmund, *Life of Josiah Quincy* (Boston, 1868).
Read, William Thompson, *The Life and Correspondence of George Read* (Philadelphia, 1870).
Reed, William B., *The Life and Correspondence of Joseph Reed* (2 vols., Philadelphia, 1847).

Bibliography

Riddell, William R., *Life of John Graves Simcoe, First Lieutenant Governor of Upper Canada, 1792-1796* (Toronto, 1926).
Rives, W. C., *History of the Life and Times of James Madison* (New York, 1868-73).
Robertson, William Spence, *The Life of Miranda* (2 vols., Chapel Hill, 1929).
Roosevelt, Theodore, *Gouverneur Morris* (Boston, 1888).
Rowland, Kate Mason, *Life of Charles Carroll of Carrollton, 1737-1832* (2 vols., New York, 1912).
——, *Life of George Mason* (2 vols., New York, 1892).
Schachner, Nathan, *Alexander Hamilton* (New York, 1946).
——, *Aaron Burr* (New York, 1937).
——, *The Founding Fathers* (New York, 1954).
Sedgwick, Theodore, Jr., *Life of William Livingston* (New York, 1833).
Shea, George, *Life and Epoch of Alexander Hamilton* (Boston, 1879).
Simms, Henry H., *Life of John Taylor* (Richmond, 1932).
Sparks, Jared, *Life of Gouverneur Morris* (Boston, 1832).
Spaulding, E. Wilder, *His Excellency, Governor George Clinton* (New York, 1938).
Steiner, Bernard C., *The Life and Correspondence of James McHenry* (Cleveland, 1907).
Stephenson, N. W., and Dunn, W. H., *George Washington* (2 vols., New York, 1940).
Thorp, Willard (ed.), *The Lives of Eighteen from Princeton* (Princeton, 1946).
Tilghman, Oswald, *Memoir of Lieutenant Colonel Tench Tilghman* (Albany, 1876).
Tolles, Frederick B., *George Logan of Philadelphia* (New York, 1953).
Tuckerman, Bayard, *Life of Philip Schuyler, 1733-1804* (New York, 1903).
Tyler, Lyon G., *The Letters and Times of the Tylers* (3 vols., Richmond, 1884-96).
Van Schaack, H. C., *Life of Peter van Schaack* (New York, 1892).
Ver Steeg, Clarence Lester, *Robert Morris: Revolutionary Financier* (Philadelphia, 1954).
Wallace, Paul A. W., *The Muhlenbergs of Pennsylvania* (Philadelphia, 1950).
Walters, Raymond, *Alexander James Dallas* (Philadelphia, 1943).
——, *Albert Gallatin, Jeffersonian Financier and Diplomat* (New York, 1957).
Warfel, H. R., *Noah Webster, Schoolmaster to America* (New York, 1936).
Wildes, Harry E., *Anthony Wayne* (New York, 1941).
Williams, John, *Life of Alexander Hamilton* (New York, 1805).

Index

absolutism, 161, 167
Adams, John, 8, 10, 49, 146, 150, 348, 359, 365, 445-446, 479, 486, 526, 528, 553, 557-558, 563; shortcomings and assets of, 220-221; elected president, 1796, 448; threatened break with H., 451; relations with H. during presidency, 457; cabinet of, 457-458; statesmanship as president, 468; as forgotten man of war effort, 481; supports McHenry against H., 482; enforcement of Alien and Sedition Acts, 484-485; names Murray as Minister to France, 493; invasion of Spanish America and, 499; runs government from Braintree, Mass., 500; ridicules H.'s predictions on France, 502; low estimate of H., 502, 523; courage and statesmanship of, 503; pardons Fries and Dutch rioters, 507; renomination of, 513-515; disloyalty of Cabinet, 517; angered at H.'s New England tour, 518; H.'s and Jefferson's criticism of, 519-520; character and popularity of, 521-523
Adams, Mrs. John, 280, 563
Adams, John Quincy, 421, 539, 542, 568
Adams, Samuel, 142
Addison, Joseph, 10
"Address to the People of New York," 209
Adet, Citizen Pierre, 449
"agrarian" vs. "fiscal" interests, 311; see also farmers; Southern planters
agriculture, capital and, 55; declining foreign markets for, 284; as economic weakness, 284; growth of, 312-313
Albany, N. Y., 23-24
Alexander, Catherine ("Lady Kitty"), 244-245
Alexander Hamilton (merchantman), 470
Alexander Hamilton (miniature ship), 213-215, 354, 439
Alien Friends Bill, 485
Alien and Sedition Acts, 483-485, 504, 509, 554; enforcement of, 489; supported in North, 491; Virginia "disunion" and, 490, 490 n.; *see also* Sedition Act
Allen, Ethan, 131
amendments, Constitutional, *see* Constitution, U.S.
American Army, *see* Continental Army; United States Army
"American empire," 100, 165
American Revolution, fundamental concepts of, 205; *see also* Revolutionary War
"Americans," vs. state citizens, 119
American shipping, *see* shipping, American
Ames, Fisher, 238, 352, 518, 525, 539, 550, 557, 561
ammunition, profiteering in, 43
Anarchiad, 148
anarchy, democracy and, 124; drift to, 143
André, Maj. John, 69-71
Anglo-American relations, 1794-95, 384-385; *see also* Great Britain
Anglophobia, demagogues and, 428
Annapolis (Md.) Convention of 1786, 136, 151
Antifederalists, 193, 196, 206, 209, 214-215, 411; at Poughkeepsie Convention, 211-213
Appeal to the American People, 449
appropriation bills, 435 n.
"Aristides," sobriquet of Jefferson, 347
aristocracy, control of democracy by, 180; H. as champion of, 19; his leanings toward, 50-51; judicial review and, 204; vs. mob action, 19; "natural" vs. "artificial," 314; "natural" rights of, 200; Paine's fear of, 49; postwar, 120; in Washington's army, 21
Aristotle, 46, 190, 196
Armed Neutrality, 418-420
Armstrong, Maj. John, 94
army, peacetime, 98-99; provisional, *see* provisional army; *see also* Continental Army; United States Army
army pay, dispute over, 91-94

641

Arnold, Benedict, 23, 65, 69, 356, 394; treason of, 69-70
Arnold, Mrs. Benedict, 70
Articles of Confederation, 40, 87, 107, 137, 147, 151, 160-161, 173, 181, 195, 198, 200, 221, 263, 392; vs. Constitution, 194; dangers of, 111-112, 190; "futility" of, 118; states' rights and, 136; weaknesses of, 116, 140, 153-155
Athens, struggle with Sparta, 115
audacity, capitalism and, 233; H.'s credo of, 227
Aurora, newspaper, see Philadelphia *Aurora*
authority, H.'s respect for, 18

Bache, Benjamin, 439, 486
Bache, Mrs. Benjamin, 486
Bacon, Lord Francis, 46
Baltic Powers, 418
Baltimore, U.S.S., impressment of seamen from, 473
banks(s), function of, 55; land, see land bank; as means of strengthening propertied class, 126-127; national, see national bank; primary purpose of, 129; see also state bank
bank competition, 128
bank dividends, taxes on, 403
bank loans, to government, 55
bank notes, issuance of, 55
Bank of England, 53-55, 270, 272 n., 274 n., 275; as model for Bank of U.S., 260; suspends specie payments, 472
Bank of Manhattan (N.Y.), 511-512
Bank of New York, 127-128, 130, 271, 274-276, 302-303, 307-308
Bank of North America, 61, 127-128, 130, 263; establishment of, 1781, 86
Bank of Pennsylvania, 127-128
Bank of the United States, 56, 115, 255-277, 296, 308, 328-329, 367, 384, 434, 439, 538; Bank of England and, 260; as balancing force in national economy, 60; bank notes issued by, 276 n.; bill signed by Washington, 267; democracy and, 120-130; dividends paid, 273 n.; idea of, 53; Jefferson's opinion of, 346; legality of, 264-265; letter to Morris on, 60; loans to government from, 55, 273; opening of, 268; private control of, 262; sale of stock in, 267-268; speculation in, 268-270; vs. state banks, 273; success of, 276-277; Washington's misgivings on, 264-265
bankruptcy, threat of, 52
bankruptcy laws, 126
bank scrip, sale of, 268-270
Barbary corsairs, 390
Barber, Dr., 7

barter, 56
Barton, William, 282 n.
Bastille, storming of, 363
Bayard, James A., 526, 529
Bayard, William, 573
Beckley, John, 341, 441, 462; dismissal and revenge of, 459 ff.
Beckwith, Maj., 223, 367-368
Bennington, Battle of, 23
Benson, Egbert, 106, 136, 190 n.
bicameral legislature, 156
bigotry, 104
Bill of Rights, absence of in Schuyler-Hamilton plan, 161; Madison and, 229; Jefferson and, 249
Bill of Rights, The, 202 n.
Bingham, Thomas, 281
Bingham, William, 237 n., 245, 526, 545 n.
blackmail, Reynolds' plot of, 333 ff.
Blackstone, Sir William, 49, 109, 140
Blanca, Florida, 557
bloodletting, in yellow fever epidemic, 380-381
Bolingbroke, Henry St. John, Viscount, 190
boom-and-bust cycle, 307
Boston Tea Party, 8, 19
Boudinot, Elias, 98, 238, 309, 438
bounties, as spur to manufacturing, 287, 289-290, 291 n., 299
Bowdoin, James, 144
boycott, colonial, 11
Brackenridge, Hugh Henry, 409-410
Bradford, David, 409-410
Bradford, William, 401, 410
Braintree, Mass., 500
branch banking, objections to, 274-275
Brandywine, Battle of, 23
bravery and heroism, H.'s statement on, 20
British-American union, economic basis for, 15: see also Great Britain
British army, underestimated by H., 21
British atrocities, in Rutgers case, 105-106
British constitution, 15, 49; as model for American, 166-167
British Empire, need for preservation of, 13; threat to from France, 370-371
"British faction," 472, 518-519
British goods, taxes on, 135
British industrialism, 288
British monarchy, as model for H.'s plan for, 165
British navy, aid from against Napoleon, 560; conquest of Spanish America and, 498; dependence on, 453, 474; as factor in war or peace with France, 471-472
British Parliament, as model for H.'s plan, 160-161, 168
British shipping, see shipping, British

Index

British West Indies, 134, 392, 422; American vessels excluded from, 422, 429; trade with, 223; *see also* French West Indies; Great Britain; West Indies
Burgoyne, Gen. John, 23, 69, 131
Burke, Edmund, 365
Burlamaqui, Jean Jacques, 106
Burr, Aaron, 170, 340, 503, 522, 537, 544, 546; as Washington's aide, 22; H.'s quarrel with, 343-360; background and character of, 355-356; affront to Washington, 356; contrasted with H., 357; appointed to Senate, 358; defeated for vice-presidency, 1788, 358-359; vice-presidential candidate, 1796, 445; placates Monroe in threatened duel with H., 461; as notorious duelist, 480; aims at vice-presidency in 1800, 510-512; contests presidency with Jefferson, 525; denounced by H., 526; background of duel, 557-570; Northern Confederacy and, 566; defeated in N. Y. governorship election, 568-569; demands satisfaction from H., 570; challenges and kills him in duel, 574-575
Burr, Theodosia (daughter), 356
businessmen, "timidity" of, 299
Butler, Pierce, 174
buying spree, postwar, 120

Cabinet loyalty, H.'s disregard of, 517
Cabinet system, H.'s idea for, 57-58
Cabot, George, 455, 477, 541
Caesar, Julius, 40, 144, 244
"Caesar," H.'s sobriquet, 185-186, 188, 347; faults as, 187
Caesarism, Continental Congress' fear of, 36-37
Callender, James T., 459, 462, 464, 485, 551, 555
Cambuskeith, Laird of, 3
"Camillus," 427-429
Campbell, Col. William, 78
Campo Formio, peace of, 466
Canada, establishment of Roman Catholicism in, 19; as "fourteenth state," 20; trade with, 428
capital, federal, site of, 248, 251, 265, 309
capitalism, "audacity" in, 233; bank as aid to, 282; vs. democracy, 122; spirit of, 286
capitalistic enterprise, manufacturing and, 286
Caribbean, French influence in, 559-560
carriage tax, 400-401; increase in, 504
"Cato," Clinton sobriquet, 185, 188
"Catullus," H.'s sobriquet, 347
Causes of Depreciation of the Continental Currency, 52
Cavalry and Infantry, School of, 482

central government, 172, 195-196; in Schuyler-Hamilton plan, 160; states as "geographical expressions" in, 162; *see also* strong central government
Champlain, Christopher, 281
Chase, Samuel, 44, 208 n., 538
checks and balances, system of, 49-50, 196; absence of in Schuyler-Hamilton plan, 161
Chesterfield, Philip Dormer Stanhope, Earl of, 66
chief executive, election of, 50-51; *see also* presidency; president
child labor, 288
Childs, Francis, 344
Christian Constitutional Society, 552
Church, Angelica Schuyler (Mrs. John Barker), 464
Church, John Barker (brother-in-law), 127, 129, 464, 547-548
Cicero, Marcus Tullius, 46
Cincinnati, Society of the, 146-147, 234
civil war, threat of, 415
Clark, Abraham, 138
Clark, George Rogers, 373
Clingman, Jacob, 337-338, 340-341, 460-461
Clinton, Gov. George, 26, 100, 107, 124-125, 132-133, 147, 149, 151, 170, 176, 184, 191, 225, 353, 357, 378, 568; Benedict Arnold and, 69-70; hatred of Loyalists, 103-104; supports Articles of Confederation against Constitution, 184-185, 209; branded by H. as "demagogue," 186, 354; threatens to withdraw N. Y. from union, 213; alignment with Livingstons, 355; *see also* Clintonians
Clinton, Sir Henry, 24, 28-29, 41
Clintonians, in Constitutional Convention, 152; attack upon Hamilton's character, 187; manhood suffrage platform of, 209; conditional ratification of Constitution by, 214
Clinton-Livingston wing, 568
clothing, dependence on Great Britain for, 11; profiteering in, 43; soldiers' lack of, 43
Cobbett, William, 384, 550
Coercive Acts, *see* Intolerable Acts
Coke, Sir Edward, 109, 205
Colbert, Jean Baptiste, 46, 293
Coleman, William, 551
colonies, economic invincibility of, 15
Columbia College (King's College), 8, 278, 383, 480; *see also* King's College
commerce, control of, 134; *see also* trade
"Commercial Propositions," Madison's, 388-389
commodities, profiteering in, 43
Compagnie des Indes, La, 53-54
Concord, Battle of, 16

Congress, U.S., appropriations for defense against France, 454; and call to arms in French crisis, 468; Supreme Court powers and, 536; *see also* Continental Congress; judicial review; Supreme Court
Connecticut Wits, 148
consent of people, as basis of government, 155, 180
"Consolato del Mare," doctrine of, 385
Constitution, U.S., as alternative to anarchy, 182; amendments to, 213-214; vs. Articles of Confederation, 194; attacks on, 187; as check on human passions, 199; contesting of in N. Y. and Virginia, 207; direct taxes and, 401 n.; exposition of in *Federalist* papers, 192; full ratification of, 215; general welfare clause, 296-297; H.'s construction and interpretation of, 267; Hamiltonian principles embodied in, 537; Jacobinism and, 563; Loyalist support of, 110; as mixture of good and bad qualities, 182; neutrality proclamation and, 371; purpose of, 195; ratification of, 181, 213, 215; Sedition Act and, 484; Supreme Court as interpreter of, 201, 537; as supreme law of the land, 202; Virginia and Kentucky resolutions and, 489-491; Yazoo land question and, 548
Constitutional Convention, Philadelphia, 51, 141, 147, 151-183, 298, 433, 561; call for, 140; compromise in, 177; first resolution for, 138; Great Compromise of July 16, 178; H.'s plan for, 59; judicial review in, 202; New York delegation at, 152; "second," 214; secrecy of, 160; stalemate on state equality, 176; *see also* New Jersey Plan; Virginia Plan
Continental Army, 23, 132, 146; as "cement of Union," 57; disbanding of, 98; "grousing" in, 35; impost and, 92-93; low morale in, 56; mutinies in, 1781, 58, 71; mutiny threats, 98; Negro slaves in, 41-42; pay grievances of, 1782, 91, 94; ragged condition of, 43; weaknesses of, 66, 143; *see also* United States Army
"Continental Association," belief in, 15
Continental Congress, 15, 18, 20, 24, 31, 36-37, 42, 131, 139, 147, 151, 221, 234, 263, 281; bankruptcy of, 55; commerce control by, 134; credit restoration and, 51-52; declining authority of, 56, 66, 99, 112, 115-116, 118, 134-136; defects and weaknesses of, 57-58, 112; deficit of, 1787, 149; denounced by Greene, 40; dispute with Rhode Island, 90; election to, 84; foreign debt of, 232; foreign policy of, 106; H.'s criticism of, 36-37; his defense of, 11; inflation and, 44-45; Seabury's diatribe against, 9-10; Second, 16; soldiers' gripes against, 35; sovereignty of, 57; "spirit of accommodation" in, 183; taxation powers of, 59, 83, 87; tax shortages and, 84; as threat to freedom, 113; threatened by Army in Philadelphia, 98; "tottering" of, 155; war- and peacemaking powers of, 108; *see also* Congress, U.S.
Continental currency, depreciation of, 44-45, 47, 56; *see also* paper money
"Continentalist, The," H.'s pseudonym, 58, 75, 89
contract, law of, 404
contraband, British confiscation of, 385
Conway, Gen. Thomas, 27-28
Cooper, Charles D., 569-570
Cooper, Rev. Myles, 17
Cooper, Thomas, 524
Cornwallis, Charles Cornwallis, Marquis of, 21, 41, 65, 71, 76; surrender of at Yorktown, 79
corruption, Republican charges of, 325
cost of living, inflation and, 45
cotton, as growing Southern industry, 313; Jay's Treaty and, 422
cotton manufacturers, 282-283; Paterson failure and, 309
cotton mills, 301
Court of St. James's, 393, 418, 496, 516
Coxe, Tench, 137, 282, 288, 523
Craigie, Andrew, 245, 305
credit, government or public, *see* government credit
"Critical Period," 143
criticism, right of, 104-105
Croesus, 86
Cromwell, Oliver, 144
Croswell, Harry, 553-554
Cruger, Nicholas, 5, 7
Cruger and Beekman counting house, 4-5
currency, depreciation of, 44-45, 47, 56
"Curtius," sobriquet of James Kent, 430

Dallas, Alexander J., 374-375
Dana, Francis, 37
Deane, Silas, 27
debt, national, *see* national debt
debt dodging, 1787, 150
debtors' legislation, 120-121, 171
debts, moratorium on, 120; sequestration of, 391-392, 416
Declaration of Independence, 268
deflation, onset of, 56; postwar, 120
Deism, 446, 552
De Lancey, Stephen, 109
Delaware, "self-defense" for, 175-176; supports H.'s plan on states, 174
Delaware River, crossing of, 21

Index

demagoguery, 126, 144, 200; Anglophobia and, 428; Burr labeled as master of, 567, 571; democracy and, 124; H.'s defeat in 1800 election and, 513; President as bulwark against, 165
democracy, anarchy and, 540; banking and, 120-130; vs. capitalism, 122; "cure" for, 565; defined, 121 n.; direct or "pure," excess of, 169; French Revolution and, 364; H.'s aversion to, 61, 156-157; House of Representatives as "hospital" for, 180; Jefferson's trust in, 315; mob rule and, 123-124; vs. property rights, 121-122, 145; in Schuyler-Hamilton plan, 164; tyranny and, 164; as "worst" of all governments, 50-51
"Democratic Man," in *Federalist* papers, 199
Democratic Societies, denounced by Washington, 413; as opponents of Hamiltonianism, 412
Demosthenes, 46, 228
Denmark, in French crisis, 418
departments, government, need for, 57-59
depreciation, inflation and, 44-45, 47, 56; postwar, 120, 126
Dickinson, John, 8
dictatorship, "constitutional," 40
diplomacy, as substitute for war with France, 454-456
direct taxes, Constitution and, 401-402
Directory, French, 451-452, 454-456, 470, 475, 492-493, 495, 500; capture of American shipping by, 466; meets Adams' demands, 501; provocation of, 469; *see also* France
distillers, internal revenue and, 398; *see also* Whisky Rebellion
disunion, threat of, 213, 238, 255-256, 490-491
domestic debt, Washington's administration, 230; *see also* national debt
domestic loan, "juggling" of, 328
Dorchester, Guy Carleton, 1st Baron of, 367-368, 390
draft, by Continental Congress, 57
Duane, James, 57, 59-60, 132, 209, 354, 355 n., 545 n.
Duane, William, 486
Duer, William, 189, 244-246, 270-271, 301, 303, 326, 337, 341, 516, 545 n.; Treasury shortages traced to, 305; imprisonment of, 306-307; manipulations of in S.U.M., 308-309; alleged link with H., 338, 340
Du Pont de Nemours, Pierre Samuel, 285
Dutch bankers, loans from, 150, 232, 301, 305, 327-328, 348

Eacker, George, 548

East India Company, 8, 17
economic individualism, 291
economic recovery, 1794, 279
economics, H.'s preoccupation with in 1778, 46-47; *see also* finance; national debt
election of 1796, 435-450; of 1800, 509-521
Electoral College, 220-221, 444, 445 n.; Burr-Jefferson vote in, 524-525; creation of, 179; vs. direct election of president, 165-166; hazards of, 567; jockeying of votes in, 221; manipulation of by H. in 1800 election, 514-516
elite, *see* aristocracy
Elizabethtown, N.J., school years at, 7-8
Ellsworth, Oliver, 503
"energetic" government, 61, 126, 135, 145, 155, 161, 438
England, Church of, 7; *see also* Great Britain
Engineers and Artillerists, School of, 482
equality, of states, 156, 174, 178, 210-211
Essex Junto, 565-566, 568
Estaing, Charles Hector, comte d', 28
European entanglements, avoidance of, 443-444
Eustice, Maj., 33-34
excise tax, armed demonstrations against, 405; constitutionality of, 399; in whisky manufacture, 396 ff.
executive, legislative and judicial functions, 49, 139-140
Executive Branch, departments of, 225
executive powers, separation of, 139-140
executive veto, 158

factions, rise of, 319, 352
factories, establishment of, 287; women and children employed in, 288
Farewell Address, Washington's, 442-443, 445
farmers, antipathy toward, 294; bank for, 128; Bank of the U.S. and, 263, 271-272; credit facilities for, 130; disaffection of with Federalists, 510; excise tax and, 397-398; Federalists' decline and, 512; Jefferson's concern for, 314; postwar plight of, 120-122; revolt of under Shays, 142-143; "ruin" of by Society of Useful Manufactures, 302; Southern bloc of, 353; vs. speculators, 240, 314; tax burden on, 222; whisky manufacture by, 397
Federal Constitution, *see* Constitution, U.S.
federal government, Articles of Confederation and, 116; capitalism and, 403; financial difficulties of, 1799, 505; "general welfare" clause as source of power, 297; national economy and, 290; vs. national government, 117-118; process of, 264-266; powers of, 403; pre-emption of excise by,

396-397; re-establishment of credit of, 281-282; separation of powers in, 139-140; vs. state sovereignty, 112; strict vs. loose construction of, 265; taxing powers of, 195; *see also* implied powers, doctrine of federalism, H.'s distaste for, 156-157; vs. nationalism, 195; *see also* states' rights; strong central government
Federalist, The, 140, 184-192, 219, 229, 235 n., 249, 289, 319, 397, 489, 497 n., 534, 536; collaboration with Madison and Jay on, 189 ff.; first issue of, 188; H.'s admission of authorship, 190 n.; as handbook for Constitution supporters, 207; impression made by, 206; number of essays written, 192; principal theme of, 195; as "second reply to Constitution," 208; solemnity of, 193; style of, 190
Federalist party, 206-208, 214, 278, 281, 332, 343, 353, 387, 413, 435-436, 438, 467, 479, 491, 524, 538, 564, 567; birth of, 193; vs. Jeffersonians, 313; disruption of, 355; New York group of, 358; and threatened war with Britain, 393-394; British respect for, 421; in election of 1796, 445; "French influence" charged against Republicans, 450; as "party of peace," 456; moderate wing of in French crisis, 471; Alien and Sedition Acts and, 483-485; "warlike" plans of, 492; feel "cheated" on French war, 494; decline of, 504, 510; absence of qualified candidates in, 512; defeat of in 1800, 513-514; in Burr-Jefferson dissolution following election of 1800, 529; in political limbo, 539; and "holocaust" of democracy, 541-542; French treaty and, 557; retreat of, 1804, 563
Federal Republic, dream of, 59
Fenno, John, 343, 349, 384, 550
Final Report to Congress, 438
Finance, Superintendent of, 59, 83, 86, 97, 244
financial collapse, threat of, 56-57
financial planning, national government and, 51; self-interest and, 92
financial system, "Hamiltonian," 235-237; *see also* fiscal policy
financiers, 127; *see also* "moneyed men"
Findley, William, 411
"fiscal faction," 311
fiscal policy, letter to Morris on, 60
fishing industry, 298-299
Fishkill, N.Y., 25
Fitzsimmons, Rep., 413
Fletcher v. Peck, 548
Fleury, Col., 65
Floridas, "empire" of, 495, 508, 557
flour, "corner" on, 44

food, profiteering in, 43
Foreign Affairs Department, creation of, 59
foreign debt, 230; debt-dodging and, 150; nonrepudiation of, 232
foreign entanglements, avoidance of, 443-444
foreign loans, 57; Bank of North America and, 87; for Bank of U.S., 55-56; juggling of, 328; *see also* Dutch bankers
foreign policy, executive control of, 370-371; test case of, 106
foreign trade, 134
Fort Stanwix, Battle of, 23
"Founding Fathers," 319
France, Alien and Sedition Acts and, 484; attacks on American shipping, 452-455; attempted crushing of Great Britain by, 451-452; attempts to "avert" peace with, 500 ff.; blockage of by Britain, 386; breakdown of negotiations with, 466; "bribe" to in XYZ affair, 466-469; deteriorating relations with, 451; expected aid from, 12; loan from, 57, 87; military alliance with, 368; peace mission to, 455-456; peace treaty with, 557; "perpetual" alliance with, 444; possible invasion of U.S. by, 467; in Revolutionary War, 370; in 1796 election, 448-449; Royal Bank of, 53
Franco-American alliance, 28
Franco-American relations, crisis in, 452 ff.
Franco-American treaties, neutral rights and, 426
Franklin, Benjamin, 68, 158, 175, 178, 206, 412, 423, 486
Fraunces, Andrew G., 340
freedom, Continental Congress as threat to, 113; as cornerstone of British-American "union," 13; French Revolution and, 365-366
freedom of the press, 488, 553; vs. license, 555
free economy, ideal of, 287
free trade, laissez faire and, 292
French army, in United States, 75
French Canada, 19-20
French citizens, in U.S., 485
"French faction," 421, 442-443, 445, 449
French fleet, in Revolutionary War, 26, 28, 44
French privateers, 373-374, 416
French Revolution, contrasted with American, 365; flight of capital in, 253; neutrality proclamation and, 363-378; threat of to Hamiltonianism, 365
French shipping, 224
French West Indies, 368, 452
Freneau, Philip, 313-345, 349, 379, 383
Fries, John, 505, 507
Frothingham, David, 487

Index

funded debt, 441
funding-assumption bill, 246-247, 249-250, 257, 263; H.'s "deal" on, 251-252
funding system, 236-237, 239, 277, 253-254, 318, 323, 381, 434; Jefferson and, 349; *see also* sinking fund

Gallatin, Albert, 411, 435, 439 n., 453, 534, 562
Gates, Gen. Horatio, 23, 28; strength and popularity of, 24-25; as "savior" of American cause, 26-27; eclipse of, 37; defection of in South Carolina, 65-66
Gazette of the United States, 270, 343, 345, 349, 384, 550
general revenue bill, 95-96; *see also* impost
"general welfare" clause, 296-297
Genêt, Citizen Edmond, 369, 372-378, 387, 412, 422
Gentleman's Magazine, 17
George II, 390
George III, 103, 112, 158, 165, 317, 344, 373, 421, 425, 502
Georgia, Yazoo land companies in, 547
Germantown, Pa., 383; Battle of, 23-24, 27
Gerry, Elbridge, 171, 187, 206, 238, 457, 492
get-rich-quick mania, 47
"getting out the vote," 513
Gibbon, Edward, 190, 539
Giles, William Branch, 312, 329-331, 453, 490 n.
Giles resolutions, 439
Gimat, Lt. Col., 77
God, human passions vs. punishment from, 199
God and Nature, Hamilton's theory of, 6, 14, 50, 121, 285, 572; judicial review and, 202
gold, corner on, 305; *see also* specie payments
good behavior, term of office dependent on, 166, 170; Senate membership and, 178
Gordon, Rev. William, treachery alleged by, 37-40
government, central, *see* central government; checks and balances in, 49-50, 161, 196; consent as basis of, 155, 180; "energetic," 61, 126, 135, 145, 155, 161, 438; federal, *see* federal government; H.'s defense of, 112, 184-205; Jefferson's opposing ideas of, 259; national, *see* national government; popularity seeking and, 552; private wealth and, 60-61, 86, 88, 143, 240, 261 n., 272-273, 314, 403; separation of powers in, 49; *see also* Continental Congress
government bonds, *see* government securities
government credit, jeopardizing of by sequestration, 391; Law's methods in, 54; national debt and, 231, 253-254; need for in Revolution, 47; restoration of, 51-52, 281-282
government departments, need for, 58-59
government powers, new faith in, 51; *see also* powers, separation of
government securities, 93; Bank of U.S. and, 261; confusion in, 1789, 232-233; "corner" on, 303-304; exchange of, 236 n.; fund for purchase of, 257-258; ownership of by Congressmen, 326; price of, 270-271; speculation in, 237, 245-246, 305, 338-339; tax on, 403
Grafton, Duke of, 44
"Grange," The, Ayrshire, Scotland, 3
Great Britain, aid from in annexation of Louisiana and Floridas, 496; avoidance of alliance with in French crisis, 472; blockade of France by, 386; commercial treaty with, 392; disdain of U.S. in impressment cases, 473-474; "economic coercion" of, 384; "economic duel" with, 11; French Directory's attempt to crush, 451-452; hatred of as prop to nationalism, 134-135; imminent invasion of by France, 472; Jefferson's "friendship" statement on, 560 n.; as model for French institutions, 363; as model for H.'s plan of national government, 166-167; "mysterious" nature of policy toward U.S., 392; national debt in, 257; peace emissary to, 393; peace treaty with, 107-108; precarious position in 1778, 28; Republican belligerence toward, 452; "second war" with, 1794-95, 384; seizure of American provision ships, 432; "self-interest" union with, 13; sequestration of debts owed to, 391; threat of war with, 1794, 415; trade with, 12, 388-389; trade war with, 222-223; "tyranny" of, 9; war with France, 1793, 385; as "workshop of the world," 293; *see also* British, seamen, impressment of
Great Compromise, in Constitutional Convention, 178
Great Lakes, armed forces on, 416
"great man" concept, 228
Greece, classical, as analogue of early U.S., 114-115, 123-124, 200
Green Mountain Boys, 131-133
Greene, Gen. Nathanael, 33, 35, 57, 68, 70; denounces Congress, 40
Greenleaf, Mrs., 487-488
Grenville, William Wyndham, Baron, 417-418, 429, 498
Griswold, Roger, 568
Grotius, Hugo, 106, 428

Hamilton, Alexander (1757-1804), birth and early years, 3-7; illegitimacy of, 3, 62; relations with father, 4; bookkeeping experience, 5; "Hurricane" letter to father, 5-6, 572; early traits disclosed, 6-7; attends Elizabethtown (N.J.) preparatory school, 7; early religious zeal, 8; enters King's College, 8; answer to Seabury as first "emergence" of, 10; as defender of colonial union and Continental Congress, 10-12; recommends establishment of clothing factories, 12; reply to Seabury, 13 ff.; urges English-speaking union, 13; on "sacred rights of mankind," 14; polemical powers, 15; saves Rev. Dr. Cooper from N.Y. mob, 17; aide-de-camp to Washington, 17-42; respect for authority and distaste for violence, 18; inveighs against Quebec Act, 19-20; as artillery captain, 20; army friendships, 22; war correspondent for New York legislature, 22-23; bargains with Gates for troops, 24-25; strictures against Gates and Conway, 27-28; loyalty to Washington, 28; heroism and heroics at Battle of Monmouth, 30-31; charges Lee with cowardice or treachery, 32; "build-up" of Washington by, 34-35; grievances against Continental Congress, 35-36; Gordon's libeling of, 37-40; urges use of Negro slaves in army, 41-42; on profiteering and moneygrubbing, 43-44; studies economics and finance at Valley Forge, 46; loses religious dogmatism, 46; studies Hume, 46-47; doubts and misgivings about American people, 49; distrust of mobs, 18-20, 49, 101, 123, 144, 425; recommends British form of government, 49; inclines toward democracy vs. "mixed government," 50; opposes direct election of president, 50-51; letter to Schuyler on dollar devaluation, 52; idea for Bank of the United States, 53; studies Law's banking methods, 54; letter to Duane on foreign loan, 57; dream of Federal Republic, 59; pleads for closer union, 1781, 59; plan for Constitutional Convention, 59; nominated as Superintendent of Finance, 59-60; letter to Morris on fiscal policy, 60; plans for "saving country," 61; inability to understand democratic ideals, 61; awareness of illegitimacy, 62; quarrel with Washington, 62-79; courtship of Kitty Livingston, 63; marriage to Elizabeth Schuyler, 64-66; affinity with Gen. Schuyler, 65; reasons for resenting Washington, 67; fluent French, 67; polished manners, 69; defense of Mrs. Benedict Arnold, 70; incivility to Washington, 72-73; quick temper and rashness displayed, 72-73; pleads with Washington for command of troops, 75; and is given command of N.Y. battalion, 76; defies British fire at Yorktown, 77-79; studies law in N.Y., 83; made receiver of taxes, 83-84; member of Continental Congress, 84 ff.; financial letters of 1780-81, 86; argues for impost, 88-90; states doctrine of implied powers, 89; upholds civilian claims, 92; urges general revenue, 95; as threat to states' rights, 96-97; as Washington's spokesman in Congress, 98; plan for peacetime army, 98-99; frustration and decision to abandon politics, 100-101; denounced in N.Y. as enemy, 101; defends Loyalists, 102-110; on bigotry, 104; defends Waddington in Trespass Act, 105-106; invokes federal judicial power, 107; upholds treaties as "supreme law of land," 108-109; urges strong union, 111; definition of government, 112; theory of history, 114; on state vs. national sovereignty, 117; fears of future of U. S., 119; advocates abolition of slavery, 122; on property rights, 123; idea of state bank, 127; opposes Livingston's land bank, 128; establishment of Bank of N.Y., 130; continued friendship with Loyalists, 130; in Vermont "independence" controversy, 132-133; at Annapolis Convention, 1786, 136-137; calls for Constitutional Convention, 138-139; mounting prestige of among nationalists, 141; on Shays' rebellion, 142; on use of force, 145; on impost, 147-148; emerges as national leader, 148; devotion to philosophy and politics at Constitutional Convention, 153; calls for new Constitution, 154-155; opposes Virginia Plan, 156-157; silence and aloofness at Convention, 159; plan for national government (Schuyler-Hamilton plan), 159-160; fundamental change in thinking revealed at Convention, 160-161; absence of checks and balances in plan, 161; urges weakening of states in favor of monarchism and strong national government as antidote to democracy, 162-164; audacity and valor as elements of success, 169; penalty for outspokenness, 170-172; relations with Franklin, 175 n.; leaves in middle of Convention for N. Y., 176; returns to Convention after public-opinion samplings, 177-178; "philosopher-President" ideal, 179; on liberty and suffrage, 180-181; accepts shortcomings of final draft of Constitution, 182-183; becomes "defender of the Constitution," 184 ff.; on inability of American people to judge Constitution's worth, 185-188;

brands Clinton as demagogue, 186; "Caesar" vs. "Publius" personalities in, 189; gives name to Federalist party, 193; further remarks on faults of American people, 197-199; sees Supreme Court as interpreter of Constitution, 201; concept of judicial review, 201-203; as true conservative, 205; enduring contribution of in supporting Constitution, 208; at Poughkeepsie ratification convention, 210-214; as first Secretary of the Treasury, 219-220; urges Washington to accept presidency, 219-220; manipulation of Electoral College by, 220; opposes trade war with Britain, 223; appearance and personal characteristics as Secretary of Treasury, 226; urge to reduce states' powers, 229-230; determination to pay foreign and domestic debt, 232; indifference to soldier vote, 234; funded national debt plan, 236-237; accused of favoring speculators, 241; names Duer assistant secretary, 245; overtures to Jefferson on funding-assumption bill, 248-250; alarmed by Virginia resolutions, 255-256; Report on the Bank, 262-263; opinion on constitutionality of Bank, 266-267; efforts to halt speculation in bank scrip, 270; champions state banks, 275-276; triumph of Bank cause, 276-277; as "golden boy" of Federalists, 278; unpopularity elsewhere, 280; in social life of Philadelphia, 281; sees self-interest as basis of capitalism, 286; on use of women and children in factories, 287-288; Report on Manufactures and mercantilist theories of, 289-291; rejects laissez faire, 292; upholds slavery in South, 294; use of "general welfare" clause for federal powers, 296-297; as "custodian" of the Constitution, 298; organizes Society of Useful Manufactures and industrial center at Paterson, N.J., 300-302; relations with Duer and Six Percent Club, 304; supports security market in panic of 1791, 305; fall of Duer, 307; takes active direction of S.U.M., 309; failure of Paterson experiment, 310; emergence of opposition to, 311-321; differences with Jefferson, 313-315; support of republicanism, 317-318; and beginnings of breakup of Federalist party, 320; charged with corruption by Jefferson and Madison, 322-342; juggling of domestic and foreign loans, 328; fails to keep Congress informed, 329; arraigned on charges of concealed shortages in Treasury, 330-331; vindicated on all counts, 332; affair with Maria Reynolds, 332-340; alleged complicity with Duer, 338; accused of speculation in government securities, 338-339; establishes innocence, 339-340; quarrel with Jefferson and Burr, 343-360; abuse from Freneau, 344-347; complains to Washington about Jefferson, 349-350; monarchical charges against, 350; in election of 1789, 352-354; early friendship with Burr, 356-357; now sees him as unprincipled demagogue, 358-359; differences with Jefferson sharpened by French Revolution, 363 ff.; urges neutrality proclamation, 369; condemns France as aggressor, 370-371; refuses funds to Genêt, 373; exposes Genêt's subversive activities, 377; stricken with yellow fever, 379-382; backs British seizure of American shipping, 385-386; rejects British Order in Council on blockade, 387; urges peace with Britain in shipping "war" but strengthens country's defenses, 390; rejected by Republicans as peace envoy, 394; upholds excise law against farmers' complaints, 396-398; internal revenue collection system of, 398-399; defends carriage tax, 402; opposes tax on government securities, 403-404; organizes militia against leaders of Whisky Rebellion, 406-409; feud with Jefferson, 412-413; stand against "Democratic States," 412-414; "invincibility" of from Washington's support, 414; instructions to Jay, 415; urges Congress to prepare for war with Britain, 1794, 417; voices disfavor with Armed Neutrality, 418-419; "sells" Jay's Treaty to public, 427; justifies Great Britain to Americans, 429; threatens to resign, 435-436; "flagrant vice" in administration charged, 435; reply to Gallatin, 436; "financial testament" of, 438; indifference to money, 440; helps write the "Farewell Address," 442-445; opposition to both Adams and Jefferson, 444-446; efforts to make Pinckney president, 448; "treachery" against Adams, 449-451; urges defense against France, 452-453; recommends diplomatic mission to France, 454-455; miscalculations about Adams' abilities as president, 458; Reynolds affair divulged by Callender, 460; incites Monroe to duel in Reynolds' affair leak, 461; publicly acknowledges marital infidelity to clear self of graver charges, 462-463; portrayed as lecherous monster in Republican press, 463; "affair" with Mrs. Church, 464-465; urges call to arms in XYZ affair, 467; seeks war with France, 470-472; appointed Maj. Gen. under Washington in French crisis, 476-477; refuses commission

in provisional army to Burr, 480; as Army Inspector General, 481-482; suspects Jefferson of treachery, 483; endorses Sedition Act, 484; sues *Argus* for libel 486-487; fears revolt in Virginia, 489-490; shocked by Adams' Jacobinism, 493; urges annexation of Louisiana and Florida territories, 495; urges Cabinet to seize control of government in Adams' absence, 500; mounting unpopularity of, 506; defeated by Burr for vice-presidency, 1800, 512-513; grieved by Washington's death, 515; political tour of New England, 517-518; openly attacks Adams, 518-520; branded as "evil genius" by Webster, 523; egotism, vanity and jealousy of, 523; Adams' final estimate of, 523; violates Sedition Act in calumniating Adams, 524; denounces Burr, 526; Supreme Court reorganization plan, 534-545; fears Jeffersonian democracy, 539; sense of impending doom, 541; builds "The Grange" in N.Y., 544; financial difficulties, 545; land speculations of, 546; death of son Philip in duel with Eacker, 549; finances N.Y. *Evening Post*, 550; assails Jefferson anew, 551-552; on "real" danger to liberties, 554 n.; last important speech, 556; defines "liberty of the press," 556 n.; plan to aid San Domingo against French, 558-560; belittles importance of Louisiana Purchase, 561; openly denounces Burr, 567-568; vindictiveness in Burr controversy, 569; refuses satisfaction, 570-571; determines to withhold fire in duel, 572-573; last letter to wife, 573; death of, 575; final tribute to, 575-576
Hamilton, Elizabeth Schuyler (Mrs. Alexander), 85, 462, 465, 573-574
Hamilton, James (father), 3-4
Hamilton, Philip (son), 548-549, 572
Hamilton Oneida Academy, 279
Hammond, George, 374, 385-386, 417-418
Hancock, John, 144
Hand, Judge Learned, 202 n.
happiness, "pursuit" of, 47-48, 83, 111, 153
Harison, Richard, 22, 69, 132, 209
Harper, Robert G., 475, 494, 508, 516, 527
Harrington, James, 140
Hawkesbury, Lord, 368
"Helvidius," sobriquet of Madison, 371
Henry, Patrick, 167 n., 240, 255
hero worship, 228
History of the United States for the Year 1796, The, 460, 462
Hobbes, Thomas, 46, 199
Holland bankers, loans from, *see* Dutch bankers

Holland Land Company, 546-547
Hosack, Dr. David, 573-574, 574 n.
House of Representatives, as check on President and Senate, 180; in H.'s plan, 166; proportional representation in, as essence of Great Compromise, 178
Howe, Sir William, 21, 23-24, 47, 375, 420
human conduct, self-interest and, 292
human nature, H.'s views on, 198-199; his skepticism on, 153; "warlike" nature of, 118
Hume, David, 46-47, 233
"Hurricane" letter, 5-6, 572
Hutchinson, Gov. Thomas, 8
Hylton, Daniel, 401

illegitimacy, awareness of, 3, 62, 65
imperialism, 290
implied powers, doctrine of, 89, 115, 267
import duties, as main revenue of new government, 222; *see also* impost
imports, increased duties on, 504
impost, 87-88, 152, 154; army as beneficiary of, 92-93; collection of by states, 96-97; Madison's aid on, 96; N.Y. speech on, 148; vetoed by N.Y., 148-149, 151
impressment of seamen, *see* seamen, impressment of
Independence, War of, *see* Revolutionary War
Indians, frontier troubles with, 143, 399
Industrial Revolution, 313
inflation, banks' responsibility in, 307; causes of, 47; controlled, 259; morals and, 48; public opinion as ultimate responsibility for, 48-49; source of, 44; struggle against, 43-61; wartime, 120
internal revenue, collection of, 398
international law, neutral rights and, 385; in Rutgers case, 106; sequestration bill and, 392
invention, 287
Intolerable Acts, 9
IOU's, army use of, 230
Iredell, James, 402
iron, tariff on, 289

Jackson, Maj. William, 461
Jacobins and Jacobinism, 424, 432, 463, 473, 496, 507, 511, 516, 518, 538-539, 542, 544, 556-557, 563, 566; Adams and, 493; Britain's fear of, 421; expected uprising in, 505; threatened revolt by in Virginia, 490; in XYZ affair, 468-469, 483
Jay, John, 10, 109, 152, 188-189, 197, 206-207, 209, 214, 256, 347, 355 n., 377, 415-434, 456, 471, 513, 516, 520, 525, 545 n., as collaborator on *Federalist*, 189-190;

Index

chosen as peace emissary to England, 394-395; treaty making with Great Britain, 415-434; assistance in writing of "Farewell Address," 444-445 n.
Jay's Treaty, denunciation and praise of, 424; effects of, 433-434; French reaction to, 452; plan to kill in House, 430; ratification of, 422-423, 449; signing of, 422; text of, 422; trade with Canada and, 428
Jefferson, Thomas, 15, 146, 170, 246, 263-264, 267, 284, 298, 313, 341, 381, 383, 392, 411, 414, 420, 428, 439 n., 441, 445, 455, 459, 464, 477, 491, 514, 516, 519, 537, 564; distaste for mob, 19; on white superiority, 41; relations with H. on funding bill, 249-250; as shrewd politician, 250-251; differences with H. outlined, 313-315; use of "monarchism" charges against H., 316-317; Republican party and, 320; quarrel with, 343-360; Freneau's praise of, 345; anonymous attack on, 345-346; alleged robbing of Dutch, 348; rebuked by Washington, 350-351; French revolution as divisive influence on, 363; sides with French revolutionaries, 366; welcomes Genêt, 373; strictures on H.'s idea of neutrality, 376; repudiates Genêt, 376; yellow fever attack, 379-380; resigns as Secretary of State, 384; opposes H. as peace emissary to Britain, 394; Whisky Rebellion and, 412; retirement of, 415; "French Faction" and, 421; as presidential candidate, 1796, 445; endorsed by France, 449; declines appointment to peace commission, 457; continued sympathy for France, 469; sponsors Virginia and Kentucky resolutions, 489; tied with Burr for presidency, 525; chosen by H. over Burr, 526-527; as "ravening wolf," 528; elected president, 1800, 529; inaugural address, 533; "crime" against Federalists, 539; Callender's attack on, 551; in Croswell libel suit, 555; abets Napoleon's aims in San Domingo, 559-560; Louisiana purchase and, 560; role of in Burr's defeat for N.Y. governorship, 569
Jeffersonian democracy, fear of, 539-540
Johnson, Samuel, 190
judicial power, vs. legislature, 202
judicial review, concept of, 108-109, 536; factors in public acceptance of, 204; principle of outlined, 201-203
Judiciary Act of 1789, 535; of 1801, 536-537
"Junius," vs. Duke of Grafton, 10, 44

Kent, James, 140, 430, 545 n., 555
Kentucky and Virginia resolutions, *see* Virginia and Kentucky resolutions
King, Rufus, 176, 207, 251, 353-355, 377, 394, 427, 471, 516, 541, 572
"King Cong," 147
King's College (Columbia College), 5, 8, 10, 46, 380
Kirkland, Samuel, 279
Knox, Gen. Henry, 21, 246, 270, 281, 327, 376, 382
Knox, Rev. Hugh, 5, 7
Kurtz, Stephen, 450

labor force, manufacturing and, 123, 287
Lafayette, Marquis de, 68, 71, 74, 76-77; French Revolution and, 363
laissez faire, 291-292
Lancaster, Pa., soldiers' riots at, 98
Lancaster Turnpike Company, 303
land bank, 128-130
land ownership, as qualification for electors, 181 n.
landowners, loans for, 128
land speculators, 243 n.; Constitution and, 548; H.'s scheme of, 545-546; *see also* speculation
Lansing, John, 171, 178, 212-213
Lansing, Robert, 152
Latin America, Anglo-American aims in, 497
Laurens, John, 22, 32, 42, 49, 64, 68, 78, 85
Lavien, John, 3
Lavien, Rachel Fawcett, "Madame Hamilton" (mother), 3
law, judicial review and, 203
Law, John, 53-55, 259
Lawrence, John, 106
league of nations, vs. national government, 153-155
Lee, Gen. Charles, 37-38, 353, 356; in battle of Monmouth, 29-31; court-martial of, 32-33; duel with Laurens, 33-34
Lee, Gen. Henry ("Light-Horse Harry"), 246, 401, 409-410, 471
Lee, Richard Henry, 187, 243, 366
legislative power, vs. judicial review, 202; *see also* judicial review
legislature, bicameral vs. unicameral, 140, 156
L'Enfant, Pierre Charles, 309
Letter from Alexander Hamilton concerning the Public Conduct and Character of John Adams, 520, 524
Lewis, Morgan, 106, 568
Lewis, William, 266
Lexington, Battle of, 16
libel suit, Croswell-Callander case, 553
liberty, defined by H., 181 n.; enthusiasm for, 20; vs. property, 122-123; "rage" for,

111-119; "real danger" to, 554 n.; vs. union, 163
"Liberty, Equality, Fraternity," 366, 476
Lincoln, Abraham, 437
Lincoln, Gen. Benjamin, 143
"Little Lion" epithet, 21, 35, 37, 68, 278, 575
Little Sarah, English brigantine, 374
living standards, raising of, 290-291
Livingston, Edward, 305, 430
Livingston, Henry Brockholst, 106, 305, 488
Livingston, Kitty, 63-64
Livingston, Maturin, 424 n.
Livingston, Philip, 309
Livingston, Robert R., 128, 306, 355 n.
Livingston, William, 7
Livingston family, 21, 152, 209, 353-355, 568
Lloyd, James, 484
loan office certificates, 230
Locke, John, 15, 123
Long Island, battles in, 20
Louis XIV, 53
Louis XVI, 27; execution of, 365, 369
Louisiana, French ambitions in, 557-560; H.'s "dream of glory" in, 495, 498, 508
Louisiana Purchase, 560-562
L'Ouverture, Toussaint, *see* Toussaint L'Ouverture
Low, Nicholas, 130, 209, 309
Loyalists, 28, 69, 100-110, 120, 142, 282, 344, 391, 464-465; disbarment of lawyers among, 110; disenfranchisement of, 104, 110; hatred of in N. Y., 101; loyalty oath required of, 104; property rights of, 105; "Troy baiting" and, 17
Loyalist tracts, Rivington and, 17
Lytton family, 3

McDougall, Gen. Alexander, 130
McHenry, James, 458, 476, 481-482, 499, 505, 507, 517, 519, 521, 525
Machiavelli, Niccolò, 13, 102 n., 199, 227-228
machinery, importing of, 287; unusable, 309-310
Macomb, Alexander, 304, 306, 545
Macpherson, Brig. Gen., 506
Madison, James, 69, 92, 99, 115, 136, 138, 140, 145, 152, 164 n., 169, 172, 178, 188, 197, 206, 214, 225, 229, 250, 263-264; 298, 304, 318, 320, 332, 341, 352, 371, 379, 381, 384, 392, 394, 415, 430, 441-442, 455, 464, 489, 509, 537; background and character of, 85-86; aids general revenue bill, 95-96; Virginia Plan of, 156; skill at Convention, 159; exasperated by H.'s plan, 172; as collaborator on *Federalist* papers, 189 ff.; first leader of House, 221; "speculative philosopher" role, 224; opposes H.'s financial program, 239-241; advocates assumption of state debts, 242; in Reynolds case, 338; Freneau and, 346; answers H.'s statements on Neutrality Proclamation, 371; "Commercial Propositions" of, 388-389; Whisky Rebellion and, 412; "French Faction" and, 421; declines to serve on French peace commission, 457; leader of loyal opposition, 491
Madisonian Society, 412
"Madison party," 320
Magna Charta, 205
majority rule, restraints on, 197
man, depravity of, 199; perfectability of, 198; warlike nature of, 118
Manhattan Company, The, *see* Bank of Manhattan
Manufactures, Report on, *see* Report on Manufactures
manufacturing, vs. agriculture, 284; bounties for, 287, 289-290, 291 n., 299; encouragement of, 282; as "political salvation," 282-283
Marbury v. Madison, 537-538
Marie Antoinette, 369
Marshall, John, 208, 238, 243, 266 n., 267, 280, 353, 366, 404, 457, 470, 492, 523, 526, 537, 548
Martin, Luther, 171
Mason, Rev. Dr., 575
Mason, Col. George, 158, 171, 187
Massachusetts, farmers' revolt in, 142
Mayor's Court, New York City, 106-107
Meade, Richard, 22
mercantilism, 47; H.'s affinity with, 290; Madison and, 222
Merchant Marine, 222; French attacks on, 1797, 452; neutral rights and, 384-386; Order in Council and, 387; *see also* seamen, impressment of
Merchants Bank of New York City, 546
middle class, plight of, 122
Mifflin, Gen. Thomas, 374, 405-406, 408, 464
military dictatorship, fear of, 36-37, 39-40
military supplies, profiteering and speculation in, 43, 46; sale of by Americans to British, 46
Million Bank, 303
"millions for defense" slogan, 467
Minerva, New York newspaper, 123
minority rights, 123
Miranda, Francisco, 496, 499
Mississippi River, navigation rights on, 393, 406, 409, 499
mob rule, distrust of, 18-20, 49, 101, 123-124, 144, 425; French Revolution and, 364
"monarchical" finance, 436
monarchism, H.'s rejection of, 211; Jeffer-

Index 653

son's charges of, 316, 350; Paine's fear of, 49
monarchy, 180; H.'s praise of, 163, 167-168; standing army and, 482
money, "creation" of by banks, 60; inflation and, 44-45; postwar scarcity of, 120; speculations in, 243-244; *see also* paper money
"moneyed men," government aid from, 55-56, 60, 86, 88, 143, 240-241, 261 n., 272-273, 314, 403; Senate as representatives of, 181 n.
Monmouth (Court House), N.J., Battle of, 28-32, 356
Monocrats, 379, 436, 534
Monroe, James, 68, 338-341, 394, 420, 449; pro-French actions of, 421; recall of from France, 452; silence on H.'s innocence in Reynolds speculation charges, 460-461
"Montague, James," 52
Montaigne, Michel, Seigneur de, 46
Montesquieu, Charles Louis de Secondat, baron de, 49, 140, 163, 211
Monticello, Va., 384
Montmorin, Count de, 372
morals, inflation and, 48
"More Power to Congress," 140
Morgan, Gen. Daniel, 24
Morris, Gouverneur, 74, 92, 97, 119, 132, 158, 173, 178, 182, 189, 201, 227, 254, 263, 280, 369 n., 372, 525, 535, 540
Morris, Robert, 60, 75, 83, 86, 91, 127, 225, 244, 280, 465, 516, 545; national bank and, 60-61
Morristown, N.J., 32, 35, 64
Mud Island, Phila., 26, 375-376
Muhlenburg, Frederick, 338-340, 460, 463
Mulligan, Hercules, 8
mutinies, in Continental Army, 58
mutiny, threat of, 71, 94, 98

Napoleon Bonaparte, 470, 503, 514, 557, 560, 562; "continental system" of, 562; and French empire in Western Hemisphere, 558; Jefferson's praise of, 453; Louisiana Purchase and, 560-562
national bank, 128; H.'s plans for, 115; Morris' plan for, 60-61; *see also* Bank of the United States
national capital (government seat), moving of to Potomac area, 251-252; transferred from N.Y. to Phila., 280
national debt, 116; at beginning of Washington's first term, 230-231; as divisive force, 255; funding of, 236-237, 239, 253-255, 281; increase of during H.'s term term as Treasury Secretary, 438; liquidation of, 438-439; Louisiana purchase and, 562; per capita, 1789, 252; "permanent," 254; reduction in, 438; in 1789, 149; sinking fund and, 257; taxation and, 88; threat of state assumption of, 117; Whisky Rebellion and, 412; *see also* domestic debt; finance; impost; manufacturing; taxation

National Gazette, 344-345, 349-350, 352, 383
national government, democracy as foe of, 125; distinguished from federal government, 117-118; H.'s hopes for, 51; vs. league of nations, 153-155; need for, 61; outlined in *The Federalist*, 195; prosperity and, 126; "pursuit of happiness" and, 153; Shays' rebellion and, 144-145; state debts and, 235
nationalism, failure of ideal of, 437; vs. federalism, 195; vs. league of nations, 153-154
Nature, "laws" of, 14-15, 121, 205; *see also* God and Nature
Navy, School of, 482
Necker, Jacques, 84, 169
Negro slaves, *see* slaves, Negro; *see also* slavery
Negro soldiers, emancipation of, 41
Negro Presidents, 563
neutral rights, 415, 426, 428; American concept of, 384-385; "death" of, in Jay's Treaty, 429; definition of, 416
neutrality proclamation, 363-378; constitutionality of, 369
Nevis Island, 3
Newburgh, N.Y., 94
New England, benefit to from Louisiana Purchase, 562-563; British attempt to cut off, 23; Northern Confederation and, 564-566; outbreak of Revolution in, 17; republicanism, bigotry and intolerance in, 19; textile industry, 301
New Hampshire, as ninth state to ratify Constitution, 213
New Jersey, retreat through, 20
New Jersey Plan, 159-160, 168; rejection of, 174
New Windsor, N.Y., 58, 60, 71
New York *Argus*, 486
New York Assembly, 147
New York City, tax delinquency in, 84; "tea party" in, 17
New York *Daily Advertiser*, 184
New York *Evening Post*, 549 n., 550, 561
New York *Herald*, 551
New York *Independent Journal*, 188
New York *Minerva*, 384
New York Provincial Congress, 20
New York State, 41; Constitutional Convention, Poughkeepsie, 212-214; Constitution of 1777, 50; delegates to Constitutional

Convention, 152; as "enemy's country" for H., 100; Federalist party in, 353; fiscal studies of, 84; importance of in 1800 election, 509-510; national capital in, 248, 251; study of law in, 83 ff.; threatened withdrawal from Union, 213; Trespass Act, 105, 107-108; Vermont border war, 131; veto of impost by, 151; votes at Convention, 158; *see also* Clintonians; Livingston family
New York–Virginia axis, 295
New York *Wasp*, 553-554
Nicholas, John, 394
"No Jacobin" essays, 377
North, Frederick, Lord, 10, 19, 260, 293
Northern Confederacy, 564-566, 568
Northern Inland Lock Navigation Company, 303
Northern ports, cession of by British, 392-393, 423, 427

office holding, good behavior and, 166
Ohio Company, 561
Ohio Valley, 19
Old West, growing power of, 561
Order in Council, June, 1793, 386; November, 1793, 389, 417-419; April, 1795, 425
Ordinances of 1785 and 1787, 149
Otis, Harrison Gray, 480, 484 n., 516, 523
Otis, James, 8

"Pacificus," sobriquet, 369-370, 372
Paine, Tom, 49, 90, 446
Pamela, 463
panic of 1791, 270-271, 307
Paoli Massacre, 78
paper money, 171, 259, 504 n.; "death" of, 56; discrediting of, 120; "flight" of, 243; inflation and, 44-45, 47; morals and, 48; worthlessness of, 230
Paradise Lost, 28
party spirit, 321
party system, cabinet system and, 58
party uniformity, 350
Passaic River, industrial community on, 300 ff., 309
Paterson, William, 160, 300
Paterson, N.J., industrial experiment at, 300-310
peace, "averting" of, 500 ff.
Peekskill, N.Y., 24
Peloponnesian War, 115
Pendleton, Nathaniel, 573-574, 574 n.
Pennsylvania, mutinies in, 71; tax riots in, 505
people, as basis of government, 180; consent of, 155; faults and poor judgment of, 185-188, 197-199; sovereignty of, 155; "voice" of, 198

per capita indebtedness, 1789, 252
personal debts, sequestration of, 391
"Peter Porcupine," 550
Petit Démocrate, 374-376
Petty, Sir William, 46
Philadelphia, 24, 44, 56, 69, 93, 100, 138, 146, 151-183, 196, 268, 300, 306, 332-340, 344, 373, 375, 381, 390, 405, 425, 461, 469, 479, 498, 514; British evacuation of, 28, 45; Howe's investing of, 23, 26; inflation and, 47; as intellectual capital, 280-281; as residence of Congress, 248, 251; soldiers' riots at, 98; yellow fever epidemic in, 379, 383; *see also* Constitutional Convention
Philadelphia *Aurora*, 486-487, 508
Philadelphia bank, 127, 128 n.
Philadelphia newspapers, 343
Philadelphia State House, 155
Philadelphia Stock Exchange, 269
"Philo-Publius," Duer's sobriquet, 189
Phocion, 102 n., 103
"Phocion" essays, 102-103
"picaroons," French, 452
Pickering, Timothy, 426, 450, 471, 473-474, 476, 481, 494, 501, 517, 519, 541, 563-565
Pinckney, Charles Cotesworth, 455, 457, 466, 476-77, 479, 492, 515, 524, 567; refused recognition by French, 452, 454; predicts war with France, 471
Pinckney, Thomas, 445-446; "loss" of, 451
Pitt, William, 226, 237 n., 386, 403 n., 485, 496
Pittsburgh, threatened distillers' attack on, 405
planters, Southern, *see* Southern planters
Plutarch, 46, 102 n., 188, 228; "code" of, 22
plutocracy, fostering of, 316
political bigotry, 104
Political Discourses, 46
Political parties, as enemy of union, 443; vs. "factions," 319
political power, Jefferson's fear of, 315
politics, Congress and, 113; as "consuming passion," 440; scurrility and, 345
poll taxes, 87
popery, tirade against, 19-20
"popular despotism," 121
popular sovereignty, vs. judicial review, 201-203
Porcupine's Gazette, 384
Postlethwayt, Malachy, 46
postwar depression, 120, 126
Potomac River, nation's capital near, 251-252, 265
Poughkeepsie, N.Y., Constitutional Convention at, 210
power, abuse of, 196; corruption through, 112; fear of, 196; sharing of between few

Index

and many, 200
powers, separation of, 49, 139-140, 156, 202
preparedness, in French crisis, 469-471
presidency, "splendid misery" of, 442
President, election of, 50-51, 178; monarchical powers of, 165; Senate as "maker" of, 179
press, freedom of, see freedom of the press
Pretensions of Thomas Jefferson to the Presidency Examined, 446
price fixing, 287
primogeniture, abolition of, 122
Princeton, Battle of, 21
Princeton College, 8, 21, 85
prisoners, exchange of, 68
private capital, government and, 55-56, 60, 86, 88, 143, 240-241, 261 n., 272-273, 314, 403; manufacturing and, 286
private property, see property
private wealth, see private capital
privateering, domestic, 43, 122
privateers, French, 417; Genêt's outfitting of, 373-374
productivity, industrialization and, 288-290
profiteering, 43, 120, 122; see also speculation
property, "crimes" against, 171; democracy and, 121-122; vs. liberty, 122-123, national government and, 140; protection of, 145; sacred nature of, 125; shipping seizures by British and, 391
proportional representation, in House of Representatives, 178
Prospect Before Us, The, 553
prosperity, and decline of Federalist party, 512; laissez faire and, 291-292; of 1794, 279; states' quest for, 121; strong central government and, 126
protective tariff, see tariff, protective; see also impost
provincialism, H.'s impatience with, 118-119
provisional army, criticism of, 504, 508; disbanding of, 508; in French crisis, 476-480; organizing of, 491-492
public bank, see Bank of the United States; national bank
public confidence, 167
public credit, see government credit
Public Credit, Report on, see Report on Public Credit
public debt, see national debt
public opinion, Constitutional Convention and, 177; fear of, 123; H.'s assessment of, 169; his disdain of, 470; his influencing of, 343; inflation and, 48-49; Jefferson's conflicting views on, 315; taxation and, 87; in XYZ affair, 468

public spirit, doubts and misgivings about, 49
"Publius," H.'s sobriquet, 44, 188, 191-199, 205-208, 210, 222, 428
Publius Valerius, 188
Pufendorf, Samuel Freiherr von, 106, 428
Putnam, Gen. Israel, 24-25

Quakers, 242, 280
Quebec Act, 19

Randolph, Edmund, 138, 156, 214, 263-264, 347, 415, 420, 425-426, 490 n.
Raritan River, 21
Ratcliffe, Judge, 488
Read, George, 137, 174
reciprocity, foreign trade and, 134
Reed, Joseph, 38
religion, see God and Nature
religious bigotry, 104
Rensselaer, Miss, 64
Report on the Bank of the United States, 262-263, 275
Report on [the Subject of] Manufactures, 278-296, 299, 319, 367, 399-400
Report on the Mint, 276 n.
Report on Public Credit, 60, 229-239, 256, 262, 265, 396
Republican bank, see Bank of Manhattan
republicanism, as "best of all governments," 50; distinguished from monarchism, 318; H.'s definition of, 164 n.; impending death of, 153; as "radically defective," 163
"Republican jealousy," vs. army pay claims, 95
Republican party, 403, 413, 417, 430, 435-436, 441, 561; rise of, 320; challenges authority of Treasury Department, 324; charges H. with "juggling" of loans, 328-329; use of informers in corruption investigations, 340; growing strength of, 352-353, 510, 516; neutrality proclamation and, 371; urges war with Britain, 1794, 390-391; rejects H. as peace emissary to Britain, 394; criticism of H. in Whisky Rebellion, 411-412; as "French sympathizers," 412; criticism of Jay's Treaty by, 423; sees H.'s retirement as "flight from justice," 439; as tool of French Jacobins, 448-450; opposes defense measures against France, 453; fear of H. as president, 458; Jacobinism in, 463 (see also Jacobins and Jacobinism); in provisional army, 479; inciting of Pennsylvania Dutch against administration, 505-506; Judiciary Act of 1801 and, 636-637; freedom of the press and, 553
requisition system, 86

revenue, general, *see* impost
revenue officers, 398
Revolutionary Army, *see* Continental Army
Revolutionary Clubs, France, 412
Revolutionary War, 17-42, 106, 118, 128, 134, 149, 198, 202, 220, 222, 260, 282, 397; British attacks in South, 40; H.'s faithfulness to ideals of, 205; hope for freedom in, 111; manufacturing and, 285; profiteering and speculation in, 43; state debt incurred during, 235, 242; sufferings of soldiers in, 35
Reynolds, James, 333-340, 458-459, 486; imprisonment of, 337
Reynolds, Maria (Mrs. James), 333-340, 458-459, 462, 464, 486, 523; H.'s public confession of adultery with, 463
Rhode Island, debtors legislation in, 121; feared "strangling" of Constitution by, 181; objections to impost in, 88-90; "reinstatement" of, 147; victory over Congress, 90-91; vote on impost, 97
rich men, *see* moneyed men
rights, vs. duties, 153
rights of man, 14, 155; Revolutionary War and, 19
Rivington, James, 17-18
Rochambeau, Jean Baptiste, comte de, 70, 74
Rodgers, Dr. John, 383
Roman Catholicism, establishment of in Canada, 19; as grounds for disbarment from public office in N.Y., 104
Roosevelt, Isaac, 130, 209
Rousseau, Jean Jacques, 46, 280
Royal Danish American Gazette, 6
Rules of Civility and Decent Behavior, 74
Rush, Dr. Benjamin, 380-381, 383
Russia, 419
Russian soldiers, 42
Rutgers, Mrs. Elizabeth, 105
Rutgers v. Waddington, 106, 109

"sacred rights of mankind," H.'s statement on, 14
St. Clair, Gen. Arthur, 326-327
St. Croix, Island of, 3-4, 7, 68
St. Méry, Moreau de, 322
San Domingo, French ambitions in, 559-562
San Ildefonso, Treaty of, 558
Saratoga, Battle of, 23, 26, 69
Scandinavian powers, in French crisis, 418-419
Schachner, Nathan, 122 n.
Schuyler, Angelica (Mrs. John Barber Church), 464
Schuyler, Elizabeth, *see* Hamilton, Elizabeth Schuyler

Schuyler, Gen. Philip, 23, 52, 56, 59-60, 64, 66, 84-85, 127, 151, 159, 244, 246, 303, 353-354, 358, 546-547
Schuyler, Margaret, 464
Schuyler-Hamilton plan, Constitutional Convention, 160
"Scioto speculation," 245
"Scourge," H.'s sobriquet, 347
scrip, *see* bank scrip
Seabury, Rev. Samuel, 9-10, 12-14, 20; kidnaping of, 17
seamen, impressment of, 422, 432, 456, 473
Sears, Isaac, 17-19
seas, freedom of the, in Jay's Treaty, 422, 429
sectionalism, inadvertent strengthening of, 434; vs. unionism, 295
security market, speculation in, 237, 245-246; *see also* government securities; speculation
Sedgwick, Theodore, 509
Sedition Act of 1798, 484, 506, 516, 524, 556; *Argus* libel and, 487; *see also* Alien and Sedition Acts
self-determination, principle of, 114
self-interest, Bank of the U.S. and, 261; capitalism and, 286-287, 291; of Englishmen in French crisis, 472; as key to fiscal planning, 92; laissez faire and, 293; U.S. foreign policy based on, 473
Senate, U.S., in H.'s Convention plan, 166; as President-maker, 179
Seneca, 46
sequestration bill, 391-392, 416
Seton, William, 130, 274, 302, 305
sharpers, paper money and, 48
Shays, Daniel, 142-143, 145
Shays' Rebellion, 142-143, 145
Sherman, Roger, 171, 257
shipbuilding, 283
Shippen, Peggy, 69
shipping, American, British seizure of, 425; French privateering and, 374, 452, 466; investment in, 310; neutral rights and, 384-386; revitalizing of, 222; pillaging of by Barbary pirates, 390
shipping, British, vs. American, 134; duties on, 222; equal footing of with French, 224; French privateering and, 374; seizure of, 432
Simcoe, Col. John Graves, 390, 393
sinking fund, 257, 308, 340, 438-439, 441
Six Percent Club, 304, 306
slaves, Negro, enlistment of in Continental Army, 41; as form of property, 326; Jay's Treaty and, 429-430
slavery, 312; abolition of advocated by H., 122; manufacturing vs., 294; Quaker petition against, 242

Index

Smith, Adam, 54, 128, 260, 288, 291-292, 403 n.
Smith, Melancthon, 212 n.
Smith, William, 389, 445, 448, 492, 516, 521
snuff, excise on, 399
Society [for Establishing] of Useful Manufactures, 300-310, 545-546
soldiers, ragged condition of, 43
soldiers' pay, dispute over, 91-92, 94
Sons of Liberty, 17
South, British attacks on, 41; H.'s antipathy toward, 294-295; injury to from manufacturing North, 294; slavery institution in, 294; war in, 76; weakness of Federalist party in, 353
South Carolina, Federalist sanctuary in, 353; proposed Negro levies in, 42; in 1796 election, 447-448
Southern planters, Bank of U.S. stock and, 269, 272; debts owed to British subjects by, 391; vs. northern capitalists, 311-312; tax burden on, 222
sovereignty, British model of, 15
Spain, H.'s empire building and, 495-496; Louisiana territory and, 557; Mississippi navigation rights and, 393; Treaty with, 447
Spanish America, British and American aspirations in, 496-497; emancipation of, 498
specie payment, boom-bust cycle and, 307; manufacturing and, 286
speculation, 122, 127, 545; in Bank of U.S. stock, 268-270; charges of against H., 338-340; government bonds and, 304; national debt and, 234, 439; profiteering and, 43; see also government securities; speculators
speculators, abetting of, 267; as new ruling class, 120; vs. patriots, 238-254
Spinoza, Baruch, 199
stamp tax, 399; Morris' recommendation of, 87; of 1798, 504
standard of living, mercantilism and, 290-291
Stanhope, Philip, see Chesterfield, Philip Dormer Stanhope
state, intervention of in national economy, 47
state bank(s), idea of, 127; vs. Bank of the U.S., 273; preservation of, 276
state courts, proposed merging of with federal, 534-535
state debts, assumption of, 242, 246-247, 255, 281, 318-319, 323, 351, 396; national debt and, 144, 234-235
state loyalty, 118
State of New York v. Frothingham, 488

state securities, decline of, 243
state sovereignty, 116-117; vs. federal government, 112; reduction of, 229-230
states, aid for from moneyed men, 143-144; "annihilation" of, 172; confiscatory acts of, 121; diverse interests of, 118; equality of, 156, 174, 178, 210-211; as geographical expressions, 172-173; inferior status of in H.'s plan, 161-162, 171, 212; small vs. large, 174-175; threat of assumption of national debt by, 117
states' rights, vs. Army solidarity, 118; Federalists and, 196; foreign trade and, 134; H.'s threat to, 96-97; minimal, 118; virtual abolition of in H.'s plan, 161-162
state tariffs, 134-135
stay laws, 120, 123, 142, 259
Steele, John, 353
Steele, Richard, 10
Sterling, William, 244
Steuart, Sir William, 46
Steuben, Friedrich Wilhelm, Baron von, 33, 77, 142
Stevens, Dr. Edward, 5, 7, 380, 383
Stirling, Gen. (William Alexander), 33, 35
stock market, collapse of, 307-308
Story, Joseph, 208
"strong central government," concept of, 126, 141, 162, 195-196; see also national government
Stuart, Gilbert, 73
sugar, excise on, 399
Sullivan, Gen. John, 59
Sully, Maximilien de Béthune, duc de, 459
S.U.M., see Society for Useful Manufactures
Superintendent of Finance, see Finance, Superintendent of
Supreme Court, U.S., 156, 297 n., 406; as archetype of democratic conservatism, 204; establishment of, 225; H.'s concept of, 535; interpretation of Constitution by, 201, 537; reorganization plan, 535; upholds carriage tax, 402; see also implied powers; judicial review
Suvorov, Gen. Aleksandr Vasilyevich, 503
Sweden, French crisis and, 418-419
Swift, Jonathan, 10

Tallyrand, Charles Maurice de, 234, 284, 292, 466, 492-493, 500; in XYZ affair, 466-469
tariff, protective, 289; increased rates of, 298; manufactures and, 285; national debt and, 232; see also impost
Tariff and Tonnage Acts of 1789, 224
tax (es), direct and indirect, 401-402; hidden, 88; import or "impost," 87-88; postwar, 120; in Schuyler-Hamilton plan, 160

taxation, colonial freedom and, 14; excise tax on whisky, 396; federal powers of, 195; as "Gordian knot," 235; lack of authority by Continental Congress in, 59, 83, 87; need for, by new government, 221-222; public opinion and, 87; rebellion and, 505; right of Congress to levy, 59; *see also* general revenue bill impost
"taxation without representation," H.'s theory of, 14
tax collections, reforms in, 84
Taylor, John, 311, 341, 401, 472, 569-570
tea, inflation and, 45
tender acts, 120-121, 142, 259
textile industry, 301
Thetis, H.M.S., 474
three-fifths rule, 563
Ticonderoga, Battle of, 23
Tilghman, Lt. Col. Tench, 22, 64
tobacco, excise on, 399
Tocqueville, Alexis de, 204
Toussaint L'Ouverture, François Dominique, 559, 562
Tontine Coffee House, 439
Tories, *see* Loyalists
trade, balance of, 290; banks and, 60; regulation of, 134-135, 264, 290
trading company, Bank of U.S. and, 55-56
transportation, 283
Treasury Department, U.S., 219 ff., 225; end of policy making by, 440-441; Gallatin's supervision of, 435-436; H. as first Secretary of, 219-220; as largest Department in 1789, 322; Neutrality Proclamation and, 372; as "sink of corruption," 437; states' contributions to, 149; supports price of government bonds, 271; *see also* Hamilton, Alexander, *passim*
Treasury notes, 504 n.; *see also* paper money
treaties, commercial, 134; neutral rights and, 384-385; as supreme law of the land, 108-109; *see also* Jay's Treaty
Trenton, second Battle of, 21
Trespass Act, 1783, 105, 107; annulment of, 108
"Triumvirate," 479-480
Troup, Col. Robert, 83, 106, 447, 513, 523, 541-542, 545, 549
Trumbull, John, 241, 278
Tryon, Gen. William, 108
Twelfth Amendment, 567
tyranny, demagogues and, 200; as last stage of democracy, 124; judicial 203

unanimity, rule of, 87
"unconstitutionality," Madisonians and, 296
union and unionism, excise as means of strengthening, 396; vs. liberty, in H.'s plan, 163; manufacturing as bulwark of, 285; positive advantages of, 196; preservation of, 443; as "rock of salvation," 59; soldiers as advocates of, 118; threatened war with France and, 468-469
United States, Bank of, *see* Bank of the United States; borrowing ability of, 230; bright outlook for 1789, 252-253; British citizens in, 485; call to arms against France in XYZ affair, 467-468; economic prospects, 1787, 149; economic recovery of, 279; first minister sent to French Directory, 493; French citizens in, 484; French influence in, 1794, 426; H.'s fears for future of, 119; importance of trade with Britain, 389; industrialization of, 289-290; Jay's Treaty with Britain, 422; "last stage of national nothingness," 149; likened to classical Greece, 114-115, 123-124, 200; "neutral rights" concept, 384; plight of outlined in the *Federalist*, 194; preparedness measures in French crisis, 469-471; present and future of discussed in "Farewell Address," 443; pro-French bias in, 372; "second war" with Britain, 1794-1795, 384; suspected as satellite of France, 421; threat of war with Virginia, 490-491; treaty obligations of, 107; treaty with France, 368-370; unbalanced economy in, 284
United States Army, birth and "fading away" of, 99; national debt and, 234; quells Pennsylvania Dutch riots, 506; reorganization act, 1799, 481; as "ruin of the country," 505; strengthening of, 1794, 390; unpreparedness of in 1797, 469; in Whisky Rebellion, 396-414; *see also* provisional army
United States Congress, *see* Congress, U.S.
United States Mint, 276 n., 389
unit rule, at Constitutional Convention, 176

Valley Forge, H.'s economic studies at, 46; winter at, 26, 35
Van Cortlandt, Col. Philip, 77
Vanderbilt, John, 130
Van Ness, William, 570-571, 574 n.
Vattel, Emerich de, 106, 428
Venable, Abraham, 338-340, 460, 463-464
Venezuela, Louisiana territory and, 496-497
Vermont, "independence" of, 131-133; joins Union, 1790, 133
vice-presidency, first, 220
View of the Manufactures of the United States, 282
violence, distaste for, 18
Virginia, Federalism in, 353; opposition to carriage tax, 400; ratifies Constitution, 213; rejection of impost by, 90; strong busi-

Index

ness interests in, 137; as threat to national union, 256; war with, threatened, 490-491
Virginia and Kentucky resolutions, Constitution and, 489-491, 505, 564
Virginia-Massachusetts coalition, fear of, 295
Virginia Plan, 155-156, 160, 168, 172-174; election of President in, 178-179; opposition to, 159
Virginia Resolutions, 1790, 255
virtue, human nature and, 199
Voltaire, François Marie Arouet de, 280
Vumenal, Baron, 79

Waddington, Benjamin, 105
Wadsworth, Jeremiah, 127, 129
war, "invention" of causes for ingrained in human nature, 118; manufacturing as safeguard against, 285
War Department, creation of, 59
War of Independence, see Revolutionary War
war powers, of Continental Congress, 108
Warville, Brissot de, 245
Washington, Bushrod, 353
Washington, George, 145, 152, 165, 173, 178-179, 206, 215, 221, 225, 520, 537; in battle of Princeton, 21; losses of, 23; "plot" by Gates and Conway, 26-28; orders attack on Clinton at Monmouth, 29-30; "fulsome" praise of Hamilton's action at Monmouth, 31-32; Laurens-Lee duel and, 34; as "Idol of America," 35; castigates profiteering and speculation, 43; fear of inflation, 45-46; recommends H. as Superintendent of Finance, 59; H.'s quarrel with, 62-79; ignorance of French language, 67-68; dependence upon H., 67-68; pride and sensitivity of, 73; self-discipline, 74; in army-civilian creditor struggle, 93-94; supports impost, 97; on Shays' Rebellion, 142; determination to establish "high-toned" government, 176-177; as Presidential choice at Convention, 179; reluctantly supports H. against Clintonians, 187; urged by H. to accept Presidency, 219-220; optimism of over administration's prospects, 238; as "aegis" of H., 246; hesitates on national bank issue, 264-265; power vacuum created by, 319-320; defends H. against Jefferson, 350-351; Burr's low opinion of, 356, 480; agrees to second term, 360; issues Neutrality Proclamation in French crisis, 369; Genêt's charge of jealousy against, 373; supports H. in Genêt controversy, 374, 377; takes action against Whisky Rebellion, 405-406; organizes militia, 407-408; denounces "Democratic Societies," 412-413; differs with H. on Armed Neutrality, 420; signs Jay's Treaty, 422-423; denies right of House to pass on treaties, 432-433; popularity impaired by Jay's Treaty, 434; refuses third term, 441-442, 514; salary and expenses of, 442; "Farewell Address," 442-443; made Commander-in-Chief in French crisis, 476; obtains appointment of H. as second in command, 476-477; Callander's slander, 486; on action against Spanish America, 499; death of, 515; land holdings of, 545 n.
Wasp, N.Y., see New York Wasp
Wayne, Gen. Anthony, 33, 35, 78
wealth, creation of through funding system, 253-254; private, see private capital
Wealth of Nations, 291, 293
Webster, Daniel, 208, 437
Webster, Noah, 320, 384, 430, 523
Weehawken, N.J., duel site, 549, 573
welfare, government and, 197; see also "general welfare" clause
West, discontent in, 398, 404-405
West Indies, 368, 388, 392, 452; commercial relations with, 15; H.'s knowledge of, 10; see also British West Indies; French West Indies
West Point, N.Y., 70, 99; Military Academy at, 482
"Westchester Farmer," see Seabury, Rev. Samuel
Western Inland Lock Navigation Company, 303, 546
whale and cod fisheries, 298-299
Whisky Boys, 406, 408-409, 411, 490
Whisky Rebellion, 396-414, 426, 435
Whitemarsh, Phila., 26
Whitney, Eli, 285, 313
Wilkinson, Gen. James, 27-28, 474, 498, 504; deceives H. on Spanish America, 499-500
Willing, Thomas, 526
Wilson, James, 92, 155, 158, 172-173, 178, 182, 407, 516, 545
Witherspoon, Rev. Dr., 8
Wolcott, Oliver, 305, 337, 339, 383, 407, 426, 440, 458-460, 476, 480, 483, 515, 519, 545, 571
women, in factories, 288

XYZ affair, 466-469, 472, 476, 492, 515

Yates, Abraham, 382
Yates, John, 152
Yates, Robert, 382
Yates, William, 171, 178, 212
Yazoo Country, Georgia, land claims in, 547
yellow fever epidemic, Philadelphia, 379
Yorktown, Battle of, 76, 79

293

JUL 05 2012
Aug 2 2012